Setting the Moral Compass

STUDIES IN FEMINIST PHILOSOPHY

Cheshire Calhoun, *Series Editor*

EDITED BY CHESHIRE CALHOUN

Setting the Moral Compass

ESSAYS BY WOMEN PHILOSOPHERS

OXFORD
UNIVERSITY PRESS

2004

OXFORD
UNIVERSITY PRESS

Oxford New York
Auckland Bangkok Buenos Aires Cape Town Chennai
Dar es Salaam Delhi Hong Kong Istanbul Karachi Kolkata
Kuala Lumpur Madrid Melbourne Mexico City Mumbai Nairobi
São Paulo Shanghai Taipei Tokyo Toronto

Published by Oxford University Press Inc.
198 Madison Avenue, New York, New York 10016
www.oup.com

Oxford is a registered trademark of Oxford University Press

Library of Congress Cataloging-in-Publication Data
Setting the moral compass : essays by women philosophers / edited by Cheshire Calhoun.
p. cm. — (Studies in feminist philosophy)
Includes bibliographical references and index.
ISBN 978-0-19-515475-7 (pbk.)
1. Ethics. 2. Feminist ethics. I. Calhoun, Cheshire. II. Series.
BJ1395.S48 2003
170'.82—dc21   2003048636

Printed in the United States of America
on acid-free paper

Preface

When I first thought about creating a collection of work in moral philosophy, this is not the collection I originally imagined. Hilde Lindemann Nelson had suggested to me that I put together an anthology of work in feminist ethics, and my first thought was to do one in feminist virtue ethics. But as I began the work of selecting contributors and writing a proposal, I found myself increasingly disinterested in that task. Instead, I began to think about all the women moral philosophers I have read since the early 1980s whom I have admired, been inspired by, and learned so much from, particularly how to write philosophy that speaks to ordinary moral experience. I wanted all of these women in one book so that I could honor (at least some of) the women who have made moral philosophy a place where women can work. And I wanted to see their work, finally, in one place because it seemed to me that there was some important way in which they are kindred philosophical minds. But there was one sizable obstacle to publishing such a collection: there didn't seem to be a rationale for bringing the diverse set of philosophers I had in mind into one collection. There was no obvious principle of unity. Some of the authors were doing explicitly feminist philosophical work addressed primarily to other feminist thinkers. Others were squarely engaged in nonfeminist philosophical conversations with other moral philosophers, most of whom were men. So this couldn't be a collection of feminist ethics. But there was no other obvious thematic unity to call upon because the sorts of moral philosophy they did were quite different. The only alternative was to envision the book as a kind of festschrift, honoring women who have contributed in important ways to moral philosophy. But this, too, was an unsatisfactory frame—not because the contributors didn't deserve to be honored (surely they do) but because what I wanted to bring into view was the nonaccidental fact that all of the philosophers I felt were kindred minds were women. So this, in the end, is the conviction that unifies this volume: gender makes a difference. The difference it makes is sometimes subtle, often unpredictable, and is compatible with deep philosophical disagreements among women philosophers. But the field of moral philosophy would not be the same without the women philosophers who helped construct it. It will be different yet in a future when it is no longer necessary to insist that the difference women make to moral philosophy is something to be prized.

I owe a debt of gratitude to the moral philosophers whose work appears in this volume—and to many others whose work does not. This collection is limited in many ways—to almost exclusively U.S. philosophers, many of whom are members of the same generation and all of whom do what might loosely be called "analytic" philosophy. Readers will probably notice many other limits.

I am grateful to my home institution, Colby College, which has, as always, provided generous research support and a sabbatical leave. That support enabled me to work with Jason Beal, a student research assistant, who cut his editing teeth on this volume. I am deeply thankful for his persistence, collaborative spirit, and hard work.

Acknowledgments

My thanks to the following publishers for granting permission to reprint essays for this volume:

Repair by Elizabeth V. Spelman. Copyright © 2002 by Elizabeth V. Spelman. Reprinted by permission of Beacon Press, Boston.

Martha C. Nussbaum, "The Future of Feminist Liberalism." *Proceedings and Addresses of the American Philosophical Association*, vol. 74, no. 2 (November 2000). Reprinted with permission of the American Philosophical Association.

Barbara Herman, "The Scope of Moral Requirement." *Philosophy and Public Affairs*, vol. 30, no. 3 (Summer 2001). Copyright Princeton University Press © 2001.

Susan Wolf, "The Moral of Moral Luck." *Philosophic Exchange*, no. 31 (2000–2001). Reprinted with permission of the Center for Philosophic Exchange.

A substantial portion of the essay "Common Decency," by Cheshire Calhoun, originally appeared in "Expecting Common Decency," *Philosophy of Education 2002: A Publication of the Philosophy of Education Society*. Copyright held by the Philosophy of Education Society, reprinted with the society's permission.

Claudia Card, "Genocide and Social Death." *Hypatia: A Journal of Feminist Philosophy*, vol. 18, no. 1 (2003). Reprinted with permission of Indiana University Press.

Alison Jaggar, "Globalizing Feminist Ethics." *Hypatia: A Journal of Feminist Philosophy*, vol. 13, no. 2 (1998). Reprinted with permission of Indiana University Press.

Michele Moody-Adams, "The Idea of Moral Progress." *Metaphilosophy*, vol. 30 (July 1999). Reprinted with permission of Blackwell Publishing Ltd.

"The Improvisatory Dramas of Deliberation," by Amelie Oksenberg Rorty, is a revised version of "The Improvisatory Drama of Decision-Making," which originally appeared in *Well-Being and Morality: Essays in Honour of James Griffin*, ed. Roger Crisp. Copyright © 2000. Reprinted with permission of Oxford University Press.

Christine M. Korsgaard, "Self-Constitution in the Ethics of Plato and Kant." *The Journal of Ethics: An International Philosophical Review*, vol. 3 (1999), pp. 1–29. Copyright © 1999 Kluwer Academic Publishers. Reprinted with kind permission of Christine M. Korsgaard, Harvard University, and Kluwer Academic Publishers.

Contents

Contributors

Annette Baier, retired from the University of Pittsburgh, lives in her birthplace, Queenstown, New Zealand, with periods of residence also in Dunedin, near the University of Otago, where she first studied philosophy. She continues to write on trust, on emotions, and on David Hume's philosophy. She is a past president of the Eastern Division of the American Philosophical Association. Her books include *The Commons of the Mind* (The Paul Carus Lectures), *Moral Prejudices*, and *A Progress of Sentiments: Reflections on Hume's Treatise.*

Marcia Baron is professor of philosophy at Indiana University. Her publications include *Kantian Ethics Almost without Apology* (1995). "Kantian Ethics and Claims of Detachment," in *Feminist Interpretations of Immanuel Kant*, ed. Robin Schott (1997) and "'I Thought She Consented,'" *Philosophical Issues*. She is currently working on battered women's self-defense claims and manipulativeness. She has served as president of the Central Division of the American Philosophical Association.

Cheshire Calhoun is Charles A. Dana Professor of Philosophy at Colby College, Waterville, Maine. She typically works at various intersections of feminist philosophy, ethics, and gay and lesbian studies. She is the author of *Feminism, the Family, and the Politics of the Closet: Lesbian and Gay Displacement* (Oxford University Press, 2000); coeditor of *What Is an Emotion?*; and has published essays on forgiveness, integrity, civility, and responsibility.

Claudia Card is Emma Goldman Professor of Philosophy at the University of Wisconsin, where she has taught since 1966. She has teaching affiliations with women's studies, environmental studies, and Jewish studies. Her most recent books are *The Atrocity Paradigm: A Theory of Evil* (2002) and *The Cambridge Companion to Beauvoir* (2003).

Robin S. Dillon is associate professor of philosophy at Lehigh University, where she also served as director of Women's Studies for six years. She has published articles on self-respect and respect, including "Self-Respect: Moral Emotional, Political," *Ethics* 107 (1997) and "Self-Forgiveness and Self-Respect," *Ethics* 112 (2001), and is the editor of *Dignity, Character and Self-Respect* (1995).

Marilyn Friedman teaches philosophy at Washington University in St. Louis. Her research falls into the areas of political philosophy, ethics, and feminist thought. She is the author of *Autonomy, Gender, Politics* (Oxford University Press, 2003) and *What Are Friends For? Feminist Perspectives on Personal Relationships and Moral Theory*; (1995), the coauthor of *Political Correctness: For and Against*; and the coeditor of *Rights and Reason: Essays in Honor of Carl Wellman* (2000), *Mind and Morals: Essays on Ethics and Cognitive Science*, and *Feminism and Community* (1995).

Virginia Held is Distinguished Professor of Philosophy at the City University of New York Graduate School. Among her books are *The Public Interest and Individual Interests (1970)*; *Rights and Goods: Justifying Social Action (1984)*; *Feminist Morality: Transforming Culture, Society, and Politics* (1993); and the edited collections *Property, Profits, and Economic Justice* (1980) and *Justice and Care: Essential Readings in Feminist Ethics (1995)*. She has served as president of the Eastern Division of the American Philosophical Association, been a fellow at the Center for Advanced Study in the Behavioral Sciences, and has had Fulbright and Rockefeller fellowships. She is currently working on a number of essays on the ethics of care and the challenge this kind of theory presents to standard moral theories.

Barbara Herman is Griffin Professor of Philosophy at the University of California, Los Angeles, and a past president of the Pacific Division of the American Philosophical Association. She is the author of *The Practice of Moral Judgment* (1996), as well as articles on Kant's ethics, issues of moral development and literacy, and the social conditions for empirical autonomy. She is currently working on the topic of moral improvisation.

Marcia Homiak is professor of philosophy at Occidental College, where she teaches philosophy, women's studies, and ancient history. Her published papers are on topics in classical ethics, the history of ethics, moral psychology, and feminist ethics. She is currently writing a book on character and virtue that seeks to show the contemporary relevance of Aristotle's discussions of these topics.

Alison M. Jaggar is professor of philosophy and women's studies at the University of Colorado at Boulder. Her books include *Feminist Politics and Human Nature* (1983); *Living with Contradictions: Controversies in Feminist Ethics* (1994); and *The Blackwell Companion to Feminist Philosophy*, coedited with Iris M. Young (1998). Currently, she is working on a book on moral justification. Alison Jaggar was a founding member of the Society for Women in Philosophy, a past chair of the American Philosophical Association Committee on the Status of Women, and now works with a number of feminist organizations.

Karen Jones is lecturer in philosophy at the University of Melbourne. She has held positions at Cornell University and at the Research School of Social Sciences, the Australian National University. She has written extensively on trust in both its epistemic and ethical dimensions.

Christine M. Korsgaard is Arthur Kingsley Porter Professor of Philosophy at Harvard University. Her primary interests are in moral philosophy and its history and the theory of practical reason. She is the author of *Creating the Kingdom of Ends*, a collection of essays on Kant's moral philosophy, and *The Sources of Normativity*, an expanded version of her 1992 Tanner Lectures on the grounds of obligation. In *Self-Constitution*, her forthcoming Locke Lectures, she explores connections among ethics, the theory of action, and personal identity.

Diana Tietjens Meyers is professor of philosophy at the University of Connecticut, Storrs. Her most recent monographs are *Self, Society, and Personal Choice*; *Subjection and Subjectivity: Psychoanalytic Feminism and Moral Philosophy*; and *Gender in the Mirror: Cultural Imagery and Women's Agency* (Oxford University Press, 2002); her most recent edited collections are *Feminists Rethink the Self* and *Feminist Social Thought: A Reader*. She is the author of the forthcoming *Encyclopedia Britannica* entry on Philosophical Feminism.

Michele Moody-Adams is currently director and Hutchinson Professor of Ethics and Public Life and professor of philosophy at Cornell University. She does research and teaching on a variety of issues in ethical theory, practical ethics, political philosophy, and the philosophy of law. She is the author of *Fieldwork in Familiar Places: Morality, Culture and Philosophy* (1997) and has published on such topics as moral relativism and moral objectivity, problems of economic and social justice, affirmative action and multiculturalism, feminism and equality, and the moral implications of reproductive technologies.

Martha C. Nussbaum is Ernst Freund Distinguished Service Professor of Law and Ethics at the University of Chicago, appointed in the Philosophy Department, Law School, and Divinity School. Her most recent books are *Women and Human Development: The Capabilities Approach* (2000), and *Upheavals of Thought: The Intelligence of Emotions* (2001). In 2002–2003, she gave the Tanner Lectures in Canberra, Australia, and Clare Hall, Cambridge, England, on "Beyond the Social Contract: Toward Global Justice."

Amelie Rorty is the director of the Program in the History of Ideas at Brandeis and Orick Visiting Professor at Yale University. Besides numerous essays on Descartes, Hume, Spinoza, and the history of moral psychology, she has edited anthologies on Aristotle, the emotions, self-deception, and most recently *Philosophers on Education, The Many Faces of Evil, The Many Faces of Philosophy.*

Elizabeth V. Spelman is professor of philosophy and the Barbara Richmond 1940 Professor in the Humanities at Smith College. She is author of *Inessential Woman: Problems of Exclusion in Feminist Thought; Fruits of Sorrow: Framing Our Attention to Suffering;* and *Repair: The Impulse to Restore in a Fragile World.*

Margaret Urban Walker is Lincoln Professor of Ethics, Justice, and the Public Sphere in the School of Justice Studies at Arizona State University. Author of *Moral Understandings* (1998) and *Moral Contexts* (2003), she writes on moral epistemology, psychology, and responsibility. She is finishing a book on moral repair, the moral psychology and social practice of responding to wrongdoing.

Susan Wolf is the Edna J. Koury Professor of Philosophy at the University of North Carolina at Chapel Hill. She is the author of *Freedom Within Reason* (Oxford University Press, 1990), a book on free will and moral responsibility, and numerous articles on ethics and the philosophy of mind. Her current research focuses on the relations among happiness, morality, and meaningfulness in life.

Setting the Moral Compass

Introduction

Cheshire Calhoun

This collection brings together nineteen of the leading women philosophers in ethics who have contributed to setting the compass in moral philosophy over the past two or three decades. The result is a set of essays that collectively display the sorts of powerful and innovative contributions to ethics that women moral philosophers have made and continue to make. It is a collection that makes visible women moral philosophers' varied conceptions of the proper subjects, texts, methods, audiences, and purposes of moral philosophy. It also invites the reader to rethink the boundaries between nonfeminist and feminist moral philosophy.

Over the past twenty-five years, the work of women philosophers has reshaped the field of moral philosophy. The most obvious difference that they have made is in the development of explicitly feminist moral perspectives. With very few exceptions, it has been women moral philosophers who have labored to produce conceptual, theoretical, and interpretive tools that make possible philosophical analyses of moral phenomena that are integrally connected with gender and other social hierarchies of power. For some, this has meant developing an alternative to Kantian, utilitarian, virtue ethical, and liberal political approaches—for example, an ethic of care or an ethic centered on trust rather than duty. For others, it has meant employing the resources of Kantian, utilitarian, and virtue ethical frameworks to address moral concerns that are most salient to persons subordinated within social hierarchies.

It would be a mistake, however, to think that women's sole—or even primary—impact on moral philosophy has been the production of an explicitly feminist ethics. Many women moral philosophers working within nonfeminist communities of scholars, for example, communities of Kantian or Aristotelian moral philosophers, have introduced distinctive perspectives to and made distinctive demands on moral philosophy. Those perspectives and demands are often continuous with those of women writing explicitly feminist ethics. It is also important to keep in mind that many women moral philosophers work within both feminist and nonfeminist intellectual communities.

Women, of course, cannot claim sole credit for the shifts in moral philosophy over the past twenty-five years. The discipline of philosophy as a whole has undergone substantial pluralization as a result of pressure from a variety of sources. Nevertheless women moral philosophers are owed much of the credit for the fact that the range of topics that are now taken to be legitimate in moral philosophy is much larger than it was in the 1970s. Women philosophers also deserve most of the credit for the fact that the politics of theory construction—whose interests do moral theories serve and not serve?—can now be part of the self-reflective business of moral philosophy. Women philosophers also deserve a sizable portion of the credit for making the use of multidisciplinary resources a component of properly done moral philosophy.

Inventive Realism

If there is any one description that captures the common character of women philosophers' work in moral philosophy, it is an *inventive realism* about moral life. By "realism" I mean attentiveness to what moral life is really like—to what moral agents are really like, to what the production and acquisition of moral knowledge is really like, to what the social practice of morality is really like, to what character development is really like, to what practical decision making is really like—*as opposed to* the conventions employed within moral philosophy for describing these same things. This is not to say that men moral philosophers are inattentive to moral truths. But it is to say that, as "outsiders-within" the profession of philosophy, women have typically been better positioned both to notice and to take up in their work moral phenomena that conventionally gets set aside.[1] Women moral philosophers, as a group, have been more willing to acknowledge and incorporate into their philosophical accounts the messiness, indeterminacy, and lucky and unlucky contingencies of moral life. That theme certainly is much in evidence in this collection. As a group, women moral philosophers have also had less patience with overly hypothetical or dramatic examples (e.g., the many drowning baby stories) and with idealized, hyperrational models of moral agents; instead, they have been insistent that moral philosophy directly addresses the actual processes, problems, and experiences of everyday moral life. Two features of everyday moral life have been particularly salient in women's moral philosophy and are also particularly salient in this volume: our vulnerabilities and dependencies on each other and the sociopolitical context in which moral life is conducted.

By "inventiveness" I mean a willingness to be imaginative about the possibilities for work in moral philosophy. That inventiveness emerges from a willingness to ask: What has moral philosophy not talked about, or said very little about, that might nevertheless be central to understanding human moral life? What distorted understandings of moral phenomena have become entrenched in disciplinary knowledge? What new concepts need naming and analyzing within moral philosophy?

Women moral philosophers have exercised their inventive realism in extending the possibilities for not only *what* the subjects of moral philosophy are but also *who* those subjects are. Women moral philosophers have explored a great variety of ways of thinking about moral agents *other* than primarily as rational beings. In this volume, for example, moral agents are described as *homo reparans* (the repairing animal), participants in improvisatory dramas, self-narrating subjects, trusting or distrusting responders to human mutual vulnerability, self-constituting unities of reason and emotion, needy animals, beings who require social vitality, and selves that cannot be detached from their unintended causal effects on others.

By "inventiveness" I also mean a willingness to be imaginative about the possible textual resources for and styles of philosophical writing. Women moral philosophers have not always assumed that moral philosophy must be addressed to academic moral philosophers. Part of being accountable to everyday life is writing moral philosophy that is accountable to the plurality of contexts in which moral philosophizing might be needed. Women moral philosophers have also not assumed that the best textual resources are necessarily academic philosophical ones. In addition to disciplinary resources, they have drawn on a wide array of literature in women's studies, psychology, psychoanalytic theory, sociology, literary theory, literature, and social and cultural history, as well as etiquette manuals and other popular texts.

That women moral philosophers have brought such originality to their work might be explained in a number of ways. First, both human activities and human cognitive and emotional capacities are gender-coded. The socialization and education of children, most of human emotionality, and the maintenance of many personal and communal relationships are coded feminine. By comparison to masculine-coded activities and capacities (e.g., combat, competitive games, the making of contractual agreements, rational decision making, and the pursuit of individual preferences), such feminine-coded activities and capacities have largely been ignored in moral philosophy. Part of what women moral philosophers have brought to the discipline is a firm sense of what those neglected activities and capacities are, as well as a vision of how moral philosophy might be improved by greater attentiveness to the full complexity of human life.

Second, although the number of women philosophers has increased over time, women remain significantly underrepresented in the discipline. Regardless of how prominent and well respected some women philosophers have become, the relative dearth of women in philosophy, particularly at more advanced levels and in the most prestigious institutions, means that women philosophers are always marked by their difference. Being already marked as different may make it more natural for women to pursue unconventional avenues in philosophy.

Finally, women philosophers, because they are members of a socially disesteemed gender, have often wanted something different and more from moral philosophy, namely, a moral philosophy that is politically responsible. This means, in part, that in its assumptions and theoretical accounts moral philosophy should not encode gender biases. In part, a politically responsible moral philosophy is one that acknowledges and is equipped to address a variety of systems of institutionalized oppression. And in part, a politically responsible moral philosophy attends to the interconnections between the social conditions under which people live and the possibilities for moral agency and knowledge.

Some of the most interesting and original work produced by women philosophers has centered around the production of richer and more complex depictions of the persons who are the agents and patients of moral action. That rich depiction has included much more careful attention to the development of moral character from childhood through adulthood and to the interpersonal, social, and political influences on character formation and moral deliberation. Women moral philosophers with feminist sensibilities have consistently challenged the tendency in much moral philosophy to begin theorizing, either implicitly or explicitly, from a picture of moral persons as fully formed adults, who are not located in inegalitarian societies, who do not experience long periods of dependency on others, whose moral life is not hedged with contingencies, whose pleasures and passions are not constitutive elements of their moral life, and for whom reason giving is unaffected by the narratives we tell of our lives or by the dynamics of social interaction. All of the essays in this volume illustrate that challenge.

Women moral philosophers have also been more inclined to abandon some familiar ways of thinking about moral character—that character is something that, once formed, is relatively static; that autonomy is the overshadowingly important moral competency; and that our conceptions of virtues and vices are not interestingly linked to social conceptions of gender. They have raised questions about what role moral education, family life, cultural gender imagery, the distribution of social resources, socially shared moral understandings, and the dynamics of social interaction play in producing morally competent (or incompetent) adults and in enabling (or disabling) individual moral progress. They have been mindful of the fact that the selves who are open to character revision and new moral understandings are always already located in a social world in which power inequalities are variously institutionalized. This fact raises important questions about how we should conceptualize the relation between the possibility of moral progress on the part of individuals and the possibility of moral and political progress at the social level.

The rich depiction of persons has also included much more careful attention to the complexity of moral psychology. Not starting from a picture of persons as ideally rational, deliberative agents has, among other things, enabled women moral philosophers to attend more carefully to questions about the role that emotions play in human moral life. In working out depictions of human moral psychology, women moral philosophers have been less attracted both to internal "combat" models—for example, those that pit reason against emotion or concern for others against concern for self—and to overly unified conceptions of the self that exclude multiplicity within the self.

Although only some women moral philosophers locate their work in the tradition of virtue ethics extending from Aristotle, many have nevertheless found analysis of particular virtues and vices to be central to a rich and complex account of persons. Investigation of virtue and vice naturally lends itself to the pursuit of questions about luck, about the social context of morality, and about morally important perceptual and emotional sensitivities. Among those character traits that have seemed particularly important to examine in inegalitarian societies are trust, self-respect, arrogance, and integrity.

Work by women philosophers has also helped to enlarge our philosophical vision of moral injury. For a complex set of reasons, including their experience of institutionalized sexism, women moral philosophers have been less inclined to focus narrowly on wrongdoing that is clearly attributable to particular individuals. When complex social arrangements and interactions are implicated in the production of moral injuries, it may be very difficult to assign individual responsibility, to mete out adequate punishment, and to focus reactive attitudes of indignation, resentment, and forgiveness on clearly defined targets. Even when individual responsibility is clear, retributive responses may be morally less important than acts and attitudes that aim at repairing broken moral relationships or reaffirming shared norms. In other cases the moral injuries are so horrific they exceed our everyday conception of moral wrongdoing and are evils for which no retributive response seems adequate. Cases in which the amount or scope of injury is excessive invite reflection on the nature of evil, the appropriateness of forgiveness, and the options for morally restorative responses.

The boundary between moral and political philosophy is not a sharp one and is especially blurred in the work of women moral philosophers. That is partly because attention to the institutions, practices, and ideologies that sustain gender inequality so often figures in their moral philosophy. Are there, for example, perspectives whose social availability should not be tolerated in the name of diversity because they are dangerous to moral development? In real-life moral discourses that aim to generate principles agreeable to all, should already socially dominant voices be muted? And given our very different social locations, who is positioned to morally criticize whose practices?

The blurring of the boundaries between the moral and the political has also resulted in part from the fact that women moral philosophers have more often included within the scope of political philosophy an attention to the justice of familial arrangements and the current distribution of care-giving work. Because women make up the majority of care givers, especially for the most needy and dependent humans at both ends of the life span, women moral philosophers have been more inclined to raise both moral and political questions about care giving. How central are caring practices to the practice of morality? How would liberal political philosophy need to be rethought in order to adequately address the centrality of care giving and care receiving to human lives?

"Woman Philosopher"?

This is a book by *women* moral philosophers. It is the authors' social location—being gendered "woman" in moral philosophy—that is central to the organization and philosophical aims of this text. It is important to be clear what this does *not* mean. Although I do think it is both legitimate and important to attend to the differences that gender makes to the production of moral philosophy (differences like the ones described above), women do not produce a "women's moral philosophy." The persistence of gender essentialism in cultural thought about women and men makes it tempting to overread the difference that gender makes. Gender essentialism is the view that all women, in virtue of being women, share a common gendered subjectivity. Those commonalities are assumed to be so pervasive that producing philosophy *as women* will result in a more or less univocal style and content of theorizing that clearly contrasts with whatever univocal style and content of theorizing men produce when they do philosophy *as men*. Feminists have by now subjected gender essentialism to extensive critique. They have argued that women's subjectivities are multiply and complexly affected by their gendered and other social identities, as well as by their personal histories and autonomous choices. Thus, that gender makes a difference to the production of philosophy does not mean that women's philosophical work elaborates a theoretically unified field, with its own set of key concepts and fundamental principles, that might then be opposed to, say, Kantian ethics or utilitarian ethics. Unfortunately, this has been how "feminist ethics" has often been misread. Especially in introductory textbooks, feminist ethics is often equated with some version of care ethics. This is simply a mistake. Feminist ethics comprises a complex and theoretically *disunified* body of work. The institutionalization of a distinct subfield of philosophy—feminist ethics or, more generally, feminist philosophy—emerged not from the theoretical unity of this work but from a political need. The point of having a distinct category of philosophy called feminist ethics or feminist philosophy is to promote the development of conceptual, theoretical, and interpretive tools that will enable philosophy to be responsive to the fact that gender and other hierarchies of power have important and damaging effects on human personal, social, and cognitive life.

In this collection, the point of using the categories *woman philosopher* and *work by women philosophers* is similarly political. I will argue, shortly, that reading women moral philosophers' work in relation to each other—rather than, say, in relation to fellow Kantians or fellow feminist philosophers—does important cognitive and practical work for the discipline of philosophy.[2] As I will explain below, the collection is intended to provide what I think is a much needed intervention in how we, philosophers, think about the relation between gender and philosophy; how we think about women's relation to both feminist and "mainstream" philosophy; and how we conventionally allow—or don't allow—women's difference to appear. Before doing so, some cautionary remarks about using the category *woman philosopher* are in order.

Presenting the work of stellar moral philosophers under the title of *Essays by Women Philosophers* is multiply problematic. To be invited to contribute to a collection devoted to work by women moral philosophers is, as Annette Baier observed, a dubious honor. "No one dreams," she wrote me, "of an anthology documenting men's contributions to recent philosophical ethics." It is as individuals with something of their own to say that men contribute to philosophy, not as examples of philosophical manhood. Toril Moi develops a similar point in her recent collection, *What Is a Woman?*

> In certain situations, I wish my female body to be considered as the insignificant background of my claims or acts. This is not the same thing as to say that I wish my body to disappear or to be transformed into a male body. My wish does not represent an attempt to escape my particularity, to be considered as a neuter, or as some kind of universalized human being. It represents, rather, a wish to deny that the fact of being a woman is of any particular relevance to my understanding of trigonometry or my capacity to compose symphonies or think ethically.[3]

In saying that the fact of her being a woman is not of any particular relevance to her capacity to think ethically, Moi is not in fact claiming that gender makes no difference to how one thinks. On the contrary, Moi denies that were she a man she would think or write exactly the same things: "I probably do read Kant or Kierkegaard," she says, "in ways I would not have done had I been a man."[4] In a society in which gender makes many differences to our lives, one's embodiment as a man or a woman is likely to make at least some difference to one's philosophical thinking. In what sense, then, is Moi's being gendered "woman" irrelevant to her capacity to think ethically? It is irrelevant in exactly the same sense that men's gender is irrelevant to their capacity to think ethically. Moi observes that when gender makes a difference to the way that men think, men are not obliged to *signify* the difference that gender makes by presenting their work as that of a male philosopher. It is a mark of sexism that whenever women's embodiment is thought to make some (even slight) difference to their philosophical thinking they are obliged to present their work as the product of a *woman* philosopher. In short, what both Baier and Moi make perspicuous is the fact that the term *woman philosopher* is part of a sexist politics of knowledge. That sexist politics of knowledge consists of regarding the effects of male embodiment on philosophical thought as unworthy of note because "philosopher" is implicitly equated with "being embodied male." That sexist politics of knowledge also consists of regarding the effects of female embodiment on philosophical thought as noteworthy because it is a deviation from the norm.

To create a collection devoted to work by *women* moral philosophers is, thus, to run the risk of implicating the contributors in this pattern of noting the effects of embodiment on philosophical thought only in the case of women and never for men. It thus risks perpetuating the very style of thinking that sustains gender inequality in the discipline.

There are other problems, too, with thematizing the gendered location of the contributors to this volume. In a discipline that is now often self-conscious about the sadly low numbers of women in philosophy and its long history of not honoring even the most deserving women philosophers, taking women's gender into account is often part of corrective practices, ranging from affirmative action to making special efforts to award to women various honors. The existence of corrective practices, however, gives women who receive awards—from jobs to American Philosophical Association presidencies—reason to wonder just what this award means. Does it mean that their talents have in fact been recognized and justly rewarded? Or does it mean that they are the token woman in a corrective practice (without which they would have received nothing)?

To create a collection devoted to work by *women* moral philosophers is, thus, to risk suggesting that they are being honored not because they are truly worthy of philosophical honor but because there has been too little honoring of women in philosophy.

Given these serious disadvantages to employing the category "woman philosopher," there had better be some strongly compelling, counterbalancing justification for constructing a collection that emphasizes that very category. I think there is.

In explicating Beauvoir, Toril Moi points out, "We are continuously making something of what the world makes of us."[5] Those who are embodied as women inevitably must make something of the fact that our social worlds make all sorts of things of our evident sex differences. And when those embodied as women come to philosophy, they must also make something of what their academic environments make of them. Women *academics* enter a world in which they constitute 36% of full-time faculty across institutions and only 25% in research universities.[6] Women *philosophers* enter a world in which their numbers are dramatically lower. It is a world in which they will inevitably be implicated in affirmative action debates (as hires, as advocates, and as members of the underrepresented group); that offers an array of opportunities for reflection on and resistance to sexism in the academy (such as women's studies programs, the Society for Women in Philosophy, and the American Philosophical Association's Committee on the Status of Women); that often presumes that any woman will represent "women's point of view"; that too often provides a basis for complaint (both on one's own behalf and on behalf of other women) about hiring, evaluation, tenure, curriculum construction, judgments about what doesn't count as real philosophy, and the distribution of resources, awards, and work (especially service work). Given the pervasive difference that gender makes to how we are received, spoken to, supported, and acknowledged, as well as to what we are expected to do or not to do, it would be remarkable indeed if gender made no difference to one's subjectivity. It would be equally remarkable if the ways in which women philosophers make something of what the world makes of us left no traces in our philosophical production. That there would be traces seems particularly likely among women philosophers who have well-formed feminist sensibilities and are attuned to the cultural difference that gender makes. It also seems particularly likely among women who are sufficiently secure in their institutional positions to be able to afford to write philosophy as they please.

The traces of an embodiment as woman show up most obviously in philosophical work about gender oppression and oppositional work critiquing masculinist bias in dominant philosophical theories. Such feminist work almost inevitably requires self-consciously positioning oneself as a *woman* philosopher.

But recall Moi's observation: she probably reads Kierkegaard or Kant differently than she would were she a man. Her point is that even when she self-consciously positions herself as simply a *philosopher*, the traces of her embodiment may show up. And this is equally true for men. Nonfeminist philosophy—what typically is thought of as philosophy "proper"—bears the traces of both women's and men's embodiment.

However, it is part of the present sexist politics of knowledge to deny that gender makes a difference to philosophy "proper." The only difference that gender is acknowledged to make is the difference that *women's* embodiment makes to an explicitly *feminist* or *woman-expressing* viewpoint. What distinguishes the present sexist politics of knowledge from the one that Beauvoir objected to is that women now are taken to be capable of producing philosophy "proper." They, like men, are assumed to be capable of entering into a process of philosophical production that is free from the traces of gendered embodiment. Such assumptions about when gender does and does not make a difference have a number of undesirable effects. First, they provide the rationale for demoting explicitly feminist—read, "deliberately gendered"—philosophy to the periphery of (or outside) philosophy "proper." Feminist philosophy, on this view, expresses a (narrow) gendered standpoint; philosophy "proper," it is imagined, does not. Imagining that men's embodiment leaves no traces in men's philosophical production (within philosophy "proper") provides the justification for not being self-reflective about the extent of gender bias in established contents and styles of philosophy. And, perhaps most worrisome, it becomes possible to think that there is no *cognitive* value in including more women in philosophy. The only value, on this view, is the value of securing equal opportunity.

The idea that gender makes a difference only to feminist philosophy, or a philosophy aimed at expressing woman's standpoint, is sustained and reinforced through two professional practices that control when and where the effects of embodiment become visible. First, there is the professional practice of using women to contribute "the woman's perspective" on some philosophical topic. It has, for example, become customary practice in anthologies and textbooks to include women philosophers as representatives of a gendered philosophy, whereas male philosophers represent all other nongendered theoretical positions. Connected with this is the practice of setting aside feminist philosophy for the expression of *women's* philosophical voice. Thus feminist philosophical conferences, anthologies, and faculty can be entirely female—in a discipline in which women probably do not constitute even one-fourth of the practitioners—without occasioning the least astonishment. Feminist philosophy is treated as the distinctive contribution of *women* philosophers and is understood to be a predictable consequence of including in the profession philosophers who are also women. Although it is no doubt true that feminist philosophy is a consequence of including women in the profession, the problem lies in the presumption that including women in the profession *has no appreciable effects on philosophy "proper" as well.* Thus there are no practices whatsoever of *both* women and men presenting gendered standpoints within philosophy "proper" (with no one articulating a gender-neutral viewpoint). Nor are there practices of bringing large numbers of women philosophers together in conferences and anthologies that are devoted to topics in philosophy "proper." So, for example, although bringing women feminist philosophers together requires no explanation, it would take significant explanation to defend bringing together all of the many notable women working on Kant's ethics into a single conference—and permitting the women to predominate on, or even constitute, the program.

This takes us to the second professional practice that sustains and reinforces the idea that gender leaves no traces on philosophy "proper." When women speak simply as philosophers—for example, as Rawlsians, Kantians, or Aristotelians—the professional practice is to limit the number of women who appear in any one place. It is now common practice for women to be included in philosophy departments, in conferences, and in collections of nonfeminist philosophical work. But their inclusion in these venues of philosophy "proper" is routinely tokenistic— often only one woman in an otherwise male lineup. So commonplace is this that it occasions not the least astonishment. Rarely does anyone think to ask, for example, "Is there really only one prominent woman working on moral epistemology who could have spoken at this conference?" So entrenched is the tokenistic inclusion of women in philosophy "proper" that affirmative action battles have to be perpetually fought (if they are fought at all) within departments for each additional woman hired beyond the first. The effect of a practice of, at worst, tokenistic inclusion and, at best, far less than equal inclusion of women is to ensure that the difference that embodiment might make to philosophy "proper" remains invisible.

This book is an intervention into these professional practices. It is premised on the assumption that embodiment makes a difference to the philosophy one does, whether one is doing explicitly feminist philosophy or not. This book aims to render visible the difference that gender makes by allowing many women philosophers to appear together in the same conceptual space as *philosophers*, not as spokeswomen for a "different voice" or a feminist ethics. Making such interventions is politically important. If we can see that embodiment does make a difference in the production of philosophy generally, then the very low numbers of women in philosophy gains added significance. It signals not just the persistence of gender inegalitarian practices. It also signals a cognitive loss to philosophy.

This book is also an intervention in practices that isolate feminist philosophy from philosophy "proper" and render invisible the connections between what women write as explicitly feminist scholars and what they write as philosophers with feminist sensibilities. Rather than clearly demarcating a feminist philosophy expressive of women's gender difference from a nonfeminist philosophy in which gender is imagined to leave no traces, I propose that we think in terms of a feminist continuum. At one end of the continuum is explicitly feminist philosophical work. At the other end is philosophical work that is not designed to contribute to feminist scholarship but that would not have been written in exactly the same way absent feminist sensibilities.[7] The essays by Claudia Card and Robin Dillon in this volume are particularly illustrative of the latter point. Both essays might easily be located in philosophy "proper" rather than feminist philosophy; but both authors describe how their essays express feminist sensibilities. Attending to the feminist continuum in philosophy will, I hope, have a double payoff. On the one hand, it encourages us to be mindful of the differences that gender may make in all philosophical production and thus the importance of a more equal inclusion of women. On the other hand, it may encourage greater cross-fertilization between explicitly feminist philosophy and other philosophical work by women.

The Essays of *Setting the Moral Compass*

The first two essays in this volume, by Marcia Homiak and Elizabeth V. Spelman, illustrate central themes and styles in women's moral philosophy. Among the themes that emerge in these and later essays are a resistance to elitism and inegalitarianism in both social life and philosophical work, an appeal to everyday activities of ordinary people for one's central examples, an emphasis on moral evaluation of social *practices* (rather than social institutions or individual acts), and attention to our dependence both on other people and on a decent sociopolitical context for a humanly good life. These first essays also illustrate common stylistic features of women's moral philosophy. Both essays draw heavily on literature outside academic philosophy; they thus work from an expanded conception of what counts as a philosophically useful text. They also show the range of women's philosophical work—from academic philosophy addressed to professional philosophers to philosophy designed for a multidisciplinary and not exclusively academic audience. Finally, these two essays illustrate two ends of the continuum that feminist philosophical work takes, Marcia Homiak positioning her work as a contribution to Aristotle scholarship and Elizabeth Spelman positioning her work within feminist philosophy.

In "Virtue and the Skills of Ordinary Life," Marcia Homiak develops a reading of Aristotle's views on the best human life that enables her to challenge his claim that the best life is available only to an elite few, and thus the state may tolerate the assignment of many to a life of menial labor. Drawing on Michael Baxandall's *Painting and Experience in Fifteenth-Century Italy*, Marcia Homiak observes that Florentine art patrons applied the mathematical knowledge used in their business lives in new ways to the interpretation of art, and did so within a community of patrons and artists who supported the continuous development of these skills of judgment. Art patrons' interpretative activities, like the contemplation that Aristotle sees as key to the good life, are continuous, relatively unimpeded, self-realizing, and require the cultivation of social virtues.

Elizabeth V. Spelman looks at a different dimension of everyday life—repair. Humans are as much repairing animals (*homo reparans*) as rational and political animals (*homo sapiens*). Masculinity is often defined in terms of skills at manual labor, whereas women's repair labor is paradigmatically the repair of people from the wear and tear of everyday life and the repair of relationships and the social fabric. It is in the household that we are first taught informal lessons about what can be repaired, how it can be repaired (e.g., through apology), and what is irreparable. It is also in the household that we are prepared and repaired for our lives as citizens, consumers, workers, moral agents, and friends.

Given human fragility and need for repair, it is a good thing that at least some humans are skilled at attending to individuals' context-specific needs. The themes of human fragility and contextual, rather than rule-driven, judgment have been central to the ethics of care. In "Taking Care: Care as Practice and Value," Virginia Held critically examines various conceptions of caring. She argues that care is a kind of work. But it is not just an activity of meeting objective needs. (This would bring an ethics of care too close to utilitarianism.) Caring labor is intrinsically relational; and caring is, in addition to being a form of labor, also an attitude toward others and a motive for one's action. Care is also a fundamental value and thus, like justice, can be incorporated into social practices ranging from mothering to social welfare to the repair work Elizabeth Spelman describes. Social practices of caring can, however, be morally deficient. One important task of an ethics of care is to evaluate existing caring practices.

Although care and justice are different values and invoke different clusters of moral considerations, both values are typically relevant in evaluating social practices and institutions. In "The Future of Feminist Liberalism," Martha C. Nussbaum takes liberal political theory to task for failing to provide for individuals' need for care in times of extreme dependency. For Rawls, for example, persons with extreme dependencies are not among the original contractors, and variations among need (created, e.g., by handicaps, pregnancy, and childhood) are not factored into the distribution of primary goods. The dependencies of infancy, childhood, old age, temporary or chronic physical or mental illness, and long-term disabilities mean that "any real society is a care-giving and a care-receiving society, and must therefore discover ways of coping with these facts of human neediness and dependency that are compatible with the self-respect of the recipients and do not exploit the caregivers." Martha Nussbaum recommends that liberal theory would do better to begin with a more Aristotelian conception of humans that can accord dignity to our animality, and not just our moral personality, and that takes neediness to be a basic feature of human life.

Both Elizabeth Spelman and Virginia Held drew attention to caring practices conducted within families. But the family, as Martha Nussbaum observes, has often been exempted from evaluation and regulation in liberal political theory. She argues that both political protections and regulations of the family should be guided by attention to the ways in which families may both enable and undermine human capabilities.

The needs, both large and small, of strangers and persons with whom we have ongoing relationships provide endless opportunities for beneficence. How to balance a duty of beneficence against concern for one's own happiness has been a recurrent theoretical problem in moral philosophy. And for any version of an ethics of care, a major task has been justifying a robust moral attention to others' needs without overburdening the caretaker. Barbara Herman takes on just this theoretical task in "The Scope of Moral Requirement." Contrary to Martha Nussbaum, Barbara Herman argues that Kantian philosophy can ground serious moral attention to human neediness, both because of the value attached to rational agency in Kantian philosophy and because others' happiness is an obligatory end. In the course of working out the relationship between our own and others' happiness, Barbara Herman argues that it is a mistake to see them as competing considerations. In growing up and living in a moral culture, we learn to take both our own moral perfection and others' interests into account in the process of choosing our own conception of happiness. And in the course of deciding how many and what kinds of relationships we will have with others, we shape the level of relational burden that we must assume. In taking on relationships, however, we also make ourselves vulnerable to others' bad luck, which generates unexpected emergency needs and limits what we would otherwise desire to do.

Susan Wolf's essay takes up, in a different way, the topic of how luck partially determines what we ought to do for others. She invites us to reexamine our intuitions about Bernard Williams's well-known example of moral luck—the case of the truck driver who negligently fails to repair his brakes and, unluckily, hits a child who darts into the road. Whereas the rationalist position that blameworthiness should track the degree of recklessness, not actual consequences, is intuitively appealing, we may also feel that the truck driver's emotional and practical response should track the level of harm done, not just the degree of negligence. Susan Wolf argues that these mixed intuitions are best explained if we assume that there are *two* kinds of responsibility at issue in cases of moral luck—*accepting* responsibility for the degree of moral fault, and *taking* responsibility for the unintended and unchosen effects of one's acts. Such responsibility taking is a necessary virtue given how "thoroughly in the world with others" human agents are.

In my contribution, I approach the question of what we ought to do for others from yet a different direction. In addition to giving others what we owe them, commonly decent people also give others "moral gifts" of mercy, forgiveness, needed directions, pleasantries, and the like. Acts of common decency, however, have an oddly hybrid character. They are not obligatory, but they are not fully morally elective either: one *ought* to treat others with common decency. I suggest that local gift-giving conventions determine which acts count as common decencies. Once in place, those conventions convert formerly supererogatory acts into ones that are simply to be expected from any minimally well-formed agent.

Margaret Walker, in "Resentment and Assurance," also takes up the theme that our moral expectations of each other are shaped by shared norms that are constitutive of our common life. Taking issue with the narrowness of philosophically familiar analyses of resentment, Margaret Walker argues that resentment registers threats to expectations based on shared norms or to one's standing to insist on those norms. The relevant norms are not all ones that philosophers typically take to be moral ones. Resentment is occasioned by a wide array of social boundary violations that involve harm, loss, exploitation, impropriety, status demotion, slights, and social offense. Walker thus invites us to contextualize moral wrongs within a broad spectrum of boundary violations occasioning the reactive attitude of resentment. She also reminds us that expressions of resentment play a crucial role in the "ongoing definition and enforcement of the standards of many types by which we live."

In a different way, Claudia Card also stresses our normative stake in preserving the shared world in which we have a social identity. In "Genocide and Social Death," she explains why it is important to include genocide on the list of war crimes even though the acts that occur in genocidal programs (e.g., rape, torture, and degradation) are already war crimes. The distinctive harm inflicted by genocide is *social* death. Genocide aims at the destruction of individuals' culture through such acts as mass murder, war rape, forcible sterilization, and removing and reeducating a group's children. The intolerability of the harm of social death is constitutive of genocide's evilness.

Survivors of genocide and terrorist attack, those subjected to highly inegalitarian social regimes, neglected and traumatized children, and the homeless and starving are all likely to lack basic trust in their social environments. In "Demoralization, Trust, and the Virtues," Annette C. Baier argues that trust in one's fellow humans is the starting point for developing moral virtues. The virtues themselves are best understood as regulating our attitude toward some aspect of our mutual vulnerability to others' good and ill will in ways that sustain a climate of trust. Demoralization occurs when we lose the social confidence that made it possible to "keep going as a functioning member of a group with a shared life." Thus the peculiar horror and viciousness of terrorism is not the destruction of life but the demoralizing destruction of trust.

For Annette Baier, trust is the Ur-virtue. For Robin S. Dillon, arrogance is the Ur-vice. Starting from an array of examples of arrogance drawn from everyday life, Robin Dillon examines three interpretations of what makes arrogance both irrational and a vice. It is especially the third interpretation that illuminates what makes arrogance so strikingly vicious: arrogance involves arrogating to oneself the authority to pass off as moral law standards that in fact merely serve to falsely boost one's self-esteem. To the extent that the arrogant demand others' self-abasement, arrogance is also the vice of seeking to corrupt others' moral standards. Thus arrogance impedes both the arrogant person's capacity for moral agency and the agency of those whom he treats as his inferiors.

A person's arrogance, then, provides one very good reason for not trusting his or her moral judgments. But are there other bases for distrusting others' moral understandings? The question is an important one in educational contexts, where liberal and multicultural projects assume that it is important to be exposed to socially different others' moral values and interpretations but where we sometimes lack the resources to critically evaluate those viewpoints. When we cannot evaluate the merit of another's moral viewpoint, what is the appropriate attitude to adopt? Trust? Wonder? Distrust? In "Diversity, Trust, and Moral Understanding," Marilyn Friedman explores just this question.

Open, inclusive discussion of a plurality of moral perspectives has also been an ideal in both discourse ethics and feminism. But in real discourse situations, inequalities of power have often motivated nonhegemonic groups to close, rather than open, their practices to outside moral scrutiny. As Alison M. Jaggar observes in "Globalizing Feminist Ethics," African women have often rejected Western feminists' entitlement to criticize clitoridectomy. Alison Jaggar argues that temporarily closing off external scrutiny may be essential for nonhegemonic groups to develop a shared moral language and perspective adequate to express the group's interests. In creating a global feminist discourse community, Western feminists in particular will need to be mindful of the effects of power inequalities on the possibilities of constructing a shared feminist agenda.

It is tempting to equate the moral progress that is supposed to result from open and inclusive discussions of alternative moral perspectives with the acquisition of better moral *beliefs* and a more adequate system of moral *concepts*. Michele Moody-Adams challenges this conception of moral progress, arguing that real moral progress is better measured by changes in individual *behavior* and in social *practices*. Real moral progress involves broad-scale social change, and such change is unlikely to be spurred merely by philosophical theorizing. It is instead the actions of engaged social critics and political actors—"moral gadflies," who take potentially severe personal risks—that enable moral progress in a society. Social failure to develop appropriately deep moral understandings is less likely a result of inadequate moral concepts than of incentives to critically scrutinize existing social practices.

The essays by Marilyn Friedman, Alison Jaggar, and Michele Moody-Adams draw attention to the variety of social factors that impede or facilitate moral understanding in inegalitarian societies. In "The Improvisatory Dramas of Deliberation," Amelie Oksenberg Rorty argues that the actual practice of both deliberation and philosophic reasoning is shaped by uncontrolled contingencies that are inevitable aspects of real dialogic process. Reasoning (even seemingly solitary reasoning) is best viewed as an improvisatory, dialectical, accident-prone drama, shaped, among many other things, by one's opponent's rhetorical skills, attitude, and credentials and one's own background agendas. But if real deliberation is affected by psychological and sociological factors, what does this imply for philosophers' idealized normative theories of deliberation? Amelie Rorty explores the ideas that idealized models cannot be regulative for beings like us, that more sophisticated normative models will incorporate sensitivity to the dramatic elements of decision making, and that normative theories are themselves produced within improvisatory dramas.

Reasoning selves are not only participants in improvisatory dramas, they are also authors of self-narratives about their lives as moral subjects. Diana Tietjens Meyers asks why narrative theory is especially attractive at this moment in history.

One reason, she suggests, is that self-narratives easily incorporate themes from competing philosophical models of the self—the unified self, the communitarian self, the psychoanalytic self, the feminist relational self, and the embodied self—enabling a more complex account of deliberation and agency. Narrative theory also clarifies how people can be shaped by internalized oppression "and yet retain their capacity to shape self-determined moral lives." Diana Meyers extends narrative theory by offering an account of the competencies that enable individuals to tell credible narratives about themselves.

By drawing attention to political, psychological, social-structural, and sociological factors, several essays challenge idealized and hyperrational accounts of deliberating agents (see especially the essays by Jaggar, Moody-Adams, Rorty, and Meyers). The essays by Christine M. Korsgaard, Karen Jones, and Marcia Baron call into question a different feature of hyperrational accounts—the opposition of emotion to rationality.

The familiar Combat Model pits reason against emotion as rivaling motivating forces in a person and explains bad action as the result of emotion overcoming the person. This model, however, as Korsgaard observes, gives us no account of the *person* who is supposed to choose between these two forces. The Constitutional Model, originating with Plato but adopted by Kant as well, gives a better account of the person, reason, and passion. Just as a *polis* can act because it has a constitution that unifies its parts by assigning to them different functions, so persons act by giving themselves a "constitution" that assigns to reason and emotion different functions. Bad action results not from an *emotion* pushing the person around but from the *person's* choice to constitute herself according to a principle that subordinates morality to inclination rather than assigning inclination its proper role of making proposals that reason must then decide to act on or not.

Christine Korsgaard implies that emotions are neither rational nor irrational, persons are. Even so, there is room to evaluate the rationality of emotions according to the "proposals" they make. Karen Jones pursues this line of inquiry in "Emotional Rationality as Practical Rationality." Starting from the assumption that emotions are constituted by patterns of perceptual salience, interpretation, and inference that affect how we frame choice situations and thus what situational considerations we take to be reason giving, she argues that emotional rationality is best understood as the rationality of good, practical perception—or framings. Correct framings latch onto those situational features that are reason giving because they fit with what one should value. A person's emotions, then, might be said to be rational to the extent that they reliably focus her attention on what she should take to be reason-giving considerations.

It is just this sort of account of the rationality of emotions that is useful in understanding the nature of the heat of passion defense in killings. Marcia Baron argues that this defense should not be seen as simply a (partial) excuse that appeals to the overpowering force of emotion (akin to temporary insanity) and a resultant loss of self-control. The idea of provocation has been and, Marcia Baron argues, should continue to be central to heat of passion defenses. What provokes are situational features that merit extreme distress or anger. Heat of passion defenses, then, are best understood as hybrid defenses, offering a partial excuse of impaired agency but, equally important, a partial justification: "This is how a good person would (or in other cases, might well) react." If so, the burden falls on the legal system to eliminate sexist biases in what it does and does not count as provocation.

Notes

1. "Outsider-within" is Patricia Hill Collins's term for black women intellectuals in the academy. The term seems apt for women generally in philosophy. See Collins, *Black Feminist Thought*, 2nd ed. (New York: Routledge, 2000).

2. Sally Haslanger, "Gender and Race: (What) Are They? (What) Do We Want Them to Be?" *Nous* 34 (2000): 31–55, has suggested that one way of getting at what gender and race *are* is to begin by asking what we want those categories *for*: "What is the point of having these concepts? What cognitive or practical task do they (or should they) enable us to accomplish?" She argues that, at least from a feminist point of view, we want those concepts for the purpose of conducting theoretical inquiries that will enable us to understand racial and sexual oppression and to work toward equality. Because we need them for primarily political purposes, the concepts of gender and race that will be most useful are themselves political—those that, for example, see gender not primarily as an aspect of personality or subjectively experienced identity but as a feature in virtue of which one is systematically subordinated along some dimension (economic, political, legal, social, etc.). I want to pursue the analogous idea that employing the category *woman philosopher* does desirable cognitive and practical work. Here, too, it will be useful to ask what particular conception of *woman philosopher* will be most useful in accomplishing that cognitive or practical task.

3. Toril Moi, *What Is a Woman? And Other Essays* (Oxford: Oxford University Press, 1999), 204.

4. Ibid., 205.

5. Ibid., 117.

6. *Harvard Magazine*, March–April 2002; www.harvard-magazine.com.

7. The echo of Adrienne Rich's classic distinction between a lesbian continuum and lesbian existence is intentional. See "Compulsory Heterosexuality and Lesbian Existence," in *The Signs Reader: Women, Gender, and Scholarship*, ed. Elizabeth Abel and Emily K. Abel (Chicago: University of Chicago Press, 1983).

I

An Ethics for Ordinary Life and Vulnerable Persons

1

Virtue and the Skills of Ordinary Life

Marcia Homiak

Surely one reason that Plato's *Republic* endures as a central text in undergraduate philosophy classes is that it asks and answers questions that remain critical for us today. Like Plato and his students, we and our students want to know why it's better to be just than to be unjust. Why, asks the *Republic*'s Glaucon at 365b–c, aren't most people right to think it's better merely to appear to be just and virtuous? Perhaps justice is for fools and simpletons, as Thrasymachus suggests at *Republic* 343c–e. When Plato asked and answered questions about the value of justice in the *Republic*, he was not being merely speculative. On the contrary, he was responding to a set of issues much debated in the Athens of his day. Fifth-century Athenian democracy required that wealthier citizens have some concern for law, justice, and the good of the entire city. But some sophists and radical critics of democracy thought, as Thrasymachus did, that the wealthy had good reason to overthrow democracy and take power for themselves. Democracy, they argued, was a violation of nature and justice was a matter of convention. Toward the end of the fifth century, these radical critics were among the leaders of two oligarchic revolutions in the city of Athens. So it mattered what the answers to Plato's questions were, for in Plato's day theoretical disputes about the nature and value of justice had political consequences.

But when we reach Aristotle's ethical writings, the tone and focus seem to have changed. Although we are still concerned with the question of how to live, the task of defending a virtuous life against critics of morality seems to have vanished. In the *Nicomachean Ethics*, for example, Aristotle does not seem to provide any argument to show that a virtuous life is good. Instead, he seems to assume that the virtues are good and that his students know and accept this. What arguments, he asks, could reform people who haven't tasted what is fine and truly pleasant, for "it is impossible, or not easy, to alter by argument what has long been absorbed as a result of one's habits."[1] For his lectures, Aristotle expects to have those who have been properly brought up and who are thus already receptive to virtue.

Aristotle's suggestion that ethical argument is best addressed to those who have already come to appreciate virtue has led some interpreters of Aristotle to view him as claiming that ethical argument takes place from within ethics itself, that virtue cannot be understood outside the perspective of virtue. For example, Jonathan Lear maintains that the "point of the *Nicomachean Ethics* is not to persuade us to be good or to show us how to behave well in the various circumstances in life: it is to give people who are already leading a happy, virtuous life insight into the nature of their own souls. The aim of the *Ethics* is to offer its readers self-understanding, not persuasion or advice."[2] If Aristotle is directing his lectures to the converted and not meeting the critical challenge directly, one may think it is a mistake to look to Aristotle for direction in how to live.[3]

In this essay I approach Aristotle's ethical views from what many may view as a hopelessly naive direction. And if it's not naive, it is surely unfashionable. I argue that Aristotle's views on the best life will be appealing not only to those who are already interested in virtue but also to those whose lives are focused around the more explicitly self-interested aims of ordinary life. Even someone like Thrasymachus, I claim, can be attracted to Aristotle's views.

My discussion is inspired by Aristotle's view that the best life is a life of unimpeded, continuous activity. As such, it is a life in which we fully realize our abilities to think and to know. The more unimpeded and continuous our activity, the more fully realized and pleasant our life is. If one cares about unimpeded activity, then one has good reason to be interested in virtue, for unimpeded activity requires virtue. So the best life is fully realized, most pleasant, and virtuous. Now Aristotle thinks we all care about unimpeded activity, for we all pursue pleasure. But ordinary human lives, he thinks, fall short of the best life because most human beings cannot fully realize their abilities to think and to know. I think Aristotle is right to think that we all care about unimpeded activity, for unimpeded activity is both pleasant and a genuine good. But I think Aristotle went wrong in thinking that ordinary human life is, or must be, far removed from it. I argue, in contrast, that reasonably unimpeded activity is within most people's grasp and that most people, once they experience unimpeded activity, will be attracted to virtue.

My essay is organized as follows: I begin with a summary of Aristotle's views on unimpeded, continuous activity. Then I offer a historical explanation of what such activity may involve. I use the class of art patrons in Renaissance Florence to show how skills acquired in everyday life can be applied to widely differing tasks for which the skills were not originally intended. As patrons extend their skills in these ways, their activities become more self-realizing and hence more continuous in Aristotle's sense. Moreover, I argue that the activities of the Florentine patron class conform to some critical features of Aristotle's notion of a life lived well and happily, and I also argue that these activities, to be sustained over time, require many of Aristotle's virtues. They also require a specific kind of political community, which Renaissance Florence did not provide. So though these activities are reasonably unimpeded, they do not fully satisfy Aristotle's conditions for unimpeded activity. Nevertheless, I argue that examples like this show that reasonably unimpeded activity is an important human good and that it is genuinely desirable to, and within the grasp of, ordinary people, even those who, like Thrasymachus, claim no interest in virtue. Aristotle's texts then, I argue, do provide direction in how to live—direction that we are well advised to take.

The Activity of the Best Life

I begin with a brief summary of, but not an argument for, some of Aristotle's claims about "activity." I try only to set Aristotle's remarks into an acceptable sequence of ideas. Although there are various ways in which Aristotle uses the words commonly translated as "action" or "activity,"[4] for my purposes the crucial distinction is between actions that Aristotle calls "complete" (or "perfect") activities (*energeiai* or *praxeis*) and actions that are mere "movements" (*kinēseis* or *poiēseis*).[5]

Aristotle discusses this distinction at *Metaphysics* 1048b18–35 and *NE* 1174a14–b14. These passages suggest that when an action is its own end or when the point of an action lies in its very exercise, it is a *praxis* or *energeia* (usually translated as an "activity"). On the other hand, when an action aims at an end outside itself or when the point of an action lies in a result that is produced, it is a *poiēsis* or *kinēsis* (variously translated as a "production," "doing," or "movement"). Of doings, their point is to bring it about that *p*. When they bring it about that *p*, they come to a definite end (they have a limit) and are finished. Doings are specified by their ends, so the different states of affairs they bring about serve to distinguish them. Learning, walking from one place to another, and house building are examples Aristotle gives of doings. Unlike doings, activities have themselves as their ends, and so they are what they are at each moment of their being. In this sense they are "complete" or "perfect" (*teleios*). Because activities contain their own ends and do not merely aim to bring it about that *p*, they do not have limits and can be continued indefinitely. Understanding, thinking, living well or happily, and enjoying are examples Aristotle gives of activities.

In the *Nicomachean Ethics* Aristotle writes that pleasure is closely associated with activity[6] and is asserted of activity. Any exercise of our capacities or faculties is a form of activity and so is pleasant (*NE* 1153a10–11). When something gets in the way of our activity and hinders its exercise, the activity is impeded. The more unimpeded an activity, the more pleasant it is (*NE* 1153b16–17). An activity that goes on wholly unimpeded is complete or perfect[7] and so is most pleasant. Aristotle notes some obvious impediments to activity such as illness, the body's natural deterioration from age, and the environment (*NE* 1153b17–19), as well as moral corruption (*NE* 1154b11–15; cf. 1176a15–19). So a morally vicious person's activity is never full and unimpeded. Since pleasure is a sign of the perfection of activity, a morally vicious person's life is less pleasant than the life of a virtuous person— and less happy, for living happily is perfect and unimpeded activity. To the extent, then, that one's life is one of unimpeded activity, to that extent it is virtuous, happy, and pleasant.

Aristotle realizes that in many actions there is an element both of activity and of doing. In such cases, the end includes both the activity itself and some result beyond the activity. Aristotle's examples include the activities of the statesman and the general (NE 1177b4–18). The general's action has as an end the exercise of his knowledge of military strategy (so his action is an activity), but he also aims to win the battle, so his action also has as an end a result beyond the exercise of his skill (so his action is also a doing). Similarly, although the statesman's action has as an end the exercise of the statesman's knowledge of how to organize and administer the city's life (an activity), the statesman also has as an end to secure the best life for the city and its citizens (a doing).

Now Aristotle thinks that the best life for a human being is a life of activity, not of doing (NE 1098a16–17). So the point of our life (our final end) cannot be to bring something about, for if it were, then what would we do when the end is attained? Most of the time Aristotle writes as if the exercise of the moral virtues is our end and constitutes the best life for human beings. But, as the examples above suggest, Aristotle also seems to think that if the general's courage served to bring about the end of hostile action, so that no further military courage were necessary, this would be to bring the general's activity to an end, and inactivity is tantamount to being asleep or being dead. Similarly, if the statesmen's justice and other virtues actually secured the best city and best citizens, the statesman's activity would come to an end. Aristotle's response to this problem is to find some activity that, by containing its own end, does not also aim to bring something about. In this sense, it is complete in itself and continuous. It does not come to an end and so is "endless."

Aristotle seems to think that in ordinary human life we do not have fully unimpeded or continuous activity (NE 1175a4–5). Our activity always contains an element of doing and so fails fully to contain its own end. Nevertheless, we can get close to fully unimpeded activity. We get as close as we can when we engage in a special kind of intellectual activity that aims only at its own exercise. This is theōria (contemplation), which Aristotle describes late in the Nicomachean Eth- ics, in Book X. When we engage in this activity, we contemplate the eternal truths of the universe and come as close as we can to the gods, whose lives consist wholly of contemplation. Theōria thus becomes Aristotles candidate for a human beings final end. In NE X.7 it is the best activity of which we are capable, for it is most continuous. It is also most pleasant. And it is most continuous and most pleasant because it is the activity that fully realizes the characteristic abilities of the human being, which are abilities to think and reason. So it is fully self- realizing activity and hence most self-sufficient.

Many readers are disappointed by Aristotle's claims in NE X. Contemplative activity seems far too restrictive to count as the best human life. And as something approaching the divine, it seems too far removed from ordinary life to be the best life for mortals.[8] Moreover, the suggestion is that only some will succeed in contemplating, in fully realizing their abilities to think and to know. One way out of this difficulty is to argue that the best life is a composite of different goods, with contemplative activity being the best of the various goods within the best life.[9] I take a different approach. Aristotle thinks that we all want to think and to know (*Metaphysics* 980a21). Indeed, we all enjoy engaging in activity, and there is some element of Aristotle's activity in most of what we do. We should not then, I think, expect a great gap between the best life and the goods and pleasures of ordinary life. I argue that the unimpeded activity of ordinary life is not far removed from the activity Aristotle views as most continuous and best. So the best human life is within most people's grasp and can be seen by them as desirable and good. It's in this way that Aristotle's texts offer us direction in how to live.

A Historical Example

First we need a better sense of what unimpeded activity may actually involve. Because Aristotle's discussions of unimpeded activity are brief and schematic, I'll put them aside for the moment. I'll turn, instead, to an example of activity that is neither ancient nor modern. It is drawn from Michael Baxandall's study of Florentine art patronage in *Painting and Experience in Fifteenth-Century Italy*.[10] Baxandall's discussion is useful for my purposes because it shows how ordinary human activity can be reasonably unimpeded and how such activity can become even more unimpeded under the right social conditions. Moreover, because it is ordinary activity—activity within almost anyone's grasp—it is activity that persons of varying moral persuasion may find attractive.

Baxandall's central contention is that the way in which we perceive complicated pictorial images depends on the cognitive skills we happen to possess—our interpretive categories and models, our habits of inference and analogy. Baxandall's aim is to show that the fifteenth-century Florentine client class for art (and especially for paintings) had a distinctive set of interpretive skills that they used in observing works of art and that accounts for their artistic tastes. Moreover, Baxandall argues, artists, having the same skills themselves, knew clients had these skills and expected that clients would use them in their observations of art. This mutual dependence of painters' and clients' skills explains the aesthetic tastes of Florentine patrons, for the paintings clients enjoyed were those that demanded the use of the skills they were accustomed to employ in ordinary life. Baxandall describes the relationship between painting and viewer in this way:

> A fifteenth-century man looking at a picture was curiously on his mettle. He was aware that the good picture embodied skill and he was frequently assured that it was the part of the cultivated beholder to make discriminations about that skill, and sometimes even to do so verbally. The most popular fifteenth-century treatise on education . . . reminded him: "The beauty and grace of objects, both natural ones and those made by man's art, are things it is proper for men of distinction to be able to discuss with each other and appreciate." Looking at [a specific] painting, a man with intellectual self-respect was in no position to remain quite passive; he was obliged to discriminate. . . . A man's capacity to distinguish a cer-

tain kind of form or relationship of forms will have consequences for the attention with which he addresses a picture. For instance, if he is skilled in noting proportional relationships, or if he is practiced in reducing complex forms to compounds of simple forms . . . these skills may well lead him to order his experience of [a specific painting] differently from people without these skills, and much more sharply than people whose experience has not given them many skills relevant to the picture. . . . Much of what we call "taste" lies in this, the conformity between discriminations demanded by a painting and skills of discrimination possessed by the beholder. We enjoy our own exercise of skill, and we particularly enjoy the playful exercise of skills which we use in normal life very earnestly. If a painting gives us opportunity for exercising a valued skill and rewards our virtuosity with a sense of worthwhile insights about that painting's organization, we tend to enjoy it: it is to our taste. (p. 34)

What skills did clients acquire in ordinary life that they later used in discriminating among paintings? In fifteenth-century Florence, the art patron was most likely a wealthy businessman. He was also a devout Christian, who regularly attended religious services and festivals. He may also have been a theatergoer and a social dancer. Baxandall argues that from all these ordinary activities—of business, religion, and social life—the art patron acquired skills relevant to his observations of art. Of the various interpretive skills discussed by Baxandall, I will focus on the specific mathematical skills used in Florentine business life, for it's this mathematical knowledge that can be most usefully understood in Aristotelian terms.

To begin, it will help to distinguish the Florentine's acquisition of mathematical knowledge from its later use.[11] As Baxandall notes, acquisition took place in the schools. After learning to read and write in the primary schools, most boys moved on to secondary school, where the focus was on mathematics. Their command of mathematics included nothing more and nothing less than elementary geometry and arithmetic: geometry to gauge volume and arithmetic to determine proportions and to measure distance and ratios. Though some students went on to university, most middle-class people ended their formal education with the mastery of elementary mathematics. Later, Baxandall explains, these same mathematical skills of categorization, analogy, and inference were deployed by merchants and bankers in their business dealings. Businessmen used geometry to reduce irregular masses and voids to combinations of manageable geometric bodies in order to measure the volume of nonstandardsized containers such as barrels, sacks, and bales. And both merchants and bankers used arithmetic to determine the ratios required for solving the problems of currency exchange.

Although it is not Baxandall's aim to explain further what is involved in either acquisition or application, we can isolate some important features shared by both.[12] (1) The first, perhaps obvious point to note is that there is some purpose to both acquisition and use. An aim of acquisition is to learn how to measure volume and how to determine proportions and distances, and an aim of application is to facilitate business dealings. Competent others then decide whether these aims have been accomplished more or less well. So (2) during both acquisition and application, individuals exhibit their knowledge in ways that are observed and judged by others. (3) Neither acquisition nor application is without challenge because specific problems, both in school and in business, are varied, complex, and unpredictable. Finally, (4) when acquired skill is used and assessed competently in the ways described above, its use is self-realizing, and the satisfaction gained from competent use enhances self-esteem.

Baxandall argues that the same interpretive skills acquired for use in business—the mathematical skills of gauging volume and of determining proportions and ratios—were given new application in assessing works of art. The points we noted above apply here as well: (1) looking at a picture had a purpose that could be more or less well achieved. The purpose was to figure something out about the picture and to communicate that insight. (2) Competent others determined how well the purpose was achieved. This is what Baxandall means when he says that a fifteenth-century beholder of a picture was on his mettle. The observer knew that other competent observers expected him to make judgments of the picture. (3) That looking at a picture tested the use of his skills in ways that competent others could assess indicates that looking at the picture posed a challenge that could be met. (4) Finally, if the beholder was acknowledged to have used his skills well, his use of his skills was self-realizing and enhanced his self-esteem.

The beholder's use of his skills is actually more complicated. Because better pictorial art was not ready-made, patrons had to commission paintings, and pictures were designed to meet the client's specifications. Baxandall notes that a client's interpretive skills often influenced the specifications he provided in the process of commissioning the painting and that painters were aware of this.[13] In many cases painters expected, for example, that clients could recognize and appreciate painters' use of mathematical perspective and proportionality.[14] That clients often wanted paintings to provoke the use of their business skills added a dimension of personal choice and self-expression to the commissioning of art that was absent from business dealings. It also served to add another dimension of competent judging to the client's experience of art. When clients were judged to have chosen well by both painters and by other patrons, these two different positive forms of assessment heightened the satisfaction clients received from reflecting about art.

Once our businessman has applied his interpretive skills successfully to art—both in commissioning it and in observing it—we can say that he is more fully realized than he was before, for he has extended his mathematical knowledge to areas for which it was not originally intended. His knowledge has proven to be highly adaptable.

The businessman's use of mathematics suggests a view of self-realization according to which an individual need not develop and apply *new* skills in order to be more fully realized over time. Rather, an individual can become more fully realized by continuing to use his acquired skills in varied contexts that pose difficulty and challenge, where success or failure can be assessed by competent judges. Although the stereotypical picture of the "Renaissance man" suggests the utopian Marxist idea[15] of someone who has developed all (or many) of his *different* powers, the picture I've drawn from Baxandall's study is of someone who has developed a *highly adaptable* set of skills that can be applied to widely different tasks and situations.

Happiness and Continuous Activity

Now we are better positioned to return to Aristotle's views on doing and activity. When the Florentine businessman uses his mathematics to conduct business transactions, this use seems to be a "doing" in Aristotle's sense. The aim of the use is to bring it about that a transaction is successfully completed. When the application of his knowledge reaches that end, the application is finished. But his business dealings also contain an element of "activity" in Aristotle's sense. As we have noted, the irregularly shaped commodities used in international commerce and banking presented difficult geometrical problems of measurement. Currency exchange posed complex arithmetic problems since each city had its own currency and its own weights and measures. Surely when the businessman responds successfully to these challenges, he takes pleasure not only in having brought his dealings to a successful conclusion but also in the very exercise of his knowledge. He enjoys discovering how to solve the mathematical problems posed by business, and he also enjoys having understood.

When the businessman applies his mathematical knowledge to art appreciation, we find another combination of doing and activity. Here the aim is to discover and communicate some insight about a painting. When that aim is accomplished, that particular application of his knowledge (the doing) is finished. And when that aim is accomplished, the businessman has figured out something about the painting. He has solved a different sort of problem, as it were. Here, too, he enjoys having understood. But an interesting thing about his having enjoyed understanding the painting is that there seems no nonarbitrary point at which this communication or understanding will stop. Rather, it makes sense to think that his having figured out something about the painting will lead him to want to figure out something else. The desire to understand and the activity of understanding do not seem to have any natural termination points. Our businessman enjoys both having understood and understanding.

These points are not simply speculative. Baxandall notes that mathematics held a central place in Florentine life and that Florentines prided themselves on their prowess in mathematics. Mathematics figured centrally not only in business and art but in other leisure activities as well (in puzzles, games, jokes, and reading).[16] One must add to these uses politics, for fifteenth-century Florence was an oligarchy ruled by bankers and businessmen, where both city officials and taxpayers needed mathematical skill to determine the value of taxable property in accordance with Florence's elaborate tax system. When the banker Giovanni Rucellai remarked of arithmetic that "it equips and spurs on the mind to examine subtle matters,"[17] he suggested not only that the use of mathematics was valued but also that it was indefinitely extendable. So the application of mathematical knowledge looks to be an example of an activity that, from Aristotle's perspective, is continuous and pleasant because it is self-realizing.

Still, even if we grant that the Florentine businessman's use of his mathematical knowledge is a continuous and pleasant activity in Aristotle's sense, this does not seem to get us very far. One might ask what all this has to do with Aristotle's views on the activity of the best life. Such a life, we remember, is lived well and happily, its activity not impeded by moral vice. So among our first questions must be this one: is there any reason to think there is a relationship between the pragmatic or playful use of mathematical knowledge and living happily or virtuously?

It is not hard to see a relationship if we focus on the question of living happily, for the Florentine businessman's life is characterized by many of the features Aristotle considers crucial to a life lived happily.[18] According to Aristotle, the happy person has a particular attitude toward himself and his life: he likes who he is and is glad to be alive (NE 1168b33–34). He is not miserable and filled with self-hatred (NE 1166b11–26). Moreover, his life contains the major good things, such as wealth, honor, family, and friendship (NE 1099a31–b7, 1153b17–19). Of the Florentine businessman, we have good reason to think he likes who he is and is not miserable and that he possesses some major good things. We have good reason to think this if other things are equal—and because I am in no position to speculate on other parts of his life (such as his relations with his family or with his god), I will assume that they are. First, as we have seen, the Florentine enjoys the activities in which he regularly participates, for he enjoys the mathematical thinking that is a large part of his business and social life. Second, as a citizen of a community that prizes the exercise of mathematical skill, he believes that enjoying his intellectual abilities is a good and he knows he possesses this good. Third, as someone who is "on his mettle" before a painting, he enjoys the respect of others whom he esteems, including his fellow art patrons and the skilled artists whose work he appreciates. Fourth, his life contains some important major goods, such as material resources, a political community that supports his values and aims, and a social life. In short, his major aims (as far as we are aware of them) are being accomplished, he recognizes this, and he is satisfied with how things are going. But we can go further. Fifth, according to Aristotle, an individual who is living happily thinks that his life is genuinely rewarding because it is a fully human and self-realizing life (NE 1097b24–1098a17). Our businessman does lead a reasonably self-realized life because he has sufficiently developed his capacities to think and judge and he has achieved sufficient understanding of his world such that he desires to continue to think and judge and to gain further understanding. There is no natural stopping point for these activities, so our businessman has an ongoing source of enjoyment and of esteem from others who think and judge and understand. His activities, then, are reasonably unimpeded.

Leisure and Continuous Activity

We have shown that the Florentine businessman's life is characterized by many of the features Aristotle considers crucial to a life lived happily and well. Still, we face two problems. The first I have already mentioned. It is that there seems to be no relationship between the Florentine businessman's life and virtuous activity. The second problem explains why we face the first. I've been looking for indefinitely extendable activity on the assumption that that's the kind of interest to ordinary persons with explicitly self-interested aims. But if the indefinitely extendable activity turns out to be morally neutral, as the use of mathematical knowledge is, then why isn't it a mistake to look for a relation between such activity and virtue? The answer is that Aristotle's texts suggest precisely this — namely, that there is an ethical dimension to highly adaptable thinking. Although these suggestions are brief and undetailed, we can find them in two places — in Aristotle's discussion of leisure and "music"[19] in the *Politics* and his discussion of tragedy in the *Poetics*.

First, let's consider the discussion of leisure in *Politics* VII 14–15, which will help us see the point of the later discussions of music and tragedy. In *Politics* VII Aristotle is concerned to explain the place of leisure in the best state. In other, deviant states, according to Aristotle, rulers mistake both the nature and importance of leisure. In militaristic states, on the one hand, rulers consider the point of leisure to provide needed rest so that renewed military activity is possible. Considered in itself, leisure is passive, inactive, and not viewed as a good; it does not provide an occasion for the exercise of virtue and is only a necessary means to achieve the best life, which is one of activity devoted to war and military supremacy (*Pol.* 1334a2–9, 36–b2). In vulgar states, leisure is also viewed as inactive, but in these states inactivity is viewed as a good. In fact, here the life of leisure, which is devoted to passive enjoyment and pleasure, is considered the best life; it brings a freedom from work that only the ruling class can achieve (*NE* 1095b19–22). But in Aristotle's view, leisure is not passive, for it provides the opportunity for the exercise of important virtues. It is important, Aristotle says, not only that we "work properly" (*ascholein orthōs*) but also that we "be capable of being at leisure well" (*scholazein dunasthai kalōs*), for leisure is the "one beginning of everything" (*archē pantōn mia*) (*Pol.* 1337b31–32).

How is being at leisure well the beginning of everything? Aristotle's discussions of music and tragedy help us see what he means. First, let's consider music. Aristotle writes that there are three possible social roles for music: (1) Music is a form of amusement or relaxation like sleep or drinking (*Pol.* 1339a16–17). (2) It is also a crucial ingredient in the process of character formation (*Pol.* 1339a24). Musical modes serve to express the character of the individuals depicted in poetic texts, and when someone performs, he comes to experience the sorts of emotions appropriate to particular character states.[20] Finally, (3) there is a more cognitive role for music: music is for "intellectual enjoyment" (*Pol.* 1338a22, 1339b5), for "practical wisdom" (*phronēsis*), and for "learning" (*mathēsis*) (*Pol.* 1339a26, 36). As explanation, Aristotle says that we ought to learn music — that is, both to perform it and to appreciate it—so that we can develop the ability to "judge" (*kritein*) musical performances correctly, especially of good dispositions and noble actions (*Pol.* 1340a13–18). By engaging our reflective powers, music aids in the development of our interpretive skills and practical knowledge, so that we can better judge and understand what we see and hear.[21]

We find more explicit comments on the importance of acquiring interpretive skills in the *Poetics*. In Book IX Aristotle writes that the learning involved in actively watching a play, like training in music, sharpens our ability to judge correctly. In attending to poetry we develop some grasp of the "universals" (*ta katholou*) that govern human activity; we learn "what such or such a kind of man will probably or necessarily say or do."[22] At the beginning of *Poetics* IV, Aristotle broadens the idea that actively attending to cultural performances sharpens our interpretive skills; he suggests that all learning develops and strengthens our ability to judge critically and properly the nature of the world. Representation, he says here, is natural to human beings. We learn from it and delight in works of representation. In explaining why this is true, he writes that "to be learning something is the greatest of pleasures not only to the philosopher but also to the rest of mankind, however small their capacity for it; the reason of the delight in seeing the picture is that one is at the same time learning—gathering the meaning of things" (*Poet.* 1448b13–17).

Here Aristotle does not elaborate on what he means. I read the point of these passages to be overarching: that training in music and poetry, indeed in cultural activities generally, helps us sharpen our interpretive skills so that we can gather the meaning of things and achieve some insightful understanding of the world. This reading is consistent with other general comments Aristotle makes about the arts and artists. In the famous beginning of the *Metaphysics*, he writes that we can gain knowledge of particulars from experience, but from art we can learn the "universal," the "why," and the causes of things (*Met.* 981a1–b10). These interpretive skills, of learning to find the universal and the cause, are ones we will also use in our ethical lives. So it is no surprise that Aristotle said about music at *Politics* 1339a26 that one of its functions is for "practical wisdom" (*phronēsis*).

These passages from the *Politics*, *Poetics*, and *Metaphysics* indicate that Aristotle does recognize the value of acquiring and developing highly adaptable interpretive skills of judgment and discrimination. There is no natural stopping point in using these skills, and as we've seen, Aristotle is quite explicit about their eventual use in ethical situations. Here, then, as in the Florentine case, we have an example of continuous activity, yet the activity is ordinary and within the scope of any rational being.

Virtue and Continuous Activity

With Florentine art patrons and with Aristotelian music students and theater spectators, we have found examples of "endless" activity that is highly pleasurable to those who engage in it. Since Aristotle thinks we all take pleasure in learning (or, perhaps more correctly, in successfully applying what we've learned), we have no reason to think such pleasure is experienced only by paragons of virtue: to the extent that our life is one of continuous and unimpeded activity, to that extent it is virtuous. The key to the relationship between activity and virtue lies in understanding the sociopolitical conditions that serve to foster continuous activity. These conditions themselves require virtue. Both the sociopolitical conditions and the role played by virtue in sustaining them are clear from the Florentine example.

The first social condition required for continuous activity is the right kind of companionship. We learned from Baxandall that in fifteenth-century Florence art patrons were expected both by other patrons and by painters to apply their mathematical knowledge to paintings. Often patrons were accustomed to discussing art among themselves, and they were judged by other patrons on their success at interpreting what they saw. The activity of judging occurred in public, so to speak, because it took place among others who could competently assess both the pictures and the judging. This public context of discussion and assessment kept both patrons and painters on their mettle and thus provided an opportunity for patrons to develop their interpretive skills even further.

In the examples we drew from the *Poetics* and *Politics*, Aristotle does not mention a public context of discussion or debate, but we know that he saw the importance to an individual of having stimulating companionship. A solitary person's life is hard, he says in the *Nicomachean Ethics*, "since it is not easy for him to be continuously active all by himself; but in relation to others and in their company it is easier. Hence his activity will be more continuous" (NE 1170a4–6). Even the individual who is contemplating "does it better with colleagues" (NE 1177a34). Competent others who share our interests and abilities provoke us to think more and to achieve greater understanding of what we observe.

Given that activity is made more continuous in the company of competent others, it behooves the Florentine art patron to maintain friendly relations with others who share his interests. Thus he needs at least a small circle of associates with whom he can exchange ideas, for if he is someone who cannot maintain friendly relations with others, his activity will be impeded. This suggests that he needs some of the virtues Aristotle mentions in *Nicomachean Ethics* IV.6–8. These social virtues characterize the general ways in which we are to treat people who are not our friends and intimates; with affection added, they characterize relations among friends (NE 1126b21). The individual with these virtues is not prone to churlishness, flattery, boastfulness, or mock modesty, for these social vices make people insufferable or unfit partners in social endeavors.

But the Florentine will also need to be concerned about wider social relations that extend beyond his circle of associates. Because wider social relations can also impede his activity, he will need to take an interest in the governance of the city. He will need material resources adequate to sustain his own engagement with mathematics and with art. So he will want the city to protect and to support his own and others' commercial success, and he will want the city to encourage the creation of the leisure activities he enjoys. Given these interests and needs, it is not surprising that Florence was an oligarchy governed and administered by the same class that valued the use of mathematical knowledge and that commissioned works of art. Because the city sustained and encouraged the kind of life merchants enjoyed, we shouldn't be surprised to find the Florentine businessman willing to sacrifice his personal well-being to aid the city in times of danger and difficulty. Like Aristotle's magnanimous person, he's prepared to contribute financially to the city's defense (cf. *NE* 1122b19–23).[23] Justice is another virtue he is unwise to ignore. Greed will disrupt the friendly social relations he needs for the full development and continuity of his activities, and greed will disrupt the smooth functioning of the city.

These remarks suggest that the Florentine businessman who enjoys reasonably endless activity will take at least an instrumental interest in many of Aristotle's moral virtues, for they are needed to sustain the friendships and the political community that maintain and promote such activities. But Aristotle thinks moral virtue has more than instrumental value. It is also valuable for its own sake. Is it reasonable to think that the Florentine businessman has more than an instrumental interest in virtue? Yes, I think that it is, for as an individual comes to enjoy reasonably endless activities, he will develop new desires and motivations that will *cause* him to act virtuously. Yet these desires won't be his *reason* for acting virtuously, so they won't provide an instrumental explanation of his interest in virtue.

Consider again the Florentine businessman's interests as I have described them. I have said that, given that he enjoys reasonably endless activity, he will need to take an interest in a variety of the Aristotelian virtues, for these virtues serve to sustain and promote both the narrow and the wide social relations that are themselves needed to maintain and encourage such activity. He needs at least a small circle of associates with whom he can share his interests in mathematics or painting, for discussion with others will stimulate and enliven his own observations and use of his skills. But it would be odd to think he sees these relations in an instrumental way. He does not say to himself, "I have got to form at least one friendship in order to render my activity more continuous." Indeed, if that were his motivation, most likely he would not attain his aim, for a friendship isn't the sort of thing that he can both knowingly and intentionally bring about. Rather, close social ties are the result of activity he performs for a different reason—in this case, that he enjoys thinking about mathematical puzzles or paintings. As Aristotle remarks in the *Rhetoric*, we feel friendly toward those "whom we admire or who admire us. And also those with whom it is pleasant to live and spend our days."[24] Once these ties are formed, their nature will affect his other desires and tendencies. Presumably he will not be inclined to disrupt his relationships and so won't tend to exhibit the kind of behavior Aristotle associates with churlish, irritating, and boorish people. He may realize that boorish behavior will have consequences he wishes to avoid, but his desire to avoid these consequences won't be the reason he engages in friendly behavior. He won't say to himself, "To render my activity more continuous, I can't afford to irritate or offend anyone in my circle of associates." Instead of viewing the social virtues as an instrumental good, he will naturally wind up being less likely to irritate others because he has formed a set of enjoyable relationships. It is more reasonable to view him as enjoying thinking and talking with his close associates in a spirited and friendly way for its own sake.

These examples help us understand the businessman's attitude toward some of Aristotle's virtues. He may, if he is sufficiently reflective, recognize that the virtues are means to the end of reasonably continuous activity, which is an end he desires and recognizes as good. But this does not mean that he acts virtuously in order to achieve that end. As we have seen, it is more reasonable to think of virtuous action as arising naturally in him as a result of his having enjoyed reasonably continuous activity. Nor is the enjoyment he takes in continuous activity his reason for engaging in it. It is true that the enjoyment he experiences may be anticipated, for the businessman may be aware that engaging in such activity will bring enjoyment. It would be odd if he weren't so aware, for he knows that he enjoys looking at paintings. Moreover, the enjoyment may be desired, in that the businessman may realize this kind of activity is a genuine good. But that the enjoyment is both anticipated and desired does not mean the activity is undertaken for the purpose of experiencing enjoyment. The reason for engaging in the activity, as I have noted, is different—to solve the puzzle or to figure out the painting.

Can we extend the businessman's desire for continuous activity further than this? As we've seen, Aristotle thinks that a delight in learning can have profound effects because this delight tends to widen and become more general in scope. We always begin with what is familiar to us but not well understood. In ordinary life we gradually come to understand the familiar and to explain its causes. Artists know causes and why things are done as they are, and so, Aristotle writes at *Metaphysics* 981a24–b9, we think they are wise. As our understanding grows, we are able to provide explanations of broader, more wide-ranging phenomena, until we achieve some grasp of first principles that fully explain the nature of things: "For it is owing to their wonder that men both now begin and at first began to philosophize; they wondered originally at the obvious difficulties, then advanced little by little and stated difficulties about the greater matters, e.g., about the phenomena of the moon and those of the sun and the stars, and about the genesis of the universe" (*Met.* 982b11–17). In ordinary life, the Florentine businessman comes to understand how to manage his own household, to see what material and personal goods he needs and why. These reflections may prompt him to consider the role the city should take in maintaining and distributing material resources. He may even participate in these deliberations. What is to stop him from becoming someone who thinks about questions of needs and goods on an even broader scale, who enjoys thinking about and solving ethical problems? From that point, it is not too far to Aristotle's notion of the political leader whose aim is to build the best community. Or the businessman's thinking might take a different direction— from solving mathematical problems in commerce to wondering about the mathematical structure of his everyday world to thinking about the causes of the universe. We are reminded of the banker Rucellai's insight about arithmetic—that it "equips and spurs on the mind to examine subtle matters." And from there it is not too far to Aristotle's notion of the philosopher who enjoys contemplating the truths about the universe. That we can extend the businessman's thinking in these two ways—into becoming a political thinker, on the one hand, or a metaphysician, on the other hand—shows that the goods and pleasures of ordinary life are not far removed from Aristotle's vision of the best life.[25]

Yet, from Aristotle's perspective, the chances that the businessman's thinking will take either of these two directions is still low, for Florence itself is an impediment. As we have noted, Aristotle thinks that because the rulers of deviant states believe that the acquisition of external goods is an end in itself, they mistake leisure for passive enjoyments such as consumption and accumulation (NE 1095b19–21). In promoting these passive aims, deviant consumptive states tend to discourage continuous activity. Unimpeded activity is possible only in an ideal state, where, when political leaders deliberate about the community's health, education, defense, finance, and other matters, their aim is to promote the conditions under which citizens can be fully active (Pol. 1325b14–32).

In important respects, Florence is like Aristotle's deviant consumptive states. Although Florence prized mathematical knowledge and encouraged its application to noncommercial activities, these tendencies were offset by others that Aristotle associates with deviant states. The commercial success of the city promoted a desire for material accumulation and encouraged the view that wealth in itself was good.[26] Moreover, merchants ruled in their own interests and not in the interests of all citizens. Their political decisions encouraged the exploitation of labor and of the poor and sustained class division, so that civic discontent was frequent and occasionally violent. Thus fully unimpeded activity was not possible in Florence, even for those best suited pragmatically to achieve it.

One might note in concluding that neither does fully unimpeded activity seem possible in the United States, where consumerism has reached dangerous new heights, affecting every social class. As private consumptive spending has intensified over the past decades, support for public goods has eroded. Quality public education, social services, public recreational opportunities, and public cultural events are less available, which prompts middle-class families to spend money on education, security, recreation, and culture. Financial pressures on the middle class reduce their willingness to spend money on taxation and on transfer programs to the poor.[27] The pressures of a heightened consumption have served to lower quality of life and to foster the kinds of desires for a passive existence that run counter to the desire for "intellectual enjoyment" that Aristotle saw in unimpeded activity.

Concluding Remarks

This essay began by asking whether Aristotle's ethics held any attraction for someone like Thrasymachus, who thought virtue was for fools and simpletons. I hope I have shown that it does. Although Aristotle's discussions often suggest that only a few human beings can live lives of unimpeded activity, I have argued that reasonably unimpeded activity is within most people's grasp. From the example of Renaissance Florence, we saw how persons of varying moral persuasion might come to enjoy reasonably unimpeded thinking and interpreting, how they might view it as a good, and how it might function in a life that they are prepared to think of as happy. Moreover, we saw how enjoyment in reasonably continuous activity could easily give rise both to some virtuous action and to a recognition that virtuous action is needed to sustain and promote continuous activity. But we also saw that as an individual engages in reasonably continuous activity, new desires and motivations are formed. These new desires and motivations cause the individual to act virtuously, but they are not the reason the individual gives or would give for acting virtuously. Though the Florentine businessman may desire, and realize that he needs, a circle of associates in order to enjoy conversation and thinking about pictures, this isn't his reason for being mild-tempered and friendly or his reason for not being boorish and rude. He may have no reason in a commonplace sense, for his actions are a natural product of his having enjoyed thinking and conversing with his associates. The kind of life lived by the Florentine businessman, and the recognition of that life as good, is within reach of the moral critic because that life involves the development and extension of skills and desires that we have as a part of ordinary life. We are all stimulated by wonder to reflect and to understand the causes of things. We cannot argue the critic into pursuing greater continuous activity and being more virtuous, for it is not easy "to alter by argument what has long been absorbed as a result of one's habits" (NE 1179b16–18). But we can expect that, as a result of the critic's ordinary activities and relationships, he develops a desire for greater continuous activity and that this desire will eventually lead to virtue. Aristotle seems aware of this possibility when in the Categories he writes, "For the bad man, if led into better ways of living and talking [will make progress toward being better]. . . . For however slight the progress he made to begin with, he becomes ever more easily changed toward virtue, so that he is likely to make still more progress; and when this keeps happening it brings him over completely into the contrary state, provided time permits."[28]

Provided time permits. We must also say provided his community permits. Aristotle holds that reasonably unimpeded activity requires a special kind of political community, in which all citizens can receive the education and the material resources that are needed to preserve and promote unimpeded activity. Aristotle's ideal state has features that modern readers are right to find unacceptable. To achieve the best life for citizens requires, according to Aristotle, that others (e.g., manual laborers, women, and slaves) be exploited. But even if we should accept his view that a life of menial labor has moral dangers, it is a further question whether Aristotle is committed to thinking that fully unimpeded activity requires the exploitation of others.[29] If we agree with Aristotle that fully continuous activity is a good and can be the basis of a good human life, then it is more reasonable to think that the state best structured to bring about fully continuous activity secures education, health care, and a proper level of material resources for all citizens. In addition, it secures the liberties and opportunities citizens need to pursue and perform meaningful work, for meaningful work is the work we do when our activity is unimpeded.[30] These issues take us to difficult and much debated matters in contemporary political philosophy, which is not surprising. Like Plato before him, Aristotle recognized that ethics is a part of politics. Thus he ends the *Nicomachean Ethics* with the directive to study constitutions—to see what causes some states to be well and others ill administered; only then, he thinks, will we be able to see which constitution is best and what laws and customs it must use.

Notes

I am grateful to Barbara Herman, Janet Levin, and Charles Young for helpful comments on earlier versions of this essay. I also owe thanks to my colleague Eric Frank for introducing me to the study of Florentine art patronage in a course we taught together on Periklean Athens and Renaissance Florence.

1. Aristotle, *Nicomachean Ethics*, 2nd ed., trans. T. H. Irwin (Indianapolis, Ind.: Hackett, 1999), 1179b16–18. Subsequent references in the text will be to *NE*.

2. Jonathan Lear, *Aristotle: The Desire to Understand* (Cambridge: Cambridge University Press, 1988), 157. In a similar vein, Bernard Williams, *Ethics and the Limits of Philosophy* (London: Fontana Paperbacks, 1985), 51, writes that an Aristotelian agent, when he thinks about ethical and other goods, thinks from a point of view that gives special significance to ethical goods: "Looked at from the outside, this point of view belongs to someone in whom the ethical dispositions he has acquired lie deeper than other wants and preferences." See also Julia Annas, "Aristotle on Pleasure and Goodness," in *Essays on Aristotle's Ethics*, ed. Amelie Oksenberg Rorty (Berkeley: University of California Press, 1980), 290.

3. Perhaps his interest lies elsewhere: for example, in providing some sense of a virtuous person's ethical perceptions and of how she responds to the complexities of the particular situations she faces, when these complexities are often a matter of working with incommensurable or conflicting human goods. So Thomas Nagel, "The Fragmentation of Value," in *Mortal Questions* (Cambridge: Cambridge University Press, 1979), 135, lauds Aristotle for recognizing that practical dilemmas are not resolved or even adequately addressed by using general principles. And Sarah Broadie, *Ethics with Aristotle* (Oxford: Oxford University Press, 1991), denies that Aristotle argues for a "grand end" that we should strive to achieve.

4. For a helpful summary of these various uses, see the glossary of Irwin's translation of the *Nicomachean Ethics*, 315–316 ("action" and "activity").

5. My presentation of the distinction between *praxis* and *energeia*, on the one hand, and *poiēsis* and *kinēsis*, on the other hand, is inspired by the following discussions of this topic: G. C. Field, *Moral Theory* (London: Methuen, 1923), chap. viii; Antony Kenny, *Action, Emotion and Will* (London: Routledge & Kegan Paul, 1963), chap. viii; J. L. Ackrill, "Aristotle's Distinction Between *Energeia* and *Kinesis*," in *New Essays on Plato and Aristotle*, ed. R. Bambrough (London: Routledge & Kegan Paul, 1965), 121–141; Warner Wick, "The Rat and the Squirrel, or The Rewards of Virtue," *Ethics* 82 (1971): 21–32; L. A. Kosman, "Substance, Being, and *Energeia*," *Oxford Studies in Ancient Philosophy* 2 (1984): 121–149; and Irwin's discussion in Aristotle, *Nicomachean Ethics*, 315–316.

6. With this language, I try to avoid addressing the general question of whether Aristotle believes pleasure is an activity or whether he believes it is something separa-

ble from the activity that "completes" or "perfects" (*teleioi*) activity. The first view seems suggested by *NE* VII, the second by *NE* X. Aristotle seems willing to accept my position when he writes, "But do we choose life because of pleasure, or pleasure because of life? Let us set aside this question for now, since the two appear to be combined and to allow no separation; for pleasure never arises without activity, and, equally, it completes every activity" (X.4 1175a18–21). For important discussions of these issues, see G. E. L. Owen, "Aristotelian Pleasures," *Proceedings of the Aristotelian Society* 72 (1971–1972): 135–152; and J. C. B. Gosling and C. C. W. Taylor, *The Greeks on Pleasure* (Oxford: Clarendon Press, 1982), esp. chap. 11.3.

7. I follow Gosling and Taylor (see note 6, above) in thinking that Aristotle makes the same point in calling activities unimpeded and perfect.

8. For this reason Martha Nussbaum, *Fragility of Goodness* (Cambridge: Cambridge University Press, 1986), 373–377, argues that contemplation cannot be Aristotle's vision of the best life for human beings.

9. Many commentators argue that Aristotle at least sometimes takes happiness to be a composite of all intrinsic goods. Some important defenses of this view include John M. Cooper, *Reason and Human Good in Aristotle* (Cambridge, Mass.: Harvard University Press, 1975); W. F. R. Hardie, *Aristotle's Ethical Theory*, 2nd ed. (Oxford: Clarendon Press, 1980); and T. H. Irwin, *Aristotle's First Principles* (Oxford: Oxford University Press, 1988). This view has been recently challenged by Richard Kraut, *Aristotle on the Human Good* (Princeton, N.J.: Princeton University Press, 1989).

10. Michael Baxandall, *Painting and Experience in Fifteenth-Century Italy* (Oxford: Oxford University Press, 1972).

11. For a description of Florentine mathematical education and the role of mathematics in Florentine cultural life, see ibid., 86–108.

12. My discussion in this and the next paragraph is indebted to the account of self-realization offered in Jon Elster, "Self-Realization in Work and Politics: The Marxist Conception of the Good Life," in *The Main Debate: Communism vs. Capitalism*, ed. Tibor R. Machan (New York: Random House, 1987), 111–138.

13. Baxandall, *Painting and Experience*, 23.

14. Ibid., 102.

15. A famous statement of Marx's views is in *The German Ideology*. Marx writes that under capitalism labor is divided, causing each individual to have "a particular, exclusive sphere of activity, which is forced upon him and from which he cannot escape. He is a hunter, a fisherman, a shepherd, or a critical critic, and must remain so if he does not want to lose his means of livelihood; while in communist society, where nobody has one exclusive sphere of activity but each can become accomplished in any branch he wishes, society regulates the general production and thus makes it possible for me to do one thing today and another tomorrow, to hunt in the morning, fish in the afternoon, rear cattle in the evening, criticise after dinner, just as I have a mind, without ever becoming hunter, fisherman, shepherd or critic." From Robert C. Tucker, ed., *The Marx-Engels Reader*, 2nd ed. (New York: Norton, 1978), 160.

16. Baxandall, *Painting and Experience*, 101.

17. Quoted ibid., 94.

18. In my understanding of Aristotle's view of happiness, I have been influenced by Richard Kraut's treatment of "subjectivist" and "objectivist" views of happiness in "Two Conceptions of Happiness," *The Philosophical Review* 88 (1979): 167–197. I disagree with him that the standard by which Aristotle evaluates human lives is too rigid. Part of

the aim of this essay is to show that the standard is broader and more flexible than one might think.

19. "Music" is more a transliteration than a translation of the Greek *mousikē*, for which there is no English equivalent. *Mousikē* is considerably wider than what we think of as music and includes any performances that are accompanied by music, such as poetry, song, and dance. See Plato, *Republic* 376e–403c, for a sense of this wide understanding of music. In my discussion of the philosophical importance of music and tragedy, I have been influenced by David Depew, "Politics, Music, and Contemplation in Aristotle's Ideal State," in *A Companion to Aristotle's Politics*, ed. D. Keyt and F. Miller, Jr. (Oxford: Basil Blackwell, 1991), 346–380. For a general discussion of *mousikē* in Greek education, see F. A. G. Beck, *Greek Education 430–350 B.C.* (London: Methuen, 1964).

20. For a discussion that emphasizes music's role in the formation of proper emotional responses, see Nancy Sherman, *The Fabric of Character* (Oxford: Clarendon Press, 1989), chap. V, 7–8.

21. Although Aristotle devotes most of his discussion in *Politics* VIII. 5–8 to music's role in the formation of proper emotional responses, some interpreters argue that his most important contribution is in suggesting this cognitive role for music. David Depew argues that some musical forms "have a *cognitive* dimension that transcends mere entertainment, psychological catharsis, and character building by inducing reflection and learning. . . . Apparently the ability to judge music implies knowing it in a technical way; and this technical knowledge is crucial to the subsequent development of both practical and theoretical knowledge" (emphasis in original). See Depew, "Politics, Music, and Contemplation," 368.

22. As translated by I. Bywater in Jonathan Barnes, ed., *The Complete Works of Aristotle*, 2 vols. (Princeton, N.J.: Princeton University Press, 1984), *Poetics* 1451b8–9. Subsequent references in the text will be to *Poet*.

23. Aristotle's citizen would be prepared to sacrifice his life on the battlefield to defend the city he loves. But the Florentine businessman need not manifest Aristotle's physical courage, for he and his fellow city officials can (and did) use their wealth to finance mercenary armies.

24. As translated by W. R. Roberts in Barnes, *Complete Works of Aristotle*, 1381a29–31.

25. In fact, these two ways of extending the businessman's thinking correspond roughly to the two kinds of admirable lives Aristotle describes in *NE* X.7.

26. The great effort expended at this time by intellectuals to find justifications for the possession of material wealth points to the emergence of a strong desire to possess, accumulate, and display it. These justifications were often based on texts attributed to Aristotle. See Hans Baron, "Franciscan Poverty and Civic Wealth as Factors in the Rise of Humanistic Thought," *Speculum* 13 (1938): 18–25.

27. For a discussion of the social, psychological, and political effects of heightened consumerism on values and the quality of life, see Juliet B. Schor, *The Overspent American: Upscaling, Downshifting, and the New Consumer* (New York: Basic Books, 1998).

28. As translated by J. L. Ackrill in Barnes, *Complete Works of Aristotle*, 13a23–24, 25–31.

29. I argue in "Feminism and Aristotle's Rational Ideal" that Aristotle is not committed to the view that the best state requires the exploitation of some so that others can live fully unimpeded lives. See *A Mind of One's Own: Feminist Essays on Reason and*

Objectivity, ed. Louise Antony and Charlotte Witt (Boulder, Col.: Westview Press, 1993), 1–17.

30. In this connection it is interesting to note an almost casual remark at the end of John Rawls's A *Theory of Justice*, 2nd ed. (Cambridge, Mass.: Harvard University Press, 1999), 464. Rawls writes that once a just constitutional system has been established, which secures basic liberties and opportunities and the material resources needed to make these liberties and opportunities effective, no one need choose "between monotonous and routine occupations which are deadening to human thought and sensibility," and work can be made meaningful for all.

2

The Household as Repair Shop

Elizabeth V. Spelman

The human being—the entertainer formerly known as Man—is the repairing animal. Repair certainly isn't the only work humans do, nor are we the only animals that do it. And no doubt there already are plenty of venerable and captivating portraits of *Homo sapiens*—as the rational animal, the political animal, the social animal, the animal that really-and-not-just-apparently uses language, the only thinking thing that also has emotions, the only thinking thing that worries about whether it is the only thinking thing. But there is a powerful and fascinating case for regarding *Homo sapiens* as *Homo reparans*.

Repair is ubiquitous, something we engage in every day and in almost every dimension of our lives. Perhaps the most obvious kinds of repair are those having to do with the inanimate objects with which we surround ourselves—the clothes crying out for mending, the automobiles for fixing, the buildings for renovating, the works of art for restoring. But our bodies and souls also are by their very nature subject to fracture and fissure, for which we seek homely household recipes for healing and consolation or perhaps the expert ministrations of surgeons, therapists, and other menders and fixers of all manner of human woes. Moreover, relationships between individuals and among nations are notoriously subject to fraying and being rent asunder. From apologies and other informal attempts at patching things up, to courts of law, conflict mediation, and truth and reconciliation commissions, we try to reweave what we revealingly call the social fabric. No wonder, then, that *H. reparans* is always and everywhere on call: we, the world we live in, and the objects and relationships we create are by their very nature things that can break, decay, unravel, fall to pieces.

But if, across the human landscape, some kind of repair or restoration or mending or rehabilitating or reconciling is bound to be going on—or at least being considered, even if in the end rejected—pray who is doing all this work? Should we expect there to be a division of the labor of repair, just as we find some such division historically in almost every other human labor? Are some groups or "types" of people assigned certain kinds of tasks, other such groups assigned others? Is there, for example, any repair work that has a claim to being "women's work"? Is there repair work that has been considered off limits to women? Off limits to some women but not others?

Women and the Question of Tools

The broader inquiry into repair of which these reflections are a part[1] begins with a description of the work of Willie, the crackerjack mechanic in rural upstate New York who is carefully and lovingly featured in Douglas Harper's *Working Knowledge*.[2] Willie—we never learn his last name—specializes in Saab automobiles, but he also works on tractors, furnaces, and other equipment necessary for life in a remote and seasonally snow-bound part of the United States. People come to Willie for repairs, not for new cars, not to have their old ones restored to mint condition. His job is to make sure that once again the engine runs, the wheels move, the doors and windows open and close, the roof doesn't leak. If it's hard to imagine work that seems more quintessentially the work of repair, it's also hard to imagine a better candidate for the quintessential repair person. It comes as no surprise that Willie is working class, white, and male, facts faithfully reflective of the several dimensions of the division of labor that govern the kind of work he does. There are no doubt African-American, Latino, Asian-American, and Native-American repairmen across the United States. But the various construction and repair trades—especially those involving skilled labor—have historically been notoriously eager to remain lily-white. And their ranks to this day include only low numbers of women of all races and ethnicities, making it shocking to be reminded by some guild records from feudal England that female carpenters and saddlers were not uncommon[3] or to learn that the circular saw was invented by a woman.[4]

Indeed, for the most part women are much more likely to appear in pinup calendars in the offices and shops of repairmen—mechanics, plumbers, carpenters, cobblers, and so on—than as partners in such work. Graphic and pornographic depictions of women are sometimes displayed precisely in order to make the few females on the job feel uncomfortable and unwelcome[5]—only one sign that this particular area of repair in human life (at least in a country like the United States) is brimming with anxiety about whether women can and should do such work. In both new and used bookshops it's not hard to find home repair guides addressed specifically to women.[6] It's not unusual for them to begin with a bit of a pep talk:

> The fact is that women don't have to be unhandy. They are *not* inherently nonmechanical; they have been educationally deprived by their society and then trained to believe that their aptitude is low. What is most needed is authoritative assurance that "educationally deprived" does not mean "uneducable," and that, in general, the business of making repairs is far easier than most women believe.[7]

The very existence of such books and their messages of "There's no reason you can't do this stuff too, ladies!" signal a history in which women are considered unsuitable for such work, on the grounds that it is too demanding, or is something that would compromise their claim to femininity. Sometimes what slips out is an undisguised assertion of entitlement: if women take these jobs, men won't have them. For example, Mary Baird, trained as a phone repair technician, reports being admonished, "You're taking a job away from a man who must provide for his wife and children."[8] Many of her male colleagues felt cramped by and resentful of her presence: "Now girly magazines had to be confined to their trucks, language had to be 'toned down' and, even worse, they had to cope with the idea that perhaps a female—who at five-foot-five and one hundred twenty pounds was clearly not an Amazon—could master *their* job."[9] There has also come to be a whole genre of writing about repair and its plethora of pleasurable accoutrements and special perks—power tools, duct tape, and long trips to the hardware store—being a "guy thing" that women just don't or can't understand.

None of this, of course, means that all men are brought up to unreservedly embrace a masculinity defined in terms of skilled manual labor. It is not unusual for middle-class, male, white-collar professionals to think of the repair of cars or houses as perhaps something they should be able to do on the weekends but yet not embrace as a career. Indeed, as Steven Gelber has shown, this version of what he has called "domestic masculinity" was on a firm footing in the United States by the 1950s.[10] A century earlier, industrialization had put many men out of the house, leaving them with scant time or incentive to develop basic skills of household maintenance and repair. But, according to Gelber, by mid-twentieth century a potent mix of forces made the possession of "do-it-yourself" skills nearly de rigeur for such men. It was both masculine, expressing mastery over tools, and yet distinctly domestic—something done around the house, perhaps in the male-defined space of a workshop. Moreover, Gelber adds, such domestic masculinity seems to have been attractive not only to middle-class homeowners, whose ordinary workweek did not involve manual labor: do-it-yourself activities "were performed by middle-class men acting like blue-collar workers and blue-collar workers acting like middle-class homeowners."[11]

Mainstream American culture is awash in reflection on the kind of repair skills domestic masculinity is thought to include. Dave Barry, for example, has carved out a handsome career by making fun of male do-it-yourselfers bumbling through home repair jobs so badly that they have to call in the professionals—the need for which, Barry wryly acknowledges, is what their wives suggested in the first place[12] and which has spawned companies such as Rent-a-Husband.[13] Continued uneasiness about the tension between domestic masculinity and class status pops up with some regularity in the popular television program *Frasier*. In one recent episode, for example, Frasier and Niles Crane, who pride themselves on their Harvard educations and their extensive knowledge of Bordeaux vintages, appear to be quite embarrassed by their inability to fix automobiles and their failure to do well in night classes for car repair. But they quickly banish such embarrassment by reverting to their always ready contempt for that kind of labor. Such disdain underscores their difference from the two working-class members of the household: from Daphne, who is thrilled by the prospect of her man, Niles, being able to rescue her in the breakdown lane and thereby, she says, show how much he really cares for her, and from their father, Martin, the retired cop for whom it is a momentous and very intimate act to be able to offer his tools, at long last, to his sons.[14]

But whether we focus on tool use at the workplace or at the home, we aren't likely to find many women on the scene. Perhaps the only skilled manual repair work that easily comes to mind as something that historically has fallen to women—or *some* women—to do, even if it is not entirely off limits to men, is mending clothing (and in rural fishing areas, mending nets). The profession of male tailors has a long history, and in a pinch at least some men exhibit perfectly adequate sewing skills: "Many a man in military service has had to darn a sock at a crucial time. I never yet saw such a man pretend to know how to use a needle, and yet I've watched dozens in the barracks secretly stitching rips in their clothing when they thought no one else was looking. It may have taken them longer than a woman to repair their torn clothing, but they did it!" And Una Robertson has pointed out that in early nineteenth-century Yorkshire it was commonly recognized that men as well as women knitted.[15] Still, mending family clothing seems almost always to have been the task of the women of the house (in recent Western cultures). So even if much of what counts as ordinary repair work—in the workplace or at home—seems to have become thought of as men's and not women's work, the mending of clothing has historically been ordinary repair work that is the work of women, or at least of women whose social standing did not require that their hands remain soft and free of the evidence of labor. But is that all? Just how generic is the *Homo* in *Homo reparans*?

The case for the ubiquity of repair rests in part on the use of "repair" and its close cousins in connection with a vast and motley range of activities: fixing automobiles and mending clothing, yes, but also repairing human relationships and reweaving rips in the social fabric. When we think of repair in this larger sense, it can seem as if women spend—or anyway are expected to spend—an enormous amount of time doing repair work.

The Household as Repair Shop

I would like to venture the idea that the history of the housewife—especially after industrialization isolated the household, and the women in it, from the rest of the economy[16]—suggests that women's work in the household has been to the larger society what the combined work of gas station, car wash, and repair shop is to automobiles. Though at the beginning of the twenty-first century there are severe cracks in its façade, the household (at least in what we breezily call Western industrial society) is designated as the default location for people to fuel up and get washed, clothed, and reclothed; it's where they're to receive the daily doses of repair and restoration necessary for them to keep on going, physically, mentally, and emotionally, to keep on functioning as social animals (the continued importance of such tasks assigned to the household is signaled by the use of the word "homeless"). Such activities, after all, have to occur *somewhere*.

Saying this doesn't require us to decide among competing views of the home as "haven in a heartless world"[17] or as the scene of horrendous abuse and violence or as neither haven nor horror chamber but bulwark against racist hostility and humiliation.[18] (The continuing debate over the proper description of the household is reflected in Miss Manners's recognition that if she is going to argue that "the traditional idea of a cheerful household is worth salvaging," she has to acknowledge how hard it is for its inhabitants to control "large and small impulses that do damage to others in the household."[19]) The general idea is that whatever else it has been or has been meant to be, the household, in its nuclear and nonnuclear varieties, has had to serve as a veritable repair shop (indeed, it is against that backdrop that domestic violence seems particularly shocking).

There is, first, the repair of the human body. The body has an awesome capacity to repair itself, in ways that are to the ordinary observer both visible (e.g., the healing of a cut) and invisible (e.g., the continual self-repair of DNA or the recently discovered capacity of the human heart to repair itself).[20] But it can't do that, and will cease doing it, without being fed and watered. So even though we might think of the feeding and watering of human beings as simple maintenance, rather than repair, such maintenance is necessary for the self-repair of the body. And that bodily repair is helped along by the knowledgeable household creation and use of salves and medicines.[21] There also is, or was, the "eternal mending"[22] of clothing—absolutely crucial when there is not likely to be anything soon to replace it, whenever holes are thought inconvenient or embarrassing, or when one wants to keep a beloved item wearable or usable for as long as possible.

Then there is the repair necessitated by the steady flow of crises arising from the vulnerability of the human heart and from the fragility of the web of human relationships. A child is heartbroken over the death of a grandmother or, for that matter, of a goldfish. A friendship breaks up or is slowly falling to pieces. A young person's confidence in her abilities has been shattered (this, of course, assumes that she lives in a larger context in which such confidence could have been established to begin with). The family tries to figure out how to deal with its own breakup from separation or divorce. Children need to learn what an apology is and when, how, and to whom to make one. They need to think about what it means to keep or break a promise. They need guidance in identifying what constitutes damage to themselves and others and help in reflecting on what it is possible to fix and what is not, as well as what is desirable to fix and what is not. (If Melanie Klein is right, the need for such guidance arises in humans long before it can be provided: Klein argues that babies fantasize about destroying their mothers, conflate the desire with its accomplishment, and then "find support against these fears in omnipotent phantasies of a restoring kind": "If the baby has, in his aggressive phantasies, injured his mother by biting and tearing her up, he may soon

build up phantasies that he is putting the bits together again and repairing her."[23])
At the same time, children may also be called upon to mend rifts in family relationships that adults can't accomplish themselves.[24]

The household functions as a multipurpose repair site. It offers a pretty good
microcosm of the variety of repair activities humans engage in, providing services
on a nonprofessional basis that in many cases migrated outside the household to
become the professional work of seamstresses, doctors, therapists, spiritual counse-
lors, mediators, and judges. Arlie Hochschild has recently argued, though, that

> capitalism and technological developments have long been gradually
> deskilling parents at home . . . [the] main "skill" still required of family
> members is the hardest one of all—the ability to forge, deepen, and
> repair relationships. Under normal circumstances the work of tending to
> relationships calls for noticing, acknowledging, and empathizing with
> the feelings of family members, patching up quarrels, and soothing hurt
> feelings.[25]

But relationships among family members are not the only ones that are likely to
need repair, and the household perforce provides apprenticeship in such skills:
because of the variety of ways in which humans are called upon to mend themselves, others, and the relationships they are in, they need some kind of rehearsal
for and training in that task long before and certainly during their school years.

So, then, like cars, human beings suffer wear and tear; like cars, humans
need not just maintenance but also repair if they are to keep on functioning; and
in the provision of such repair the household, by default if not by design, for
better and for worse, is to the larger society what the auto repair shop—along with
the gas station and car wash—is to the world of automobiles. Sometimes these
home repair shops do a decent job; sometimes they don't. And of course the
analogy is imperfect: although apprentices in the household and in the repair
shop can learn to repair, cars cannot (though cars can have self-corrective mechanisms, and there are some new materials that "know" how to go back to their
original shape after a collision).[26] Although cars can't be violated by attempts to
repair them (except in the sense that their structural integrity might be violated),
there are moral constraints on our attempts to repair others, to "straighten them
out" against their will. Debates over the appropriateness of corporal punishment
of children, for example, are a reminder of the ongoing process of trying to determine what those constraints ought to be.

Repairing People for What?

If there is any analogy at all between the repair of automobiles and the repair of
persons, we ought to be able to specify what function is being restored when the
repair of persons or some aspect of them is taking place; for what makes the
working on a car a matter of repair is that the function of the car or some part of
it is being restored. The car now works again: it can be used to perform the

function of getting its occupants relatively safely and efficiently from one place to another. But what functions of humans are restored when humans are repaired? Is the household the place for the production, maintenance, and repair of humans' functioning as citizens? Consumers? Workers? Well-lubricated cogs in the social machine? All of the above?

The analogy between the repair of a car and the repair of a person suggests that there is a kind of repair of humans that restores them to a state of basic functioning, of being able to use their energies and skills as they see fit. After all, when the mechanic restores the basic function of a car as a relatively safe and efficient moving vehicle, the idea is that the owner then can use it as she wishes. So it would seem that just as cars are repaired so that people can use them as they desire, people are repaired so that they can get back in basic working order, in order to get on with what they want to do.

But we cannot assume that repair is neutral in this sense, as we can see from the case of Willie. Willie repairs cars without regard to how they will look in their postreparative state and, to a certain extent, without regard to the original design of the car. He'll get your Saab purring again like a kitten and make sure the back door opens and shuts tightly and easily, but he won't guarantee that the door he ends up using will be the same color as the rest of the car, nor will he promise not to violate the original design of the door handle or the engine. He is going to repair your car in a much different fashion than someone you hire to repair it in a way that will preserve or restore it as a particular vintage of Saab automobile. Either way, your car will once again function as a relatively safe and efficient moving vehicle. But Willie's repair is likely to complicate future attempts to restore the car as closely as possible to its original condition. Repairing a hip so that someone can walk again might under some conditions get in the way of repairing it so that the person can run.

When, then, we think about the work of the household as including the repair of humans from the wear and tear of everyday life, where repairing means restoring them to some kind of functional state, we surely ought to ask whether repairing them to be able to function in some ways is compatible with repairing them to be able to function in others. For example, to the degree to which the household provides respite for those who work outside it from the wear and tear of that work and performs the repair necessitated by such wear and tear, it restores humans to their functions as workers. And indeed a good chunk of the scholarship on the function of the household since industrialization has been on its role in the production and reproduction of the work force—the creation, maintenance, and, we would now add, repair of people so they are not just physically but psychologically ready and able to take on the work demanded of them, day after day after day. Under harsh conditions of labor—that is, under conditions of labor that are the norm rather than the exception in most parts of the world—the kind of maintenance and repair work done by the household resembles nothing so much as preparation for a demolition derby, in which an auto is repaired just enough so it can be entered in an event the point of which is to smash the car to smithereens. The analogy will be more or less close, depending on the extent to which workplace owners don't want to have to replace their work force at frequent intervals.

But is repairing the worker to be able to function in the workplace compatible with repairing him or her to be able to function as citizens? They might not be incompatible, but we cannot assume that one repair suits all functions. Certainly repairing the worker to be able to function in a destructive workplace is not the same as repairing the workplace; and it may or may not repair the worker in her struggle to make the workplace less destructive. As did all the Black girls growing up in the cotton-mill town of Kannapolis, North Carolina, in the 1950s, Katie Geneva Cannon assumed she would follow her mother and become a domestic worker for white people: "We were not only supposed to know how to keep house but also how to cook perfect meals and not burn food up. . . . How to mop the floors, how to pick the strings up after the mop, how to dust so that you don't break things, how to wash windows and wipe down the blinds, the whole mechanical system of how to clean a house. I knew all that by the time I was eight."[27] Because her mother was working for white families all day, Katie Cannon's sister was responsible for teaching her how to clean. Though Katie and her sisters were supposed to keep their own house in top shape—"There is nothing that would irritate a black woman more than to clean a white woman's house all day long and then come home to a dirty house"[28]—the work they did at the white people's house was, as we have learned so well from Judith Rollins and others,[29] performed in such a way and under such conditions that the superiority of the whites to the Blacks would be affirmed. "Most of the white people in Kannapolis didn't clean their houses. That was what Black women were for. That was how Black women would get their income, how they survived."[30] Challenging their employers in hopes of making conditions of work less toxic[31] was likely to cut off the supply of that necessary income. Katie Cannon's case is not pertinent here because she was doing repair work—indeed, cleaning house is typically thought of as maintenance, not repair, and as involving unskilled rather than skilled labor—but because some of the very good "repair work" she got at her own home was to enable her to go back day after day to damaging labor outside it.

In thinking about the household as a multipurpose repair shop, it's important to consider not only the kinds of repair that are undertaken there but also the kinds of discussions that take place, the lessons handed down, about the varieties of damage there are in the world, and what one can or can't and should or should not do about it. Indeed there are implicit lessons in civics, morality, economics, and politics that are passed on in household discussions and decisions about to whom one has and has not to apologize, whether and how one is responsible for damage to the environment, when a marriage or partnership has frayed beyond the point of repair, and what kinds of repair it is deemed appropriate for men and women of one's class or ethnicity to engage in. In certain circumstances something as seemingly simple as whether or not one should mend clothing is fraught with social and political significance: "My mother always said, 'A patch, my dear, is never a disgrace, but a hole . . . that is.' In 1943 a neatly mended patch or a darned hole in a sock is a badge of patriotism. But no matter what the date or year—even if the threads or material do not match—a patch or a darn will always mean a badge of self-respect."[32]

Obviously the household is not the only place where such lessons are passed on or such questions brought up. But whether households are good at it or lousy at it, they are places where people are supposed to get prepared for lives as citizens, consumers, workers, moral agents, and friends. Steven Gelber reports that one of the messages given to a certain class of Victorian boys was that the aggressiveness and competitiveness they'd need in the workplace would have to be learned away from the household—though paradoxically that lesson about the proper place to receive such instruction might come from the household itself.[33] One not only needs basic repair to keep functioning in the various ways demanded of us in and outside the household; functioning in those capacities itself involves all manner of judgments about the possibility and impossibility, the desirability and undesirability, of repair. Slave testimonies and other historical sources also remind us that the household is one of the places where people are given lessons, implicitly or explicitly, about their role in the maintenance and repair or the subversion and destruction of the current social and political order: the steady maintenance and repair of white supremacy and the system of slavery, for example, required the unceasing work among whites of attempting to break the spirits and dash the hopes of slaves.[34]

The repair women do in the home—including the lessons about reparability and irreparability they explicitly or implicitly pass down—does not constitute all of their work; it is not always easily distinguishable from the rest of their work; and they are not necessarily alone in the household in doing it.[35] But they are on the whole managers by default of such repair work, whatever the size or extent of their household and however many adults there are in it. If central to domestic masculinity is the repair of material objects and the passing down of lessons about such repair, central to domestic femininity is the repair of persons and relationships and the imparting of lessons about that kind of repair. There is no particular training for such repair, and the world outside the household may be geared to undermining it. For example, part of slavery and its legacy in the United States was the assumption that Black women who were working for white people should put the needs of the white families ahead of those of their own.[36]

The analogy between the household and the automobile repair shop reminds us, too, that repair can be dangerous work. It can severely hurt the repairer, and it can destroy rather than fix the object meant to be mended. Mechanics need to learn how to anticipate dangerous situations and to protect themselves, their fellow workers, and the cars in their care from the many kinds of accidents that might occur in a shop. The propane torch with which one does reparative welding could severely burn one's hand or set the car, the shop, and all its inhabitants on fire. To the extent to which women become the repairers of choice in the household—including being healers of rifts, menders of hearts—there are dangers both for them and for the other members of it. It is a crucial part of a relationship for those in it to be able to tend to its cracks and fissures themselves, to not turn automatically to a third party for rescue. For example, the author of a recent book about the social and moral development of boys reports his realization that when tension between him and his son got high, both he and his wife tended to rely on her to mediate, thereby not only relieving father and son of the need to figure things out on their own but also depriving them of the chance to deepen their relationship by having to deal with its fault lines.[37] But if the presence of a repairer-on-call threatens to stunt the growth of reparative muscle in others, it may also leave the ever reliable repairer in short supply of help when she is in need herself.

Repair and the "Ethics of Care"

Carol Gilligan famously proposed some twenty years ago that there are two distinct orientations involved in conceptualizing and resolving moral puzzles and problems, one more likely to be found among men than women, the other more likely to be found among women than men.[38] Suppose, for example, that Henry and Ruth have a fifteen-year-old daughter, Jackie. Jackie comes to her parents in tears with news that she is pregnant. Should she get an abortion?

According to an early version of the Gilliganian view, men, more likely than not, treat moral deliberation as a matter of seeking out relevant principles or rules and applying them to the case at hand. We can expect Henry to think about Jackie's predicament in terms of whether or not an abortion would violate or be in accord with some relevant moral law or principle. Such law provides the kind of steady compass that in this view is the hallmark of morality: in its absence our moral thinking would be without proper direction, without consistency, and all too partial. Unless there are rules and laws telling us what to do, we won't know how to reach a decision; we will remain without moral direction. It's the following of rules that assures us of consistency—that when another case comes along it will be treated in the same way. It's the adherence to rules that promises impartiality—that we are guided not by our current whims or fears or loves or hopes but by the steadiness of a rule that applies no matter how we happen to feel and no matter to whom or to what we happen to be attached. Wanderers in the confusing and treacherous moral wilderness need a compass—an instrument that gives clear directions, that points in the same direction every day, no matter who the wanderer is and no matter how much he might wish it to point in another direction.[39]

Women, Gilligan et al. argued, are likely to pose and to try to resolve moral problems in quite a different way. Persons are by their very nature bound up in relation to others, and tensions and conflicts in those relations are at the heart of moral dilemmas. To resolve such conflicts one must focus on the specific situation of the persons involved, on the web of their relationships to people, and on how to keep those relations intact. What is the best thing for Jackie to do, given the nature of her relationship to the man involved and her social and economic condition? How might her decision affect her relation to her parents? What kind of life would the child have? What kind of emotional and economic support does Jackie need?

Women, on this view, do not share the assumption that the proper resolution of Jackie's dilemma requires the application of a governing law or principle. Moral direction is something to be figured out by the moral travelers in the thicket of their relations with others, not something they can determine by reference to a sure and steady compass. Attention is to be given to the specifics of Jackie's predicament, not to the ways it is like or unlike that of other girls. Jackie needs the partiality of her parents' love, not the carefully kept distance of a stone-sober observer.

The first orientation, dubbed an "ethics of justice," emphasizes the autonomy of moral agents, their capacity to govern themselves and not be swayed by people around them or by powerful emotions of the moment. It insists on the importance of the ways in which acting from principle ensures consistency and impartiality. The second, referred to as an "ethics of care," emphasizes the embeddedness and specificity of moral agents in relationships with others and embraces a kind of care for people that is unapologetically partial and apparently unconcerned with consistency across cases.

The idea that there are such distinct orientations in moral thinking and that they can be tidily mapped onto distinctions between men and women, no matter their class, racial, or ethnic identity or their nationality, has been subject to intense scrutiny. In the ever-growing body of literature about these claims, there have been probing and fruitful questions about just what ethnographic group of men and women Gilligan et al. had in mind, about whether a robust sense of justice would include care, and whether any care worthy of the name would be concerned with justice.[40] Some commentators have expressed worries that the ways in which women are said to care for others may reflect and strengthen their political and economic subordination to men[41] or obscure patterns of such subordination among women (e.g., between female employers and the domestic workers they "care for").[42] Our interest here, however, is whether the kind of caring activity highlighted in these examinations—*whoever* engages in it—provides a window into some of the work of *Homo reparans*. How much is what is called an ethics of care about repair?

The language of repair occurs hardly at all in the various discussions of what these moral orientations are, how distinct they are, and the strengths and shortcomings of each. True, it is not unusual to find reference to the maintenance of relationships—for example, women are said to "undertake to resolve conflicts by maintaining or strengthening their connections with those with whom they are in conflict";[43] their moral thinking is said to involve "a responsiveness to others that dictates providing care, preventing harm, and maintaining relationships";[44] and a reference to repair is clear in the idea that the "emotional work" women are supposed to do in the household involves "soothing tempers, boosting confidence, fueling pride, preventing frictions, and mending ego wounds."[45] But in fact there appears to be a striking similarity between the kind of knowledge and skills involved in care ethics thinking and those involved in doing careful repair work. Let me return for a few moments to Willie.

Though Willie has been working on Saabs, other vehicles, and farm machinery a good part of his life, he doesn't expect any two cases to be alike. He is not inclined to turn to instruction manuals or even diagnostic equipment since as far as he is concerned they are of limited usefulness, especially compared to what he has learned about the nature of the materials he works with from long years of handling them, wrestling with them, and letting them speak to him. He has intimate knowledge of the parts he deals with, the stuff of which they are made, and their actual and potential relationships to each other. This knowledge prepares him to deal with the problems his customers bring to him, but not because he sees the same problems again and again. One of the reasons he enjoys his work and is regarded as so skilled is that he comes up with nifty case-specific solutions to the constant stream of unique challenges.

The ethics of care highlights the intimacy of the knowledge of the moral agent as problem solver: intimate both in the sense of having or seeking for specific, nuanced, and contextualized knowledge of the people involved and the situations they are in and in the sense of acknowledging or creating a close relationship to the people involved. Insofar as Ruth has a care orientation toward Jackie, she thinks of Jackie as her daughter, not just another fifteen-year-old, not just another generic human being faced with an important moral decision; she knows her not just as a pregnant teenager but also as, say, someone who got involved with this young man as a way to get back at the boy she broke up with three months ago.

Willie's handling of machinery and Ruth's deliberations about Jackie call upon highly contextualized knowledge. But it is not that alone that prompts the idea that Ruth, like Willie, is doing a kind of repair work. What makes it repair work is that Jackie's world has, as we often say, fallen apart, and she needs help in putting it back together again. That web of existing and future relationships that are said to be central to Ruth's thinking about Jackie's predicament is by its very nature fragile, something that is bound to need not just maintenance but also repair. At the same time, unless Ruth is determined to counsel Jackie that any and all relationships need to be sustained and restored (something some critics of an ethics of care worry is being urged), Jackie is going to need help in thinking about which of her relationships are possible and desirable to repair and which are not: for example, what if her father says he'll disown her if she has an abortion, and her boyfriend says he'll break up with her if she doesn't? If Jackie feels shame at being pregnant and unattached, she may need help in thinking about whether she can or should try to restore the picture she had of herself before the pregnancy.

Insofar as an ethics of care is about understanding people as being in relationships with others, and about seeing conflicts as threatening such relationships, surely a large part of moral deliberation as understood under an ethics of care is about repairing those relationships or judging that it is not possible or desirable under the circumstances to do so. If we think about the possible appropriateness of the language of repair for the kinds of situations to which an ethics of care turns our attention, it certainly looks as if the nature of the care being underscored is a concern for harm to persons, to beings understood as, by their nature, in breakable relation to each other. Indeed what has been called an ethics of care implies that at the core of morality is a response to the fact of fragility, a fragility in the relationships in which and through which persons lead their lives. And then, in turn, the language of breakability, fragility, and repair suggests that one way to characterize the difference between the care and the justice orientations is that the care orientation focuses on morality as about relationships, which can collapse, whereas the justice orientation focuses on morality as about principles, the force and authority of which can be eroded. If that's the case, then it's not that care is about repair and justice isn't but that a crucial difference between them is where our reparative efforts ought to go—to relationships among people or to the principles by which they should live.

Conclusion

If we think about repair as something that must involve tools, at least the kind of tools found in hardware and plumbing supply stores or at construction sites, our cast of repair characters is mostly going to involve men—not because all men have them or use them even if they have them or even because all men are supposed to have them or be able to use them: differences in social and economic class among men are at least roughly correlated with the degree to which they use such tools to make a living. Not all working-class men make a living using such tools; still, making a living by using such tools is one version of a male working-class life. But though not all men have been welcomed into or expected to aspire to the brotherhood of tool users, women of all classes and complexions need not even apply.

However, many repair activities don't involve such tools. It's not just cars or toilets or phone lines that break and need fixing. We humans don't just live in a world of breakables; we *are* breakables, our bodies and souls by their very nature subject to fracture and fissure. And we are social animals, our dependency upon each other given shape by the connections we find and forge among ourselves. These relationships are by their very nature subject to damage, dissolution, collapse—sometimes for the better, sometimes for the worse.

Repair work must be on and done by humans on a more or less daily basis. Though some of that repair is taken care of without our direction and without our knowledge by the miraculous, mundane workings of the human organism, much of it has to be made to happen. Exploring some aspects of the lives of women has led to the suggestion that the household is a veritable repair shop. It is by default the institution for aiding and abetting the natural bodily processes of repair; for mending spirits frayed or broken by the wear and tear of life, by the damaging effects of its pleasures as well as its pains; and for providing informal lessons about the reparable and the irreparable.

Notes

1. Elizabeth V. Spelman, *Repair: The Impulse to Restore in a Fragile World* (Boston: Beacon Press, 2002).

2. Willie (no last name provided) is the subject of a loving and illuminating study by Douglas Harper, *Working Knowledge: Skill and Community in a Small Shop* (Berkeley: University of California Press, 1987).

3. Catherine Hall, "The History of the Housewife," in *The Politics of Housework*, ed. Ellen Malos (London: Allison & Busby, 1980), 49.

4. Edward Deming and Faith Andrews, *Work and Worship: The Economic Order of the Shakers* (Greenwich, Conn.: New York Graphic Society, 1974), 153–156; cited in Autumn Stanley, "Women Hold Up Two-Thirds of the Sky: Notes for a Revised History of Technology," in *Machina ex Dea: Feminist Perspectives on Technology*, ed. Joan Rothschild (New York: Pergamon, 1983), 9.

5. See Susan Eisenberg, *We'll Call You if We Need You: Experiences of Women Working Construction* (Ithaca, N.Y.: Cornell University Press, 1998), passim.

6. For example, Bruce Cassiday, *The New Practical Home Repair for Women: Your Questions Answered* (New York: Berkley Windhover, 1972); Jim Webb and Bart Houseman, *The You-Don't Need-a-Man-to-Fix-It Book: The Woman's Guide to Confident Home Repair*, introduction by Erma Bombeck (Garden City, N.Y.: Doubleday, 1973). A much more recent book alludes to an earlier absence of women authors: Lyn Herrick, *The Woman's Hands-on Home Repair Guide. Written by a Woman for Women* (Pownal, Vt.: Storey Books, 1997).

7. Webb and Houseman, *You-Don't Need-a-Man-to-Fix-It Book*, 3. They also guess that "about four out of five men seem to be washouts as home repairers" (2).

8. Mary Baird, "Phone Repair Technician," in *Hard-Hatted Women: Stories of Struggle and Success in the Trades*, ed. Molly Martin (Seattle, Wash.: Seal Press, 1988), 249.

9. Ibid.

10. Steven Gelber, "Do-It-Yourself: Constructing, Repairing, and Maintaining Domestic Masculinity," in *The Gender and Consumer Culture Reader*, ed. Jennifer Scanlon (New York and London: New York University Press, 2000), 70–93.

11. Ibid., 75.

12. See, for example, Dave Barry, "The Tool Man Cometh," *Ellsworth American*, June 27, 1997, 9–10; Phil McCombs, "Tooling Around Town," *Washington Post*, March 8, 1996, B5.

13. See Rent-a-Husband.com, described on its Web site as an organization "dedicated to meeting your needs as a homeowner, and enhancing the image of skilled craftsmen in the process."

14. "Frasier," NBC, March 20, 2001. Is the brothers' contempt a defense against embarrassment over incompetence, or is their incompetence the intended fruit of their contempt?

15. Cassiday, *New Practical Home Repair for Women*, 1; Una Robertson, *The Illustrated History of the Housewife, 1650–1950* (New York: St. Martin, 1997), 152–153.

16. This happened first among the urban middle classes, but it eventually reached rural and working-class populations as well. See Tamara K. Hareven, "The Home and the Family in Historical Perspective," in *Home: A Place in the World*, ed. Arien Mack (New York: New York University Press, 1993), 246ff.

17. Christopher Lasch, *Haven in a Heartless World: The Family Besieged* (New York: Basic Books, 1979).

18. See, for example, Carol Stack, *All Our Kin: Strategies for Survival in a Black Community* (New York: Harper & Row, 1974); Eleanor Leacock, "Postscript: Implications for Organization," in *Women's Work: Development and the Division of Labor by Gender*, ed. Eleanor Leacock and Helen I. Safa (South Hadley, Mass.: Bergin & Garvey, 1986), 253–265.

19. Judith Martin, *Miss Manners' Guide to Domestic Tranquility: The Authoritative Manual for Every Civilized Household, However Harried* (New York: Three Rivers Press, 1999), 2.

20. Stephanie Nano, "Doctors Find a Hint Hearts Can Self-Repair," *Boston Globe*, January 3, 2002, A2.

21. See descriptions of healing practices in, for example, Lewis Mehl-Madrona, M.D., *Coyote Medicine* (New York: Scribner, 1997); Gay Wilentz, *Healing Narratives: Women Writers Curing Cultural Disease* (New Brunswick, N.J.: Rutgers University Press, 2000).

22. Describing the ongoing work of 1920's British working-class women in the 1920s even in the last stages of pregnancy, Marjorie Spring Rice, "Working Class Wives," in *The Politics of Housework*, ed. Ellen Malos (London: Allison & Busby, 1980), 92, pointed out, "Even if she is in bed, she . . . can direct operations, even perhaps doing some of the 'smaller' jobs herself—like drying crockery, ironing, and of course the eternal mending."

23. Melanie Klein and Joan Riviere, "Love, Guilt and Reparation," in *Love, Hate and Reparation* (New York: Norton, 1964), 61. The sense that reparation is successful may be hard to achieve: "The desire to control the object, the sadistic gratification of overcoming and humiliating it, of getting the better of it, the *triumph* over it, may enter so strongly into the act of reparation (carried out by thoughts, activities, or sublimations) that the benign circle started by this act becomes broken. The objects which were to be restored change again into persecutors, and in turn paranoid fears are revived." Klein, "Mourning and Its Relation to Manic-Depressive States," in *The Selected Melanie Klein*, ed. Juliet Mitchell (New York: Free Press, 1986), 153.

24. See Sally Greene, "Mending Webs: The Challenge of Childhood in Elizabeth Spencer's Short Fiction," *Mississippi Quarterly* 49, no. 1 (1996): 89–98.

25. Arlie Russell Hochschild, *Time Bind: When Work Becomes Home and Home Becomes Work* (New York: Henry Holt, 1997), 209–210.

26. Guy Gugliotta, "'Self-Healing' Plastic Reported," *Boston Globe*, February 15, 2001, A7: "Using high-tech materials and a low-tech concept inspired by the human body, the scientists devised a process that can continuously repair and regenerate the chemical soup that makes up most plastics by activating special resin-filled capsules stored within the material itself."

27. Katie Geneva Cannon, in *Hard Times Cotton Mill Girls: Personal Histories of Womanhood and Poverty in the South*, ed. Victoria Morris Byerly (Ithaca, N.Y.: ILR Press, 1986), 36

28. Ibid.

29. See Judith Rollins, *Between Women: Domestics and Their Employers* (Philadelphia: Temple University Press, 1985).

30. Cannon, in *Hard Times Cotton Mill Girls*, 38–39.

31. The notion of the toxic workplace is highlighted in Barbara Reinhold, *Toxic Work: How to Overcome Stress, Overload, and Burnout and Revitalize Your Career* (New York: Penguin Plume, 1997).

32. Linda Marvin, *Housekeeping Made Easy: More than 2,000 Shortcuts for Daily Household Living* (New York: Vanguard, 1943), 237.

33. See, Gelber, "Do-It-Yourself," 73.

34. See, for example, Harriet Jacobs, *Incidents in the Life of a Slave Girl, Written by Herself,* ed. Jean Fagan Yellin (Cambridge, Mass.: Harvard University Press, [1861], 1987).

35. This recitation of the daily or weekly tasks of the English housewife until surprisingly recently is not atypical: "cooking, cleaning, fetching water and fuel, making candles, washing and ironing, producing food from the garden, looking after poultry, pigs, or bees, going to market to sell products of her own making or to buy in what was required, supervising servants [many of them also females of the household], caring for children and other dependents." See Una Robertson, *The Illustrated History of the Housewife, 1650–1950* (New York: St. Martin, 1997), 150. My inquiry into the kinds of repair women do in the household is meant to complement such a list.

36. See, for example, Cannon, in *Hard Times Cotton Mill Girls;* Jacqueline Jones, *Labor of Love, Labor of Sorrow: Black Women, Work and the Family, from Slavery to the Present* (New York: Random House, 1986), 4.

37. Daniel Robb, *Crossing the Water: Eighteen Months on an Island Working with Troubled Boys* (New York: Simon & Schuster, 2001). Comment heard on "Talk of the Nation," National Public Radio, May 30, 2001.

38. Carol Gilligan, *In a Different Voice: Psychological Theory and Women's Development* (Cambridge, Mass.: Harvard, 1982).

39. The metaphor of a moral compass is a bit misleading since there is no debate about the possibility of more than one "true north," whereas there are ongoing debates about whether there might be equally valid moral laws pointing in conflicting directions.

40. For sustained discussion, see Robin West, *Caring for Justice* (New York and London: New York University Press, 1997); Joan Tronto, *Moral Boundaries: A Political Argument for an Ethic of Care* (New York: Routledge, 1993).

41. See, for example, Barbara Houston, "Prolegomena to Future Caring," in *A Reader in Feminist Ethics,* ed. Debra Shogan (Toronto: Canadian Scholars Press, 1992), 109–127.

42. See, for example, Rollins, *Between Women,* Cannon, in *Hard Times Cotton Mill Girls;* Jacobs, *Incidents in the Life of a Slave Girl.*

43. See Houston, "Prolegomena to Future Caring," 113.

44. Eva Feder Kittay and Diana T. Meyers, "Introduction," in *Women and Moral Theory,* ed. Eva Feder Kittay and Diana T. Meyers (Totowa, N.J.: Rowman & Littlefield, 1987), 3.

45. Cheshire Calhoun, "Emotional Work," in *Explorations in Feminist Ethics: Theory and Practice,* ed. Eve Browning Cole and Susan Coultrap-McQuin (Bloomington: Indiana University Press, 1992), 118.

3

Taking Care: Care as Practice and Value

Virginia Held

The last words I spoke to my older brother after a brief visit and with special feeling were "take care." He had not been taking good care of himself, and I hoped he would do better; not many days later he died, of problems quite possibly unrelated to those to which I had been referring.

We often say "take care" as routinely as "goodbye" or some abbreviation and with as little emotion. But even then it does convey some sense of connectedness. More often, when said with some feeling, it means something like "take care of yourself because I care about you." Sometimes we say it, especially to children or to someone embarking on a trip or an endeavor, meaning "I care what happens to you so please don't do anything dangerous or foolish." Or, if we know the danger is inevitable and inescapable, it may be more like a wish that the elements will let the person take care so the worst can be evaded. And sometimes we mean it as a plea: "Be careful not to harm yourself or others because our connection will make us feel with and for you." We may be harmed ourselves or partly responsible, or if you do something you will regret we will share that regret.

One way or another this expression, like many others, illustrates human relatedness and the daily reaffirmations of connection. It is the relatedness of human beings, built and rebuilt, that the ethics of care is being developed to try to understand, to evaluate, and to guide.

For a little over two decades now, the concept of care as it figures in the ethics of care has been assumed, explored, elaborated, and employed in the development of theory. But definitions have often been imprecise, or trying to arrive at them has simply been postponed, as in my own case, in the growing discourse. Perhaps this is entirely appropriate for new explorations, but the time may have come to seek greater clarity. Of course, to a considerable extent, we know what we are talking about when we speak of taking care of a child or providing care for the ill. But care has many, many forms, and as the ethics of care evolves, so should our understanding of what care is.

A seemingly easy distinction to make is between care as the activity of caring for someone and the mere "caring about" of how we feel about certain issues.[1] But the distinction may not be as clear as it appears since when we care for a child, for instance, we certainly also care about her. And if we really do care about world hunger, we will probably be doing something about it—such as, at least, giving money to alleviate it or to change the conditions that bring it about—and thus establishing some connection between ourselves and the hungry we say we care about.[2] And if we really do care about global climate change and the harm it will bring to future generations, we imagine a connection between ourselves and those future people who will judge our irresponsibility, and we change our consumption practices or political activities to decrease the likely harm.

Many of those writing about care agree that the care that is relevant to an ethics of care must at least be able to refer to an activity, as in taking care of someone. Most, though not all, of those writing on care do not lose sight of how care involves work and the expenditure of energy on the part of the person doing the caring. But it is often thought to be more than this.

There can, of course, be different emphases in how we think of care. I will be trying to clarify the meaning of care in contexts for which taking care of children or those who are ill are in some ways paradigmatic. But the caring relations I will be thinking about will go far beyond such contexts.

It is fairly clear that engaging in the work of taking care of someone is not the same as caring for them in the sense of having warm feelings for them. But whether certain feelings must accompany the labor of care is more in doubt.

Nel Noddings focuses especially on the attitudes of caring that typically accompany the activity of care. Close attention to the feelings, needs, desires, and thoughts of those cared for and a skill in understanding a situation from that person's point of view are central to caring for someone.[3] Carers act in behalf of others' interests, but they also care for themselves since without the maintenance of their own capabilities, they will not be able to continue to engage in care. To Noddings, the cognitive aspect of the carer's attitude is "receptive-intuitive" rather than "objective-analytic," and understanding the needs of those cared for depends more on feeling with them than on rational cognition. In the activity of care, abstract rules are of limited use. There can be a natural impulse to care for others, but to sustain it persons need to make a moral commitment to the ideal of caring.[4] For Noddings, care is an attitude and an ideal manifest in activities of care in concrete situations. In her recent book, *Starting at Home*, she explores what a caring society would be like. She seeks a broad, near universal description of "what we are like" when we engage in caring encounters, and she explores "what characterizes consciousness in such relations."[5]

Care is much more explicitly labor in Joan Tronto's view. She and Berenice Fisher have defined it as activity that includes "everything that we do to maintain, continue, and repair our 'world' so that we can live in it as well as possible," and care can be for objects and for the environment, as well as for other persons.[6] This definition almost surely seems too broad: vast amounts of economic activity could be included, like house construction and commercial dry cleaning, and the distinctive features of caring labor would be lost. It does not include the sensitivity to the needs of the cared for that others often recognize in care, nor what Noddings calls the needed "engrossment" with the other. And, Tronto explains, it excludes production, play, and creative activity, whereas a great deal of care, for instance, child care, can be playful and is certainly creative.

If one accepts Marx's distinction between productive and reproductive labor and then sees caring as reproductive labor, as some propose, one misses the way caring, especially for children, can be transformative rather than merely reproductive and repetitious. Although this has not been acknowledged in traditional views of the household, the potential for creative transformation in the nurturing that occurs there, and in child care and education generally, is enormous. Care has the capacity to shape new *persons* with ever more advanced understandings of culture and society and morality.[7] Only a biased and damaging misconception holds that caring merely reproduces our material and biological realities, and what is new and creative and distinctively human must occur elsewhere.

Diemut Bubeck offers one of the most precise definitions of care in the literature: "Caring for is the meeting of the needs of one person by another person, where face-to-face interaction between carer and cared for is a crucial element of the overall activity and where the need is of such a nature that it cannot possibly be met by the person in need herself."[8] She distinguishes between caring for someone and providing a service; on her definition, to cook a meal for a small child is caring, but a wife who cooks for her husband when he could perfectly well cook for himself is not engaging in care but rather providing a service to him. Care, Bubeck asserts, is "a response to a particular subset of basic human needs, i.e. those which make us dependent on others."[9]

In Bubeck's view, care does not require any particular emotional bond between carer and cared for, and it is important to her general view that care can and often should be publicly provided, as in public health care. She seems to think that care is almost entirely constituted by the objective fact of needs being met, rather than by the attitude or ideal with which the carer is acting. Her conception is then open to the objection that, as long as the deception is successful, someone going through the motions of caring for a child while wishing the child dead is engaged in care of as much moral worth as that of a carer who intentionally and with affection seeks what is best for the child. For me this objection is fatal. I suppose a strict utilitarian might say that if the child is fed and clothed and hugged, the emotional tone with which these are done is of no moral significance. But to me it is clear that in the wider moral scheme of things, though I cannot argue it here, it is significant. A world in which the motive of care is good will rather than ill will (plus any self-interest that may additionally be needed to motivate the care giver to do the work) is a better world. Even if the child remains unaware of the ill will, an unlikely though possible circumstance, and even if the child grows up with the admirable sensitivity to the feelings of others that would constitute a better outcome, even on a utilitarian scale, than if she doesn't, the motive would still matter. An important aspect of care is how it *expresses* our attitudes and relationships.

Sara Ruddick sees care as work but also as more than this. She says that "as much as care is labor, it is also relationship . . . caring labor is intrinsically relational. The work is constituted in and through the relation of those who give and receive care. . . . More critically, some caring relationships seem to have a significance in 'excess' of the labor they enable."[10] She compares the work of a father who is bringing a small child to a day-care center and that of the day-care worker who is receiving the child. Both can perform the same work of reassuring the child, hugging him, transferring him from father to worker, and so on. But the character and meaning of the father's care may be in excess of the work itself. For the father, the work is a response to the relationship, whereas for the day-care worker, the relationship is probably a response to the work. So we may want to reject a view that equates care entirely with the labor involved.

To Bubeck, to Noddings in her early work, and to a number of others who are writing on care, its face-to-face aspect is central. This has been thought to make it difficult to think of our concern for more distant others in terms of caring. Bubeck, however, does not see her view as leading to the conclusion that care is limited to the context of the relatively personal, as Noddings's view suggested, because Bubeck includes the activities of the welfare state in the purview of the ethics of care. She thinks the care to be engaged in, as in child-care centers and centers for the elderly, will indeed be face-to-face, but she advocates widespread and adequate public funding for such activity.

Bubeck rejects the particularistic aspects of the ethics of care. She advocates generalizing the moral principle of meeting needs, and thus the way in which an ethic of care can provide for just political and social programs becomes evident. But this comes too close, in my view, to collapsing the ethics of care into utilitarianism. In addition to being the meeting of objective needs, care seems to be at least partly an attitude and motive, as well as a value. Bubeck builds the requirements of justice into the ethics of care. But this may still not allow care to be the primary moral consideration of a person, say, in a rich country, who is engaging in empowering someone in a poor country, if there will never be in this engagement any face-to-face aspect. And this is troubling to many who see care as a fundamental value, with as much potential for moral elaboration as justice, but doubt that justice can itself be adequately located entirely within care or that care should be limited to relatively personal interactive work.

Peta Bowden has a different view than Bubeck of what caring relations are like. She starts with what she calls an intuition: that caring is ethically important. Caring, she says, "expresses ethically significant ways in which we matter to each other, transforming interpersonal relatedness into something beyond ontological necessity or brute survival."[11] Adopting a Wittgensteinian approach to understanding and explicitly renouncing any attempt to provide a definition of care, she carefully examines various examples of caring practices: mothering, friendship, nursing, and citizenship. In including citizenship, she illustrates how face-to-face interaction is not a necessary feature of all caring relations, though it characterizes many.

In his detailed discussion of caring as a virtue, Michael Slote thinks it entirely suitable that our benevolent feelings for distant others be conceptualized as caring. "An ethic of caring," in his view, "can take the well-being of all humanity into consideration."[12] Where Bubeck rejects the view of caring as motive, he embraces it. To him, caring just is a "motivational attitude."[13] And in the recent volume *Feminists Doing Ethics*, several contributors see care as a virtue.[14]

I think feminists should object to making care entirely a matter of motive or of virtue since this runs such a risk of losing sight of it as work. Encouragement should not be given to the tendency to overlook the question of who does most of this work. But that caring is not only work is also persuasive, so we might conclude that care must be able to refer to work, to motive, to value, and perhaps to more than these.

In her influential book *Love's Labor*, Eva Kittay examines what she calls "dependency work," which overlaps with care but is not the same. She defines dependency work as "the work of caring for those who are inevitably dependent," for example, infants and the severely disabled.[15] When not done well, such work can be done without an affective dimension, though it typically includes it.[16] Kittay well understands how dependency work is relational and how the dependency relation "at its very crux, is a moral one arising out of a claim of vulnerability on the part of the dependent, on the one hand, and of the special positioning of the dependency worker to meet the need, on the other."[17] The relation is importantly one of trust. And since dependency work is so often unpaid, when dependency workers use their time to provide care instead of working at paid employment, they themselves become dependent on others for the means with which to do so and for their own maintenance.

Ann Ferguson and Nancy Folbre's conception of "sex-affective production" has much to recommend it in understanding the concept of care. They characterize sex-affective production as "childbearing, childrearing, and the provision of nurturance, affection, and sexual satisfaction."[18] It is not limited to the labor involved in caring for the dependent but also includes the provision of affection and the nurture of relationships. Ferguson and Folbre are especially concerned with analyzing how providing this kind of care leads to the oppression of women. But one can imagine such care as nonoppressive, for both the carers and the cared for. Bubeck and Kittay focus especially on the necessary care that the dependent cannot do without. But when we also understand how increasing levels of affection, mutual concern, and emotional satisfaction are valuable, we can aim at promoting care far beyond the levels of necessity. So understanding care as including rather than excluding the sharing of time and attention and services, even when the recipients are not dependent on them, seems appropriate.

Sara Ruddick usefully notes that "three distinct though overlapping meanings of 'care' have emerged in recent decades. 'Care' is an ethics defined in opposition to 'justice'; a kind of labor; a particular relationship."[19] She herself argues for a view of care as a kind of labor, but not only that, and advocates "attending steadily to the relationships of care."[20] Ruddick doubts that we ought to define an ethics of care in opposition to an ethics of justice since we ought to see how justice is needed in caring well and in family life. But then she wonders how, if care is seen as a kind of labor rather than an already normative concept contrasted with justice, it can give rise to an ethics. Her answer follows, and these passages are worth quoting extensively:

> The "ethics" of care is provoked by the habits and challenges of the work, makes sense of its aims, and spurs and reflects upon the self-understanding of workers. The ethics also extends beyond the activities from which it arises, generating a stance (or standpoint) toward "nature," human relationships, and social institutions. . . . First, memories of caring and being cared for inspire a sense of obligation. . . . [And] a person normatively identifies with a conception of herself as someone who enters into and values caring relationships, exercising particular human capacities as well. Neither memory nor identity "gives rise" to an "ethics" that then leaves them behind. Rather there is an interplay in which each recreates the other.[21]

I think care is surely a form of labor, but it is much more. The labor of care is already relational and can for the most part not be replaced by machines in the way so much other labor can. Ruddick agrees that "caring labor is intrinsically relational,"[22] but she thinks the relationship is something assumed rather than necessarily focused on. I think that as we clarify care, we need to see it in terms of *caring relations*.

I doubt that we ought to accept the contrast between justice as normative and care as nonnormative, as the latter would be if it were simply labor. I think it is better to think of contrasting practices and the values they embody and should be guided by. An activity must be purposive to count as work or labor, but it need not incorporate any values, even efficiency, in the doing of it. Chopping at a tree, however clumsily, in order to fell it, could be work. But when it does incorporate such values as doing so effectively, it becomes the practice of woodcutting. So we do better to focus on practices of care rather than merely on the work involved.

Practices of justice such as primitive revenge and an eye for an eye have from earliest times been engaged in and gradually reformed and refined. By now we have legal, judicial, and penal practices that only dimly resemble their ancient forerunners, and we have very developed theories of justice and of different kinds of justice with which to evaluate such practices. Practices of care, from mothering to medical care to teaching children to cultivating professional relations, have also changed a great deal from their earliest forms, but to a significant extent without the appropriate moral theorizing. That, I think, is what the ethics of care should be trying to fill in. The practices themselves already incorporate various values, often unrecognized, especially by the philosophers engaged in moral theorizing, who ought to be attending to them. And the practices themselves as they exist are often riddled with the gender injustices that pervade societies in most ways but that especially characterize most practices of care. So, moral theorizing is needed to understand the practices and to reform them.

Consider, for instance, mothering, in the sense of caring for children. It had long been imagined in the modern era, after the establishment of the public-private distinction, to be "outside morality." Feminist critique has been needed to show how profoundly mistaken such a view is. Moral issues are confronted constantly in the practice of mothering, and there is constant need for the cultivation of the virtues appropriate to this practice. To get a hint of how profoundly injustice is embedded in the practice of mothering, one can compare the meaning of "mothering" with that of "fathering," which historically has meant no more than impregnating a woman and being the genetic father of a child. "Mothering" suggests that this activity must or should be done by women, whereas, except for lactation, there is no part of it that cannot be done by men as well. Many feminists argue that for actual practices of child care to be morally acceptable, they will have to be radically transformed to accord with principles of equality, though existing conceptions of equality should probably not be the primary moral focus of practices of care. And this is only the beginning of the moral scrutiny to which they should be subject.

This holds also for other practices that can be thought of as practices of care. We need, then, not only to examine the practices and discern with new sensitivities the values already embedded or missing within them but also to construct the appropriate normative theory with which to evaluate them, reform them, and shape them anew. This, I think, involves understanding care as a value worthy of the kind of theoretical elaboration justice has received. And understanding the value of care involves understanding how it should not be limited to the household or family; care should be recognized as a political and social value also.

We all agree that justice is a value. There are also practices of justice: law enforcement, court proceedings, and so on. Practices incorporate values but also need to be evaluated by the normative standards values provide. A given actual practice of justice may only very inadequately incorporate within it the value of justice, and we need justice as a value to evaluate such a practice. The value of justice picks out certain aspects of the overall moral spectrum, those having to do with fairness, equality, and so on, and it would not be satisfactory to have only the most general value terms, such as "good" and "right," "bad" and "wrong," with which to do the evaluating of a practice of justice. Analogously, for actual practices of care we need care, as a value to pick out the appropriate cluster of moral considerations, such as sensitivity, trust, and mutual concern, with which to evaluate such practices. It is not enough to think of care as simply work, describable empirically, with "good" and "right" providing all the normative evaluation of actual practices of care. Such practices are often morally deficient in ways specific to care, as well as to justice.

If we say of someone that "he is a caring person," this includes an evaluation that he has a characteristic that, other things being equal, is morally admirable. Attributing a virtue to someone, as when we say that she is generous or trustworthy, describes a disposition but also makes a normative judgment. And it is highly useful to be able to characterize people and societies in specific and subtle ways, recognizing the elements of our claims that are empirically descriptive and those that are normative. The subtlety needs to be available not only at the level of the descriptive but also within our moral evaluations. "Caring," thus, picks out a more specific value to be found in persons' and societies' characteristics than merely finding them to be good or bad or morally admirable or not on the whole. But we may resist reducing care to a virtue if by that we refer only to the dispositions of individual persons since caring is so much a matter of the relations between them.

Diana Meyers examines the entrenched cultural imagery that can help explain the hostility often encountered by advocates of the ethics of care who seek to expand its applicability beyond the household and to increase care in public life:

> Oscillating sentimentality and contempt with regard to motherhood and childhood fuel this problem. If motherhood and childhood are conditions of imperfect personhood, as they are traditionally thought to be, no one would want to be figured as a mother or as a child in relations with other persons. This perverse constellation of attitudes is enshrined in and transmitted through a cultural stock of familiar figures of speech, stories, and pictorial imagery.[23]

As she explores various illustrative tropes, she shows that the myth of the "independent man" as model, with mothers and children seen as deficient, though lovable, is part of what needs to be overcome in understanding the value of care.

The concept of care should not in my view be a naturalized concept, and the ethics of care should not be a naturalized ethics.[24] Care is not reducible to the behavior that has evolved and that can be adequately captured in empirical descriptions, as when an account may be given of the child care that could have been practiced by our hunter-gatherer ancestors, and its contemporary analogues may be considered. Care as relevant to an ethics of care incorporates the values we decide as feminists to find acceptable in it. And the ethics of care does not accept and describe the practices of care as they have evolved under actual historical conditions of patriarchal and other domination; it evaluates such practices and recommends what they morally ought to be like.

I think, then, of care as practice and value. The practices of care are, of course, multiple, and some seem very different from others. Taking care of a toddler so that he does not hurt himself but is not unduly fearful is not much like patching up the mistrust between colleagues that will enable them to work together. Dressing a wound so that it will not become infected is not much like putting up curtains to make a room attractive and private. And neither is much like arranging for food to be delivered to families who need it half a world away. Yet all care involves attentiveness, sensitivity, and responding to needs. It is helpful to clarify this, as it is to clarify how justice in all its forms requires impartiality, treating persons as equals, and recognizing their rights. This is not at all to say that a given practice should involve a single value only. On the contrary, as we

clarify the values of care, we can better advocate their relevance for many practices from which they have been largely excluded.

Consider police work. Organizationally a part of the "justice system," it must
have the enforcement of the requirements of justice high among its priorities. But
as it better understands the relevance of care to its practices, as it becomes more
caring, it can often accomplish more through educating and responding to needs,
building trust between police and policed, and thus preventing violations of law
than it can through traditional "law enforcement" after prevention has failed.
Sometimes the exclusion of the values of care is more in theory than in practice.
An ideal market that treats all exchanges as impersonal and all participants as
replaceable has no room for caring. But actual markets often include significant
kinds of care and concern, of employers for employees, of employees for customers, and so on. As care is better understood, the appropriate places for caring
relations in economic activity may be better appreciated.[25]

At the same time, practices of care are not devoted solely to the values of
care. They often need justice also. Consider mothering, fathering in the sense of
caring for a child, or "parenting" if one prefers this term. This is probably the
most caring of the caring practices since the emotional tie between carer and
cared for is characteristically so strong. This practice has caring well for the child
as its primary value. But as understanding of what this involves becomes more
adequate, it should include normative guidance on how to avoid such tendencies
as mothers may have to unduly interfere and control, and it can include the
aspect well delineated by Sara Ruddick: "respect for 'embodied willfulness.'"[26]
Moreover, practices of parenting must include justice in requiring the fair treatment of multiple children in a family and in fairly distributing the burdens of
parenting.

Ruddick worries that if we think of justice and care as separate ethics, this
will lead to the problem that, for instance, responding to needs, as economic and
social rights do, cannot be part of the concerns of justice. To hold this position
would be especially unfortunate just as the economic and social rights of meeting
basic needs are gaining acceptance as human rights at the global level (even if
not in the United States, where having such needs met is not recognized as a
right). I believe Ruddick's concern is not a problem and that the difference here
is one of motive. The motive for including economic and social rights among the
human rights on the grounds of justice is that it would be unfair and a failure of
equality, especially of rights to equal freedom, not to do so.[27] When meeting needs
is motivated by care, on the other hand, it is the needs themselves that are responded to and the persons themselves with these needs that are cared for. This
contrast is especially helpful in evaluating social policies, for instance, welfare
policies. Even if the requirements of justice and equality would be met by a
certain program, of payments let's say, we could still find the program callous and
uncaring if it did not concern itself with the actual well-being, or lack of it,
brought about by the program. One can imagine such payments being provided
very grudgingly and the recipients of them largely disdained by the taxpayers

called on to fund them. And one can imagine the shame and undermining of self-respect that would be felt by the recipients of these payments. Except that the amounts of the payments and the range of recipients of them never came close to what justice would require, the rest of this description is fairly accurate about welfare programs in the United States. One can compare this with what a caring program would be like. In addition to meeting the bare requirements of justice, it would foster concern for the actual needs of recipients, offer the needed services to meet them, and express the morally recommended care and concern of the society for its less fortunate and more dependent members.

It seems to me that justice and care, as values, each invoke associated clusters of moral considerations and that these considerations are different. Actual practices should usually incorporate both care and justice, but with appropriately different priorities. For instance, the practice of child care by employees in a child-care center should have as its highest priority the safeguarding and appropriate development of children, including meeting their emotional, as well as physical and educational, needs. Justice should not be absent: the children should be treated fairly and with respect, and violations of justice such as would be constituted by racial or ethnic discrimination against some of the children should not be tolerated. But providing care rather than exemplifying justice would be the primary aim of the activity. In contrast, a practice of legislative decision making on the funding to be supplied to localities to underwrite their efforts to improve law enforcement should have justice as its primary aim. Localities where crime is a greater threat should receive more of such funding so that equality of personal security is more nearly achieved. Care should not be absent: concern for victims of crime and for victims of police brutality should be part of what is considered in such efforts. But providing greater justice and equality rather than caring for victims would be the primary aim of such legislative decision making.

Sara Ruddick does not consider justice inherently tied to a devaluation of relationships. I think justice and its associated values are more committed to individualism than she seems to think. It seems to me that it is on grounds of care rather than justice that we can identify with others enough to form a political entity and to develop civil society.[28] Moreover, relations of care seem to me to be wider and deeper than relations of justice. Within relations of care, we can treat people justly, as if we were liberal individuals agreeing on mutual respect. This can be done in more personal contexts, as when friends compete fairly in a game they seek to win or when parents treat their children equally. Or it can be done in public, political, and social contexts, as when people recognize each other as fellow members of a group that is forming a political entity that accepts a legal system. When justice is the guiding value, it requires that individual rights be respected. But when we are concerned with the relatedness that constitutes a social group and is needed to hold it together, we should look, I think, to care.

My own view, then, is that care is both a practice and a value. As a practice, it shows us how to respond to needs and why we should. It builds trust and mutual concern and connectedness between persons. It is not a series of individual actions but a practice that develops, along with its appropriate attitudes. It has attributes and standards that can be described, but more important, that can be recommended and that should be continually improved as adequate care comes closer to being good care. Practices of care should express the caring relations that bring persons together, and they should do so in ways that are progressively more morally satisfactory. Caring practices should gradually transform children and others into human beings who are increasingly more morally admirable.

Consider how trust is built, bit by bit, largely by practices of caring. Trust is fragile and can be shattered in a single event; to rebuild it may take a long time and many expressions of care, or the rebuilding may be impossible. Relations of trust are among the most important personal and social assets. To develop well and to flourish, children need to trust those who care for them, and the providers of such care need to trust the fellow members of their communities that the trust of their children will not be misplaced. For peace to be possible, antagonistic groups need to learn to be able to trust each other enough so that misplaced trust is not even more costly than mistrust. To work well, societies need to cultivate trust between citizens and between citizens and governments; to achieve whatever improvements of which societies are capable, the cooperation that trust makes possible is needed. Care is not the same thing as trust, but caring relations should be characterized by trust, and caring is the leading contributor to trust.

In addition to being a practice, care is also a value. Caring persons and caring attitudes are valued, and we can organize many evaluations of how persons are interrelated around a constellation of moral considerations associated with care or its absence. For instance, we can ask of a relation whether it is trusting and mutually considerate or hostile and vindictive. I disagree with the view that care is the same as benevolence because I think it is more the characterization of a social relation than the description of an individual disposition, and social relations are not reducible to individual states. It is caring relations that ought to be cultivated between persons in their personal lives and between the members of caring societies. Such relations are often reciprocal over time if not at given times. The values of caring are especially exemplified in caring relations, rather than in persons as individuals. Caring relations form the small societies of family and friendship on which larger societies depend. And caring relations of a weaker but still evident kind between more distant persons allow them to trust one another enough to live in peace and to respect each others' rights. For progress to be made, persons need to care together as a group for the well-being of their members and of their environment.

The ethics of care builds relations of care and concern and mutual responsiveness to need on both the personal and wider social levels. Within social relations in which we care enough about one another to form a social entity, we may agree on various ways to deal with one another. For instance, for limited purposes we may imagine each other as liberal individuals, independent, autonomous, and rational, and we may adopt liberal schemes of law and governance and policies to maximize individual benefits. But we should not lose sight of the deeper reality of human interdependency and of the need for caring relations to undergird or surround such constructions. The artificial abstraction of the model of the liberal individual is at best suitable for a restricted and limited part of human life rather than for the whole of it. The ethics of care provides a way of thinking about and evaluating both the more immediate and the more distant human relations with which to develop morally acceptable societies.

Notes

I wish to thank especially Sara Ruddick and Hilde Nelson for helpful comments and the American Society for Value Inquiry for the occasion to present this essay at its session at the meeting of the Central Division of the American Philosophical Association in Chicago in April 2002. I am also grateful to the Philosophy Department at Vanderbilt University where the essay was presented and discussed in April 2003.

1. Jeffrey Blustein, *Care and Commitment* (New York: Oxford University Press, 1991); and Harry G. Frankfurt, *The Importance of What We Care About* (Cambridge: Cambridge University Press, 1988).

2. Joan C. Tronto, *Moral Boundaries: A Political Argument for an Ethic of Care* (New York: Routledge, 1993).

3. Nel Noddings, *Caring: A Feminine Approach to Ethics and Moral Education* (Berkeley: University of California Press, 1986), esp. 14–19.

4. Ibid., 42, 80.

5. Nel Noddings, *Starting at Home: Caring and Social Policy* (Berkeley: University of California Press, 2002), 13.

6. Tronto, *Moral Boundaries*, 103; and Berenice Fisher and Joan Tronto, "Toward a Feminist Theory of Caring," in *Circles of Care*, ed. E. Abel and M. Nelson (Albany: SUNY Press, 1990), 40.

7. Virginia Held, *Feminist Morality: Transforming Culture, Society, and Politics* (Chicago: University of Chicago Press, 1993).

8. Diemut Bubeck, *Care, Gender, and Justice* (Oxford: Oxford University Press, 1995), 129.

9. Ibid., 133.

10. Sara Ruddick, "Care as Labor and Relationship," in *Norms and Values: Essays on the Work of Virginia Held*, ed. Joram C. Haber and Mark S. Halfon (Lanham, Md.: Rowman & Littlefield, 1998), 13–14.

11. Peta Bowden, *Caring* (London: Routledge, 1997), 1.

12. Michael Slote, *Morals from Motives* (New York: Oxford University Press, 2001), ix.

13. Ibid., 30.

14. See chapters by Lisa Tessman, Margaret McLaren, and Barbara Andrew in *Feminists Doing Ethics*, ed. Peggy DesAutels and Joanne Waugh (Lanham, Md.: Rowman & Littlefield, 2001).

15. Eva Feder Kittay, *Love's Labor: Essays on Women, Equality, and Dependency* (New York: Routledge, 1999), ix.

16. Ibid., 30.

17. Ibid., 35.

18. Ann Ferguson and Nancy Folbre, "The Unhappy Marriage of Patriarchy and Capitalism," in *Women and Revolution*, ed. Lydia Sargent (Boston: South End Press, 1981), 314.

19. Ruddick, "Care as Labor and Relationship," 4.

20. Ibid.

21. Ibid., 20–21.

22. Ibid., 14.

23. Diana Tietjens Meyers, *Gender in the Mirror: Cultural Imagery and Women's Agency* (New York: Oxford University Press, 2002), 65.

24. Virginia Held, "Moral Subjects: The Natural and the Normative," Presidential Address, American Philosophical Association, Eastern Division, *Proceedings and Addresses of the American Philosophical Association* (Newark, Del.: APA, November 2002).

25. Virginia Held, "Care and the Extension of Markets," *Hypatia* 17, no. 2 (Spring 2002): 19–33.

26. Sara Ruddick, "Injustice in Families: Assault and Domination," in *Justice and Care: Essential Readings in Feminist Ethics*, ed. Virginia Held (Boulder, Col.: Westview, 1995).

27. Virginia Held, *Rights and Goods: Justifying Social Action* (Chicago: University of Chicago Press, 1989), esp. chap. 8.

28. Virginia Held, "Rights and the Presumption of Care," in *Rights and Reason: Essays in Honor of Carl Wellman*, ed. Marilyn Friedman, Larry May, Kate Parsons, and Jennifer Stiff (Dordrecht: Kluwer, 2000).

4

The Future of Feminist Liberalism[1]

Martha C. Nussbaum

Giribala, at the age of fourteen, then started off to make her home with her husband. Her mother put into a bundle the pots and pans that she would be needing. Watching her doing that, Aulchand remarked, "Put in some rice and lentils too. I've got a job at the house of the *babu*. Must report to work the moment I get back . . . "

Giribala picked up the bundle of rice, lentils, and cooking oil and left her village, walking a few steps behind him. He walked ahead, and from time to time asked her to walk faster, as the afternoon was starting to fade.[2]

It will be seen how in place of the *wealth* and *poverty* of political economy come the *rich human being* and *rich human need*. The rich human being is . . . the human being *in need of* a totality of human life-activities.[3]

I. Liberalism and Feminism

During the 1950s and 1960s, it was widely believed that political philosophy had come to a stop. The normative tradition of theorizing about justice that extended, in Western thought, from Plato through Sidgwick and T. H. Green was con-demned as "nonsense" by those under the sway of positivism, since it pursued neither conceptual analysis nor empirical factual inquiry. Young American philos-ophers were discouraged from pursuing projects in this area, unless they confined themselves to analyzing the function of moral and political language.

By now all this has dramatically changed. Theorizing about justice is one of the most fertile areas of work for young philosophers, and there is virtually no department that would condemn all such work as soft and unphilosophical. Two distinct sources of creativity in this area must be credited with the shift, and it is the tense relationship between them that I wish to consider.

On the one hand, writers in the tradition of Kantian liberalism must surely be given much of the credit for the turn back to substantive political philosophy.

John Rawls and Jürgen Habermas, in particular, have become central points of reference, and both must surely be counted as among the most distinguished philosophers of our century.

On the other hand, the most creative movement in the revival of theorizing about justice, I would argue, has been feminist philosophy, which has put new questions on the agenda of moral, political, and legal thought, and has pursued those questions with a prophetic sense of urgency that can be lacking in our sometimes all too detached profession. Important though issues of gender justice are now agreed to be, they were simply not addressed in most major works of political philosophy in the Western tradition; or, as in the case of Rousseau, they were addressed in a perverse and unhelpful manner. Plato and Mill are major exceptions; Mill's *The Subjection of Women* is still one of the major works in the subject, alongside the work of Mary Wollstonecraft and other feminist women. But systematic investigation of justice in the family, of domestic violence and child abuse, of sexual harassment and full workplace equality—all these awaited the modern feminist movement, and have been illuminated by its insights.

As the names of Wollstonecraft and Mill indicate, liberalism and feminism have not always been at odds in our philosophical tradition. Even today, some of our most influential feminist philosophers are liberals. But on the whole liberalism has not fared well in feminist circles. Leading feminists have denounced liberalism as a theoretical approach with insufficient radical potential to expose the roots of women's subordination or to articulate principles for a society of gender justice.

I have argued in the past that some of these feminist criticisms are based on a misunderstanding of the deepest and most appealing liberal conceptions, and that other criticisms, while based on an adequate understanding, should themselves be rejected in favor of liberal conceptions by those who seek full justice for the world's women.[4] Here I shall not return to those arguments. Instead, I shall investigate two areas of political thought in which liberalism, even in its strongest forms, has not yet given satisfactory answers to deep problems exposed by feminist thinkers. Those areas are: the need for care in times of extreme dependency; and the political role of the family. I shall argue that the failure of current liberal theories to solve these problems does not mean that we should reject liberalism; it does mean, however, that we need to recast it in some major ways. I'll conclude that a form of liberalism based on ideas of human functioning and capability can carry us further than we have been able to go so far.

II. Need and Dependency

All theories of justice and morality based on the idea of a social contract adopt a fictional hypothesis that appears innocent, but that ultimately has problematic consequences. This is the fiction of competent adulthood. Whatever differences there are among the different founders of that tradition, all accept the basic Lockean conception of a contract among parties who, in the state of nature, are "free, equal, and independent."[5] Thus for Kant persons are characterized by both freedom and equality, and the social contract is defined as an agreement among persons so characterized. Contemporary contractarians explicitly adopt this hypothesis. For David Gauthier, people of unusual need are "not party to the moral relationships grounded by a contractarian theory."[6] Similarly, the citizens in Rawls's Well Ordered Society are "fully cooperating members of society over a complete life."[7]

Life, of course, is not like that. Real people begin their lives as helpless infants, and remain in a state of extreme, asymmetrical dependency, both physical and mental, for anywhere from ten to twenty years. At the other end of life, those who are lucky enough to live on into old age are likely to encounter another period of extreme dependency, either physical or mental or both, which may itself continue in some form for as much as twenty years. During the middle years of life, many of us encounter periods of extreme dependency, some of which involve our mental powers and some our bodily powers only, but all of which may put us in need of daily, even hourly, care by others. Finally, and centrally, there are many citizens who never have the physical and/or mental powers requisite for independence. These citizens are dependent in different ways. Some have high intellectual capabilities but are unable to give and receive love and friendship; some are capable of love, but unable to learn basic intellectual skills. Some have substantial emotional and intellectual capabilities, but in a form or at a level that requires special care. These lifelong states of asymmetrical dependency are in many respects isomorphic to the states of infants and the elderly.

In short, any real society is a caregiving and care-receiving society, and must therefore discover ways of coping with these facts of human neediness and dependency that are compatible with the self-respect of the recipients and do not exploit the caregivers. This is a central issue for feminism since, in every part of the world, women do a large part of this work, usually without pay, and often without recognition that it is work. They are often thereby handicapped in other functions of life.

It must be said at the outset that in this particular area a Kantian starting point is likely to give bad guidance. For Kant, human dignity and our moral capacity, dignity's source, are radically separate from the natural world. Morality certainly has the task of providing for human neediness, but the idea that we are at bottom split beings, both rational persons and animal dwellers in the world of nature, never ceases to influence Kant's way of thinking about how these deliberations about our needs will go.

What's wrong with the split? Quite a lot. First, it ignores the fact that our dignity just is the dignity of a certain sort of animal. It is the animal sort of dignity, and that very sort of dignity could not be possessed by a being who was not mortal and vulnerable, just as the beauty of a cherry tree in bloom could not be possessed by a diamond. If it makes sense to think of God as having dignity (I'm not sure— magnificence and awe-inspiringness seem more appropriate attributes), it is emphatically not dignity of that type. Second, the split wrongly denies that animality can itself have a dignity; thus it leads us to slight aspects of our own lives that have worth, and to distort our relation to the other animals. Third, it makes us think of the core of ourselves as self-sufficient, not in need of the gifts of fortune; in so thinking we greatly distort the nature of our own morality and rationality, which are thoroughly material and animal themselves; we learn to ignore the fact that disease, old age, and accident can impede the moral and rational functions, just as much as the other animal functions. Fourth, it makes us think of ourselves as atemporal. We forget that the usual human lifecycle brings with it periods of extreme dependency, in which our functioning is very similar to that enjoyed by the mentally or physically handicapped throughout their lives.

Political thought in the Kantian social-contract tradition (to stick with the part of the tradition I find deepest and most appealing) suffers from the conception of the person with which it begins. Rawls's contracting parties are fully aware of their need for material goods. Here Rawls diverges from Kant, building need into the foundations of the theory. But he does so only to a degree: for the parties are imagined throughout as competent contracting adults, roughly similar in need, and capable of a level of social cooperation that makes them able to make a contract with others. Such a hypothesis seems required by the very idea of a contract for mutual advantage.

In so conceiving of persons, Rawls explicitly omits from the situation of basic political choice the more extreme forms of need and dependency human beings may experience. His very concept of social cooperation is based on the idea of reciprocity between rough equals, and has no explicit place for relations of extreme dependency. Thus, for example, Rawls refuses to grant that we have any duties of justice to animals, on the grounds that they are not capable of reciprocity;[8] they are owed "compassion and humanity," but "[t]hey are outside the scope of the theory of justice, and it does not seem possible to extend the contract doctrine so as to include them in a natural way."[9] This makes a large difference to his theory of political distribution. For his account of the primary goods, introduced, as it is, as an account of the needs of citizens who are characterized by the two moral powers and by the capacity to be "fully cooperating," has no place for the need of many real people for the kind of care we give to people who are not independent.

Now of course Rawls is perfectly aware that his theory focuses on some cases and leaves others to one side. He insists that, although the need for care for people who are not independent is "a pressing practical question," it may reasonably be postponed to the legislative stage, after basic political institutions are designed:

> At this initial stage, the fundamental problem of social justice arises between those who are full and active and morally conscientious participants in society, and directly or indirectly associated together throughout a complete life. Therefore, it is sensible to lay aside certain difficult complications. If we can work out a theory that covers the fundamental case, we can try to extend it to other cases later.[10]

This reply seems inadequate. Care for children, the elderly, and the mentally and physically handicapped is a major part of the work that needs to be done in any society, and in most societies it is a source of great injustice. Any theory of justice needs to think about the problem from the beginning, in the design of the most basic level of institutions, and particularly in its theory of the primary goods.

More generally, variations and asymmetries in physical need are simply not isolated or easily isolable cases: they are a pervasive fact of human life. Pregnant or lactating women need more nutrients than non-pregnant persons, children need more protein than adults, and the very young and very old need more care than others in most areas of their lives. Even within the clearly recognized terrain of the "fully cooperating," then, the theory of primary goods seems flawed if it does not take such variations into account in measuring who is and is not the least well off, rather than, as the theory recommends, determining that status by income and wealth alone. Amartya Sen has used the example of a person in a wheelchair, who will certainly need more resources to be fully mobile than will a person whose limbs work well. Rawls can't consistently exclude this person, who surely has the mental and moral powers. But even if he should exclude these physical disabilities, as some of his remarks suggest, the problem of variation in need is pervasive. So even in order to take account of the physical needs of non-disabled citizens—which the theory seems bound, even on its own terms, to take account of—Rawls will need a way of measuring well-being that does not rely on income and wealth alone, but looks at the abilities of citizens to engage in a wide range of human activities.

Thomas Scanlon confronts these problems facing a Kantian contract doctrine much more directly than does Rawls. I am unable here to discuss the subtleties of his view, which in any case is a moral and not a political contract doctrine; but, taking cognizance of the problem posed for such a theory by people with various handicaps, he concludes that we may recognize facts of extreme dependency in such a doctrine in one of two ways. Either we may persist in our pursuit of the contract doctrine, and say that the contracting parties are also trustees for those who are incapable of participating in that process; or we may say that the contract doctrine offers an account of only one part of morality: we will need a different account to cope with the facts of extreme dependency.[11] Applied to the Rawlsian project of selecting principles of justice that will form the basic structure of society, this would mean that we either take the parties in the Original Position to be trustees for the interests of all dependent members of society, as they currently are trustees for future generations—or else we should grant that the Original Position is not a complete device for designing political justice, and that other approaches are also required.

The first solution seems unsatisfactory. To make the "fully cooperating" trustees slights the dignity of physically and mentally handicapped people, suggesting that they are worthy of respect in the design of basic political institutions only on account of some relationship in which they stand to so-called "fully cooperating" people. Furthermore, the move also means making the "fully cooperating" trustees for their own infancy and senility, and perhaps other stages of their own lives. Gauthier puts the problem most starkly, when he says that the elderly have paid for their care by earlier periods of productive activity, but the handicapped have not.[12] In other words, for the contractarian only productivity justifies, ultimately, a claim to support, and the elderly get support only because at one time they were not elderly. Animality all on its own cannot justify a claim to support. Rawls's theory, though more subtle, still suffers from something like this problem. To require of the parties that they split their thinking in this way, conceiving of themselves as made up of two parts, the rational and the animal, is to force into their thinking a Kantian splitting that may well prejudice their thinking about the dignity of animality in themselves. Are we not in effect saying that animality gets support only in virtue of its contingent link to "fully cooperating" adulthood? And doesn't this slight the dignity and worth that needy human animals surely possess even when they are not fully cooperating? Surely, if it is not necessary to require such split thinking, we should avoid it.

Thus, like Scanlon, I prefer the second solution: the contract doctrine does not provide a complete ethical theory. But this reply, while fine for Scanlon because he is doing ethical theory, creates large problems for the contract doctrine in the area of political theory. Any approach to the design of basic political institutions must aim at a certain degree of completeness and finality, as Rawls's doctrine explicitly does. We are designing the basic structure of society, those institutions that influence all citizens' life-chances pervasively and from the start. So it is not open to us to say: we have done one part of that task, but of course other parts, equally basic, based on completely different principles, will come along later. If we leave for another day not only our relations to the non-human animals, but also the needs entailed by our own animality, that would leave huge areas of political justice up for grabs and would entail the recognition of much indeterminacy in the account of basic justice as so far worked out.

What, then, can be done to give the problem of care and dependency sufficient prominence in a theory of justice? The first thing we might try, one that has been suggested by Eva Kittay in her fine book, is to add the need for care during periods of extreme and asymmetrical dependency to the Rawlsian list of primary goods, thinking of care as among the basic needs of citizens.[13]

This suggestion, if we adopt it, would lead us to make another modification: for care is hardly a commodity, like income and wealth, to be measured by the sheer amount of it citizens have. Thus adding care to the list would cause us to notice that Rawls's list of primary goods is already quite heterogeneous in its structure. Some of its members are thing-like items such as income and wealth; but some are already more like human capabilities to function in various ways: the liberties, opportunities, and powers, and also the social basis of self-respect. Along with this suggestion, we might propose understanding the entire list of primary goods as a list not of things but of basic capabilities. This change would not only enable us to deal better with people's needs for various types of love and care as elements of the list, but would also answer the point that Sen has repeatedly made all along about the unreliability of income and wealth as indices of well-being. The well-being of citizens will now be measured not by the sheer amount of income and wealth they have, but by the degree to which they have the various capabilities on the list. One may be well off in terms of income and wealth, and yet unable to function well in the workplace, because of burdens of caregiving at home.

If we accepted these two changes, we would surely add a third, highly relevant to our thoughts about infancy and old age. We would add other capability-like items to the list of basic goods: for example the social basis of health, and the social basis of imagination and emotional well-being.

Suppose, then, we do make these three changes in the list of primary goods: we add care in times of extreme dependency to the list of primary goods; we reconfigure the list as a list of capabilities; and we add other pertinent items to the list as well. Have we done enough to salvage the contract doctrine as a way of generating basic political principles? I believe that there is still room for doubt. Consider the role of primary goods in Rawls's theory. The account of primary goods is introduced in connection with the Kantian political conception of the person, as an account of what citizens characterized by the two moral powers need. Thus, we have attributed basic importance to care only from the point of view of our own current independence. It is good to be cared for only because care subserves moral personality, understood in a Kantian way as conceptually quite distinct from need and animality. This seems like another more subtle way of making our animality subserve our humanity, where humanity is understood to exclude animality. The idea is that because we are dignified beings capable of political reciprocity, therefore we had better provide for times when we are not that, so we can get back to being that as quickly as possible. I think that this is a dubious enough way to think about illnesses in the prime of life; but it surely leads us in the direction of a contemptuous attitude toward infancy and childhood, and, a particular danger in our society, toward elderly disability. Finally, it leads us strongly in the direction of not fully valuing those with lifelong mental disabilities: somehow or other, care for them is supposed to be valuable only for the sake of what it does for the "fully cooperating." They are, it would seem, being used as means for someone else's ends, and their full humanity is still being denied.

So I believe that we need to delve deeper, redesigning the political conception of the person, bringing the rational and the animal into a more intimate relation with one another, and acknowledging that there are many types of dignity in the world, including the dignity of mentally disabled children and adults, the dignity of the senile demented elderly, and the dignity of babies at the breast. We want the picture of the parties who design political institutions to build these facts in from the start. And this may well mean, as Scanlon has suggested, that the theory cannot be a contractarian theory at all.

Such a conclusion should be reached with caution. Rawls's theory has often been wrongly criticized, because critics have not noticed that his model of the person in the Original Position is complex: his account of the person is not simply the account of the rationality of the parties, but that account *combined with* the account of the veil of ignorance, which is a complex way of modeling benevolence. Thus it is incorrect to say that he has not included concern for others in the conception of the person that forms the foundation of his theory—as he has noted, discussing Schopenhauer's similar critique of Kant. What this mistake shows us is that the contract doctrine has many ways of modeling the person; so we should not rule out the possibility that some device may be found through which a doctrine basically contractarian in spirit could model need and animality, just as it has modeled benevolence.[14] There is, however, some reason to doubt that this can be done. For any such model would still involve a split of just the sort I've objected to, one that makes our rationality trustee, in effect, for our animality. And that, as I've argued, is inadequate for the kind of dignity and centrality we want to give to the problems of asymmetrical need.

Thus, while not denying that some determined contractarian might possibly solve this problem, I think it best to proceed as if it has not been solved. When we add to our worries the fact that Rawls's contract doctrine uses a political concept of the person at a number of different points, most of them not in association with the complex model of the original position, we have even more reason to want the political concept of the person to be one that does justice to temporality and need. So I believe we need to adopt a political conception of the person that is more Aristotelian than Kantian, one that sees the person from the start as both capable and needy—"in need of a rich plurality of life-activities," to use Marx's phrase, whose availability will be the measure of well-being. Such a conception of the person, which builds growth and decline into the trajectory of human life, will put us on the road to thinking well about what society should design. We don't have to contract for what we need by producing; we have a claim to support in the dignity of our human need itself. Since this is not just an Aristotelian idea, but one that corresponds to human experience, there is good reason to think that it can command a political consensus in a pluralistic society. If we begin with this conception of the person and with a suitable list of the central capabilities as primary goods, we can begin designing institutions by asking what it would take to get citizens up to an acceptable level on all these capabilities. I cannot say more here about the detail of that project.

In this area, then, liberal theory needs to question some of its most traditional starting points—questioning, in the process, the Kantian notion of the person. That does not disable the enterprise. It seems to me that a theory basically liberal—building in a central role for choice and liberty—can survive this critique. But it does entail substantial changes in the shape and intuitive grounding of the theory.

III. Justice in the Family

The most difficult problem liberal theory faces in the area of women's equality is the problem of the family. On the one hand, the family is among the most significant arenas in which people pursue their own conceptions of the good, and transmit them to the next generation. This fact suggests that a liberal society should give people considerable latitude to form families as they choose. On the other hand, the family is one of the most non-voluntary and pervasively influential of social institutions, and one of the most notorious homes of sex hierarchy, denial of equal opportunity, and sex-based violence and humiliation. These facts suggest that a society committed to equal justice for all citizens, and to securing for all citizens the social bases of liberty, opportunity, and self-respect, must constrain the family in the name of justice. Most liberal theories (Mill being the honorable exception) have simply neglected this problem, or have treated the family as a "private" sphere into which political justice should not meddle. As Catharine MacKinnon has observed, the public-private distinction has typically functioned to protect *male* privacy, and not female privacy, and thence the unlimited sway of men over women in a protected domain; thus liberal rhetoric about the sanctity of privacy should strike us as "an injury got up as a gift."[15] Rawls from the first has denied that the family is a space exempt from the claims of justice, by asserting that it is part of society's basic structure, ergo one of those institutions to which principles of justice would apply. But, having granted this, he then has to solve one of the most difficult of problems: how to render this institution compatible with justice.

In "The Idea of Public Reason Revisited," Rawls has finally addressed the problem.[16] He makes two claims, which are difficult to render consistent. On the one hand, he asserts that the family forms part of society's basic structure. At the same time, however, he claims that the two principles of justice, while they apply directly to the basic structure, do not "apply directly to the internal life of families." In fact, he continues, the principles apply to families in just the way that they apply to society's many voluntary associations, such as churches and universities. That is, the principles supply external constraints on what the associations can do, but they do not regulate their internal workings. A university, for example, cannot violate basic provisions of the criminal law, or of political justice more generally; but it may assign functions in accordance with its own criteria, whatever they are. So too with the family: the principles of justice do supply real constraints, by specifying the basic rights of equal citizens. The family cannot violate these rights. "The equal rights of women and the basic rights of their children as future citizens are inalienable and protect them wherever they are. Gender distinctions limiting those rights and liberties are excluded."[17] And yet, citizens are not required to raise their children in accordance with liberal principles; we may have to allow for some traditional gendered division of labor in families, "provided it is fully voluntary and does not result from or lead to injustice."[18]

In practical terms, Rawls thinks that we cannot make rules for the division of labor in families, or penalize those who don't comply. But at the legislative stage we can introduce laws that protect women's full equality as citizens, for example divorce laws of the sort favored by Susan Okin: "It seems intolerably unjust that a husband may depart the family taking his earning power with him and leaving his wife and children far less advantaged than before . . . A society that permits this does not care about women, much less about their equality, or even about their children, who are its future."[19]

These proposals raise three large questions. First of all, if the family is part of the basic structure, how can it also be a voluntary institution, analogous to a church or a university? The institutions of the basic structure are those whose influence is pervasive and present from the start of a human life. The family is such an institution; universities, and churches (except as extensions of families) are not. For adult women, membership in a family may be voluntary (though this is not always clear), and Rawls's protection of their exit options may suffice to ensure their full equality. But children are simply hostages to the family in which they grow up, and their participation in its gendered structure is by no means voluntary. Granted, it is not terribly clear what it would mean to apply the principles of justice to the family *as part of the basic structure*: for surely the principles apply to the basic structure taken as a whole, and this does not entail that they apply piecemeal to every institution that forms part of the basic structure. And yet the fact that the family is part of the basic structure, and universities, etc. are not, ought to make *some* difference in the way in which the principles apply; Rawls ought to have given us some account of that difference.

Second, Rawls does not acknowledge the parochial character of the Western nuclear family. Surprisingly, he still seems to regard some such unit as having a quasi-natural status, and as characterized by what he continues to call "natural affections"; although he has broadened his account to include non-traditional nuclear groupings, such as same-sex couples, he nowhere acknowledges the parochial character of the whole idea of raising children in a nuclear family. Village groups, extended families, women's collectives, kibbutzim, these and other groups have been involved in raising children; the contracting parties, not knowing where they are in place and time, should not give preference to a Western bourgeois form over other possible forms. They should look at the issues of justice with an open mind, giving favor to those groupings that seem most capable of rearing children, compatibly with other requirements of justice.

Third, Rawls does not recognize the extent to which, in all modern societies, the "family" is a creation of state action, enjoying a very different status from that of a church or a university. People associate in many different ways, live together, love each other, have children. Which of these will get the name "family" is a legal and political matter, never one to be decided simply by the parties themselves. The state constitutes the family structure through its laws, defining which groups of people can count as families, defining the privileges and rights of family members, defining what marriage and divorce are, what legitimacy and parental responsibility are, and so forth. This difference makes a difference: the state is present in the family from the start, in a way that is less clearly the case with the religious body or the university; it is the state who says what this thing *is* and controls how one becomes a member of it.[20]

To see this more clearly, let us consider the rituals that define a person as a member of an association: in the (private) University, matriculation (and, later, the granting of a degree); in a religious body, baptism, conversion, or some analogous entrance rite; in the family, marriage. Now it is evident that the State has some connection with university matriculation/graduation and with religious baptism/conversion: it polices these rites on the outside, by defining the institution as enjoying tax-free status, by preventing the use of cruelty or other illegalities in the ritual, and so forth. But marriage is from the start a public, state-administered rite.

There are state laws defining it, which restrict entry into that privileged domain. The state does not police marriage on the outside, it marries people. Other similar people who don't meet the state's test cannot count as married, even if they satisfy all private and even religious criteria for marriage. (Thus, same-sex couples whose unions have been solemnized by some religious body still are not married, because the state has not granted them a license.) All human associations are shaped by laws and institutions, which either favor or disfavor them, and structure them in various ways. But the family is shaped by law in a yet deeper and more thoroughgoing way, in the sense that its very definition is legal and political; individuals may call themselves "a family" if they wish, but they only get to be one, in the sense that is socially significant, if they satisfy legal tests. In short, the political sphere cannot avoid directly shaping the family structure, by recognizing some and not other groupings as families. Rawls tends to treat the family as an organization that has an extrapolitical existence, and to ask how far the state may interfere with it. If, instead, he had recognized the foundational character of the state's presence in the family, he might have granted that it makes good sense for principles of justice to recognize and favor any units, traditional or non-traditional, that perform the functions associated with family in ways that are compatible with political justice.

My feeling is that in this delicate area Rawls has been too ready to recognize what are, in effect, group rights: the right of families, conceived of as pre-political, to protection against state action. Put another way, his distinction between external and internal regulation recreates the problematic features of the very distinction he questions, the distinction between the public and the private sphere. If we really acknowledge the equal worth of all citizens, and the profound vulnerability of children in families, we should, I believe, conceive of the entire issue in a subtly different way: by thinking how we may balance adult freedom of association, and other important interests in pursuing one's own conception of the good, against the liberties and opportunities of children as future citizens. Once again, beginning from citizens' needs for a wide range of human capabilities puts the problem on a subtly different footing from the start and enables us to move forward. No group gets special privileges qua group. But all persons deserve support for a wide range of capabilities—prominently including not only the capabilities of freedom of religion and freedom of association, but also the capability to form relationships of affection and care.

If we proceed in this way, and recognize in addition that there is no group that exists "by nature," and that the family is more a state creation than most other associations, then the natural question will be: What forms of state action, and what forms of privilege given to certain groupings, will best protect the liberties and opportunities of women and children, within limits set by the protection of adult freedom of association and other important liberties? In posing this question, we do not assume that any one affiliative grouping is prior or central in promoting those capabilities. People have needs for love and care, for reproduction, for sexual expression; children have needs for love, support, and education; and people also enjoy a wide range of associational liberties. But at this point I believe we need to look and see how different groupings of persons do in promoting these capabilities. In some nations, for example India, women's collectives play a valuable role in giving women love and friendship, in caring for children, and in fostering the other capabilities. Conventional families often do less well. Sometimes a women's collective appears to be more truly a child's family than its nuclear home, as when, as often happens, women's collectives protect children from sexual abuse, or arrange for children at risk of abuse, or child marriage, to be protected through state-run schools. There need not even be a presumption that all the functions we now associate with family will be bundled under a single institution. Thus France has acted wisely, I believe, when it asks why the definition of household for the purposes of inheritance should be at all the same as the account of who gets to adopt and raise children. Brothers and sisters who live in the same house may be a household for the former purpose but not for the latter. My approach would urge that such decisions be contextual, asking how, in the given history and circumstances, public policy can best promote the claims of the human capabilities. The only thing that stops state intervention is the person and the various liberties and rights of the person, including associative liberties, the right to be free from unwarranted search and seizure, and so forth. The family has no power to stop this intervention on its own, as though it were a mystical unity over and above the lives of its members.

Similarly, my approach urges us to question whether the distinctions relied upon by Rawls's current position—distinctions between external and internal regulation, and between state action and inaction, are really coherent. Laws governing marriage, divorce, compulsory education, inheritance—all are as internal as anything can be in the family. Nor should the criminal justice system know a distinction between inside and outside, in the definition and ranking of criminal offenses: it should treat rape as rape, battery as battery, coercion as coercion, wherever they occur. To let things take their status quo ante course is to choose a course of action, not to be completely neutral. In short, the state's interest in protecting the dignity, integrity, and well-being of each citizen never simply leads to external constraints on the family structure, whatever appearances may be; it always leads to positive constructing of the family institution. This constructing should be done in ways that are compatible with political justice.

In practical terms, my approach in terms of the promotion of capabilities and Rawls's approach, which views the two principles of justice as supplying external constraints on the family, will give many of the same answers. Laws against marital rape, laws protecting marital consent, laws mandating compulsory education, laws banning child marriage and child labor, laws ensuring an appropriate material recognition of the wife's economic contribution to the family, laws providing child care to support working mothers, laws promoting the nutrition and health of girl children—all these laws, I think, we would both support as appropriate expressions of state concern for citizens and future citizens. But the grounds on which we will support them will be subtly different. Rawls sees the laws as supplying external constraints on something that has its own form, the way laws constrain a university or a church; I see them as contributing to the constitution of an institution that is in the most direct sense a part of the basic structure of society.

Furthermore, my approach, like Rawls's, would permit the state to give conventional family groupings certain special privileges and protections, just as it gives religious bodies certain privileges and protections. It will probably do so in many cases, since the family does promote the rearing of children, as well as serving other needs of citizens. Thus parents may be given certain limited kinds of deference in making choices regarding their children. And tax breaks for family units are not ruled out, insofar as these units promote human capabilities. But for me, the reason the state will choose such policies is to protect the central capabilities of individuals; the definition of family, and the policies chosen, should be chosen with this aim in view. Rawls does not ask how "family" should be defined, nor does he make it clear on what basis it should have special privileges, although the state's interest in its future citizens would appear to be one such basis.

Most important of all, because Rawls takes the family as given, he does not ask what my approach urges us to ask at all times: What other affective and associational ties deserve public protection and support? It is not at all clear, then, what role non-traditional affective groupings such as Indian women's collectives, or French Pacts of Civil Solidarity, could play in his account of society's basic structure. And yet he proceeds as if, at the level of the Original Position, the account is historically neutral, not biased in favor of the status quo in any given place and time. In my approach, at that basic level we have only the capabilities to consider, and we may consider any institutional grouping that can promote them. At a later, more concrete level—corresponding to Rawls's constitutional and legislative stages—such inquiries will rightly become contextual, although even at that point this will not mean that the traditional form of a practice will have exclusive privileges.

Notice, then, that my approach leaves for fine-tuned contextual judgment of certain matters that Kantian liberalism wishes to settle in a definite way before lauching into the currents of history, including the all-important question of what forms of human organization shall be favored for the care and education of children. I urge that these questions be left to the contextual deliberation of citizens, in the light of their history and their current problems, and in the light of the capability list, which remains relatively constant over time. Such an approach will strike the Rawlsian as dangerously "intuitionistic"; and yet we should not purchase definiteness at the price of falsehood, by stating or implying that a parochial grouping is ahistorical and universal.

Again, my approach would forbid certain types of interference with the family structure that Rawls's approach would also forbid. For me as for Rawls, it is wrong for the state to mandate the equal division of domestic labor or equal decision-making in the household. But again, the reasons for this shared conclusion will differ. Rawls judges that it is wrong to interfere with the internal workings of a particular institution, deemed to exist apart from the state—whereas I judge simply that there are associational liberties of individuals, and liberties of speech, that should always be protected for citizens, no matter where they occur. (Rawls might have reached a result similar to the one he does reach by relying on the priority of liberty; but, significantly, he does not use that argument.) It just seems an intolerable infringement of liberty for the state to get involved in dictating how people do their dishes. But for me, dubious conduct gets less prima facie protection if it is in the family than if it is in a purely voluntary association, since the family (for children at any rate) is a non-voluntary institution that influences citizens' life chances pervasively and from the start.

In a wide range of areas, our approaches will support different choices of public policy. In my approach, the central capabilities always supply a compelling interest for purposes of government action. Thus it will be all right to render dowry illegal in India (as has been done), given the compelling evidence that the dowry system is a major source of women's capability failure. I believe that Rawls would have a difficult time justifying this law—because he is thinking of the family as pre-political, and dowry as one of the choices it makes in its pre-political state. For me, by contrast, the family is constituted by laws and institutions, and one of the questions to be asked is whether dowry-giving is one of the things it should be in the business of doing. Permitting dowry is not neutral state inaction toward an autonomous private entity; it is another (alternative) way of constituting a part of the public sphere. Again, interference with traditional decision-making patterns in the family will be much easier to justify on my approach than on Rawls's. Consider the Mahila Samakhya project in Andhra Pradesh, in southern India. This project, funded and run by the national government, is explicitly aimed at increasing women's confidence and initiative, and empowering them in their dealings with employers, government officials, and husbands, and extending a wide range of life options to their female children. There is no doubt at all that the government is attempting to reconstruct the family by altering social norms and perceptions. No community and no individual is forced to join, and this is a reservation I would support. Nonetheless, it seems likely that there is more in the way of endorsing a particular conception of family governance than Rawls would consider acceptable. Apart from the content of the teaching, the very existence of the women's collectives as a focus for women's affective lives transforms the family profoundly, making it no longer the sole source of personal affiliation. It seems likely that Rawls would oppose government support for such collectives on that account, thinking of it as the endorsement of one conception of the good over another—for much the same reason that he has opposed government support for music and the arts. For me, the fact that women's capabilities are in a perilous state, together with the fact that empowerment programs have succeeded in giving them greater control over their material and political environment, gives government a compelling interest in introducing such programs.

Or consider governmental programs that focus on giving women access to credit and economic self-sufficiency, together with education in confidence and leadership. (Such programs are common in developing countries; at least some such programs are governmental.) I surmise that for Rawls such programs would be an impermissible interference by government into the family structure. The very idea that government would support an all-women's bank, for example, would be highly suspect. For me, while I think it's very important for a program like this to be non-coercive, it seems quite all right for government to act in ways that aim at changing social norms that shape the family, and at promoting capabilities in those who lack them. For after all, and this is the crux of the matter, government is already in the business of constructing an institution that is part of the basic structure of society. It had better do this job well.

The largest difference in the two approaches will be in the treatment of female children. It is here, especially, that my approach recognizes the pervasive and non-voluntary nature of family membership, and gives the state broad latitude in shaping perception and behavior to promote the development of female children to full adult capability in the major areas. This means not only the abolition of child marriage and (where practically possible) child labor, and (where practically possible) compulsory primary and secondary education for all children. Rawls would presumably also favor these changes. It also means encouraging the public perception that women are suited for many different roles in life, something that Rawls is likely to see as too much promoting of a definite conception of the good. Thus the content of public education should include information about options for women, and about resistance to women's inequality. In addition to regular schooling, the Indian government also supports residential programs for young girls who are at risk for child marriage, to remove them from home and give them education and job training. Rawls would be likely to see this as too much state intervention, even if the mothers consent to the girls going away: after all, government is saying, "I will support you if you leave this dangerous structure." My approach judges that the protection of girls' capabilities warrants an interventionist strategy.

Rawls's approach to the family and mine are very close. Both of us take our bearings from the idea of the dignity and worth of humanity, and the idea that no human being shall be used as a mere means for the ends of others. Both of us define the person as the basis of distribution; both of us see an important role for liberties of association and self-definition; both of us recognize the intrinsic value of love and care. But Rawls, while rejecting the public/private distinction, remains half-hearted in that rejection. I have tried to show how an approach through the central capabilities would capture the value of family love and care, while nonetheless rejecting more consistently a distinction that has disfigured the lives of girls and women through the ages.

IV. A Liberal Future?

Liberal political thought has not yet realized its full potential. In two areas crucial to women's equality there are basic problems with liberal doctrines as so far developed. These difficulties give us good reason to try out new liberal alternatives; one that deserves a hearing is a neo-Aristotelian liberalism based on an idea of human capabilities as central political goals.

It seems clear that a theory basically liberal in spirit can meet the problems of need and dependency. The difficulties pertaining to the family raise more troubling issues: for they seem to threaten the very project of a political liberalism, an approach committed both to respecting each person as an end and to respecting the fact of reasonable pluralism among comprehensive views of life. There is no doubt that some of the major comprehensive views of what gives life meaning are dead set against the kind of revisionary treatment of family structure that my approach sees required by political justice. Extending the privileges of marriage to previously unrecognized couples is at least on our political agenda; radical rethinking of the institutions of marriage and family will be much more difficult to achieve, although nations such as France and India have been able to go further. It is no accident that in a sphere that is the home both of intimate self-definition and also of egregious wrongdoing the search for liberal justice should encounter difficulties: for liberal justice is committed both to protecting spheres of self-definition and to ending the wrongful tyranny of some people over others.

But the failure to have a fully satisfactory solution to these difficulties is not a failure of liberal justice, because the liberal is right. Self-definition is important, and it is also important to end wrongful tyranny. The tension that results from these twin principles is at the heart of liberalism, but it is a valuable and fruitful tension, not one that shows confusion or moral failure. In general, tension within a theory does not necessarily show that it is defective; it may simply show that it is in touch with the difficulty of life. And that, I believe, is the case here. Reflection on the tension ought to lead us, over time, to figure out how to design a society that balances these competing values as well as they can be balanced, and to provide institutional protections for women and children who currently suffer from unresolved conflicts between them. This effort would do well to begin by imagining and studying the many ways in which groups of people of many different types have managed, in different places at different times, to care for one another and to raise children with both love and justice.

Notes

1. I am grateful to Ann Cudd, John Deigh, Chad Flanders, Charles Larmore, Thomas Scanlon, and Cass Sunstein for comments on a previous draft and to Geof Sayre McCord, Tom Hill, Jr., and other members of the Research Triangle Ethics discussion group for extremely helpful discussion of these issues.

2. Mahasweta Devi, "Giribala," Translated from the Bengali by Kalpana Bardhan, in *Women, Outcastes, Peasants, and Rebels: A Selection of Bengali Short Stories* (Berkeley, CA: University of California Press, 1900), 274.

3. Marx, *Economic and Philosophical Manuscripts of 1844*.

4. See my "The Feminist Critique of Liberalism," chapter 2 of *Sex and Social Justice* (New York: Oxford University Press, 1999); also published as a Lindley Lecture, 1997, University of Kansas Press.

5. Locke, *Second Treatise of Government*, 1869, chapter 8.

6. David Gauthier, *Morals By Agreement* (New York: Oxford University Press, 1986), 18, speaking of all "persons who decrease th[e] average level" of well-being in a society.

7. John Rawls, *A Theory of Justice* (Cambridge, MA: Harvard University Press, 1971).

8. Ibid., 504–505.

9. Ibid., 512.

10. John Rawls, "Kantian Constructurism," in *Moral Theory*; *The Dewy Lectures* 1980. Journal of Philosophy, V. 77 1980, 515–572.

11. T. M. Scanlon, *What We Owe to Each Other* (Cambridge, MA: Harvard University Press, 1999).

12. David Gauthier, *Morals By Agreement* (New York: Oxford University Press, 1986), 18 n. 30.

13. Eva Kittay, *Love's Labor: Essays on Women, Equality and Dependency* (New York: Routledge, 1999).

14. I owe this point to Geof Sayre-McCord, who pointed out that I myself have criticized feminists who don't see the Veil of Ignorance as part of the model of the person: see my "Rawls and Feminism," in *The Cambridge Companion to Rawls*, ed. Samuel Richard Freeman (Cambridge, MA: Cambridge University Press, 2002)

15. Catharine MacKinnon, "Privacy N. Equality," *Feminism Unmodified: Discourses on Life and Law* (Cambridge, MA: Harvard University Press, 1987), 100.

16. John Rawls, "The Idea of Public Reason Revisited," *University of Chicago Law Review* 64 (1997): 765–807.v

17. Ibid., 791.

18. Rawls understands the fact that it is chosen on the basis of one's religion as a sufficient condition of voluntariness, in background conditions that are fair (Ibid., 792 and n. 68); he notes that the question needs a fuller discussion

19. Ibid., 792.

20. See Martha Minow, "All in the Family and In All Families: Membership, Loving, and Owing," in David Estlund and Martha Nussbaum, eds., *Sex, Preference, and Family: Essays on Law and Nature* (New York: Oxford University Press, 1997). See also Frances Olsen, "The Family and the Market: A Study of Ideology and Legal Reform," *Harvard Law Review* 96 (1983): 1497–1577, and "The Myth of State Intervention in the Family," *University of Michigan Journal of Law Reform* 18 (1985): 835–864.

II

What We Ought to Do for Each Other

5

The Scope of Moral Requirement

Barbara Herman

The subject of this article is the duty of beneficence: the obligation we have to promote one another's good. It is generally agreed that there is a duty of easy rescue; we are required to provide aid when that will prevent or relieve dire conditions for someone, when the cost to us is slight or moderate. And also that there is a companion duty of consideration or helpfulness, a requirement that we "lend a hand" to persons whose permissible activities or projects would founder without some small help we might easily provide. What is less clear is the nature and scope of the moral requirement in other cases. It is difficult to be sure about the sorts of need that fall under beneficence, how much can be required of us, and toward whom.

In moral theories that take the promotion of well-being as their core value, beneficence comes naturally. The philosophical and practical challenge is to bring it under control.[1] Once the claim of need is acknowledged, it is not easy to see what, morally, can constrain its demand. In theories whose core value does not refer to well-being, while it may be obvious that there is a duty of beneficence, its source is often not so clear. Typically, something about the value of persons is said to support a concern for well-being directly, or as a weighty derivative value. Here too it has not been easy to specify the duty's scope and a level of reasonable response.

In many accounts of beneficence, a great deal of work tends to be done by the intuition that the duty cannot be very demanding: it can neither absorb large amounts of our resources, nor require a great deal of practical attention. But a slippery slope threatens. If it is allowed that the duty might be even somewhat demanding, might impose real costs on our activities and plans, then given any reasonable account of the need that might trigger beneficence, there is no well-founded stopping point on the demand up to the point of reducing the aid-provider to comparable neediness. Even with the introduction of a lateral requirement, for example, that we cannot be called on to assume more than our fair share of the burden of meeting need, it remains an open empirical question whether that share might not be large.[2]

The issues here reflect two independent currents in our moral understanding. One is the relation of fit between morality and ordinary life: that whatever morality requires of us, it should not make our lives unlivable, or too severe. The other is the conviction that we must negotiate a decent response to the irrefutable facts of need—of hunger, disease, and poverty. The tension between them plays out in many ways: it can, for example, seem reasonable to think that we have different and perhaps special obligations to persons in need who are in one sense or another local to us—to friends, family, or coworkers—than we do to those at a distance; we also recognize a continuum of need to which we seem obligated to respond impartially, regardless of relation or locale. If we regard these currents as reflecting independent values, of human well-being and the moderation of moral demand, or of the local and the global, the resources for resolving the tensions between them seem limited to some sort of balancing. But it is hard to imagine striking a balance that will not seem or be arbitrary.

My own view is that neither the intuitions about cases, nor the tensions within morality they point to, make available sufficient resources of argument to take us past this point. Whether the problems associated with beneficence are intractable, or turn out to be expressions of parochial sentiment, or something else, will depend on how things look when they are located in a more comprehensive moral view. We should not, for example, just assume that questions about the limits of obligation, about the fit of obligations in a decent life, are to be negotiated by appeal to extra-moral value, as if it were obvious that morality cannot get it right about what reasonably matters to us. Nor should we just assume that there is (or is not) some natural division in obligation that tracks group affiliations or relationships.

What I propose to do here, after a brief canvass of some of the intuitions that generate the tensions, is to introduce a theoretical framework for thinking about them drawn from a comprehensive moral view: specifically, Kant's account of obligatory ends and the imperfect duties they support. It is an avenue not much tried, and there are some obvious advantages to be hoped for in reframing scope questions in the terms of an agency-sensitive theory such as Kant's. Obligatory ends turn out to be a useful axis of inquiry because they present beneficence, the duty to take others' happiness as one's end, within a unified account of duties to self and others. Somewhat unexpectedly, their way of carving up moral space makes some sense of our bias toward the local in beneficence, as well as offering a very different perspective on the demandingness of the duty.

I will treat as a separate question how such an agency-based account of beneficence fits with the different obligation to need we have in justice. Though both justice and beneficence can have the same object—human welfare—they negotiate distinct domains of concern. What I hope to show is that in a variety of interesting ways justice and beneficence both limit and complete one another.

In any discussion of need, questions of injustice, both rectificatory and distributive, can swamp other issues. But the moral tensions the facts of need introduce are not necessarily the product of injustice, though injustice can surely make them more complicated. Philosophically, there is a prior, independent issue concerning our moral relations to one another: a question about the moral standing of one's own life, and how one is to think about this in a decent way.

The Primacy of the Local

If one thought there were a single, general duty of beneficence, the equal moral standing of persons would bring all who had need within its scope, and the most needy, wherever they are, would have the largest prima facie claim. The current combined resources of technology and the capacity for large-scale projects makes global beneficence practicable. People can be fed, medicine delivered, technology and expertise exported.

A competing perspective on beneficence arises from the ways in which everyday morality is inherently local.[3] Two parameters structure this perspective: the fact that ordinary beneficence has the form of a duty of mutual aid, and, something more fundamental, the ideal fit of morality in everyday activity. Mutual aid is not the idea that in helping one thereby banks some good will or gratitude that can be called on for one's own need, like insurance. It is a conception of a moral relationship we are in when we live among others. The fact that *we* stand ready to help makes it an intelligible normal act to ask for aid. The obligation is no doubt felt most strongly where we are closest to each other, and it follows out lines of connection and affiliation.

The place of morality in everyday life is ideally marked by a certain seamlessness, an absence of conflict between morality and interest. It is not just that we have internalized norms and so no longer notice them; we depend on the stability and structure of a morally configured world for the possibility of normal action. As a matter of course, we count on each other not only not to harm or deceive, but also for help. This is not to say that no conflicts occur between what morality requires and goals we may pursue. However, morality is hardly unique in posing challenges to our efforts to integrate diverse principles and ends. The normal agent develops skills to manage potential conflicts, and to recuperate when there is loss. Some ends and values are not negotiable, and for the normal agent, moral values are chief among these.

The seamlessness of everyday morality, however we account for it, partly explains why the encounter with need at a distance will seem to have a different moral character than that with local need.[4] We are connected in more complex ways to those around us: personal interactions, shared institutions, claims of social justice introduce overlapping reasons to attend to the needs of local others that do not apply at a distance. There are also various internal features of beneficence, of the relation of providing aid or help, that push toward the weightiness or priority of the local. To be responsive to need requires that one know what it looks like. Some aspects of need are universal: the integrity of life and limb; disease and disability; the necessities of human sustenance. But once we go beyond urgent need, the nature and status of different needs becomes increasingly local and context dependent. Think of the range of things a person might require to be an effective member of her community: from literacy to clean and presentable clothes.[5] Locally, for the most part, need—or the need that counts—is a well-recognized part of everyday life. If we are attentive, we often can act directly and with confidence. We divide a task; make a call; offer a loan. In more specific settings of family or work or voluntary association, other needs will present themselves, and we have more nuanced resources to offer.

In responding to need at a distance, providing appropriately tailored help is difficult: there are special burdens of investigation and on creativity of response. The line between beneficence and paternalism may be harder to draw, conditions of dependence harder to see. Often we just contribute money. Need at-a-distance can also be less visible. This is not to say that salience is the condition of obligation; rather, what is differently salient, *if* we are not at fault for not seeing, will have a different place in the configuration of obligations.[6]

There also appear to be differences in the extent of our obligation. Normally, in providing aid, we take on new responsibilities. You have a headache; I offer aspirin, but by mistake give you antacid. Even if it is now harder to give you the aspirin you need than it would have been, because I started helping I now have to do more. If the aspirin I give you makes you suddenly ill, I am at the front of the line of those who should get you help.[7] While just such extensions of responsibility often make people hesitate to help in the first place, they also mark out the contours of what it means to be members of a community. We see this easily in the context of family relationships. But even with strangers: if I have dialed 911 for help and no one comes, I have taken on a further reason to see things through.

That we do not seem open to comparable extensions when we aid at a distance may be a function of the fact that we most often meet these obligations through contributions to charitable and public institutions. To be sure, using an intermediary gives rise to *other* responsibilities. We ought to investigate the helping institutions we support: ask about their expense-to-donation ratio, their decision-making process, or even about how responsible they are in the way they provide aid. However, if the aid they deliver on our behalf is not right, or not enough, we do not seem responsible for more *because* we contributed to the failed effort. That this may also be the case wherever there is large-scale aid suggests that the metric of local-global may not provide an independent basis for getting a clear picture of the obligation.

In both spheres, taxation and institutional tithing make the demanding more ordinary by making it less intrusive; but, as we well know, that something can be made ordinary does not show we have an adequate moral account of it.

I do not mean to insist on any of these intuitions about cases. They can be disputed; different accounts can be given of their conclusions. I do think that collectively these and other such reports indicate the presence of a subject matter: something to be explained, or explained away. This is a good enough reason to turn to a more comprehensive moral theory.

The Familiar Kantian Account

Kant's account of beneficence is found in two places: the last of the examples illustrating the formulations of the categorical imperative in the *Groundwork of the Metaphysics of Morals*, and the doctrine of obligatory ends in the second part of the *Metaphysics of Morals*. For present purposes, I will be less concerned with reconstructing the details of Kant's arguments than with describing the shape and structure of the duty of beneficence they advance.

The *Groundwork* pattern of argument tells us that we may not act in ways (on maxims) that cannot be universally or rationally willed. In the example about beneficence, Kant argues that we may not adopt, because we cannot rationally will, a maxim of never helping anyone.[8] However, the duty that follows, that we must adopt a maxim of sometimes helping, is by itself too minimal to give guidance about when we are to act.

We can derive a bit more content for the duty from an assumption needed to make the argument work. General facts about human vulnerability and limited efficacy indicate that our very agency can be threatened or undermined in ways we may not, on our own, be able to resist. Such facts are used to explain why no one could rationally will or assent to a universal principle of nonbeneficence. Suppose they do explain it. Then, if it is because of the ineliminability of agency vulnerability that we have a duty of beneficence, it is reasonable to think that threats to agency are the needs to which the duty of beneficence requires us to respond. This is enough to shift the burden of justification in such cases to reasons for not helping. But it is not clear how it secures more than easy rescue when life is in danger. We get no guidance about the range of agency needs that might trigger beneficence, nor about how much we must sacrifice when such needs are threatened.

The best explanation for this indeterminacy is that the point of the first *Groundwork* argument is directed elsewhere. Rather than setting parameters for the casuistry of beneficence, the purpose of the argument is to show that and also why need, or a category of need, is morally salient. It cannot just be assumed that the needs of others must be our moral concern. This is not a quirk of Kantian rationalism. Even for Hume, while sympathy brings need to our attention, something else is necessary to show that attending to need (or to some kinds of need) is a moral virtue, not a fact we may, if we will, develop strategies to ignore.

The *Groundwork*'s formula of humanity has more to say about beneficence.[9] In explicating the injunction to treat humanity (rational nature) as an end, Kant concludes that we must take the fact that happiness is the natural end of human beings as a reason to strive, as much as we can, to further the ends of others. This is because "[t]he ends of a subject who is an end in himself must as far as possible be my ends also." The implications for a duty of beneficence could be clearer. Taken literally, these terms for the duty would render it incoherent. For everyone to strive to make all ends of all others their ends also would not leave enough of ends that are truly a person's own to form a conception of the happiness others are to promote.

So we might ask: what could it sensibly mean for the ends of others to be ends for me—to be, as much as possible, my ends also? There is a continuum of ways to connect with the ends of another: noninterference, joint action for the end, support of your action for your end, support for your action for your reasons. Ends and reasons may also have a place within a conception of a life, and be (partly) valued as they do. Most ends we pursue we value conditionally: vacations matter, but less (or more) if we are supporting an aged parent, or have just finished a major piece of work. What we can make of another's ends will vary with our situation and our relationship. So Kant's "as much as we can" might be relative in its practical import. We can take on very little of a stranger's end; in such cases, a limited yet stringent duty of easy rescue makes sense. With regard to our child or partner, the situation is quite different; indeed, we easily err in the other direction, making their ends too much our own. So *if* we must attend to the happiness of others by "making their ends our own," a relationship-sensitive account of the obligation eliminates some of the conceptual difficulty. It would also give beneficence something like a point of view.

Elaborating the idea of beneficence in this way suggests the shape casuistical principles might take. My being part of complex cooperative or affiliative relations connects me in many different ways to needs as they bear on ends or a way of life that I can share. It might explain why needs of those close to us have priority, or why, when our helping causes harm locally, our responsibility for the harm is typically much greater, and the fault more likely to shade toward negligence than inadvertence. Moreover, if intimacy and dependence articulate beneficence, our obligations will more easily fit in everyday life. They can come to be among the things we just do: as we look both ways before crossing the street, we hold a door for someone burdened with packages, or leave work to take a friend to the hospital, or attend a school play.

If a relationally specified duty helps make sense of the requirement that we make others' ends our own, it leaves many questions unanswered. What moral grounds are there for accepting this specification? It is not that our capacity to help is limited in this way. Since even relationally specified beneficence cannot reasonably require response to all needs that arise from the pursuit of ends, what sets the limit? We seem to have left behind the thought that the needs at issue connect to the vulnerabilities of rational agency. And just as we have reason to worry that open-ended beneficence abroad would constrain the kinds of caring we could permissibly allow ourselves, unfettered beneficence at home would surely introduce its own disruptive demands.

Once again the best explanation for the limited result lies in what Kant was trying to do. As I read it, the formula of humanity argument is designed to show only that obligations to others are conceptually connected to the fact of our pursuit of ends generally, and so to our end of happiness. How this result fits with the earlier argument about the vulnerability of rational agency, and what significance it has, if any, for limiting the duty of beneficence, remains to be worked out. To take on this task we must first address a more fundamental question: how to think about the moral standing of our own ends—our happiness—in the mix of ends we are to make our own. Providing tools to answer this question is one of the signal accomplishments of Kant's doctrine of obligatory ends.

Obligatory Ends

Let me begin this section with a few general remarks about the *Metaphysics of Morals*, since its purpose and method are less familiar than that of the *Groundwork*. In the *Metaphysics of Morals* the kinds of duties and obligations that apply to us are arrived at as "specifications" of the moral law. The structure of argument is not one of direct derivation; instead, the moral law, as the constitutive principle of practical rationality, determines specific conditions on rational willing for our kind of rational being (finite, limited), in the particular circumstances in which we act (a shared material world of moderate scarcity). The specification proceeds in stages. It begins with the facts that human agents do not naturally coordinate their use of things (or each other) and yet require coordinated conditions of use to act effectively. To meet this need, the first principle of right secures the moral idea of positive law: that a part of morality (the conditions and norms of externally free action) is to be worked out in terms of civic order and legal sanction. These conditions make the institutions of property and contract morally possible, and provide a framework for institutional rules that dictates their consistency with the (external) freedom of all. One striking consequence of Kant's argument is that ownership is not (morally) more fundamental than citizenship. Conditions for the latter may therefore constrain the permissions that come with the former (e.g., making morally mandatory taxation for public education and welfare).

A second sequence of specification is drawn from the first principle of virtue, which sets possibility conditions for good willing. For human rational agents, a condition for *internal* freedom, for good willing, is that there be ends it is obligatory to have. Otherwise, Kant argues, morality cannot unconditionally direct agents' action. The first principle of virtue sets two obligatory ends: our own perfection and the happiness of others.[10] They neither replace our natural interest in our own happiness nor compete with it as independent goals. As ends we must have, they are to give form to the way we conceive of our happiness. If the first principles of right create a normative social world fit for human activity (a world of right, not merely force), so, analogously, we can say that obligatory ends make the natural end of happiness an end fit for autonomous human agents: an end of rational choice, not merely desire. They are the beginning of an account of why and how "own-happiness" (for want of a better term) has weight in our moral deliberations.

We do not normally think of Kantian theory as having morally positive things to say about own-happiness. This should strike us as paradoxical, in Kant, or in any nonconsequentialist theory that extends beneficence beyond rescue. Why would we have moral concern for each others' happiness when our own happiness lacks moral significance for each of us, except insofar as it is the object of restriction and constraint, a cause of temptation, and the like? Rights and perfect duties protect our liberty, not our happiness. This may be part of the reason why, beyond rescue, negative tasks and small efforts tend to be the focus of attention in many nonconsequentialist discussions of aid, and why any more substantial engagement with the happiness of others is frequently located in the space of supererogatory actions, though even that makes little sense in a moral theory that does not give own-happiness a place. Impartial morality seems to be indifferent to the success or failure of our projects as such because, from the moral point of view, there is no loss if we wind up doing one permissible thing rather than another. Of course *we* most often don't have that view of what we do.

One familiar way to fix this is through special relations and obligations: to fellow citizen, family member, coworker, friend. They place us in distinctive settings of cooperative activity or coordinate concern that give us moral interest in the success of the ordinary projects of some specific others, and they in ours. However, the logic of the fix is strange. Of course it matters to us that we have special relations, and our having them gives us reasons. But if mattering to us is sufficient to secure moral standing, then one wouldn't need to be talking about *special* relations and obligations. It would be odd to think that if morality is indifferent to what I care about, it gains an interest in what I care about because I stand in some relation to someone else.[11] This lack of argument makes itself felt in a disturbing adhocery in the assignment of relative weights among special obligations, and between them and impartial beneficence.[12]

There are obvious and sound reasons to resist the partitioning of value between own-happiness and morality. Even if, analytically, morality and happiness are separate, the way a normal adult functions does not keep them so. If happiness is the province of own-interest, it is not populated merely by natural desire. Part of the social effect of a moral culture is to transform our desires and so our idea of own-happiness. We teach honesty, and expect normal agents not to covet what belongs to others. We restrain a child's impulse to strike out when angry or hurt, and expect adults in distress to desire sustained connection rather than violent resolutions.

It is in just this moral space that obligatory ends do their work. They introduce *positive* moral conditions into the pursuit of happiness, requiring that the activities and ends we choose for the sake of happiness must also, in the ways that they can, be valued as they promote our perfection (natural and moral) and the happiness of others. And, as I will argue, because the moral work of obligatory ends is done through shaping the pursuit of happiness from the inside, they draw own-happiness into the space of moral reasons.

Before going on, I should note that it has been customary to interpret Kant's doctrine of obligatory ends differently. They tend to be regarded as the source of positive duties, though duties that are defeasible if in conflict with our interests. Kant's idea that obligatory ends leave a "playroom (*latitudo*) for free choice in following . . . the [moral] law"[13] is seen as an attractive invitation to the agent to decide for herself when and to what extent she will act for an obligatory end. Less attention is paid to the more rigorous claim that the latitude of duty is "not to be taken as permission to make exception to the [prescribed] maxim of actions but only as permission to limit one maxim of duty by another (e.g., love of one's neighbor in general by love of one's parents)."[14] One can see why it is tempting to downplay this aspect of the latitude. By emphasizing free choice, interpreters credit Kant with seeking a sensible way to fit positive duties into a plausible moral schema without swamping out our own concerns. I satisfy the obligatory end of the happiness of others by committing myself to provide help sometimes.[15]

However, the idea of an obligatory end that gives us a "do something sometimes" duty cannot be right. If the needs of others support moral reasons, it is not credible that just *any* interest of ours is sufficient to set them aside (so long as we sometimes help someone, or even plan to). A more promising idea is to take seriously Kant's striking claim about the latitude of obligatory ends: that it is only a permission to limit one maxim of duty by another, the effect of which, he says, is to *widen* the field for moral action, and not to create room to decline to act.

To understand this claim, a good place to start is with some formal features of obligatory ends. If an end is obligatory, and as such a source of duties, it is one that in some way we must always have. As Kant presents them, it is clear that obligatory ends not only establish moral conditions for the pursuit of happiness, they also jointly constitute the material final end of human action: that is, they are ends for the sake of which we are to act *and* in light of which other ends are to be chosen. (It is in this role that they answer to the possibility condition of unconditionally good action: absent obligatory ends, all actions would be chosen for the sake of contingent ends, and no action could be unconditionally good.)[16] As to why the obligatory ends are just the two (our own perfection and the happiness of others) Kant's answer is, if not simple, direct: "What, in the relation of a human being to himself and others, *can* be an end [for pure practical reason] *is* an end for pure practical reason."[17] Of the four candidate kinds of to-be-promoted ends (our own and others' happiness, our own and others' perfection), it makes no sense to have a duty to adopt an end we necessarily have (the end of our own happiness),[18] nor an end we can only indirectly promote (correctness in end-adoption by others: their perfection);[19] what remains is our own perfection and the happiness of others.

We can think of the two obligatory ends as the complete material specification of rational nature as an end in itself for human rational agents. They are permanent and ubiquitous: permanent because obligatory, ubiquitous because jointly final and materially exhaustive. It follows that a condition on my acting for my own happiness (being beneficent to myself) is taking the happiness of others as an end, and also that a condition of my acting for the sake of the happiness of others is some attention to myself.[20]

It does *not* follow that everything I do must be in the service of promoting one or another obligatory end. To have an obligatory end is to be committed to a set of considerations as always deliberatively salient; they will not always direct one to action. It is in this sense that obligatory ends give rise to imperfect duties: there can be no rule specifying "precisely in what way one is to act and how much one is to do by the action for an end that is also a duty."[21] The "latitude" for choice that comes with an imperfect duty is not about frequency of acting for the end, but a space for judgment as to how (and how much), in appropriate circumstances, the end might be promoted.

As an imperfect duty, beneficence will have its content determined by judgment directed at the value its supporting obligatory end expresses. The object of beneficence, human well-being, is not the value that sets the duty. Neither the satisfaction of desire per se nor the promotion of any arbitrary conception of happiness could obligate us. If well-being matters, it will be because of its connection with the core value of rational agency. The appeal to that value in the *Groundwork* yields (at least) a duty to aid when agency is threatened. What remains to be explained is how less urgent projects could matter in a way that allows us to claim from others some of the cost of pursuing them, or, correlatively, to resist the claims of others on resources we want for our purposes. At issue is why, in the face of need, a human life is not to be regarded as a warehouse of potentially distributable skills and possessions.

The resistance to this use of persons should come from the same features of human agency and happiness that make beneficence beyond rescue a duty. A likely account of what they might be goes this way. It takes some doing to become an effective agent, and some more to sustain agency. Our agency arises in ordered stages; it is the result of a process shaped by natural and social resources, completed by our own choices. Within a range of normal variation, there are general conditions for effective agency. Many of the resources that support successful or developing agents cannot be made available for use by others without undermining the agency from which they would be withdrawn. Think of what a parent gives a child, or education, or the stuff of physical and cultural identity. I could have shifted my parenting activities to a child needier than my son. But (let us assume) because I could not have done that without damaging him, it is not the sort of thing I could have sensibly been required to do (or him to forego) for the sake of benefitting others, regardless of how well off my son was on many measures. Compare this with an nth year of recreational dance lessons, or a summer hiking in the mountains; these are important goods for those who have them, but it is less shocking to imagine that they (in the form of the resources that support them) are in principle available for transfer. Because effective agency is not like getting one's adult teeth, it will not just happen with time and food, a moral theory that prizes the value of rational agency has to be especially sensitive to its social and material conditions as it goes about the business of parceling out goods.

Now, the vehicle that drives the development of human rational agency is the natural interest we have in our own happiness.[22] To be a creature with happiness as an end is to have a practical interest in one's life going well. But this bare interest gives no object of action; it rather sets a practical task of working out an idea of how one's life is to go, which in turn is the basis for developing specific projects and objects of action. In doing the work of articulating a conception of own-happiness, we become a particular agent: we develop needs (and interests), executive skills, special vulnerabilities and strengths. Clearly, then, whatever is involved in making the happiness of others my end, it cannot much resemble what is involved for me in having my own happiness as an end.

For these and related reasons, the adjustment negotiated between own-happiness and morality is complex. It is not just that in the pursuit of happiness we cannot violate moral requirements. If we do not care enough about ourselves, we may become less able agents: we can lose the courage to act well or the strength to resist temptation. We may also undervalue our happiness by exaggerating the nature and extent of moral requirement. The vices of moral fanaticism and avarice, Kant argues, violate a duty to oneself insofar as they are assaults on the healthy pursuit of our interests, and prevent us from enjoying life.[23] But why should denying oneself enjoyment be a vice—I mean, a Kantian vice? Enjoyment is not a kind of minimum wage to keep moral workers happy so that they won't go on strike. The thought is rather that unless one is willing and to some degree able to enjoy life, one cannot appreciate and so correctly evaluate the range of human concerns. One will not make wise judgments about either one's own needs as an agent, or about the happiness of others.

In thinking about the conditions for sound judgment, it is perhaps less difficult to grasp how impairment of the capacity to suffer, or to feel pain, might disable someone's ability to discern what matters morally. Kant's point here is that a healthy capacity for enjoyment is the positive side of this same practical ability. The instrumental role of enjoyment does not make enjoyment instrumental. It rather explains why morality takes it seriously.[24]

The role of own-happiness in the moral story is in this way extended. If the drive to happiness prompts the development necessary for rational agency, and so for moral action, the positive experiences of free enjoyment enable moral judgment. Time and cultural space are therefore part of the conditions of effective moral agency. We require safety and stability, material well-being sufficient to support the pursuit of an idea of happiness, freedom to learn through repetition and mistakes, the opportunity to acquire the evaluative skills for assessing complex arrays of greater and lesser goods. (Kant adds the need to be acquainted with beauty: to apprehend, through aesthetic enjoyment, pleasure that is not the pleasure of satisfied desire.)[25] Confidence in one's abilities as a moral agent is not gained through moral action alone; it comes through the myriad small things we experience and do, projects we take on, long-term goals that we care about and enjoy. In an environment in which we cannot enjoy what we do, we do not flourish as agents. The conditions for effective moral agency are not, then, to be regarded as luxuries. Although to an extent contextually specific, and very often resource-demanding, the cultural conditions of moral agency are matters of moral necessity.[26]

This pattern of argument not only permits but can require agency-based concerns for oneself to have priority over needs-claims of others. But because the needs on which agency depends are situationally specific, we may not be able to say in advance or in the abstract where the line is to be drawn between what we require for ourselves and what can permissibly be made available for others. Resolving this indeterminacy calls for judgment that attends to particulars, not merely the balancing of competing values. So someone's judgment that she should continue her education rather than send money to Oxfam can be a moral judgment, not a limitation on the reach of moral requirements. In such a case, the obligatory end of one's own perfection limits action for the end of others' happiness.

To get this result it might seem as though one must resort to some sort of balancing after all. But such an objection misses the point. It is true that different considerations are in play: one person's education, others' needs. But the argument does not ask for their relative weights. *If* education is a necessity in some context for effective agency, then it (or the wherewithal to support it) is not available for distribution to others. Whether one may sacrifice such a resource for the sake of others is not, then, entirely discretionary.

In moving elements of own-happiness into the space of moral reasons for each agent, happiness is not subsumed by morality, as if the determination of what makes my life go best is to be made impersonally. What is absorbed into morality is the *status* of the pursuit of happiness. This is not just about finding moral space for our own happiness; without the status argument, we would lack an account of why the happiness of others matters morally—how it *could* matter—in a theory that does not accord satisfaction of desire intrinsic moral value. The happiness of others matters morally for the same reasons that my happiness matters: the pursuit of happiness is the organizing principle of our kind of agency.[27]

One of the dangers in treating emergencies as central cases of beneficence is that they distort the picture of what the duty of beneficence is about. Emergency cases make vivid the scale of human suffering as if it required no argument to show that relief of suffering is a first-order moral obligation. In the Kantian account of beneficence, point of the help we may be required to give, in both emergency and normal cases, is not to alleviate suffering per se, but to alleviate suffering because of what suffering signifies for beings like us. In the face of unnecessary suffering one naturally thinks: how could it not be better that it cease? And if someone can easily make it stop, what good reason can one have not to do so? There is no reason to deny that. Nor to deny that relief of suffering per se is the proper object of our kindness and compassion. Even if suffering per se is not the object of beneficence, responsiveness to suffering comes with it. Bringing a sphere of human concern into the space of moral attention changes the way we look at things intimately related to it. Given that we have moral reason to be concerned with the happiness of others, we will have reason to be concerned with their pain and suffering. What is at issue is the *order* of concern.

The Latitude of Beneficence

Having brought own-happiness into the space of moral reasons, we are in a better position to consider what the latitude of beneficence, as an imperfect duty, amounts to. As we shall see, the salutary effect of locating the argument for beneficence under an obligatory end is to transform the way concern for self is connected to concern for others so that judgment need not be about adjudicating between own- and others'-happiness by means of the weighing and balancing of kinds of interests and numbers of persons.

It is a consequence of the developmental role of own-happiness that we are open to the shaping effect of ends. Given ends of importance and presence, the reasons they provide become salient across a wide range of a person's practical concerns, becoming part of what makes one this person rather than that one. The combined facts of the ubiquity and requiredness of obligatory ends place them among the central shaping norms for a human life. Whether or not we must act frequently for their sake, they will be strongly directive. To take on as obligatory the end of the happiness of others calls for the development and deployment of skills of interpersonal awareness: perceptiveness about other lives; judgment about the fit of one's abilities and resources with the needs of others; the acquisition of dispositions of appropriate helpfulness (attitudes of humility and respect; wariness about paternalism and dependence, and so forth). It is not as though we have a duty to become social beings, as if that were contrary to our nature, but as with the more familiar duties of respect, our social connections are to be formed and framed by these (among other) moral attitudes. However, as we develop more beneficence-related skills, our opportunities to act for the sake of others' happiness will increase. This need not be a burden, for the development of the skills that reveal need typically involves enhanced capacities of attachment, care and concern.

The obligations of parents provide a useful intuitive guide in thinking about the shape of duties under obligatory ends. For example: once responsibility for a child is taken on, one gains ends whose standing in deliberation is not discretionary. They may be onerous or not. It is unlike a job one may not find fulfilling and so leave, or even a friendship, which though it gives nondiscretionary ends, if outgrown, can, with care, be eased away from. And because the occasions to act on parenting ends are pervasive and the ends nondiscretionary, being a parent often becomes central to who one conceives oneself to be. When the role is welcomed, the concerns that belong to the obligation enter the space of reasons of own-happiness, effecting a link between morality and the actions of everyday life. Of course it need not be so; and when it is not, the obligations can exact a heavy toll, not just on time and energy, but also, sometimes, as a cause of shame.

The point of the analogy is to suggest that we get it wrong about obligatory ends if we think of them as setting a parallel and competing agenda to our own. Obligatory ends provide positive norms for how one should treat oneself and others while going about the business of one's life. When all works well, moral deliberation can be coincident with the contours of reasonable ambition, attachment, and interest, while such ends, in turn, can routinely support our moral well-being. And just as it is not always wrong to let a child cry, for the interests of children, important as they are, are not the only interests that should matter to those who care for them, simply doing more for an obligatory end is no sure sign of virtue. Self-sacrifice will be a vice if it leads to the neglect of activities and attachments that keep us effectively engaged with the world. How this will work out in a life is not easy to say. Given our different abilities and tolerances, where the line is drawn is neither fixed nor certain. Though one can state the rule, it remains a task of judgment to assess the relevant particulars.

If we stopped here, it might look as though all that has happened is a shift in the balance point between own and other interests: more for own-happiness because, morally, we require it. Indeed the balance has shifted, but not in that way. Facts about us, personal as well as social, may call for more (or less) attention to own-happiness, but also, the degree and kind of our moral involvement with the happiness of others will partly be a function of how we live with them. As relationships become closer, the field for the practice of beneficence typically widens. Those with extensive families and dependencies, wide networks of friends and associates, will bring into their lives, via these relationships, extensive areas of concern. Those with more solitary lives will not be free of moral concern for others, but the interests of others will be less pervasive because others are less important in the way such a life is lived. Indeed, having made certain decisions about how to live one's life, say, ones that require the focused development of special talents, one may have closed off, morally speaking, certain ways of living with others. That is, such decisions affect not just obligations, but permissions as well. We can now understand why it is that how often and how much I might offer help could in a sense be up to me and it be the case that "I don't feel like it" is not a reason for not helping.

If, as you run frantically down the path I could easily step aside to let you through, I think that I need not because I am as entitled as you are to be there, I simply fail to understand how the needs of others provide reasons for me. Where I am more involved with others, I have greater opportunity to have an impact on their happiness. We know a lot more about the conditions of happiness or well-being of those with whom we live or work, and those to whom we are closest are often those we can most easily harm by our neglect. When I do not help a stranger with his project, I am not neglecting him. But when a coworker or friend is similarly needful, the threshold of neglect is much lower.

It follows that, independently of the relationships we are in, we cannot say what the full content of our imperfect duty toward others will be. Whether we take on greater relational burdens is up to us; it belongs to the space of decisions about our lives over which we have authority. Some of the goods of a human life will increase the shared terrain of morality and happiness. It works both ways. In making adjustments for one's own concerns and the needs of one's friends, one works out what kind of friendship one has. If we extend ourselves into relations with others, our moral involvement with their happiness and well-being widens.[28] Among the reasons why general charity or welfare can be taken care of by public institutions is that, though we each stand to the need of strangers under the duty of beneficence, they require help, not our help.

Strangers, Inherited Obligations, and Moral Triage

Once strangers appear on the scene, we are immediately faced with other complicating factors. Not all strangers are related to us in the same way; not all their claims of need point to beneficence. Some strangers are our fellow citizens, some are not. Some needs ought to be met as a matter of justice. The task of elaborating and keeping track of these sometimes conflicting currents of claim and relation is considerable, and not something one should expect from the resources of an argument for beneficence. There is, however, a more limited question in the arena of these issues that we are in a position to examine, and that is whether the general structure of obligation to self and other based on obligatory ends has any bearing on the scope of moral requirement once we leave the space of relationships. This is a question about the connections between the argument for beneficence and justice. In discussing this, I consider only an approximately Kantian or liberal account of social justice, based in something like a nation or state. Both assumptions are controversial. I make them because of their fit with Kant's own arguments about these matters, but also because the conclusions have some bearing on the circumstances in which we currently live.

Let me start with claims of justice for fellow citizens. In any complex social order, it is not always possible to tease apart the sources of need. Sometimes it arises directly from the distribution of benefits and burdens: the n percent unemployment that is supposedly necessary to a healthy economy; sometimes there are those whose abilities and skills simply do not fit the available forms of productive life. A just system of social rules ought, morally, to include some program of public support for those in need to remedy the imperfections of human-designed institutions and to extend the benefits of social cooperation to those whom misfortune hinders from making their own way. Most of what is required of us individually in this way of helping strangers falls under the general obligation to support just institutions. The demand on our resources may or may not be considerable, but in modestly decent social circumstances it is neither unfair nor undermining of the possibility of one's having a whole and healthy life.

However a community works this out, there will be residual individual obligations to aid that belong to beneficence. One has direct responsibilities for pressing needs that arise outside of or in the crevices of the institutional framework of support. Someone falls and is hurt; an elderly neighbor suddenly needs help getting to the doctor. Locating individual responsibility for the needs of others in the places institutions cannot reach, the residual obligation is respectful of the life intruded on, and if demanding, it is only so as circumstances are in some way unusual. If, living in a just society, one happens to be the person in front of whom large numbers of people trip and fall, then one is unlucky, and large demands are indeed made on one's time and resources. There can be no moral guarantee that one will get to live the life one wants.

What, then, is the status of those outside our framework of relationships and political institutions? Typically, those not in our own community to whose need we might attend are members of other societies: some, perhaps, lacking resources and unable to meet their citizens' needs, others, perhaps, unjust and unwilling to do so. One natural thought is that such local failures give rise to or trigger global or general obligations. That is, legitimate needs that fail to be met within a society might be the basis of claims against all of us who might help: a secondary claim of beneficence. If they were, there would be a moral connection to need at-a-distance, though we could not straightaway conclude that we simply inherit all of the moral work. Not every moral failure that calls for remedy warrants a response of the same kind. Failures of the educational system in our own community don't burden us to teach, or repair classrooms, though they do burden us with some responsibility for the unmet need. Sometimes *how* a failure comes about affects the obligations others inherit.

Inherited obligations belong to a rather interesting if not much examined class: obligations that are satisfied by persons other than those who originally bear them. Some obligations can be contracted out. Other obligations move on to others in less sharply defined ways: they can be passed on or down; they can be individually obligating, and yet be shared; they can (literally) be inherited. One can act as an obligation-surrogate (grandparents raising their children's children), or substitute (child-care workers); one can be a relief worker (taking a neighbor's children to school on a hectic morning). In many cases, the derived obligation will not be the same as the primary obligation. One may take on only an aspect of another's more general obligation (if the child I am driving to school has a fever, I am not thereby obligated to take him to the doctor); it may not be appropriate in some circumstances for the holder of the derived obligation to act; in some cases, the derived obligation is only to forestall some bad effect that would occur were the original obligation to be unmet. Some cases might generate a derived obligation to help restore the primary obligation holder to full functioning. One can imagine cases in which the obligation (or what it can require) weakens as it descends; in other cases (easy rescue, for example) it may be the same at all declined positions.

What is the bearing of this on the duty to aid? If a class of need first imposes moral obligations on local social institutions (claims of justice), and general obligations to meet distant need are inherited from them (secondary beneficence), it is not likely that the inherited obligation will have the shape of open-ended, universal beneficence. The shape of the secondary duty of beneficence will depend on, among other things, whether inheritance here preserves the scope and stringency of the primary obligation in justice, and whether it makes any difference if the failure that triggers the inherited obligation is moral (injustice, corruption) or merely practical (resource insufficiency, earthquake). However, if our obligations to need at a distance are inherited, one thing we do know is that the delivery of aid should not interfere with sound local institutions; and where those do not exist, we should not act in ways that make their development less likely. Otherwise we do not adequately respect the priority of the local, primary obligation. We now recognize that in some disaster situations, direct palliative aid addressed to individual need can be hazardous. Heroic food-aid creates refugee camps, encourages abandonment of the land, and promotes dependency and corruption. Many conclude that we must therefore adopt alternative models of aid such as training in new farming techniques, establishing local markets, promoting female literacy, which, while not directed at immediate suffering, do more, over time, to diminish overall need and to create the possibility of effective local responsibility.

Suppose this is right. Would those whose current needs are not met have grounds for complaint against us when resources are diverted from aid to the project of institution building? If we had a direct obligation to meet their needs, then a rationale of balancing present suffering against future benefits to possible future persons would fail to address the claims on help that present persons make. But if our moral relation to need at-a-distance is inherited, what is inherited is not individual obligations to meet need, but a society's failed welfare obligation. We inherit a complex set of derived obligations that require us to respond to a situation in which there is both institutional failure and unmet welfare needs. We are obliged to attend to both.

Inherited obligations serve two masters. They respect the content of the primary obligations they take over, and they reflect the conditions that engage inheritance (consent, in some cases, beneficence in the case at hand). This can make specifying the inherited obligation a complex business. With respect to need, the primary obligation of a society consists in the use of its resources to insure, first, that food, shelter, and basic health care are available to all citizens. It is reasonable to think that the primary obligation extends beyond that, to those things necessary for adequate social and economic functioning, as these are understood locally. The values of agency Kantian beneficence is responsive to suggest that the line for the inherited obligation should also be drawn at this higher level of functioning. The derived general obligation will therefore reflect the social conditions in the locale of the primary obligation. It should in any case be no more extensive than the extended primary social obligation, but it may be less. A society can generate "needs" for very high levels of well-being, but it is not likely that meeting such needs is a part of secondary beneficence, any more than contributing to the pet projects of this or that person is among the things we must do if we have their happiness as our end.

A few caveats. Nothing in this account speaks to the issue of equality (within and between societies) or to claims of global justice. So to say that we might have only a limited secondary obligation under beneficence to provide aid to strangers at-a-distance is not to deny that we might be otherwise obligated to take steps to reduce global inequality, or to rectify instances of global injustice. Moreover, I have been talking mainly about individual obligations to aid, which, obviously, are not the only obligations to aid or to ameliorate states of need (or inequality) there may be. If the primary obligation for social welfare is one of justice, it belongs to members of a society collectively, as the bearers of benefits and burdens of social cooperation. As individuals, we have a duty to support just institutions and to supply backstop aid. Obligations toward need at-a-distance are often met through institutions (to take advantage of economies of scale, and the like), but I do not think these derived obligations are institutional or held by us collectively: there does not seem to be a natural collectivity to receive the obligation short of all of us—that is, all who are capable of assuming the inherited obligation.

If our individual obligation to persons in need at-a-distance were an inherited secondary obligation, that would provide some explanation of otherwise puzzling moral facts, especially the limitedness of the obligation, and the special sensitivity that seems warranted to social and institutional effects. I have not argued directly for the inherited individual obligation, and the moral facts, if they are facts, might be explained some other way. But apart from exploitation or other injustice, it is hard to see how a society, whose raison d'être and authority derive from its role in securing the fair distribution of the burdens and benefits of social cooperation for its members, would inherit failures of obligation from other cooperative schemes and so warrant to tax its own members on their behalf.[29] A secondary (inherited) obligation to aid *can* devolve on us as individuals because, given the obligatory end of the happiness of others, we already have an indeterminate obligation to all persons that bears on their need. The secondary obligation is not one we would have but for failure elsewhere to meet an obligation of justice. Such failures partly specify the content of our otherwise indeterminate obligation.

Difficult questions remain. Even if it were only failures of primary obligations that oblige us to provide aid at-a-distance, and even if only at a subsistence level, when we consider both episodic and chronic global emergency conditions, the demand on our resources could be considerable. The empirical claims here are not uncontroversial. But for purposes of this discussion, I want to assume a high level of demand, for this puts the most pressure on the argument.

It is sometimes suggested that we may limit our response because it is not possible to live a life where we may be drawn this way and that by moral demands. This isn't quite right. Where we have strong bonds of relationship, or are members of a cooperative endeavor, prolonged emergencies may dramatically alter the shape of our lives, limiting, by demands on our resources and time, much that we would like to do. It is not unreasonable that unchosen events shape our ends and lives, or that relationships and social connections extend our vulnerability (they also offer protection). Most of us organize our ends and activities knowing this, minimizing or eliminating activities that cannot survive interruption. Because we have strong reason to avoid conditions where the intrusion of repeated and different demands can cumulatively undermine normal goals and projects, some of our positive obligations are best met through the mediation of political and nonpolitical institutions. The more finite burdens of paying for insurance, or paying taxes, can free us from the costs of having to weigh our needs against the lives and needs of others, but only to a limited extent.

If, however, our duties to others at-a-distance fall under beneficence as an inheritance of defaulted social obligations, the inherited obligations must fit with the structure of relational duties we already have, and also with our morally required concern for ourselves. For this reason, not only will the general duty to others be limited, in order to meet our primary duties of beneficence, we may also be required to expend resources on higher-function needs close to us rather than on more basic needs at a distance.

One might straightaway object that morality always requires equal concern. But equal concern does not require equal action. Parents have equal obligations to their children to help them develop and flourish, though what they are required to do for each depends on the needs and interests each has. Teachers make extra efforts to improve the work of weaker students, or provide special assignments for those who would benefit from additional challenges. This is all familiar, and easily resides within the space of equal concern.

The issue seems much more difficult in cases of chronic and extensive need. Consider, by way of analogy, a family with two children, where one child has such enormous physical and psychological needs (for health care, special training, and the like) that there are no nonsubsistence resources in the family that could not be absorbed in bringing the first child toward normal self-sufficiency. Beyond some baseline of reasonable care, it is not obviously impermissible to expend resources on some of the higher-order needs of the second child (piano lessons, college). And this may be done without having to balance overall costs and benefits. If this intuition can be generalized, it would suggest that something like moral triage may have a role to play in adjudicating claims of need.[30]

Triage is a way of sorting needs to be met according to values other than urgency. In medicine, triage protocols direct that some needs not be addressed because a person cannot be made well; others because resources can be used elsewhere to better effect; lesser needs go unmet because they can be borne. The Kantian duty of beneficence, though derived from the obligatory end of others' happiness, neither directs us to bring about the greatest good, nor to meet only the most urgent needs. It directs us to attend to the well-being of persons as we can, because and insofar as it is in and through the pursuit of happiness that persons create and sustain themselves as agents. If agency-related needs are the object of aid, then triage may well be an appropriate model for judgment.

One of the attractions of thinking in terms of triage is that its rules trim at both ends. So if a principle of triage permits agency-sensitive direction of resources on the one side, it should also require something analogous to need that can be borne. And it can. There are levels of luxury that are morally gratuitous, however much coveted, and the felt need for such things does not enter the space of beneficence. To be sure, the line between culture, high culture, and mere luxury is not easy to draw. But from the point of view of morality, culture is not just another preference; it is a morally protected good, even though it creates new needs, and transforms some of the new needs into necessities. The culture of luxury is another matter. This does not seem to be an impossibly difficult judgment to make.

Conclusion

Kantian obligations of beneficence are not additive; we are not always obliged (or permitted) to help the greatest number; some robust level of concern for oneself is obligatory. Indeed, for each of us, coming to recognize what is possible *sub specie* beneficence is a moral demand on self-knowledge: of understanding the conditions and limits of our own moral agency. When Kant asks, "How far should one expend one's resources in practicing beneficence?" and answers, not to the point of needing help oneself, he is not arguing that you ought to go that far, but that you may *not* go farther.[31] Or at least may not on grounds of beneficence.

What we *must* do to meet the needs of others is to be worked out primarily through the relational specifications of beneficence, but also local institutions of justice, and secondary obligations to strangers at-a-distance. Whether the duties of aid singly or in sum turn out to be demanding, and if demanding, intrusive, is in part up to us and how we manage our lives, but in any case not anything that is or ought to be determinable in advance. The upshot of locating beneficence in the space of obligatory ends is not tidy answers about what to do, but a wide-ranging deliberative resource. This is the kind of result one should hope for if moral theory is to cohere with real-world moral complexity.

A last point. Kant remarks that, as a matter of fact, most of the burdens of poverty are the result of injustice. Much of what we do to meet need only repairs injustice — not our law-breaking, but our being party to and beneficiaries of unjust laws and unfair practices, past and present.[32] Such reparative action does not belong to beneficence, and so does not fall under the rules of moral triage. To the extent that this is so, the argument for the space of own-happiness within beneficence may provide more of an ideal than a sufficient guide to what we are obligated to do now for need we could meet.[33]

Notes

1. The *locus classicus* of the modern challenge is Peter Singer, "Famine, Affluence, and Morality," *Philosophy & Public Affairs* 1, no. 3 (1972): 229–243. Singer, of course, was not seeking to bring the duty under control.

2. For the best recent account of these issues, see Liam B. Murphy, *Moral Demands in Nonideal Theory* (Oxford: Oxford University Press, 2000).

3. The beginnings of a more general account of the importance of the social and so local bases of morality can be found in my "Morality and Everyday Life," *Proceedings and Addresses of the Amerian Philosophical Association* 74, no. 2 (2000): 29–45.

4. I do not mean to suggest that these metaphors mark a single, uniform metric. I am in many ways closer to my son across the country than to a neighbor down the street. On the other hand, distance matters. An important argument for the significance of spatial distance is to be found in F. M. Kamm, "Does Distance Matter Morally to the Duty to Rescue?" *Law and Philosophy* 19 (2000): 655–681.

5. Amartya Sen develops this idea (which he associates with Adam Smith's notion of "necessaries") in his *Development as Freedom* (New York: Random House, 1999), chap. 3.

6. A very different sort of problem of salience is introduced by the televised cause du jour.

7. It is a mistake, I think, to treat such cases as about fault or negligence. In some contexts, responsibility can be extended simply by embarking on a course of action.

8. The argument is found at *Groundwork* 4:423. The page numberings for all Kant quotations are from the German "Akademie" edition of his work (volume and page).

Translations from the *Groundwork* and the *Metaphysics of Morals* are, with some modifications, from Immanual Kant, *Practical Philosophy*, trans. and ed. Mary J. Gregor (Cambridge: Cambridge University Press, 1996).

9. *Groundwork* 4:429–430.

10. Perfection concerns the cultivation of an agent's natural and moral capacities, those needed for the furthering of ends in general, and whatever is necessary for virtue. Cf. *Metaphysics of Morals*, 6:391–393. Happiness, for Kant, names the set of objects, whatever they are, the realization of which matches our idea of a life that will please us. Cf. *Groundwork* 4:417–419; *Critique of Practical Reason* 5:22–26.

11. It is only odd (or empty) if it is the mere fact of the relationship that makes it matter; it is circular if it matters morally because it is a relation to others that I care about.

12. One might suppose that it is not merely the fact that others are related to us that gives rise to special obligations but the additional fact that closeness creates special vulnerabilities. Where there is vulnerability we must be concerned not to harm, but not helping will count as a harm in these contexts only if it is independently the case that happiness matters.

13. *Metaphysics of Morals* 6:390.

14. Ibid. An exception is Onora O'Neill, "Instituting Principles: Between Duty and Action," *Southern Journal of Philosophy* 36 (1997): 79–96; see also her *Towards Justice and Virtue* (Cambridge: Cambridge University Press, 1996), chap. 7. For other accounts of obligatory ends, see Thomas E. Hill, Jr., "Kant on Imperfect Duty and Supererogation," in his *Dignity and Practical Reason* (New York: Cornell University Press, 1992); and Marcia Baron, *Kantian Ethics Almost Without Apology* (New York: Cornell University Press, 1995), chaps. 4 and 5.

15. However, since on such a view there is no act of helping that must be performed (setting aside easy rescue) and since it is likely that every act of helping that one does perform one was free not to do, all or almost all such acts turn out to be supererogatory.

16. *Metaphysics of Morals* 6:382.

17. Ibid., 6:395.

18. Happiness seems to be a naturally necessary end for us because we not only have desires, we also have desires about our desires (singly, and over our whole life).

19. One might think we must also have the end of developing the moral character of others: providing them with moral instruction, training for their natural faculties, such as memory, imagination, judgment, and understanding. We will have concern for the character of others, but it falls under the end of their happiness. To act from the obligatory end of others' happiness is not just a matter of helping them get a lot of what they want. We should want that they get things right (e.g., that they not crave what they ought not have, that they be able to act for their ends effectively, that they not use others merely as a means) and so be concerned with the elements of their natural and moral perfection. Cf. *Metaphysics of Morals* 6:394.

20. Ibid., 6:451.

21. Ibid., 6:390.

22. I give a fuller account of the developmental role of happiness in "Rethinking Kant's Hedonism," in *Facts and Values: Essays for Judith Thomson*, ed. R. Stalnaker, R. Wedgwood, and A. Byrne (Cambridge, Mass.: MIT Press, 2001).

23. *Metaphysics of Morals* 6:408, 433–434.

24. There is an inevitable question here about high-end enjoyments: surfing in exotic locales, expensive pleasures, and the like. There are several things to say. Introducing enjoyments into an account of moral agency is not about raising the baseline for what we get to keep for ourselves, but about introducing a different set of reasons for having access to resources, and with them, an additional moral burden in acquiring preferences. On the other hand, one need not be simplistic about how enjoyments fit into lives. Some high-end activities are more sustaining, even if infrequently pursued.

25. Kant, *Critique of Practical Judgment* 5:353–354.

26. There are those who are "by nature" well-suited to morality. Instinctual demands may be modest; sympathetic attunement with others high. From the fact that in the most dire circumstances such persons may act well, it does not follow that the normal conditions for the development of moral agency are not to be regarded as necessities.

27. That is why Kant locates duties of *respect* among the duties concerned with happiness (*Metaphysics of Morals* 6:462f). It bears saying that giving happiness moral status does not supplant the more familiar ways that happiness of self and others matters to us.

28. To be sure, not every element of every conception of happiness is one that has to be realized. Because I very much want something, have hung my hat on it, it does not follow that you or anyone has reason to help me get it. Set-backs are normal. We are or should be capable of adjusting our ends in the face of reversals; a healthy agent has significant recuperative powers.

29. There are many issues to be sorted about injustice and its effects on group-to-group obligations. A society that is not an exploiter might incur obligations if some of its members are or have been. Exploitation (or other injustice) as a cause of need might alter the status of one society's claim on others, regardless of causal responsibility. And so on. Given this complexity, I have tried to restrict my remarks as much a possible to the circumstances of individuals who could provide help and their moral relation to those who need it.

30. Although the example supports the intuition about triage, it is doubtful that triage is the best way to think about extreme burdens on families. They more plausibly generate a secondary obligation going in the other direction, from the individual or family to the community or state. If there are good reasons for families to take primary responsibility for some kinds of needs, there are equally good reasons for the community to be responsible for extreme conditions of individuals.

31. *Metaphysics of Morals* 6:454.

32. See ibid., 6:454, and *Lectures on Ethics* (Collins lecture notes), ed. Peter Heath and Jerome Schneewind, trans. Peter Heath (Cambridge: Cambridge University Press, 1997), 27:416.

33. Earlier versions of this article were presented at the Harvard Center for Ethics and the Professions, Dartmouth College, University of California, Davis, University of California, Santa Barbara, the Southern California Philosophy Conference, and the Southern California Law and Philosophy Group. I thank members of those audiences for their many good questions. My thanks also to members of those audiences, and to Miles Morgan, Carol Voeller, and the Editors of *Philosophy & Public Affairs* for their helpful questions and suggestions.

6

The Moral of Moral Luck

Susan Wolf

In 1976, Bernard Williams coined the phrase "moral luck" to refer to the range of phenomena in which our moral status—how good or bad we are and how much praise or blame we deserve—is significantly determined by factors beyond our control.[1] Whether we are naturally sociable or irritable, whether we find ourselves faced with particularly explicit or burdensome moral challenges, whether the arrows of our actions hit their targets—all constitute ways in which things we cannot control affect the moral quality of our lives. All, then, serve as examples of moral luck, which, taken as a group, make up one of the most philosophically perplexing and troubling features of ordinary moral experience.

To accept the phenomena uncritically is to allow that one can be praised or blamed for what one cannot help. This goes against a very deep commitment most of us have to the idea that you should be morally judged only for what falls within the sphere of your will. Yet to reject the judgments and practices that seem unavoidably to lead to these phenomena would require a radical, and perhaps practically impossible, revision of ordinary moral evaluation.

In this essay, I am concerned primarily with one type of moral luck, luck in "how things turn out." A paradigmatic case is that of the truck driver (or, in Williams's essay, "a lorry driver") who accidentally runs over a child. Let us assume that the driver is guilty of a minor degree of negligence—he has not had his brakes inspected as recently as he ought—and that this negligence contributes to the accident. What makes this a case of moral luck, if it is a case, is that this truck driver has much more about which to feel guilty—he has much more moral weight on his shoulders, so to speak—than other drivers who, though equally negligent, had no children run across their paths.

I discuss this example and variations of it at great length in this essay, and I occasionally refer to one or two other instances of moral luck. It should be noted at the outset, however, that the phenomenon in question is ubiquitous. Every day, people in laboratories, government offices, corporations, and universities sign off on things to which they ought to put a stop, or they bend the rules for the sake of convenience or laziness or misplaced generosity. Rarely, but occasionally, such acts of flawed reasoning, weakness, or negligence blow up in someone's face. What is philosophically in question is how we should judge the perpetrators of these acts and how the perpetrators should judge themselves. Specifically, the question is whether those whose acts actually lead to serious harm deserve the same treatment and the same judgments as those who, but for fortune, would have caused as much damage.

The Problem of Moral Luck

In the discussions of this issue that I have heard, only a few people (including perhaps Williams himself) seem to accept the idea of moral luck more or less wholesale. That is, only a few seem to hold in a perfectly unqualified way that a person whose actions have morally worse effects is herself worse or more blame-worthy than one whose equally faulty behavior has less harmful consequences. The majority tends to reject the idea that there really is such a thing as moral luck, drawing instead the conclusion that many of the judgments we make in day-to-day life are simply inconsistent. According to the majority's position, although we may in fact blame the driver whose recklessness causes a death more than we blame the equally reckless driver who causes no harm, the blame they deserve is equal. We would be more just and more rational, according to this view, if we were to regard these agents, and if these agents were to regard themselves, as equally faulty and equally blameworthy.

The latter view, according to which equal recklessness deserves equal blame, I call the rationalist position. To mark the opposition, I call the former view the irrationalist position. These labels, however, should not keep anyone from assessing these positions on their merits.

I myself have some sympathy, if also some dissatisfaction, with each position. The rationalist view, that equal recklessness deserves equal blame, seems to me, on first reflection, the more justifiable. Yet the ideal of justice and rationality that would have us regard two agents whose actions have had drastically different moral consequences as being in precisely the same moral position, and especially, the ideal that would have the two agents regard themselves as being in the same position, strikes me as not just unrealistic but as positively eerie.

Something, it seems to me, is wrong with the rationalist position—or perhaps I should say that something is missing, for, as will become clear, I do not believe that the rationalist position is, strictly speaking, false. Rather, it is incomplete. It fails to capture, or even to acknowledge, something morally significant in the phenomenon of moral luck, something that suggests some grain of truth in the irrationalist response. My goal in this essay is to bring out more clearly what is unsatisfying about the rationalist position and to find an acceptable way of expressing the grain of truth in the irrationalist response. In short, I hope to find the moral in the phenomenon of moral luck.

The Rationalist Position Considered

Let us begin by looking more closely at the rationalist position, according to which luck in how things turn out is irrelevant to blameworthiness. According to this position, how much blame one deserves depends on how wrongly one has acted, on how much moral fault is revealed or expressed or instantiated in the action one has performed (or in one's failure to act). Of course, assessing how wrong or morally faulty an action (or failure to act) is is itself a highly complex matter,[2] but one thing moral faultiness is not a function of, according to this position, is how the action turns out. The robber who tries to shoot a storekeeper in the heart is as blameworthy as the robber who succeeds, at least if the only difference is that the former's pistol misfired. The parent who breaks his child's jaw in a fit of rage is as blameworthy as the parent who kills his child, if the only difference lies in the fortuitous angle of the child's fall.

This position, as I have already noted, seems by far the most natural one. Why should we even hesitate to accept it? To be sure, our actual judgments and attitudes do not always conform to rationalist principles. But, a defender of rationalism will suggest, these data can be explained without thereby being justified. Indeed, when we consider the circumstances in which such judgments and attitudes are formed, several possible and plausible explanations suggest themselves.

First and most obvious, we are more apt to know of someone's attempt at murder, assault, or theft if her attempt has been successful, and we are more apt to know of someone's reckless behavior or negligence if the act or omission resulted in the harm the potential for which made the behavior reckless or negligent in the first place. Since we can only blame people for actions or omissions of which we are aware, we will more often blame people whose wrongful actions or faulty behavior lead to bad results than those whose actions cause no harm.

Second, many if not most morally faulty actions are such that it is difficult to assess *how* morally faulty they are. Faultiness is at least partly a function of how great a risk of harm and how great a harm one's actions can be expected to incur. But we often lack the information that would allow us to fix on even an approximate range of expected harm. How reckless was the truck driver's driving? How negligent was the doctor who failed to diagnose her patient's rare disease? Since we cannot be maximally careful, thoughtful, sensitive, and protective of others all the time and since it is hard to weigh the costs of uncertain risks against the benefits, the question of when and how much our actions fall below the line of our duty is not easy. When damage is done—a child is run over or a patient falls into a coma—we tend to suspect that the behavior that led to it was faulty. Chances are, the driver was driving recklessly and the doctor was cutting corners. When things turn out all right, we are less certain of whether and how much blame was deserved.

Third, whether or how much we actually blame people varies not only with how blameworthy we think they are (how much blame, in other words, we think is deserved and appropriate) but also with how much we are inclined or motivated to "go in for" blaming. If an act results in harm, we are not only more likely to be aware of its faultiness but also more likely to be upset or angered by it. The impulse to blame often provides victims and those who sympathize with them with a way to direct the emotional energy aroused by their suffering. If a building that was not up to the standards of the fire code catches fire and burns to the ground with tenants trapped inside, we are, of course, more apt to find out that the landlady and the inspector she bribed have acted wrongly. But our blame might also be harsher than our blame in another case in which a similar violation was caught before any damage actually occurred, for the urge to blame may be greater as a response to the greater shock, anger, and sorrow at the victims' actual losses.

These and other differences in our epistemological and motivational positions with respect to acts with morally important differences in outcome go a long way in explaining our differential reactions to these acts. Importantly, they help to explain the reactions not only of the victims of these acts and of third parties who hear of them but also of the agents themselves. The question, however, is whether they explain enough to put the matter of how to respond to differential harm to rest. Can our tendency to blame people differentially on the basis of harm caused rather than fault exhibited be completely explained by appeal to our imperfect knowledge and our nonrational emotions?

If so, it seems that we should accept the rationalist position in its entirety and conclude that, at least under conditions of more perfect knowledge, it would be more just and simply morally better to blame people equally if they exhibit equal fault and, indeed, that it would be more just and simply morally better if people whose behavior was equally faulty blamed themselves equally. Pretheoretical reflection about cases, however (even cases in which the epistemological problems are absent and in which our emotional reactions are subdued), resists this conclusion.

A Problem with the Rationalist Position

To see why, let us return to the two hypothetical truck drivers, this time explicitly assuming the epistemological problems away by stating that the drivers had possessed equal reason to get their brakes checked and had equally neglected it, with the result that the risk of accident they were incurring was 10% higher than it would otherwise have been. In the case of the one driver, a child runs into the street and is killed. The other reaches his destination without incident. The position we are considering says that the two drivers are equally blameworthy for driving under these conditions, whatever the difference in the consequences of their behavior.

The suspicion that there is a problem with this position emerges when we follow it up with what seems to be the natural question: the two drivers, we are told, are equally blameworthy—but how blameworthy is that? We may partially answer this question with further comparative claims: this sort of reckless driving is less wrong, less faulty, than increased degrees of recklessness (not to mention less wrong than intentional homicide) and more faulty than other instances of driving under some less impaired conditions. But we also seem to want some non-comparative assessment, some more or less determinate measure of wrongness, on the basis of which we might establish some appropriate degree of punishment or scolding or even of anger or resentment to be directed toward the wrongdoer. It is quite unclear, however, how one could go about providing it.

Let us look in particular at the question of what level of blame would be appropriate for the drivers to assign to themselves. We may imagine that the driver whose recklessness led to the child's death feels terrible about what he did. He knows that he did not mean to kill anyone and that it was an unlucky coincidence that the child ran out when she did. Still, he keeps mentally confronting the fact that if he had had his brakes checked the week before, the accident might have been prevented. He feels a need to do something significant to help the family of the child, or at least symbolically to express his guilt and to offer penance. He is plagued by nightmares about the crash, and he cannot drive again for many weeks.

The second driver, let us imagine, arrives home safely and goes to bed. The next morning he reads a story of the first driver and the accident in the paper. Realizing that, but for fortune, that might have been he, he immediately makes an appointment to fix his brakes, taking the time from his busy schedule that he had not previously found. Moreover, he, like the first driver, has learned his lesson once and for all—never again does he let time slip away before checking or repairing his brakes. Still, he gets into his truck that very day and drives without difficulty; he suffers no nightmares and feels no need to donate time or money either to the cause of safer driving or to the family of the deceased child.

It seems only natural to summarize these descriptions by saying that the first driver blames himself more than the second one does. If the simple rationalist position on moral luck is correct, this would imply that at least one of these men is not acting, or at least is not feeling, as he ought. According to that position, since these two men are equally blameworthy, they should blame themselves to an equal degree. To what degree? The defender of rationalism has several options: she can say that they both ought to feel as the first driver does feel, that they both ought to feel as the second driver does feel, or that the right amount of blame falls somewhere in between. All of these answers seem wrong, however.

In fairness to the rationalist, we should note that she may allow what pretheoretical reflection suggests—namely, that there need be no single, uniquely correct reaction in any case, no precise quantity of blame, anger, or punitive suffering that it would be exclusively proper for the agents to impose on themselves. Rather, rationalists may admit that there is a range of reactions each of the agents might have which would seem normal, acceptable, and healthy. The range, however, is not so broad as to stretch, for either agent, across the entire span I have described. If the first driver, who had actually killed the child, responded as I described the second driver doing, we would, I think, be appalled and condemning. Yet if the second driver reacted as the first driver did, inflicting himself with equal guilt, we would also find this disturbing, indicative perhaps of a psychic imbalance. These judgments might draw one to the third option—that the right degree of blame, guilt, and so on lies somewhere in between. If so, however, I suspect that it is the appeal of the rationalist view in the abstract that draws us. Were it not for the fact that the drivers' reactions are so different from each other, there would be nothing internal to their separate reactions that would seem in the least inappropriate or odd.

The Irrationalist Position Considered

If one is moved by these considerations, one may be tempted simply to embrace the opposite position, the position I earlier labeled the irrationalist position. For if one thinks it clearly appropriate that the driver who killed the child blame himself more than the driver who didn't, must not this be because he deserves more blame? Following this train of thought, one point seems fairly to leap out in support and explanation of it—namely, that the first driver did something worse than the second: *he ran over a child.* According to this position, we may suppose, both drivers deserve equal blame for reckless driving. But, in addition, the first driver deserves blame (presumably, a lot of blame) for running over a child. Since the second driver did not run over a child, he cannot deserve blame for that. And so the first driver deserves more blame than the second.

Despite a certain rhetorical strength to this elaboration of the irrationalist position, its force as an argument is superficial at best. It seems as if a linguistic trick is being used in support of a moral claim. For although it must be granted that the one driver did something that the other driver did not, the explanation for this difference lies wholly in events outside of the drivers' control. Since the issue in question is precisely whether blameworthiness can legitimately depend on differences in outcome that lie beyond the agents' control, an appeal to this difference between the two drivers' actions simply asserts the irrationalist position—it does not justify it.[3]

Moreover, whatever intuitive support the irrationalist position gains from taking the points of view of the reckless drivers seems to vanish when we turn our attention to the question of how others ought to feel and how they ought to judge them.

I earlier suggested that we would expect the truck driver who runs over a child to feel very bad about what he has done, much worse than we would expect or want an equally reckless but much luckier driver to feel. Yet, as the drivers' friends or even sympathetic observers, it would be appropriate to try to make the first driver feel less bad to emphasize how limited was his faultiness and how large the element of luck. In other words, it would be appropriate for third parties to bring out the equal faultiness in the two drivers—this, despite our sense that the two drivers themselves ought not, at least to begin with, feel equally bad. The point is not that we expect the first driver to feel worse than we think he *ought* to feel, and therefore third parties are required to bring his guilt feelings down to the appropriate level. Rather, it seems, we want the first driver to feel worse—he ought, at least initially, to feel so bad that some soothing, some appeals to "reason" are necessary to stop him from judging himself too harshly.[4]

Reconciling Our Intuitive Responses

From the standpoint of impartial observers, the rationalist position seems to assert itself. Yet there seems to be a certain appropriateness to the phenomenon of unequal blame in the self-imposed feelings and judgments of the agents themselves. Can we make rational sense of this pair of intuitive responses? Is there any way to reconcile the thought that the equally reckless drivers are equally deserving of blame with the thought that it is nonetheless right for them to feel differently—for the one, as one naturally puts it, to blame himself more than the other?

Since the salient difference between the two drivers is that one caused a great harm that the other did not, the question is whether it makes sense to believe that one ought to feel bad about causing harm over and above what one feels for the recognition of one's faultiness in acting in a way that brought about the harm. The issue may seem puzzling because once one's faultiness is factored out, it is unclear why one's special connection to the harm isn't factored out as well. Of course, any decent person will be sorry to learn that a child has been run over, that a woman has fallen into a coma, or that a building with tenants inside has burned to the ground. But this will not account for the specific "agent-regret," to use Williams's term, that we approvingly imagine the relevant driver, physician, or building inspector to feel. The second driver, who reads of the other's accident, has both reason to blame himself for his own reckless driving and reason to grieve over the poor child's death—but the feelings these reflections arouse will not add up to the feelings of the first driver, whose behavior actually brought about that death. If we cast this puzzle aside, however, and simply accept the judgment that the first driver reasonably feels worse than the second about himself, a different puzzle confronts us—namely, how can it be right for the driver to feel worse about himself and yet not right for us to feel worse toward him?

An answer worth considering is that the unlucky driver has reason to feel bad because things have turned out badly for him, much worse than they turned out for the equally reckless but luckier driver. He has killed a child, and this is something he presumably would very much have preferred to avoid. At the expense of stretching a term, we might say that he has failed in one of his projects. At any rate, we may liken the driver's reaction to the reaction of one who has failed in a project—one who has ruined his marriage, botched an experiment, or fumbled the ball. It seems perfectly natural that a person should feel bad about failing to reach his goals. Moreover, it seems natural that others do not feel anger or resentment toward him on these accounts. It is too bad for him if his goals are not met, but he does not deserve blame for it.

There are two problems with the offered analogy. The first is that it assimilates the driver's regret for having killed the child to the case of someone feeling sorry for himself, as if, in addition to the blame he feels for having driven recklessly, he is sorry about *his* bad luck: "Why did the child have to run across my path, rather than the other guy's?" But this is not the content of the extra bad feeling that we had imagined as both natural and proper. Second, the propriety of the driver's regret does not depend on the fact that the harm he caused was unintended, on its being a failure of one of his projects or an event in conflict with one of his values. It would be proper, albeit unlikely, for the successful murderer to feel worse than the unsuccessful one. (Nor is this thought *wildly* unlikely, for a person may pull the trigger and then think, "What have I done?" In such a case, he may blame himself not for failing in a project but for having had the project and having succeeded.)

Unacceptable as this proposed answer is, two aspects of the analogy between the unlucky, faulty moral agent and the unlucky spouse or scientist or ballplayer are worth noting. First, these cases call to mind the variety of negative attitudes we may have toward ourselves that are not species of guilt or primarily expressions of blame. We may be angry, frustrated, and disappointed with ourselves in ways and for reasons that have nothing to do with moral fault or vice or harm. Second, these cases remind us of how natural and apparently appropriate it is for our attitudes toward ourselves to be affected by contingencies beyond our control. It seems natural and appropriate to be proud when one is awarded an honor or has proved a theorem or has fixed a faucet without having to call in the plumber. It seems natural and appropriate to be disappointed or annoyed with oneself when one doesn't make the team or the shortlist or when one screws up the faucet even worse. To be sure, one shouldn't be too proud or too self-critical on the basis of these successes and failures—the element of luck that enters into these things is considerable. But as we find fault with the person who takes too much credit or discredit for the successes and failures that are partly due to luck, we also find fault with the person who distances herself too much from all these events.

With these remarks in the background, let us return to the case of the unlucky driver who has run over a child. This time, however, imagine that, moved by considerations that support the rationalist position, he *is* able to detach his feelings and judgments about himself from the unfortuitous consequences of his recklessness. "To be sure, I was at fault," he thinks. "I should have had those brakes checked last week. But thousands of others are similarly negligent every day. My behavior was no worse than theirs, and I am no more a 'murderer' than any of them."

Earlier, I suggested that such a response would strike us as appalling. I now want to consider why it would strike us that way. Perhaps we suspect that the driver is trying, or succeeding, in judging himself less harshly than he deserves—that he is disclaiming responsibility for an act or a harm for which he is objectively responsible. But I believe that there is something else that is disturbing, not about the level of self-assessment that his detachment from the accident makes possible for him, but rather about the detachment itself. There is something disturbing about the agent's thought that the child's death, sorry as he may be about it, has relatively little to do with him.

The concern is not that his thoughts or judgments are, strictly speaking, false. Indeed, they may not be. He is right that his negligence is no different from the negligence of thousands of others, and if he feels considerably guilty and blames himself to a significant extent, then it may well be that his sense of his own blameworthiness is within the range that accuracy requires. What is problematic is his failure, beyond this, to take the consequences of his faultiness to have consequences for him, to be a significant part of his personal history, in a way in which witnessing, much less reading about, an accident would not be. The problem is not that he refuses to accept what responsibility he objectively has for the child's death; it is that he fails to take responsibility for it in a way that goes beyond that. He reveals a sense of himself—his real self, one might say—as one who is, at least in principle, distinct from his effects on the world, whose real quality and value, for better and for worse, is at best impurely indicated but not at all constituted by the goods and the harms, the successes and the failures, that make up his life in the physical world. It is as if he draws a circle around himself, coincident with the sphere of his will.

If one contemplates this attitude, not just as a single reaction to a single incident but also as a way, if you will, of being in the world, one might well question the intelligibility of the conception of identity that lies at the heart of it. Here, however, I am concerned to make a more purely normative point—namely, that even if this attitude toward life can be made out to be conceptually coherent, it defines an approach to life that is unhealthy and undesirable.

A Nameless Virtue

Let me elaborate on the slightly paradoxical claim I made two paragraphs ago— that what is troubling about the fully rationalist truck driver is not that he refuses to accept what responsibility he objectively has for the child's death; it is that he fails to take responsibility for it in a way that goes beyond that. It is this thought and the virtue to which it refers that I believe properly lies at the heart of the solution to the problem of moral luck.

There is a virtue that I suspect we all dimly recognize and commend that may be expressed as the virtue of taking responsibility for one's actions and their consequences. It is, regrettably, a virtue with no name, and I am at a loss to suggest a name that would be helpful. It involves living with an expectation and a willingness to be held accountable for what one does, understanding the scope of "what one does," particularly when costs are involved, in an expansive rather than a narrow way. It is the virtue that would lead one to offer to pay for the vase that one broke even if one's fault in the incident was uncertain; the virtue that would lead one to apologize, rather than get defensive, if one unwittingly offended someone or hurt her. Perhaps this virtue is a piece or an aspect of a larger one, which involves taking responsibility not just for one's actions and their consequences but also for a larger range of circumstances that fall broadly within one's reach. One may offer to pay for the vase one's child broke or offer to take the blame for the harm someone suffered as a result of the practices of an agency of which one is the head. Like other virtues, this one is a matter of offering the right amount (whether it be of compensation, apology, or guilt) at the right time to the right person in the right way. It is not the case that the more responsibility one takes for the harms that lie at increasing distance from one's control, the better.[5] Yet one ought to take responsibility for more than what, from a bystander's point of view, would be justly impersonally assigned.

If I am right in thinking that this is a virtue, and one, moreover, that most of us at least implicitly recognize, then it gives us a way of understanding our responses in moral luck cases: equally reckless drivers, equally negligent building inspectors, and so on deserve equal blame for their faulty behavior. But those who cause harm are called upon to feel and to do something more that others are not similarly called upon to do and to feel. It is, in other words, the occasion for the one agent to display his (nameless) virtue or lack of it, whereas it is no such occasion for the other.

The idea that we regard an expansive sense of responsibility (when costs are involved) as a virtue provides a coherent explanation of the pair of intuitive responses that earlier appeared to be in tension. Whether these responses are justified, however, depends on the further question of whether we *ought* to regard this as a virtue—whether, if you will, it *is* a virtue. There seem to me to be two reasons for thinking that it is.

Perhaps the more obvious reason for regarding it as a virtue is that, when applied to harmful actions, this trait is a species of, or at least akin to, the well-established virtue of generosity. Generosity generally involves a willingness to give more—more time, more money, more love, more lenience, more, in one way or another, of oneself than justice requires. In offering to pay for the broken vase or in trying to ease the pain or provide comfort to the grieving family beyond what a rationalist assignment of liability would demand, an agent voluntarily benefits or tries to benefit others at cost to herself. That this should be seen as virtuous is not hard to understand.

There is another aspect to the character trait in question, however, that is worthy of support as well. This aspect comes more sharply into view if we contrast a mere witness to the breaking of the vase who offers to replace it with the person who, innocently or not, actually broke the vase. In either case, the offer to pay would seem to be an act of generosity. But whereas we might appreciate and even admire the bystander's offer, we might also be slightly puzzled by it or even in certain cases resent it. On the other hand, we are apt positively to expect the offer from the agent who broke the vase and to be puzzled or disturbed by his failure to offer to pay. We expect the vase breaker, like the truck driver who hit the child, to acknowledge that the consequences of his behavior have something specifically to do with him. We expect the vase breaker to offer to pay, then, not only because we want him to be generous but also because we expect him to accept contingency in the determination and assessment of who he is.

Whereas generosity is a thoroughly moral notion, this other aspect of the virtue I am discussing is not so clearly or narrowly moral. The reason for objecting quite generally to an attitude of greater detachment and for commending an embrace of at least some of what lies beyond the sphere of one's will has less to do with a benevolent concern for others than with a view about what, for lack of a better word, might be called psychic health. The desirability of this trait comes partly from its expression of our recognition that we are beings who are thoroughly in the world, in interaction with others whose movements and thoughts we cannot fully control and whom we affect and are affected by accidentally, as well as intentionally, involuntarily, unwittingly, inescapably, as well as voluntarily and deliberately. To form one's attitudes and judgments of oneself and others solely on the basis of their wills and intentions, to draw sharp lines between what one is responsible for and what is up to the rest of the world, to try in this way to extricate oneself and others from the messiness and the irrational contingencies of the world, would be to remove oneself from the only ground on which it is possible for beings like ourselves to meet. If we define ourselves in ways that aim to minimize the significance of contingency and luck, we do so at the cost of living less fully in the world, or at least at the cost of engaging less fully with the others who share that world.

The Moral of Moral Luck

In my introductory remarks, I mentioned that something seemed to be missing in the rationalist response to the phenomena that the concept of moral luck concerns, something that suggests a grain of truth in the irrationalist response. The conclusion to which the train of thought in this essay has been leading is that what is missing is an acknowledgment of the nameless virtue that urges us, as a matter both of moral character and of psychic health,[6] to recognize and accept (to an appropriate degree) the effects of our actions as significant for who we are and for what we should do. By explicitly including a description and endorsement of this virtue in our response to the phenomena at issue, we reach a position that we may think of as falling between the starker alternatives of rationalism and irrationalism as I initially presented them. With the rationalists, this position holds that equal fault deserves equal blame and that, therefore, an impartial observer ought to judge equally faulty actions to be equally blameworthy. Yet, with the irrationalists, it allows that different effects call for different responses, so that the faulty—or, for that matter, the nonfaulty—agent's attitude toward herself, as well as her deliberations about what to do from here on, are properly affected by her actions' effects.

This proposal is abstract and leaves many questions open. The proposal of the nameless virtue to which I alluded, for example, calls out for further refinement: how much and what kinds of difference in agents' emotional and practical responses should the contingent and uncontrollable differences in the effects of their voluntary behavior make? How, if at all, does this alleged virtue apply or appear in connection with the positive or beneficial effects of actions that are at least partly not traceable to the quality of the agents' wills? Should we restrict the scope of this virtue or of the evaluative judgments relating to it to the realm of moral luck in "how things turn out," or does the position sketched in this essay have implications for our responses in other areas of moral experience where we must also confront the considerable role played by luck (e.g., luck in one's circumstances or luck in one's natural moral endowments)?

These questions are intrinsically interesting, practically important, and apt, I suspect, to arouse much controversy. Without answering them, it may be said, we cannot claim to have "solved" the problem of moral luck or laid it, once and for all, to rest. Still, I believe that if we can agree on the basic features of the admittedly abstract position for which this essay has been arguing, considerable progress will have been made. We will be able to identify much more in common in the intuitions and theoretical positions that formerly may have seemed diametrically opposed. Disagreements will have been narrowed and conceptually sharpened.

The framework of the abstract position advocated here leaves room, then, for many variations in response to more detailed questions concerning the range of phenomena involving moral luck. I end by discussing one pair of such variations that seems to me particularly curious and that may be especially closely tied to a contrast in sensibilities that might formerly have attracted people respectively to rationalist and irrationalist positions on moral luck.

Blame, Guilt, and Agent-Regret

The position for which I have argued states (in agreement with the rationalist) that blameworthiness is solely a function of faultiness. In other words, equal fault deserves equal blame. At the same time, my position holds (in agreement with the irrationalist) that different effects call for different responses—including different emotional responses in the agents whose behaviors bring about these effects. A question that arises is how the difference in appropriate emotional response is related to the equality in appropriate blame—for blame, it would seem, especially blame of oneself, is itself an emotional matter.

One response to the question involves the claim that there are two distinct emotional responses at issue that sit, as it were, side by side. The emotional response to beliefs about one's blameworthiness is traditionally called guilt. The emotional response to beliefs about the badness of the effects of one's actions is what Bernard Williams labeled "agent-regret." According to this first position, guilt is the emotion one feels or should feel in proportion to how much one judges oneself blameworthy. Agent-regret, by contrast, is a special form of sadness or pain accompanying the wish that things had been otherwise with regard to something with which one's agency was somehow involved. This position allows us to be pure and simple rationalists with respect to the issue of blame while also supporting the view that it is reasonable and appropriate that two agents whose acts turned out very differently should, in some way, feel differently about themselves and their acts. How much guilt one would feel, on this view, would be a function of how blameworthy one judged oneself to be; how much "sadness" would be a reflection of the nameless virtue.

This proposal neatly addresses the tension between the equality in appropriate blameworthiness and the inequality in appropriate negative feelings that depend on the consequences of one's actions by assigning the appropriate responses to separate emotional categories. To some, however, including myself, this proposal seems *too* neat. Our emotions do not seem to sort themselves out as clearly as this position suggests. This thought gives rise to a second proposal.

This position, like the earlier one, acknowledges a distinction between guilt and agent-regret. Guilt is at least partly a function of judging oneself to be blameworthy. In cases in which we judge ourselves to have done something wrong but which—luckily—have no bad effects, guilt, and not agent-regret, is an appropriate response. Moreover, guilt is not appropriate when we have done nothing wrong. In cases in which we are not at fault but which nonetheless—unluckily—lead to serious harm, agent-regret, and not guilt, may be appropriate. However, when a faulty action causes a harm, our feelings tend to get all mixed together—several sources for feeling bad about oneself and for being motivated to engage in certain sorts of actions combine to produce a mental state that is not itself analyzable into component states. Moreover, in light of a point I made earlier about the indeterminateness of the proper "amount" of blame to be assigned to a given act, this phenomenon seems logically, as well as psychologically, inevitable.

Earlier, I pointed out that although one can sensibly make some comparative judgments among wrongful actions, noting that one act is more blameworthy than another, and that some acts are very blameworthy and others only slightly blameworthy, it is unclear how fine-grained and precise such judgments can meaningfully be. Equally important, there is no apparent principle correlating degrees of blameworthiness with uniquely appropriate amounts of pain, punishment, or guilt. Because of this, it is inevitable that how one feels in connection with an acknowledgment of blameworthiness will depend on more than the degree of blame one acknowledges oneself to deserve. How much one blames oneself, in other words, must be a function of more than how blame*worthy* one thinks one is—for how blameworthy one is cannot supply a complete answer of how much blame one should get. Thus, the fact that the truck driver who kills a child blames himself more than the other driver need not indicate that he judges himself to be more blameworthy than the other, for how much he blames himself is a function not only of his judgment of blameworthiness but also of his reasons for agent-regret.

The recognition that the amount of blame and guilt that it is appropriate to direct toward an agent is significantly indeterminate—the recognition, that is, that blame and guilt cannot exclusively be a function of blame*worthiness*—may be combined with an endorsement of the nameless virtue to support this second response to the tension with which we have been concerned. Whereas the first response emphasizes the difference between guilt and agent-regret, this one emphasizes the complexity of the phenomena of blame and guilt—the different reasons and reasonable factors that shape whether and how much blame we allot, both to others and especially to ourselves. This position would endorse the idea that one person might properly blame herself more than another whose action was equally faulty, and so it may be said to concede more to the initial irrationalist position than the previous one. At the same time, it retains the notion that lies at the core of the rationalist view that how much blame one *deserves,* or, perhaps better, how deserving of blame a person is, is purely a function of faultiness in action and not at all a function beyond that of how one's actions turn out.

According to this view, then, moral luck—at least the sort of moral luck we have been discussing, luck in how our actions turn out—is a reality, rather than an illusion, in this sense: that how good or bad a person should feel about herself, how much she should blame herself (or pat herself on the back) and how much or how little it is morally incumbent on her to do, is in part a function of how her actions turn out in ways that are beyond her control. And yet it is not, as the irrationalist position would suggest, because one's moral record, as it were, that establishes one's goodness or badness as a person is determined by these nonvoluntary matters. Rather it is because, as creatures of a physical and social world, we have among our responsibilities, or perhaps less moralistically, among our given projects, one that urges us to recognize the effects of our actions as things that connect significantly to us, that have repercussions for who we are and what we should do.

The Moral of Moral Luck, Again

What is the moral of moral luck? I regret that I do not have a slogan of twenty-five words or less that sums it up beautifully. However, if I am right about my analysis and assessment of the phenomenon in question, then the moral is one that must recognize the considerable truth in both the rationalist and the irrationalist positions. It is that a morally conscientious approach to life, as well as a humanly conscientious approach to morality, must strike a balance between an interest, on the one hand, in attaining the kind of justice that comes from limiting the significance of that which is independent of the power and the quality of our wills with an interest, on the other hand, in acknowledging our earthly character and maintaining our connection to the social and physical world. The paradoxical quality of the phenomenon of moral luck comes from the fact that this latter interest can only be served if we affirm the significance that the former interest seeks to limit.

Notes

I wrote this essay an embarrassingly long time ago, and for no good reason let other things take precedence over finding the time to make the changes I wanted to make before sending it out for publication. I am indebted to Douglas MacLean; Galen Strawson; Susan Hahn; audiences at MIT, Georgetown University, the University of Michigan, the Australian National University, and the University of Santa Clara; and participants of the Society for Ethics and Legal Philosophy and Philamore for their stimulating and insightful comments and suggestions. Some, I hope, have led to improvements in the present essay. Others spur me to work more in the future on related topics.

1. Bernard Williams, "Moral Luck," in *Moral Luck* (Cambridge: Cambridge University Press, 1981), 20–39. See also Thomas Nagel, "Moral Luck," in *Mortal Questions* (Cambridge: Cambridge University Press, 1979), 24–38.

2. It is, for example, a function not only of how serious a moral breach is involved, which itself is a complex matter, but also of the degree to which the agent could have been expected to appreciate the seriousness of that breach and how free she was to govern her actions according to her appreciation of its moral status.

3. There is another reason to be dissatisfied with this "linguistic" defense of the irrationalist position I have presented—namely, that the linguistic point cannot easily be made about other cases that seem morally analogous to the case of the reckless drivers. In the drivers' case, our language readily and naturally provides different descriptions of what blameworthy things the two drivers have done. But other examples with the same moral structure may not lend themselves to similar differences in description. Consider a woman who has a clandestine affair with a married man, whose spouse, upon discovering the deception, commits suicide, and compare her with the woman, who, having no more and no less reason to worry about her lover's spouse, sees the relationship through without the wife ever knowing. As with the truck drivers, the women in these two cases might naturally and appropriately feel very differently about themselves. The one, after all, has been involved in something that has led to an innocent woman's death, and the other has not. But one wouldn't say that the lover in the first case had killed the wife or even caused her death. We might say that her actions contributed to events that led to the suicide, but that description does not in itself make clear that she acted in a way that was blameworthy at all. (What triggers a suicide in a sufficiently troubled person may be totally innocent, after all.) The most natural description of what the first woman did wrong applies just as well to the second— she failed to take the wife's interests sufficiently into account. And yet, I submit, it is perfectly natural that, given the way things turned out, the one woman should blame herself more than the other.

4. Bernard Williams, "Moral Luck," makes a similar point in the article that introduced this example. (His point was addressed to the lorry driver whose driving was entirely faultless.) The point that when we take the observer's point of view we are less sympathetic to the irrationalist position seems even clearer when we consider intentionally immoral acts and their equally faulty attempts. For example, in the case of the murderer and the attempted murderer, the inclination to judge and to blame them equally seems to me even stronger, or more clearly strong, than in the case of the reckless drivers. Perhaps this is because the indeterminacy of blameworthiness (and also of badness and wrongness) is less problematic in the case of murder and attempted murder than in the case of—pardon the expression—middle-of-the-road recklessness. We all know that murder and attempted murder are very bad indeed and that a great deal of blame in either case is appropriate.

5. Thus, for example, it is far from obvious that it would be a virtue for all Germans to feel responsible for the consequences of the Third Reich.

6. From an Aristotelian point of view, there is no distinction between these values.

7

Common Decency

Cheshire Calhoun

Charles Dickens's Ebenezer Scrooge is a portrait of a man without common decency. Scrooge's central failing is not his miserliness or callousness toward suffering. His sometimes spectacularly contemptible failings—as when he suggests that the poor should simply get on with dying and reduce the surplus population—are connected to a less spectacular but more pervasive failing: Scrooge has removed himself from the daily commerce of favors, mercies, small kindnesses, forgivings, expressions of gratitude, and social pleasantries that are the stuff of common decency. He gruffly rebuffs his nephew's invitation to Christmas dinner. He grumbles at being expected to let his employees off on Christmas day. He threatens to take a ruler to a Christmas caroler. And he refuses even the smallest compliance with the convention of charitable giving during the Christmas season. Though we see Scrooge's faults at the Christmas season, his failing is not seasonal. Scrooge routinely fails to behave like a decent human being, and for that reason no one ever stops "him in the street to say, with gladsome looks, 'My dear Scrooge, how are you? When will you come to see me?' No beggars implored him to bestow a trifle, no children asked him what it was o'clock, no man or woman ever once in all his life inquired the way to such and such a place, of Scrooge."[1]

That Scrooge has no truck with simple favors, such as telling others the time or giving them directions, signals his lack of common decency. Paying Bob Cratchit barely a living wage, relentlessly collecting debts from the already impoverished, and displaying an indecently callous attitude toward the destitute are simply more egregious examples of Scrooge's general inability to live up to our moral expectations about how minimally well-formed agents will behave.

In disappointing expectations about how a minimally well-formed agent will behave, Scrooge does not invite others' resentment or moral indignation. Nor is guilt what he comes to feel about his past bad behavior. In *A Christmas Carol*, Scrooge's lack of common decency is most often met with surprise, pity, contempt, mockery, and cooled affections. What Scrooge himself comes to feel about his lack of common decency is not guilt but a mixture of shame and loss of human connection.

But for all that Scrooge is "an odious, stingy, hard, unfeeling man,"[2] there is no one whom he clearly *wrongs*. It may be indecent to insist that his employees work on Christmas day, but he correctly observes that since they also expect to be paid, he does not owe them this day off. Nor does he owe his nephew pleasantries, Christmas carolers something for their cheer, Bob Cratchit higher wages than agreed upon, his debtors a grace period in meeting their debts, or any particular charitable organization a donation. These are all gifts that he is within his rights to refuse to bestow. As for what Scrooge owes others, Dickens gives us no reason to think that Scrooge fails to render what is due. On the contrary, Scrooge is obsessed with debts. He wants nothing more from others than exactly what they owe him. In return, he will give others exactly what he owes and not a bit more. His business and moral ledgers carefully track debts payable to and by him, making no allowance for giving or receiving that exceeds the obligatory. And this is the source of his failure of common decency. For Scrooge, others are morally entitled to expect only what is rightfully theirs. He is unable to see the moral legitimacy of their expectation that he will give them the grace periods, sympathetic ear, relief from work duties, livable wages, the time of day, and sociability that are just matters of common decency. Scrooge sees nothing morally objectionable about removing himself from commerce with others' needs. "It's not my business," he says. "It's enough for a man to understand his own business, and not to interfere with other people's."[3]

The common decencies and failures of common decency at the center of Dickens's *A Christmas Carol* are familiar ones. Yet, from a philosophical point of view, common decency is puzzling. Acts of common decency seem to occupy a shadowy territory between the obligatory and the supererogatory. On the one hand, Scrooge seems within his rights to withhold the kindnesses and mercies that are emblematic of common decency. He in fact doesn't owe his debtors grace periods or his nephew pleasantries upon their meeting. Yet those around him also seem justified in responding with moral contempt and a severing of social bonds. They rightfully find moral fault with his behavior. *But how can one be faulted for failing to give what was never owed?* What sense can be made of our treating acts of common decency as though they were not obligatory but not purely elective either?

In what follows, I suggest that the normative expectations connected with common decency do not derive from a conception of what we owe each other. Instead, they derive from a constructed conception of what can be expected of a minimally well-formed moral agent.

Two Species of Common Decency

Since the term "decency" has many uses, let me say a bit about what I have in mind by "common decency." Then we can turn to the puzzling normative status of common decencies.

The term "decent," like the terms "good" and "mediocre," is a grading term. Anything that can be graded could receive the grade of "decent." We speak, for example, of a decent cup of coffee, a decent selection of items, a decent society, a decent system of law, and decent housing. The core meaning of "decent" in all of these cases is *adequate* or *minimally acceptable as good*. What is decent just satisfies the standard for items of a particular kind. A decent cup of coffee is a good cup, but only just. "It's decent" offers only faint praise and draws attention to what is only a cut above the shamefully inadequate.

Sometimes what is minimally acceptable and only a step from shamefulness is the agents' *moral performance*. The notion of minimally acceptable moral performance —and thus of common decency—can be understood in two different but related ways. First, we sometimes equate common decency with fulfilling one's *minimal moral duties*. Philosophers in particular tend to construe common decency in this way, although they disagree on whether all duties or just some duties are "minimal."[4]

Doing what morality minimally requires is, I think, an important form of common decency.[5] But it is not the philosophically most interesting form of common decency. Think back to Ebenezer Scrooge. Scrooge lacks common decency not because he shirks his minimal moral obligations but because he fails to live up to others' very strong expectations about the moral gifts—pleasantries, mercies, kindnesses, and favors—they can count on receiving from any agent who is at least minimally well-formed. This second form of common decency is, as John Kekes puts it, especially connected with "moral attitudes that call upon one to go beyond the rules."[6] It "involves good will toward fellow members of the society, a reluctance to injure others in pursuit of our own ends, *even if we have the right* to pursue our ends. It is the attitude opposite to extracting our pound of flesh."[7] Thus although it is true that we sometimes say of a person, "At least she had the common decency to do what she agreed to do," common decency is not simply a matter of living up to minimal moral obligations. "Common decency" also names the basic sorts of things that we expect any minimally well-formed agent will *elect* to do for others *absent any requirement* to do so.[8]

These two forms of common decency—fulfilling minimal moral duties and giving those "moral gifts" that are only to be expected—have a common core: common decency has to do with what can be expected from any *minimally* well-formed moral agent. To have common decency is to be a good or acceptable moral agent, but just barely.

I now set aside the common decency of fulfilling minimal moral obligations and turn exclusively to the common decency of giving those moral gifts of kindness, mercy, pleasantness, and so on that are only to be expected of a minimally well-formed agent.

Common Decency, Supererogation, and Obligation

Common decencies appear to occupy a shadowy territory between the supererogatory and the obligatory. Consider first their relation to supererogation. Common decencies differ from typical supererogatory acts because they are *expected* of agents and are *shameful* to omit. But common decencies share with supererogatory acts the feature of being *nonobligatory*.[9] As Scrooge understood so well, common decencies are elective—gifts one is morally free to give (or not). Because of this, the kindnesses, mercies, favors, and the like that constitute common decency seem to fit quite naturally within the basic categories of supererogatory acts:[10] (1) favors; (2) acts of beneficence; (3) volunteering; (4) mercy and forgiveness; (5) praisings, congratulating, and honorings; (6) gratitude; (7) gift givings; and (8) saintliness and heroism.[11]

Saintly and heroic acts are obviously not matters of *common* decency. But each of the remaining seven categories contains some mixture of common decencies that are expected of all minimally well-formed agents and especially virtuous acts that could only be expected from unusually well-formed agents and thus are left fully to the agent's discretionary judgment. How do we determine *which* acts are common decencies? Let me propose for the moment that, as a general rule, any act falling into categories (1) through (7) that has been socially conventionalized—so that it is just "what is done"—will be a matter of common decency. Giving one's child a birthday present is, for example, socially conventionalized. So, too, in many organizations is volunteering to take one's turn at some undesirable task (e.g., serving as department chair). Holding a stranger's place in line, giving directions or the time to those who ask, opening the door for those whose hands are full, and giving up one's bus seat to the elderly are familiar conventionalized favors. Such conventionalized giftings, volunteerings, and favors are matters of common decency.

Although common decencies resemble supererogatory acts in being morally good but nonobligatory, they also differ in one important respect: they are not fully morally elective. An act is fully morally elective when

1. Omitting the act is not morally criticizable.
2. No "ought" stronger than an "ought" of moral advice giving is appropriately used to recommend it.
3. Choosing the act is meritorious—something we commend or admire the agent for doing rather than take as owed or simply to be expected.
4. Gratitude untempered by any thought that one has some moral title to the gift bestowed is the proper response to the act.

Common decencies are not fully morally elective in any of these senses. First, people who don't manage to do what is just a matter of common decency are criticizable. They are not criticizable for *wronging* others, but their failure to give expected moral gifts does open them to the charge of being petty, mean-spirited, contemptible, disappointing, irritating, and a poor excuse for a moral agent.[12] Such criticism underlines the sub par nature of the moral performance. Contempt, pity, cooled affections, resentment, and (the agent's) shame are all appropriate reactive attitudes to failures of common decency. By contrast, supererogatory acts are ones whose omission does not warrant moral criticism or negative reactive attitudes.

Failures of common decency thus have an odd status. On the one hand, they are not wrongs. On the other hand, they are not morally acceptable omissions. Scrooge's mercilessness toward his debtors, for example, was clearly taken by others to be an offense, yet one that he was not morally obligated to avoid. Failures of common decency thus seem to have the interesting status of being morally disvaluable acts that are nevertheless permitted rather than forbidden. Chisholm has called acts having these features "permissive ill-doings" (or "offenses"),[13] and Julia Driver has described them as "suberogatory."[14]

Second, common decencies are not fully morally elective because even if the "ought" of obligation does not apply to common decencies, an "ought" that is considerably stronger than mere advice giving does apply. Joel Feinberg is perhaps best known for making this observation.[15] Feinberg uses the example of one kind of common decency—simple favors—to argue that "there are some actions which it would be desirable for a person to do and which, indeed, he *ought* to do, even though they are actions he is under no *obligation* and has no *duty* to do." He invites us to imagine being approached by a stranger who politely asks for a light. "Ought I to give him one?" he asks, and replies, "I think most people would agree that I should, and that any reasonable man of good will would offer the stranger a match."[16] The sense of "ought" here falls somewhere between a command to do one's duty and the observation that this is one among many morally good acts that one might elect.

Third, common decencies are not fully morally elective, because they establish our minimal acceptability as a moral agent; they do not signal our achievement of a virtuously high standard of moral agency. This is why omitting common decencies is criticizable. It is also why choosing to behave with common decency is not meritorious—something that we commend or admire the agent for doing rather than take to be owed or simply to be expected. In the United States, for example, tipping waitpersons 15% to 20% is a common decency, only to be expected of any minimally well-formed agent who is familiar with tipping conventions. It is not an indication of commendable virtue.[17] By contrast, supererogation is the domain of commendable and admirable virtue.

Fourth, the proper response to a fully elective moral gift is gratitude. The proper response to being shown common decency is at most perfunctory gratitude. Because we are normatively entitled to expect common decency from others, gratitude in excess of simple thanks for commonly decent treatment would be misplaced. Given this difference between common decencies and supererogatory moral gifts, a good way to discern which favors, mercies, volunteerings, and so on are just matters of common decency is to ask oneself, "What favors (mercies, volunteerings, etc.) could I ask of others without putting myself in the position of incurring a debt of gratitude for a meritorious display of goodwill?" Some ways of filling in requests such as "Would you do me the favor of . . . ?" "Could you spare . . . ?" "Would you mind letting me . . . ?" and "Could you tell me . . . ?" clearly impose on others' goodwill and would, if granted, incur a debt of gratitude. In other cases, we simply assume that others should be willing to grant our request because we aren't asking for a meritorious display of goodwill—just common decency.

Utilitarian and Kantian Obligation to Show Common Decency

In sum, common decencies appear to occupy a hybrid category, sharing some features of obligation and some of supererogation. One might, however, balk at this idea. In particular, one might object that if common decencies are what we *ought* to do, then common decencies are obligatory.[18] Both utilitarians and Kantians would probably insist that the injunction "You ought to do that; it's just common decency" points to an obligation. A utilitarian might take common decencies to be strictly obligatory, as a rule, because they benefit others but cost the agent little. And utilitarians think that we are always obligated to do whatever will maximize welfare.

Kantians would probably categorize common decencies among imperfect duties. If common decencies are imperfect duties, this would explain why the "ought" recommending common decency seems weaker than the "ought" of obligation. No act fulfilling an imperfect obligation is strictly required. Imperfect obligations simply require that one perform *some* acts of a particular kind—for example, some possible favors. The "ought" recommending, for example, doing someone the favor of holding her place in line is thus not the strong "ought" of perfect obligation that commands what we must do now. It is the weaker "ought," requiring that we do some favors but not necessarily this one now.

Both utilitarian and Kantian approaches solve the puzzle over the normative status of common decencies by denying there ever was a puzzle: the "ought" recommending common decency just is the "ought" of obligation. Neither approach, however, enables us to retain much of the ordinary conception of common decency. Consider, first, the utilitarian view. A utilitarian would have to insist that common decencies are obligatory in just the way that keeping promises and telling the truth are obligatory. Thus the utilitarian would have to insist that Scrooge wasn't just criticizable for not giving his debtors a grace period, but he actually *wronged* them. A utilitarian would also have to drop the idea that common decencies are more strongly required than are saintly mercies and kindnesses but are less strongly required than minimal promise keeping, truth telling, and so on. All acts that maximize utility—whether acts of promise keeping or of common decency or of saintly beneficence—are equally obligatory. Of course, a utilitarian could try to argue that our commonsense distinctions between the strictly obligatory, the commonly decent, and the saintly are useful fictions to preserve.[19] Perhaps we gain something when people are left free to elect to be decent, and freer yet to be saintly, rather than feeling obliged. But this still amounts to jettisoning, at the metalevel, our everyday distinctions between different degrees of "oughtness."

The Kantian, too, must reject the idea that there are different degrees of "oughtness." First, both common decencies and unusually virtuous moral gift givings are simply different ways that agents might elect to discharge their imperfect obligations. The same "ought" of imperfect obligation applies to both types of act. There is thus no obvious way of capturing the idea that common decencies are normatively expected in a way that other moral gifts are not. Second, the Kantian cannot capture the idea that *particular, individual* acts of common decency are what we ought to perform. One might ordinarily think that absent a special excuse, you really ought to give the match to the person who asks you for one, and you are criticizable if you refuse. From a Kantian point of view, however, what is criticizable is adopting a *policy* of refusing to render assistance. Omitting a *particular* act that would discharge an imperfect obligation cannot be criticized. Within a Kantian framework, the only way to capture the individually criticizable nature of failures of common decency would be to treat common decencies as matters of perfect obligation. That move, too, has a serious drawback. One of the distinguishing features of common decencies is that they involve not standing on one's rights when one is entitled to. This is most obvious for the common decency of not insisting on taking one's fair share; it is also obvious for the common decency of being merciful or forgiving.

In sum, if common decencies are governed by the "ought" of obligation—either strict or imperfect—then much ordinary talk about common decency must be set aside as confused. The alternative is to see if we can make sense of there being an "ought" that is weaker than the "ought" of obligation and stronger than the "ought" of moral advice. Is there some way of making sense of the idea that there are *elective* acts that we would be *criticizable* for not performing?

Constructing the Category of the Decent

What I want to propose is that the category of the decent—with its peculiarly hybrid properties—is constructed out of an antecedently determined domain of supererogatory acts. What I have in mind is this: we begin from some moral theory that enables us to determine what acts are obligatory and what acts are supererogatory. The determination of the domain of the obligatory sets boundaries to what could possibly be a matter of common decency. Something that is itself obligatory cannot be a matter of common decency, a moral gift that we are within our moral rights not to give. Nor can violations of obligation be common decencies since they are morally prohibited.[20] Only supererogatory (elective and morally valuable) acts are *candidates* for common decencies. The actual list of commonly decent acts is constructed from those candidates. By "constructed" I mean that unlike the obligatory and the supererogatory, norms of common decency emerge only from within a social practice of morality. Those norms articulate what moral gift-giving participants in a particular social practice of morality are expected to elect.[21] The expectation here is normative. It is not just that we happen in point of fact to expect other people to be willing to do us simple favors, forgive us for small failings, or volunteer to take a turn. We also take ourselves to be justified in having these expectations and to have a legitimate basis for criticizing those, like Scrooge, who disappoint us.

This takes us to the central question. From what source does this subset of nonobligatory, morally good acts that we call common decency get its heightened normativity?

Conventions

One account (which I will ultimately reject) of the heightened normativity attached to common decencies draws on the value of having and sustaining social conventions of moral gift giving. The argument goes like this:

It is often remarked within moral philosophy that securing the reliable performance of some acts has a special urgency. Our ability to carry out any life plan at all would be seriously undermined if we could not rely on others not to injure or kill us, to keep their agreements, to respect our privacy and property, and to communicate with us truthfully. This form of reliability—reliable forbearance from undermining others' security or agency—is, indeed, of great moral importance, and the concept of moral obligation works to secure that reliability. However, our need to rely on others extends well beyond matters of basic security and nonmanipulated agency. Like Blanche Dubois, we find that we unavoidably depend on the kindness of strangers. We need help in carrying out our plans, emotional support, occasional release from promises, forgiveness and mercy for errors, a grace period for repaying debts, and so on. That is, we depend on people electing to give us moral gifts. Personal planning and social coordination are enhanced, however, if some of what others might elect to do for us is routinized so that we can have advance knowledge of the contexts in which we can or cannot depend on others to help out. For example, when giving directions, telling the time, and lending a match are converted from fully elective, supererogatory gifts into socially institutionalized, expected gift givings, we can venture out in the world unburdened with maps, watches, and lighters. Or, for example, when forgiving those who are five or ten minutes tardy for appointments is conventionalized, we are spared from always having to allow extra time to arrive. In short, optimal social functioning depends not only on individuals fulfilling their moral duties toward others but also on the reliable exchange of moral gifts. Converting fully elective supererogatory acts into normatively expected ones by institutionalizing them in the shared, everyday moral practice of a group of people produces that reliability. When socially institutionalized, formerly fully elective acts such as picking up items dropped by another, giving up one's seat on a bus to the elderly, and letting those with only a few items go ahead of oneself in line become things that a decent person *ought* to do, even if others cannot demand them as a right.

Drawing on this idea that acts of common decency are part of an institutionalized practice of moral gift giving, we can explain the heightened normativity of common decencies in one of two ways. First, it is *advantageous* for there to be moral gift-giving conventions rather than leaving it entirely up to individual discretion which, if any, favors, mercies, forgivings, volunteerings, and the like they will do for others. Supporting those conventions thus has moral value because those conventions are useful ones.

Alternatively, one might observe that the fact that common decencies are *institutionalized* practices of moral gift giving from which everyone benefits means that those who insist on their right to refuse to be decent are a kind of free rider.

Whether they wish to or not, they in fact benefit in myriad ways from others' participation in the practice of bestowing those moral gifts that constitute common decency. Indecent people, like Scrooge, reap the benefits of moral gift-giving conventions without doing their part in this system of reciprocal favors, mercies, volunteerings, and forgivings. And that is unfair.

Now, here is what I think is the problem with this way of explaining why we ought to treat others with common decency and are criticizable if we don't. An appeal to the social utility of moral gift-giving conventions and the unfairness of free riding on those conventions justifies too much. Common decencies turn out to be not just obligation-*like*. They are *obligatory*. Many have argued, for example, that the usefulness of a conventionalized practice of promising and the unfairness of free riding on that practice ground an obligation to keep promises. So, if we are going to make sense of the electiveness of common decencies, we need an account of their normativity that does not draw on the moral value of sustaining useful conventions or of avoiding free riding on them.

Minimal Agency

A second account—which I think is the better one—shifts our attention from the status of norms that recommend decent *conduct* to the status of the *identity* that behaving decently sustains. Scrooge doesn't just behave badly. He disappoints our expectations for how any minimally well-formed agent will behave. The moral importance of the identity "minimally well-formed agent" generates the normativity of common decency. That identity is morally important because any functioning practice of morality must presume that its practitioners are capable of meeting a minimal standard of moral performance. I now turn to a more detailed explication of the central ideas in this second account of the normativity of the "ought" that recommends common decency.

The thought that we can expect any minimally well-formed agent to do x, y, and z arises both for obligations and for elective moral gifts. That is why there are, as I observed earlier, two related forms of common decency—one pertaining to minimal moral obligations and one pertaining to minimal moral gift giving. Consider, first, our expectations about obligatory moral performance. Although everyone stands under the obligation to do one's duty and moral failures meet with criticism, we nevertheless tolerate a good deal of moral backsliding. We tolerate it in the sense that much wrongdoing seems unsurprising and a normal hazard of everyday moral practice. We expect to meet with and accommodate a good deal of moral misbehavior that results from a variety of character shortcomings. We know that variations in natural and acquired dispositions, moral education, and strength of will result in variation both in individuals' moral performances and in their overall "success" as moral agents. There is, however, a baseline that we expect agents, no matter their individual character and temptations, to be able to manage to achieve. Even if it would be unreasonable to expect that fellow moral agents will always do what they ought, there are at least some things it is reasonable to expect.[22] Those who disappoint these expectations compound the wrongfulness of what they do with the senselessness of subjecting others to what even the most minimally well-formed agent should have been able to manage to avoid.

In general, acts that are reasonably expected of even *minimally* well-formed agents are, first, acts that are not motivationally taxing. They cost the agent very little. Doing them is, as it were, no skin off one's nose. Nor do they presuppose any appreciable degree of virtue. As a result, excuses appealing to temptation or understandable failures of virtue are unavailable. Second, they are acts whose moral value in the situation at hand is obvious and unambiguous. So such excuses as "I didn't realize I should . . ." or "I wasn't sure I ought . . ." are not plausible. Third, in virtue of their being motivationally nontaxing, obvious, and unambiguous, they are the sorts of acts whose omission is not open to standard excuses, and this is why we so strongly expect people *not* to omit them.

Some obligatory acts are like this. Some supererogatory acts are like this, too. The domain of the supererogatory covers acts that vary widely in the degree to which they tax agents' motivational resources. Some supererogatory acts, particularly the saintly and the heroic, entail significant losses for the agent. Because of that, their performance requires exceptional motivational resources. So we understand why people do not usually elect these forms of supererogation. The domain of the supererogatory, however, also includes many unspectacular acts that are motivationally nontaxing. Although everything in the domain of the supererogatory is elective, the further one moves away from the saintly and heroic, the more reasonable it becomes to wonder why one would *not* elect to do this or that morally valuable act. As we imagine motivationally less and less taxing supererogatory acts—such as doing favors or engaging in idle pleasantries—we find it increasingly difficult to make sense of a person's refusing or neglecting to elect them. This is, in part, because the level of goodwill, concern for others' welfare, and commitment to the value of rational agency that moves a person to satisfy her minimum obligations should also move her to elect some morally good but nonrequired acts. Someone who *only* did what duty required and elected no supererogatory acts would, thus, not be a plausible candidate for a minimally acceptable agent.[23] On the contrary, when someone like Scrooge doesn't elect even the least motivationally taxing supererogatory acts, we have to suppose that something has gone wrong with his moral psychology. He suffers, perhaps, from excessive self-absorption or deficient sympathies. In this way, reflection on what can be expected of a minimally well-formed moral agent leads us to construct a conception of commonly decent moral gift givings from the larger domain of the supererogatory.[24] Those gift givings retain their elective character, but their incorporation into our conception of what any minimally well-formed moral agent would elect heightens their normativity.

Clearly, however, not every supererogatory act that is motivationally nontaxing is a matter of common decency. There are endless favors, mercies, kindnesses, forgivings, volunteerings, praisings, and present givings that we could do for others that are relatively cost-free. Most are not expected of all minimally well-formed agents. Stooping down to tie a stranger's shoelace when his hands are full of packages, for example, is no more motivationally taxing than stepping forward to open the door for him. Yet shoe tying is not a matter of common decency, whereas door opening is. So why are some motivationally nontaxing moral gifts matters of common decency but others are not? The obvious difference between shoe tying and door opening is that opening doors for others is a socially conventionalized moral gift giving. Tying strangers' shoelaces is not. Such conventions convert supererogatory acts into common decencies.

Social conventions can convert supererogatory acts into common decencies in part because they make it obvious and unambiguous what it would be good to elect. When there are no conventions, giving people moral gifts can be problematic in all the ways that giving people ordinary material gifts sometimes is. We may give the appearance of bribing, currying favor, being paternalistic, taking liberties, showing favoritism, or seducing. This was the problem with tying the stranger's shoe. What was intended as a kindness may come across as an invasion of privacy, presumptuousness, paternalism, or a bit of seduction. So although tying the stranger's shoe may be motivationally nontaxing, its uncertain reception makes it neither obviously nor unambiguously a good thing to do. Conventions disambiguate. They render obvious and unambiguous the desirability of, say, opening doors for strangers with their hands full.

Conventions also affect what agents do and do not take to be motivationally taxing. When there are moral gift-giving conventions in place, agents expect the costs associated with them. When you board a bus, you expect to give up your seat to elderly passengers. When you go to a dinner party, you expect to bring a token gift. When you teach a course, you expect to give some grace periods. Such expected costs are not burdensome because our plans and expectations for ourselves already include their possibility. We don't feel particularly burdened by giving up our seat because doing so is not an additional cost of riding the bus. It comes with the territory of riding the bus. So, too, bringing a token gift comes with the territory of dinner parties, and showing occasional mercy to students comes with the territory of teaching.

In short, gift-giving conventions determine which elective acts will be motivationally nontaxing and obviously and unambiguously desirable. But this means that there is no one standard for being a minimally well-formed moral agent. The moral gift-giving conventions of actual moral practices supply the standard. Common decency is thus always a local construction.

Decent people are, then, like decent cups of coffee or decent housing. Their decency is relative to local standards. A decent cup of coffee in Nebraska is not a decent cup of coffee in Italy. Decent housing in rural South Carolina is not decent housing in San Francisco. This is not to say that there are no objective *limits* to what could count as decent housing or coffee. Any decent housing must provide some protection from the elements. Any decent coffee must use noncontaminated water. But these are very general guidelines. Local conventions supply the substantive content, and they may set the bar for decent coffee or decent housing higher or lower.

So, too, local moral gift-giving conventions supply the substantive content for the concept of common decency. Here also there will be objective limits to what could count as common decency. Common decencies cannot strain human nature with their motivational demands. But just as the standard for a decent cup of coffee may vary with locale, so may the standard for common decency.

Conceptions of common decency can vary *horizontally*. Among the vast array of motivationally nontaxing supererogatory acts, different moral practices might conventionalize different sets. So, for instance, California Bay Area residents conventionally gift each other with enormous forbearance in wearing perfumed products, but they have no conventions for doing drivers who wish to change lanes the favor of permitting them to do so. Elsewhere, one finds conventions of doing fellow drivers favors but none of forbearing to wear perfume.

Conceptions of common decency might also vary *vertically*. Some locales may have lower standards all around for commonly decent behavior. The villagers in Le Chambon during World War II constructed what seems to us an extraordinarily high standard of decency. They clandestinely assisted approximately 3,000, largely Jewish refugees, when doing so was potentially severely punishable. What to us seems like grave risk taking to protect Jewish strangers from Nazi capture came to be simply what was to be expected. As Lawrence Blum observes, knowing that many others were involved in aiding the refugees had a double effect: it made the worthwhileness of taking the risk to help more obvious and unambiguous *and* it reshaped the villagers' sense of undue burden, making it motivationally easier to choose to take those risks.[25]

Conclusion

This, now, is what we might say to Scrooge: you take yourself to be a minimally well-formed moral agent. Indeed, you pride yourself on paying your debts and exacting the debts from others that they owe you. But you have misconceived what it means to be a minimally well-formed moral agent. If you really had the basic competence to practice morality with others, including caring about others' well-being and agency, you would at least elect those supererogatory acts that are motivationally nontaxing and obviously and unambiguously desirable. Being pleasant to your nephew, giving your employees Christmas off, and showing some mercy to your most destitute debtors should have been obvious, unambiguous, and easy moral gifts for you to give because they are conventional practices in your social world. In refusing to give those gifts, you show yourself to be a shamefully inadequate moral agent—a being without common decency.

Notes

Special thanks to Michael Smith and Julia Driver for conversations about this essay, as well as to the faculty and graduate students at Macquarie University, the Australian National University's Research School for Social Science, Indiana University, and Colby College. Work on this essay was in part made possible by a grant from the National Endowment for the Humanities.

1. Charles Dickens, *A Christmas Carol and Other Haunting Tales* (New York: Doubleday, 1998), 260–261.

2. Ibid., 316.

3. Ibid., 268.

4. Susan Wolf observes that "the goal of a theory of duty is to set minimal standards of moral decency." Those standards "tell people who wish to be decent that they must *at least* do this much": "Above and Below the Line of Duty," *Philosophical Topics* 14 (1986): 131–248, 139–140, 145. Even some utilitarians try to specify the minimal moral obligations that are matters of common decency; see, for example, J. O. Urmson, "Saints and Heroes," in *Moral Concepts*, ed. Joel Feinberg (London: Oxford University Press, 1969). This conception of decency also appears to be at the heart of Avishai Margalit's *The Decent Society* (Cambridge, Mass.: Harvard University Press, 1996). A decent society, in his view, is one in which people are treated in nonhumiliating ways in the basic institutions of society.

5. Susan Wolf, "Above and Below the Line of Duty," points out that moral philosophers who formulate theories of duty typically see themselves as setting up "a standard that will tell people who wish to be decent that they must *at least* do this much." Two basic positions on how many of our moral duties are minimal ones are these: (1) one might think that all moral duties are minimal because morality is not very demanding and does not require much of us by comparison to the full range of morally good things that we might do for others. If morality is not demanding, then one can expect any minimally well-formed agent to be able to do her duty. This will be just common decency. (2) Alternatively, one might think that some moral duties are quite demanding, and that our minimal duties are those that do not tax the motivational capacities of a minimally well-formed moral agent.

6. John Kekes, "The Great Guide of Human Life," *Philosophy & Literature* 8 (1984): 236–249, 243.

7. Ibid., 248; my emphasis.

8. The *O.E.D.* for example defines a decent person as someone who is "kind, accommodating, pleasant"—not as someone who does her minimal duties (*O.E.D Online*, definition 5b). Acts of common decency in this sense belong on the same scale with George Bailey's uncommonly decent acts in the movie *It's a Wonderful Life* (1947). Both common and uncommon decency involve "interfering" for the better in others' lives through moral gifts of kindness, compassion, generosity, charity, mercy, forgiveness, patience, pleasantness, thoughtfulness, and the like.

9. David Heyd's observation in *Supererogation: Its Status in Ethical Theory* (Cambridge: Cambridge University Press, 1982), 148, about one kind of common decency— favors—applies generally to acts of common decency: "They may be deserved or undeserved, done spontaneously or as a response to a request. Yet they are never deserved as a matter of right, and a refusal to do a favour cannot be criticized as morally wrong. We can ask for a favour, but never claim it."

10. These categories are derived, with some alteration, from Heyd's list, ibid.

11. Obviously, there is some overlap among these categories. Gift givings (particularly charitable gifts), favors, and volunteerings can be forms of beneficence.

12. Common decency thus does not fit Heyd's familiar description in *Supererogation*, 175, of the supererogatory: decisions that concern the truly supererogatory are "free not only from legal or physical compulsion, but also from informal pressure, the threat of moral sanctions, or inner feelings of guilt. It is purely optional."

13. Roderick M. Chisholm, "Supererogation and Offence: A Conceptual Scheme for Ethics," *Ratio* 5 (1963): 1–14.

14. Julia Driver, "The Suberogatory," *Australasian Journal of Philosophy* 70 (1992): 286–295. Driver's category of the suberogatory is possibly a bit broader than what I have in mind by the decent. For her, the suberogatory are bad acts that involve a failure to act on an ideal (e.g., the ideal of nonwastefulness). I want to stress that they are failures to live up to the standard of being a minimally acceptable moral agent. The differences here, however, are not large, and her article is full of important insights about the nature of these types of acts.

15. Joel Feinberg, "Supererogation and Rules," *Ethics* 71 (1961): 276–288.

16. Ibid., 276–277.

17. An agent could not *omit* common decencies and still claim to have a virtue like generosity. But to be generous is to be disposed to treat others also in some ways that exceed mere common decency. Purchasing the prize goose for Bob Crachit's family exceeds common decency, and it provides some evidence of Scrooge's commitment to becoming a better, more generous person.

18. Heyd, *Supererogation*, 150, raises this worry in connection with Feinberg's description of favors, but the point applies equally to all common decencies. Heyd points out that, "if the 'ought' means just 'the best thing to do'—an advice—then favours *are* supererogatory; and if 'ought' means a kind of requirement, how can Feinberg say that favours are never obligatory?"

19. Urmson, "Saints and Heroes," for example, tries to give a utilitarian justification for preserving a distinction between the obligatory and the "higher flights" of morality that constitute the supererogatory. I thank Michael Smith for reminding me that these are still fictional distinctions.

20. I thank Julia Driver for the latter point.

21. It is conceivable that a social practice of morality might operate without a conception of common decency. In that case, it would not treat any supererogatory acts as ones that agents are *expected* to elect; and it would not supply any basis for criticizing agents who stand on their rights and refuse to show mercy, volunteer, forgive, do favors, and help out when doing so is not obligatory.

22. Failures to meet that baseline typically meet with a different response than do other sorts of moral failures. Our reactive attitudes of resentment, indignation, and contempt are typically calibrated to the expectation that the moral agents with whom we share a daily practice of morality will behave as minimally adequate moral agents. Failures of common decency and failures to fulfill minimal moral obligations generally meet with heightened indignation, resentment, and sometimes contempt.

23. An analogy may help press this point. It would be odd to equate a minimally adequate professor with one who only does what duty requires. Suppose duty requires that a faculty member have *some* office hours, give *some* written evaluation of student papers, and do *some* committee service but leaves as a matter of election how much. Those who meet with students as little as possible, who return papers with hardly a word of comment, and who decline to serve on all but the least demanding committees shirk no professional obligations. However, they also do not live up to the expectations for minimally adequate professorial performance. More is expected of them precisely because the same commitment to academic ideals that provides a reason to fulfill their professorial obligations also provides a reason for discretionary elections that advance those ideals. In short, a minimally well-formed professor would choose more

than what her obligations require. Similarly, a minimally well-formed moral agent would choose more than what her obligations require. A commitment to the values that provide a reason to fulfill her moral obligations should also provide a reason for discretionary elections that advance those values.

24. Lawrence Blum, "Community & Virtue," in *How Should One Live: Essays on the Virtues*, ed. Roger Crisp (Oxford: Clarendon Press, 1996), 235, also draws a somewhat similar distinction between levels of virtue—noteworthy virtue and ordinary virtue. He describes ordinary virtue in a way that captures what I have in mind by common decency. Acts of ordinary virtue "are simply what are to be expected of a normal moral agent"; they are "not regarded as meriting distinct praise or esteem."

25. Ibid.

III

The Normative Importance
of a Shared Social World

8

Resentment and Assurance

Margaret Urban Walker

Resentment is a kind of anger. It is widely agreed that resentment predicates some kind of wrong at others' hands and that it is in some way a defensive emotion in its operation or its manner of expression. The most widely cited contemporary account of resentment, Jean Hampton's, renders the anger, wrong, and need for defense in a particularly colorful way.[1] Hampton's is an individualistic and agonistic account of resentment. Beings acutely aware of their "value and rank" are moved to anger by injuries to themselves that challenge their presumed standings, and they are mobilized in *fearful* defense of the self-esteem these standings underwrite. Hampton uses this agonistic picture to make resentment itself look somewhat shabby and misguided, a defensive reaction based on dubious views that one's own human worth can actually be diminished by others' actions.

An older account of resentment paints a more social and less self-referring picture of it. In his sermon "Upon Resentment," Joseph Butler describes "deliberate anger or resentment" in this way:

> The natural object or occasion of settled resentment then being injury, as distinct from pain or loss; it is easy to see, that to prevent and to remedy such injury, and the miseries arising from it, is the end for which the passion was implanted in man. It is to be considered as a weapon, put into our hands by nature, against injury, injustice, and cruelty.[2]

Butler viewed deliberate resentment, when not groundless, extravagant or vengeful, as "one of the common bonds, by which society is held together; a fellow-feeling, which each individual has in behalf of the whole species."[3] It is that by which "Men are plainly restrained from injuring their fellow-creatures by fear" when virtue would not suffice.[4]

I argue that resentment is a versatile and economical emotion that serves the negotiation of shared lives pervaded by norms and the expectations to which they give rise. Shared life requires mutually recognized boundaries and fairly reliable expectations based on them. Responses that target violations and prompt violators to reconsider and to beware or those that signal the need for this sort of action are thus important, and resentment plays, I argue, this sort of role.[5] Occasions of resentment are in fact many and more varied than either Hampton's or Butler's discussions would suggest. I claim that what best explains the extent and variety of possible occasions for resentment is that resentment responds to perceived *threats to expectations based on norms* that are presumed shared in or justly authoritative for common life. In some cases resentment also responds to experienced *threats to one's standing* to assert or insist upon those norms. Possibilities for resentment are many because the field across which intelligible resentments range is as broad as that of behavior to which norms are taken to apply. This range of behavior includes table manners and modes of dress and address, as well as styles of life and social interaction and matters of justice and basic decency among human beings. While resentment registers anger at threats to expectations underlain by norms, or to one's standing as a competent judge of operative norms, it targets others' intentional acts as the source of threat and tends to impugn their motives and attitudes. Resentment is an accusing anger, one that calls others to account, as P. F. Strawson argued in calling resentment a "reactive" attitude that attributes responsibility.[6] But at the same time, as I explain below, resentment not only sends a message but also invites a response: it seeks assurance from offenders or from others that they can be (or be again) trusted to reaffirm and respect the boundaries that norms define, boundaries that offer protection against harm or affront, as well as the security of membership and reliable expectations in a community of shared normative judgment.

I see my account as being in the spirit of Butler's, endorsing his insight into the deeply social and expressive aspects of resentment. Butler's characterization of resentment as a "fellow feeling" is multiply apt. Resentment extends to injuries or exclusions of those one takes to be one's fellows, but it can also forge a sense of fellowship where it had not been felt before. In addition, it can be prompted by threat to one's sense of belonging with others in a community of judgment that shares standards. When Butler speaks of resentment as a "weapon" against injury, injustice, and cruelty, however, he not only draws the defended territory too narrowly but is also sanguine about our equal entitlements to bear and brandish these emotional "arms." And he is hasty in supposing that the effects of so doing are likely to be uniform or as intended. Attention to a fuller array of examples will help to show this.

It is Hampton's more widely known contemporary analysis, however, that I will examine first, using limitations in her account to draw out features of my own view. To be clear at the outset: I don't take Hampton (or Butler) to be attempting an account of necessary and sufficient conditions of resentment, nor do I attempt one. I take it that Hampton's account, as does my own, aims at a "normal form" characterization of a syndrome of feelings and expressions that in certain kinds of contexts is likely to be identified as resentment. I believe the grammar of emotion terms is somewhat rough and ready. This means that not much is settled simply by butting intuitions about individual cases against one another. Our emotion vocabularies are not that neatly regimented, and whether someone is willing to call one scenario or another a case of resentment is not so significant as the reasons that we are inclined to describe cases in that way or in some other way. Descriptively, the point is to achieve a characterization that covers the *widest* class of common cases and, better still, that sheds light on why contested examples cause disagreement. Explanatorily, a plausible account should make sense of the roles that the experience and expression of the emotion play in our shared lives. The view I develop here is meant to address those descriptive and explanatory challenges. The question of when resentment is justified and deserves to receive the satisfaction it seeks is not my topic here.

Getting Resentment in Broader View

For Hampton, resentment "is an emotion whose object is the defiant reaffirmation of one's rank and value in the face of treatment calling them into question in one's own mind."[7] In her view, resentment serves at once as a protest and defense.[8] The occasion of resentment for Hampton is "being wronged," which is not only being damaged or hurt but also being so in a way that "insults" or is "disrespectful of" one's worth, however that is conceived (e.g., as relative or absolute or fixed or variable).[9] "Resentment," she says, "is an emotion which reflects their judgment that the harmful treatment they experienced should not have been intentionally inflicted on them by their assailants insofar as it is *not* appropriate given their value and rank."[10] A resentful victim of wrongdoing is thus *angry*—more particularly "defiant" or "battling" against the lower standing imputed to him or her by the culpably disrespectful harming.[11] But at the heart of resentment, Hampton sees something defensive in another sense; she believes its angry defiance reveals a *fear*. It is feared that the offender is right to think that the victim's worth *is* as implied in the insulting treatment or that it is *permissible* to lower the victim in rank by means of such an action ("putting her in her place").[12] So resentment combines *anger* and *fear*.

Hampton draws a distinction between resentment and indignation, claiming that indignation is an impersonal anger at a challenge to "someone's value," which threatens a standard of value, whereas resentment is personal anger and defends oneself "against the action's attack on one's self-esteem" and is "normally an emotion experienced only by the one who has been harmed."[13] One's self-esteem is threatened by the possibility that the action has revealed one is or has now been made lower in rank or value than one was or had assumed.

So, for her, the occasion of resentment is being culpably wronged. The constitutive belief in resentment is that one's deserved or true rank and value have been impugned or imperiled. The feeling of resentment embodies anger at insult and its implications and fear that one's status is lowered or one's diminished status is revealed. The object or aim of resentment is to defend and protect self-esteem.

Hampton's view of resentment is narrow in several ways. Consider her limitation of resentment to reactions in defense of oneself when it is oneself who is wronged. This seems implausibly restrictive, for we commonly enough speak of resentment at the way others are treated or looked at, nor must these others be ones with whom we have personal connections or prior identification. One can, looking on, resent a sales clerk's rude treatment of a shabbily dressed person, the condescension of a teacher to a girl in a physics class, or the self-congratulatory attitude of a wealthy political candidate who is discussing problems of "the poor" when these actions involve or refer to strangers or groups to which one does not belong. Furthermore, the distinction Hampton makes between supposedly impersonal indignation and allegedly personal resentment is unconvincing. Diners badly served their suppers or employees failing to receive their anticipated bonuses may be the very type of the indignant individual. So indignation is quite commonly a reaction to injuries to oneself taken very personally indeed, whereas resentment can just as well take the cause of others to heart. Resentment and indignation, in fact, may not be distinct emotions; in the modern but older usage of Butler (or Adam Smith), the two are not distinguished and the terms are used interchangeably, as when Butler spoke of resentment as "the indignation raised by cruelty and injustice." But even without settling the precise nature of the difference between indignation and resentment, I think there are enough examples to confute the alignment of resentment and indignation, respectively, with what is "personal" and "impersonal" or what concerns "self" and "other" for reasons I expand below. No doubt to resent something is to "take it personally," but the sense in which this is true remains to be spelled out.

Hampton wants to see resentment and indignation as distinct but parallel, with resentment as the personal version and indignation as the impersonal version of angry *fear* at wrongdoing. But this doesn't seem to work either, for straightforward cases of indignation don't seem to be marked by the fearfulness that Hampton, and not she alone, associates with resentment. The indignant person is characteristically the picture of confident or unreserved righteousness. For that matter, not all cases of resentment seem to involve fear. A gentleman who is spoiling for a fight may coolly brandish his resentment at an insult as a provocation to a contest—say, a duel—he has little fear of losing. A dominating husband may resent and expressly avow resentment of his wife's wage earning, confidently and correctly surmising that the fact of his resentment will cause her to quit her job.

Yet the term "resentment" seems tinged for many people with associations of someone cringing or sulking in gnawing and roiling anger that is tamped down or turned inward, as if out of fear. I have no doubt that Nietzsche's memorable creation of the image of *ressentiment*—a kind of seething, angry envy of the powerful by the powerless, who must nonetheless hang back in their despicable weakness—has had an impact, and not only on philosophers. But it is well to remember that Nietzsche is not talking about resentment in any commonplace sense. He coins a novel term of art to advance an imaginative scenario in which morality itself emerges as a kind of brilliant trick of the weak, who remain nonetheless despicable in their weakness. The fictional Nietzschian drama is propelled by what we would more usually describe as *envy* of the superiority of the strong.[14]

I return below to some ways in which resentment can be inflected by envy or fear, as also by disgust or bitterness, and to some reasons that resentment is apt to be differently inflected for those in positions of relative weakness. But the examples above of the insulted but confident gentleman or the successfully dominating but irritated husband, as well as a very broad array of cases of *resentment at offense* that I discuss shortly, suggest a different explanation of what prompts resentment. What is central to resentment on this explanation is a perceived *threat*, whether or not one has reason to fear what is threatened and whether or not one in fact does fear it. A threat suggests a prospect of damage to or loss of something valued, and people can get *angry* at the suggestion that someone is inclined to act in a way that might damage or get in the way of what they count on or deem important, even if they have no fear of heading off the threat. The sometimes in-turned or tamped quality of resentment in many cases may have more to do with the position the resenting one is in: one is not always in a position to give forthright expression to one's anger at a perceived threat. The nature of the *display* of this kind of anger is sensitive to the *position*—situational, emotional, social, and institutional—one is in to show how one feels or to anticipate a desired response to that display.[15]

Another questionable claim in Hampton's account is that resentment is a strategy aimed at defending self-esteem (or "self-respect," which she uses interchangeably in this context). This seems to require that a resenting person has some modicum of self-esteem to defend. She says that "the ability to feel resentment following a wrong-doing depends upon one's having enough sense of one's own worth to believe that the treatment is inappropriate and worthy of protest."[16] Similarly, Jeffrie Murphy, her interlocutor in *Forgiveness and Mercy*, holds expressly that resentment defends one's self-respect and that proper self-respect is essentially tied to resentment, so that "a person who does not resent moral injuries done to him . . . is almost necessarily a person lacking in self-respect."[17] Yet there is a lot of everyday evidence that people need not hold themselves highly, indeed, not respect or esteem themselves at a basically decent level, to be great resenters. Self-abasing flatterers, cringing self-despisers, and miserable sellouts, or people beaten down or those consumed with self-hatred of their powerlessness, are quite capable of resentments, including resentment of others to whom they self-abasingly bow or of others who maintain dignity or integrity under circumstances similar to their own. Unless one wants to award the honorific "self-respect" to anyone who won't bridle at *something*, it seems resentment need not imply self-respect in even a modestly positive sense. On the other hand, whereas resentment is possible and common for those who fail to respect themselves, those who enjoy robust self-respect may be magnanimous or respond with confidence or determination rather than resentment, even when they are themselves treated ill or are the object of neglect or undeserved indifference. Self-respect, then, is not obviously either necessary or sufficient for experiencing resentment when threatened or even when injured or affronted.

Finally, it is questionable to narrow the response of resentment to harmful and insulting treatment intentionally inflicted. This description calls up vivid images of abusive or disrespectful treatment that would make one wince to observe, as well as to suffer. Cases like this surely merit resentment if any do. But this identification of occasions for resentment with damage and injury both pushes aside the pervasiveness of resentment in everyday life and tends, misleadingly, to moralize it. Resentment is often provoked by the good, generous, fair, or even simply decent treatment of others when the resentful one feels convinced that she would not have fared as well or perhaps remembers an instance in which she did not, or when she thinks that it is she and people like her, and not those others, who are entitled to the treatment or rewards in question. And there is also the familiar case of charged and evident resentment felt in response to those perceived as exceeding their places, prerogatives, and authority, those who are "uppity," "arrogant," or "too big for their britches." They seem to illustrate that it can be just as threatening to see some others claim respect and receive good or dignifying treatment as it is for oneself to be shown to the lower rung of the status ladder. More surprising, perhaps, is the extent to which resentment arises at the behavior of others that simply upsets established patterns and expectations.

Resentment and Threat

My objection to Hampton's view is not that she has not identified and explored insightfully the ways in which resentment results from perceived injuries that are insults to status (her "rank and value"). My objection is that she has ignored the broader field in which being demeaned by being treated below one's status consti- tutes *one* kind of occasion for resentment that can be placed within a more gen- eral account. Here I make a start on that.

In my view, resentment is best explained as a defensive response of anger (and in some but not all cases, fear or other negative feelings) to others' inten- tional actions perceived as violating boundaries defined by norms. Sometimes the violation is an actual injury, but even then it is not only the harm caused but also the sense of *wrongfulness* of the behavior causing the harm that is characteristic of resentment (in distinction to other kinds of anger, which may arise from frustra- tion or thwarting that need not issue from another human agent or can be di- rected at human agents whose motives we need not impugn). The wrong is de- fined by some supposed rule or standard, a norm. The constitutive belief is: they *should not* have acted in that way. Strawson points out that the pain may be as unpleasant in a case in which someone treads on my hand accidentally as when one does so out of contempt, but it is the latter case that is ground for resentment because of "the very great importance we attach to the attitudes and intentions toward us of other human beings."[18] But before we get so far as attitudes and intentions, notice how various are perceived wrongs to which resentment is a response.

Resentment is occasioned not only by *harms* and *losses*, as when one is as- saulted, cheated, made to suffer, or forcibly relieved of one's goods, but also by cases in which some ride free or manipulatively profit in excess ways from roles, systems, or cooperative practices in which others comply without extra profit; call these *exploitations*.[19] Resentment can also be provoked by someone's assuming a position or being treated as entitled to a status that disturbs a presumed status ordering; call these *improprieties*. If the disturbance makes the resenter's position or status lower or less valuable than it had been or than he or she believed it to be, we might call these *demotions*. Then there are cases in which one endures treatment beneath his or her proper status—*slights*. Finally, resentment is often enough prompted by rule breaking, norm violating, or simply behavior seen as "out of bounds," even without evident profit to the violator or harm or expense to others; call these *offenses*. These are things "not done" or "unacceptable." Harms, losses, exploitations, improprieties, demotions, and slights may be my own or others, and they may inspire resentment on my own or on others' behalf. Offenses may be apparently victimless social fouls.

The category of offenses is vast but significant not only for that reason. It also reveals something about what can occasion resentment and thus about what can be at issue in it. People seethe and prickle with resentment at those who laugh too loudly, speak too freely, fail to say "please" or "thank you," or utter other conventional formulas; at fashion fads, the piercing of body parts (now, other than ears), and weird haircuts;[20] at the yelps of other people's children and at people's sitting closer on a bench or bus than they must; and the list goes on and on. One explanation of many of these "offending" occasions given by William Miller is the enormous social importance of "disattendability," explored so acutely by sociologist Erving Goffman, by which what is ordinary, routine, and normal generates "normative expectations" to which we hold people accountable, if only in the medium of untoward feelings like disgust, alarm, pity, contempt, embarrassment—and, of course, resentment.[21] Cases of offense or affront are revealing, for what we see in them is not a harm or injury in the usual sense but an occurrence construed as a threat either to a norm or familiar pattern imbued with some prescriptive force by the perceiver.

In all cases of resentment, it seems we are angry because (we think) we or others are injured or because we are (we think justifiably) affronted by the actions of some who have gotten out of bounds. Someone has made free with what we thought were the rules, crossed boundaries we supposed intact, ignored claims we believed authoritative, or rendered idle or ridiculous our hope that things will go on in any of the many ways we believe they should. The sense of threat in resentment, as Strawson claimed, tends to go to the agent's apparent malice or indifference, when we suppose he or she might have shown the good will, attention, due care, respect, or understanding that would have led to proper behavior. In many cases, although perhaps not all, the proper will, care, or attitude is what we had expected to be shown; in all cases, we must think that it *could* have been. As Strawson noted, resentment is a feeling that impugns the agent and imputes responsibility, and so culpability, for some kind of wrong. There is threat both in a norm's being tested by overt noncompliance and in the presumption that the agent in getting out of bounds displays irresponsibility or worse. There can also be a threat to the resentful perceiver's sense of authority and competence as a judge of what "is done" or "goes" or is acceptable "among us" if one's resentment is not shared or its eliciting violation is not recognized by others.

In cases of direct injury and insult, one is not so likely to be wrong in thinking that something unacceptable has occurred. But the case of offenses is again not only revealing but instructive as well. For in the case of offenses, many a resented behavior is seen as "out of bounds" not only in the absence of any actual injury, and even when the behavior is in no apparent way "aimed" at the one who resents it, but also when ill intent by the agent is undetectable by reasonable observers. These are the cases in which as onlookers we feel inclined to say to someone wrought up with resentment, "What's it to you?" This question is exactly the right one, for it requests an interpretation that at least specifies the transgression (what is wrong here, which may not be obvious to others) if not the faulty attitude it may seem to embody. One common resentful response, however, is also apt: "Who do they think they are to . . . ?" This goes to the heart of the matter of resentment. The offender is taken to be "thinking" that he or she is exempt from some requirement he or she must or ought to know applies. Resentment carries this implication of a faulty attitude on the actor's part.

This is a danger inherent in resentment. We may not have independent reasons to believe people bear us ill will or are indifferent or careless when we find that what they do threatens our sense of a prevailing order, but it is very easy, and it seems very common, to translate one's own sense of threat back into an attribution of fault or malice in the intentions of others. Resentment embodies a sense, or an implicit and presumptive imputation, of fault that can be difficult to dislodge, and one gripped by resentment may be far more disposed to *find* fault in others rather than to question whether one's own resentment might be misplaced or exaggerated. And it is also true that when people resent hearing "foreign" languages spoken, encountering people of racial or ethnic groups other than theirs in their neighborhood, or seeing evidence of gay and lesbian households, there is usually a prior belief that some kinds of people aren't to be trusted or accepted to begin with, and the fact that people like that are intruding where they don't belong is additional evidence of their inappropriate presumption or aggressiveness. Those already resented are likely to arouse yet more resentment for behaving as if they don't know—and shouldn't they?—that they aren't the kind who belong.

Whether it is correct or not in particular cases to infer that an agent's attitude is faulty, though, the central matter of resentment is an injury or affront that is threatening in disappointing expectations, or dimming or dashing hopes, for others' conduct that in some sense we think we had a "right" to.[22] The best explanation of that "right," I claim, is the belief in an operative norm of *some* kind, although *not* necessarily a moral norm. The huge category of resented offenses alone suggests that resentment should not be "moralized." What threatens is the *license* taken by some with what others of us take to be the operating understandings, limits, or rules. In the case of injury or cruelty, for example, the sense of threat is urgent because actual harm is the result of an offender's failure to abide by or to be restrained by a norm, and more such harm might be forthcoming. Or if someone receives treatment inappropriate to his kind in a system carefully arranged around appropriate responses to kinds of people, that rankles but also threatens those faithful to that system: where will this breakdown of order lead? This is as true when a murderer goes free on a technicality as when a member of a despised racial group is treated with respect.

The threat that prompts resentment, made fully explicit, is of *license with impunity*. The transgression announces a possibility that is at least annoying, often alarming, or even fearsome—a possibility that might persist unless something forecloses it. So the fact of the transgression puts in question, even threatens, whatever confidence, trust, assurance, or hope allowed one to be unconcerned about such injuries or affronts or unburdened by their unsettling implications. This is the sense in which we "take personally" what we resent. It is not that what we resent necessarily is an injury or insult to us ourselves or even an affront aimed specifically at us. Rather transgressions against boundaries cause us concern when they announce the possibility of something we might have to reckon with—a factor that throws us uncomfortably out of our normative expectations, moral and otherwise, or undermines our ability to assert with confidence what and where certain social, moral, or interpersonal boundaries lie. In that threat lies a *potential* for fear, as for other negative feelings, that can flavor resentment or compound it.

Resentment is itself a "weapon" (using Butler's image)—an unpleasant, accusing, and potentially threatening response when expressed overtly at the offender. When apparent to others, it is also, to continue the image, a kind of "call to arms." Where there is opportunity and ability to get transgressors back within bounds, to impose some corrective action on them, or at the very least to summon support from others for a clear repudiation of what transgressors have done, resentment may be relieved as the threat is diminished. It is something at least if the rules and boundaries are reiterated, even if the individual offenders go unpunished and are no longer trustworthy. It is better, of course, if we can be assured that punitive treatment of transgressors serves as an informative and possibly deterring example to others. It is best if those who have broken the rules can actually be brought to reaffirm their subscription to them. Yet often the opportunity or ability to correct offenders or to inflict reprisals on them is uncertain or unavailable. Worse, sometimes repudiation is not forthcoming from any others, from enough others, or from others with authority. Then the threat of license with impunity is fulfilled. In such cases, there is a basis for resentment at a transgression to turn disgusted, bitter, envious, shamed, or fearful.

Resentment can be *disgusted*, for example, in a case in which one has ceased to be surprised at certain goings on and has given up any thought that one can forestall their occurrence or defend against them.[23] Consider the situation of a lone female office clerk in a welding shop who has failed to become inured to pinup calendars and continuing sexual insults and challenges. If she no longer rises to the bait emotionally she might still disapprove of her coworkers' conduct. What is missing if she ceases to resent it? She might without any longer experiencing resentment continue to disapprove of her coworkers' conduct and continue to believe that the norms that define it as rude, insulting, and hostile are valid and that her coworkers know very well that what they do is at least some of these things. But if she still *resents* these goings-on—if she still gets angry about the wrong these goings-on inflict on her, or on women in general, and does not merely shrug and think, "It's not supposed to be that way, but who can do anything about it?"—her resentment reveals that she continues, quite precisely, to "take it personally." The wrongfulness of their behavior gets a grip on her and moves her emotionally and motivationally in the direction of her own hostile display—a kind of accusing anger that puts her in the expressive position of rebuking them. Her resentment *is* that rebuke.

But even if she feels resentment, she might not show it. Even though resentment disposes her to show her anger in overt and confrontationally angry displays, actually showing anger in her situation may not be a sane or safe option. She may know that this leads to escalation or attracts reprisals. She may then find that her anger takes the form of a withdrawal or recoil in disgust from the situation. She might begin to experience her coworkers to some extent as a kind of noxious substance in the environment, rather than as fully fellow agents who can and should be confronted with their knowing misbehavior; she may also experience self-disgust at her own sense of powerlessness or her failure to recruit others to negative judgment or rectifying action. Her resentment may mingle with disgust, or disgust may simply replace it. Her resentment itself may move her in directions that in turn provoke other feelings that modify the expression and course of the resentment or perhaps cause resentment to give way to other, less stressful, costly, or defensive feelings, where active resistance isn't going anywhere.[24]

Bitter resentment might similarly involve scenarios in which one cannot stop blaming some others for failing to supply at least a community of confirming judgment, if not actual protection, from injuries or affronts that one cannot or will not "learn to accept." Sometimes people are supposed to accept the treatment they protest, and sometimes they are supposed to accept the futility of their protesting that treatment. People are called "bitter" who can't seem to stop complaining, those whom others see as stuck in an accusation that is not (in the eye of the beholder) going to change anything. Those who find themselves increasingly isolated, justly or not, in their accusation may find that resentment acquires a brittle quality, less an accusing display than a kind of choked protest that already anticipates it will be ignored or refused by others.[25]

Resentment may mingle with *envy* when one repudiates what others do but at the same time wishes one had the power, nerve, or panache to get away oneself with what they do. This is the variation on resentment that Nietzsche's *ressentiment* captures and inflates to mythic proportions. But although envious resentment (or resentful envy) is real, it would be a mistake to think that all resentment involves envy. That would be to deny that anyone ever burns with anger at wrongdoing without actually, perhaps secretly or unconsciously, wishing that one could get away with what wrongdoers do or could themselves have the attributes that make wrongdoers capable of violating norms. Resentment might invite *shame* when one wants to be able to express one's anger in a way that rebukes someone's behavior but is too timid or prudent or ingratiating to do so. The shame accompanying resentment is more poignant, though, when one is invisible or so negligible in others' eyes that the protest one's resentment reveals is beneath the notice or concern of others. It is easy to see how shamed resentment could breed envy: the miserably treated servant might rather be the tyrannical master, if those are the only positions available in certain social worlds. But it would be dangerous to assume that those oppressed or slighted necessarily yearn to turn the tables; often, they want to overturn those particular tables and level the ground for future relations.

On my account of resentment, when people cease to resent things they once did it reveals some kind of resignation, a kind of "normative surrender." This might involve ceasing to believe that a norm is valid, losing expectations that a valid norm will be honored and letting go of a personal stake in that norm, or losing conviction that one is in a position to assert shared norms, or at least certain ones, with any effect. But when people continue to resent certain behavior even as they recognize that their normative investment is neither shared nor enforceable (at least locally), the residual resentment preserves and expresses a personal "normative stake," an insistence on the validity and importance of a norm, a repudiation of the prevailing situation of dereliction or insouciance, and so a continuing normative protest of what exists in favor of what should be. They continue to take it personally.

Resentment can also be fearful. The association of resentment with *fear* is common, as noted above, and with reason. Fear comes in with resentment especially in cases of (standing or passing) vulnerability and inadequate or unreliable defense—that is, when one does not expect one's resentment to constitute an effective accusing and restraining signal. Worse, in some weak positions, one might fear that one has invited additional harm or threat for having *shown* resentment—a kind of anger—in response to the original harm or threat. In any case, fearful (and perhaps disgusted or bitter) resentment can involve *second-order fear*. It is bad to be injured or affronted, and so as a result to be under threat of, even in fear of, further injury or affront because what protected you from it is destroyed or in doubt. It is worse to see no way to reestablish security, for now you are afraid that you are going to have to be afraid, to live in fear, without assurance or protection of a community of shared boundaries that one's fellows are willing to assert and enforce. Second-order fear is understandable in continuing situations of weakness, including situations of continuing subordination by role or status. Members of oppressed, stigmatized, or despised groups are continuously vulnerable in such ways, across many social situations and encounters. Second-order fear might be one of the conditions in which resentment assumes a "roiling" or "gnawing" quality, an accusing anger that can't, because it must not, get "out" expressively.

Resentment that is fearful feeds on exposure to injury in virtue of one's demonstrated vulnerability or exposure to affront in view of the apparently negligible importance or authority of one's expectations or hopes. Yet I have argued that even resentment that is not fearful turns on a sense of *threat*. This suggests an explanation of why some injuries to others can excite resentment whether or not one "identifies" with those injured or offended. Indeed, it explains why the perception of another's being injured or affronted can sometimes *prompt* identification with him or her that was not there to begin with. In some cases the breach of bounds that reveals the vulnerability of others causes us to recognize that we, too, are exposed and that we have something in common with them. If what threatens us is license with impunity, then those upon whom objectionable action is visited are not the only ones threatened, for the offender who will go beyond bounds could be a future menace or a dangerous example to others. In the case of victimless offense to presumed standards, the authority of the standards we rely on is jeopardized, and our confidence in proceeding on the basis of these standards, or even a hope that these standards will be respected, is undermined. In other cases we may feel that our group membership is threatened, either because we are no longer sure that our community is one whose operative standards we can accept or respect or because we feel defeated in our attempt to grasp and apply standards that are operative. Is a community that harbors or tolerates this sort of thing really one I can call *mine*? Or is my competence as a judge or the authority of the standards I assume are common put in question here? Am I "out of it"? There are significant resentments of alienation and marginality, in which one's protest simply places one outside serious consideration: one is an old fogie, a wacko, a malcontent, a whiner.

Resentment as Moral Address

To come back to the central point, whether or not resentment is further driven or infused by other feelings, it is a kind of *accusing anger at something done*. The anger is directed at the doer of what is out of bounds, with the implication that the doer knows, or ought to know, better. Does the anger of resentment have an aim? If expressions of resentment tend to play as protests, rebukes, or demands ("I resent that" or "How dare you/he/she?" or "There ought to be a law"), what satisfaction does resentment seek? To ask this question is to assume that some emotional responses have not only an etiology in certain perceptions but also an expressive point or communicative direction. Resentment seems to be one such emotion. Hampton claims that in resentment the victim "would have it" that *rank and value* are not lower or lowered because that is on her account what is threatened. Butler seems to think that resentment seeks or threatens the punishment of the offending party in order "to remedy or prevent harm."[26] On my account, what resentment calls out for is *assurance of protection, defense, or membership* under norms brought in question by the exciting injury or affront. What can assuage resentment of actual *injury* is renewed trust or hopefulness that people, including oneself, will be defended or protected. And what reassures us in the face of *affront* is confirmation that our sense of boundaries is shared; it is those who offend who are up for negative appraisal, rebuke, or exclusion, not we who will be ignored, ridiculed, or silenced. Now, to whom are resentment's rebukes or demands expressed?

I have already mentioned Strawson's famous article on resentment and other reactive attitudes. Strawson considered resentment a "reactive attitude," and these, it has been pointed out, are a kind of *moral address*: they are expressive not only because they reveal something going on in the one who experiences them but

also because they are a kind of communicative display that invites a kind of response.[27] They address those at whom they are directed and often others, bidding
them to recognize the existence or the possibility of a kind of relationship. In the
case of resentment, the appeal or invitation for assurance of protection, defense,
or membership might sometimes be addressed *to the offender*: The angry display
"sends a message" to the offender about the unacceptability of the offender's behavior. This sort of case is what Butler had in mind, and it seems to be the
response now characteristically read as indignation, overt rebuking anger. But the
assumption that one's accusing and reproving anger and the possible reprisal it
portends will be effective supposes one is in a position to accuse, reprove, and
threaten the transgressor. Many of us in many situations are not in this position.
When resentment is fearful because of vulnerability, fear would be the wrong
message to address to an offender when the offense displays ill will or bold indifference (rather than neglect), and so when the victim's fearful vulnerability might
constitute exactly the wrong sort of invitation, that is, an invitation to further
aggression, bad treatment, ridicule, or contemptuous flouting of rules.

    Yet insofar as resentment, like other reactive attitudes, can be read as a mes-
sage or signal, resentment's anger, even if fearful, is not unwisely addressed to
others who are not the offender but who might be in some position to reaffirm
standards and so ratify the resenter's judgment, to act in defense of the victim in
the form of intervention or reprisal; or to protect the victim (and perhaps others,
including themselves) from repetitions of the injury. These are the responses that
create or recreate the basis for confidence, trust, or hope that the boundaries that
include and protect us are as we believe and need them to be. Seen in this way,
the "aim" of resentment is, ideally, to activate protective, reassuring, or defensive
responses in some individuals or community that can affirm the victim's being
within the scope of that community's protective responsibilities or the resenter's
being in fact competent in grasping and applying the community's normative
expectations. The transgressor can reassure by "getting the message" and responding with acceptance of rebuke or with apology or amends. Allies can reassure
by joining in confirming or corrective action. The sought-for "answer" to being
"addressed" in the mode of resentment is "be assured, trust again" or "be assured,
we judge as you do."

    Commonly enough, however, resentment turns inward, festers or roils, and
is not appropriately answered. So the association of resentment with the weak,
with those whose vulnerability is confirmed by the fact of their exposure to harm,
exploitation, demotions, and slights, is understandable. The weak will be in harm's
way precisely because their weakness invites predation or indifference. Worse,
they look forward to living with injuries and slights and with the second-order fear
of having always to be angry and afraid. A weak position—socially, whether structural or situational—portends that one's resentment is less likely to be "heard," or
if heard to be answered. Alternatively, it is more likely when heard to attract
reprisals or ridicule for its presumption rather than protection from what prompts
it. The resentment of subordinates and victims can outrage their betters and tor-
mentors when it does not amuse them. An expression of resentment can invite

ridicule from those in a position to disqualify the one resenting as a judge. Not everyone is in a position to brandish Butler's weapon; the likely results of doing so, at any rate, are not a constant across situations or social positions. The seductive glimmer of truth about resentment in Nietzsche's account of *ressentiment* is that the weak might have to be "expert in silence, in long memory, in waiting, in provisional self-depreciation, and in self-humiliation."[28] Nietzsche was right to call this corrosively fearful anger "poisonous." Thwarted resentment can do damage. But it is easier to understand the nature and depth of the damage if we appreciate the degree to which resentment both expresses a sense of wrong and calls for recognition and a reparative response.

I have argued here against limiting resentment to a response to *actual* injury, to specifically *moral* injury, or to injury to *oneself*. Resentment functions as a reactive attitude for those who believe themselves or others injured or affronted, whether in fact they are and whether or not such injury or affront is morally objectionable. What is at stake in resentment is the mutual recognition of norms that define our society and our claims to membership in it. That is what begs to be examined when someone's resentment reveals a sense of threat. Of course, in particular cases resentment may be baseless, exaggerated, or misdirected, as other emotions can be in some instances. Even when it is, however, it serves as an extremely sensitive indicator and revealing expression of people's personal investment in what they understand to be, or what they believe should be, prevalent norms and people's investment of some social patterns with normative force. Resentment is not pleasant or attractive, but it has an important role to play in social and moral life, focusing our attention on the ongoing definition and enforcement of the standards of many types by which we live.

Notes

This essay has evolved through many presentations as part of a project on the moral psychology of responses to wrongdoing by victims, offenders, and third parties. I have presented versions at many places, and at every one I have received challenging feedback that moved me to reconsider and recast my claims. I thank audiences at the University of South Florida, State University of New York at Buffalo, Pennsylvania State University, Queens University, Dalhousie University, Syracuse University, University of Connecticut at Storrs, the Research School of Social Sciences at Australian National University and Arizona State University. Special thanks to Peggy DesAutels, Robert Richardson, and Mitchell Haney, who steered me away from a mistake about resentment and fear early on; and to Norvin Richards, whose commentary at a colloquium version of the paper at the American Philosophical Association Pacific Meeting was especially insightful and helpful.

1. Jeffrie G. Murphy and Jean Hampton, *Forgiveness and Mercy* (New York: Cambridge University Press, 1988).

2. Joseph Butler, *Butler's Fifteen Sermons Preached at the Rolls Chapel and A Dissertation of the Nature of Virtue*, ed. and with intro. and additional notes by T. A. Rob-

erts (London: Society for Promoting Christian Knowledge, [1726] 1970), 76. A companion article, "Upon Forgiveness of Injuries," argues that this naturally designed "remedy" for deficiencies of wisdom and virtue is a painful one whose satisfaction in revenge defeats its own aim of diminishing human misery. Even so, it is only the "excess and abuse" of resentment in malice and revenge, and not the emotion itself, that is to be avoided (81).

3. Ibid., 75.

4. Ibid., 78.

5. See Frans de Waal, *Good Natured: The Origins of Right and Wrong in Human and Other Animals* (Cambridge, Mass.: Harvard University Press, 1996), esp. chaps. 3 and 4, on responses in nonhuman social primates that look very much like gratitude, indignation, and so on.

6. P. F. Strawson, "Freedom and Resentment," in *The Philosophy of Thought and Action*, ed. P. F. Strawson (New York: Oxford University Press, 1968).

7. Murphy and Hampton, *Forgiveness and Mercy*, 59–60.

8. Ibid., 55, 56.

9. Ibid., 44, 52.

10. Ibid., 54.

11. Ibid., 57, 58.

12. Ibid., 57.

13. See ibid., 56, n. 16, for Hampton's comment that there are exceptions that nonetheless prove the rule. Another account that makes injuries to oneself the core of resentment is William E. Young, "Resentment and Impartiality," *Southern Journal of Philosophy* 36 (1998): 103–130.

14. See R. Jay Wallace, *Responsibility and the Moral Sentiments* (Cambridge, Mass.: Harvard University Press, 1996), 246–247, for a succinct discussion of why Nietzschean *ressentiment* is not the same as resentment. See also Claudia Card's discussion of Nietzsche in *The Atrocity Paradigm* (New York: Oxford University Press, 2002), chap. 2. Nietzsche's own discussion is in his *On the Genealogy of Morals*, trans. Francis Golffing (New York: Doubleday/Anchor Books, 1956).

15. I believe that many emotional expressions are sensitive to position in this way and that this is one of the complications of tracking the grammar of emotion concepts. One innovative and searching discussion of the issue of identifying emotions and of emotions commonly identified is in Sue Campbell, *Interpreting the Personal: Expression and the Formation of Feelings* (Ithaca, N.Y.: Cornell University Press, 1997). Campbell argues that expression individuates feelings, with the important consequence that public uptake controls possibilities of expression. See also María Lugones's remarkable "Hard-to-Handle Anger," in *Overcoming Racism and Sexism*, ed. Linda A. Bell and David Blumenfeld (Lanham, Md.: Rowman & Littlefield, 1995), on the communicative dimensions of anger and the difference it makes whether one expresses anger from a position of social strength or one of oppression or marginality.

16. Murphy and Hampton, *Forgiveness and Mercy*, 55.

17. Ibid., 16.

18. Strawson, "Freedom and Resentment," 75.

19. Unfair advantage is included in the description of resentment in Murphy and Hampton, *Forgiveness and Mercy*, 16.

20. Alan Gibbard points out, "Weird haircuts . . . make people angry, regularly and normally," although "our anger is mistaken," in *Wise Choices, Apt Feelings: A Theory*

of Normative Judgment (Cambridge, Mass.: Harvard University Press, 1990), 187. Yet it would seem, if this kind of "offense" really is "regular and normal," that there is some description under which it is not *just* a mistake.

21. William Ian Miller, *The Anatomy of Disgust* (Cambridge, Mass.: Harvard University Press, 1997), 198–199. Miller doesn't mention resentment in this passage, although a good deal of what he says about the social valence of disgust and contempt is relevant to resentment as well. Civil disattendability shades off rather too readily into norms of "respectability" that load hierarchical social arrangements, sheer prejudice, and socially sanctioned contempt for and exclusion of certain groups or their "ways" from specific social locales. See Iris M. Young, *Justice and the Politics of Difference* (Princeton, N.J.: Princeton University Press, 1990), 136–141, on the oppressive force of "respectability." See also Susan Wendell, *The Rejected Body* (New York: Routledge, 1996), on the situation of those with some kinds of disabilities who are not disattendable to the "normal."

22. Wallace, *Responsibility and the Moral Sentiments*, develops a somewhat similar view about resentment being a reflection of expectations in the context of developing a view of responsibility with affinities to Strawson. See esp. chap 2 and app. 1.

23. Norvin Richards pointed out to me the important possibility of disgusted resentment, where one resents what one nonetheless fully expected.

24. The interaction and synergy of emotions in context is a topic that deserves more treatment, especially as it may highlight the rather loose grammar of emotion concepts and some consequently fuzzy individuation of emotions. When does one emotion precipitate another, modulate another, or emerge as a kind of transformation of another? Contempt, for example, might come about in some instances as a transformation of resentment when being mobilized in anger becomes exhausting. One might start out resentful and then (as in the hostile, sexist work environment) become resentfully disgusted but finally become disgusted to the point where one depersonalizes and objectifies the unruly offenders. Then a kind of contemptuous revulsion might emerge that sees its objects as trivial or low, not as something to defend against and call to account so much as something to scorn or recoil from.

25. Two insightful discussions of bitterness are in Campbell, *Interpreting the Personal*, 167–172; and Lynne McFall, "What's Wrong with Bitterness?" in *Feminist Ethics*, ed. Claudia Card (Lawrence: University Press of Kansas, 1991).

26. Murphy and Hampton, *Forgiveness and Mercy*, 57, 74–76.

27. See Jonathan Bennett, "Accountability," in *Philosophical Subjects*, ed. Zak Van Straaten (New York: Oxford University Press, 1980); Gary Watson, "Responsibility and the Limits of Evil," in *Responsibility, Character, and the Emotions*, ed. Ferdinand Schoeman (New York: Cambridge University Press, 1987); and Barbara Houston, "In Praise of Blame," *Hypatia* 7 (1992): 128–147, on reactive attitudes as forms of address. The phrase seems to be Watson's.

28. Nietzsche, *Genealogy of Morals*, 172.

9

Genocide and Social Death

Claudia Card

This essay develops the hypothesis that social death is utterly central to the evil of genocide, not just when genocide is primarily cultural but even when it is homicidal on a massive scale. It is social death that enables us to distinguish the peculiar evil of genocide from the evils of other mass murders. Even genocidal murders can be viewed as extreme means to the primary end of social death. Social vitality exists through relationships, contemporary and intergenerational, that create an identity that gives meaning to a life. Major loss of social vitality is a loss of identity and consequently a serious loss of meaning for one's existence. Putting social death at the center takes the focus off individual choice, individual goals, individual careers, and body counts and puts it on relationships that create community and set the context that gives meaning to choices and goals. If my hypothesis is correct, the term "cultural genocide" is probably both redundant and misleading—redundant if the social death present in all genocides implies cultural death as well, and misleading if cultural genocide suggests that some genocides do not include cultural death.

What Is Feminist about Analyzing Genocide?

The question has been asked, what is feminist about this project? Why publish it in a work devoted to feminist philosophy? The answer is both simple and complex. Simply, it is the history behind the project and the perspective from which it is carried out, rather than a focus on women or gender, that make the project feminist. Some of the complexities are as follows.

The evil of genocide falls not only on men and boys but also on women and girls, typically unarmed, untrained in defense against violence, and often also responsible for care of the wounded, the sick, the disabled, babies, children, and the elderly. Because genocide targets both sexes, rather than being specific to women's experience, there is some risk of its being neglected in feminist thought. It is also the case that with few exceptions,[1] both feminist and nonfeminist philosophical reflections on war and other public violence have tended to neglect the impact on victims. Philosophers have thought mostly about the positions of perpetrators and decision makers (most of them men), with some feminist speculation on what might change if more women were among the decision makers and if women were subject to military conscription. The damage of war and terrorism is commonly assessed in terms of its ruin of individual careers, body counts, statistics on casualties, and material costs of rebuilding. Attention goes to preventing such violence and the importance of doing so but less to the experience and responses of the majority of victims and survivors, who are civilians, not soldiers. In bringing to the fore the responses of victims of both sexes, Holocaust literature stands in sharp contrast to these trends. Central to Holocaust literature is reflection on the meaning of genocide.

Women's studies, in its engagement with differences among women, has moved from its earlier aim to train a feminist eye on the world and all kinds of issues (such as evil) to the more limited aim of studying women and gender. I return here to the earlier conception that recognizes not only the study of women, feminism, or gender but also feminist approaches to issues of ethics and social theory generally, whether the word "feminist" is used or not. My interests move toward commonalities in our experiences of evil, not only commonalities among women differently situated but commonalities shared with many men as well. Yet my lens is feminist, polished through decades of reflection on women's multifarious experiences of misogyny and oppression. What we notice, through a feminist lens, is influenced by long habits of attending to emotional response, relationships that define who we (not just women and girls) are, and the significance of the concrete particular.

Centering social death accommodates the position, controversial among genocide scholars, that genocidal acts are not always or necessarily homicidal (on which more below). Forcibly sterilizing women or men of a targeted group or forcibly separating their children from them for reeducation for assimilation into another group can also be genocidal in aim or effect. Such policies can be aimed at or achieve the eventual destruction of the social identity of those so treated. It may appear that transported children simply undergo a change in social identity, not that they lose all social vitality. That may be the intent. Yet, parents' social vitality is a casualty of children's forced reeducation, and in reality transported children may fail to make a satisfying transition.

The Holocaust was not only a program of mass murder but also an assault on Jewish social vitality. The assault was experienced by hidden children who survived, as well as by those who died. Hitler's sterilization program and Nuremberg laws that left German Jews stateless were parts of the genocide, not just preludes to it. Jews who had converted to Christianity (or whose parents or grandparents had done so) were hunted down and murdered, even though one might think their social identities had already changed. This pursuit makes a certain perverted sense if the idea was to extinguish in them all possibility of social vitality, simply on grounds of their ancestral roots. Mass murder is the most extreme method of genocide, denying members of targeted groups any degree or form of social vitality whatever. To extinguish all possibility of social vitality, child transportation and reeducation are insufficient; it may be necessary to commit mass murder or drive victims mad or rob them of dignity, all of which were done to Holocaust victims.

Although I approach genocide from a history of feminist habits of research and reflection, I say very little here about the impact of genocide on women and girls as opposed to its impact on men and boys. I would not suggest that women suffer more or worse than the men who are also its victims. Nor am I especially interested in such questions as whether lifelong habits of care giving offer survival advantages to segregated women. (In fact, the evidence appears to be that no one survives without others' care and help.) My interest here is, rather, in what makes genocide the specific evil that it is, what distinguishes it from other atrocities, and what kinds of atrocities are rightly recognized as genocidal. Feminist habits of noticing are useful for suggesting answers to these questions.

Genocide, War, and Justice

Genocide need not be part of a larger war, although it commonly is. But it can be regarded as itself a kind of one-sided war. Precedents for regarding one-sided attacks as wars are found in the idea of a war on drugs and in the title of Lucy Dawidowicz's *The War Against the Jews*.[2] If genocide is war, it is a profoundly unjust kind of war, perniciously unjust, an injustice that is also an evil.

John Rawls opened his first book on justice with the observation that justice is the first virtue of institutions, as truth is of systems of thought. No matter how efficient and well arranged, he wrote, laws and institutions must be reformed or abolished if they are unjust.[3] As did critics who found these claims overstated, even Rawls noted that although these propositions seem to express our intuitive conviction of the primacy of justice, no doubt they are expressed too strongly.[4] Not all injustices, even in society's basic structure, make lives insupportable, intolerable, or indecent. Reforms are not always worth the expense of their implementation. Had Rawls made his claim about abolishing unjust institutions in regard to *pernicious* injustices, however, it should not have been controversial: laws and institutions must be abolished when they are evils.

Not all injustices are evils, as the harms they produce vary greatly in importance. Some injustices are relatively tolerable. They may not affect people's lives in a deep or lasting way, even though they are wrong and should be eliminated— unjust salary discriminations, for example, when the salaries in question are all high. An injustice becomes an evil when it inflicts harms that make victims' lives unbearable, indecent, or impossible or that make victims' deaths indecent. Injustices of war are apt to fall into this category. Certainly genocide does.

The Concept of Genocide

Genocide combines the Greek *genos* for "race" or "tribe" with the Latin *cide* for "killing." The term was coined by Raphael Lemkin, an attorney and refugee scholar from Poland who served in the United States War Department.[5] He campaigned as early as the 1930s for an international convention to outlaw genocide, and his persistence resulted in the United Nations Genocide Convention of 1948. Although this convention is widely cited, it was not translated into action in international courts until the 1990s, more than forty years later. The first state to bring a case to the World Court under the convention was Bosnia-Herzegovina in 1993. It was not until 1998 that the first verdict under that convention was rendered, when the Rwanda tribunal found Jean-Paul Akayesu guilty on nine counts for his participation in the genocide in Rwanda in 1994.[6] The United States did not pass legislation implementing ratification of the 1948 genocide convention until 1988, and then only with significant reservations that were somewhat disabling.[7] Such resistance is interesting in view of questions raised during the interim about the morality of U.S. conduct in Vietnam. By the time the United States ratified the convention, ninety-seven other UN members had already done so.

The *term* "genocide" is thus relatively new, and the Holocaust is widely agreed to be its paradigmatic instance. Yet Lemkin and many others find the *practice* of genocide ancient. In their sociological survey from ancient times to the present, Frank Chalk and Kurt Jonassohn discuss instances of apparent genocide that range from the Athenians' annihilation of the people of the island of Melos in the fifth century B.C.E. (recorded by Thucydides) and the ravaging of Carthage by Romans in 146 B.C.E. (also listed by Lemkin as the first of his historical examples of wars of extermination) through mass killings in Bangladesh, Cambodia, and East Timor in the second half of the twentieth century.[8] Controversies are ongoing over whether to count as genocidal the annihilation of indigenous peoples in the Americas and Australia (who succumbed in vast numbers to diseases brought by Europeans), Stalin's induced mass starvation of the 1930s (ostensibly an economically motivated measure), and the war conducted by the United States in Vietnam.

The literature of comparative genocide—historian Peter Novick calls it comparative atrocitology[9]—so far includes relatively little published work by philosophers. Here is what I have found. Best known is probably Jean-Paul Sartre's 1967 book, *On Genocide*, written for the Sartre-Russell International War Crimes Tribunal, which was convened to consider war crimes by the United States in Vietnam.[10] In 1974 Hugo Adam Bedau published a long and thoughtful article, "Genocide in Vietnam?" responding to Sartre and others who have raised the question of whether the United States was guilty of perpetrating genocide in Vietnam.[11] Bedau argues for a negative answer to that question, relying primarily on intent as an essential factor. His view is that the intent of the United States in Vietnam was not to exterminate a people, even if that was nearly a consequence. Berel Lang's article, "The Concept of Genocide" and the first chapter of his book, *Act and Idea in the Nazi Genocide,* are helpful in their explorations of the meanings and roles of intent in defining genocide.[12]

Other significant philosophical works include Alan S. Rosenbaum's anthology, *Is the Holocaust Unique? Perspectives on Comparative Genocide,* which discusses the Nazi assault on Jews and Romani during World War II, the Atlantic slave trade, the Turkish slaughter of Armenians in 1915, and Stalin's induced famine.[13] Legal scholar Martha Minow reflects philosophically on measures lying between vengeance and forgiveness taken by states in response to genocide and mass murder.[14] Jonathan Glover's *Humanity: A Moral History of the Twentieth Century,* in some ways the most ambitious recent philosophical discussion of evils, includes reflections on Rwanda, Stalin, and Nazism.[15] The Institute for Genocide Studies and the Association of Genocide Scholars (which holds conventions) attract an interdisciplinary group of scholars, including a small number of philosophers. And the Society for the Philosophic Study of Genocide and the Holocaust sponsors sessions at conventions of the American Philosophical Association.

On the whole, historians, psychologists, sociologists, and political scientists have contributed more than philosophers to genocide scholarship. Naturally, their contributions as social scientists have been empirically oriented, focused on such matters as origins, contributing causes, effects, monitoring, and prevention. Yet, philosophical issues run throughout the literature. They include foundational matters, such as the meaning of genocide (which appears to be a highly contested concept), and such issues of ethics and political philosophy as whether perpetrators can be punished in a meaningful way that respects moral standards. If adequate retribution is morally impossible and if deterrence is unlikely for those who are ideologically motivated, then what is the point in punishing perpetrators? If there is nevertheless some point sufficient to justify doing so, then who should be punished, by whom, and how?

Controversies over the meaning of genocide lead naturally to the closely related question of whether genocide is ethically different from nongenocidal mass murder. The practical issue here is whether and, if so, why it is important to add the category of genocide to existing crimes against humanity and war crimes. Crimes against humanity were important additions to war crimes in that, unlike war crimes, they need not be perpetrated during wartime or in connection with a war, and they can be inflicted by a country against its own citizens. But given that murder of civilians by soldiers is already a war crime and a human rights violation, one may wonder whether the crime of genocide captures anything that they omit.

If the social death of individual victims is central to genocide, then, arguably, genocide does capture something more. What distinguishes genocide is not that it has a different kind of victim, namely, groups (although it is a convenient shorthand to speak of targeting groups). Rather, the kind of harm suffered by individual victims of genocide, in virtue of their group membership, is not captured by other crimes. To get a sense of what is at stake in the hypothesis that social death is central, let us turn briefly to controversies over the meaning of "genocide."

The definition of "genocide" is currently in such flux that the Association of Genocide Scholars asks members on its information page (which is printed in a members directory) to specify which definition they use in their work. A widely cited definition is that of the 1948 UN Convention on the Prevention and Punishment of the Crime of Genocide:

> Genocide means any of the following acts committed with the intent to destroy, in whole or in part, a national, ethnical, racial or religious group, as such: (a) killing members of the group; (b) causing serious bodily or mental harm to members of the group; (c) deliberately inflicting on the group conditions of life calculated to bring about its physical destruction in whole or in part; (d) imposing measures intended to prevent births within the group; (e) forcibly transferring children of the group to another group.[16]

Every clause of this definition is controversial.

Israel Charny and others criticize the UN definition for not recognizing political groups, such as the Communist Party, as possible targets of genocide.[17] Political groups had been, in fact, recognized in an earlier draft of the genocide convention, and Chalk and Jonassohn do recognize political groups as targets of genocide in their historical survey.[18] Some scholars, however, prefer the term "politicide" for these cases and reserve the term "genocide" for the annihilation of groups into which one is (ordinarily) born—racial, ethnic, national, or religious groups. Yet, one is not necessarily, of course, born into one's current national or religious group, and either one's current or one's former membership can prove fatal. Furthermore, some people's political identity may be as important to their lives as religious identity is to the lives of others. And so, the distinction between genocide and politicide has seemed arbitrary to many critics. A difficulty is, of course, where to draw the line if political groups are recognized as possible victims. But line drawing is not a difficulty that is peculiar to political groups.

The last three clauses of the UN definition—conditions of life intended to destroy the group in whole or in part, preventing births, and transferring children—count as genocidal many acts that are aimed at cultural destruction, even though they are not homicidal. Preventing births is not restricted to sterilization but has been interpreted to include segregation of the sexes and bans on marriage. Social vitality is destroyed when the social relations, organizations, practices, and institutions of the members of a group are irreparably damaged or demolished. Such destruction is a commonly intended consequence of war rape, which has aimed at family breakdown. Although Lemkin regards such deeds as both ethnocidal and genocidal, some scholars prefer simply to call them ethnocides (or cultural genocides) and reserve the term "genocide" (unqualified) for events that include mass death. The idea is, apparently, that physical death is more extreme and therefore, presumably, worse than social death. That physical death is worse or even more extreme is not obvious, however, but deserves scrutiny, and I will return to it.

Even the clauses of the UN definition that specify killing group members or causing them serious bodily or mental harm are vague and can cover a wide range of possible harms. How many people must be killed for a deed to be genocidal? What sort of bodily harm counts? (Must there be lasting disablement?) What counts as mental harm? (Is posttraumatic stress sufficient?) If the definition is to have practical consequences in the responses of nations to perpetrators, these questions can become important, for example, with respect to issues of intervention and reparations.

Although most scholars agree on including intention in the definition of genocide, there is no consensus about the content of the required intention. Must the relevant intention include destruction of all members of a group as an aim or purpose? Would it be enough that the group was knowingly destroyed as a foreseeable consequence of the pursuit of some other aim? Must the full extent of the destruction even be foreseeable if the policy of which it is a consequence is already clearly immoral? Bedau makes much of the content of the relevant intention in his argument that whatever war crimes the United States committed in Vietnam, they were not genocidal because the intent was not to destroy the people of Vietnam as such, even if that destruction was both likely and foreseeable.[19]

Charny, however, objects to an analogous claim made by some critics who, he reports, held that because Stalin's intent was to obtain enough grain to trade for industrial materials for the Soviet Union, rather than to kill the millions who died from this policy, his famine was not a genocide.[20] Charny argues that because Stalin foresaw the fatal consequences of his grain policies, those policies should count as genocidal. As in common philosophical criticisms of the doctrine of the double effect, Charny appears to reject as ethically insignificant a distinction between intending and merely foreseeing, at least in this kind of case.

The doctrine of double effect has been relied on by the Catholic Church to resolve certain ethical questions about life-and-death issues.[21] The doctrine maintains that under certain conditions it is not wrong to do something that has a foreseeable effect (not an aim) that is such that an act *aiming* at that effect would have been wrong. The first condition of its not being wrong is that the act one performs is not wrong in itself, and the second is that the effect at which it would be wrong to aim is not instrumental toward the end at which the act does aim. Thus, the church has found it wrong to perform an abortion that would kill a fetus in order to save the mother but, at the same time, not wrong to remove a cancerous uterus when doing so would also result in the death of a fetus. The reasoning is that in the case of the cancerous uterus, the fetus's death is not an aim; nor is it a means to removing the uterus but only a consequence of doing so. Many find this distinction troubling and far from obvious. Why is the death of a fetus from abortion not also only a consequence? The aim could be redescribed as to remove the fetus from the uterus in order to save the mother, rather than to kill the fetus to save the mother; and at least when the fetus need not be destroyed in the very process of removal, one might argue that death due to extrauterine nonviability is not a means to the fetus's removal, either.

The position of the critics who do not want to count Stalin's starvation of the peasants as a genocide would appear to imply that if the peasants' deaths were not instrumental toward Stalin's goal but only an unfortunate consequence, the foreseeability of those deaths does not make Stalin's policy genocidal, any more than the foreseeability of the death of the fetus in the case of a hysterectomy performed to remove a cancerous uterus makes that surgery murderous. Charny's position appears to imply, on the contrary, that the foreseeability of the peasants' mass death is enough to constitute genocidal intent, even if it was not intended instrumentally toward Stalin's aims.

Some controversies focus on whether the intent was to destroy a group as such. One might argue with Bedau, drawing on Lang's discussion of the intent issues,[22] that the intent is to destroy a group as such when it is not just accidental that the group is destroyed in the process of pursuing a further end. Thus, if it was not just accidental that the peasant class was destroyed in the process of Stalin's pursuit of grain to trade for industrial materials, he could be said to have destroyed the peasants as such, even if peasant starvation played no more causal role in making grain available than killing the fetus plays in removing a cancerous uterus. Alternatively, some argue that the words "as such" do not belong in the definition because, ethically, it does not matter whether a group is deliberately destroyed as such or simply deliberately destroyed. Chalk and Jonassohn appear to take this view.[23]

Furthermore, one might pursue the question of whether it is really necessary even to be able to foresee the full extent of the consequences in order to be accurately described as having a genocidal intent. Historian Steven Katz argues in *The Holocaust in Historical Context* that the mass deaths of Native Americans and Native Australians were not genocides because they resulted from epidemics, not from murder.[24] The suggestion is that the consequences here were not reasonably foreseeable. David Stannard, American studies scholar at the University of Hawaii, however, finds the case less simple, for it can be argued that the epidemics were not just accidental.[25] Part of the controversy regards the facts: to what extent were victims deliberately infected, as when the British, and later Americans, distributed blankets infected with small pox virus? And to what extent did victims succumb to unintended infection stemming from ordinary exposure to Europeans with the virus? But, also, part of the controversy is philosophical: if mass deaths from disease result from wrongdoing and if perpetrators could know that the intolerably destructive consequences had an uncontrollable (and therefore somewhat unpredictable) extent, then does it matter ethically whether the wrongdoers could foresee the full extent of the consequences? One might argue that it does not, on the ground that they already knew enough to appreciate that what they were doing was evil.

What is the importance of success in achieving a genocidal aim? Must genocide succeed in eliminating an entire group? An assault, to be homicide, must succeed in killing. Otherwise, it is a mere attempt, and an unlawful attempted homicide generally carries a less severe penalty than a successful one. Bedau and Lang point out, however, that genocide does not appear to be analogous to homicide in that way. There may still be room for some distinction between genocide and attempted genocide (although Lang appears not to recognize any such distinction) if we distinguish between partially formed and fully formed intentions or if we distinguish among stages in carrying out a complex intention. But in paradigmatic instances of genocide, such as the Holocaust, there are always some survivors, even when there is clear evidence that the intention was to eliminate everyone in the group. There is general agreement that at least some mass killing with that wrongful intention is genocidal. The existence of survivors is not sufficient to negate fully formed genocidal intent. There may be survivors even after all stages of a complex genocidal intention have been implemented. Bedau observes, however, that there is a certain analogy between genocide and murder that enables us to contrast both with homicide. Both genocide and murder include wrongfulness in the very concept, whereas a homicide can be justifiable. Homicide is not necessarily unlawful or even immoral. In contrast, genocide and murder are, in principle, incapable of justification.

On my understanding of what constitutes an evil, there are two basic elements: (1) culpable wrongdoing by one or more perpetrators and (2) reasonably foreseeable intolerable harm to victims. Most often the second element, intolerable harm, is what distinguishes evils from ordinary wrongs. Intentions may be necessary in defining genocide. But they are not always necessary for culpable wrongdoing, as omissions—negligence, recklessness, or carelessness—can be sufficient. When culpable wrongdoing *is* intentional, however, its aim need not be to cause intolerable harm. A seriously culpable deed is evil when the doer is willing to inflict intolerable harm on others even in the course of aiming at some other goal. If what is at stake in controversies about the meaning of genocide is whether a mass killing is sufficiently evil to merit the opprobrium attaching to the term "genocide," a good case can be made for including assaults on many kinds of groups inflicted through many kinds of culpable wrongdoing. Yet that leaves the question of whether the genocidal nature of a killing has special ethical import and, if so, what that import is and how, if at all, it may restrict the scope of genocide. I turn to these and related questions next.

The Specific Evils of Genocide

Genocide is not simply unjust (although it certainly is unjust); it is also evil. It characteristically includes the one-sided killing of defenseless civilians—babies, children, the elderly, the sick, the disabled, and the injured of both genders, along with their usually female caretakers—simply on the basis of their national, religious, ethnic, or other political identity. It targets people on the basis of who they are rather than on the basis of what they have done, what they might do, or even what they are capable of doing. (One commentator says genocide kills people on the basis of *what* they are, not even *who* they are.)

Genocide is a paradigm of what Israeli philosopher Avishai Margalit calls indecent in that it not only destroys victims but also first humiliates them by

deliberately inflicting an utter loss of freedom and control over their vital interests.[26] Vital interests can be transgenerational and thus survive one's death. Before
death, genocide victims are ordinarily deprived of control over vital transgenerational interests and more immediate vital interests. They may be literally stripped
naked; robbed of their last possessions; lied to about the most vital matters; witness
to the murder of family, friends, and neighbors; made to participate in their own
murder; and if female, likely to also be violated sexually. Victims of genocide are
commonly killed with no regard for lingering suffering or exposure. They, and
their corpses, are routinely treated with utter disrespect. These historical facts, not
simply mass murder, account for much of the moral opprobrium attaching to the
concept of genocide.

Yet such atrocities, it may be argued, are already war crimes if conducted
during wartime, and they can otherwise or also be prosecuted as crimes against
humanity. Why, then, add the specific crime of genocide? What, if anything, is
not already captured by laws that prohibit such things as the rape, enslavement,
torture, forced deportation, and the degradation of individuals? Is any ethically
distinct harm done to members of the targeted group that would not have been
done had they been targeted simply as individuals rather than because of their
group membership? This is the question that I find central in arguing that genocide is not simply reducible to mass death, to any of the other war crimes, or to
the crimes against humanity just enumerated. I believe the answer is affirmative:
the harm is ethically distinct, although on the question of whether it is worse I
wish only to question the assumption that it is not.

Specific to genocide is the harm inflicted on its victims' social vitality. It is
not just that one's group membership is the occasion for harms that are definable
independently of one's identity as a member of the group. When a group with its
own cultural identity is destroyed, its survivors lose their cultural heritage and
may even lose their intergenerational connections. To use Orlando Patterson's
terminology, in that event, they may become socially dead and their descendants
natally alienated, no longer able to pass along and build upon the traditions,
cultural developments (including languages), and projects of earlier generations.[27]
The harm of social death is not necessarily less extreme than that of physical
death. Social death can even aggravate physical death by making it indecent,
removing all respectful and caring rituals, social connections, and social contexts
that are capable of making dying bearable and even of making one's death meaningful. In my view, the special evil of genocide lies in its infliction of not just
physical death (when it does that) but also social death, producing a consequent
meaninglessness of one's life and even of its termination. This view, however, is
controversial.

African-American and Jewish philosopher Laurence Mordekhai Thomas argues that although American slavery natally alienated slaves—that slaves were
born severed from most normal social and cultural ties that connect one with
both earlier and later generations—the Holocaust did not natally alienate Jews.[28]
He does not explicitly generalize about genocide and natal alienation but makes
this judgment in regard to the particular genocide of the Holocaust. Yet the appar-

ent implication is that a genocide no more successful than the Holocaust (an accepted paradigm of genocide) is not natally alienating because enough victims survive and enough potential targets escape that they are able to preserve the group's cultural traditions. Thomas's analyses of patterns of evil in American slavery and the Holocaust are philosophically ground breaking and have been very helpful to me in thinking about these topics. Yet I want to question this conclusion that he draws. I want to consider the Nazi genocide in light of the more fundamental idea of social death, of which natal alienation is one special case, not the only case.

Thomas's conception of natal alienation is more specific and more restricted than Patterson's conception of social death. Thomas seems not to be thinking of lost family connections and lost community connections, the particular connections of individuals to one another, but rather the connections of each individual with a culture in general, with its traditions and practices. He finds members of an ethnic group natally alienated when the cultural practices into which they are born forcibly prevent most of them from fully participating in, and thus having a secure knowledge of, their historical-cultural traditions.[29] He notes that after seven generations of slavery, the memories of one's culture of origin are totally lost, which is certainly plausible. Patterson uses the term "natal alienation" for the extreme case of being *born* to *social death*, with individual social connections, past and future, cut off from all but one's oppressors at the very outset of one's life. Hereditary slavery yields a paradigm of natal alienation in this sense. Slaves who are treated as nonpersons have (practically) no socially supported ties not only to a cultural heritage but even to immediate kin (parents, children, and siblings) and peers. As a consequence of being cut off from kin and community, they also lose their cultural heritage. But the first step was to destroy existing social ties with family and community, to excommunicate them from society, as Patterson puts it.[30] In Rawlsian terms, they were first excluded from the benefits and protections of the basic structure of the society into which they were born and in which they must live out their lives. Loss of cultural heritage follows.

Those who are *natally* alienated are *born* already socially dead. Natal alienation might be a clue to descent from genocide survivors (although not proof, insofar as genocide depends also on intent). Thus, the natal alienation of slaves and their descendants, when slavery is hereditary, is one clue to a possible history of genocide committed against their ancestors.

Thomas recognizes that alienation is not all or nothing. A lost cultural heritage can be rediscovered, or partially recovered, later or in other places. Those who were alienated from some cultures may become somewhat integrated into others. Still, he denies that the Holocaust natally alienated Jews from Judaism because the central tenets of Judaism—the defining traditions of Judaism—endured in spite of Hitler's every intention to the contrary.[31]

The question, however, should be not simply whether the traditions survived but also whether individual Jewish victims were able to sustain their connections to those traditions. Sustaining the connections meaningfully requires a family or community setting for observance. Many Jews, of course, escaped being victimized because of where they lived (e.g., in the United States) and because of how the war turned out (the defeat of the Axis powers), and they were able to maintain Jewish traditions with which survivors might conceivably connect or reconnect. But many survivors were unable to do so. Some found family members after the war or created new families. Many did not. Many lost entire families, their entire villages, and the way of life embodied in the *shtetl* (Russian village). Some could not produce more children because of medical experiments performed on them in the camps. Many survivors lost access to social memories embodied in such cultural institutions as libraries and synagogues.

Responding to the observation that entire communities of Jews were destroyed and that the Yiddish language is on the way out, Thomas argues that members of those communities were destroyed not as such (e.g., as shtetl Jews), but more simply as Jews, and that the entire community of Jews was not destroyed. He concludes that the question must be whether the Holocaust was natally alienating of Jews as such, without regard to any specific community of Jews.[32] In answering negatively, he is apparently thinking of survivors who reestablished a Jewish life after the war, rather than of non-European Jews, potential victims whose positions might be regarded as somewhat analogous to those of unhunted and unenslaved Africans at the time of the African slave trade.

Some European Jews survived, however, only by passing as Christians. Some hidden children who were raised by strangers to be Christians only discovered their Jewish heritage later, if at all. If they were full members of the societies in which they survived, Thomas does not consider them natally alienated. Those who pass as members of another religion need not be socially dead, even if they are alienated from their religion of origin. Still, if they were originally connected in a vital way with their inherited religion and if they then experienced no vital connection to the new one, then arguably they do suffer a degree of social death. More clearly, those who were made stateless before being murdered were certainly treated socially as nonpersons. National Socialist decrees robbed them of social support for ties to family, peers, and community; stripped their rights to earn a living, own property, attend public schools, and even ride public transportation; and on arrival at the camps they were torn from family members. Although they were not *born* to social death, they were nevertheless intentionally deprived of all social vitality before their physical murder.

For those who survive physically, mere knowledge and memory are insufficient to create social vitality, even if they are necessary. Those who cannot participate in the social forms they remember do not actually have social vitality but only the memory of it. Furthermore, from 1933 to 1945, many children were born to a condition that became progressively more *natally* alienating. Contrary to the apparent implication of Thomas's hypothesis about the differences between American slavery and the Holocaust, social death seems to me to be a concept central to the harm of genocide, at least as important to what is evil about the Holocaust as the mass physical murder.

Although social vitality is essential to a decent life for both women and men, the sexes have often played different roles in its creation and maintenance. If men are often cast in the role of the creators of (high?) culture, women have played very central roles in preserving and passing on the traditions, language, and (daily) practices from one generation to the next and in maintaining family and community relationships. Where such generalizations hold, the blocking of opportunities for creativity (e.g., being excluded from the professions) would fall very heavily on men. But disruptions of family and community, such as being alienated from one's family by rape or being suddenly deported without adequate provisions (or any means of obtaining them) into a strange environment where one does not even know the language, would also fall very heavily, perhaps especially so, on women.

Most immediate victims of genocide are not born socially dead. But genocides that intentionally strip victims of the ability to participate in social activity prior to their murders do aim at their social death, not just their physical death. In some cases it may appear that social death is not an end in itself but simply a consequence of means taken to make mass murder easier (e.g., concentrating victims in ghettos and camps). When assailants are moved by hatred, however, social death may become an end in itself. Humiliation before death often appears to have been an end in itself, not just a means. The very idea of selecting victims by social group identity suggests that it is not just the physical life of victims that is targeted but also the social vitality behind that identity.

If the aim, or intention, of social death is not accidental to genocide, the survival of Jewish culture does not show that social death was not central to the evil of the Holocaust, any more than the fact of survivors shows that a mass murder was not genocidal. A genocide as successful as the Holocaust achieves the aim of social death both for victims who do not survive and, to a degree and for a time, for many survivors. Thomas's point may still hold that descendants of survivors of the African diaspora produced by the slave trade are in general more alienated from their African cultures of origin than Holocaust survivors are from Judaism today. Yet it is true in both cases that survivors made substantial connection with other cultures. If African Americans are totally alienated from their African cultures of origin, it is also true that many Holocaust survivors and their descendants have found it impossible to embrace Judaism or even a Jewish culture after Auschwitz. The survival of a culture does not by itself tell us about the degree of alienation that is experienced by individual survivors. Knowledge of a heritage is not by itself sufficient to produce vital connections to it.

The harm of social death is not, so far as I can see, adequately captured by war crimes and other crimes against humanity. Many of those crimes are defined by what can be done to individuals considered independently of their social connections, for example, rape (when defined simply as a form of physical assault), torture, and starvation. Some crimes, such as deportation and enslavement, do begin to get at issues of disrupting social existence. But they lack the comprehensiveness of social death, at least when the enslavement in question is not hereditary and is not necessarily for the rest of a person's life.

Still, it is true that not all victims of the Holocaust underwent social death to the same extent as prisoners in the camps and ghettos. Entire villages on the

Eastern front were slaughtered by the *Einsatzgruppen* (mobile killing units) without warning or prior captivity. Yet these villagers were given indecent deaths. They were robbed of control of their vital interests and of opportunities to mourn. Although most did not experience those deprivations for very long, inflicted en masse these murders do appear to have produced sudden social death prior to physical extermination. The murders were also part of a larger plan that included the death of Judaism, not just the deaths of Jews. Implementing that plan included gradually stripping vast numbers of Jews of social vitality, in some places over a period of years, and it entailed that survivors, if there were any, should not survive as Jews. The fact that the plan only partly succeeded does not negate the central role of social death within it or the importance of that concept to genocide.

If social death is central to the harm of genocide, then it really is right not to count as a genocide the annihilation, however heinous, of just any political group. Not every political group contributes significantly to its members' cultural identity. Many are fairly specific and short lived, formed to support particular issues. But then, equally, the annihilation of just any cultural group should not count either. Cultural groups can also be temporary and specialized, lacking in the continuity and comprehensiveness that are presupposed by the possibility of social death. Some mass murders—perhaps the bombings of September 11, 2001—do not appear to have had as part of their aim, intention, or effect the prior soul murder or social death of those targeted for physical extermination. If so, they are mass murders that are not also genocides. But mass murders and other measures that have as part of their reasonably foreseeable consequence or as part of their aim the annihilation of a group that contributes significantly to the social identity of its members are genocidal.

Notes

1. Robin Schott, "Philosophical Reflections on War Rape," in *On Feminist Ethics and Politics*, ed. Claudia Card (Lawrence: University Press of Kansas, 1999); Claudia Card, "Rape as a Weapon of War," *Hypatia* 11, no. 4 (1996): 5–18; and Claudia Card, "Addendum to Rape as a Weapon of War," *Hypatia* 12, no. 2 (1997): 216–218.

2. Lucy W. Davidowicz, *The War Against the Jews, 1933–1945* (New York: Holt, Rinehart, & Winston, 1975).

3. John Rawls, *A Theory of Justice*, rev. ed. (Cambridge, Mass.: Harvard University Press, 1999), 3.

4. Ibid., 4.

5. Raphael Lemkin, *Axis Rule in Occupied Europe: Laws of Occupation, Analysis of Government, Proposals for Redress* (Washington, D.C.: Carnegie Endowment for International Peace, Division of International Law, 1944).

6. Diane F. Orentlicher, "Genocide," in *Crimes of War: What the Public Should Know*, ed. Roy Gutman and David Rieff (New York: Norton, 1999), 153.

7. Berel Lang, "Genocide," in *Encyclopedia of Ethics*, vol. 1, ed. Lawrence C. Becker with Charlotte B. Becker (New York: Garland, 1992), 400.

8. Frank Chalk and Kurt Jonassohn, eds., *The History and Sociology of Genocide: Analyses and Case Studies* (New Haven, Conn.: Yale University Press, 1990).

9. Peter Novick, *The Holocaust in American Life* (Boston: Houghton Mifflin, 1999).

10. Jean-Paul Sartre, *On Genocide* (Boston: Beacon, 1968).

11. Hugo Adam Bedau, "Genocide in Vietnam?" in *Philosophy, Morality, and International Affairs*, ed. Virginia Held, Sidney Morgenbesser, and Thomas Nagel (New York: Oxford University Press, 1974), 5–46.

12. Berel Lang, "The Concept of Genocide," *Philosophical Forum* 16, nos. 1–2 (1984–1985): 1–18; and Berel Lang, *Act and Idea in the Nazi Genocide* (Chicago: University of Chicago Press, 1990).

13. Alan S. Rosenbaum, ed., *Is the Holocaust Unique? Perspectives on Comparative Genocide* (Boulder, Col.: Westview, 1996).

14. Martha Minow, *Between Vengeance and Forgiveness: Facing History After Genocide and Mass Violence* (Boston: Beacon, 1998).

15. Jonathan Glover, *Humanity: A Moral History of the Twentieth Century* (New Haven, Conn.: Yale University Press, 2000).

16. Nehemiah Robinson, *The Genocide Convention: A Commentary* (New York: Institute of Jewish Affairs, World Jewish Congress, 1960), 147.

17. Israel Charny, "Toward a Generic Definition of Genocide," in *Genocide: Conceptual and Historical Dimensions*, ed. George Andreopoulos (Philadelphia: University of Pennsylvania Press, 1997).

18. Chalk and Jonassohn, *History and Sociology of Genocide.*

19. Bedau, "Genocide in Vietnam?"

20. Charny, "Toward a Generic Definition of Genocide," 64–69.

21. William David Solomon, "Double Effect," 268–269.

22. Lang, *Act and Idea in Nazi Genocide*, 3–29.

23. Chalk and Jonassohn, *History and Sociology of Genocide.*

24. Steven Katz, *The Holocaust in Historical Context: Vol. I: Mass Death Before the Modern Age* (New York: Oxford University Press, 1994).

25. David E. Stannard, *American Holocaust: The Conquest of the New World* (New York: Oxford University Press, 1992); and David E. Stannard, "Uniqueness as Denial: The Politics of Genocide Scholarship," in *Is the Holocaust Unique?* ed. Alan S. Rosenbaum (Boulder, Col.: Westview, 1996).

26. Avishai Margalit, *The Decent Society*, trans. Naomi Goldblum (Cambridge, Mass.: Harvard University Press, 1996), 115.

27. Orlando Patterson, *Slavery and Social Death* (Cambridge, Mass.: Harvard University Press, 1982), 5–9.

28. Laurence Mordekhai Thomas, *Vessels of Evil: American Slavery and the Holocaust* (Philadelphia: Temple University Press, 1993), 150–157.

29. Ibid., 150.

30. Patterson, *Slavery and Social Death.*

31. Thomas, *Vessels of Evil*, 153.

32. Ibid.

10

Demoralization, Trust, and the Virtues

Annette C. Baier

Hume famously wrote that "we must look within to find the moral quality."[1] He took the inner moral qualities of persons and their actions to be lasting character traits, or virtues, expressed in their behavior, both intentional action and spontaneous reaction. Some have recently doubted that persons have such dependable traits of personal character but rather claim that we all, uniformly, behave according to the situation we find ourselves in. So, for instance, we obey authority figures who order us to administer severe electric shocks to others or refuse help to the injured when we are late for an important appointment, regardless of our previous reputation for consideration or kindness. What is "within," on such a view, is uniform human nature, adapting itself to the particular situations in which particular persons find themselves. Such "situation ethics," as we might facetiously call it, eschews the attribution of individual character traits that purport to sort the generous from the stingy, the kind-hearted from the callous, the brave from the cowardly, the tactful from the blunt, the honest from the dishonest. Virtue ethics would then rest on a mistake, the "fundamental attribution error."[2] For all of us, regardless of how glowing the testimonials we may have received, it will then be true that only the grace of lucky circumstance keeps us from showing the worst that human nature can show—what it regularly shows in desperate battle, in enraged revenge, and in the callous torture chambers of overzealous "intelligence" services.

It is certainly true that there will always be some conditions that threaten to rob a person of the good qualities she had been reputed to possess. These conditions include not just war, plague, and famine but also private shock and misfortune. The previously confident and cheerful person may become broken-spirited after personal tragedy, or gross betrayal, or violent assault. She may become demoralized, lose her moral nerve for a while, and need help if she is to recover her old self and its moral qualities. But this fact does not deter parents from trying to encourage children to be considerate, patient, brave, honest, and generous rather than violent, impatient, cowardly, and greedy. As long as we are not in a moral "state of nature," there will be normal conditions in which good habits of the heart can be cultivated and more or less survive. Even when these conditions fail, when a person is subjected to more than she can take, the broken habits may be restorable. Of course, it will still be a matter of luck that a given person was brought up in a way that gave her good initial habits, whereas another was not, or that she gets the support she needs after psychological trauma. We do not need the infamous Milgram experiments to convince us that it is always true that "there, but for the grace of God, go I" and so to curb our tendency to be unfairly judgmental of those who show unwelcome qualities.

I propose an analysis of good moral quality that takes it to lie in the mental attitude a person has, either on a particular occasion or on a succession of like occasions, to an ever present fact about our human situation, namely, our mutual vulnerability. I will speak as if there are more or less lasting character traits that show on these occasions; but since the crucial thing, on my analysis, is the sort of thoughts about oneself, others, and mutual vulnerability that are in a person's head on a particular occasion, virtue and virtues could in theory come and go rather than being habitual. What makes an attitude to mutual vulnerability virtuous, or morally welcome, I suggest, is its contribution to the climate of trust within which the person lives. A one-shot exhibition of great bravery and calm in face of danger by a normally timid person may make a great contribution, preventing dangerous panic, although usually it will be dependable, lasting traits that do this job of maintaining interpersonal security, a climate of trust that combines due caution with some willingness to give as well as to meet trust. The moral "mother thought," I suggest, is the thought of our power over each other, for good or ill.

When I say that it is thoughts about mutual vulnerability and mutual protection that count when virtue and vice are the issue, I do not intend to overintellectualize the virtues. The thoughts I am concerned with are what Hume would call "lively" thoughts, giving content to desires, emotions, and intentions.[3] Nor do I intend to require an explicit thinking of some particular form to go on in the head of, say, the brave person or the generous one when they display their courage or their generosity. Often the thought of power and vulnerability will be implicit only; sometimes virtue will show in its silencing. My thesis is that the moral virtues regulate, sometimes by increasing the volume of, sometimes by silencing, some variant of the mother thought of our power over each other, for good or ill, and that the point of such attempted regulation is improvement and maintenance of a climate of trust.

This role for trust does not reduce all virtues to trustworthiness, let alone to willingness to trust. To see where we properly trust, we must map the contours of our distrust.[4] Due vigilance, especially in those responsible for the safety of others, will be a virtue, just as much as helpfulness and friendliness. No reductive project is afoot here; indeed, part of my aim is to get an account that can do justice to the full variety of morally excellent traits (a variety I can here only gesture at). There is a sense in which what I am doing here is reexamining an old moral compass and its setting since I will be accepting a fairly traditional list of virtues.

And we can turn to old Thomas Hobbes for suggestions about the plurality of attitudes that may require regulation. The thought of mutual vulnerability is "by divers circumstances diversified," and its due virtuous forms will be equally diverse.[5] Hobbes gives us marvelous analytical lists of passions along with the verbal forms expressing them, and he takes virtues to regulate our desire for preponderance of power over others and our fear of their power. He relies mainly on diversity of grammatical mood to get the variety of verbally expressed passions that may need moral regulation, but he rightly allows that words may be insincere and that "the best signs of passions present are in the countenance, motions of the body, actions and ends or aims which we otherwise know a man to have."[6] Virtues are regulated passions and intentions toward those whom we have some power to help or harm and who have that power over us. Their recognized presence or absence necessarily affects our mutual willingness to be in each other's power and so necessarily affects the climate of trust we live in. (I am here assuming that trust is the absence of apprehension when in another's power, confidence that the trusted will not use that power against us.)

Once we have our list of virtues, taken as regulated attitudes to mutual vulnerability, the question will arise of whether demoralization consists in loss of any of them or whether it is only some, such as fortitude, that are lost to the demoralized person. Fortitude may have a special place among the virtues, and there may be others—some version of faith, hope and love—whose role includes staving off demoralization in stressful times, keeping us steadfast, and enabling us to endure. But before we can consider that, we need some list of virtues and some analysis of the varied ways in which they contribute to a climate of mutual trust by regulating the threats, promises, offers, orders, acceptances, and so on that we make to each other and what we feel toward them.

I begin with what, on this account, become central virtues: thoughtfulness and considerateness. The considerate person is appropriately aware of how her attitudes and actions affect those around her, and if necessary she alters them so as not to cause fear, hurt, annoyance, insult, or disappointment in others, particularly in those who hoped for cooperation or help. If she has more power over the other than that one has over her, she will not flaunt it or use it ruthlessly for her own ends. (She will, for example, silence any thought of the power her knowledge of facts about the other that he would not want made public gives her.) In conversation she will be courteous, willing to listen to others and not force her views upon them. This is the old virtue of doing to others as we would have them do to us if roles were reversed. It is pretty obvious that its presence in people makes for a good climate of trust. Indeed, like its Christian and Kantian versions, this virtue threatens to swallow up all the others, leaving us with no need for a list.

However, a person can have this will to treat others as she hopes herself to be treated but not notice the particular vulnerabilities of those around her. If she is herself thick-skinned, she may not realize how hurtful some of her wit is to the thinner-skinned subjects of it. Or if she is intrepid in adventure, she may drag more timid companions with her on her escapades. She might desist if she were made aware of their distress, but she may fail to notice it. Such a person is thoughtless and imperceptive rather than inconsiderate. Rightly do those who know her come to distrust her moves, become uneasy around her.

The vice of cruelty, deliberately hurting others or threatening to do so, is of course a graver failing than lack of considerateness, thoughtlessness, and lack of perceptiveness. The cruel or malicious person relishes the opportunity and power to inflict disgrace, ridicule, and other more deadly hurt; and even a few such people around can, as anthrax scares have shown us, have dramatic effects on a climate of trust. When the hurt is inflicted in the name of some cause or as part of a "holy war," and when the one inflicting it is ready to share the fate of his or her victims, then fear will verge on terror, and the thought of our vulnerability will be loud and clear. The terrorist is clearly aware of her power to do harm and has made herself invulnerable by her will to martyrdom. It is difficult for us, whose religion respects its own crusaders, to find that the will to kill and to die for a cause is vicious; but there can be no doubt that it ruins a climate of mutual trust. The ruthlessness of the suicide attacker's determination to sacrifice lives, including her own, to her cause leaves us helpless and horrified. The horror is part admiration of such dangerous courage and determined devotion since we have been trained to admire such traits in our own crusaders and martyrs. We are nonplussed by suicide attackers, and that increases our loss of nerve. We look desperately around for some moral high ground, find only swamp, and so flail around. The terrorist planner knows this and so delights in imitating our own cultural heroes, and using, as refuge from our counterattacks, the underground tunnels we ourselves prepared, just as his suicide attackers show the military vir-tues we recognize in our own heroes: "He is bloody minded, and delights in death and destruction. But if the success be on our side, our commander has all the opposite good qualities, and is a pattern of virtue and good conduct. His treachery we call policy. His cruelty is an evil inseparable from war."[7]

The terrorist's violent, deliberate attack on our moral nerve and self-confi-dence must indeed, on this analysis, count, on the face of it, as especially vicious since it aims not to improve but to worsen a climate of trust. But if that attacked climate was a microclimate, that of a privileged group who ignored or refused to alleviate the distress of those outside it or profited from their oppression, then the moral status of terrorism alters. For moral purposes, nothing human can be alien to us, and the climate of trust we should be improving cannot have merely na-tional borders. This does not condone the ruthlessness of terrorist action but rather points us to its causes, to the circumstances that propagate such desperation. The dreadful insecurity that may demoralize the terrorists' surviving victims is the nor-mal condition of life for those on whose behalf some terrorists act. We cannot expect moral virtue from the homeless and starving. Such wretched or oppressed people are not so much demoralized by their conditions of life as never moralized. Morality and moral training presuppose some degree of security of life. If that is absent, then such pockets of security as more fortunate groups may have enjoyed must be at risk from the resentment of those outside their comfort zone. What is a national climate of trust without international justice but a conspirator's cell writ large? Demoralization is a disease of the morally fortunate, a bit like other occupational diseases of the affluent. It is a fall from a state of moral health that the really unfortunate never attain. Their activist groups may have superb morale, but that involves only a few virtues or apparent virtues, in particular courage, discipline, and solidarity. Demoralization may involve loss of these, and so include loss of morale, but it is a more general loss, just as moralization involves more than achievement of reasonably high morale. Morale is the approximation to morality that people in insecure conditions, such as battlefields and disaster zones, can possess. It presupposes a very limited trust, trust in fellow members of one's cadre. It nourishes selected virtues, such as dedication, loyalty, and endurance, but can be accompanied by cruelty, ruthlessness, and disregard for human life.

On this analysis, all moral virtues—those possessions of the morally lucky—contribute to a climate of trust. Respect for the lives and property of others, as virtues, makes a vital contribution to a climate of trust by blocking any thought of resorting to manslaughter or theft in those who might have motive to do so. Some awareness of how easily anyone can be harmed by such acts is proper, and vigilance for one's own security of person and property requires such awareness; but the person who sees every stranger, let alone every acquaintance, as a possible attacker, robber, or thief contributes, just as much as the criminal, to a climate of distrust. Those traumatized by terrible experiences may display such generalized fear and overvigilance; and children, such as those from Romanian orphanages, who have never known emotional or any other sort of security, have an understandable habit of distrust that may be difficult to break. War orphans, who had to scavenge to survive, might also be less than fully respectful of others' property and have an understandable tendency to grab any tempting, easily taken good that lies to hand, even after their conditions of life have improved. Until they not merely are but also feel secure, skills for survival in a state of nature will continue to be exercised. And until they trust their human environment, they cannot be expected to be themselves trustworthy. The relation between trust and the virtues is a two-way dependence. A climate of trust must first exist before we can expect the virtues that sustain it. Aurel Kolnai wrote that "trust in the world . . . can be looked upon, not to be sure as the starting point and very basis, but perhaps as the culmination and epitome of morality."[8] This seems to me exactly wrong. Some degree of trust in the social world is the starting point and very basis of morality.

Those who study the brains of traumatized or neglected children find underdevelopment of the frontal cortex, responsible for emotional regulation. The cingulated gyrus is apparently the brain locus of moral quality and will not develop unless some parent figure talks and plays with the infant. A trusting relationship must initiate the child into normal social interaction. Brain scans and cranial measurement show the lasting, but in principle reversible, damage of "adverse" infant experience.[9] Earlier I spoke of parents as "encouraging" their children to have the wanted attitudes to themselves and others; and if this sort of encouragement from trusted care givers is lacking, then the developing child will literally lack the courage needed to function as a social being, the courage to let others control some aspects of his well-being, to cooperate, and to trust. He may not lack all forms of courage—he may be stoical in physical suffering—but what he will lack is what we could call social courage, the willingness to take the risks that relying on others always involves, the faith or hope that others will not treat him badly. If his infant dealings with people have discouraged him from any trust in them, then he will, of course, be fearful and lacking in social courage.

Courage is a traditional virtue, but as Hume warned, we need to distinguish different versions of it. Military courage, the sort that gets medals, may contribute to death and destruction, not to a secure climate of trust. And that sort is shown as much by the terrorist as the counterterrorist. (This is what high morale involves.) What the "girdle" around the frontal lobes of the brain gives us is a regulation of basic emotions like fear, which can be felt not only on battlefields but also whenever the perceived threat is another person, a social situation, or some other form of our human and human-made environment. (As a child of nine or so, I was fearless in athletic activities and quite at ease in the classroom but terrified of shops and shopkeepers, and when sent to do simple household shopping, I felt as if I were struck dumb at the counter. To me the world of commerce was an alien and threatening place. Only after I, with my parents' encouragement, took a vacation job as a shop attendant, when I was thirteen, did my fear of shops begin to go away. Facing one's demons is the tradition-recommended way to banish them.)

The virtues of self-respect and respect for other persons, proper pride and appropriate modesty, can be seen as Hume saw them, as awareness of one's own strength and its limits, especially in comparison with the strength and power of others. These virtues are essential to a climate of trust in which, given a division of labor, each can count on the competence and goodwill of those whose competence is different from one's own and whose power to affect others is also different. Demoralization can lead to a feeling of total incompetence, helplessness, and loss of self-respect, along with an exaggerated respect, bordering on fear, of others and their power.

Patience with the common failings of others, with their lack of punctuality, tact, consideration, or good sense, is a virtue that allays expectation of anger and, like forgiveness of repentant offenders, restores a tolerable interpersonal atmosphere. Just when we should refuse to forgive and allow our anger expression is a question admitting of no general answer. We do deplore the overmeekness of those who let themselves be trampled on or abused, who forgive the same offense too many times, even when they do so out of love. Is this because such acceptance of wrongs by their victims encourages the wrongdoer, rather than deterring him? Protest at wrongs one has suffered is as much a duty to others who may suffer such wrongs as a matter of self-protection; and the virtue of slowness to anger must be accompanied by that of the courage to resist the abuser if our climate of trust is to be tolerable—at home, in police cells, or in the workplace.

It is fairly obvious how honesty in speech and in voluntary exchanges such as promises and contracts contributes to a climate of trust; indeed, the plausibility of contractarian theories of morality relies on it. As Hume pointed out, promises and contracts allow us to extend secure reliance on delivery of goods or services from simultaneous exchange to nonsimultaneous exchange and future delivery. The whole of commerce and banking rests on this useful "artifice"; but to see the whole of morality as resting on it distorts relationships such as love and friendship—which do not rest on deals, fair or unfair—and equally distorts relations, such as that of benefactor to beneficiary, where the virtues of beneficence and generosity, not that of any sort of agreement keeping, are shown. A tactful benefactor will allow for the pride of the beneficiary and not expect even gratitude in return for her help, or she will make her gift anonymously or somehow disguise it. This is not to deny that graciousness in acceptance of gifts and aid is a virtue and contributes to a climate of trust but merely to recognize that the virtue of gratitude, as Hume and Kant agreed, is a hard one and in some conflict with that of proper pride. As feeding stray cats has shown me, the neediest are the likeliest to bite the hand that feeds them, out of understandable insecurity. It takes time for the really needy to come to trust the one who meets their need.

The virtues of fairness and a sense of social justice are also distinct from fidelity to promises and contracts and from generosity to the needier. These virtues should regulate what particular contracts get made and mitigate the need for people to depend on others' generosity. In a very inegalitarian society, where the gap between the rich and the poor is huge and blatant, there will likely be resentment, leading to theft, robbery, and other illegal acts by the poorest or those who act on their behalf, and a justified feeling of insecurity in the rich. A decent climate of trust demands some measure of equality, not just among citizens of one nation but among nations. Some redistributing of the earth's resources and wealth, rather than a jealous hanging on to what are often ill-gotten gains at the individual or the national level, seems a fairly obvious prerequisite for peace and any reasonable level of mutual trust. We know how, by graduated taxation, to redistribute at the national level, and it should not be beyond us to institute some form of international taxation. The individual virtues we need to cultivate in order to get greater equality are not merely a sense of fairness and the willingness to protest (and relinquish) unfair advantages but also the vision to design workable institutions, both national and international, or to extend existing ones in ways that improve our overall climate of trust.

Hobbes' third "law of nature," that men perform the covenants they have made, would be idle unless there is obedience to his first and second laws: that men seek peace and be willing, in certain conditions, to risk making a covenant, and so to renounce some right or power for the sake of peace. The virtue he called "justice" (keeping agreements) comes in to play only after the prior ones of being peace seeking and tractable enough to enter into a covenant have prepared the way for it. (His fifth law requires a more general tractability.) Such fundamental virtues obviously regulate our attitudes to our power over each other: power to attack, to refuse to renounce power, to wreck the efforts of peacemakers, and to be "stubborn, insociable, forward, intractable." A climate of trust that a person with the Hobbesian virtues will not, by his very virtue, make himself "a prey to others" requires that there be general cultivation of these virtues, that they be the rule, not the exception.

The virtue of conscientiousness, doing what others are counting on us to do, is close to but not the same as doing what one promised or contracted to do. Conscientious parents have not, in having children, contracted with anyone to rear their children carefully. Such duties as parental ones and filial ones are not founded on any sort of agreement, and not all duties of the workplace are taken on in a contract of employment. Others are always vulnerable to our discharge of such duties as we are, for whatever reason, expected to do, and the climate of trust is worsened if duties are neglected. In some conditions, such as industrial disputes or oppressive forms of marriage, the needed virtue may be the spirit to refuse to do what one is unfairly expected to do, but then fair warning will need to have been given so that innocent third parties to the dispute will not be harmed.

Discretion is also distinct, as a virtue, from keeping to agreements since not all of those who confide in us, trusting our discretion, ask for promises of secrecy, and the person of discretion may not always keep such confidences secret but rather show good judgment about when to divulge them. If in the confidence of a suicidal teenager, she may show her discretion in divulging her confidant's intentions to someone who can counsel and help, rather than in keeping quiet. Discretion is good judgement in what we do with sensitive knowledge we have about others. The gossip, the blabbermouth who cannot keep secrets, the industrial spy, the blackmailer, all in different ways misuse the knowledge they have of others' private affairs.

It might be granted that cultivation of the virtues on Hobbes's and Hume's and other lists do contribute to a decent climate of trust without agreement that their very essence lies in this connection. What I am suggesting is that, as trust itself can be seen as the acceptance of vulnerability to the trusted—along with confidence that by trusting in this instance one will not in fact become the prey of the trusted—so each virtue regulates our attitude to some aspect of the mutual vulnerability that makes trust, distrust, and meeting and betraying trust possibilities for us, and does so in a way that preserves and improves our climate of trust. This thesis may seem more plausible with such virtues as fidelity to promises, veracity, and conscientiousness than with others such as respect for life, where, it might be said, the wrong done by the one without the virtue is simply manslaughter, not the inducing of fear for their own lives in survivors of the killer's threats or acts. The latter may be granted to be an ancillary evil done by the killer but not the main evil. What's wrong with murder, it will be claimed, is the taking of a life, whether or not that harms the climate of trust of survivors. But why, then, do we regard the terrorists' disregard for life with such peculiar horror? Lives were taken ruthlessly by those who bombed Dresden and Hiroshima, but they at least could say that they did what they did to hasten surrender and peace. Their commanders may also have intended to demoralize, as a means to that end, and if they did, their killing is to that extent like the terrorists' in that the effect on survivors was essential to their intention. Admittedly my thesis that the moral evil of murder is the terror caused by the murderer, the fear of death rather than the death itself, is counterintuitive. But the history of English criminal law shows that for a long time (until Henry II's reforms) murder was treated as disturbance of the king's peace and as loss of manpower to the victim's family, that is, as a kind of theft; so our common contemporary view that inflicted death mainly wrongs the one whose life is ended may rest more on indoctrination by right-to-lifers than on any insight into eternal moral truths. Respect for life is, of course, generally taken to regulate our attitudes to our power of life or death over each other, but to claim that it does so primarily to improve a climate of trust in security of life, rather than simply to protect and prolong life, is admittedly a controversial thesis. It has the advantage that the assistance in hastening death given to those terminally ill persons who request it can be seen as kindness, not wrongful killing. Once we give up the implausible view that cutting off a human life is always wrong, whether or not the one who dies wants to die, we can see how a climate of trust in hospitals and hospices would be improved, not worsened, if such assistance could be counted on. Of course, there are practical problems about ensuring that the patient's consent has been given, but provided proper safeguards were in place, there would be less, not more, to fear in hospitals were voluntary euthanasia an option. There are fates reasonably deemed worse than death, and continued life with severe disability, dependence, and suffering has a strong claim to be so judged. We should allow those who in their own case do so judge it the right to assistance in ceasing to go on living if our main aim is a decent climate of trust, including trust in health-care workers. Respect for human life is respect for a person's opportunity to make something worth having of her life, and if the ability to do so is gone, respect for the person should include respect for her wish to die.

There are other traditional virtues besides respect for life and property that on the face of it do not seem to have much to do with a climate of trust since they seem to concern primarily the virtue possessor, not her fellow persons. How is our climate of trust the worse if I am greedy in my eating habits, or lazy, or unnecessarily morose? Of course, I will be worse company with such vices, but if I overeat, laze, and gloom away in secret rather than in company, what harm do I do to society? One answer open to me to save my thesis is "none—these are pseudovices." I do not, however, think that matters are quite so clear-cut since these "self-regarding" traits usually connect with other society-related ones. Indeed, eating disorders, inactivity, and depression can signal that demoralization that is fundamentally a loss of social confidence, of the courage to keep going as a functioning member of a group with a shared life. To "resign" from that shared life does affect others, and it will affect a climate of trust if too many become holed up, indulging their solitary vices. So my answer to this objection is not to deny that these matters are moral ones but rather to reject a sharp distinction between what concerns others and what concerns self. One might also explore the notions of self-trust and see self-respect as a sort of private climate of properly regulated self-trust, but I will not do that here.

Suppose it were granted that there is some plausibility in taking virtues to be essentially regulated attitudes to our mutual power and vulnerability, where the regulation serves to improve a climate of trust. What is gained by taking them in this way? A loose unity is thereby given to the virtues, making them more than a mere bundle but not reducing the variety to any one comprehensive virtue. We might even get a little structure into our bundle if some virtues serve to protect others against loss in adverse conditions, and others, those needed for good morale, can, unlike gentler virtues, be cultivated in bad conditions. I suggested that some strengthening "girdle" of social hope, faith, and love might provide the strength not to go to pieces when terrible things happen or the resilience to put ourselves back together, morally speaking, after a temporary collapse. Any virtue can be lost when we are demoralized: our courage, our self-respect, our self-control over fear and anger, our good sense about what to eat and how much, our sociability, our personal cleanliness, even possibly our honesty. In such bad times we tend to lose self-trust, as well as trust in others. We may need to be "retamed," as would an animal after a bad experience at human hands, and this takes extra patience, love, and tact in those who provide support.

I said that I was examining an old compass when I advanced my thesis about the role and essence of moral virtues, but the test of any such thesis is not merely "saving the phenomena" that are already recognized but pointing us to previously overlooked or not sufficiently looked-at ones, as well as relations among them. Do new virtues or new relations between virtues come into view once we see them as I have encouraged us to see them? Well, there is a special importance that accrues to the virtues of social faith, hope, and love, but that is an adaptation of an old thesis. Are there some new virtues protected by these special ones? One is the social inventiveness that enables some to design new trust-extending social "artifices" and to see what reforms of imperfect laws might improve society. Another is the diplomatic skill and understanding that allow some to become good mediators or peacemakers. Hobbes's fifteenth law, to allow mediators safe conduct, is without point unless some are able and willing to perform this vital role of facilitating agreement and peace. Then there is a virtue that as far as I know only Hume has noticed, namely, expressiveness, the complementary virtue to perceptiveness. And inscrutability does become a vice if we must rely on others' facial and other bodily or verbal expressions to know how they are affected by our own actions, expressed feelings, and intentions. John Banville, in his novel *The Untouchable*,[10] has his main character, a spy modeled on the art historian Anthony Blunt, observe that the poet T. S. Eliot had an immobile face, perfect for dissembling. With such people, we do not know where we are and so are uneasy and suspicious. But even with expressive people, we can go wrong in our assumptions about what thoughts and intentions their faces, body language, and actions show. If virtue is an inner quality, then one such virtue must be diffidence in judging others since we can never be sure what exactly was in their head and heart and we do not have infallible access even to our own.

Many virtues come in complementary pairs, like scrutability and perceptiveness. There are helpfulness and gratitude, trustworthiness and some willingness to trust, willingness to enter into mutually beneficial agreements and fidelity to them, willingness to apologize and try to make up for harms done to others and willingness to accept such overtures, self-respect and respect for others, perhaps respect for life and making the most of life, and respect for property and using one's property in a socially responsible manner (including the capitalist virtue of giving gainful employment to others). Putting the emphasis on our mutual dependence encourages us to note such complementarities, the virtue ethics parallel to the complementarity of the deontologists' rights and obligations. Some virtues, such as consideration for others, tact, gentleness, good temper, serenity, patience, and reluctance to condemn, do not need any complement, and new forms of them will come into play as conditions of life and technology change. (Good email manners are not the same as politeness in old-style letters.)

Taking the virtues to be attitudes to those to whom we are vulnerable and who are vulnerable to us is not so very different from taking virtue, singular, to lie in the "maxim" behind one's action or inaction. Taking the crucial thing to be a contribution to the climate of trust that we share is not so different from comembership in a "realm of ends." Hobbes, Hume, and Spinoza may be the more obvious sources for the view I have taken here, but I hope that no reflective moral philosopher is altogether alien to me, so I am happy to note this partial agreement with Kant. My debt to the utilitarians and contractarians is also clear. I have narrowed the aim of morality from the utilitarian's "happiness" to one vital component of it, a good climate of trust, since I do not want to include all personal traits that contribute to human happiness (wit, musical and poetic genius, etc.) as moral virtues, nor do I want to restrict these latter to qualities of will. I have tried to generalize the contractarian's emphasis on reciprocity of contribution and yield, specified in a hypothetical agreement, to something more actual, our sharing in one climate of trust, which each can worsen or make better. Cultivating the virtues is making a contribution to a common good, although there is no way of ensuring that all will equally benefit from it, that none will exploit and damage it. Trying to more closely approximate equality of returns is one of the virtues we will recognize, and this requires vigilance against exploiters and wreckers of the climate of trust.

"Give me my scallop shell of quiet, my staff of faith to walk upon, my scrip of joy . . . my gown of glory, hope's true gage, and thus I'll take my pilgrimage." We may need some secular equivalent of Walter Raleigh's faith and hope if we are to have his joy, his glory (in Hobbes's sense of confidence in power?), and his calm in a world where terror always threatens and death is a certainty. The world has always been like this, so we can use old moral compasses to set our course in it: those of Socrates, who taught us how to die; Aristotle, who taught us how much we need friends and gave us a useful revisable list of social virtues; the Stoics, who taught us serenity and highlighted vulnerability even while denying it; Aquinas, who saw the role for faith, hope, and love; Hobbes, whose perception of morality's main concern with attitudes to power I have relied upon here; Descartes, who taught us that *generosité* that makes us always courteous, affable, and of service to each other; Spinoza who saw how an ethics of cooperation could show us how to increase our power and so show us how to live, as well as to die; Hume, who saw how vital to morality are those social institutions that enable an extension of mutual trust; and so on. With a little judicious tinkering and updating, these old compasses can still guide us.

I have in this essay sketched a method of taking familiar virtues in a slightly new way, as contributors to a good climate of trust. Since I have in other places defended an account of trust that sees it to lie in the attitude of the one who trusts to being in some respect in the power—sometimes but not always the voluntarily given power—of the trusted, and trustworthiness as the ability and willingness to use such power for the expected good, not the harm, of the one who trusts, I take the virtues to include good judgment about when to trust and willingness to meet such reasonable trust, but also to include many other qualities that affect such judgment and such willingness, all of them attitudes to mutual power and vulnerability. I take a climate of trust to be good to the extent that persons can safely trust others, including strangers, officials, makers of machines, builders, and those who issue licenses, control airports, and so on. Some may agree with me about virtues being contributors to a climate of trust but reject my presupposed account of trust, and so perhaps see the inner quality of what persons contribute to its climate differently. Others may more or less accept the account of trust but deny that a good climate of trust is the point of cultivation of the virtues. Some may reject or amend my incomplete list of virtues—for instance, ask how or if integrity and avoidance of hypocrisy fits into this account. (Are they part of self-respect?) Some may think I have quite misunderstood demoralization. There is much more work to be done to defend and elaborate the suggestions I have advanced, especially when it comes to the three descendants of the old "theological" virtues of faith, hope, and love, to which I have assigned an important role. I once did explore "secular faith," and those of us who have written about an ethics of care have to some extent addressed the sort of loving concern a secular morality needs to cultivate, but hope is for me a whole new territory to explore.[11] One of the good things about virtue ethics is that there is always something more to be said and that nothing, neither the list of virtues nor analysis of them, is ever final.

Notes

I am grateful to Karen Jones for drawing my attention to the topic of demoralization and to her and to Kurt Baier for helpful comments on a draft of this paper.

1. See David Hume, *A Treatise of Human Nature*, ed. Peter H. Nidditch and L. A. Selby-Bigge (Oxford: Clarendon Press, 1990), 477.

2. For a good discussion of this debate, see Peter Goldie, *The Emotions, a Philosophical Exploration* (Oxford: Oxford University Press, 2000), 160–175.

3. James Martineau, *Types of Ethical Theory* (Oxford: Clarendon Press, 1886), 468, called emotion "thought in a glow."

4. Ajay Close's heroine, in her novel *Official and Doubtful* (London: Secker & Warburg, 1996), 272–273, is said to trust her lover "enough, which is to say she'd comprehensively mapped the contours of her distrust."

5. See Thomas Hobbes, *Leviathan*, chap. 6, para. 13.

6. Ibid., para. 56.

7. See Hume, *Treatise of Human Nature*, 348.

8. See Aurel Kolnai, "Forgiveness," in *Ethics, Value and Reality*, ed. Bernard Williams and David Wiggins (Indianapolis, Ind.: Hackett, 1978).

9. The research is being done by Bruce Perry, at the Child Trauma Academy in Houston, and Peter Fonagy, University College, London, as reported by Jo Carlowe in the *Observer* January 2002, 19–20.

10. John Banville, *The Untouchable* (London: Picador, 1997).

11. On our bookshelves we have three so far unread German volumes about it by Ernst Bloch, so I have little excuse.

IV

Achieving Adequate Moral Understandings

11

Kant on Arrogance and Self-Respect

Robin S. Dillon

The driver who refuses to wait his turn at the merge point; the self-proclaimed expert who dismisses your views without even considering them or treats your ignorance with contempt; the coworker who regards his project as so much more important than yours and demands an unfair share of the resources; the administrator who tries to impose his vision on the department without consulting the department members; the boss who makes it clear that his way is the only right way; the person who insists that you drop what you are doing and attend to his needs *now*; the church official who says, in defense of a priest accused of child molestation, that the negligence of the six-year-old boy and his family contributed to the abuse;[1] the doctor who disdainfully dismisses the idea that you might know something about your own condition; the telemarketer who assumes you have nothing better to do with your time than listen to his sales pitch;[2] the relative who insists that he knows what's best for you and acts for you without your knowledge or consent—the arrogance of some people can be irritating, frustrating, enraging, even dangerous. And it doesn't take a Kantian to see the disrespect that arrogance expresses. It also doesn't take much to see that being arrogant can be a very effective way to get what one wants. "Bad for you, perhaps," the arrogant person might say as he blithely disregards my rights, "but good for me." But is it? Is there no self-regarding reason to not be arrogant?

When writing about different kinds of self-respect, I once claimed that there is such a reason—a reason of self-respect. In particular, I claimed that arrogance is the vice of excess, as servility is the vice of deficiency, in relation to which one kind of self-respect is the mean; thus, inasmuch as a person has strong self-regarding reasons to be self-respecting, she has as strong a reason to not be arrogant as she does to not be servile.[3] I derived this picture of arrogance and self-respect not from Aristotle, as might be expected (although I would argue that it is there), but from Kant. As part of a larger project of understanding the nature and moral importance of self-respect, I want in this essay to revisit Kant's account of arrogance. For a more careful examination of what Kant has to say reveals that the connection between arrogance and self-respect is more complex than I had previously suggested; indeed, arrogance is opposed in several different ways to several kinds of self-respect. But there is more than conceptual tidiness of interest here. What Kant has to say about arrogance and self-respect makes it clear that arrogance is the deadliest of moral vices and why self-respect is the very core of morality.

I am interested in arrogance and so in what Kant has to say about it not only as someone who is professionally and personally interested in questions of self-respect but also as a feminist. For arrogance is quite clearly a gendered concept. As I have been reading around—in philosophy, in dictionaries, in newspapers and magazines, in literature—for help in understanding arrogance, it has struck me that women are rarely called arrogant. Women are called proud, vain, supercilious, haughty, disdainful, imperious, and presumptuous; but even though women can exhibit characteristics that would make it appropriate to call them arrogant, the epithet is rarely applied. The very few examples I have come across suggest why. For instance, the PBS series, "The Roman Empire in the First Century," quotes Tacitus's judgment of Agrippina, wife of and effectively coruler with the emperor Claudius: "This was a woman without feminine frivolity. She was openly severe and often arrogant. [Her] dominance was almost masculine. Agrippina turned her back on Roman ideals of feminine virtue by seizing power directly and using it proudly."[4] Arrogance is a decidedly a masculine trait, one quite obviously about power. Feminists thus have reason to ask, "To what extent are the mainstream conceptions of arrogance and its opposites reflections of, and to what extent is arrogance itself an instrument of, sociopolitical arrangements of domination and subordination?"[5] I suspect that "arrogance" functions in the way Catherine MacKinnon showed us that "rape" has functioned legally: understood as "using more force than usual," it secretly legitimizes unjust treatment and relationships.[6] That is, I suspect that arrogance typically involves claiming more than one's already illegitimate share of power, rights, and authority. Developing this suspicion unfortunately lies outside the scope of this essay. However, taking a cue from Agrippina, and reflecting on the everyday effectiveness of the power of arrogance in getting what one wants raises a rather different question to which Kant's account can speak: might arrogance in women and in other subordinated people be valuable in struggles against domination? I have argued elsewhere that one kind of self-respect is a virtue that subordinated people need in order to deal effectively with oppression.[7] But we might wonder if it isn't arrogance that's the virtue in such circumstances, the virtue of unsubordinating insubordinance. If Kant is right, however, arrogance, though potentially unsubordinating, is not a trait that self-respecting feminists could wholeheartedly embrace.

Interpersonal Arrogance and Respect for Others

Kant discusses arrogance throughout his ethical works.[8] One striking aspect of these discussions is that what he is talking about on some occasions is clearly rather different from, though not unrelated to, what he is talking about on other occasions.[9] He does not consistently draw explicit distinctions regarding arrogance, but his treatment does correspond roughly to the contemporary tendency to think of arrogance in two different, though not unrelated, ways. Consequently, I shall say that Kant discusses two different, though not unrelated, kinds of arrogance, which I'll call "primary arrogance" and "interpersonal arrogance." Kant explicitly contrasts primary arrogance with self-respect and interpersonal arrogance with respect for others. However, his account of interpersonal arrogance reveals that it also arises from a failure of self-respect. Thus arrogance, on Kant's view, always involves a violation of the core moral duty of self-respect.

Let us begin with interpersonal arrogance. I expect that most of us think first of arrogance as essentially interpersonal, a matter of how someone regards and interacts with other people.[10] This arrogant individual is generally thought to be someone who treats other people contemptuously, disdainfully, peremptorily, or without consideration, making it clear that he views them as less important, less valuable than his very important, very valuable self. His opinions must, of course, be accepted by benighted others; his needs, desires, and projects must take priority over their trifling ones. This view of arrogance is expressed in the definition given in the *American Heritage Dictionary*: "a sense of overbearing self-worth or self-importance, marked by or arising from an assumption of one's superiority towards others."[11] The dictionary lists as synonyms "proud," "haughty," "disdainful," and "supercilious"; all involve "an inflated ego and disdain for what one considers inferior."[12] Arrogance thus contrasts with mere conceit. Whereas the conceited person has an excessively high opinion of his worth, the arrogant person not only has a high opinion of his worth—which may be but need not be (if we are talking about the worth of his personal merits or accomplishments) unjustifiably high—but also views himself as superior to other people, not only superior in merit but superior in status, and hence as entitled to treat them as his inferiors: to disdain them, dismiss their views and perspectives out of hand, ignore their concerns, make demands on them, and expect their deference. The infuriating people with whom this essay began exemplify interpersonal arrogance.

Kant develops a view of interpersonal arrogance as one of the vices that violate our duty to respect other human beings as such. Although I said it doesn't take a Kantian to see that arrogance is profoundly disrespectful, it is useful to look at Kant's explanation of just how it is disrespectful. In the *Metaphysics of Morals* he writes, "Arrogance [*Hochmut*][13] (*superbia* and, as the word expresses it, the inclination to be always *on top*) is a kind of *ambition* [*Ehrbegierde*] (*ambitio*) in which we demand that others think little of themselves in comparison with us . . . arrogance demands from others a respect it denies them. . . . Arrogance is, as it were, a solicitation on the part of one seeking honor for followers, whom he thinks he is entitled to treat with contempt" (AK 6:465; MM 581). This presumptuous "lack of modesty in one's claims to be *respected* by others," which Kant also calls "self-conceit [*Eigendünkel*] (*arrogantia*)" (AK 6:462; MM 579), is "therefore a vice opposed to the respect that every human being can lawfully claim" (AK 6:465; MM 581).

The respect that arrogance denies others is what I have elsewhere called "interpersonal recognition respect": the basic respect that, on Kant's view, is owed to each person by every person.[14] As rationally autonomous moral agents—beings with the capacity to choose freely to act on purely rational motives—persons have dignity, an intrinsic absolute and incomparable worth that is independent of personal qualities, social status, and accomplishments and failures, including one's record as a moral agent. In virtue of this dignity, persons are ends in themselves, each fundamentally equal to every other. The moral law categorically forbids treating persons as if they were things, that is, treating beings of absolute intrinsic worth as if they had value only relative to someone's feelings or desires, treating ends in themselves as if they were at best merely means to be used to get something else that someone happens to want or need. The dignity of each person must always be acknowledged by every person, in attitude as well as in action; interpersonal recognition respect is the practical acknowledgement of dignity. In particular, interpersonal recognition respect for someone as a person among persons involves recognizing that she is a being with dignity, valuing her as an end in herself, understanding at least implicitly the moral constraints on moral agents to which the dignity of persons gives rise, having the attitudes that such appreciation involves, and acting in regard to her only in morally appropriate ways out of this appreciation of her as a person. Interestingly, what Kant emphasizes in discussing the duties of respect for others is not actions we must or must not perform but attitude, and, in particular, the way we are to value ourselves in light of the way we are morally obligated to value others. As Kant puts it, respect for others is "to be taken in a practical sense (*observantia aliis praestanda*), as a *maxim* of limiting our self-esteem by the dignity of humanity in another person" (AK 6:449; DV 116–117). The duty of respect is a negative one "of not exalting oneself above others," which is "contained in the maxim of not abasing any other man to a mere means to my end (not demanding that the other degrade himself in order to slave for my end)" (AK 6:450; DV 117). In fulfilling this duty I "contain myself within certain limits in order to detract nothing from the worth that the other, as a man, is entitled to posit in himself" (AK 6:450; DV 117). What this last point makes clear is that what is at stake in the duty to respect others is their self-respect. All persons have a moral right to posit an absolute inner worth in themselves; but more than this, they have a moral duty to value themselves as ends in themselves and equals among equals. The duty to respect others thus includes the duty to refrain from anything that would threaten another person's right and duty to respect themselves and to do this out of modesty, that is, by willingly restricting our claims to be valued by others (AK 6:462).[15]

Arrogance is one of several vices that Kant discusses as violating the duty to respect others. Insofar as they involve "deny[ing] them the respect owed to human beings in general" (AK 6:463; MM 579), these vices are forms of contempt, which is "judging something to be worthless" (AK 6:462; MM 579). Arrogance involves contemptuous disrespect in several ways. First, the arrogant person does not regard others as his equals in moral importance whose rights, projects, views, or feelings he has to take into consideration when deciding how to act. Rather, he regards them as annoying obstacles he has to deal with, as incompetent or dim-witted idiots that he has to take in hand, as things he might use to further his desires, or simply as morally irrelevant. He thus does not see them as sources of moral constraints on getting what he wants. Second, what the arrogant person wants is not merely to have his view accepted, get resources for his project, advance his car a few feet more a few seconds sooner, and so on but also and more importantly to heighten his own self-esteem. He does this in two ways: by, as Kant says, "demanding," "extorting," or "compelling" respect from others (AK 27:409, 27:620, 27:666; L 174, 363, 400) or, more accurately, the appearance that they value him highly, and by making explicit the lower esteem in which he holds them. Their deference marks for him their "respect"; his disdainful glance, contemptuous snort, obstinately blank look, or refusal to engage marks for them his disesteem. In the *Lectures*, Kant makes it clear that the kind of self-worth the arrogant person cares about is essentially comparative and competitive. Arrogance is an inclination to think highly of oneself, but it asks "not what one is worth, but how much more one is worth than another"; the arrogant person "already believes in his own worth, but he esteems it solely by the lesser status of other people" (AK 27:241; L 17). The arrogant person can't have the worth he values unless others manifestly have little worth in comparison to him; hence he is moved both to demand esteem from others and to make it clear to everyone how little he values them.

The third way in which arrogance involves contemptuous disrespect is that the arrogant individual demands not only that others value him more highly than he deserves but also that they value themselves much less than they deserve. Specifically, he demands not just that they think of themselves as, for example, less intelligent or their projects as less worthwhile but also that they think of themselves as having a fundamentally lower status than he does, as deserving less in the way of basic respect and common courtesy. What he demands is that they willingly acquiesce to his demands, that they acknowledge in their unhesitating submission to him the rightness of his priority and their status as inferior. The arrogant individual, that is, requires that others sacrifice their self-respect in order to advance his self-interest and boost his self-esteem. And he demands this of them because, with their acquiescence in their devaluing, the arrogant person can "think he is entitled to treat [them] with contempt" (AK 6:465; MM 581). There is moral sleight of hand here. He could be entitled to treat others with contempt only if they are in fact worthless (or at least worth less), and if they are worthless, then he is not arrogant: his attitudes toward and treatment of them are nothing but just. If they accede to their fundamental inferiority, then his self-esteem gets an additional boost: his just assessment and treatment of them attests to his greater moral merit.

Arrogance is a violation of respect for others because it both denies the intrinsic dignity of others and strikes at their self-respect. Thus, since we have a categorical moral obligation always to acknowledge that others are ends in themselves and never to hinder them in fulfilling their duty to respect themselves, we have the strongest other-regarding reason to not be arrogant. But it does not seem, from what I've said, that a person has any self-regarding reason of self-respect to not be arrogant. Indeed, it seems that just the opposite is true: the increase to self-esteem that arrogance seeks is a strong self-regarding reason to be arrogant. However, in his discussion of interpersonal arrogance, Kant hints that things are not as they seem. For he contrasts arrogance not only with respect for others but also with "pride proper [*Stolz*] (*animus elatus*), which is *love of honor* [*Ehrliebe*], that is, a concern to yield nothing of one's human dignity in comparison with others (so that the adjective '*noble*' [*edlen*] is usually added to 'pride' in this sense)" (AK 6: 65; *MM* 581). And in the *Lectures* he tells us that true noble pride [*wahre edle Stolz*] is one of two elements of proper self-respect (AK 27:348; *L* 129).[16] But to fully understand how interpersonal arrogance involves a lack of self-respect, we need first to examine what Kant has to say about the other kind of arrogance.

Primary Arrogance, Servility, and Self-Respect

Interpersonal arrogance essentially involves regarding and treating others as if they were one's inferiors. But not all forms of arrogance involve relating to others this way. Indeed, some forms of arrogance don't involve relating to others at all. Consider the following examples.

1. A newspaper story about an exhibit of the photographs of Alfred Stieglitz relates that Stieglitz met artist Georgia O'Keeffe, who later married him, when he exhibited her charcoal drawings without her knowledge or permission.[17] "When she protested, he replied: 'You have no more right to withhold those pictures than to withdraw a child from the world.'" A series of photographs of O'Keeffe is said to exhibit "the same sort of charming arrogance" in two ways. First, Stieglitz "directed her as a performer in still movies. Here she is, modeling the steely androgyny of Gertrude Stein. Here she is, exuding the granite-chinned saltiness of a Winslow Homer sailor. Here her hand is caressing an animal skull as if it she's playing an instrument of nature." Second, as one photo historian remarks, Stieglitz tried through 350 photographs "to know his wife" but failed "because of who she was." "More complicated" and "far more sophisticated artistically then he was," O'Keeffe "wasn't a guy's wife, she was a titan!" The arrogance of Stiegliz and his photographs did not involve regarding or treating O'Keeffe as in any way inferior to him. Rather, Stieglitz was arrogant, first, for acting as if he had the right to show her work without her permission and, second, for assuming he had the ability to understand and capture her in his photographs. The photographs themselves seem to depict arrogance insofar as they portray O'Keeffe as powerful, aloof, manly, and capable of compelling nature to serve her.

2. The Lehigh Valley, where I live, comprises numerous small cities, boroughs, and townships spread across two counties. One of the three chambers of commerce that serve businesses in the area recently changed its name from the Lehigh County Chamber of Commerce to the Lehigh Val-

ley Chamber of Commerce, thereby claiming to represent all businesses in a much larger geographic region. It did this without consulting either the businesses it had not previously served or the other two chambers of commerce. This unilateral move prompted the chairman of one of the other chambers to call the renaming "arrogant and pretentious." "How can they think they can fairly represent the areas?"[18]

3. A young, beginning investor bought stock only to watch the price fall. Reflecting on lessons learned, he "concedes that it probably was 'good for me in the long run that it went down. I did kind of have this arrogance that because I owned it, it was going to go up.'"[19]

4. Physicist Subramanyan Chandrasekhar ascribed the inability of most physicists to do innovative work as they get older to "a certain arrogance toward nature. . . . These people had great insights and made profound discoveries. They imagine afterwards that the fact that they succeeded so triumphantly in one area means that they have a special way of looking at science that must be right. But . . . nature has shown over and over again that the kinds of truth which underlie nature transcend even the most powerful minds."[20]

5. Soon after John F. Kennedy, Jr., his wife, Carolyn Bessette Kennedy, and her sister Lauren Bessette were killed when the private plane he was piloting crashed, I read, on the one hand, numerous eulogies of Kennedy that spoke of his humility and modesty, surprising in one so famous and privileged, and, on the other hand, several criticisms blaming his arrogance for the crash. The arrogance lay, it was said, in his trying to fly a too-powerful plane in bad visibility conditions without having been trained to fly by instruments and with a recently-broken ankle that was too weak to work the pedals that controlled the plane. The arrogance lay, that is, in the apparent assumption that he was capable of transcending constraints that might hamper others, that he was somehow immune to the laws of physics and the realities of nature that evening.[21]

6. Writing not long after the September 11, 2001, terrorist attacks on the United States, columnist Roger Rosenblatt criticized those who "would like to think that God is on our side against the terrorists, because the terrorists are wrong and we are in the right, and any deity worth his salt would be able to discern that objective truth." This, he said, is "good-hearted arrogance . . . the same kind of thinking that makes people decide that God created humans in his own image. (See the old *New Yorker* cartoon that shows a giraffe in a field thinking, 'And God made giraffes in his own image.')"[22]

7. Young wizard-in-training Harry Potter, who had been forbidden to leave Hogwarts School for his own protection, was caught sneaking out by Professor Snape, who snarled, "Famous Harry Potter is a law unto himself. . . . Famous Harry Potter goes where he wants to, with no thought for the consequences. . . . How extraordinarily like your father you are, Potter. . . . He too was exceedingly arrogant. . . . Your father didn't set much store by rules either. . . . Rules were for lesser mortals."[23] Later, thinking he had saved Harry from being murdered by someone whom Harry then defends,

Snape repeated the charge: "You would have been well-served if he'd killed you. You'd have died like your father, too arrogant to believe you might be mistaken."[24]

In none of these examples do we see someone who believes himself to be superior to others and consequently looks down on them and treats them with disdain or contempt. These are thus not cases of interpersonal arrogance. Rather, they are cases of primary arrogance. This kind of arrogance is what the *O.E.D.* defines as "the taking of too much upon oneself as one's right; the assertion of unwarrantable claims in respect of one's own importance; undue assumption of dignity, authority, or knowledge; aggressive conceit, presumption, or haughtiness."[25] This definition makes it clear that to be arrogant is to arrogate, that is, "to assume as a right that to which one is not entitled; to lay claim to and appropriate (a privilege, advantage, etc.) without just reason or through self-conceit, insolence, or haughtiness (from L., to ask or claim for oneself)."[26] Stieglitz claims the right to exhibit O'Keeffe's pictures; Snape thinks that Potter assumes he has a right to act however he wants, never mind the rules; the chamber of commerce assumes the authority to represent all businesses in a larger geographic region; theists claim the prerogative to make God in their own image. To label them arrogant is to say both that they have no such right or authority and that they ought to know that they don't. Stieglitz also claims a certain artistic ability; Potter and the physicists are said to assume that they have a certain intellectual power and knowledge; Kennedy and the investor claim both a certain power and an immunity from foreseeable harms—to call them arrogant is to say that the abilities they do have give them no reason to think that they are able to do what they claim to be able to do, and that any reasonable person would know that. Arrogance is not, however, a matter of mistake, stupidity, or irrationality. The arrogant person always has subjectively the strongest reason for claiming and assuming what he does: he wants it. What distinguishes the arrogant person from the merely desirous person is that the former presumes entitlement: that he wants it gives him a right to it, and so he shall have it. Primary arrogance is thus the exercise of a certain kind of power in the service of desire, masquerading as a perfectly reasonable entitlement claim.

Interpersonal arrogance, it should be clear, is a type of primary arrogance. The disdain for others in the former rests on several unwarrantable claims: the claim to have greater worth than others, the claim to have superiority over them, the claim to be entitled to their deference. Interpersonal arrogance can develop out of primary arrogance. For example, the unjustified assumption that one is unusually intelligent might lead one to suppose that one is intellectually superior to others; the assumption that intellectual superiority is what really matters might give rise to a presumption that one occupies a loftier position overall. The appropriation of superior status might in turn engender, on the one hand, contempt for others that one deems inferior in intellect and status and, on the other hand, the assumption that one is entitled to their deference.[27] The sphere of arrogation expands through a series of inferences,[28] each step being a matter not of explicit reflection on the reasonableness of such a move but, rather, of taking more for granted, each implicit taking motivated by a desire for what the next step provides. And it is the first unwarranted taking, the step of primary arrogance, that is the really big one.

As we saw, Kant's discussion of interpersonal arrogance in the *Metaphysics of Morals* explicitly identifies it as opposed to our duties to respect others. Earlier in the book he treats arrogance in connection with servility, one of the vices opposed to our duties to respect ourselves, and this time it is primary arrogance that is in focus. It is this discussion that had suggested to me the view of arrogance and servility as the vices of excess and deficiency in relation to the proper valuing of oneself that is the virtue of self-respect.

Kant's discussion of servility begins, as did the discussion of interpersonal arrogance, by emphasizing the dignity, or absolute inner worth, that persons have simply as persons. Each person has equal dignity and so is owed respect from all other persons; but each of us also has a duty to respect ourselves, that is, a duty to pursue our ends always with consciousness of our dignity and status as persons. Servility, which Kant also calls false or lying humility, is deliberate self-abasement: "the disavowal of all claim to any moral worth in oneself" either to "acquire a borrowed worth" or "merely as a means to acquiring the favor of another"(AK 6: 435–436; DV 100–101). This, he says, "is contrary to one's duty to oneself since it degrades one's personality" (AK 6:36; MM 558). That is, in conveying to others a sense of himself as something less than a being with dignity, the servile person violates the duty of self-respect.

The kind of self-respect in focus here is what I have elsewhere called "interpersonal recognition self-respect," the application to oneself of the kind of respect one owes all persons. It involves properly acknowledging and valuing oneself as a being with fundamental worth, an equal person among persons and an end in oneself. Those with interpersonal recognition self-respect regard certain forms of attitude and treatment from others as their due as a person and other forms as degrading and beneath the dignity of persons; and, other things equal, they are not willing to be regarded or treated by others in ways that mark them as less than a person. This aspect corresponds to Kant's "proper pride," with which, as we saw earlier, he contrasts interpersonal arrogance and which he identifies as love of honor, "a concern to yield nothing of one's human dignity in comparison with others" (AK 6:65; MM 581). But this is precisely what the servile individual does yield as he invites others to regard him as a being of a lesser kind. Servility conveys the view that the moral community is not a relation of equals but a hierarchy of two moral castes, one composed of beings with higher fundamental worth and the other, to which one belongs, of beings with lower fundamental worth who deserve much less in the way of consideration and respect. Servility thus involves a false valuation of the self.

As Kant makes clear, however, servility is not simply a matter of misunderstanding human worth; it is motivated self-abasement. Kant calls what he is discussing "lying humility" (AK 6:436; MM 558), and this lie is motivated, as lies typically are, by a desire for something else. The servile person disavows his true moral worth because he wants to be valued in some other way. Perhaps the individual claims to be of little importance compared to others in order, like Uriah Heep in *David Copperfield*, to gain their trust so as to take advantage of them; perhaps the individual pretends, as did a quite talented girl I knew in junior high school, to be insignificant in the belief that others admire and like humble people; perhaps the individual is willing to be bossed around by others or to be their lapdog in exchange for their protection or financial support. But whatever the specifics, the servile person makes himself "a plaything of the mere inclinations and hence a thing" (*AK* 6:420; *MM* 545). Two sets of inclinations dominate here: the servile person's own desires, such as the desire to be liked by others or to think well of himself for his humility or cleverness, and the feelings and desires of those whose favor he seeks, especially their desire for a self-esteem that feeds on the deference of others. What, at bottom, makes servility wrong, Kant explains, is that it is a violation of the "prohibition against depriving [oneself] of the *prerogative of a moral being*, that of acting in accordance with principles, that is, inner freedom" through the willingness to let one's choices be determined by the inclinations rather than by reason (*AK* 6:420; *MM* 545). Thus, as Kant describes it here, servility is not the possibly blameless misunderstanding of one's basic rights and status as a person that might, for example, characterize someone who was raised to believe she was a lesser sort of being than others.[29] It is rather the deliberate and so culpable devaluing of oneself, and it is self-devaluation twice over. Servility is the devaluation of one's moral worth and status vis-à-vis others, the lying denial that one is a being with dignity whose status as an end in oneself must always be acknowledged in attitude and action, one's own as well as those of others. And insofar as it involves the subjection of one's power of rational choice to inclinations, servility devalues that which, on Kant's view, is most truly one's self: the rationality that makes one a person. As a doubly false valuation of the self, then, servility is the failure to have interpersonal recognition self-respect.

Kant introduces arrogance in the midst of his analysis of servility, contrasting it explicitly with (genuine) humility and servility and so implicitly with self-respect:

> The consciousness and feeling of the insignificance of one's moral worth *in comparison with the law* is humility [*Demut*] (*humilitas moralis*). A conviction of the greatness of one's moral worth, but only from failure to compare it with the law, can be called *moral arrogance* [*Tugendstolz*] (*arrogantia moralis*).—Waiving any claim to moral worth in oneself, in the belief that one will thereby acquire a borrowed worth, is morally false *servility* [*Kriecherei*] (*humilitas spuria*). (*AK* 435; *MM* 558)

This is a puzzling paragraph, and there are at least three ways to interpret what Kant is saying about arrogance here, which I'll consider in turn. Each interpretation links primary arrogance with a different kind of self-respect.

Primary Arrogance and Interpersonal Recognition Self-Respect

One question on which the different interpretations hang is about what Kant means by "moral worth" [*moralischen Wert*], of the greatness of which the arrogant person is convinced. The first interpretation looks to the surrounding discussion of servility and interprets "moral worth" as fundamental worth or dignity [Würde].[30] Whereas servility is claiming too little fundamental worth, arrogance is claiming too much; both contrast with the mean in basic self-valuing, which is interpersonal recognition self-respect. The arrogant person, on this reading, shares with the servile person the view of the moral community as organized hierarchically, but he sees himself as a member of the upper caste, with all the rights and privileges pertaining thereto. In particular, as we saw earlier, the arrogant person sees himself as entitled—by virtue of his dignity and higher status—to respect from others that they do not deserve from him. In valuing himself too highly, the arrogant person values himself just as falsely as does the servile person. And like servility, arrogance is motivated by desire, but in a more straightforward fashion: the arrogant person inflates his worth vis-à-vis others in order to heighten his self-esteem. Thus arrogance also involves the subjection of the will to the inclinations; the arrogant person makes himself a "plaything of the mere inclinations and hence a thing" and so fails to respect himself as an end in himself. The servile person sets his value in relation to others too low, the arrogant person sets it too high, and each does so because he wants to esteem himself and thinks, wrongly, that this self-valuation is more important. By contrast, the person with interpersonal recognition self-respect knows the real value of himself and of the different forms of self-valuation and he values himself vis-à-vis others correctly.

However, this mean-and-extremes picture is actually misleading, for arrogant false self-valuation isn't really too much of a good thing. The arrogant person does not posit in himself too much of the right kind of worth. The failing is deeper than this. Because dignity is a noncomparative, nonscalar form of worth—all persons have it equally and absolutely—the arrogant person can't claim more dignity than his due. Rather, what he claims isn't dignity at all. The valuation of self at the heart of arrogance is thus much more seriously false than a mere measurement error; it manifests a warped view of the worth of persons. The only worth he understands and values, recall, is scalar—comparative and competitive. So, the problem is not just that he does not regard others as ends in themselves or is motivated by considerations of self-esteem to deny that others are his equals in fundamental worth and status, making him liable to treat them disrespectfully. The deeper problem is that he cannot regard any being as an end in itself, as unconditionally deserving of respect, himself included. Thus, Kant says, the arrogant person is always "*mean* [*niederträchtig*] in the depths of his soul. For he would not demand that others think little of themselves in comparison with him unless he knew that, were his fortune suddenly to change, he himself would not find it hard to grovel and to waive any claim to respect from others" (AK 6:466; MM 582). And "meanness" or self-abasement [*Niederträchtigkeit*], as Kant says in the *Lectures*, is the opposite of self-respect (AK 27:349; L 129).[31] Servility and arrogance, which seemed so far apart, are in fact not so very different underneath.

The interpersonal arrogance that disrespects others thus arises from a primary arrogance—an unwarranted claim to moral worth—that at bottom does not respect the self. So, even if the arrogant person was scrupulous in treating others morally appropriately (through, e.g., prudence or fear), his primary arrogance would still be intrinsically morally bad and a direct violation of the categorical imperative inasmuch as it involves a failure of interpersonal recognition self-respect: not valuing an absolutely valuable being—himself—as he morally ought to be valued.

This interpretation of primary arrogance applies to many of our everyday examples of arrogance, including Stieglitz, rude drivers, Snape's "Potter the rule breaker," dictatorial bosses and administrators, authority-grabbing theists[32] and chambers of commerce, and paternalists, all of whom claim to have rights or status that they don't in fact have. It also makes it clear that interpersonal arrogance, insofar as it arises from primary arrogance, needn't always involve contempt for others. Indeed, arrogance not only can benefit others, as Stieglitz's showing of O'Keeffe's drawings did, but also can be motivated by a desire to benefit others, as in the case of paternalism. This analysis also highlights the self-regarding danger of primary arrogance (while not downplaying the other-regarding wrong of disrespect in interpersonal arrogance). For those who claim rights or a status they don't have don't get the goods without paying a stiff price: not only do they fail to appreciate something of utmost importance about themselves, but the sense of worth underlying their claims is precarious, subject to deflation should their fortunes change. Moreover, arrogance is ultimately self-defeating. For as Kant points out, in trying to exercise power over others by demanding their esteem and deference, the arrogant person actually hands them power over his self-valuation, thus giving up on *self*-respect (AK 27:666–667; L 400), and ensures that they will not give him the esteem that he wants, "for the more he shows that he is trying to obtain respect, the more everyone denies it to him" (AK 465; MM 582).[33] Interpersonal recognition self-respect, which acknowledges the equality, rights, and dignity of others in the acknowledgment of its own proper dignity and status, not only is our moral duty but also promises unconditional security of self-worth, which seems to be what the arrogant person is really after.

Primary Arrogance and Evaluative Self-Respect

The first way to interpret Kant's reference to arrogance in the passage from the *Metaphysics of Morals* focused on the contrast with servility and tied the discussion of primary arrogance in connection with our duty of self-respect to that of interpersonal arrogance in connection with our duty to respect others. However, Kant frequently discusses arrogance without linking it to disrespect of others. The second interpretation of the *Metaphysics of Morals* passage connects it to these other discussions by focusing on the contrast Kant draws between (primary) arrogance and (genuine) humility. This interpretation also brings in a second concept of moral worth and a second kind of self-respect. Recall the contrast: "The consciousness and feeling of the insignificance of one's moral worth [*moralischen Werts*] *in comparison with the law is humility* [*Demut*] (*humilitas moralis*). A conviction of the greatness of one's moral worth [*Werts*], but only from failure to compare it with the law, can be called *moral arrogance* [*Tugendstolz*] (*arrogantia moralis*)."

What Kant says about humility might seem puzzling, for in the immediately preceding paragraph he argues, in effect, that persons have dignity in virtue of the ability to create moral law through our willing, which is the function of morally practical reason. So it seems odd to be struck by the insignificance of one's moral worth in comparison to the law of which one is the author. But the oddness dissolves if we understand "moral worth" to be not dignity but what I'll call "moral merit." Whereas dignity is the absolute and unconditional worth that all persons have equally simply in virtue of being persons, that is, beings capable of freely choosing to act through a purely rational motive, moral merit is conditional worth, which individuals earn more or less of through virtue, that is, by willing maxims in accordance with the categorical imperative and so realizing our capacity to act rationally.[34] As Kant explains in the *Lectures*, when we compare our moral performance to the standard of perfection set by the moral law, even the morally best of us fall short, so that moral humility—having a low opinion of our moral merit—is appropriate. Humility, which "presupposes a *correct estimation* of self" (AK 27:39; L 16), is "the curbing of any high opinion of our moral worth, by the comparison of our actions with the moral law" (AK 27:350; L 129). By contrast, arrogance [*Tugendstolz*, literally, "virtue pride"] involves claiming great moral merit, a claim greater than anyone is entitled to make.[35]

Moral merit is grounds for a kind of self-respect different from that grounded on dignity, which I call "evaluative self-respect."[36] Evaluative self-respect involves the judgment that one's character and conduct at least come up to scratch in the absence of significant moral demerit; it may also include thinking well of oneself on account of positive moral merit.[37] Self-judgment is always liable to warping by inattention, blindness to one's flaws, bias, self-deception, and so on,[38] but warranted evaluative self-respect involves judging correctly that one is genuinely trying to live morally appropriately while also acknowledging that one still falls far short in comparison with what is morally required. The moral value of evaluative self-respect lies in the importance of the disposition to appraise one's conduct and character and to regulate oneself in light of one's findings to moral motivation, moral self-development, and reflective self-government. Evaluating oneself and caring enough about the results of the survey to stake one's sense of self on them is essential to keeping oneself on track, morally speaking, and to getting oneself back on track when one strays off. Moreover, the clear-sighted assessment of successes and failures both motivates further moral effort and wards off "timorousness," "dejection," or "despondency" [*Mutlosigkeit*])—the fear that takes a moral failure as proof that one lacks altogether the strength to comply with the moral law—which could inhibit moral conduct and efforts at self-improvement (AK 27: 350, 611; L 130, 355). Kant discusses something like evaluative self-respect in connection with "the first command of all duties to oneself," which is "*know* (scrutinize, fathom) *yourself* . . . in terms of your moral perfections in relation to your duty," to examine not only our actions but also our motives and patterns of motivation in light of the moral law to which we hold ourselves (AK 6:441; MM 562). From this command follows the duties of "impartiality in appraising oneself in comparison with the law, and sincerity in acknowledging to oneself one's inner moral worth or lack of worth" (AK 6:442; MM 563), which Kant identifies as "*love of honor [Ehrliebe] (honestas interna, justum sui aestimium),*" the virtue that is opposed to the vice of disrespect of oneself (AK 6:420; MM 545).

On the second interpretation, then, the arrogance opposed to genuine humility is primary arrogance, an unwarranted claim to much more moral merit than one has actually earned, and it is the excess with regard to which well-grounded evaluative self-respect is the mean. Although this form of primary arrogance could give rise to interpersonal arrogance,[39] the two are not essentially connected. There need be no inference from this inflated sense of merit to claims about what one is entitled to vis-à-vis others, no expression of contempt for others or demand that they demean themselves in the service of one's self-valuation. Hence this form of primary arrogance need not give rise to any violation of one's duty to respect others. But it is a false valuation of oneself that is opposed to a kind of self-respect that one has a duty to deserve by striving to be good and a duty to maintain through just self-assessment.

Kant discusses this vice on numerous occasions. It is the "*egotistical* self-esteem [*eigenliebegen Selbstschätzung*]" which takes mere wishes—wishes that, however ardent, always remain empty of deeds—for proof of a good heart" (AK 6: 441; MM 563); the "*arrogantia* [or] pride [*Stolz*], when we presume to a value [*Wert*] that we do not possess" that differs from the haughtiness [*Hochmut*] of "lay[ing] claim to precedence over others . . . put[ting] down the other and deem-[ing] him lesser and lower than we are" (AK 27:458; L 211);[40] the self-regard that is self-satisfaction [*Wohlgefallens an sich selbst*] (*arrogantia*) or self-conceit [*Eigendünkel*], in which one's "claims of self-esteem . . . precede conformity to the moral law" (AK 5:74; C 76); the self-conceit [*Eigendünkel*] in which a person "build[s] too much on his own powers . . . [being] such a fool as to think he can fulfill [the moral law in its full purity] quite purely by his own efforts" (AK 27:351; L 130); the moral self-conceit [*moralische Eigendünkel*] of believing oneself "to be perfect in comparison to the law," which is far worse than believing oneself superior to other people (AK 27:349; L 129); the "arrogance, or moral self-conceit [*Arroganz, moralischen Eigendünkel*]" that "makes an unwarranted pretension to merit" and is a "far more damaging defect" than *philautia*, or moral self-love [*Eigenliebe*], which is "an inclination to be well-content with oneself" and "devoid of self-reproach" (AK 27:357; L 135); the "moral self-conceit [*moralischen Eigendünkel*] of thinking [oneself] morally good, and having a favorable opinion of [one]self," a "dream-like condition" that is one of the "tendencies to evil" in us that we must "constantly contend against" (AK 27:464; L 216); the complacent self-love[41] that rests on the failure to assess our true moral worth and is "the cause of great harm" (AK 27:621–623; L 364–365) and a "source of all evil" (AK 6:46; R 66–67).

We can see a connection between moral arrogance so understood and some of our examples of everyday arrogance, including the arrogance imputed to the physicists who believe they have the power to unlock the secrets of the universe, to Harry Potter whom Snape regards as being unable to believe he could be mistaken in his judgments of other people, and to the pilot Kennedy who had overly high esteem for his flying abilities. And just as the moral arrogance Kant focuses on puts the individual "in danger of being incapable of examining or amending his faults" (AK 27:621; L 364), so unwarranted claims to knowledge or ability can make it impossible for the individual to recognize errors in his judgments, both about himself and about other things, which can lead to failure to make intellectual progress or to tragedy. In each case, the arrogant person sacrifices honest self-assessment—a clear view of what one is and can do in comparison to what one regards as very important to be and do—in exchange for a more easily obtained enhancement of self-esteem, being able to think highly of oneself. Thus, although the two forms of primary arrogance so far identified relate to different kinds of self-worth and different kinds of self-respect, they are motivated in the same way. In both cases, the arrogant person is driven by his desire for self-esteem, thereby making himself a "plaything of the inclinations" and subjugating his rational freedom (including his ability to follow the best reasons) to his desires. Well-grounded evaluative self-respect, resting on impartial self-scrutiny and honest appraisal of the merit one has actually earned or lost through the exercise of one's rational will, puts one in a better position to achieve and sustain success in the attainment both of secure moral worth and of one's intellectual or other goals— which is what the arrogant person is really after—while preserving his autonomy, which is what any rational agent should want.

Primary Arrogance and Agentic Recognition Self-Respect

There is a puzzling aspect to Kant's repeated discussions of the second form of primary arrogance. Although it is clear how it involves a failure of evaluative self-respect, it is not clear why claiming unwarranted merit is not merely foolish but rather is a "very damaging defect" far worse than disrespect of others, a "cause of great harm" and a "tendency to evil," indeed, a "source of all evil." There is a third way of interpreting the relevant *Metaphysics of Morals* passage that resolves the puzzle by identifying a form of primary arrogance that is a much more serious vice than misjudging one's moral merits, a form that is linked to a third kind of self-respect. Recall the contrast between humility and arrogance: "The consciousness and feeling of the insignificance of one's moral worth *in comparison with the law is humility* [Demut] (humilitas moralis). A conviction of the greatness of one's moral worth, but only from failure to compare it with the law, can be called *moral arrogance* [Tugendstolz] (arrogantia moralis)."

The third interpretation focuses not on the kind of worth claimed but on the source of the self-ascription of worth. Given, on the one hand, the ineluctable imperfection and inevitable failings of every human and, on the other hand, the high standards for conduct and character set by the moral law, it is reasonable to suppose that an accurate assessment of one's moral merit in comparison with the law would yield humility; thus any high opinion of self-worth would be unjustifiably high. Nevertheless, moral arrogance lies, Kant says, not in overestimating one's moral merit but in doing so "*only* from failure to compare it with the law." This suggests that any claim to merit, even if it happens to be accurate, is unwarranted if it doesn't come from comparing oneself against the standards of moral excellence contained in the law. The arrogance of claiming great moral merit is thus not merely the conceit that results from poor self-assessment skills but rather is the elevation of one's desire to think well of oneself (self-esteem) to the level of the standard of moral virtue. That is, moral arrogance is the refusal to acknowledge the moral law as the only standard for self-evaluation. The real problem, then, is not an unjustified opinion of merit but the refusal to submit one's desires for and judgments of self-worth to the authority of the moral law. Conceit rises to the level of arrogance inasmuch as it involves the arrogation to one's desire for self-esteem of the authority to determine virtue. This is primary arrogance, and it contrasts not, as on the first interpretation, with both servility and recognition self-respect, and not, as on the second reading, with both an unjustifiably low opinion of one's moral merit and proper evaluative self-respect, but with a third kind of self-respect, which I call "agentic recognition self-respect."

As persons, on the Kantian view, we have dignity and so both the moral right and the moral duty to value ourselves as ends in ourselves in virtue of our capacity for rationally autonomous agency. Whereas interpersonal recognition self-respect is the practical appreciation of oneself as a person among persons, agentic recognition self-respect is the proper acknowledgment and valuing of oneself specifically as a moral agent. This involves, among other things, taking seriously the responsibilities of moral agency; and for Kant, the most central of these is the responsibility to realize one's capacity for autonomy by choosing to act from purely rational motives. This is possible only through submitting oneself to the authority of the moral law, that is, to the dictates of one's own rationality unimpeded by the importuning of the inclinations. One claims too much merit out of the arrogant claim of moral authority for one's inclinations and so the subordination of one's capacity for rational judgment. This debasement of one's dignity as a rational being is a failure of agentic recognition self-respect: no self-respecting moral agents would not subordinate their rational autonomy to their desire for self-esteem.

Kant discusses this form of arrogance, revealing how serious a vice it is, in the second *Critique's* explication of how the moral law can be an incentive, that is, how it can directly determine our choice of action independently of our wants, needs, desires, and emotions. There Kant contrasts two forms of self-regard [*Selbstsucht*] (*solipsismus*), which is what he calls the sum of our inclinations. The first is "self-love [*Selbstliebe*], which is a predominant benevolence towards oneself [*Wohlwollens gegen sich selbst*] (*philautia*)," which is also called "selfishness [*Eigenliebe*]"; the second is "self-satisfaction [*Wohlgefallens an sich selbst*] (*arrogantia*)" or "self-conceit [*Eigendünkel*]" (AK 5:73; CB 76). The moral law becomes an incentive through the effect on selfishness and self-conceit of our consciousness of the law. The two are affected differently. The natural desire of self-love is "checked," or reigned in, by pure practical reason so that one's self-benevolent actions are restricted to those in agreement with the law. But pure practical reason "*strikes down* self-conceit altogether, since all claims to esteem for oneself that precede accord with the moral law are null and quite unwarranted because certainty of a disposition in accord with this law is the first condition of any worth of a person . . . and any presumption prior to this is false and opposed to the law" (AK 5:73; CG 199).

Self-conceit, or arrogance, has to be struck down and not just constrained as is selfishness because it poses a unique and insidious threat:

> Our nature as sensuous beings [is] so characterized that the material of the faculty of desire (objects of inclination, whether of hope or fear) first presses upon us; and we find our pathologically determined self, although by its maxims it is wholly incapable of giving universal laws, striving to give its pretensions priority and to make them acceptable as first and original claims, just as if it were our entire self. This propensity to make the subjective determining grounds of one's choice into an objective determining ground of the will in general is called self-love [*Selbstliebe*]; when it makes itself legislative and an unconditional practical principle, it can be called self-conceit [*Eigendünkel*] . . . self-conceit . . . decrees the subjective conditions of self-love as laws. (AK 5:74; CB 77)

As Lewis White Beck puts it, arrogance is "the inclination to take one's own subjective maxims and interests as having the authority of law."[42] That is, arrogance effects a dramatic transformation of one's inclinations: what are in fact merely contingent features of one's personal psychology, a matter of what one alone happens to want, are cast as rationally justified principles of action with unconditional authority over all agents. Arrogance involves the supplanting of the moral law by inclination; it is thus the chief obstacle to morality and must therefore be "dislodged" (AK 5:75; CB 78) by being struck down to make possible the acknowledgment of the authority of the moral law. This striking down of arrogance is experienced first as humiliation (for it lowers our estimate of our worthiness of esteem) and then as respect both for the profoundly superior moral law and for ourselves as authors of the law (AK 5:74; CB 76). And respect for the moral law and for ourselves as authors are, Kant maintains, among the subjective grounds of the possibility of morality—if we did not experience them, morality would be impossible (AK 6:399–403; MM 528–531).

Unchecked arrogance is the unwarranted pretension to merit; how what seems like merely foolish conceit ends up posing such a threat to morality becomes clear when we understand its mode of operation.[43] An agent can't think well of himself morally without acknowledging moral standards and taking his conduct, motives, attitudes, or character to conform to them. Someone of modest merit, great demerit, and a compelling desire to think well of himself arrives at a high opinion of himself not by ignoring the moral law or thumbing his nose at it, taking himself not to be bound by it (for Kant regards this as impossible for a rational being; AK 6:35; R 58), but by taking himself to meet the demands of the law which he "flatters himself that he inwardly reveres" (AK 430; MM 553). Though he does not meet the law's standards, his inclinations "secretly work against" the law (*AK* 5:86; *CB* 89) in at least three ways to produce a judgment of high merit. First, the arrogant person deceives himself about the standards for moral conduct, "conceiv[ing] the moral law to be indulgent" (*AK* 27:350; *L* 130) and "narrow" (*AK* 27:357; *L* 135), pretending that the law only advises rather than commands inescapably and unconditionally the strict performance of all duties (*AK* 27:623; *L* 365). Judging himself by such lax standards, he can't but look good. Second, he deceives himself about himself, both about the moral quality of his actions and, very importantly, about his motives for acting, which, as Kant argued in the *Groundwork*, are the real source of moral merit. Not only does the "partisan" moral judge within him evaluate him indulgently, excusing or turning a blind eye to his inadequate performance (*AK* 27:357; *L* 135), but he also pretends to himself (as he has to) that his motive for acting is the motive of duty—which is the only motive that gives actions moral worth—when his real motive is his desire to think well of himself.[44] Through this self-corrupting double self-deception, the arrogant person's conduct and motives can appear morally worthy to him. Third, he "tinkers with the moral law, till he has fashioned it to suit his inclinations and convenience" (*AK* 27:465; *L* 216), craftily "fabricat[ing] such a law for oneself, whereby one may do evil under the aegis of the true law" (*AK* 27:359; *L* 137). Out of the desire to heighten or maintain his self-esteem, the arrogant person adjusts the law and its standards to his actions so that he can think well of himself as doing his moral duty, no matter what in fact he does.

This last move is the most seriously wrong; indeed, Kant identifies it as the deepest source of evil in human nature, in which "the mind's attitude is . . . corrupted at its root" (*AK* 6:30; *R* 54). For it involves, not merely the frailty of wanting to do right but being too weak to resist temptations, nor the impurity of needing to be pushed by our inclinations to do what we know we ought to do, but the "depravity" or "perversity" of subordinating the incentives of the moral law to those of the inclinations (*AK* 6:29–30; *R* 53–54). The deepest source of evil involves not the fact that one pays attention to one's inclinations in deciding what to do but in their insubordination. It lies, that is, in "revers[ing] the moral order of his incentives in incorporating them into his maxim," making "the incentives of self-love and their inclinations the condition of the compliance with the moral law" (*AK* 6:36; *R* 59). In this way the arrogant person is able to pass off what he wants to do for what he ought to do, representing as law something that encourages him to do what he wants and calls it right. The desire for self-esteem thus makes self-love a "legislative and an unconditional practical principle," usurping for itself the kind of authority that is possessed only by the moral law generated by pure practical reason.

From the perspective of the desire for self-esteem, arrogance is a bargain hunter's dream: it promises what we want at a very low price. Rather than having to work hard morally to earn moral merit by bringing one's conduct and character into line with the demands of the moral law, the arrogant person can, with just some mental manipulation, bring both the law and his self-assessments into line with his desires. And what results from this process are the two distinctive characteristics of arrogance: the arrogant person gets both the high self-esteem he craves and the claim of objective justification for what he wants and does that underwrites confidence in his opinion of his moral worth.

Although I have identified three forms of primary arrogance, the third is truly primary. It underlies all other forms of arrogance as the necessary first step, in which one's subjective reasons for action and attitude ("I want") are magically transformed into objective reasons ("I am entitled") that claim authority and demand the respect of everyone else. This form of arrogance is the ultimate exercise of power—over morality and reason itself—in the service of the desire for self-esteem. Not only can we see it playing out in our everyday examples of the other forms of primary arrogance, but we can now see another dimension of interpersonal arrogance. That form of arrogance, recall, is not simply the claim to greater respect from others than is one's due; it is also the demand that others value themselves less than they deserve, that they not respect their dignity as persons but abase themselves to serve as mere means to the arrogant person's desire for self-exaltation. Not content with its own moral corruption and flouting of the moral law, arrogance seeks the moral corruption of others—the deformation of their valuing capacity and so the perversion of their rational agency through their willed and flagrant violation of the categorical command to treat all persons, oneself, as well as others, always as ends in themselves. Arrogance not only makes unwarranted claims to the respect of others but also wrongly claims authority over their valuing activities and agency. It expresses the lack of agentic recognition self-respect and seeks to annihilate the agentic recognition self-respect of others.

The person with agentic recognition self-respect values intrinsically and unconditionally the autonomous exercise of rational judgment and will, takes seriously the responsibilities that lie on moral agents in virtue of their capacity for rational autonomy, and regards morally worthy conduct as the only fitting expression of the consciousness of one's dignity as a moral agent. The arrogant person values self-esteem intrinsically and unconditionally; consequently, his judgment is perverted, his agency corrupted, his rational autonomy undermined, and his dignity degraded.

Understood as an excessively high opinion of one's moral merit, as in the second interpretation, arrogance seems to be one moral flaw among many others to which imperfect humans are inevitably liable. But understood, as on the third interpretation, as claiming for one's inclinations the authority both to set the standards of moral virtue and to determine how one fares by their light—to regard one's subjective interests as having the authority of objective moral law—primary arrogance is the most serious of vices: an improper valuing of oneself, not only of one's merit but, more importantly, of one's capacity for autonomous rational agency, which stands as the chief obstacle to morality. It is The Vice that must be eliminated before proper exercise of moral agency and rational judgment is possible. It is not an excess of which agentic recognition self-respect is the mean; rather, it is a radically deformed value system altogether different from self-respect. As the contrary of this form of arrogance, agentic recognition self-respect is thus the first condition of the possibility of genuine moral agency and judgment.

Could Arrogance Be a Virtue?

Let me return briefly to the feminist concern I raised at the beginning of this essay. It seemed that the cultivation of arrogance in oppressed people promised to be a powerful tool in their struggles to end subordination. But if Kant and I are right about arrogance, then the answer to the question "Could arrogance be a virtue of unsubordinating insubordinance?" is . . . no, sort of but not really, perhaps, and yet no.

First, insofar as arrogance is contempt for the moral law and for one's own autonomy that masquerades as respect for both, the false valuation of one's dignity and moral merit, and contempt for others that requires their self-abasement and thus their moral corruption through their willed and flagrant violation of their duty of self-respect, it is irredeemably vicious and is the failure of interpersonal recognition self-respect, evaluative self-respect, and agentic recognition self-respect. Cultivating arrogance for the purposes of empowerment in the struggles for liberation might well result in the overthrow of oppression, but it is likely to result both in the formerly oppressed people simply becoming oppressors themselves and, more importantly, in their own inner self-subordination and the abdication of a form of autonomy that is arguably more valuable than political autonomy.

Second, it is inevitable that the attempts of subordinated people to unsubordinate themselves will appear to dominant people to be arrogant.[45] For in claiming the authority for themselves to redefine their status and worth, those struggling for liberation are usurping the authority of the dominant norms and values. From the perspective of the dominant norms, their claims are unwarranted, hence arrogant; but to the extent that their claims are in fact rationally justified, they are not arrogant. The liability to be labeled "arrogant" is not necessarily the result of the possession of any of the forms of arrogance; it can result simply from the fact that application of concepts like arrogance is relative to moral outlooks,[46] and the moral outlook of dominants is quite different from the outlook of those seeking to end their dominance. Indeed, what is in fact self-respect can seem like arrogance to those whose moral outlook is itself perverted by arrogance, and so to some, the virtues of self-respect will appear to be the vices of arrogance.[47] But they aren't. Nevertheless, while those who struggle for liberation should not be afraid of the epithet "arrogant" or its kin, they should be wary of the strong possibility, highlighted in Kant's analysis, of self-deception about the justification of one's judgments and claims.

Third, there is a real sense in which those who struggle for liberation are genuinely arrogant, and their arrogance is a moral virtue. That is, the stance of independence from and superiority to the social norms and statutes that command the submission of these people to those, the stance that takes one's desires for freedom and for morally higher forms of self-valuation to set the standard by which one judges one's conduct and character and to be authoritative with respect to the norms that pass for moral law, that claims different grounds for the basic self-worth of persons and requires that some people value themselves less than they have been, that takes pride in efforts to destroy a whole way of life—this stance is, arguably, genuinely arrogant. For the warrant for these claims is, subjectively, no more secure than the warrant that underlies the claims against which one struggles, and the objectivity of warrant for the competing claims is precisely what the struggle is about. In this sense, the trait of arrogance can be reasonably regarded by subordinated people as a genuine virtue, although it would need to be held in check by conscious efforts to remain self-respecting and respectful of what genuinely deserves respect. Nevertheless, an endorsement of arrogance must be a cautious one, for there is danger in claiming arrogance as a virtue: it is all too easy to slip from the circumscribed arrogance that aims at political liberation to other forms of unbounded arrogance that serve only self-esteem.

In the end, however, although arrogance is potentially unsubordinating, the Kantian analysis persuades that it is not a trait that self-respecting feminists could wholeheartedly embrace. For although arrogance promises power, freedom, and a glorious pride in the self—all at a low discount price, much of which one can get others to pay—it delivers the deepest form of subjugation and it costs one's self-respect.

Notes

Versions of this essay were presented at the Pacific Division Meeting of the American Philosophical Association in Seattle, Washington, March 2002, and at the conference on "Kantian Ethics: Interpretations and Critiques," sponsored by the Values Institute at the University of San Diego, January 2003. I am grateful to Bernard Reginster, who commented on this work on both occasions, for his generous comments and development of some of the themes and to the audiences on both occasions for helpful discussions.

1. Ronald Ivey, "Cardinal's Arrogance Is Astounding," letter to the editor, *The* (Allentown, Pa.) *Morning Call*, May 2, 2001.

2. From an advertisement for *Bottom Line Yearbook* (2001). Thanks to Cheshire Calhoun, Joanne Sleigh, and Cheryl Dougan for several of the examples.

3. Robin S. Dillon, "How to Lose Your Self-Respect," *American Philosophical Quarterly* 29 (1992): 125–139.

4. Quoted in Margaret Koval, "The Roman Empire," *The Roman Empire in the First Century* (Goldfarb & Koval Productions, 2001); broadcast on PBS during 2001; text online at pbs.org/empires/romans/empire/empire3b.html. The source is apparently Tacitus's *Annals* 12.7. It may not be irrelevant to the charge of arrogance that, in addition to openly exercising political power in ways no women before her had done, Agrippina murdered Claudius so that Nero, her son from a previous marriage, would become emperor. Nero in turn had his mother murdered to escape her efforts to rule him.

5. Marilyn Frye addresses this question brilliantly in "In and Out of Harm's Way: Arrogance and Love," in *The Politics of Reality: Essays in Feminist Theory* (Freedom, Cal.: Crossing Press, 1983), 52–83.

6. Catharine MacKinnon, *Toward a Feminist Theory of the State* (Cambridge, Mass.: Harvard University Press, 1989), chap. 9.

7. Robin S. Dillon, "Toward a Feminist Conception of Self-Respect," *Hypatia* 7, no. 1 (Winter 1992): 52–69.

8. The chief discussions are in *The Metaphysics of Morals, Critique of Practical Reason*, and throughout the *Lectures*; the discussion of good and evil in *Religion Within the Boundaries of Mere Reason* is also relevant. Page references in the text are given both for the appropriate volume of *Kant's gesammelte Schriften*, herausgegeben von der Königlichen Preussischen Akademie der Wissenschaften (Berlin: Georg Reimer, 1907) (cited as AK) and for the translation used (but see note below about the *Lectures*). I've used the following translations:

The Metaphysics of Morals, Part II
- "The Metaphysics of Morals," in *Practical Philosophy*, ed. and trans. Mary J. Gregor (Cambridge: Cambridge University Press, 1996) (cited as MM).
- *Doctrine of Virtue, Part II, The Metaphysics of Morals*, trans. Mary J. Gregor (Philadelphia: University of Pennsylvania Press, 1964) (cited as DV).
- "The Metaphysical Principles of Virtue," in *Ethical Philosophy*, trans. James W. Ellington (Indianapolis, Ind.: Hackett, 1983) (cited as MP).

Critique of Practical Reason
- *Critique of Practical Reason*, trans. Lewis White Beck (Indianapolis, Ind.: Bobbs-Merrill, 1956) (cited as CB).
- "Critique of Practical Reason," in *Practical Philosophy*, ed. and trans. Mary J. Gregor (Cambridge: Cambridge University Press, 1996) (cited as CG).

Religion Within the Boundaries of Mere Reason, ed. and trans. Allen Wood and George di Giovanni (Cambridge: Cambridge University Press, 1998) (cited as R).

Groundwork of the Metaphysics of Morals
- *Groundwork of the Metaphysics of Morals*, trans. H. J. Paton (New York: Harper & Row, 1956) (cited as G).
- "Groundwork of the Metaphysics of Morals," in *Practical Philosophy*, ed. and trans. Mary J. Gregor (Cambridge: Cambridge University Press, 1996) (cited as GG).

Lecture on Ethics
- *Lectures on Ethics*, ed. Peter Heath and J. B. Schneewind, trans. Peter Heath (Cambridge: Cambridge University Press, 1997) (cited as L).
- *Lecture on Ethics*, trans. Louis Infield (Indianapolis, Ind.: Hackett, 1980) (cited as LI).

Note: The Heath translation contains four sets of lecture notes taken by students in Kant's university courses in ethics, covering the periods 1762–1764 (Herder's notes), 1784 (Collins's notes), 1784–1785 (Mrongovius's notes), and 1793–1794 (Vigilantius's notes). The Infield translation is based on Paul Menzer's 1924 German edition of notes of Kant's lectures from 1775–1780, which are indistinguishable from Collins's notes. For the German of Collins's notes I used Kant, *Eine Vorlesung über Ethik*, herausgegeben von Gerd Gerhardt (Frankfurt: Fischer Taschenbuch Verlag GmbH, 1990). The German versions for all four sets of notes included in the Heath translation are in *Kant's gesammelte Schriften*, vol. 27.

9. Between the inevitable latitude in translation and Kant's not always consistent use of synonyms, identifying passages throughout works that span thirty-some years as "about arrogance" can be difficult. Where possible I have used multiple translations and checked them against the German in the *Shriften* and the *Vorlesung*. What I am calling "arrogance" Kant variously refers to as *Hochmut, Hoffart, Tugendstolz, Arro-*

ganz, Eigendünkel, Ubermut, Stolz, Ehrbegierde, Anmaßung, and the *Selbstliebe* that is
Wohlgefallens an sich selbst. These are variously translated as "arrogance," "moral arrogance," "pride," "haughtiness," "self-conceit," "ambition," "lust/craving for honor," "pretension," "self-satisfaction," "love of good pleasure in oneself," and "love of well-liking
toward oneself." Kant often inserts the Latin term *arrogantia* in parentheses after the
German word and sometimes gives synonyms in German. In the text I have inserted
the German terms in italics in square brackets. The italicized Latin terms in parentheses are Kant's.

10. Such a view of arrogance is explicated by Valerie Tiberius and John D. Walker,
"Arrogance," *American Philosophical Quarterly* 35 (1998): 379–390, who argue that arrogance is essentially and, by implication, exclusively "an interpersonal matter. It consists
in a particular way of regarding and engaging in relations with others" (381).

11. *American Heritage Dictionary of the English Language*, 4th ed. (Boston:
Houghton Mifflin, 2000), s.v. "arrogant."

12. Ibid., s.v. "proud," "synonyms."

13. Ellington translates *Hochmut* here as "pride" (MP130).

14. See Robin S. Dillon, "Self-Respect: Moral, Emotional, Political," *Ethics* 107
(1997): 226–249. I borrow the term "recognition respect" from Stephen Darwall, "Two
Kinds of Respect," *Ethics* 88 (1977): 34–49.

15. See Mary Gregor, *Laws of Freedom* (Oxford: Basil Blackwell, 1963), 182–188.

16. *Selbstschätzung* is translated as "self-respect" by Infield and as "self-
esteem" by Heath; the latter is linguistically more accurate. However, as Kant describes
it, it corresponds to interpersonal recognition self-respect and not to either what I
would call "self-esteem" (having a high opinion of oneself based on one's belief that
one possesses qualities that one prizes) or to what others have called "moral self-
esteem" (having a positive opinion of one's moral merit), both of which have to do
with earned high merit rather than human dignity. See Primary Arrogance and Evaluative Self-Respect below.

17. Geoff Gehman, "At the Michener, an Erratic Album of Stieglitz Photos," *The*
(Allentown, Pa.) *Morning Call*, March 4, 2001, F7.

18. Hang Nguyen, "Lehigh Chamber Puts Valley in Name," *The* (Allentown, Pa.)
Morning Call, February 12, 2002, A1.

19. Matthew Harper, quoted in Steve Rosen, "Invest When You're Young and Get
Lifelong Dividends in Knowledge," *The* (Allentown, Pa.) *Morning Call*, March 4, 2001,
D2.

20. Quoted in Robert C. Roberts and W. Jay Wood, "Humility and Epistemic
Goods," in *Intellectual Virtue: Perspectives from Ethics and Epistemology*, ed. Michael
DePaul and Linda Zagzebski (Oxford: Oxford University Press, 2003). The quotation is
from Allan L. Hammond, ed., *A Passion to Know: Twenty Profiles in Science* (New
York: Scribner, 1984), 4.

21. Alas, although I kept copies of several eulogies extolling the humility, I've lost
the references for the accusations of arrogance.

22. Roger Rosenblatt, "God Is Not on My Side. Or Yours," *Time*, December 17,
2001, 92. In a similar vein, a Presbyterian minister, in an op-ed piece responding to an
essay by a syndicated religion columnist that had accused the Presbyterian Church of
apostasy for, among other things, urging Presbyterians to "respect diversity regarding belief in God," in turn criticizes "the arrogance of believing that the correct interpretation of faith is only that which is held by one's own self." Donald R. Repsher, "Colum-

nist's Inflammatory Opinion Should Be Softened with Humility," *The* (Allentown, Pa.) *Morning Call*, July 12, 2001, A21.

23. J. K. Rowlings, *Harry Potter and the Prisoner of Azbakan* (New York: Scholastic Press, 1999), 284.

24. Ibid., 361.

25. *O.E.D.*, s.v. "arrogant." This kind of arrogance is the focus of Roberts and Wood's analysis of intellectual arrogance in "Humility and Epistemic Goods."

26. *O.E.D.*, s.v. "arrogate."

27. Interestingly, Kant admits to this pattern of arrogance in his often-quoted reflection on the effect Rousseau had on his view of human worth: "I am an inquirer by inclination. I feel a consuming thirst for knowledge, the unrest which goes with the desire to progress in it, and satisfaction at every advance in it. There was a time when I believed this constituted the honor of humanity, and I despised the people, who know nothing. Rousseau set me right about this. This blinding prejudice disappeared. I learned to honor humanity" (*AK* 20:44). Quoted by Allen Wood, "General Introduction," in *Practical Philosophy*, ed. and trans. Mary J. Gregor (Cambridge: Cambridge University Press, 1996), xvii.

28. On the inferences that arrogance involves, see Tiberius and Walker, "Arrogance"; Roberts and Wood, "Humility and Epistemic Goods"; and Gabriele Taylor, *Pride, Shame, and Guilt: Emotions of Self-Assessment* (Oxford: Clarendon Press, 1985), 43ff.

29. In "Servility and Self-Respect," *Monist* 57 (1973), Thomas E. Hill, Jr., identifies two forms of servility: one that involves misunderstanding one's basic rights and status as a person and another that values them improperly. By calling servility *lying* humility, Kant indicates that he is talking only about the latter. However, since Kant thinks that persons are always aware of their dignity and status as persons, even if some individuals sometimes ignore it or act as if they weren't aware, it is not unreasonable to think that for Kant all servility involves lying, to others and perhaps to oneself.

30. Kant identifies *Würde* as *"einen absoluten inner Wert"* (e.g., AK 435).

31. The idea that "meanness" underlies arrogance corresponds with the contemporary view that the arrogant person, deep down, is quite the opposite of how he wants to appear: far from being powerful and confident about his superiority, the arrogant person is actually insecure about his self-worth and so seeks to make himself look bigger by cutting others down. Kant develops this view in the *Religion*, where he explains that there is a form of self-love that necessarily involves comparison; we can know we are happy or unhappy, for example, only in comparison with how others are doing. From this form of self-love,

> originates the inclination *to gain worth in the opinion of others*, originally, of course merely *equal worth*: not allowing anyone superiority over oneself, bound up with the constant anxiety that others might strive for ascendancy; but from this arises gradually an unjust desire to acquire superiority for oneself over others. . . . [The] vices of secret or open hostility to all whom we consider alien to us . . . do not really issue from nature as their root but are rather inclinations, in the face of the anxious endeavor of others to attain a hateful superiority over us, to procure it for ourselves for the sake of security, as a preventive measure. (AK 27; *R* 51)

But, of course, only those who do not value themselves as ends in themselves would think that others could acquire any superiority that really matters over them. That is, only someone who lacked interpersonal recognition self-respect would fear the ascendancy of others or seek ascendancy over them. Arrogance, on this view, is thus the disposition to make preemptive strikes against others' self-worth in order to bolster an insecure sense of one's own self-worth. (It is worth noting that there is another view of the matter: arrogance is not a coverup for weak self-esteem but a straightforward manifestation of a too-powerful self-esteem. See, for example, Solomon Schimmel, *The Seven Deadly Sins: Jewish, Christian, and Classical Reflections on Human Psychology* (New York: Oxford University Press, 1992), chap. 2, esp. p. 39. I develop this second view below.)

32. In the *Lectures*, Kant identifies as a violation of our duty to God the "error in divine veneration" of "arrogance (an apotheosis of humanity in our own person) or the claim to an immediate intercourse, fellowship and social connection with God" (*AK* 27:727; *L* 448).

33. See also *Lectures*, AK 27:409, 458; L 174–175, 211.

34. Moral merit is the moral worth Kant is talking about, for example, in the *Groundwork* discussion of the moral worth of actions done from duty (AK 4:398–399; G 65–67). I should note that in the *Lectures* Kant distinguishes between the worth [*Wert*] that one has because one has done one's duty, for example, by being honest, and the merit [*Verdienst*] one earns by going beyond duty, for example, through kindness. In virtue of one's *Wert* one deserves respect [*Achtung*]; in virtue of one's *Verdienst* one deserves high esteem and honor [*Hochschätzung und Ehre*] (AK 27:410; L 175). I merge these two forms of worth into one category, moral merit, focusing on the fact that both are earned through activity of the will, in contrast to the worth of dignity, which is unearned.

35. It might seem that interpreting "moral worth" as moral merit makes the *Metaphysics of Morals* passage puzzling in a different way. For there appears to be a shift in subject which Kant seems not to notice, and it is not clear what humility and arrogance with regard to one's moral merit have to do with servility with regard to one's dignity. But the topics are in fact related. For as Kant makes clear in the *Lectures*, "proper self-esteem" [*geziemenden Selbstschätzung*] includes both humility, which in turn is the opinion of our moral merit that comes from comparing ourselves with the moral law, and true noble pride, which is valuing ourselves highly and as equal with others, which in turn is interpersonal recognition self-respect (AK 27:348–349; L 129). Since in Kant's view, proper self-valuing requires an appreciation of both our dignity and our moral merit, it would be natural for him to discuss humility, arrogance, and servility in the same breath, though the first two relate to merit and the last to dignity.

36. I take this term from Stephen D. Hudson, "The Nature of Respect," *Social Theory and Practice* 6 (1980): 69–90. Darwall's term in "Two Kinds of Respect" is "appraisal self-respect."

37. On coming up to scratch, see Elizabeth Telfer, "Self-Respect," *Philosophical Quarterly* 18 (1968): 114–121.

38. For which reason Kant argues that we have need of the judgments of others: "Prudence teaches us that we should weigh our conduct by the judgment of our fellows so that we may not act purely from self-love; our own judgment of our conduct may have a corrupting effect, but the judgments of others are a corrective" (AK 408; LI 187). Kant identifies the prudential desire for the respect of others as "love of honor" [*Ehrliebe*] and contrasts it with the "craving for honor" (L) or "lust for honor" (LI) [*Ehrebegierde*] or "ambition" [*Ambition*], which "yearns to be an object of high esteem to others" (AK 27:408; L 174).

39. Kant does link the two once in the *Lectures*: the "improper love of well-liking to-

ward oneself" [*unrechtmäßige*] that "rests, without examination, on a judgment of one-self," and "without assessment of our true moral worth" is the arrogance [*Arroganz*] "whereby the agent makes himself an object of the respect that we require from others, and enhances his worth, without justification, over others" (AK 27:621–622, L 364–365). Elsewhere, Kant treats the unwarranted claim to moral merit independently of the claim to superiority in status over others.

40. This is the one occasion when Kant explicitly distinguishes two kinds of arrogance: *Hochmut*, interpersonal arrogance, and *Arrogantia*, primary arrogance.

41. This is the "love of well-liking towards oneself" [*Selbstliebe des Wohlgefallens gegen sich selbst*] of the *Lectures*, which is contrasted with the "love of well-wishing towards oneself" [*Liebe des Wohlwollens gegen sich selbst*] [AK 27:621–622; L 364–365], and the "love of good pleasure in oneself" [*Liebe des Wohlgefallens an sich selbst*] or *complacentiae* of the *Religion*, contrasted with the "love of good will" [*des Wohlwollens*] or *benevolentiae* [note, AK 6:45; R 66].

42. Lewis White Beck, *A Commentary on Kant's Critique of Practical Reason* (Chicago: University of Chicago Press, 1960), 291; see also 100, n. 20.

43. I am indebted to Bernard Reginster for calling my attention to and helping me to understand this process.

44. The idea that the arrogant person cannot, in principle, acknowledge his true motives for acting is Reginster's.

45. But if I'm right about the power dimensions of arrogance, then dominants won't use the word "arrogance" to describe subordinates. Instead they'll talk about how subordinates are uppity, presumptuous, make unreasonable demands, take liberties, and don't know their place.

46. See Roberts and Wood, "Humility and Epistemic Goods."

47. Sethe, in Toni Morrison's novel *Beloved* (New York: Alfred A. Knopf, 1987), illustrates this: her attempts to claim self-respect are interpreted by Paul D and by neighbors on several occasions as arrogant pride.

12

Diversity, Trust, and Moral Understanding

Marilyn Friedman

Diverse Viewpoints

Dialogue with people who hold diverse points of view has been championed by various theories and traditions as an important means of moral development. John Stuart Mill, for example, famously argued that a crucial task for a lively intellect is to engage continually with views different from one's own, particularly with those at odds with one's own.[1] These encounters offer both sides a win-win situation. Each side to any dispute gains either by learning about new truths one had not formerly grasped or by being stimulated to recall or recognize the reasons supporting one's own perspectives. No encounter with viewpoints different from one's own is an intellectual waste of time, in Mill's assessment.

The latest version of this long-standing emphasis on encountering viewpoint diversity is the now familiar educational focus on *multiculturalism*. Learning about cultures and subcultures other than one's own is now widely championed as an important way to gain a critically reflective standpoint as a citizen of today's world.[2] The multicultural movement, addressed to an audience of mainstream Westerners, has particularly emphasized the study both of non-Western cultures and of subcultures within the West that deviate from standard, mainstream Eurocentric traditions and perspectives. Cross-cultural viewpoint diversity, of course, is not the only sort of viewpoint diversity there is. Gender, sexuality, religion, age, and varieties of ableness can each contribute to diversity of outlook.[3] The movement known as multiculturalism tends to encompass these alternative forms of diversity along with those of more strictly cultural types. According to the multicultural view of education, *any* viewpoint diversity is a good thing.

Diversity can emerge in at least two different aspects of interpersonal relationships. First, other *persons* can be different from oneself in some socially significant way, such as gender or religion. Second, other persons who may not be especially different from oneself in socially significant ways may nevertheless hold *views* that differ significantly from one's own. Diversity of persons in regard to their socially significant traits or group memberships is neither necessary nor sufficient for diversity of viewpoint. Yet most champions of multiculturalism probably assume, as do I, that when people differ in socially significant ways, they will very likely have substantially different social experiences as a result. Differences among people would probably not be socially significant in the first place unless they manifested themselves somehow in differences in people's experiences and perspectives. Thus encountering diverse sorts of persons is likely, even if not certain, to acquaint one with views different from one's own.

One crucial realm of understanding that is enhanced by encountering the diverse views of others is that of morality. One can learn about the morally significant features of people's lives, the moral problems they face, and the moral values they bring to the resolution of those problems. Diverse sorts of people tend to have somewhat different moral needs and problems and may adopt different moral values based on their diverse experiences. One important sort of moral communication a person can make to others is to report her experiences, what situations she faces, what she does about them, and what happens as a result.

Someone else's experiential reports about morally significant matters in her life constitute what we might call her moral testimony. Learning about others involves accepting their moral testimony. As Karen Jones notes, the acceptance of the moral testimony of others is a necessary part of a mature moral outlook.[4] Reliance on moral testimony is far more pervasive than we might think upon first considering the idea. It is not simply a matter of thinking about the occasional, controversial front-page figure who testifies before the Senate Judiciary Committee.[5] Learning about others is an omnipresent feature of daily life. People casually discuss with their kinfolk, friends, coworkers, and other acquaintances the ordinary and trivial conditions and occurrences of their lives, the events of momentous importance, and the norms and values they invoke to cope with those conditions. It is commonplace to hear from friends and acquaintances how things are going with them and what they think should be done about it. In everyday life, there are probably very few actions people take without relying in part on the testimony of friends, relatives, coworkers, and acquaintances for information about what is happening and what conditions are like in other parts of the world, the country, the workplace, the neighborhood, and even their very own homes. It is probably not possible to survive by relying only on the beliefs and values generated by first-hand experience.

What liberalism, and especially multiculturalism, emphasizes is the importance of hearing from those whose views *differ* from our own. Views that differ from our own challenge us in various ways. We may have to work to recognize how, if at all, they are warranted. If they are in any way opposed to views or values we already hold, we have to negotiate those conflicts. To benefit from exposure to alternative viewpoints, one may have to take up a particular attitude toward them. One must not simply regard other viewpoints as if they were specimens at a zoo, members of different species that are entertaining to behold but cannot teach us what to think. To benefit from diversity in the rich sense called for by multiculturalism and certain liberal traditions, one must really engage with alternative views; one must take them seriously and be open to being convinced by them.

One crucial question, then, in the project of encountering the views of diverse others is this: what is involved in taking seriously the views of others and in approaching them with genuine openness to the possibility of finding them appealing or convincing? What are the qualities, attitudes, or habits one needs in order to be able to carry out the liberal and multicultural educational directive of engaging seriously with viewpoints other than one's own? What traits or attitudes make possible the acceptance of views of others that one had not accepted before?

I can identify at least four stages in the sequence of encountering the viewpoints of others and begin to see in rough outline how to approach each stage in order to be most open to the newly encountered views. First, one must obviously become *acquainted* with viewpoints that differ from one's own. Depending on the degree of insularity in one's own life and the homogeneity of one's social milieu, one may have to search actively to find diverse viewpoints. Second, one must be sure one really *understands* the new view.[6] Dialogue with those who hold the view may allow one to ask questions, an effective way to check one's degree of understanding. One may also need to adopt a respectful attitude toward dialogical partners who hold the view in order to encourage them to convey their views openly and honestly and also to correct one's own misunderstandings.

Third, one must give the new view genuine reflective *consideration*. To do this, one may have to suspend for a time any tendencies to criticize or reject the alternative viewpoint. If one starts the inquiry with commitments that directly conflict with the new view under consideration, one may have to bracket somehow or set aside those commitments. Fourth, one may *assess* the new view. One may accept it as true or reliable, reject it as false or unreliable, reinterpret the subject matter, or evaluate it in some other way. Such conclusions can become dogmatic and unrevisable, but they need not do so. We may hold our assessments tentatively, open to the possibility of future revision, perhaps in the light of still newer moral views gleaned from still other persons we encounter subsequently.

Accepting, in the end, the moral view of another person involves regarding it as true, convincing, warranted, justified, or reliable. I have identified at least four stages in this process: (1) *acquaintance* with a new view, which can occur by chance or as a result of active searching; (2) *understanding* of the new view, which may also require self-consciously active effort; (3) *consideration* of the new view, which may require special attitudes so that the new view gets a fair hearing; and (4) *assessment* of the new view, in a manner which may be open to future revision.

Karen Jones, as noted earlier, has explored what is involved in accepting the moral testimony of other persons. In Jones's discussion, "testimony" is not limited simply to someone's reports of her moral experiences. Jones explores how to evaluate any of the moral communications of others. Of special importance are all the moral communications that one is unable to assess independently and which one therefore accepts because the one communicating them "vouches" for them.[7]

Jones emphasizes that finally accepting someone's moral testimony in this way requires trusting the one who offers it.[8] Two different grounds for such trust are important. One pertains to the sincerity, or absence of any intention to deceive, on the part of the one reporting her experiences. As Jones puts it, one needs to trust the *goodwill* of the testifier. The other ground of trust is the *competence* of the one reporting her experiences. She must have some minimal capacity to understand the circumstances about herself and her situation that she recounts and some minimal level of skill in representing those circumstances accurately in the medium in which she reports them to others. Thus, trusting someone's moral testimony involves trusting both her goodwill, or sincerity, and her competence in being able to testify reliably.[9] As it turns out, Jones does not recommend a generalized trust in the diverse moral views of others; quite the contrary. We will explore her reasons below, but first let us consider a more positive recommendation for encountering diverse others.

Iris Young interprets the concept of moral respect in a manner that goes beyond mere trust in the goodwill or competence of others. Young begins by emphasizing the importance of listening to what others have to say about their experiences from a "stance of moral humility" in which one recognizes that one can never truly adopt the other person's perspective.[10] This attitude reflects the idea that moral understanding is a difficult process, which is exacerbated by social distance. The more diversity there exists between two people, the harder it will be for the one trying to understand the other to be sure she has done so adequately.

Although we cannot, in Young's opinion, adopt another person's perspective, we can nevertheless gain some understanding of it and give it some consideration. Young argues that to do this, especially for points of view different from one's own, we have to get "out of ourselves" and learn "something new." Someone is able to understand a "new expression" to the extent that she is "open" and will "suspend" her "assumptions in order to listen."[11] Borrowing from Luce Irigaray,[12] Young suggests that we interpret the important concept of moral respect in terms of the attitude of *wonder*. This is the attitude, beyond mere trust, that Young recommends we bring to our communicative encounters with others. Young emphasizes that one should have "a respectful stance of wonder" toward the other person and of "openness to the newness and mystery of the other person." This stance also involves seeing "one's own position, assumptions, perspective as strange, because it has been put in relation to others."[13]

Before evaluating the attitudes of trust and wonder toward newly encountered moral views, let us note that considering and assessing the acceptability of viewpoints different from one's own is not the only way one can approach them. One can also approach them *strategically*. One can regard them as *"enemy"* and believe that it is prudent to "know thine enemy." On that approach, one may set out to learn what the enemy thinks, all the while being under no illusions about taking that view seriously. One merely studies it in order to figure out, say, how to refute it or how to suppress it. There is certainly a sort of learning that can go on in this way, but it does not involve opening oneself to the possibility of adopting a new view. Learning about a view with the aim of better combating it does not generally promote greater moral understanding of it. One is likely to learn only its weak points or to misunderstand it altogether, to miss what makes it plausible to the one who holds it, and to regard it as mere prejudice, irrationality, or fanaticism.

Of course, we are not fully in control of our epistemic leanings. The newly apprehended views of others can surprise us with a semblance of unexpected credibility that leads us, in spite of ourselves, to change our minds. We may approach the views of diverse others expecting to find irrational fanaticism and be surprised to find justified rage instead. To the extent that such transformations of moral understanding are surprising and out of one's control, one can, by definition, do little to promote or prevent them. Yet there may be aspects of the process of encountering moral testimony and moral views in general that we may be able to influence in certain ways. Thus, we return again to the question of *how* we should prepare ourselves to be influenced.

So multiculturalism and some strands of liberalism recommend that, in order to cultivate one's moral understanding, one should seek both to understand viewpoints different from one's own and to be open to them in a way that allows for the possibility of accepting divergent views. Yet we need to ask, what traits or attitudes should we cultivate in order to do this? Is Young's attitude of wonder or the attitude of trust mentioned by Jones epistemically sufficient for encountering diverse views or diverse experiential reports? Is there any problem with either of these attitudes?

A Problem

Mill, as we know, had a wildly optimistic view of the value of encountering perspectives different from one's own. Mill thought that even the most corrupt of them might contain some germ of truth we may have overlooked, and those that are entirely false still prompt us to engage in an ever crucial defense of our own views, thereby deepening our understanding of the merits of our own positions.[14] Mill does not seem to worry enough about the possibility that views one encounters might be not merely unwarranted or unreliable but also injurious to anyone who lives accordingly or to those with whom she interacts.

One of the most obvious things about diversity is that it is very . . . diverse. There are an indeterminate number of ways in which people's views can differ from each other. The problem is that not all viewpoints are equally nice. The fact that a type of viewpoint has been socially marginalized does not necessarily mean that it was silenced unjustly or that it is in fact credible and reliable. Stephen Macedo notes that "diversity and difference are not always to be celebrated" because "some groups have been pushed to the margins of society for good reason," for example, Nazis in the United States today.[15]

At least two distinct problems affect the attitude of openness toward views different from one's own. One problem pertains to the credibility or reliability of such views. (I discuss the second problem in the next section.) Some views different from one's own are warranted and reliable, whereas others are unwarranted and unreliable; still other views are mixtures of both. As noted earlier in the discussion of trust, Jones observes that the views that someone expresses may be unreliable for at least one of two possible reasons. Someone may report her views incompetently, in which case one would risk relying on her misjudgment. Or someone may be prevaricating, in which case one would risk relying on her insincerity. Someone's competence and sincerity are two features of someone's moral communication that can clearly go wrong.

Thus, the very attitude of trust that enables us to take seriously viewpoints different from our own is, at the same time, an attitude that makes us vulnerable to persuasion by viewpoints that are unwarranted or unreliable. It seems, then, that we cannot simply ask, what traits or criteria will lead one to accept diverse views? We must also ask, what traits or attitudes enable one to accept the *reliable* views of others while rejecting the *un*reliable views? That is, what traits or attitudes enable one to *differentiate* the warranted from the unwarranted in the views expressed by others?

Mere experiential reports can be incompetent in several distinct ways. For one thing, experiential reports can be—perhaps are always and necessarily—theory-laden. The experiences that someone reports are laden with theoretical commitments about norms, values, and the way the world is. Sometimes the theoretical commitments of others are obvious, and one can decide to accept or reject their moral testimony based on one's level of confidence in the underlying theoretical commitments. For some of us, for example, third-person claims to have seen ghosts, vampires, and (after 1977) Elvis are easy to reject. Other sorts of moral testimony, however, are much harder to assess, for example, conflicting claims made by enemies in a war zone.

Someone's experiential reports may also be affected by the experiential reports of others who have influenced *her* viewpoint. Someone may think she saw a ghost because her friends had made similar, previous claims that she trusted. Thus, what we get from the testimony of any one person may well be an amalgamation of what she has experienced in some pure sense, if there is such a thing, and the influence of both the theoretical commitments that shape her thinking and the moral testimony she herself has heard and accepted about conditions of the sort she is reporting. In trusting someone's testimony, one therefore accepts a good deal more than the unvarnished report of her "brute" experiences. Many of these background commitments and secondhand testimonies may be unarticulated and inaccessible to the reflective scrutiny or correction of those to whom the testimony is communicated.

It seems that there is no clear-cut line demarcating (mere) experiential reports from the expression of more full-blown views. Rather, there may only be blurred boundaries. In considering the moral views of others, we should be wary of trying to differentiate pure experiential reports from other sorts of views. At any rate, both multiculturalism and liberalism urge broader sorts of intellectual encounters with diverse others than simply that of attending to experiential reports. We are encouraged to encounter whole viewpoints different from our own, ranging from narrowly experiential testimony to the most abstract moral theories.

Perhaps a useful, although rough, distinction can be drawn between, on the one hand, the moral views and expressions of others that one has the resources and capacities for assessing and, on the other hand, the moral views and expressions of others that one lacks the resources or capacities for assessing.[16] If someone presents a moral conclusion along with evidence that is supposed to support it, one can explore the logic of the argument by using one's own reasoning skill to see whether the evidence really supports the conclusion. Assessing the logic of the argument may not require accepting anything on trust. Yet the moral communications of others are usually not this simple to assess. Often one has to consider the reliability of factual claims. If a moral viewpoint is to any extent beyond one's resources or capacities to assess critically, to that extent one's trust in the one who communicates it may be the primary or sole basis on which one can determine its acceptability. The line between accepting on trust and accepting on other grounds is not based on a distinction between different sorts of moral claims made by others (pure experiential testimony versus theoretical claims). Rather it is based on a distinction between what the listener has the resources to assess in its own terms and what she lacks the resources to assess in its own terms. Young moral learners with few epistemic resources have to accept even moral norms and values on trust if they are to accept these moral generalities at all.[17]

Consider again what is involved when accepting any moral viewpoints on trust. Should we go beyond trust to the attitude of wonder recommended by Young? If trust is risky, wonder would seem to be even more so. To be sure, Young recognizes that the attitude of wonder, which she urges us to adopt as the attitude of moral respect toward others, has some dangers. She notes that it can lead one to hold inappropriate views of another person—for example, a view of the other as "exotic," feeling such awe before her that she becomes inscrutable, or a "prurient curiosity" that prompts one to intrude too forcefully into her life.[18] Thus, Young worries about the harms that may befall those who are the targets of the wonderment of others.

Young does not, however, mention the sort of harm that may affect those who *harbor* the attitude of wonder. Wonder is far from a neutral attitude. Dictionary definitions include "the feeling of surprise, admiration, and awe which is excited by something new, unusual, strange, great, extraordinary, or not well understood." Dictionary synonyms of wonder include "admiration, appreciation, astonishment, reverence, surprise, and amazement."[19] Whereas several of these terms are neutral ("surprise" and "not well understood"), the great majority of them incline toward acceptance and approval. To regard a new moral view with wonder right from the start is thus to accept it partially right from the start and, perhaps, even to revere it. An attitude of wonder that is not balanced by any methods of critical assessment thus constitutes, at a minimum, a default stance of trust or acceptance. At a minimum, the attitude of wonder seems to provide no screen for filtering out moral communications expressed by others that are insincere or inaccurate.

We must remember that depraved views can be carefully masked. Before one has encountered a particular form of depravity, one may not know what that "other" is really like. By the time one knows what the other is really like, it may be too late to ward off her influence. One may have come to trust and be corrupted by what the other believes or values. Even nasty groups try to sell themselves by good deeds. Recently in Missouri, the Ku Klux Klan "adopted" a section of a state highway, that is, the KKK formally registered with a state program to take on the responsibility for keeping a stretch of highway clean. Notice that the Klan was not engaging in racist activities, nor was it even expressing any racist ideas. It was trying to do a "good deed," admittedly one that would bring it some free publicity. A legal challenge to the Klan's involvement in the program went all the way to the U.S. Supreme Court, which ruled, on First Amendment grounds, that the KKK could not be denied the opportunity to adopt a section of highway. (The Missouri Department of Transportation later threatened to rescind the privilege anyhow because the KKK did not keep its section of highway clean.[20])

Thus diverse groups may hold corrupt and depraved views, but mask their messages with genuine good deeds and promote a favorable public image of themselves and their views. If one were prompted to approach the KKK with wonder, would one be able to be sufficiently critical later on after learning their views about race? We will return to the question of what traits, attitudes, or guidelines will enable us to differentiate what is reliable from what is not reliable in viewpoints different from our own.

A Second Problem

Before we try to answer the question of discernment, we should note that there is a second problem with the attitude of unguarded intellectual openness. The first problem—the risk of accepting unreliable views and of being harmed by relying on them—affects everyone. The second problem is selective; it affects only some of us. This problem is the potential loss of self-respect that might occur in people who are the targets of the pervasive and demeaning attitudes of others.

Could it really be good for, say, a member of a scorned or despised minority group to contemplate in wonder and trust the perspectives of dominant, majority group members who scorn her? For a scorned minority group member to gain genuine understanding of the views of, say, the dominant group members who don't want her moving into their neighborhood, she would have to open herself up in wonder to their ideas and their concerns. She would have to make herself vulnerable to their points of view, *their* worries, *their* fears, their derogatory attitudes about *her*. If I am from a disadvantaged minority or national group and the "diverse" other is someone from a privileged majority or nation, do I really stand to benefit from lowering my intellectual guard, setting aside my distrust, and contemplating in wonder the perspectives of those who despise the sort of person I am? People who are already marginalized, disadvantaged, and the brunt of social stereotypes thus take an added risk by trying seriously to entertain viewpoints different from their own.

Therefore, whereas anyone takes an epistemic risk when approaching new views with unguarded intellectual openness, some people face an additional risk: the internalizing of scorn or hatred directed at themselves. Those who are socially devalued or stigmatized are thus particularly vulnerable to harm if they approach viewpoints different from their own with the attitude of wonder. Young recognizes that the oppressed will have problems if they try to "take the perspective" of socially privileged others, and she rejects the idea that doing so is required for moral respect. She fails to note, however, that the attitude of wonder, which she defends in its place, poses similar difficulties for those who are socially stigmatized.[21]

Because of this second problem, it seems that the current multicultural call for us all to learn about viewpoints other than our own cannot seriously be a call for *all* of us to do this with the same degree of intellectual openness toward *all other views.* The multicultural educational imperative is, I believe, really meant to be an intellectual wake-up call mainly for privileged social groups in Western societies whose views fully controlled the Western educational agenda until recent decades. In U.S. society, these groups include, among others, the white majority, men, Christians, and heterosexuals. These are the persons who might develop in moral discernment and understanding from an open, unguarded intellectual encounter with viewpoints different from their own. The "different" views would be those of minority races, minority religions, women, and other groups that were until recently silenced in much of the larger Western culture and whose perspectives were excluded from nearly all of the educational curriculum.

This is not to say that there are *no* ways in which members of stigmatized groups can benefit from encountering views different from their own. Oppressed or subordinated groups might benefit from mutual understandings they can forge with each other since they might discover that they face similar social problems and injustices. What stigmatized minorities have to worry about is an attitude of wonder toward those who scorn them.

Jones's Proposal

If most of us have to rely at least sometimes on what others say about moral matters, then we need to devise habits or tools for distinguishing the reliable from the unreliable in what others have to say. The problem is to determine which moral views are worth accepting and which are not and to articulate general guidelines for this discernment.

Jones argues that the appropriate stance to take toward moral testimony depends on at least four context-sensitive conditions: "climate," "domain," "consequences," and one's own trusting or distrusting "tendencies." Thus, according to Jones, attitudinal *climates* vary in the degree to which there is "strong motive to be untrustworthy." The traits that incline people to be trustworthy in some *domains* of knowledge or activity may be very widespread and easily attained so that one can have high confidence that people will tend to be trustworthy in those domains. Once a domain is specified, we should consider the *consequences* of trusting or not trusting someone in that domain: what are the risks either way? Finally, people should check their own trusting or distrusting *tendencies* for biases such as tendencies "to distrust young African-American men" or tendencies toward "self-interest."[22]

Jones, however, believes that these factors are difficult to assess in any situation. She therefore argues that "the appropriate default stance toward testifiers about morality is one of distrust." According to Jones, one should have a general, although not universal, "presumption against accepting moral testimony, where this presumption can take the form of either disbelieving such testimony, or withholding judgment." To move from this position of distrust toward one of trust in the testimony of a particular person or group of people, one should want "good evidence about the person's character, about possible hidden agendas, and about whether she has the sort of experiences that contribute to the kind of competence we are counting on her to have. We would also want to know that our witnesses have appropriate epistemic self-assessment," which means that they themselves do not exaggerate the epistemic reliability of what they have to say. Jones muses: "Perhaps the most trustworthy testifiers about moral matters are those who are least inclined to offer such testimony."[23]

An interesting contrast thus emerges between Jones and Young on the question of how to approach the moral communications of others. The attitude that Jones recommends is quite far from the "admiration," "awe," "appreciation," and "reverence" that inflect Young's recommended attitude of wonder. On Jones's view, one is to begin by considering new moral views with suspicion and distrust and to be open only to counterarguments that are convincing enough to overcome this initial barrier. Her overall emphasis is on keeping the *bad* or *unreliable* moral views *out* and on the attitudes a moral knower may employ to screen them. It appears that Young, on the other hand, pays special attention to attitudes a moral knower may use to let in and be *receptive* to the *good* or *reliable* moral viewpoints.

Both Jones's and Young's attitudes can give rise to mistakes. The default distrust that keeps bad moral testimonies out may also keep good moral testimonies out. Jones's default distrust may thus give rise to false negatives, viewpoints we should have relied on but instead dismissed because the evidence in their favor was not sufficient to overcome her default distrust. On the other hand, the attitudes that make someone receptive to good moral testimonies may also make them receptive to bad moral testimonies. Young's method of wonder may thus give rise to false positives, viewpoints accepted by someone whose wonderment did not sufficiently detect the unreliability of the new views. Is there some basis for saying that one of these two attitudes, default distrust or default wonderment, is in general more warranted or worthwhile than the other in the encounter with diverse moral viewpoints?

The views of Jones and Young may be separated at bottom by one or more quasi-factual assumptions—"quasi" because there is probably no way to confirm or disconfirm them, and their acceptance may therefore rest ultimately on faith.

One possible assumption has to do with how many of the diverse moral views in the world are warranted or reliable as compared to the number that are unwarranted or unreliable. Jones may be covertly assuming that moral views are more often wrong than right (so that default distrust will give good guidance more often than not), whereas Young might be covertly assuming the reverse. Or Jones may concede that diverse views are more often right than wrong, but she may worry that the wrong views can be so depraved or treacherous that it is better to rely on fewer really reliable people than to risk accepting even one bad moral view. Again, Young by contrast may worry less about our accepting a depraved view than about our rejecting the views of those who are reliable and deserve to be heard.

There may also be a difference in the political agendas of the two theorists. Jones refers to sexism and racism as examples of moral mistakes but is not focused on presenting a political viewpoint; her primary concern is with an issue of moral epistemology. Young, by contrast, has long been known to champion in her philosophical writings the public credibility of certain social groups such as women, racial minorities, and sexual minorities,[24] and the issues of abstract moral theory per se seem to be secondary.

Thus, notice that Young does not defend the attitude of wonder on abstract grounds alone. She bolsters her account with examples of testimonies she believes it would be genuinely worthwhile to accept, including Anita Hill, American Indians, and disabled people.[25] These specific examples are landmarks on a map of leftist sentiments in the United States today. They serve to give a certain substantive definition to the range of perspectives Young would want us to approach with wonder. Leftist audiences already find those particular viewpoints credible and would be happy to see other people approach them with wonder. Audiences not already so favorably inclined are not likely to be convinced.[26] Even leftist audiences should *wonder* whether wonder is the best attitude to bring to the contemplation of a viewpoint that is truly unknown and that has as much chance of being like Nazism as it has of being like Anita Hill's testimony. Should I really approach with "appreciation," "admiration," "awe," and "reverence" a view that, *for all I know*, might ultimately call for mass atrocities to be perpetrated against some innocent human community?

Suppose we scale back the intensity of Young's recommended attitude of wonder but still imagine a positive reaction. Two alternative possibilities are default trust and mere openness. Default trust involves accepting a newly encountered view unless good reasons become apparent for not doing so. Default trust is strongly positive but not so much as wonder in that it lacks the reverence that wonder connotes.

More weakly still, we can imagine an attitude of mere openness; Young herself uses this term along with "wonder." Openness is a matter of letting down one's guard. It involves an absence of trust, as well as an absence of distrust. At the same time, it is mildly positive. One is not shielded from the persuasive power of the new view by prejudgment or other biases that prevent a full and considered assessment of what the new view has to offer. One is intellectually unguarded, so to speak. The contrast to openness is to be closed to diverse moral views, to shut them out altogether. Openness lacks an adversarial posture of any sort, and no burden of proof is assigned.

Before drawing conclusions about whether any of these attitudes can promote reliable differentiation among diverse moral views, let us explore an important political dimension to this entire issue.

Politics

Young's wonder seems excessive. At the same time, Jones's default distrust, despite her political examples, may take insufficient account of the politics involved in the social grounding of moral knowledge.

Jones's fourth criterion for assessing moral testimony is about our own trusting or distrusting tendencies. Do I tend automatically to trust the testimony of some types of people but distrust that of other types? Tendencies such as these often reflect socially pervasive stereotypes and established cultural narratives. Stereotypes and cultural narratives usually accompany and reinforce patterns of political hierarchy and domination. Some groups are prejudged, say, as having criminal tendencies and are subjected to judicial violations based on that assumption. Jones's discussion of our personal trusting tendencies omits mention of the way in which these tendencies are culturally sustained and reinforced. To examine our trusting and distrusting tendencies, we should attend not merely to our own individual inclinations but also to the political forces at work in our larger social contexts.

As Lorraine Code argues, different groups in a society may have quite different degrees of social credibility. Evaluating testimony as if it were merely neutral empirical evidence ignores the social distribution of "cognitive authority," which is based partly on power.[27] The problem is much bigger than that of mere random individual biases. Gender, race, ethnicity, class, religion, sexuality, educational background, and other factors may influence the societal extent to which someone's moral (or other) testimony is considered credible by others. There are many groups at any time that have high society-wide credibility; their views, reports, explanations, and perspectives gain acceptance and influence in many important institutional processes, such as those of law and science. The voices of those with, say, little or no access to communications media are unable to gain the credibility they need in order to overcome default distrust and win assent for their moral views. Those voices need special support simply to be heard in the first place. A naive listener who, for example, sorts through the moral testimonies that appear in articles in the mass media may have no way to tell whether or not the articles represent all points of view involved in any particular affair. Unless someone can become acquainted with marginalized views in the first place, she will have no opportunity to try to understand or consider them.

Not only do people vary in the degree to which they themselves are believable to others; they also vary in the degree of influence they have over social practices in which the testimony of still *other* persons is under consideration. As Code notes, some people have the social power to promote or undermine the testimony of others,[28] at least to some audiences on some issues, for example, by controlling the mass media that help to shape stereotypes and cultural narratives. In the most extreme cases, some people can create institutional rules and norms that formally discredit the moral views or testimonies of particular groups of people. Legal theorist Kit Kinports writes, for example, about the way in which, "until recently, the uncorroborated testimony of the victim was an insufficient basis for a rape conviction in many states," something that was not true of uncorroborated testimony in cases of assault or theft.[29] Rape victims are typically female.

Macedo, as noted earlier, is right to recognize that being marginalized, oppressed, or silenced is no guarantee that one's views are credible or reliable. Yet being marginalized is no guarantee that one's views are noncredible or unreliable either. There is no shortcut to assessing diverse moral views. There is no way to avoid having to discriminate among the (often mutually contradictory) moral views of others.

Unfortunately, to have a reliable way of screening out untrustworthy moral views while letting in trustworthy moral views, someone would already have to have a justified political outlook. If having a justified political outlook requires having already wisely discriminated among the contradictory moral views of others, then a circularity problem looms large.[30] If someone needs an astute politics to begin to filter moral communications well, then there is no systematic way she can get herself started on the task. A new moral knower by definition does not yet have a justified political outlook that could warrant a sophisticated political screen. A mature moral reasoner can only hope she had wise—or correctable— early socialization.

Conclusions

Openness is appropriate in the early stages of encountering new and diverse moral views.

We have eliminated wonder and are left with openness, default trust, and default distrust as attitudes that might facilitate the encounter with new moral views.[31] Openness is distinctive in this group in appearing to be best suited to the early stages of encountering new moral views, the stages of acquaintance, understanding, and consideration. These stages mainly involve learning about the new view, and learning might not occur at all unless one suspends one's critical tendencies. Openness is an attitude that motivates one to move forward through these stages, where one sets aside one's preconceptions and biases, either for or against a new view (and those who hold it), and becomes familiar with the view in its own terms and with the reasons that support it in the estimation of its advocates. These stages of learning seem best facilitated by lowering one's guard, actively seeking acquaintance with and understanding of new views, and bracketing for awhile one's critical tendencies—in other words, by openness.

At the assessment stage, if one lacks relevant preconceptions,
one should withhold judgment as long as practical exigencies
allow it.

At some later point, one may have to move on to the fourth stage of encountering
a new moral view, that of assessment. At this stage, one should raise one's guard
once again and invoke criteria of assessment to see whether there are reasons for
or against the new view. Notice that Jones actually defines default distrust as "either disbelieving [moral testimony] . . . or withholding judgment."[32] I suggest that
we pry these two notions apart. They represent important, distinct attitudes. Thus
our assessment choices are at least three in number: default trust (accepting a
view unless good reasons appear for rejecting it), default distrust (rejecting a view
unless good reasons appear for accepting it), and indecisiveness. In the absence
of all knowledge about what to expect in a new viewpoint, there is no more reason
to prefer an attitude of default distrust than there is to prefer one of default trust.
These two attitudes seem equally warranted, or unwarranted, in the abstract.
Withholding judgment, however, is more warranted still in case one is able to
postpone reaching a conclusion. One thereby avoids making unnecessary mistakes. If one lacks preconceptions about a new view and there is no need to rush
to judgment, one should remain undecided and wait for good reasons on either
side.

If practical exigencies require conviction of some sort, one
should opt for default trust or default distrust as determined
by those of one's preconceptions that seem most warranted
and have proven most reliable in the past.

What if one has preconceptions that incline one in a certain direction regarding
a new moral view? We all come to self-consciousness with habits of trust toward
some individuals and groups and against trust toward other individuals and
groups. When we reach the stage of self-consciously reflecting on whom to believe, we are already entrenched in habits of trusting in the credibility of some
sources and rejecting the credibility of others. Our reactions to moral diversity constitute another "ship afloat," which we must repair piecemeal while still sailing.

When one has preconceptions about the perspective one is encountering,
withholding judgment may no longer be warranted or even possible. If one has
no reason to think one's own preconceptions are flawed and if one is required by
exigencies to make an assessment, one should lean as heavily as possible on one's
own (trustworthy) inclinations. If nothing else, the coherence of one's outlook
calls for consistency with the attitudes and norms one already holds until good
reasons appear for rejecting them. There is something to be said for being true to
oneself in the form of loyalty to one's existing convictions, as long as they have
not been discredited. Yet since we do not all share the same preconceptions and
predispositions to trust or not, we cannot, as Jones recognizes, generalize about
which views to accept and which not to accept.

*If one is a political activist, one should not call for wonder
or trust toward all diverse views in general.*

The public realm is filled with what we can call epistemic activists, each trying
to win credibility for her selected groups. A lot of political work on issues of
injustice and oppression consists simply of trying to promote societal trust in previously discredited groups. One of the primary aims of feminist work, for example,
is to make the case for the credibility of diverse sorts of women. Feminists work
actively to combat misogynist biases in all social domains.

Anyone who is trying to promote the societal credibility of the viewpoints of
particular groups is ill advised to defend a general attitude of trust or wonder
toward *all* diverse others or their viewpoints. If one really cares about improving
the credibility of a particular social group, one would not want people to approach
all views with wonder, especially those invoking distrust, scorn, or hatred toward
the group one is defending. One should be prepared, however, to accept openness
toward all new views at the *early* stages of encountering them. To argue that only
certain views or groups of persons should be approached with openness (or trust
or wonder, for that matter) is to draw distinctions that one's audience may not yet
be entitled to follow.

Of course, the exigencies of life and the need to act quickly may sometimes
force one to make rapid assessments of new moral views. Being open to new and
diverse moral views is a luxury that not all can afford at all times. Yet default trust
and default distrust probably occur more often than they have to. We should strive
to recognize those valuable opportunities when we can afford the time to learn
from and with others and to reassess where we stand morally in our worlds.

Notes

A much earlier version of this essay was presented under the title "Diversity and Moral
Character: Cultivation or Suffocation?" at a conference on "Moral Cultivation," University of Santa Clara, Santa Clara, California, April 14, 2001.

1. John Stuart Mill, *On Liberty*, ed. Elizabeth Rapaport (Indianapolis, Ind.: Hackett, 1978), 33–50.

2. See, for example, Martha C. Nussbaum, *Cultivating Humanity: A Classical Defense of Reform in Liberal Education* (Cambridge, Mass.: Harvard University Press, 1997).

3. These categories are, of course, not unrelated to culture.

4. Karen Jones, "Second-hand Moral Knowledge," *Journal of Philosophy* 96 (February 1999): 55–78, 56.

5. Both Iris Young and Lorraine Code refer to the debate surrounding the credibil-
ity of Anita Hill's testimony before the U.S. Senate Judiciary Committee in 1991
against Supreme Court nominee Clarence Thomas: Iris Marion Young, "Asymmetrical
Reciprocity: On Moral Respect, Wonder, and Enlarged Thought," in *Intersecting
Voices: Dilemmas of Gender, Political Philosophy, and Policy* (Princeton, N.J.:
Princeton University Press, 1997), 43, 52; Lorraine Code, *Rhetorical Spaces: Essays on
Gendered Locations* (New York: Routledge, 1995), 60–61, 75–77.

6. In this essay, the term "new view" refers to a view that has been *newly encountered* by the one who is considering it. Obviously, it need not be radically new in human history at the time of that encounter.

7. Jones, "Second-hand Moral Knowledge," 57.

8. Ibid., 67.

9. Ibid., 68–69.

10. Young, "Asymmetrical Reciprocity," 49.

11. Ibid., 53.

12. Luce Irigaray, *The Ethics of Sexual Difference* (Ithaca, N.Y.: Cornell University Press, 1984), 14.

13. Young, "Asymmetrical Reciprocity," 56.

14. Mill, *On Liberty*, 33–50.

15. Stephen Macedo, *Diversity and Distrust: Civic Education in a Multicultural Democracy* (Cambridge, Mass.: Harvard University Press, 2000), 12, 24–25.

16. To say that one has resources and capacities of one's own for assessing the moral views of diverse others is not necessarily to say that one does this entirely *alone*. A mature moral reasoner may assess new moral views by herself or in company with others. Moral assessment in either case is grounded in social practices and relationships.

17. A point made by Jones, "Second-hand Moral Knowledge," 55.

18. Young, "Asymmetrical Reciprocity," 56

19. *Webster's New Twentieth Century Dictionary of the English Language, Unabridged*, 2nd ed. (New York: Prentice Hall, 1983), 2103.

20. Staff and wire reports, "High Court Allows KKK to Adopt a Highway," March 5, 2001, p. 4, www.cnn.com/2001/LAW/03/05scotus.kkk.02/.

21. Young, "Asymmetrical Reciprocity," 48.

22. Jones, "Second-hand Moral Knowledge," 71–72.

23. Ibid., 72–73.

24. See, for example, Iris Marion Young, *Justice and the Politics of Difference* (Princeton, N.J.: Princeton University Press, 1990).

25. Young, "Asymmetrical Reciprocity," 41–44. Macedo also makes this observation about Young's arguments in *Diversity and Distrust*, 24–25.

26. Journalist David Brock published an influential article in the *American Spectator* and a subsequent best-selling book about Anita Hill that viciously assailed Hill's credibility, as well as her character. Since then, however, he has acknowledged that his attack was based on outright lies; see *Blinded by the Right: The Conscience of an Ex-Conservative* (New York: Crown Publishers, 2002). Unfortunately, the damage done to Anita Hill at the time is unlikely to be repaired by this belated recantation.

27. Lorraine Code, *Rhetorical Spaces: Essays on Gendered Locations* (New York: Routledge, 1995), 62.

28. Ibid., 60.

29. See, for example, Kit Kinports, "Evidence Engendered," *University of Illinois Law Review* 1991, no. 2: 413–456, 437.

30. Helen E. Longino notices this problem with regard to "standpoint epistemology" in *Science as Social Knowledge: Values and Objectivity in Scientific Inquiry* (Princeton, N.J.: Princeton University Press, 1990), 12.

31. This part of my discussion is based on conversations with Linda Nicholson and Helen Power. In these final remarks, I ignore the possibility of reinterpretation as a response to newly encountered moral views.

32. Jones, "Second-hand Moral Knowledge," 73.

13

Globalizing Feminist Ethics

Alison M. Jaggar

Global trade and interaction are not new, but their current intensification is unprecedented. Local communities have never been completely closed, but now their boundaries have become so porous that people speak of community disintegration. Economies have never been entirely self-sufficient, but never before has international trade been so crucial to the prosperity and even the survival of local economies. These developments have raised new problems for moral and political philosophy and so for feminist ethics.

Women are located at the center of these contemporary developments. They constitute a large and increasing portion of the labor force in many newly industrializing, as well as industrialized, countries; they (with their children) constitute 80% of the world's refugees; they are trafficked in a worldwide prostitution trade; and their bodies are the site of technological interventions designed both to promote and to control fertility. At the same time, women are frequently taken as emblems of cultural integrity, so that defending beleaguered cultures becomes equated with preserving traditional forms of femininity, especially as these are manifest in traditional female dress and practices of marriage and sexuality. Thus, women are situated in the vortex of contending social forces: on the one hand, centripetal tendencies toward increasing globalization and integration and, on the other hand, centrifugal tendencies toward nationalism and fragmentation.

Contemporary moral theory reproduces these tensions, counterposing a universalistic discourse of human rights against such approaches as communitarianism and postmodernism, which emphasize the local and so are often construed as relativist. In this context, philosophers' increasing rejection of moral foundationalism makes it difficult to see how conventional and local norms may be subjected to systematic moral critique. My larger project, from which this essay emerges, is to develop an account of practical moral reason that shows how respect for cultural difference may be combined with claims to postconventional moral objectivity. In developing this account, I draw on the dialogical tradition in

Western moral theory that stretches from Plato, through Locke and Kant, to Rawls and Habermas, and I take seriously the values that lie at the heart of this tradition, including the values of discursive equality, openness, and inclusiveness. In addition to being inspired by this philosophical tradition, my own understanding of practical discourse is also shaped by reflection on the discursive practices of recent feminist grassroots activism in North America.[1]

As developed by Karl-Otto Apel and Jurgen Habermas, classical discourse ethics defines moral justification in terms of universal consensus in conditions of domination-free communication. This definition is often derided as utopian—and so ultimately skeptical—for reasons that include not only practical difficulties of establishing universal discourse but also what appear to be insurmountable difficulties of principle, notably the impossibility of implementing anything like domination-free communication. Yet even though such problems are even more conspicuous in global than in local contexts, the beginnings of a global discourse community nevertheless seem to be emerging among feminists. These beginnings are most visible in official and semiofficial venues, such as the several UN conferences on women since 1975 and their accompanying nongovernmental organization (NGO) fora, but they are also evident in a multitude of ongoing interactions among grassroots groups, such as the Network of East/West Women and the Women's Global Network for Reproductive Rights.

One respect in which a feminist conception of practical moral discourse differs from that of classical discourse ethics is that it addresses directly issues of discursive equality and openness in situations inevitably structured by power. This essay begins to explore the role played by small communities in feminism's attempts to reconcile a commitment to open discussion, on the one hand, with a recognition of the realities of power inequalities, on the other hand.

Illustrating the Problem

My own conception of practical moral discourse seeks to reconstruct the norms guiding the discursive practices of many late twentieth-century groups of North American feminist activists. These groups have often limited discursive openness in two related ways. One way is by limiting their agendas: activist groups typically come together around certain moral convictions, such as opposing militarism or violence against women; rather than debating these basic moral commitments, they devote themselves to exploring their implications. Unquestioned within the group, such commitments become foundational for the groups' moral perspectives. The second way in which groups have often limited discursive openness is by restricting participation in their discussions, excluding individuals who do not share the basic commitments of the group or who do not have "standing" because they are outsiders.

The exclusion of outsiders or the closure of moral agendas are sometimes de facto but can be matters of explicit and fierce insistence. For example, some prostitutes' groups have emphatically rejected middle-class feminist analyses of them as victims of sexual exploitation; African-American women have sometimes asserted that domestic violence and rape by African-American men are topics that are off-limits to European Americans; some lesbian women have sought to exclude heterosexual women from discussing certain lesbian practices; and, outside the West, some North African women have objected to Western feminist criticisms of the practices of clitoridectomy and infibulation. One especially bitter controversy arose around an article co-authored by two Australian women, an anthropologist of European descent and a "traditional" Aboriginal. This article exposed astronomical rates of violence and rape, including frequent gang rapes, committed by Aboriginal men against Aboriginal women. The truth of the allegations was undisputed, but some Aboriginal women objected that it was inappropriate for this topic to be broached by a white woman, even in collaboration with an Aborigine.[2] Closing some debates and excluding some topics from some people's intervention seem to run entirely counter to the ideal of free and open discussion as that has been understood in Western moral philosophy. I suggest, however, that a feminist conception of moral discourse may be able to justify such exclusions without denying that ideal and may even do so in its name.

Groups of women who have sought to remove their lives from the critical scrutiny of outsider feminists have offered a number of rationales for their desire. Prostitutes' groups have argued that middle-class feminists are ignorant of the real conditions of prostitute life, and some North African women have argued that Western feminists do not understand the role of clitoridectomy and infibulation in African cultures. In both cases, the groups whose practices have been challenged by outsiders allege that the criticism is inadequately informed. Sometimes they also express concern that open discussion of certain issues may have deleterious consequences for their community; for instance, some lesbians worry that drawing attention to controversial lesbian practices may encourage attacks from homophobes, and some African-American women fear that their community may be divided by discussions of violence inflicted by African-American men.

Outsider feminists whose interventions are rejected often remain unconvinced by these arguments.[3] Some may respond by asserting their familiarity with the cultures or subcultures in question; others may argue that first-person experience is not authoritative, noting that victims frequently rationalize their abuse, as well as their "choices" to remain in abusive situations. The outsiders may also object to what they perceive as misplaced concern for "the community" as a whole at the expense of some women within it. They may even argue that ignoring the plight of such women is racist or ethnocentric, insofar as it suggests a moral double standard according to which high levels of abuse and exploitation are regarded as "culturally acceptable" for some women but not for others.

In evaluating these difficult and complex issues, it is important to notice that these examples all share some significant features. In each of the foregoing cases, those who seek to protect their lives from scrutiny belong to a group that is socially stigmatized and/or is a cultural minority and/or has a history of colonization, whereas those whom they wish to exclude belong to more powerful or hegemonic groups. Each of the groups whose practices are in question is struggling under external pressure to maintain a sense of self-respect and cultural integrity; more-over, each has been a frequent object of study by psychologists, sociologists, anthropologists, and even criminologists from outside that group. These social scientists have typically assumed that their studies have made them experts on the lives of those studied, whom they have often presented as exotic, as victims, or as pathological.

In this context, some communities' resistance to opening their lives for critical feminist examination from the outside may be interpreted less as an attempt to limit the discursive autonomy of others than as a claim to discursive autonomy for themselves. Women from nonhegemonic groups have good reason to suppose that if their lives were to become the subject of feminist discussion, their own perspectives might be discounted. The views of feminists with professional credentials would probably be taken as authoritative, especially if they were published in scholarly journals, where authors are positioned as experts and those studied become "informants" whose opinions are merely data for expert analysis. One critic of the white Australian anthropologist Diane Bell observed that even though Bell's controversial article was officially coauthored with an Aboriginal woman, Topsy Napurrula Nelson, Nelson's words were placed in italics and framed by Bell's prose, a device that distinguished Nelson's input from "the dominant White voice controlling the shape and tone of the academic text."[4]

Objections to the discursive intervention of feminist outsiders do not necessarily depend on any particular hypothesis about the outsiders' motivation. Outsiders may wish to advance their professional reputations by becoming recognized as experts on some group of marginalized women, they may enjoy posing as the rescuers of victimized women, or they may care deeply for the welfare of the women about whose lives they speak. Regardless of the speakers' motivations, the structure and context of their discursive interventions may have the consequence of positioning the subjects of their discourse as less than equal. In these circumstances, discussion of some issues by some feminists may not only mute the voices of other women but even suggest that they are incapable of speaking for themselves. Ironically, it was precisely the recognition of these kinds of oppressive dynamics that led Western women to form the feminist groups in which they developed the sorts of discursive practices that I now call Feminist Practical Dialogue.

Reflection on the previous examples reveals that idealized understandings of practical discourses as politically innocuous exchanges of ideas occurring in some timeless domain are seriously misleading. To address the moral and political issues surrounding empirical discourse, feminists must recognize that practical discussions are historical events with real-life consequences, not all of which may be controlled or foreseen. In addition, we must never forget that empirical discussions are always infused with power, which influences who is able to participate and who is excluded, who speaks and who listens, whose remarks are heard and whose dismissed, which topics are addressed and which are not, what is questioned and what is taken for granted, and even whether a discussion takes place at all. These aspects of moral discourse should be considered not only in feminist practice but also in philosophical theory. For instance, philosophers can appeal to them in explaining why inclusive participation and an open agenda may, on some occasions, impede rather than promote unconstrained discussion. Such considerations also help to explain the epistemological indispensability of closed communities of discourse.

The Epistemological Indispensability of Closed Communities

Themes of voice and silencing have been central to twentieth-century Western feminism, and by now there is an extensive feminist literature that dissects women's domination in or exclusion from discourse. One classic discussion is Gayatri Chakravorty Spivak's "Can the Subaltern Speak?" in which the author details how "subaltern" Third World women have been represented in discourse in ways that have obscured their subjectivity while promoting the interests of the authors of the texts.[5] In Spivak's example, Indian widows immolated on their husbands' funeral pyres in the practice of *sati* were represented by some British colonizers as victims who must be saved from the slaughter of "backward practices" and by some Indian men as heroes loyal to "Indian" cultural traditions.[6] In both Marxist structuralist and poststructuralist accounts, the widows' subjectivities were equally invisible. Meanwhile, Spivak asserts, the subaltern woman remains mute because she herself "cannot know or speak the text of female exploitation."[7]

Why the subaltern woman cannot *speak* of her exploitation at first does not appear mysterious; perhaps this is Spivak's rhetorical way of saying that her indigenous language is incomprehensible to intellectuals or that she cannot produce "texts" because she is illiterate. But why can't she even *know* about her exploitation? Even if she is unfamiliar with classic texts of exploitation, such as Marxism, surely she must be aware that there is something wrong with her situation. How can she be content in her oppression? One answer to this puzzle is suggested by Indian feminist Uma Narayan:

> Girls (of my grandmother's background) were married off barely past puberty, trained for nothing beyond household tasks and the rearing of children, and passed from economic dependency on their fathers to economic dependency on their husbands to economic dependency on their sons in old age. Their criticisms of their lot were articulated, if at all, in terms that precluded a desire for any radical change. They saw themselves as personally unfortunate, but they did not locate the causes of their misery in larger social arrangements.[8]

Narayan's words suggest that the subaltern woman's muteness is rooted not in slavish contentment but in her inability to conceptualize the injustice to which she is subjected. Like all diagnoses, this analysis implies the appropriate remedy: what the subaltern woman needs is a conceptual framework, a language capable of articulating her injuries, needs, and aspirations. The existing discourses or texts of exploitation do not provide such a language: even when they promise explicitly to liberate the subaltern, they obscure the distinctive nature of her oppression;

indeed, by purporting to speak for her, they position her as mute. To articulate her specific exploitation, the subaltern woman must create her own language.

Language is a public construct, and its absence is a public, not a private, deficit. Creating a new language is by definition a collective project, not something that can be accomplished by a single individual; if the subaltern woman seeks to enter practical discourse alone, therefore, her experience is likely to remain distorted and repressed. She can overcome her silence only by collaborating with other subaltern women in developing a public language for their shared experiences. She must become part of a group that explicitly recognizes itself as sharing a common condition of oppression—in Marxist terms, a group that constitutes itself as a class for itself, as well as in itself. She must claim a collective identity distinct from her identification as the particular daughter, wife, and mother of particular others. Only by creating a collective identity with other women in similar situations, perhaps with other daughters, wives, and mothers, can the subaltern even come to see herself as subaltern, and only in this way can she break through the barriers to her speech. Articulating women's distinctive interests requires a language and this, in turn, requires a community. Without either of these, the emergence of counterhegemonic moral perspectives remains impossible.

Small communities, whose members are known personally to each other, have been indispensable to the development of Western feminist moral perspectives. They have enabled Western feminism to offer alternative understandings of social phenomena expressed in a distinct vocabulary that includes expressions like "sexism," "womanism," "sexual objectification," "date rape," "othermother," "the double day," "sexual harassment," "the male gaze," "*mestizaje*," and "emotional labor." Such communities have typically focused on some specific aspect of what they have taken to be women's subordination, and they have taken some beliefs for granted, as given within that group. They may have accepted as given the wrongness of militarism or rape or domestic violence or pornography, or they may have accepted as given the value of lesbianism or peer counseling or woman-produced music or erotica. Assuming some such beliefs as foundational for them, the members of the community then have gone on to explore the implications of these beliefs and to elaborate a distinctive moral perspective. For example, once the moral legitimacy of lesbianism was accepted, lesbians went on to raise questions about why people, especially women, are heterosexual; about the social and political consequences of a norm of heterosexuality; about the ways in which heterosexuality is implicated in Western conceptions of gender; and about prevailing definitions of sexuality and family.

It is not only feminists or even moral thinkers whose systems of ideas have been developed in the context of small personal communities united by adherence to certain beliefs or methods. The history of science is full of accounts of "invisible colleges," or groups of scientists working from shared assumptions. David L. Hull calls such groups "demes," by analogy with local populations of organisms sufficiently isolated that they play an important role in biological evolution.[9] The notion of "schools" of artists, such as the Bauhaus, is commonplace, and philosophers have frequently worked in such groups as the Jena Circle (to which

Hegel belonged), the Vienna Circle, the Frankfurt School and the Oxford philosophers. All these small, usually face-to-face communities functioned as intellectual crucibles in which systems of ideas were explored and elaborated.

Helen Longino notes that progress in science would be impossible unless certain questions were closed to debate, at least temporarily: "The knowledge-extending mission of science requires that its critical mission be blocked. Were the critical dimension of science not controlled, inquiry would consist in endless testing; endless new proposals and new ideas would be subjected to critical scrutiny and rejected."[10]

Developing systems of moral and political ideas also requires that certain premises be held constant. By uniting around certain shared assumptions, moral and political communities provide intellectual space in which members are continually freed from pressure to defend their premises and explain their technical vocabulary. Because they are typically small and the members known personally to each other, communication within such communities is likely to be informal and rapid. Half-formed ideas may be tried out and sometimes may be developed by members literally thinking together.

When the ideas involved are heretical by the standards of the larger society, such communities provide emotional, as well as intellectual, support for their members. Patricia Hill Collins asserts that a "realm of relatively safe discourse, however narrow, is a necessary condition for Black women's resistance."[11] A single dissenting individual is likely to be labeled crazy, if not wicked, and in the absence of support she may even come to regard herself as wicked or crazy. María Lugones observes that "unless resistance is a social activity, the resister is doomed to failure in the creation of a new universe of meaning, a new identity, a *raza mestiza*. Meaning that is not in response to and looking for a response fails as meaning."[12] When others share the dissenter's views or endorse her methods, the conditions exist for developing an oppositional identity that individuals often find validating, even emancipatory. Sarah Hoagland writes that "coming out (as a lesbian) was, for me, coming home. I experienced the sensation of landing and centering. It is lesbians who inspire me, lesbian energy which enlivens me."[13] Within the safety of her community, the dissenter may feel that finally she has the freedom to "be herself." She no longer has to be on guard or to dissemble. Finally, she is free to be "authentic," to say—and therefore discover—what she "really" thinks. Paradoxically, however, the same features that enable small moral communities to liberate the thinking of their members often simultaneously operate to limit it.

Moral and Epistemological Hazards of Closed Communities

Although it is liberating for the members of closed communities to be freed from having to defend their basic assumptions, their thought is also restricted by the constraints on what may be questioned within those communities. In scientific communities, shared assumptions often remain hidden and only idiosyncratic beliefs are challenged.[14] The same is true in moral and political communities of right, left, and center, all of which appeal to foundational values often thought to be enshrined in documents taken as authoritative, such as the Bible, the Communist Manifesto, or the U.S. Constitution. In consequence, intragroup disagreement is typically cast as debate over how to interpret the community's foundational values or texts.

Although it would be impossible to develop systems of moral and political ideas unless certain assumptions were temporarily taken for granted, it is equally true that, if those assumptions are never opened to challenge, the system based on them becomes a form of dogmatism. Members of the community find themselves forced to express questions and disagreements obliquely, perhaps even to suppress them entirely, at best to articulate them in the approved language, larded with references to the approved texts. People on the outside may regard the community as a cult, especially if the ideas to which it is committed are heretical or unorthodox.

All communities exert pressure on their members to conform to the prevailing interpretation of their unifying assumptions and values. These pressures are likely to be especially intense in small oppositional communities beleaguered by pressures from the larger society. Fearful of assimilation or defeat, such communities may regard internal conformity as a necessary condition of their survival, and in these circumstances dissent may appear as betrayal. Community resistance to challenge and change is also likely to be stronger when the members' self-definitions are centrally bound up with the community as constituted since dissent challenges more orthodox members of the community to modify their cherished beliefs and threatens values integral to their sense of who they are. When members regard their identities as inseparable from the community, they may also fear that change in the values of the community will not only affect the way the community is perceived by outsiders but also reflect on the members personally. If the community has a leader or leaders, they are likely to feel their authority threatened by dissenters, a challenge they are especially likely to resist if their work with the community is central to their life activity.

Most small communities encourage conformity through formal or informal sanctions, even if these are no more than chilliness toward or ridicule of certain ideas. Often, such communities also seek to strengthen group loyalty by developing a sense of superiority in relation to the larger society. Community members are encouraged to view themselves as an enlightened elite, dismissing those who disagree with them as sinful, ignorant, or victims of false consciousness. This perception may be used to justify different standards of behavior toward those within and those outside the community. The sense that the community is an ingroup enjoying a privileged religious, scientific, political, or moral perspective also strengthens the community's ultimate weapon for enforcing conformity, namely, the threat of expulsion. Not merely excluded from the group, a nonconformist may be defined as unworthy to belong to it. She is labeled a heretic or a pagan, a quack or a charlatan, a traitor, a renegade or a counterrevolutionary—no longer a "true" feminist or communist, unprofessional, or un-American.

The threat of expulsion is the ultimate sanction, enforcing conformity in most communities. How far the threat is successful in suppressing dissent depends on how much community members fear exclusion, and this fear varies according to the type of community in question, its relationship to the larger society, the needs it satisfies for its members, and the dependence members feel on that community. If the members of a religious community believe that excommunication will result in an eternity of hellfire, they have an extremely powerful incentive to conform; so do members of a professional organization for whom expulsion will result in the loss of their occupational licenses. By contrast, the prospect of expulsion from a neighborhood swimming club is likely to be unpleasant but not especially frightening because club membership does not represent the only way in which members can fulfill their needs for exercise and social affiliation.

When belonging to a particular community is central to a member's sense of her own identity, the threat of expulsion is likely to loom extraordinarily large. Leaving the community may represent losing connection with the religious, moral, political, or cultural values that have given meaning to her life. It may represent losing her emotional home; her sense of belonging; her colleagues, comrades, friends, and lovers. Such fears are especially intense for members of racial or ethnic and oppositional communities because no comparable alternatives are likely to be available. This is one reason that community loyalty and discipline are often especially strong among ethnic and cultural minorities and on both the right and the left of the political spectrum.

Some communities may seek to forestall challenges to their beliefs or values by limiting diversity among those they admit, excluding people thought likely to hold disruptive opinions or values or even people with an unacceptable image. Ethnic or cultural minorities may refuse to admit "half-bloods" or people who have been "Westernized"; lesbian communities may refuse to admit bisexuals; gay groups may exclude drag or leather queens. Conscious policies of exclusion reinforce the tendencies toward cultural homogeneity that exist in all small communities whose members rely on each other for emotional, as well as intellectual, support.[15] Policing the boundaries of the community serves to maintain the "purity" of its beliefs and values by insulating its members from the challenge of alternative thinking.[16]

Endemic to closed communities are a number of closely related epistemological and moral dangers. They include the dangers of repression and denial of autonomy, dogmatism, intellectual dishonesty and self-deception, elitism, and partialism. For these reasons, I contend that, although temporarily closed communities are indispensable for the development of systematic alternatives to hegemonic moral systems, the alternatives they produce eventually must be subjected to wider moral evaluation. To increase the degree to which their moral agreements are justified, communities ultimately must open their basic commitments to critical scrutiny from the outside.

Globalizing Feminist Discourse

For contemporary Western feminists to open our basic commitments to critical scrutiny requires considering or reconsidering perspectives we have hitherto excluded. This may mean that we reconsider the views of those Western antifeminists who assert that a woman's place is in the home and that date rape and harassment are figments of paranoid feminist imaginations. It may also mean that we take account of Nonwestern perspectives, especially those ignored or demonized by Western media. Most immediate and urgent, however, it requires that Western feminists learn to hear and consider respectfully the views of Nonwestern women from the so-called Third World, including women whose voices are muted even within their own nations.[17] Most especially, we should pursue critical engagement with those members of Nonwestern communities who share some of our own commitments but who may have disagreements or different perspectives on particular issues. Critical dialogue between members of communities that have significant differences but still share some basic concerns is likely to be more immediately useful in promoting reassessments of our own commitments and refinements of our own views than "dialogue" with those whose commitments and worldviews are far removed from our own. Dialogue with those who share many of our values and commitments is also almost indispensable for making social change within democratic contexts.

Some would challenge the possibility of global feminist dialogue on the grounds that feminism is not a worldwide movement. Such a view has often been held by Western feminists, who have assumed that the lot of Nonwestern women can be improved only through the introduction of Western feminist ideas. Chandra Talpade Mohanty observes that Western feminist images of the "average third world woman" have often portrayed her as leading "an essentially truncated life based on her feminine gender (read: sexually constrained) and her being 'third world' (read: ignorant, poor, uneducated, tradition-bound, family-oriented, victimized, etc.)." Mohanty contrasts this representation of Nonwestern women with the implicit self-representation of Western women "as educated, as modern, as having control over their own bodies and sexualities, and the freedom to make their own decisions."[18]

Nonwesterners, as well as Westerners, have often portrayed feminism as an exclusively Western phenomenon. Kumari Jayawardena observes:

> The concept of feminism has . . . been the cause of much confusion in Third World countries. It has variously been alleged by traditionalists, political conservatives and even certain leftists, that feminism is a product of "decadent" Western capitalism; that it is based on a foreign culture of no relevance to women in the Third World; that it is the ideology of women of the local bourgeoisie; and that it alienates or diverts women from their culture, religion and family responsibilities on the one hand, and from the revolutionary struggles for national liberation and socialism on the other.[19]

The belief that feminism is primarily a Western phenomenon, ironically shared by both Nonwestern antifeminists and many Western feminists, is in fact mistaken. Kumari Jayawardena documents how women in Asia and the Middle East have fought collectively against their subordination from the late nineteenth century on, though Nonwestern women have been less likely than Western women to form autonomous women's organizations and have been more likely to express their feminism in the context of nationalist struggles, working-class agitation, and peasant rebellions.[20] Uma Narayan writes that the pain that motivated her Indian feminism "was earlier than school and 'Westernization,' a call to rebellion that has a different and more primary root, that was not conceptual or English, but in the mother-tongue."[21]

Chandra Talpade Mohanty observes, "No noncontradictory or 'pure' feminism is possible."[22] Today, in the world beyond the industrialized West both small groups and large, government-sponsored organizations dedicated to improving the status of women are proliferating, and in Nonwestern as in Western contexts, the beliefs of these groups reveal tensions between conservative and radical ideas. For instance, some Nonwestern movements that assume the label of feminist have failed to address forms of domination affecting the lives of poor and peasant women or to challenge the ideology of the middle-class family; meanwhile, other Nonwestern movements concerned with increasing the self-reliance of poor women and enlarging their choices nevertheless refrain from direct challenges to male privilege[23] or eschew the label of feminist because they perceive it as a white, middle-class movement narrowly defined as a struggle against gender discrimination.[24] Everywhere in the world, feminism is maligned and contested.

Whether or not they call themselves feminist, innumerable groups outside the West are currently working to promote what Maxine Molyneux calls women's gender interests. Molyneux defines gender interests as "those that women (or men for that matter) may develop by virtue of their social positioning through gender attributes."[25] She distinguishes practical from strategic gender interests. The former emerge directly from their concrete life situations and include such immediately perceived necessities as food, shelter, water, income, medical care, and transportation. Molyneux notes that demands for these "do not generally . . . challenge the prevailing forms of subordination even though they arise directly out of them."[26] Indeed, addressing women's practical gender interests may even reinforce the sexual division of labor by reinforcing the assumption that it is women's responsibility to provide for their families. By contrast, women's strategic gender interests are defined as necessary to overcoming women's subordination. According to Molyneux, they may include all or some of the following, depending on the social context:

> the abolition of the sexual division of labor; the alleviation of the burden of domestic labor and childcare; the removal of institutionalized forms of discrimination such as rights to own land or property, or access to credit; the establishment of political equality; freedom of choice over childbearing; and the adoption of adequate measures against male violence and control over women.[27]

It is groups working to promote women's strategic gender interests that are most likely to share the basic commitments held by many Western feminists.[28]

Because of their potentially challenging nature, local grassroots groups dedicated to addressing women's strategic gender needs in the Third World are largely unsupported either by national governments or bilateral aid agencies.[29] They may be seen as communities of resistance comparable in many ways to Western feminist communities. Like some Western feminist groups, which may open women's health centers or run automobile or home maintenance workshops, many Nonwestern groups find that they can develop the skills and motivation necessary for addressing women's strategic gender interests by working immediately on practical gender interests. One example is the Forum Against Oppression of Women, which in 1979 began campaigning in Bombay to draw attention to such issues as rape and bride burning but soon shifted its focus to housing, which was an especially acute problem for women deserted or abused by their husbands in a culture where women by tradition had no access to housing in their own right. Organizing around homelessness raised awareness of the male bias in inheritance legislation, as well as in the interpretation of housing rights, and ultimately ensured that women's strategic gender needs related to housing rights were placed on the mainstream political agenda.[30]

Even if we grant a significant base of similar commitments between Western feminists and Nonwestern women committed to advancing women's strategic gender interests, there are many obstacles to dialogue that is genuinely egalitarian, open, and inclusive.[31] Still, these are not insuperable barriers to the possibility of global feminist discourse.

Who May Participate in Global Feminist Discourse?

If feminism is committed to inclusiveness, one might reasonably infer that everyone concerned about ending the subordination of all women is eligible to participate in global feminist discourse. To draw this inference, however, is to forget our earlier recognition that discourse is not an ahistorical abstraction but rather a series of discrete encounters that occur at specific places and times among specific individuals, who stand to each other in a variety of specific social, as well as power, relations. Even though I contend that equality, openness, and inclusiveness are central norms of feminist moral discourse, we have seen that they are not incompatible with limiting some people's access to some discussion about some topics on some occasions.

In putting the ideals of openness and inclusiveness into practice, it is necessary to remember both the social constitution of moral rationality and the vast power inequalities between the present Western and Nonwestern worlds. The first point entails that it is reasonable to exclude from specific moral discussions people who seem to share no common convictions on the basis of which rational discussion could occur; such people indeed exclude themselves. The second point suggests that it is sometimes reasonable for a beleaguered moral community to exclude members of more powerful communities, especially when the beleaguered community is addressing certain internal or domestic issues, such as the earlier example of Aboriginal violence against women. Members of subordinated groups may not wish to discuss problems affecting their community with members of more powerful communities, especially if the powerful communities already claim cultural superiority. Criticism of one's own cultural practices in the hearing of outsiders may be experienced as a form of betrayal, and the presence of outsiders who are perceived as more powerful may inhibit discussion among insiders. That the ideal of unconstrained discourse may sometimes permit or even require members of dominant groups to be excluded from the discourse of subordinated groups does not entail, of course, that it is equally legitimate for the members of dominant communities to exclude members of subordinated groups from their discussions, especially when the dominant groups are discussing practices that have a significant impact on the subordinated groups.

Even though there may be reasonable grounds for excluding members of dominant groups from specific occasions of discourse, outsiders' concerns about the situation of women in specific cultures are not necessarily illegitimate. When cultural relativism is espoused by the relatively powerless and impoverished, it may be a means of expressing resistance to cultural imperialism; when it is advocated by the wealthier and more powerful, however, cultural relativism is just as likely to express imperial arrogance as an ethnocentric insistence on the absolute superiority of the norms of the wealthier culture. For instance, it is certainly presumptuous for Western feminists to assume that they are already aware of the most important problems faced by women outside the West or that they are experts on how those problems should be solved, but it does not manifest genuine cultural respect to assume without question that Nonwestern women are content with lives that Western women would find constraining, exhausting, or degrading. Conversely, it is equally legitimate for Nonwestern women to raise questions about the moral permissibility of practices widely accepted by Western feminists, practices that might include sex work or the integration of women into the military. Global feminism requires concern for women in other communities and nations, and raising questions about the moral justifiability of foreign practices is very different from peremptorily condemning them, let alone intervening unilaterally to change them.

In an interesting discussion of the relative advantages and disadvantages of insiders and outsiders who engage in social criticism, David Crocker argues that insiders are not exclusively privileged in morally evaluating their own cultures. Insiders enjoy the advantages of understanding the cultural meaning of their own society's practices, of being able to express their evaluations in language accessible to their community, and of possessing undisputed standing for engaging in social criticism; but they also suffer characteristic disadvantages, such as possible ignorance of alternative ways of seeing and doing things and susceptibility to social pressures that may inhibit their freedom to express their criticisms. Outsiders suffer the disadvantages of unfamiliarity with cultural meanings, the perception that they are not entitled to intervene discursively in the affairs of another culture, and the possibility of ethnocentric arrogance or its inverse, romanticization of the culture in question. But they also enjoy the advantages of external perspectives, which may reveal things hidden from insiders; familiarity with novel moral ideas; and relative social freedom to say what needs to be said.[32]

Despite the difficulties and dangers of cross-cultural moral discourse, it is not impossible for outsiders to participate in evaluating the internal practices of another culture. Advocates of women's strategic gender interests in both the West and the Third World, therefore, should not regard questions and criticisms of our own cultural practices by our foreign counterparts as inevitably presumptuous or unwarranted but rather should view them as moral resources. For feminism to become global does not mean that Western feminists should think of themselves as missionaries, carrying civilization to primitive and barbarous lands, but neither does it mean that people concerned about the subordination of women in their own culture may dismiss the plight of women in others. At least on the level of morality, global feminism means that feminists in each culture must reexamine their own commitments in light of the perspectives produced by feminists in others so that they may recognize some of the limits and biases of their own beliefs and assumptions. Of course, the moral evaluations of any cultural practice must always be "immersed" rather than "detached," taking account of "the practices, the perceptions, even the emotions, of the culture."[33] Elsewhere, I suggest that a feminist conception of discourse, with its emphasis on listening, personal friendship, and responsiveness to emotion and its concern to address power inequalities, is especially well suited to facilitate such an immersed evaluation.

We have seen already that the more conformist members of any community are likely to challenge dissenters' status as insiders; in a Third World context, attempts have sometimes been made to discredit the voices of African feminists or Western-trained medical personnel when they have been raised in opposition to traditional practices such as female genital surgery, portraying such critics as no longer authentic members of their communities. But community membership is partly, though not entirely, a matter of self-definition, and it is rarely clear who is entitled to define others as inside or outside moral communities or by what process. All communities change, and there is no reason to identify a community with its most conservative elements or to assume that individuals who dissent from some of their community's moral beliefs thereby renounce their membership in that community.

Recognizing the possibility—indeed, the inevitability—of disagreement *within*, as well as *among*, moral communities complicates our hitherto simple model of insiders and outsiders. For instance, if we were to determine that issues that appeared to concern only a single group might be assessed solely by members of that group, so that only prostitutes could evaluate prostitution and only African women could discuss clitoridectomy and infibulation, we would immediately encounter new problems of identity, authorization, and legitimization. Who is entitled to speak for a group as a whole and whence derives her authority?[34] Can ex-prostitutes speak for prostitutes who are currently working? Can an African woman who has received a Western education fairly represent other African women? There is no reason to suppose that African women, prostitutes, lesbians, or African-American women all think alike, and dissenters in these groups may be silenced by women who claim to speak for the whole. It is interesting to notice

how the urban Aboriginal women who participated in the Bell controversy delegit-
imized the voice of Topsy Naparrula Nelson by labeling her "traditional," even
though it could well be argued that Nelson was better qualified than her Western-
educated challengers to speak for other Aboriginal women precisely by virtue of
her traditional identity. Some Aboriginal women who had no opportunity to participate in the published debate might have agreed with Nelson in welcoming the
intervention of an outsider whose professional credentials enabled her to be heard
while their own voices were ignored.

Most people actually belong to more than one community, and as the world
becomes increasingly integrated through international trade, population migra-
tion, and electronic communication, communities are increasingly likely to overlap and individuals to be multicultural or multilingual. Poet Meena Alexander,
born in India, educated in North Africa and Britain, currently living in New York
City, describes herself as a "woman cracked by multiple migrations":

> Everything that comes to me is hyphenated. A woman poet, a woman
> poet of color, a South Indian woman poet who makes up lines in En-
> glish, a postcolonial language, as she waits for the red lights to change
> on Broadway. A Third World woman poet, who takes as her right the
> inner city of Manhattan, making up poems about the hellhole of the
> subway line.[35]

In the circumstances of the contemporary world, even women who never
physically leave their communities of origin are increasingly likely to evaluate
their own lives in light of what they know about the situation of women in other
cultures—though it remains true that Nonwestern women are likely to know
much more about Western cultures than vice versa. When external influences
operate through a local response to things learned elsewhere, Nussbaum and Sen
argue, it is still an internal rather than an external evaluation of the practices of a
given culture. They contend that "criticizing the position of women in, say, today's Iran by reference to freedom enjoyed by women elsewhere is no more 'external' than reference to the position of women in Iran's own past."[36]

Although cultural communities are not fictions, they are set increasingly in a
larger global context in which moral traditionalists often bemoan the impossibility
of banishing external or foreign influences. Not only do many direct forms of economic and political intervention exist but also, when global communications are
so rapid and extensive, the sheer existence of alternative ways of life itself becomes
a moral intervention. Once again, it must be noted that the external pressure for
change is much stronger on Nonwestern than on Western cultures and that Western economies and politics inevitably will undermine some aspects of Nonwestern
cultures while reinforcing others. Because nothing seems likely to prevent these
eventualities, it is especially important for Western feminists to seek ways of being
allies to Nonwestern women who are seeking to affect these developments so that
they may promote rather than undermine the strategic gender interests of women
in their communities.

What Is on the Global Feminist Agenda?

Western feminists have often assumed that priority in international feminist discourse must be given to what they perceive as horrific Nonwestern practices such as polygamy, the sex-selective abortion of female fetuses, female seclusion, arranged and child marriage, unilateral divorce, bride price and bride burning, female infanticide, and currently the most popular topic of all, so-called female circumcision, or female genital surgery. The last, in particular, has now become a stock example in Western classroom discussions of moral universalism versus cultural relativism, and consideration of this issue has generated an extensive literature on such topics as discursive incommensurability and moral relativism.

Nonwestern women naturally resent what they regard as a sensationalized Western focus on non-Western marital and sexual practices.[37] Western discussions are typically predicated on the assumption that female genital surgery is morally unjustified, thus framing the issue as one of balancing the threats to the health and welfare of Third World women against the evils of maternalism or cultural imperialism. A related problem is that so much focus on these practices encourages Western feminists to regard themselves as missionaries, spreading the civilizing word of feminism, while simultaneously positioning Nonwestern women as backward, barbarous, and victimized. Finally, Western discussions of female genital surgery and similar Nonwestern practices often misleadingly homogenize Nonwestern communities and ignore the existence of indigenous forms of dissent.[38]

Regardless of the circumstances in which it may become legitimate for outsiders to involve themselves in the domestic affairs of another community or nation, our increasingly integrated contemporary world does not lack issues that affect women more globally. Some cluster around the worldwide phenomenon of gendered violence against women; this phenomenon was explored at a global tribunal of women's NGOs, which met in Vienna in 1993 in conjunction with the Second World Conference on Human Rights to urge that violence against women be recognized as a violation of human rights, as well as to highlight the connection between the murder, torture, and sexual coercion and abuse of women and their economic vulnerability. Many other issues are much less comfortable for Western feminists to address since discussion may reveal that most Westerners are on the wrong side of the moral divide. Central to these uncomfortable questions is the justice of the global system itself, a question that has been addressed directly by few Western feminists, especially feminist philosophers.

There are many ways in which what occurs on one side of the world affects women on the other; even if Third World women's oppression cannot be reduced to imperialism, it nevertheless exists in a context of economic domination reinforced by Western military interventions, either directly or by proxy. Matters of international feminist concern therefore include not only explicitly gendered issues—such as efforts by Western agencies to include Third World women in "development" or to control their fertility by linking so-called aid with prohibitions on abortion or insistence on contraception—but also less evidently gendered issues about the nature of development and the forces that currently define it.

Most pressing among these issues may be the debt owed by the Third World to the West. During the late 1960s and 1970s, when interest rates were low, the Third World engaged in massive borrowing to finance economic and social development. By the end of the 1970s, with interest rates rising, the Third World had increasing difficulty in paying the interest on its loans, and a world debt crisis resulted. Since 1982, severe "structural adjustment" policies have been imposed on the Third World by Western-controlled financial institutions such as the World Bank and the International Monetary Fund, whose primary concerns are to ensure that the debt to Western banks be serviced. These institutions' insistence on export-led development in the Third World and on sharp reductions in the economic and welfare functions of these states resulted, as early as 1986, in a net annual outflow from the Third World to the West three times as large as the amount received in aid from all Western sources. This hemorrhage of wealth has inevitably had catastrophic consequences for the living standards of most Third World women, though it has benefited its elites.[39] Related issues of global feminist concern include plant relocations by multinational corporations from the West to the Third World, multinational extraction of Third World resources, and Western conceptions of development and patterns of consumption.[40] These provide a context for discussing issues such as environmental degradation in both the Third World and the West;[41] the trade in heroin and cocaine;[42] militarism;[43] tourism, including sex tourism;[44] population control;[45] and the international traffic in women.

Western and Third World women are not affected equally by recent changes in the world economic order: Third World women are generally affected more adversely than Western women. A tiny minority of Third World women and a much larger proportion of Western women benefit from these changes, at least in some respects; but in both worlds the poorest women suffer most. In both worlds, moreover, the contemporary structure of the world economic order affects the lives of women differently from, and generally more harshly than, the way it affects men's lives. Thus these superficially ungendered matters are actually issues of the most urgent feminist concern.

Is There a Global Feminist Discourse Community?

Many Western accounts of moral rationality invoke idealized conceptions of moral community.[46] Idealizations offer simplified theoretical models that are often illuminating but may also mislead. My own project of developing a feminist conception of practical moral discourse is motivated by the conviction that the idealized communities postulated by many Western moral philosophers obscure several crucial features of empirical moral discourse, including considerations of social power.

Some authors have suggested that global feminism should be understood in terms of an "imagined community."[47] This expression gained its contemporary currency from Benedict Anderson's book *Imagined Communities*, which describes the myths and practices used by builders of modern nation-states to create a sense of common national identity and patriotism among disparate peoples.[48] Drawing on Anderson's insight that all communities are bound together by a shared conception of their history, traditions, ideals, and values, Ann Ferguson suggests that thinking of global feminism in terms of an imagined community might inspire individual feminists to see themselves as part of a global sisterhood. Ferguson emphasizes that such identification must be more than a fantasy, requiring engagement in actual meaning- and value-making rituals with women who are not of one's own national origin.[49] Margaret Walker, however, worries about the hazards of imagining a global feminist community: "Imagined communities are seductive because they yield real psychic comforts, powerful feelings of belonging and mattering; imagined communities are irrelevant or dangerous because they distract our attention from actual communities."[50]

Frequently overlooked features of actual communities include their fluidity and internal heterogeneity. The boundaries of empirical communities are shifting, permeable, and frequently contested; empirical communities are often riven by dissent, and their members often belong simultaneously to other communities. Ignoring these aspects of empirical communities encourages what Narayan calls "cultural essentialism," that is, images of national and cultural contexts as "sealed rooms, impervious to change, with a homogenous space 'inside' them inhabited by 'authentic Insiders' who all share a uniform and consistent account of their institutions and values."[51] "Cultural essentialism" has often been used to serve colonial purposes, but Narayan observes that today it is sometimes adopted uncritically by Western feminists in well-meaning efforts to recognize "Difference." Narayan argues that cultural essentialism is problematic not only because of its empirical inadequacy but also because it promotes sharp oppositions, which, like all binaries, overvalue one pole while disparaging the other. Cultural essentialism typically draws contrasts between Western and Nonwestern cultures. One version assigns to the West a commitment to such values as liberty and equality, despite innumerable examples of Western subjugation and inequality, while portraying such appalling but exceptional practices as *sati* as central to Indian culture;[52] another version accepts a romanticized picture of Nonwestern cultures as spiritual and harmonious while representing Western culture as exclusively materialist and genocidal. Cultural essentialism reifies selected differences between East and West, and in so doing exaggerates the difficulties of discourse between feminists from each world.

Other dangers of imagining a global feminist discourse community include the temptation to imagine some transnational feminist counterpublic, within which varying local interpretations of women's subordination receive final and authoritative adjudication. This could encourage acceptance of a model of moral rationality, according to which local communities would generate distinct moral perspectives that would be assessed by "the" global community and perhaps finally ratified by a consensus of all feminists. Such a model would be misleadingly simple and mechanistic, relying on a neopositivist distinction between "discovery" and "justification" while ignoring the inevitably provisional nature of feminist agreements. Finally, the notion of imagined community might distract feminists from recognizing the real and continuing inequalities of power both within and among communities. Walker notes the danger of "responding to an imagined (international or global) community of women or of feminists, while failing to take account of, and so responsibility for, the many ways our actual national and cultural communities make the imagined community simply impossible, and the invocation of it irrelevant, if not insulting."[53] Despite the real dangers of imagining communities, I suggest that they be taken not as conclusive objections to any feminist imaginings of community but rather as warnings against inventing romanticized, discursive utopias. If all communities are imagined, in the sense that they depend on a shared self-conception, then reinventing and reimagining communities becomes a crucial political task for feminists at the local, national, and global levels.[54] In imagining a global feminist discourse community, however, we must avoid generating feminist versions of the naively apolitical idealizations produced in mainstream moral theory; for instance, we must avoid premature postulations of a global sisterhood. Instead, we must recognize that global feminist discourse communities are not philosophical or political fantasies but real entities that already have begun to exist. Innumerable feminists are engaged already in discussing issues that cross national borders, and they are increasingly cooperating in working to address these issues. "The" global feminist discourse community is not singular, because global feminist discourse occurs in multiple and overlapping networks of individuals and communities and with varying and changing agendas. Indeed, it is a community in the making, and in this sense, it is not only both ideal and imagined but continually being reimagined. Feminist imaginings offer ideals toward which to aspire; imagining a global feminist discourse community that seeks constantly to be more inclusive, open, and equal may serve as a heuristic for feminist moral discourse and a basis for feminist political action.

Notes

This essay draws on several sections of my book in progress, *Sex, Truth and Power: A Feminist Theory of Moral Reason*. I read the first version at an invited symposium of the Pacific Division of the American Philosophical Association in Berkeley, California, in March 1997; the topic was "Cultural Relativism and Global Feminism," and I thank its organizer, Dean Chatterjee. I read the second version at Socialist and Feminist Philosophers in Action, and I thank all those who participated in the discussion, especially my introducer, Bat Ami Bar-On. Many people have offered valuable comments on the ideas presented here, but in preparing this version I am grateful for help from Ann Ferguson, Sandra Harding, Jim Maffie, Linda Nicholson, and Margaret Walker. Special thanks go to Uma Narayan, who has discussed these issues with me over several years and who went carefully and sympathetically through an originally rambling draft, providing extremely helpful suggestions for organizing and focusing it.

1. For a first account of my conception of feminist practical discourse, see "Toward a Feminist Conception of Moral Reasoning," in *Morality and Social Justice: Point/Counterpoint*, ed. James Sterba (Lanham, Md.: Rowman & Littlefield, 1995).

2. Diane Bell, "Reply [to Huggins et al.]," *Anthropological Forum* 6, no. 2 (1990): 158–165; Diane Bell, "Intraracial Rape Revisited: On Forging a Feminist Future Beyond Factions and Frightening Politics," *Women's Studies International Forum* 14, no. 5 (1991): 385–412; Diane Bell, letter to the editor, *Women's Studies International Forum* 14, no. 5 (1991): 507–513; Diane Bell and Topsy Naparrula Nelson, "Speaking About Rape Is Everyone's Business," *Women's Studies International Forum* 12, no. 4 (1989): 403–416; Jackie Huggins et al., letter to the editor, *Women's Studies International Forum* 14, no. 5 (1991): 506–507; Renate Klein, "Editorial," *Women's Studies International Forum* 14, no. 5 (1991): 505–506; Jan Larbalestier, "The Politics of Representation: Australian Aboriginal Women and Feminism," *Anthropological Forum* 6, no. 2 (1990): 143–157; and Topsy Napurrula Nelson, letter to the editor, *Women's Studies International Forum* 14, no. 5 (1991): 507.

3. Some insiders also remain unconvinced. A good example of an insider critique of exclusionary views can to be found in "Intersectionality and Identity Politics: Learning from Violence against Women of Color" by Kimberlé Crenshaw in *Reconstructing Political Theory: Feminist Perspectives*, ed. Mary Lyndon Shanley and Uma Narayan (University Park, Md.: Pennsylvania State University Press, 1995), pp. 178–193.

4. Larbalestier, "Politics of Representation," 143–157, 147.

5. Gayatri Chakravorty Spivak, "Can the Subaltern Speak?" in *Marxism and the Interpretation of Culture*, ed. Cary Nelson and Lawrence Grossberg (Urbana: University of Illinois Press, 1988).

6. Spivak notes both that the British "grotesquely mistranscribed" the names of the women and that *sati* actually translates as "good wife" and is a common name for Indian girls.

7. Spivak, "Can the Subaltern Speak?" 288.

8. Uma Narayan, "The Project of Feminist Epistemology: Perspectives from a Nonwestern Feminist," in *Gender/Body/Knowledge: Feminist Reconstructions of Being and Knowing*, ed. Alison M. Jaggar and Susan R. Bordo (New Brunswick, N.J.: Rutgers University Press, 1989), 267–268.

9. See David L. Hull, *Science as a Process: An Evolutionary Account of the Social and Conceptual Development of Science* (Chicago and London: University of Chicago Press, 1988), 433–434.

10. Helen E. Longino, *Science as Social Knowledge: Values and Objectivity in Scientific Inquiry* (Princeton, N.J.: Princeton University Press, 1990), 223.

11. Patricia Hill Collins, *Black Feminist Thought: Knowledge, Consciousness and the Politics of Empowerment* (New York: Unwin Hyman, 1990), 95.

12. Maria C. Lugones, "On Borderlands/*La Frontera*: An Interpretive Essay," *Hypatia* 7, no. 4 (1992): 31–37, 36.

13. Sarah Lucia Hoagland, *Lesbian Ethics: Toward New Value* (Palo Alto, Cal.: Institute of Lesbian Studies, 1988), 3.

14. Longino, *Science as Social Knowledge*, 223.

15. Iris Marion Young, *Justice and the Politics of Difference* (Princeton, N.J.: Princeton University Press, 1990), 235.

16. Shane Phelan, *Identity Politics: Lesbian Feminism and the Limits of Community* (Philadelphia: Temple University Press, 1989).

17. Terminology is a problem. I am especially interested in the possibility of dialogue between feminists from the wealthy industrialized or postindustrial capitalist nations, located mainly in Western Europe, Australasia, and North America, on the one hand, and, on the other hand, women from the poor rural or industrializing nations, located mainly in Africa, Latin America, the Caribbean, South and Southeast Asia, and Oceania. Some people refer to each side of this divide as North and South, respectively, but I avoid this usage here because North is often taken to include Japan, and possibly Central and Eastern Europe, and South to include Australasia. Instead, I choose to contrast Western feminisms—the Eurocentric feminist traditions of North America, Western Europe, and the Antipodes—either with Nonwestern feminisms, even though this usage linguistically gives privilege to the West, or with Third World feminisms, even though the Second World no longer exists.

18. See Chandra Talpade Mohanty, "Under Western Eyes: Feminist Scholarship and Colonial Discourses," in *Third World Women and the Politics of Feminism*, ed. Chandra Talpade Mohanty, Ann Russo, and Lourdes Torres (Bloomington: Indiana University Press, 1991), 56.

19. Kumari Jayawardena, *Feminism and Nationalism in the Third World* (London: Zed Books, 1986), 2.

20. Ibid.

21. Uma Narayan, *Dislocating Cultures: Identities, Traditions, and Third World Feminism* (New York: Routledge, 1997), 7.

22. Chandra Talpade Mohanty, "Cartographies of Struggle: Third Women and the Politics of Feminism," introduction to *Third World Women and the Politics of Feminism*, ed. Chandra Talpade Mohanty, Ann Russo, and Lourdes Torres (Bloomington: Indiana University Press, 1991), 20.

23. Kathleen Newland, "From Transnational Relational Relationships to International Relations: Women in Development and the International Decade for Women," in *Gender and International Relations*, ed. Rebecca Grant and Kathleen Newland (Bloomington: Indiana University Press, 1991), 130.

24. Cheryl Johnson-Odim, "Common Themes, Different Contexts: Third World Women and Feminism," in *Third World Women and the Politics of Feminism*, ed. Chandra Talpade Mohanty, Ann Russo, and Lourdes Torres (Bloomington: Indiana University Press, 1991), 313.

25. Maxine Molyneux, "Mobilization Without Emancipation? Women's Interests, the State, and Revolution in Nicaragua," *Feminist Studies* 11, no. 2 (1985): 227–254, 232.

26. Ibid., 232–233.

27. Ibid., 233.

28. One recent study of global feminist activism is Amrita Basu, *The Challenge of Local Feminisms: Women's Movements in Global Perspective* (Boulder, Col.: Westview, 1995).

29. Caroline O. N. Moser, "Gender Planning in the Third World: Meeting Practical and Strategic Needs," in *Gender and International Relations*, ed. Rebecca Grant and Kathleen Newland (Bloomington: Indiana University Press, 1991), 109–110.

30. Ibid., 109.

31. One question confronting those who seek global feminist dialogue is whether conceptual and moral incommensurability make moral discourse impossible across cultural boundaries. I have no space here to address this question, but I argue elsewhere that incommensurability in moral perspectives does not entail mutual incomprehen-

sion sufficient to make moral dialogue impossible. Of course, that people can communicate with each other in principle does not at all guarantee that they understand each other in practice.

32. David A. Crocker, "Insiders and Outsiders in International Development," *Ethics and International Affairs* 5 (1991): 149–173.

33. Martha Nussbaum and Amartya Sen, "Internal Criticism and Indian Rationalist Tradition," in *Relativism: Interpretation and Confrontation*, ed. Michael Krausz (Notre Dame, Ind.: University of Notre Dame Press, 1989), 308.

34. An excellent discussion of these issues is in Linda Alcoff, "The Problem of Speaking for Others," *Cultural Critique* 20 (1991–1992): 5–32.

35. Hema N. Nair, "Bold Type: The Poetry of Multiple Migrations," *Ms.*, January–February 1991, 71.

36. Nussbaum and Sen, "Internal Criticism," 321.

37. It has sometimes appeared to me that prurience is one factor that encourages this focus. For instance, a recent prize-winning "news" photograph portrayed a young woman examining herself after female genital surgery. She surely thought she was unobserved, and the angle of the photograph suggested that the photographer was hiding in a tree with a telephoto lens. In my view, the photograph not only objectified and exoticized the young woman but also grossly invaded her privacy.

38. In 1994, South Asian women's groups in Canada protested a Canadian doctor's willingness to abort female fetuses for Indian Canadians. The doctor defended himself by saying that he would be guilty of "cultural arrogance" if he criticized the practices of another ethnic community, but his critics called his attitude racist, saying that sex selection was not inherent in South Asian cultures.

39. The social consequences of these policies may be summed up in a single figure from UNICEF (the United Nations children's fund), which estimates that half a million children die every year as a direct result of the debt crisis. The suffering and death of these children, a disproportionate number of whom are girls, obviously affects women's lives much more severely than men's; it is primarily women who struggle to care for these children, who cope with the malnutrition-caused disorders of those who survive, and who bear more children at the cost of their own health and sometimes their lives. See Susan George, *A Fate Worse Than Debt* (New York: Grove, 1988); and Susan George, *The Debt Boomerang: How Third World Debt Harms Us All* (London: Pluto, 1992).

40. Cynthia Enloe, *Bananas, Beaches and Bases: Making Feminist Sense of International Politics* (Berkeley: University of California Press, 1990); Maria Mies, *Patriarchy and Accumulation on a World Scale: Women in the International Division of Labour* (London: Zed Books, 1986); Maria Mies and Vandana Shiva, *Ecofeminism* (London: Zed Books, 1993); Maria Mies, Veronika Bennholdt-Thomsen, and Claudia von Werlhof, *Women: The Last Colony* (London: Zed Books, 1988); Catherine V. Scott, *Gender and Development: Rethinking Modernization and Dependency Theory* (Boulder, Col.: Lynne Rienner, 1996); and Vandana Shiva, *Staying Alive: Women, Ecology and Development* (London: Zed Books, 1988).

41. Shiva, *Staying Alive*.

42. George, *The Debt Boomerang*.

43. Enloe, *Bananas, Beaches and Bases*.

44. Ibid.

45. Ruth Dixon-Mueller, *Population Policy and Women's Rights* (Westport, Conn.:

Praeger, 1993); Betsy Hartmann, *Reproductive Rights and Wrongs: The Global Politics of Population Control and Contraceptive Choice* (New York: Harper & Row, 1987); and Jodi L. Jacobson, *The Global Politics of Abortion* (Washington, D.C.: Worldwatch Institute, 1990).

46. For instance, Kant contends that a necessary condition of moral agency is membership in a community of equals, but he views this not as a specific empirical community but rather as an idealization, an imagined transhistorical community, comprising all rational beings. John Rawls's community of parties in the original position is also a thought experiment that is explicitly unrealizable. Habermas's communicative ethics is apparently more naturalistic in postulating an empirical discourse community, but because this community is defined in terms of conditions that are inevitably counterfactual, I would argue that it, too, turns out to be an idealized community. At first sight, communitarianism appears to be even more naturalistic than discourse ethics because it posits a variety of historically specific communities that have emerged organically and are characterized by adherence to distinctive moral traditions. I would contend, however, that communitarianism deals also in idealized communities because it works from a romanticized and essentialist vision of community.

47. See Mohanty, "Under Western Eyes," 4; and Ann Ferguson, "Feminist Communities and Moral Revolution," in *Feminism and Community*, ed. Penny A. Weiss and Marilyn Friedman (Philadelphia: Temple University Press, 1995).

48. Benedict Anderson, *Imagined Communities: Reflections on the Origins and Spread of Nationalism* (London: New Left Books, 1983).

49. Ferguson, "Feminist Communities and Moral Revolution," 385.

50. Margaret Urban Walker, "Global Feminism: What's the Question?" *APA Newsletter on Feminism and Philosophy* 94, no. 1 (1994): 53–54, 54.

51. Narayan, "Project of Feminist Epistemology," 33.

52. Ibid.

53. Walker, "Global Feminism."

54. Narayan, *Dislocating Cultures*.

14

The Idea of Moral Progress

Michele Moody-Adams

I want to defend a constructive account of the nature and sources of moral progress and a cautious optimism about its possibility. But any such view must acknowledge skepticism about the very idea of moral progress. Some critics will argue that we cannot know whether moral beliefs and practices are headed in the right direction until we know what the "destination" is, and that we cannot know what the destination is without proof of access to an objective standard of moral rightness.[1] Those who combine this claim with skepticism about moral objectivity, as many do, will insist that the idea of moral progress has no content.[2] Others will urge that even if we could establish the existence—and perhaps also the substance—of an independent standard against which to test relevant beliefs and practices, it would be difficult (if not impossible) to identify a single direction in which those beliefs and practices, on the whole, are clearly headed. On this view, even if the idea of moral progress has any content, it is unlikely to have any plausible uses.

Moral Progress Is Always Local

Yet we do not discern moral progress by reference to some fully specifiable destination toward which we can say that all beliefs and actions ought to be headed. Changes that are reasonably deemed to constitute moral progress occur locally, in relatively circumscribed domains of concern.[3] Moral progress in belief, for instance, is progress in grasping what Mark Platts calls the "semantic depth" of particular moral concepts.[4] This involves coming to appreciate more fully the richness and the range of application of a particular moral concept (or a linked set of concepts), as well as understanding how some newly deepened account of a moral concept—some new moral conception—more adequately captures features of experience which the concept aims to pick out.

As Platts rightly urges, moral concepts pick out features of the world that are "of indefinite complexity in ways that transcend our practical understanding."[5]

This means that no single conception of a complex moral idea, such as justice, can adequately capture its semantic depth.[6] It also means that we cannot fully specify a "proper" destination for moral beliefs, not even for a single moral concept. Yet we have no reason to lament these facts or to assume that they warrant skepticism about moral objectivity. They are simply evidence of morality's complexity. In view of that complexity, we must heed C. D. Broad's advice not to expect any one account of morality to yield "the whole truth, and nothing but the truth" about morality.[7] We must also reject the notion that substantive moral progress requires convergence on some one moral theory or some one substantive moral view.

Moral progress in practices results when some newly deepened moral understanding is concretely realized in individual behavior or social institutions. In the treatment of women, for instance, moral progress has often been constituted by practices embodying deepened understandings of justice and related moral notions. Of course, even within a single moral domain, moral progress may be limited or incomplete. Moreover, moral progress within one domain may be accompanied by moral regression in some neighboring domain. But since moral progress is always local, we need not establish that beliefs and practices are all headed in a single direction in order to identify particular instances of moral progress.[8] Understanding the local character of moral progress thus helps to clarify both the content and the plausible applications of the idea.

I have claimed that moral progress in belief is a matter of deepening our grasp of complex, already existent, moral ideas. Yet it has been urged that moral progress frequently requires the discovery or invention of fundamentally new moral ideas and that such accomplishments demand the special expertise of moral philosophers. Thus Michael Slote argues that on matters such as slavery and the treatment of women, for instance, "the development of moral thought and the realization of virtue" required fundamentally new moral ideas.[9] Slote further contends that, in views as varied as eighteenth-century utilitarianism and Rawls's twentieth-century democratic egalitarianism, moral philosophy has been a reliable source of "totally new," wholly "original" moral ideas which have furthered the development of moral thought.[10]

Cheshire Calhoun relies on Kuhnian terminology to defend a related claim. Calhoun argues that we must distinguish "normal moral contexts," in which the rightness or wrongness of action is socially "transparent," from "abnormal moral contexts," which "arise at the frontiers of moral knowledge." Abnormal moral contexts emerge, she continues, "when a subgroup of society (for instance, bioethicists or business ethicists) makes advances in moral knowledge faster than they can be disseminated to and assimilated by" the rest of us.[11] Echoing Slote's understanding of the conditions for progress in the treatment of women, Calhoun adds that feminist theorizing tends to give rise to abnormal moral contexts that are "particularly resistant to normalization."[12]

Yet as I argue in the second section, we cannot recognize that some new conception constitutes moral progress unless it can be made intelligible as a defensible development in moral thinking.[13] New moral insights can be "assimilated" only if they can somehow be expressed in terms of familiar moral concepts. Moreover, only those insights which can be assimilated can serve as the foundation of moral progress in practices. If "ought" implies "can," as I think it does, fundamentally new moral ideas—as distinct from new insights about how to understand fundamental moral concepts—could never be realized in individual action or social institutions.[14] I show in section three that newly deepened moral understandings can be widely "disseminated" only if engaged social critics and political actors can get others to confront and reject their shallow grasp of moral concepts, and then to contemplate ways of embodying some deeper understanding in everyday experience. I have a "not yet extinguished faith"—as one critic describes it—that moral philosophy can play an important role in the processes that stimulate moral progress.[15] But that faith is rooted in philosophy's capacity to inspire political actors and social critics who struggle to disseminate new moral understandings and to influence the practice of those persons who are able to translate new insights into social practice.[16] Finally, in section four, I articulate some epistemological commitments of the claim that moral progress in belief is a matter of deepening our grasp of existing moral concepts and that it does not (indeed cannot) teach anything fundamentally new about morality. I thus extend and refine a longstanding conviction, defended elsewhere, that the principal barrier to moral progress in beliefs is not ignorance of a revolutionary new moral idea, but affected ignorance of what can, and should, already be known.[17]

The Assimilation of Moral Progress

The notion that moral philosophy is regularly a source of "totally new" moral ideas conflicts with the self-conceptions of its most important practitioners. With very few exceptions, moral philosophers claim to reformulate central elements of ordinary moral consciousness, in order to reveal its unstated regulative commitments.[18] In *The Principles of Morals and Legislation*, for instance, Bentham insists that the principle of utility is deeply rooted in the "natural constitution of the human frame."[19] In response to complaints that the *Groundwork* offers no new moral principle, Kant wondered: "Who would want to introduce a new principle of morality and, as it were, be its inventor as though the world had hitherto been ignorant of what duty is or had been thoroughly wrong about it?"[20] Still further, in A *Theory of Justice*, Rawls insists that the difference principle best captures one of the "fixed points" of our considered convictions. He also claims that the principle expresses a "natural meaning" of fraternity and gives content to the familiar idea of reciprocity.[21] The self-conception that underwrites such claims rests on two important assumptions: first, that philosophical moral inquiry must be continuous with everyday moral inquiry, and second, that, even in philosophy, the most important component of constructive moral inquiry is the reinterpretation of existing moral ideas.[22] Together, these assumptions amount to an implicit denial that philosophical moral inquiry could provide totally new moral ideas or make paradigm-shattering advances in moral knowledge.

Any account of a moral concept's regulative commitments may generate claims about its semantic depth which, if followed, would have profound consequences for everyday practice. Utilitarianism is a frequent source of such claims. For instance, Peter Singer's understanding of the scope of the duty to aid, if widely accepted, would drastically change the nature of existence in contemporary consumer societies. But Singer relies on assumptions about the regulative commitments of existing moral concepts and explicitly appeals to familiar elements of ordinary moral consciousness.[23] He expects agreement on the notion that we have a duty to respond to suffering and that this duty can have overriding moral significance. Moreover, he expects his readers to agree that alleviating the suffering of a drowning child is morally more significant than keeping one's suit clean or being on time for a routine appointment. Of course, Singer also believes that well-off inhabitants of wealthy societies typically have an inadequate grasp of the duty to respond to suffering—one which allows them to deny morally relevant similarities between the suffering of a nearby child and the suffering of a child who simply happens to be distanced by geography, culture, or political membership. Yet the idea that we have a basic duty to respond to suffering was not "totally new," or in any way "original," with utilitarianism. Thus Mill could reasonably claim that utilitarianism reveals the regulative commitments of the Judeo-Christian tradition which helped define conventional morality in nineteenth-century England. "To do as you would be done by" and "to love your neighbor as yourself," Mill argued, constitute the "ideal perfection of utilitarian morality."[24]

Such claims implicitly recognize that the position of the person trying to assimilate a new moral insight is a lot like that of an explorer or anthropologist trying to make sense of a cross-cultural confrontation with unfamiliar moral practices. Even in the most serious cross-cultural moral disagreement there is always substantial agreement about the basic concepts that ought to shape any reflection properly deemed moral. Cross-cultural moral disagreement is possible only because "fundamental" moral disagreement across cultures is not.[25] Moreover, the careful analysis of specific cases of disagreement consistently bears out this observation.[26] What the methodology of moral interpretation teaches, in such cases, is that a judgment or belief counts as moral only if it fits into a pattern of beliefs and judgments that, in fundamental respects, resembles one's own.[27] But the same constraint on moral interpretation is at work when we confront some new moral insight—even when that insight comes from sources that are culturally "close to home." We can contemplate a new insight as a moral insight, and attempt to assimilate it in everyday moral thinking, only if it fits into a complex pattern of belief and judgment that to a large extent resembles the current one.

My account of the intelligibility of moral progress must be distinguished from a superficially similar view defended by Joseph Raz. Raz attempts to show that a change in moral thinking can be intelligible only if some unchanging normative principle explains the change. He defends this claim as part of an attempt—with which I am otherwise sympathetic—to challenge social relativism about morality.[28] Yet Raz's challenge presupposes that principles are the fundamental elements of moral understanding. On my view, in contrast, what is fundamental to moral understanding are complex concepts such as justice, compassion, or righteousness. Ideals or principles may be advanced as reasonable interpretations of such concepts. Given the nature of human understanding, fundamental moral concepts could not be fully applicable in everyday practice unless they were frequently interpreted in this way. But no single conception of a complex fundamental moral notion can adequately capture its semantic depth. This means that no ideal or principle offered as an interpretation of a fundamental moral concept — say, the concept of justice — could ever serve as an unchanging guide for discerning moral progress in belief. The Enlightenment ideal of equality, for instance, was an important attempt to deepen the understanding of justice.[29] But the nineteenth and twentieth centuries have shown, I think, that the ideal of equality cannot by itself capture the richness and complexity of justice.[30]

Yet while there are no unchanging moral principles to guide the evaluation of moral interpretations, there are some fairly common signs of moral progress. Moreover, the predictive value of these signs is dependable across a broad range of social practices and in quite varied cultural and historical circumstances. For instance, if we can predict that some institution or practice can be preserved without extreme violence and with a minimal amount of coercion, we can often conclude that an interpretation which recommends it constitutes moral progress.

But the absence of extreme coercion and excessive violence in social practices is not an unimpeachable guide to moral progress. A set of social practices might persist without them because all of its critics have been forcibly eliminated; such practices would not thereby become instances of moral progress. Still further, coercion and violence may be unavoidable when we seek to create, or to recreate, institutions which embody an appropriately deep grasp of fundamental moral concepts. Indeed there are circumstances — for instance, the American Civil War or the Allied effort in World War II — in which extremes of coercion and violence may constitute part of the regrettable, but morally necessary, conditions for responding properly to an indefensibly shallow moral conception, or to a profoundly terrifying moral regression.[31]

In this context, the emergence of an international culture of human rights in the aftermath of World War II proves to be one of the great, but fortunate, ironies of history. For that culture embodies an important attempt to formally recognize the link between minimizing coercion and socially sanctioned violence and encouraging moral progress in human practices. Like any culture, the culture of human rights is not a seamless web. There is frequent disagreement about what constitutes conformity to its central norms; there is something less than universal agreement about the value of conformity; and conformity may be spotty even where there is widespread agreement about what conformity to the norms really requires. Yet the tendency of human rights doctrine is to support institutions which minimize social coercion and stigmatize state-sanctioned violence. Thus the fact of broad international agreement on the doctrine is grounds for cautious optimism about the possibilities for moral progress.

The need for cautious optimism is underscored by the extraordinary complexity of constructive moral inquiry. A central task of such inquiry, as I understand it, is to show us when and how we must sometimes enlarge the class of things—entities, actions, institutions, or states of affairs—to which some fundamental moral concept applies. As Singer's arguments suggest, this usually requires getting us to confront important similarities between characteristics of items already included under the concept and characteristics of others not yet so included. But this is frequently no simple matter.

Any subject of moral judgment is always embedded within what Karl Duncker described as a "concrete pattern of situational meanings."[32] Moreover, any pattern of situational meanings will be a complex set of factual beliefs about, and affective associations concerning, some action, entity, institution, or state of affairs. Any phenomenon—for instance, an action such as the killing of aged parents—will be the subject of moral evaluation only as it is embedded in a particular pattern of situational meanings. A people who believe that killing one's aged parents is the only way to ensure the parents' entry into a promised heaven will evaluate the action differently, as Duncker points out, from those for whom the intentional killing of aged parents is a malicious attack on the sanctity of human life. As a rule, then, moral inquiry can change our moral understandings, and constructively enlarge our grasp of moral concepts, only if it can alter some of the constituent beliefs and affective associations that structure important patterns of situational meanings.

But effecting change in situational meanings, and encouraging new understandings of fundamental moral concepts, may require one or more of several argumentative strategies. First, it may involve pointing out the under-appreciated relevance of empirical facts. Singer reminds us, for example, that advances in the technology of communication and travel require us to rethink the notion of who is in proximity to us. But second, a moral critic seeking to change the situational meaning of some phenomenon may need to articulate and analyze problematic emotions that are unreasonably generated by some action, person, or thing in question. It is thus that an argument about the morality of practices governing AIDS victims might try to dispel irrational fears about the transmission of the disease. Third, we are sometimes convinced to see some phenomenon in a new light when we are compelled to confront important inconsistencies in beliefs and practices regarding it. A critic of contemporary American legal practices, for instance, might challenge the morality of allowing harsher sentences for the sale and possession of crack cocaine than for the sale and possession of other forms of cocaine. Fourth, bringing about a change in situational meanings may require supplying a new metaphor, or some other imaginative structure, in an attempt to reshape our conception of a particular phenomenon. In this regard, Singer's defense of the sharing ethic might have more influence were it linked with some re-imagining of human life compelling enough to counter Hardin's image of wealthy countries as lifeboats already filled to carrying capacity. Finally, because the patterns of situational meanings most resistant to change are those concerning the self, one of the most important tasks of constructive moral inquiry is to try to break down the common human resistance to self-scrutiny.[33] New moral understandings can be widely disseminated only if we can be made to confront and to reject some shallow grasp of a particular moral concept.

The Dissemination of Progressive Moral Beliefs

I have maintained that in spite of these difficulties, moral progress sometimes occurs. I have also claimed that moral philosophy is not the principal vehicle through which morally progressive insights are broadly disseminated. Critics who share the conception of moral expertise defended by Slote and Calhoun will wonder exactly how, on my view, the broad dissemination of moral insight occurs. My answer is that only socially and politically engaged moral inquirers—which moral philosophy rarely produces—can effectively disseminate new moral insights in ways that are likely to produce moral progress in social practices.[34] Thus I second Michael Walzer's contention that moral progress in social institutions results from "workmanlike" social criticism and political struggle, not from "paradigm-shattering" philosophical speculation.[35]

Engaged moral inquirers have four essential characteristics. First, they must have a committed personal engagement with the everyday consequences of the moral arguments they advance. This engagement often develops in response to the personal experience of hardships traceable to the moral shallowness of some current practice. But it may sometimes result from moral outrage at the hardships suffered by others. Second, engaged moral inquirers must be willing to assume great personal risk in order to advance the causes they advocate. Such willingness is typically an unavoidable consequence of the seriousness of their engagement with the cause. But, as I argue more fully below, advocacy can be genuinely moral only if the advocate attempts to minimize its risks to others, especially to unwitting or innocent others. That is, deliberately exposing others to risks of great harm can be moral only as an extraordinary measure of last resort. Thus, the third characteristic of the engaged moral inquirer is a commitment to the idea that the deliberate exposure of others to risk is allowable only as a morally necessary—though regrettable—means for combatting dangerously shallow or regressive practices.[36] Fourth, engaged moral inquirers must be willing to rely on methods not typically recognized by philosophers as methods of rational persuasion—including offering their own lives and practice as moral examples and relying on nonviolent public protests and demonstrations.

Many contemporary moral philosophers will agree with emotivists like Stevenson, who claims in *Ethics and Language* that nonviolent civil disobedience and reliance on personal example are forms of "non-rational persuasion."[37] But it is far from clear that the evidence justifies this stance. Many of us are familiar with Martin Luther King's "Letter from Birmingham Jail," in which King argues that participants in the civil rights movement sought, by their protest, to create a "tension in the mind"—an intellectual "crisis"—through which segregationists

might be compelled to acknowledge inconsistencies between the liberal democratic ideal of equality and the reality of legally sanctioned segregation and discrimination.[38] Less familiar is the fact that segregationists sometimes complained
of "violence" allegedly wrought by nonviolent protests embodying these goals.[39]
How should we understand such complaints, since there is ample evidence that
the only violence involved was the violence too frequently directed against the
protesters? In my view, these false reports of violence are best explained as unreflective reactions to the experience of being required to confront something from
which one has spent a lifetime averting one's glance.[40] More precisely, the "violence" which some Southern whites claimed to find in nonviolent protest was
simply the experience of being rationally compelled to confront the inconsistency
between segregation and the ideals of American political morality.

But nonviolent direct action is only one of a vast array of methods at our
disposal to express, reveal, or reiterate the failure of some pattern of situational
meanings, and existing moral understandings, to survive rational scrutiny. A work
of art, for instance, may reiterate the relevance of under-appreciated facts—much
as Picasso's *Guernica* reiterated the horrors of war and Harriet Beecher Stowe's
Uncle Tom's Cabin reiterated the shamefulness of slavery. A memoir or an ethnog-
raphy may confirm the irrationality of certain emotions and affective associations—much as nineteenth-century slave narratives confirmed the irrationality of
the notion that slavery might be an expression of "concern" for the slaves. First-
person social experience may force us to confront inconsistencies in belief and
practice that we would otherwise ignore or deny. A retired military officer whose
daughter is sexually harassed as she completes an officers' training program may
be forced, for the first time, to admit the inconsistency between democratic principles and sexual discrimination. The tendency of such experiences to deepen
moral understanding informs the growing trend toward "service learning" in secondary and postsecondary education. As we should expect—if my view is right—
none of these methods will teach fundamentally new moral concepts. But they
provide unmatched opportunities for experience and rational reflection which
help us articulate the requirements for a sufficiently deep appreciation of the
meaning of our existing moral concepts. In the end, they may be rationally compelling intimations of a moral truth that transcends human experience—though
one need not have such Platonic sensibilities to recognize the value of the many
methods of argument available to the engaged moral inquirer.

I have offered a list of quite varied methods for revealing the shortcomings
of situational meanings and existing moral understandings. Many philosophers
will want to resist my claims about the rationality of these methods, methods
which generally do more to show than to say what is deficient about situational
meanings and moral understandings. But this is precisely why, in my view, philosophy is unlikely to produce many engaged moral inquirers, or to have much
direct influence in broadly disseminating the insights most likely to produce
moral progress.

Being a moral philosopher is not intrinsically incompatible with being an
engaged moral inquirer. If we are to believe Plato's account—as I do—Socrates

may be one of the purest examples of such an inquirer. Moreover, the theoretical underpinnings of the American civil rights movement owe as much to the Platonic Socrates as to Gandhi's views or to the Judeo-Christian religious commitments of many of its participants. Still further, utilitarians such as Bentham and Mill might well qualify as perfect examples of moral philosophers who were also engaged moral inquirers. But it seems clear that contemporary academic moral philosophy is unlikely to produce many engaged moral inquirers. Even when its practitioners display the appropriate levels of personal engagement, and a willingness to assume personal risk, they are typically bound by too narrow a conception of the methods of rational persuasion, and indeed of rationality itself.

Thus my notion of the engaged moral inquirer must not be confused with Richard Posner's concept of the "moral entrepreneur," defended as part of his recent attack on "card-carrying academic moralists."[41] In "The Problematics of Moral and Legal Theory," Posner argues that contemporary academic moral philosophy lacks the "intellectual vitality" and the "emotional power" to have any influence in the processes which produce genuine changes in moral belief and practice.[42] Such changes, he claims, are always the work of "moral entrepreneurs," who understand the challenge of "selling" their view and who meet that challenge by mixing appeals to self-interest with emotional appeals that "bypass our rational calculating faculty." Indeed he claims that the most influential moral entrepreneurs are those with a mastery of techniques of nonrational persuasion that are not part of the "normal equipment of scholars."[43] Posner acknowledges that the moral entrepreneurs make arguments. Yet he insists that the influence of the moral entrepreneurs is never a function of the quality of their arguments, but of their skill at nonrational or irrational persuasion.[44]

There is an unexpected element of truth in Posner's concept of the moral entrepreneur, for it rightly suggests a link between moral advocacy and risk. Just as the entrepreneur in business (ideally) assumes a series of risks in order to sell a particular product or service, the engaged moral inquirer assumes extraordinary personal risk in order to carry out her advocacy. Civil rights workers who were murdered for advocating racial equality in the American south, like Chinese students killed for their advocacy of democracy in Tiananmen Square, were not performing some postmodern experiment in performativity or trying out some Rortean redescriptions. They were risking their lives in order to promote moral progress.[45]

Yet Posner's conception remains deeply problematic, because it is rooted in a fundamentally implausible skepticism about morality and moral progress. Posner believes that any committed advocacy of social change can be characterized as moral advocacy, and thus he never acknowledges the plausibility of the idea of moral progress as something distinct from social change. In keeping with this skepticism, Posner classifies Hitler as a moral entrepreneur—one who sought to narrow the bounds of altruism, he claims, in contrast to figures like Bentham or Jesus who sought to expand them.[46] But the engaged moral inquirer, as I have argued, seeks to minimize deliberate risks to others—and believes that extreme coercion and state-sanctioned violence are justified only as regrettable last resorts. Few eras in human history have involved more coercion and violence, and more deliberate exposure of others to death and other grave personal harm, than the era of Nazism. Thus, on any plausible understanding of the notion, no one whose advocacy supported or furthered the aims of that era can properly be deemed a moral advocate.

Philosophers who make normative moral claims can indeed be moral advocates, though their moral advocacy will never be the main engine of moral progress. Further, even the advocacy of engaged moral inquirers seldom directly brings about moral progress in social practices. The task of embodying some new moral insight in social practices involves the slow and steady work of persons (unlike most philosophers and even most engaged moral advocates) whose actions can directly reshape social practices and institutions. Political leaders and policymakers; educators, parents, and religious leaders; doctors and hospital administrators; lawyers and judges—these are the sorts of people who must work to reshape everyday social life in accordance with a newly deepened grasp of some fundamental moral concept. Engaged moral inquirers sometimes function well in these roles, but the painstaking work of trying to reshape everyday social life tends to be incompatible with the engagement, and the tolerance of personal risk, required to constitute an effective moral advocate. This means that engaged moral inquirers who undertake this work must frequently divorce their activities as moral advocates from their efforts to reshape everyday life. Sometimes they must simply give up, altogether, their activities as advocates.

Those who are well placed to reshape social life must usually rely on the method of trial and error in carrying out various morally progressive social experiments. But social experiments may be incomplete, and their results in one domain may be improperly linked to relevant results in another.[47] Still further, social experiments undertaken in the name of progress may go wrong—sometimes even producing results antithetical to the progressive moral insights which initially underwrote them.[48] The complexity of social experiments undertaken in the name of moral progress thus provides further reasons for adopting a cautious optimism about the possibility of moral progress.

Yet advocacy conducted within the conventional bounds of contemporary moral philosophy may nonetheless be quite effective in giving shape to the right kinds of social experiments. Moreover, as Martha Nussbaum has recently suggested, there are several routes by which philosophers may influence social practice—from political activity to service on hospital ethics boards, as well as in advisory and consulting roles in various government agencies.[49] But philosophical moral advocacy is also important for its capacity to inspire engaged moral inquirers, and the American civil rights movement is just one recent example of how important this inspiration can be. Posner's dismissive attack on the intellectual vitality of moral philosophy is simply inconsistent with the facts of philosophy's obvious—though admittedly complex—influence in the moral dimensions of human life.

Moral Progress and Moral Ignorance

I have claimed that the main engine of moral progress is the advocacy of engaged moral inquirers—mainly because of the richness and complexity of their conceptions of rationality and rational persuasion. I have also described five argumentative strategies available to the engaged moral inquirer seeking to change the situational meanings of particular phenomena and to deepen our grasp of the meaning of moral concepts. It may be wondered about the compatibility of this account with arguments I have made elsewhere that the main obstacle to moral progress in social practices is the tendency to widespread affected ignorance of what can and should already be known.

But I have always maintained that one cannot assimilate a newly deepened grasp of a moral concept unless one is first willing to see oneself and one's place in the world in a new light.[50] Thus, in describing the five argumentative strategies available to the engaged moral inquirer, I note that none of the first four can be effective without the fifth. That is, the first four strategies will not work unless the moral inquirer is able to break down her audience's resistance to self-scrutiny. Such efforts can be successful, moreover, only if the arguments of others can get us to admit that some unscrutinized element of our practice or belief is not quite as immune to criticism as we hope to claim. We frequently avoid self-scrutiny because we expect it to yield insights that we are not prepared to obey. Yet the moral importance of self-scrutiny is the one aspect of moral truth, in my view, that is clearly accessible to all. Moreover, it is accessible as soon as we become capable of sustained self-reflection, and whatever the level of sophistication in our grasp of other moral notions.[51]

It is true that the efforts of the engaged moral inquirer are often indispensable to our attempts to give direction and constructive comment to our moral inquiry. But we do not need engaged moral inquirers to tell us the things we most need to know in order to be moral. We already know that for any being capable of critical scrutiny, the life worth living must be an examined life—even though we frequently find ways to ignore this central element of moral truth.[52] Moreover, the practice of ordinary persons bears out the truth of this view. For example, when we attempt to teach our children to be moral, we count on them to learn how to examine their conduct. Given the unpredictable complexity of human life, and the fact that moral situations are rarely exactly reproduced, unless children learn to be sufficiently self-critical, they will eventually be unable to follow the right examples, or to appreciate and conform to the right rules, or both. Thus parents or caretakers who fail to encourage self-examination—as some, unfortunately, do—will simply fail as moral educators.

A commitment to the examined life is a necessary, though not a sufficient, condition of the life worth living. Moreover, an indefinite number of more specific moral commitments are embedded in the ideal of the examined life. One task of constructive moral inquiry is to try to articulate some of these commitments. Still further, since the whole truth about morality is complex, reasonable and defensible efforts to articulate that truth may differ in important and serious dimensions. In particular, not all defensible answers to the question about how to lead a human life worth living will give precisely the same emphasis to self-scrutiny. Yet the ideal of the examined life is essential to a proper grasp of the moral concept of righteousness—a concept which, along with justice and compassion, is surely among the fundamental moral concepts. The practices of human beings—in every culture and in every era—consistently reveal the morally foundational role of self-examination.[53]

All human beings have at their disposal important nonmoral knowledge that underscores the moral importance of self-scrutiny. Some of the most important nonmoral knowledge, in this regard, is the knowledge of human fallibility—particularly knowledge of the possibility that any human practice could always be wrong. Even if we were to concede the possibility that some person claiming divine (and infallible) inspiration might be correct in doing so, it would still be an inescapable fact that the content of any such inspiration must be interpreted if it is to be applied in human life. Further, any humanly generated interpretation, even of a presumably infallible inspiration, may always be morally wrong—or may be applied in a morally condemnable fashion. This is why human beings have compelling reasons to be cautious about the kinds of practices and institutions they support. Practices which deliberately maim, kill, or drastically limit the central freedoms of other persons are especially dangerous. Indeed this is why social changes which minimize or eliminate extremely coercive or violent practices are so frequently instances of moral progress: such changes embody a clear appreciation of the moral weight of self-examination and its moral and, ultimately, political implications.

The link between the capacity for self-scrutiny and the possibility of moral education is a close one—so close, in fact, that it is far too easily taken for granted. When this happens, we may come to believe that it is possible to lead moral lives by rejecting self-scrutiny and eschewing any associated critical reflection on ongoing social practices and our participation in those practices. Thus in *Rationalism in Politics*, Michael Oakeshott contends that once a society has developed sufficiently complex moral habits, we can only endanger historically established social equilibrium by encouraging critical scrutiny of our practices and of our places in those practices.[54] Yet such claims virtually provide a recipe for self-righteousness and complacency. As such, they are frequently a source of moral shallowness and morally regressive practices and beliefs.

When we relinquish self-righteousness long enough to consider the possible shortcomings of our practices, the insights of an engaged moral inquirer may be indispensable to defensibly reinterpreting the relevant moral concepts. Sometimes they may, primarily, yield a deeper understanding of why (and how) a current interpretation is, in fact, morally sufficient. Yet the engaged inquirer's assistance will not be a matter of inventing or discovering fundamentally new moral concepts or categories. This is why Bernard Williams was right to maintain, as he did in *Shame and Necessity*, that the ancient Greeks didn't need any new moral ideas—certainly not the Enlightenment ideal of equality, for instance—to be able to recognize and condemn the moral wrong of ancient slavery.[55] Still further, for all the alleged radicalism of Catherine MacKinnon's feminism, by her own account, her scrutiny of contemporary legal and social practices concerning women is an attempt to show that "women are human beings in truth but not in social reality."[56] This should not surprise us. Morally constructive feminism is not a matter of producing "new moral categories" to attempt to break the conceptual bounds of "normal moral contexts," as Calhoun has claimed.[57] Instead, it involves reiterating the very simple point that women ought to be included within the scope of existing moral categories which have been wrongly interpreted to exclude them.

Of course, people do not always willingly relinquish self-righteousness. They frequently resist critical scrutiny of social practices—and their roles in sustaining them—because they fear that such scrutiny may issue in moral claims they are not prepared to accept. But, again, the solution to this problem is not a (futile) search for totally "new" moral ideas. Instead, we must encourage the development of moral "gadflies." Moral gadflies are those persons and groups who are willing to work, sometimes at great personal risk, to generate intellectual crises in our understanding of morality—crises that can be resolved only by serious self-scrutiny and, ultimately, by genuine social change. Yet when the efforts of these moral gadflies are unsuccessful, the effort to realize moral progress in social practices may sometimes demand a judicious reliance on morally necessary—though regrettable—forms of organized coercion. Neither the engaged moral inquirer, nor the society concerned to assimilate her insights, can afford to forget this.

Finally, we should reject the poorly substantiated idea that socially widespread failures to develop sufficiently deep moral understandings "must" be explained by some sort of culturally or historically generated "inability" to see what morality required.[58] What we must do in order to understand socially widespread moral failures is simply to acknowledge that there is frequently a dearth of incentives to scrutinize social practices.[59] We must also admit the obvious fact that significant moral progress in human practices commonly has less to do with desires to promote the realization of progressive moral insights than with considerations of social expediency and enlightened self-interest.[60] But this suggests that it is possible to provide incentives to accept morally progressive practices without first deepening moral understandings. Moreover, when this possibility is realized in practice, the pace of moral progress in practices will sometimes outstrip the pace of moral progress in beliefs.[61] But this is not a reason for moral pessimism. On the contrary—given how easy it is to ignore the moral demands of self-scrutiny—the fact that progress in individual beliefs may be a consequence of prior progress in social practices is the most compelling reason we have to be optimistic about the possibility of moral progress.

Notes

A version of this essay was presented at a session of the Eastern Division of the American Philosophical Association. I thank Nicholas Sturgeon and David Wong for insightful comments and helpful criticism of that version.

1. This discussion of forms of skepticism about the idea of moral progress draws on Bury's discussion of skeptical approaches to the idea of human progress generally. See J. B. Bury, *The Idea of Progress: An Inquiry into Its Origin and Growth* (New York: Dover, 1960).

2. For an interesting contrast to this stance, see Richard Rorty's discussion of moral progress in "Solidarity or Objectivity," in *Philosophical Papers, Vol. I: Objectivity, Relativism and Truth* (Cambridge: Cambridge University Press, 1991). Rorty combines skepticism about moral objectivity with optimism about the possibility of moral progress—he simply denies that the only way to understand progress is in terms of an antecedently fixed end.

3. The notion of "relatively circumscribed" is important here. No morally relevant domain of human concern is ever entirely distinct from all others.

4. Mark Platts, "Moral Reality," in *Essays on Moral Realism*, ed. Geoffrey Sayre-McCord (Ithaca, N.Y.: Cornell University Press, 1988), 287–288, 298–299.

5. Ibid., 299.

6. I am sympathetic to Platts's claim (ibid., 289) that our grasp of fundamental moral concepts "can and should improve without limit." Yet I would substitute the notion of improving indefinitely for improving "without limit."

7. C. D. Broad, *Five Types of Ethical Theory* (London: Routledge & Kegan Paul, 1979), 1. Rationally defensible efforts to articulate moral truth may differ from one another, sometimes in quite significant ways. There will be a great deal of overlap in the content of defensible answers to the question of how we ought to lead our lives. Moreover, some answers will simply be indefensible in the whole, or in some of their defining elements. But moral objectivity simply does not require convergence on a single answer to the question of how to lead a life worth living. Indeed, given the unpredictable complexity of human experience, which demands that we continually reinterpret the terms of even familiar moral debates, convergence on a single account of morality would be the antithesis of progress. For fuller discussion of these concerns, see Michele Moody-Adams, "Feminism by Any Other Name," in *Feminism and Families*, ed. Hilde Nelson (London: Routledge, 1997).

8. We do not need to establish a single direction for moral beliefs and practices even within a single domain.

9. Michael Slote, "Is Virtue Possible?" *Analysis* 42 (1982): 70–76.

10. Ibid., 76.

11. Cheshire Calhoun, "Responsibility and Reproach," *Ethics* 99 (1989): 389–406, 396–398; cf. Tracy Issacs, "Cultural Context and Moral Responsibility," *Ethics* 107 (1997): 670–684.

12. Calhoun, "Responsibility and Reproach," 397.

13. Joseph Raz defends a similar stance in "Moral Change and Social Relativism," in *Cultural Pluralism and Moral Knowledge* (Cambridge: Cambridge University Press, 1994), 144–152. But the account defended here, as I will show, differs from Raz's account in rejecting the suggestion that fundamental moral concepts must always be understood to embody fundamental moral principles.

14. In other words, even if it were possible to come up with totally new fundamental moral concepts, it would not be possible to assimilate them. Of course, I argue in this essay that it isn't possible to come with "totally new" fundamental moral concepts. See also Michele Moody-Adams, "The Virtues of Nussbaum's Essentialism," *Metaphilosophy* 29 (October 1998): 263–272; Michele Moody-Adams, *Fieldwork in Familiar*

Places: Morality, Culture, and Philosophy (Cambridge, Mass.: Harvard University Press, 1997), 102–106, 190–201; and Michele Moody-Adams, "Culture, Responsibility and Affected Ignorance," *Ethics* 104 (1994): 291–309.

15. Richard Posner, "Reply to Critics of 'The Problematics of Moral and Legal Theory'" *Harvard Law Review* 111 (May 1998): 1796–1823, 1822.

16. Moody-Adams, *Fieldwork in Familiar Places*, 160–177.

17. Moody-Adams, "Culture, Responsibility and Affected Ignorance"; Moody-Adams, *Fieldwork in Familiar Places*; Moody-Adams, "Virtues of Nussbaum's Essentialism," 263–272.

18. I had long believed that Nietzsche was, perhaps, the most important exception. Yet my colleague Paul Eisenberg has suggested that even Nietzsche may have appealed to existing moral notions—for instance, the general rejection of unjustified resentment—to generate support for his "transvaluation" of all values.

19. Jeremy Bentham, *The Principles of Morals and Legislation* (New York: Hafner Press, [1789] 1948), 2.

20. Immanuel Kant, *Groundwork of the Metaphysics of Morals*, trans. H. J. Paton (New York: Harper & Row, [1785], 1964), 8n.

21. John Rawls, *A Theory of Justice* (Cambridge, Mass.: Harvard University Press, 1971), 102, 105. Slote is not alone in ignoring Rawls's own characterizations of his method. For instance, Michael Walzer, *Interpretation and Social Criticism* (Cambridge, Mass.: Harvard University Press, 1987), 12–13, insists that the difference principle is the result of an elaborate process of invention de novo.

22. Moody-Adams, *Fieldwork in Familiar Places*, 136–142, 146–160.

23. Peter Singer, *Practical Ethics* (Cambridge: Cambridge University Press, 1979).

24. John Stuart Mill, *Utilitarianism* (Indianapolis, Ind.: Hackett, 1979), 17.

25. This claim distinguishes the critical pluralism I defend here and elsewhere— Michele Moody-Adams, "Theory, Practice, and the Contingency of Rorty's Irony," *Journal of Social Philosophy* 25 (1994): 209–227—from the pluralism defended by David Wong, for instance in "Coping with Moral Conflict and Ambiguity," *Ethics* 102 (1992): 763–784.

26. Moody-Adams, *Fieldwork in Familiar Places*, 29–60, 74–106.

27. David Cooper, "Moral Relativism," in *Midwest Studies in Philosophy, Vol. 3, Studies in Ethical Theory*, ed. Peter French, Theodore Uehling, and Howard Wettstein (Morris: University of Minnesota Press, 1978); Peter French, *Responsibility Matters* (Lawrence: University of Kansas Press, 1992); and Moody-Adams, *Fieldwork in Familiar Places*.

28. Raz, "Moral Change and Social Relativism," 148.

29. Accompanying developments in the language of rights—developments that eventually linked the idea of rights to ordinary persons—were an equally important part of the process of deepening our grasp of the concept of justice.

30. Rawls's attempt to deepen our understanding of justice—with an interpretation combining the ideals of liberty, equality, and fraternity—is a monumental attempt to distill the lessons of that history. Even those who would challenge the details of Rawls's interpretation ought to recognize that it provides invaluable lessons about the nature of moral thinking and about plausible methods of constructive moral inquiry.

31. I follow Michael Stocker in believing that it is sometimes rational to regret doing something that morally speaking ought to be done. See Michael Stocker, *Plural and Conflicting Values* (Oxford: Oxford University Press, 1990), 110–123; Moody-Adams, "Feminism by Any Other Name," 121–130.

32. Karl Duncker, "Ethical Relativity?" *Mind* 48 (1939): 39–57, 43.

33. Michele Moody-Adams, "On the Alleged Methodological Infirmity of Ethics," *American Philosophical Quarterly* 27 (1990): 225–235; Moody-Adams, "Culture, Responsibility and Affected Ignorance," 291–309; and Moody-Adams, *Fieldwork in Familiar Places*.

34. Moody-Adams, "Culture, Responsibility and Affected Ignorance," 291–309; and Moody-Adams, *Fieldwork in Familiar Places*, 196–204, 184–186.

35. Walzer, *Interpretation and Social Criticism*, 27.

36. The failure to understand the category of actions that are morally necessary but regrettable is the source of many serious misunderstandings of the nature of moral conflict. See Moody-Adams, *Fieldwork in Familiar Places*, 121–130.

37. C. L. Stevenson, *Ethics and Language* (New Haven, Conn.: Yale University Press, 1944).

38. Martin Luther King, Jr., "Letter from Birmingham Jail," in *Why We Can't Wait* (New York: New American Library, 1964), 79.

39. Such encounters are depicted in the 1960 sit-ins at lunch counters in Louisiana, in *Eyes on the Prize, Part I*, produced and directed by Judith Vecchione, PBS Video, 1986.

40. Moody-Adams, "Culture, Responsibility and Affected Ignorance," 291–309, 298–303.

41. Posner, "Reply to Critics," 1796–1823, 1822–1823.

42. Richard Posner, "The Problematics of Moral and Legal Theory," *Harvard Law Review* 111, no. 7 (May 1998): 1638–1709, 1691; cf. 1638.

43. Ibid., 1667.

44. Ibid.

45. Moody-Adams, "Theory, Practice, and the Contingency of Rorty's Irony," 209–227; and Moody-Adams, *Fieldwork in Familiar Places*.

46. Posner, "Problematics of Moral and Legal Theory," 1638–1709, 1667.

47. The reason some women seem to feel "betrayed" by the feminist movement, for instance, seems to be a function of the gap between changes in attitudes about women's roles and changes in social institutions sufficient to allow women to comfortably assume new roles. See Moody-Adams, "Feminism by Any Other Name."

48. Some analysts of the American civil rights movement would suggest just such an account of its aftermath.

49. Martha Nussbaum, "Still Worthy of Praise," *Harvard Law Review* 111, no. 7 (May 1998): 1776–1795, 1792.

50. Michele Moody-Adams, "Alleged Methodological Infirmity of Ethics," 225–235; Moody-Adams, "Culture, Responsibility and Affected Ignorance," 291–309; and Moody-Adams, *Fieldwork in Familiar Places*.

51. Anyone who learns a natural human language learns how to say no, and thus how to consider that things might be other than they are. Further, anyone who learns how to affirm or deny a particular self-conception—to say, "Yes, this is who I am" or "No, that's not the sort of person I am"—learns how to engage in self-scrutiny.

52. Moody-Adams, "Culture, Responsibility and Affected Ignorance," 291–309; and *Fieldwork in Familiar Places*.

53. Moody-Adams, *Fieldwork in Familiar Places*.

54. See Michael Oakeshott, "The Tower of Babel," in *Rationalism in Politics and Other Essays*, expanded ed. (Indianapolis, Ind.: Liberty Press, 1991).

55. Bernard Williams, *Shame and Necessity* (Berkeley: University of California Press,

1993), 124, 137. I am far less sympathetic, however, with Williams's claims about why they didn't actually condemn slavery (112–128). See also Moody-Adams, *Fieldwork in Familiar Places*.

56. Catherine MacKinnon, "Not by Law Alone," in *Feminism Unmodified* (Cambridge, Mass.: Harvard University Press, 1987), cf. Moody-Adams, "Theory, Practice, and the Contingency of Rorty's Irony," 209–227, 217–218.

57. Thus I reject Rorty's analysis of MacKinnon's view in "Feminism and Pragmatism," *Michigan Quarterly Review* 30 (1991): 231–266. My account of morally constructive feminism helps explain how feminist moral commitments can be embedded in the practice even of women who claim not to be feminists. For further discussion of this point, see Moody-Adams, "Feminism by Any Other Name."

58. Moody-Adams, "Culture, Responsibility and Affected Ignorance," 291–309; and Moody-Adams, *Fieldwork in Familiar Places*. This is a widespread view. One of the most intriguing formulations, defended by a stalwart moral realist, is Nicholas Sturgeon, "Moral Explanations," in *Essays in Moral Realism*, ed. Geoffrey Sayre-McCord (Ithaca, N.Y.: Cornell University Press, 1988).

59. This phenomenon is especially important. In some instances, even blameworthy ignorance can be forgivable if, say, one's social circumstances provide extremely limited opportunities for reflection and debate; see Michele Moody-Adams, "On the Old Saw That Character Is Destiny," in *Identity, Character, and Morality: Essays in Moral Psychology*, ed. Owen J. Flanagan and Amelie Oksenberg Rorty (Cambridge, Mass.: MIT Press, 1991). Moreover, there are always degrees of responsibility for the collective moral failures of an entire society. Aristotle had more opportunities for debate and reflection than the average free Greek; thus his support of slavery is more condemnable than that of the average free Greek. Similarly, Jefferson had more opportunities for debate and reflection about the morality of keeping slaves and about the moral and intellectual worth of people of African descent than many of his compatriots. Jefferson's willingness to keep slaves and to derogate their abilities and worth was thus more condemnable than the same tendencies in his compatriots.

60. Solomon Asch, *Social Psychology* (New York: Prentice-Hall, 1952), 380; Moody-Adams, *Fieldwork in Familiar Places*, 96.

61. This is especially true, I would argue, in contemporary American race relations, and in gender relations as well.

V

The Dramatic and Narrative Form of Deliberation and Agency

15

The Improvisatory Dramas of Deliberation

Amelie Oksenberg Rorty

No action without interaction;
no interaction without drama;
no drama without habit and happenstance;
no philosophy without melodrama.

It's no news that the movement from decision to action and from action to outcome are contingent and accident-prone. But we tend to set aside the fact that—for good or ill—intentions, deliberations, and decisions are themselves affected by tangential and accidental contingencies. I want to explore the dynamics of the process of shared or collective decision making in which participants improvise dramatic roles that often do not represent their primary aims or views.[1] Despite the powerful role of chance and accident in decision making, despite the apparent arbitrariness of its outcome, there is (I argue an Aesopian lesson) a surprising set of norms that should govern the process.

By way of surveying the territory, we'll begin with a case study, an example of the ordinary dramas of decision making. That story should, I hope, be sufficiently vivid and familiar to convince you that "this is how things are." We'll then turn to the Aesopian moral of the story, a summary of what it reveals about the actual process that we grandly call practical deliberation. After a brief review of several contemporary models of rational deliberation, we'll turn to an Aesopian observation about the role of philosophy as critic and legislator of the ethics of deliberation.

Our story is meant to represent a wide array of ordinary and familiar types of decision making, but any resemblance to specific persons—living, dead, or imaginary—is purely coincidental.

Consider a fictional prime minister (call him Hedge) of a self-styled constitutional democracy (call it Luna) that is structured by a checks-and-balances separation of powers among its executive, legislative, and judicial branches. Although the military of Luna is under the direct command of the PM as the head of the executive branch, the legislature controls the military budget. In principle, a declaration of war must be approved by the legislative branch, but in fact the executive can mandate limited military action under special circumstances.

Let's suppose that Lunar decision makers agree on at least three reigning policy directives (call them principles): (1) Luna is—and must remain—the dominant political, economic, and military world power. (2) Although Luna does not have a mandate to intervene in the internal affairs of other nations, it has undertaken some (undefined) responsibility to preserve international peace and protect human rights (let's ignore the Lunar motivations for undertaking such a role). When this commitment appears to conflict with (what is presumed to be) Luna's national interest, the timing, focus, and strategies for exercising its presumptively humanitarian obligations should be designed to be compatible with (perceived) Lunar national interest. (3) Luna is protective of its military personnel: it is reluctant to engage its force without a reasonable assurance of attaining a well-defined objective, with minimal cost in lives.

Suppose there is a serious international crisis, one that doesn't directly involve Luna but that could indirectly affect its interests, for instance, a famine or civil war in a neighbouring nation-state. Suppose decision makers find themselves individually and collectively uncertain and conflicted about the policy priorities that Luna should adopt in such circumstances. What happens is this: without consultation or collusion, the various branches of the government adopt a division of rhetorical labor. Hedge makes belligerent and threatening speeches to confirm Lunar global dominance. Influential legislators, stressing the priority of Luna's internal financial needs and interests, take a noninterventionist stand; and the military urges caution and presses for a carefully defined objective. Beyond the immediate cast of official decision makers, there are important unofficial bit players: lobbyists who represent various interest groups, influential journalists and "experts," and powerful opponents, waiting to take advantage of every slip and failure. In short, even simple decisions occur within the context of a larger drama whose outcome will be affected by a vast array of contingencies—many of them accidental, unintended, and largely beyond the control of even the most risk-sensitive decision makers. Predictably, unintended and unforeseeable consequences follow not only every decision but also every step—every earnest or untoward aside—of the deliberative process. All this is just within Luna. The ambitions and deliberations of other nation-states (call them Mars and Venus) also affect the dynamics of Lunar decision making. Of course Martian and Venusian intentions and decisions are equally dynamic and dialectical, equally affected by a host of contingent and accidental events: the support of allies, an assassination, a terrified soldier shooting into a crowd, the reactions of an uninformed dictator. Moreover, decision makers on all sides may misunderstand one another's priorities and conventions; they may be misinformed about one another's political structures and struggles.

The role that each actor plays in the drama of his interactive deliberation depends only in part on his own priorities and judgment. The dramatic momentum of a situation may impel him to take a role-defined position in the expectation that it will be blocked by that of another group. Because each player counts on the others to represent counterbalancing and counterpoint policies, he may advance and defend a view that is actually stronger than one he would actually countenance.[2] Indeed, he may depend on other actors in their drama to check and block the policy he proposes. He—and his countering players—agree that it is strategically important to express the range of Luna's general aims even if they seem to mandate policies they intend to reject.

Sometimes the casting of policy roles may occur fortuitously, by sheer happenstance, rather than by differences in the participants' own priorities and judgments. Had a set of tangential circumstances—circumstances irrelevant to the matter at issue—been slightly different, the deliberation would have taken a different turn. If, for instance, Hedge was in the midst of a campaign to solicit support for his reelection, he may have taken a conciliatory rather than an interventionist position on foreign affairs. Similarly, legislators could have taken a belligerent stance, thinking that doing so might secure the resolution of a critical labour strike. The dynamic momentum of the decision makers' interactions—embedding as it does a wide range of extraneous factors (accidents of timing, other dominant issues at stake, and the rhetorical powers of the participants)—can lead to a decision that may not represent the preferences of any of the participants, acting individually or collectively. Needless to say, the final decision may not be in Luna's best interests, either in its own terms or objectively considered. But it may also, by happenstance, serve the players better than any of them, acting individually, collectively, or in their roles, could have imagined. Like luck, happenstance is impartial; and (what seems to be) today's beneficial happenstance may in time come to seem like disaster—and vice versa. The drama of the division of roles occurs in ordinary collective decision making. It can also occur in the very process of articulating the most general aims of an association or group.[3] It occurs in department meetings and corporate boardrooms, in families and town councils, in labor unions and law firms. The dramas of contingency and happenstance can also occur for an individual, deliberating—as she supposes—*in foro interno*. Happenstance—a chance encounter or a powerful film or novel—often redirects a train of deliberation; it can change her tolerance for risk or shift the dynamic tension among her diverse interests.

Philosophy as Collective Deliberation

However else they may differ in their aims and sometimes in their methods, philosophic reflection and practical deliberation are alike in their improvisatory, dialectical dramas. Like it or not, we cannot avoid acknowledging the distance between idealized models of rational decision making and the actual practice of deliberation. Even the most rigorous, austerely self-critical decisions are typically subject to the law of unintended consequences. But we tend to gloss over the distance between our idealized model of philosophic reasoning and the actual practices of philosophic reflection. We are so focused on our individual work—our solitary struggles in writing—that we tend to ignore the extent to which philosophy is collaborative, set in a frame of inherited and shared assumptions. Not only our views but also accepted modes of reasoning reflect the contingencies and accidents of our interactions with colleagues and opponents. Even the most sober, rigorous, and least dramatic philosophic and scientific discussions—in which neither decisions nor actions appear to be in the offing—can take this dynamic, improvisatory, dialectical, and accidental form. Philosophers and scientists develop positions that they might not have taken but for the counterpoint of their contemporaries.[4] Think of the accidental factors that affect a person's first appointment and the colleagues whose conversation will—for good and ill—affect the development of her work. The counterpoint of their interactions often represents a host of accidental, as well as intellectually germane, features. The charm, wit, and rhetorical power of a philosopher; the lineage and influence of her patrons and teachers; and the luck of getting a sympathetic commentator at an American Philosophical Association talk affect the hearing and discussion her position receives. Like decisions, philosophic positions are dramatically and substantively affected by the interactions of the current players in the field.[5]

Think of the way in which a conversation—a real conversation, a common investigation—takes place.[6] Unlike the minuets of comforting ritual speeches or exchanges of monologues, real conversation is risky: the participants do not know, ahead of time, what they will say or even sometimes what they think. We respond to a skeptical interlocutor in one way, to a confirming interlocutor in another, and to a coexplorer in yet another. To be sure, there are constraints: ideally, interlocutors want (among many other things) to arrive at what is true, and they are guided by what they presently believe is true. But at any moment in the conversation there are an indefinite number of relevant, consecutive true things they could say and think. Since every conversation carries the weight of many other projects besides that of conveying or discovering what is true, the segue of thought and speech is also affected by other ends: wooing, showing off in sheer play, or winning a hidden competition. Views and attitudes are affected by the minutiae of interactions: puzzlement or indignation on an interlocutor's face, the elation of common pursuit, or an ironic or admiring remark. As background moods change, relentless optimism can be infectious, or it can elicit skeptical reactions; frivolity can produce general merriment or provide stern gravity. Even when we think in solitude or act in character, from our deeply entrenched traits, our performances emerge from an interactive process that sometimes takes place *in foro interno*, with familiar and usually idealized figures. The configuration of a person's traits—the patterns of dominance and recessiveness—that emerges in any given situation is affected by (the embedded history of) her interactive company. Some of our interactive partners elicit our (very own) boldness; others elicit our (very own) caution. The more subtle partners in a conversation understand each other—the more they are familiar with one another's gestures, facial expressions, and reactions, the more condensed and improvisatory their conversation is likely to be. Like improvisatory jazz musicians, they sometimes lapse into a familiar habitual riff for a little rest, finding something in that riff that will lead them in a new direction. The improvisatory swerve of conversation can be changed by chance: it may have come to a different conclusion if a leading participant went to the bathroom at a critical moment in an argument. Not only conversations and music making, but also many of our basic decisions—designing a curriculum or a playground, teaching a seminar, choosing a restaurant or planning a meal, selecting a Supreme Court justice, or hanging paintings for an exhibition—take this form.

Like practical reasoning, philosophic reflection is, in its fine-grained details, implicitly dialogic.[7] True enough, the press of decision and action does not weigh on philosophers: we can—and apparently do—continue to disagree forever without being forced to closure. But though practical deliberation is constrained by the social context of action, it by no means always issues in consensus or even in consent. Even if the deliberative process does not issue in closure and disagreements remain, practical reasoning and philosophic reflection embed the influence of their dialogic partners; the process of their articulation is subject to the improvisatory contingencies and accidents of all interactions. The more discussion, the more criticism a participant receives, the more her position becomes specified and refined in a collaborative process, even when it is a polemical or antagonistic exchange. Even when arguments seem decisive, their relative importance are often denied. ("You may be right about . . . but the really important issue is. . . . ") They also often focus on aspects of issues that they believe to be neglected by their colleagues. Because they emphasize the lacunae in their opponents' views or because they attempt to complement or supplement them, their argumentative rhetoric tends—usually un-self-consciously—to become stronger and more exclusionary. Each side brackets the claims of the other in a sweeping ceteris paribus clause.

The dramatic discussions implicit in solitary philosophical reflection express the dynamics of counterpart dialectical role playing.[8] Ironically, even discussions that end by moving participants farther apart are nevertheless collaborative: each position is affected by those of others in the drama. "No thought without interaction; no interaction without drama" applies to philosophical reflection, as well as to practical deliberation.

How to Get from Familiar Models of Rational Deliberation to Improvisatory Drama

Our story raises difficult, even frightening questions: how do trustworthy decisions emerge from these accident-ridden dramas, fraught as they are with wild accidents and sheer happenstance? Notoriously, dramatists and novelists have difficulty in bringing their work to a plausible closure. Literature had once provided a set of resolutions: a deus ex machina, a marriage or death, a family reconciliation, or the return of a long-lost rightful heir. The imagination—in this case, following what it knows of life—continues to ask, "And what happened after that?" Postmodernists rejected the convention of closure and left the multiple dramas of contingency and multiple voices unresolved.

But, like responsible decision makers, the philosopher within charges, "Never mind all that psychological and sociological gossip. What aims or norms *should* govern deliberations and discussions? What *should* hail the resolution of a philosophical dispute, even though the participants tirelessly continue to express their views?" Needless to say, attempts to address these questions issue in the very sorts of dramatic discussions and deliberations they are meant to resolve. Improvisatory drama appears all the way down in the search for "fundamentals" and all the way up to the quest for "regulative norms and principles." For better or worse, the process of formulating the criteria for rationality—its basic aims, structures, and norms—is itself open to the multiperspectival, critical reevaluation. Despite its apparent rigorous internal logic and despite its determination to serve exacting critical evaluation, normative philosophy itself also abounds in the contingencies of dialectical improvisatory drama. Still, whatever their status, normative questions about decision making remain: they confront individual agents, policymakers, and ethical theorists. Of course, any sophisticated normative theory of decision making recognizes that ordinary decisions are made under conditions of uncertainty and indeterminacy. Our story seems to make the formulation of norms for sound decision making even more difficult than the (already formidable) problems of ordinary ignorance and confusion. It adds the sober reminder that, besides revising their aims, decision makers also sometimes redefine the norms for reliably sound deliberation, as well as the criteria for an appropriate time frame for evaluating it. Enlarging the scope of these normative problems to include the psychological and social dimensions of deliberation helps to explain the sobering and remarkable fact that even our most rationally self-critical, far-reaching, responsible deliberations often issue in melodramatic tragedy.

Although it may seem indirect, the best way to bypass the melodrama of the circular or regressive search for norms for responsible deliberation is to sketch some current theories of rational choice and deliberation, to note some of their shortcomings, and to show how their sophisticated reformulation embeds elements of our account. These rough sketches are not meant to be either exhaustive or mutually exclusive. And although they border on caricatures, they reveal the extent to which even their sophisticated formulation presupposes and drifts toward incorporating my story. To be sure, expanding standard theories in these directions may seem as useful and friendly as adding complicated ellipses to save a theory whose initial attraction was its simplicity. When that happens, we find ourselves in yet another domain of decisive disagreement about the proper tasks and aims of theories of decision making.

The Real Politik *Model*

In the *real politik* model, those who have the most power—however it be directed, defined, or measured and whatever their aims may be—determine policy decisions. They may do it by coercion; they may do it by limiting options in such a way as to make theirs seem the most acceptable. An astute winner typically provides incentives to elicit long-term cooperation from dissenters.

But what's power and who has it? Isn't the very definition under contention? "Power comes out of the barrel of a gun." Who has the financial power to supply armaments? And who has the power to convince the industrialists to develop electronic communication technology rather than nuclear weaponry? Who has the rhetorical and imaginative power to form the mentality of decision makers?[9] Polemical arguments about the definition and criteria of power are themselves subject to the model of decision making I that have sketched.

The First-Person–Instrumentalist Model

In the naive version of the instrumentalist model, decision makers have relatively specific preferences; it is rational for them to opt for the alternative they believe most likely to achieve satisfaction within a predetermined time frame, bearing in mind the least costly side effects of the most readily available option.

In the sophisticated, self-corrective version, in determining their preferences and calculating the probability of satisfactory outcomes, decision makers recognize that the process of decision making is enhanced by collaborative deliberation. The dynamics of such deliberation may lead them to change their initial preferences and options quite dramatically.

Such decisions—deciding to emigrate, to attend a conference, to have a child, or to embark on a course of study—could in principle be analyzed as a sequence of discrete moments.[10] To be sure, the improvisatory character of such decisions can be *analytically* subdivided as a sequence of discrete microdecisions, but they rarely take that psychological form. In any case, an analysis of this kind would not explain the rationale of the sequence of microdecisions in its entirety. It would not reveal the structure or direction of the process, taken as forming a dramatic whole, with a beginning, middle, and end.

Sophisticated versions of the instrumentalist model of rational choice are typically developed under the protection of a ceteris paribus clause. An idealized, rational decision maker has transparency of information, including a sound understanding of her own psychology—her affections and volatile instability, her (in)capacity to remain steady under stress, the extent to which her desire for harmonious cooperation is capable of overriding her dialectical aggression, and so on. In principle, rational deciders are assumed to be able to control, utilize, or coopt their various traits; their physical and psychological constitutions; their temperaments and fantasies; and so on. When that is not readily feasible, idealized, sophisticated decision makers are at least able to factor their psychology among other constraints that govern their decisions and opt for the alternative that maximizes preference satisfaction under conditions of uncertainty and indeterminacy.

As the instrumentalist model becomes more sophisticated, it adds ellipsis after ellipsis: it becomes more complex, plastic, and flexible than was promised by its original formulation. Seeing the necessity and the utility of a responsive sensitivity to her interactions with others, the rational instrumentalist recognizes the likelihood of dramatic changes in her original preferences; she not only attempts to foresee contingencies but also attempts to develop the second-order skills involved in being able to adapt to unforeseeable accidents.

The Negotiation, or "Let's Make a Deal," Model

Like the naive version of the instrumental model, the naive version of the negotiation model presupposes that the participants initially begin with a relatively fixed set of aims, staking out an area of maximal and minimal conditions of satisfaction. In the worst cases, the participants do not know their partners' priorities, habits of thought, attitudes to risk, or levels of trust. Even when they are aware of one another's bargaining range, they may be naive or ignorant of the conventions and strategies that govern one another's modes of negotiation. They may fail to perceive goodwill or fail to see the sources and depths of ill will. They may be unaware of the events, constraints, and contingencies that affect one another's negotiating practices and positions: for instance, the threat of a famine or civil uprising, the protocols of secrecy or publicity that govern public policy, or the idiosyncrasies of individual negotiators. Had the negotiating partners been aware of one another's constraints—concerns that (each from her own perspective) might seem irrational or irrelevant—they might have been able to enlarge or modify their positions. In the absence of ideal conditions, the naive negotiation model follows the instrumentalist model in counseling approximation: maximize the satisfaction of initial preferences.

The sophisticated version of the negotiation model allows a wider range of adaptability. The very process of negotiating may revise the partners' aims and attitudes by providing a clearer insight into one another's working priorities and premises. At best, they may be able to substitute collaborative for competitive solutions, removing themselves from the presumption of zero-sum constraints. Rather than each negotiator attempting to approximate her original ideal solution—that of maximizing the satisfaction of her initial preferences—she may be able to cooperate in devising a solution that enlarges or changes her conception of a satisfactory solution.[11] By incorporating an account of mutually adaptable dynamic and dialectical adjustment, the sophisticated version of the negotiation model moves toward our story.

The Deliberative and Constructivist Models

The naive version of the deliberative model is an extension of the sophisticated negotiation model. Participants present what they take to be the best policy or action, recognizing it as partially vague or indeterminate. Each offers (what she takes to be) the best reasons for adopting a specific version of her preferred options, taking into account her values and principles. Quite independently of whether the partners treat each other as equals, decision making is considered to be collaborative, allowing public deliberation about the merits of each position. Alternatives are continuously refined to accommodate new considerations. Ideally a consensus is formed: a solution emerges, one that accommodates the needs and concerns of the minority, allowing them—perhaps for reasons of their own—to cooperate as best they can, even if that only means agreeing not to obstruct the decision.

The naive version of the deliberative model typically assumes that decision makers share a relatively fixed "starting point"—a set of general values, aims, principles, or commitments. Within contestable limits, these starting points are recognized to be vague and indeterminate, open to distinctive interpretations, that permit them to be implemented in a range of different ways. Rational agents evaluate alternative ways of specifying and satisfying those preferences and select the policies that, all things considered (including their moral commitments, as well as existing social and economic constraints), seem best to realize them. They allow that the criteria for satisfaction—significantly including the time frame within which it is to be measured—may themselves be subject to further deliberation.

Sophisticated or constructivist versions of the deliberative model recognize that the presumptive starting points of deliberative decisions may themselves become the subject of deliberation. Even the normative standards of evaluation—a set of principles or values—could emerge as a late discovery or even as a late compromise decision.[12] The constructivist model is latitudinarian about including unexpected considerations as relevant. In the course of the discussion, a participant may come to treat (what had previously been merely) a tangential consideration as dominantly relevant to her decision. By sheer accident, what was, for all participants, initially considered to be only marginally relevant can become the central aim.

Most normative theories of deliberative decision making are developed by projecting a theory about idealized rational agents, in principle capable of being directly responsive to reasonable considerations and of acting in compliance with them without tangential negative reactions from such compliance. Such theories acknowledge—as they must—that their ideal model presupposes that the participants of public deliberation are not only capable of being moved by rational considerations but also have been formed and educated in a genuinely civically minded, civil society, one that is only likely to emerge as a result of such public deliberation. Like many purely idealized models, normative theories of deliberative decision making face the bootstrap problems. As Marx puts it, "Changed men are products of . . . changed upbringing . . . the educator himself needs educating."[13]

Decision makers are purportedly guided by an ideal of *all things considered*. That phrase is, of course, rhetorically inflated: *all* considerations in a decisive deliberation about building a dam on the Yangtze might include a speculative calculation of the effects of El Niño on the mean annual rainfall in Brasília. What is required is weighing factors that may reasonably be argued to be relevant. Constructivists acknowledge that quite unexpected—and, indeed, accidental—considerations may become relevant to deliberation.

When pressed, the *real politik*, negotiation, and deliberative models acknowledge that each moment or stage of decision making opens new and unexpected options; each new option brings new problems; each new problem brings new considerations whose relevance must be weighed. The constructivist model reveals what was latently present in the other models: that dialectically sensitive decision making acknowledges the possible relevance of tangential, accidental, and ironic contingencies. In sum, the extent to which current models of decision making become more descriptively sophisticated—the extent to which they add ellipses to accommodate the dramatic dynamics of decision making—marks the extent to which they move to incorporate the elements of our account.

Let's Drop Olympian Pretensions

But we've still not satisfied the philosopher within, the philosopher who says, "All this is very well as a rough description of the gory mess of decision making and philosophic disputation. What should normative theories of rational deliberation and decision making do for us and we for them? How should we—as responsible philosophers—adjudicate among competing normative criteria for rational deliberation? How much of the conditions of our psychology—our finding ourselves role-cast in dynamic, interactive dramas—should a regulative model of rational deliberation take into account?" On the one hand, norms that only idealized deliberators—angels or Martians—are capable of following cannot be regulatively binding on mere humans. On the other hand, if we are too closely guided by our current beliefs about the sociopsychological constraints on deliberative practices, we may cut off the possibility of critical, radical reforms of those practices. We seem caught between two philosophic obligations: formulating norms that (working within the "realistic" constraints) can actually guide conduct and formulating those that (projecting beyond existing conditions) criticize and reform those realistic constraints.

But if the very process of evaluating and correcting the norms that govern realistic rational deliberation is regressive—if it replicates the very drama it is meant to regulate—are we forced to abandon the idea of fixed, reliable, generalized regulative norms and directions for deliberation and decision making? Does our story mean that there are no better or worse modes of deliberation, no criteria for evaluating the deliberative process? Does it mean that the norms of every deliberation are context-bound and that the legitimacy of dialogic interventions depends on the participants' acceptance of those interventions? When does an intervention indicate an exit from the discussion, and when does it introduce a new turn within a continuing dialogue?[14] These rhetorical questions presuppose inappropriate polarities: they should be refused rather than directly addressed. Like literary dramas, deliberation does—and does not—have norms. Like them, the formulation of the criteria for its success is subject to the further dramas of deliberation: they cannot be abstracted from their historical and sociopolitical contexts.

The discussions and deliberations chronicled in the *Federalist Papers* and the documents of the Constitutional Convention provide a superb example of our story. Although each of the founders had distinctive economic, demographic, and geopolitical agendas, they all had general (and even vague) aims and principles of British and French Enlightenment philosophy. Their deliberations issued in a

set of constitutional decisions that were simultaneously substantive and methodological. In the very process of mandating a division of powers, they also defined
a set of rules and procedures for future deliberations and decision making. Those
norms regulated the scope, power, issues, and participants of federal deliberation
and decision making. They specified the method by which the members of those
bodies would be selected, thereby determining who should have a voice in various
areas of public deliberation. And crucially, they defined procedures for overriding
those decisions. But the founders did not begin de novo: at least some of the
raw materials of their principles derived from existing practices and ideals. Their
vocabulary—their definitions, analogies, and images—join, echo, and develop the
conceptual language and the deeply embedded practices of the time. The emancipation of slaves and the enfranchisement of women changed the understanding
and application of those principles and the ground rules for deliberation. The
abolitionists succeeded in changing the criteria for legitimate deliberation by appealing to biblical texts and presumedly shared Christian sentiments. The reassess-
ment and modification of criteria for deliberation and decision making are themselves subject to dramatic improvisation, and they rest on the prepared ground of
previously half-articulated presentiments.[15]

Similarly, Aristotle's normative guide for constructing tragic dramas drew on
his analysis of the "successful" dramas of the time. Changes in the heuristic norms
for writing tragedy—those of Corneille and Racine; of Dryden and Jonson; of
Adorno, Benjamin, and Brecht—presupposed and modified Aristotle's handbook.

Our characterization—our account of the accident-prone dramas of decision
making—is itself subject to the story it has sketched. Although our story is primarily descriptive, it presupposes a decision about the phenomena that should be
incorporated and acknowledged within a responsible theory of decision making.
Like other descriptions and decisions, it has been developed in dialectical response to current models of rational decision. Its details can be—should be—further
specified in different ways, accidentally affected by the interactive drama of our
discussions with our colleagues. That's how things are, boot straps all the way.

You might think that all this is nothing more than armchair sociology, mere
speculation about the psychological susceptibilities of intellectuals and politicians.
You might think that serious philosophy requires a reflective assessment of the
arguments of competing positions. For those who see philosophy as a strongly
normative enterprise, I fear that the promise—or threat—of my Aesopian moral
may be embarrassingly deflationary. Honesty recommends that we drop our Olym-
pian pretensions and admit ourselves to be role-cast in the dramas of philosophic
discussions, recognizing that our most considered reflective views and decisions
embed the chance and accidental imprints of our colleagues' role-enacting participation. This retreat to modesty goes much further than the familiar obligatory
courtesy with which we admit our fallibility ("I could be wrong, but . . . "). It
counsels against a contextless, ahistorical metatheoretical attempt to formulate
criteria or norms for evaluating ethical theories *überhaupt*.[16] It recommends that
each decision-making philosopher should not only present the best, weightiest
arguments and considerations for her views but also directly address the concerns

of her opponents and explicitly acknowledge the sources, limitations, and lacunae of her position. She may not always be able to locate her own perspectival, dialectical role, but she can at least indicate her uncertainties and hesitations, inviting further dialogue for their remedies.[17]

If this small sample of mottos in a handbook for responsible philosophic and practical deliberation sounds like a watered-down, glossy magazine version of the ethics of deliberative discourse, that is because that is what it is. When generalized, contextless, ahistorical mottos are stripped of the rhetoric of their high-flying normative ambitions, they not only sound but also are vapid. But the vacuous, heuristic mottos of handbooks have a useful place even when they parade as principles. Ambiguous as they are, they can lure—invite and bind—players to participate in the uncertain, unchartered dramas of deliberation.

Notes

I am grateful to MindaRae Amiran, Myles Burnyeat, Rudiger Bittner, Catherine Elgin, Moshe Halbertal, Virginia Held, Shirley Kaufman, Genevieve Lloyd, Clifford Orwin, Ruth Nevo, Jay Rorty, Josef Stern, Eleanore Stump, and the Van Leer Foundation and the Hartman Institute, both in Jerusalem, who generously provided hospitality for writing this essay. It is a revised version of "The Improvisatory Drama of Decision Making," which was delivered at the World Congress of Philosophy in Boston, Massachusetts, August 1998, and appeared in *Well-Being and Morality*, ed. Roger Crisp and Brad Hooker (Oxford: Oxford University Press, 1999).

1. Although the participant players may represent groups—Labor and Likud in Israel, the Congress Party and the BJP in India, or factions within the Republican Party—for the sake of convenience, I refer to players and participants in the singular.

2. See Alasdair MacIntyre, "How Virtues Become Vices," in *Evaluation and Explanation in the Biomedical Sciences*, ed. H. T. Engelheardt and S. F. Spicker (The Hague: Mouton, 1982); Amelie Oksenberg Rorty, "From Exasperating Virtues to Civic Virtues," *American Philosophical Quarterly* 33 (1996): 303–314.

3. See *The Federalist Papers*; Thucydides's reports of the Athenian debates (*The History of the Peloponnesian War*); and David Wiggins, "Deliberation and Practical Reason," *Proceedings of the Aristotelian Society* 76 (1975–1976): 29–51. Decisions about means and about ends are interwoven. The difference between them is not a difference between types of events but is about perspectives on the object of choice: every choice of means subtly affects the choice of ends; and, of course, every determination and articulation of an end constrains the range of appropriate of means.

4. See Mikhail Bakhtin, *The Dialogic Imagination*, trans. C. Emerson and M. Holquist (Austin: University of Texas Press, 1981); Mikhail Bakhtin, *Speech Genres*, ed. C. Emerson and M. Holquist (Austin: University of Texas Press, 1981); Wolfgang Iser, *Languages of the Unsayable* (New York: Columbia, 1989); Amelie Oksenberg Rorty, "The Advantages of Moral Diversity," *The Good Life and the Human Good* (Cambridge: Cambridge University Press, 1992). In focusing on the dialectically interactive character of the formation of intentions and decisions, I do not intend to discuss the social formation of x, y and z (whatever *that* might mean).

5. This is not a claim about the social construction of philosophy. For one thing, social constructionists tend to posit a homogeneous, uniform "mentality." Like practi-

cal reasoning, philosophic thought is dramatically, dynamically multivocal. We are affected by and responsive to the oppositions among our ancestors and contemporaries. Sometimes we set ourselves to reconcile them, sometimes to vanquish them. Our "own" thought is marked by the fine-grained details of those tasks.

6. See "Virtues and Their Vicissitudes," in Amelie Oksenberg Rorty, *Mind in Action* (Boston: Beacon Press, 1988).

7. See Annette Baier, *The Commons of the Mind* (Peru, Ill.: Open Court, 1997); and my "Witnessing Philosophers," in *The Many Faces of Philosophy*, ed. Amelie Oksenberg Rorty (Oxford: Oxford University Press, 2003).

8. See Bakhtin, *Dialogic Imagination*.

9. See my "Power and Powers," in *Rethinking Power*, ed. Thomas Wartenberg (Philadelphia: Temple University, 1992); and my "Imagination and Power" in Rorty, *Mind in Action*.

10. I am grateful to Stephen White for raising this objection in another context.

11. See Avishai Margalit's critique of the "approximate the ideal" model, in his "Ideals and Second-Bests," in *Philosophy for Education*, ed. Seymore Fox (Jerusalem: Van Leer Institute Press, 1983), 77–90; and Avishai Margalit, *The Decent Society* (Cambridge, Mass.: Harvard University Press, 1996), 283–284.

12. See Christine Korsgaard, *Creating the Kingdom of Ends* (New York: Cambridge University Press, 1996); Jurgen Habermas, *Moral Consciousness and Communicative Action* (Cambridge, Mass.: MIT Press, 1990); Seyla BenHabib, ed., *Democracy and Difference* (Princeton, N.J.: Princeton University Press, 1996).

13. Karl Marx, *Theses on Feuerbach* III.

14. See Albert Hirschmann, *Exit, Voice and Loyalty* (Cambridge, Mass.: Harvard University Press, 1970).

15. See Dan Sperber, "Apparently Irrational Beliefs," in *Rationality and Relativism*, ed. Martin Hollis and Steven Lukes (Cambridge, Mass.: MIT Press, 1982), esp. 166ff.

16. For a responsible attempt to locate the ethics of deliberative discourse within historical and political contexts, see Seyla Ben Habib, *Transformations of Citizenship: Dilemmas for the Nation State in the Era of Globalization* (Assen, Netherlands: Van Gorcum, 1997).

17. See T. M. Scanlon, *What We Owe to Each Other* (Cambridge, Mass.: Harvard University Press, 1998), for a subtle, carefully formulated account of this condition.

16

Narrative and Moral Life

Diana Tietjens Meyers

The last two decades of the millennium saw a surge of philosophical inquiry into the role of narrative in moral life. Why narrative? Why now?

The obvious answer to the first question is that people tell lots of stories — stories about themselves and their own experiences; about people they know and their experiences; about people, past and present, whose lives they know of secondhand; and about people whom they imagine. Schematically, intentional agency involves a purpose moving someone to act in order to bring about an outcome. Thus, intentional agency coincides with the most familiar, bare-bones narrative template — beginning/purpose, middle/act, end/outcome. It is hardly surprising, then, that people's lives are so full of stories. Personal narratives track and articulate social encounters, as well as the eddies of subjectivity. An individual's past experience may recur in the form of flashbacks, but more often people recollect their experience in narrative form. Moral relations also capitalize on narrative, for assigning responsibility and excusing misdeeds depend on identifying protagonists, characterizing their state of mind, and specifying their actions and the consequences of their actions. Phenomenologically, the answer to the question "Why narrative?" seems to be "Because it's so pervasive and ineliminable."

Since narrative is such a prominent feature of human life, ignoring narrative making, narrative telling, and narrative understanding would seem to be a case of philosophical ineptitude, if not malpractice. Yet, narration and narrativity have hardly been central topics in twentieth-century Anglo-American philosophy. Only since Charles Taylor, Martha Nussbaum, Richard Rorty, Alasdair MacIntyre, and Alexander Nehamas cast narrative in a leading role in their moral and political theories has it gained sustained attention.[1]

Building on this work, narrativity theorists have recently advanced a number of intriguing claims about the philosophical significance of narrative. According to Marya Schechtman, those individuals who "weave stories of their lives" are persons.[2] A person's identity, she adds, "is constituted by the content of her self-narrative, and the traits, actions, and experiences included in it are, by virtue of that inclusion, hers."[3] Margaret Walker makes narrative pivotal to morality. "A *story*," in her view, "is the basic form of representation for moral problems."[4] Leading a morally creditable life that is distinctively one's own requires developing and enacting narratives of "identity, relationship, and value."[5] Seyla Benhabib accents the relation between narrative and agency: "Our agency consists of our capacity to weave out of those [socially furnished] narratives and fragments of narratives a life story that makes sense for us, as unique individual selves."[6] Likewise, Hilde Nelson claims that identities are "complex narrative constructions consisting of a fluid interaction of the many stories and fragments of stories surrounding the things that seem most important, from one's own point of view and the point of view of others, about a person over time."[7] Moreover, because demeaning, culturally transmitted narratives can damage the identities and agency of members of systematically subordinated social groups, respectful counternarratives are necessary to repair these individuals' identities and to secure their agency.[8]

Is human reality (or some especially important dimension of it) itself narrative in nature? Is human reality (or some especially important dimension of it) impossible to understand except through narrative devices? Or do narratives provide a particularly felicitous and easily communicated vehicle, but by no means the primary, only, or best vehicle, for representing human reality (or some especially important dimension of it)?

There is reason to be cautious about overplaying the narrativity card in metaphysics or epistemology. A variety of nonnarrative modes of representation—pictorial imagery, poetic tropes, and dance gesture, not to mention theoretical analysis—can be expressively powerful and revealing of human reality. I would stress, moreover, that people avail themselves of all of these modes of representation, collectively, as well as individually—that is, at the level of cultural production and consumption and at the level of personal utterance and communication. In this respect, narrative is not privileged. In addition, the huge assortment of narrative forms available to Western narrators—together with the possibility that acquaintance with other cultures might reveal an even vaster array of narrative templates—raises doubts about what is being asserted when this or that is said to be narrative in structure or structured by narrative. Although I think I know a story "when I see one," I am not at all confident that anyone can distinguish narratives from theories, sequential listings of events, and other forms of representation with enough clarity to grasp what is being denied when narrativity is affirmed.[9]

Many narrativity theorists implicitly acknowledge these points by adopting very capacious views of narrative. They include story fragments and pictorial imagery in their conception of narrative; they do not exclude giving reasons from self-narratives; and they allow that autobiographical narratives need not be thematically unified or characterologically consistent and that they need not cohere as a single plot line.[10] Others mute their metaphysical claims by treating narrativity as an organizing principle of the lives persons lead or by treating personal identities as discursive constructions and distinguishing personal identities from persons or selves.[11] When fully spelled out, affirmations of narrativity sometimes prove to be less contentious than they initially sound.

I set these matters aside, however, for my purpose is not to debate the merits of particular accounts of narrative and narrativity, nor is it to assess the tenability of basing metaphysics or epistemology on narrative. Rather, I wish to pose the question "Why narrative now?" Thus, the first three sections explore the philosophical confusions, disappointments, and yearnings that motivate the turn to narrative. Philosophers invoke narrativity to underwrite conceptions of the moral subject, moral knowledge, and moral agency. I consider why these proposals are as attractive as they are. Although I think there is much to be learned from this approach to moral philosophy, I believe that there are two disturbing omissions in narrativity theory. The first section concludes by pointing out the failure of narrativity theory to account for the richness of the moral subject's constitutive experience—the material that the narrator's stories relate. The concluding section argues that excessive attention to narrative leads philosophers to overlook the capacities that make narration possible and valuable.

The Moral Subject

Moral subjects are members of moral communities. They regard themselves and one another as intentional agents, and they hold themselves and one another responsible for what they do. To those who lead this kind of life, nothing could seem more ordinary and natural. Yet, characterizing the creatures who engage in this form of interaction sparks heated controversy. An adequate account of the constitution of moral subjectivity must explain what enables people to reflect on moral problems and participate in moral relations, and there are quite a few accounts that have demonstrated their usefulness in explaining people's moral powers. I consider five of the most widely espoused and widely debated conceptions of the moral subject. Some theorists advocate the Kantian unitary self. Others embrace the communitarian social self, the psychoanalytic divided self, or the feminist relational self. The embodied self seems all but orphaned in these debates, but it seems to me that slighting the embodied self slights important forms of moral experience.

Rationality is both the essence and the triumph of the unitary self. Proponents of this conception of the moral subject hold that reason enables individuals to discover and justify moral principles for themselves. By ensuring the mutual consistency of those principles, reason ensures unity within the individual's action-guiding system and thus unity of purpose for the moral subject. Furthermore, since the unitary subject's rationally mandated desires and actions express its essential nature, those desires and actions are most genuinely its own. Equally important, rationality endows individuals with critical powers. When unitary subjects detect conflicts within their system of principles or between their principles and their conduct, they seek to resolve these conflicts by amending their principles or reforming their conduct. They may apply the same critical skills to their society's institutions, policies, and practices. The unitary self appeals to moral theorists, then, because it makes sense of people's capacity for independent judgment and also because it underwrites a life of integrity. The unitary self leaves many moral theorists dissatisfied, though. Not only does this conception screen out all of the work (largely done by women) of nurturance and training in the "arts of person-hood," as Annette Baier calls them, but also it assumes a universality of moral rationality that even a superficial acquaintance with comparative cultural studies belies.[12]

The communitarian social self addresses these concerns by underscoring the fact that moral subjects are socialized or enculturated. To become competent moral subjects, individuals must acquire a stock of cultural values, attitudes, and interpretive frameworks and learn how to use these resources to understand and negotiate social relations. They must assimilate social norms and master appropriate ways to speak and act. Internalized, this material is constitutive of the individual's identity. This cultural enmeshment of the social self injects a welcome note of realism into discussions of moral subjectivity. It demystifies the source of people's moral values and dispositions. It offers an explanation of the development of moral subjectivity that acknowledges cultural diversity and that makes sense of people's loyalty to their communities and cultures of origin. However, opponents of this view worry that, conceived as a social self, the moral subject becomes a virtual captive of her or his social context. Their critical leverage minimized, people are limited to tinkering with the norms they inherit, if they are not destined to reproduce culturally transmitted norms. Undeniable though it is that individuals cannot create their own value systems and styles of conduct ex nihilo and that individuality is parasitic on socialization and enculturation, it is also undeniable that these normalizing processes threaten independent judgment and free choice.

The psychoanalytic divided self is the psychodynamic self. Advocates of the divided self find fault with both the unitary self and the social self because these conceptions oversimplify moral subjectivity. Split between consciousness and self-awareness, on the one hand, and elusive unconscious affect and desire, on the other hand, the divided self is characterized by inner depth, complexity, and enigma. The distinctive but open-ended psychic economy of the divided self is manifest in a unique subjectivity and personality. There is no universal core humanity, but individuals do not merely sponge up their cultural environment. Since individuals process cultural inputs and since this processing is not constrained by universal rational standards, the divided self undermines moral theory's most reliable stanchions—tradition and reason. The psychodynamic conception also complicates moral subjectivity by curtailing self-supervision. As Freud memorably remarked, the ego "is not even master in its own house."[13] Beset by unconscious drive and repressed desire, people are not transparent to themselves, nor can they exert complete control over their conduct. For this reason, the divided self is the natural locus of a major species of excuses—"I couldn't help it," "I don't know what came over me," "I lost it," and the like. Because unconscious motivation can account for moral fecklessness without accusing the agent of malice, the divided self explains why many of our excuse-making and excuse-accepting practices are warranted forms of moral leniency.

The feminist relational self is the interpersonally bonded self. This view seeks to respond to several criticisms of the preceding conceptions. Like proponents of the social self and the divided self, proponents of the relational self deny that critical reason can or should fully determine the moral subject's deliberations and decisions. But proponents of the relational self object to the social self on the grounds that it abstracts and reifies society and to the divided self on the grounds that it overestimates the importance of biology. The relational self personalizes society by emphasizing the influence of interpersonal relations throughout life, including but not limited to the formative interaction between children and their care givers. The relational self interpersonalizes biology by insisting that children take their developmental cues from their care givers and by denying that anatomy is intrinsically meaningful.[14] As relational selves with lasting emotional attachments to others, people share in one another's joys and sorrows, give and receive care, and generally profit from the many rewards and cope with the many aggravations of friendship, family membership, religious or ethnic affiliation, and the like. These relationships are sources of moral identity, for people become committed to their intimates and to others whom they care about, and these commitments become central moral concerns. Invested in a circle of family, friends, or other close personal connections, the relational self anchors the patterns of moral partiality that most people regard as justified and routinely enact. Yet, morally crediting these ties poses a problem for ethical theory. Since responding to others' needs can become so consuming that the individual is deprived of any opportunity to pursue personal goals and projects, valued relationships can morph into a "plague of commitments," to borrow Margaret Walker's striking phrase.[15] Thus, proponents of the unitary self and the divided self may counter that the relational self is insufficiently separated from others—too entangled in its relational web to achieve a distinctive moral identity.

The embodied self is often ignored in discussions of the moral subject. This is strange, for people can neither take action nor partake in sensuous pleasure unless they are embodied. Also, that so much child-rearing effort is aimed at regulating the body and so much cultural machinery is dedicated to enforcing canons of physical appearance attests to society's preoccupation with bodies and their comportment. This concentration of attention heightens people's investment in their body image—their sense of what they look like and what their physical capabilities are. Since attacks on bodily integrity can be traumatic even when they are not life threatening, prohibitions on physical aggression are among the most stringent moral norms. Still, it would be a mistake to reduce the embodied self to its manipulability and vulnerability. To be sure, ingrained bodily skillfulness is crucial to personal safety, but it is also crucial to social engagement. Body language—facial and gestural expressivity—conveys much of the meaning of people's speech, as well as their nonverbal behavior. The embodied self is also a repository of memory. Experiences of well-being, as well as experiences of suffering, are viscerally encoded and shape subsequent conduct.[16] Physical misery, such as chronic hunger and back-breaking labor, often signals injustice and may catalyze social critique. Thus, the embodied self is a wellspring of moral insight and innovation as well as a vehicle of moral enactment and self-revelation.

Each of the preceding conceptions of the self captures a significant dimension of moral subjectivity—of what it's like and what it means to be a participant in a moral community. Yet, these conceptions are usually presented as mutually exclusive. A theory of moral subjectivity, it is assumed, must take a stand on which kind of self the moral subject really is and must somehow subsume the other four phenomenal selves within that conception. Indeed, because familiar theories of the self endeavor to incorporate the strengths of the five conceptions sketched above, my discussion may seem to artificially pry them apart. In my view, however, the move to synthesize these conceptions has two unfortunate consequences: (1) Each conception must be stretched and twisted to accommodate dimensions of moral subjectivity that fit far more easily into alternative conceptions, and (2) dimensions of moral subjectivity that cannot be crammed into one's preferred conception must be dismissed as peripheral or illusory. In light of these problems, it would be better to drop the synthetic imperative and to regard the five conceptions of the self as articulating five faces of the moral subject—five dimensions of subjective experience, five loci of value, five schemas for understanding oneself and others, and five foci of moral concern. Alas, this suggestion seems to amount to recommending a cumbersome, perhaps incoherent, account of the moral subject. Yet, if my dissatisfaction with theories that embrace the synthetic imperative is well grounded, parsimony and completeness may not be jointly attainable.

Here, I would urge, is where narrativity gets its purchase. In self-narratives, people effortlessly weave together the disparate themes that the unitary self, the social self, the divided self, the relational self, and the embodied self highlight.

Consider, for example, Lynne Taetzsch's autobiographical essay, "Fighting Natural," which chronicles her odyssey from poverty and unpopularity in a New Jersey high school to dissociating from herself at the University of Southern California (USC) after trying to masquerade as a California coed and finally to donning a professional getup and teaching writing at George Washington University. The pivotal motif in Taetzsch's story is dyeing her hair. Blatantly at odds with her general indifference to her appearance—she doesn't bother to wear makeup and prefers casual clothes—her dedication to this ritual baffles her.[17] In addition, it conflicts with her principles. Preparing to teach bell hooks's critique of Madonna's *Blonde Ambition* performances, she reproaches herself for betraying the cause of gender and racial equality and also for forsaking her students who need her to model an alternative to the beauty codes promulgated in the mass media.[18] With an assist from her divided self, however, she represses the contradictions her rational, unitary self descries and blithely opts for a blonder-than-blond frosting the very next day. At home after the treatment, inspecting the results, she is appalled by what she's done but loves the way she looks anyway.[19]

How could she have come to be so ambivalent about and alienated from herself? That's partly a story about her relational self—the father who agreed with the high school counselor who condemned her for thinking she was "smarter than everyone else" and the first boyfriend who dated her only to "make his old girl-friend jealous."[20] It's also a story about her social self and the stereotypes that frame perception and social positioning. At USC, men read her "California-girl look-alike attempt" as a sexual come-on, and later, at Cooper Union, fellow students and faculty members read her no-holds-barred sex-object pastiche as slutty.[21] Not surprisingly, the embodied self figures prominently, too: "I'm fifty-one years old and can't remember a day when I felt at home in my body."[22] Near the end of her story, the divided self resurfaces:

> I had nowhere to put my rage. So I took it out on my hair. . . . What I've
> done most to my hair is torture it. I've bleached it, permed it, burned it,
> cut it, tied it, and dyed it with a vengeance to disfigure, not enhance my
> appearance. The Clairol home treatment—whether silver blond or blue-
> black—has been a kind of purging for me, a tearing out of my old life
> so that I might look in the mirror and see a new person, find a new life,
> a way to be in the world that worked this time.[23]

Reacting to a gender system that identifies women with their looks, that demands that women fight their "natural" looks, and that condemns them for looking un-natural, Taetzsch turns her aggression on herself.

Without ever naming the five conceptions of the self that I have identified, Taetzsch tells a succinct, coherent story that includes every one of them. I realize that her story is an artfully crafted memoir, not an ordinary self-narrative. Still, I do not think her inclusion of these five dimensions of selfhood is atypical of the latter.

It is troubling, however, that narrative accounts of the moral subject do not so much *resolve* as *dissolve* the tensions among the five conceptions. The themes remain, and they are articulated. But the disparate origins of these identity-consti-tuting experiences remain implicit. Because self-stories do not distinguish the re-spective roles of reasoning, enculturation, interpersonal relations, bodily processes, and intrapsychic dynamics in the constitution of moral subjects, the analytical incompatibilities and incongruities of the corresponding conceptions of the self disappear. Thus, narrativity theory provides the sought-after synthesis, but at the cost of explanatory power. Taetzsch's story depicts the experiences of a remarkably complex individual, but it does not purport to explain what kind of being is capa-ble of undergoing the many kinds of experience she describes. If "a story-telling being" is not an informative characterization of such individuals, it seems to me that narrativity theory must retain the five conceptions of the self that I have sketched.

Moral Knowledge

Twentieth-century Anglo-American philosophy puts a premium on codifying moral knowledge. According to Margaret Walker, however, this epistemological demand has not always held sway. She traces its assent to Henry Sidgwick's monumental survey, *The Methods of Ethics*.[24] Subsequent to Sidgwick's schematization of ethical thought, the approach to moral philosophy that Walker dubs the "theoretical-juridical model" came into currency.[25] Henceforth, moral philosophy's foremost tasks include articulating a finite set of action-guiding principles, organizing them into a hierarchical system, and defending this system. Correlatively, possession of a rationally justified system of principles is conceived as the key to moral deliberation. To figure out how they should act, moral subjects must distill morally significant information from their circumstances and identify relevant moral principles. Using these materials as premises, they must then construct deductive arguments that yield judgments about what they ought (or ought not) to do. Thus, the theoretical-juridical model aspires to bring theory and practice into alignment.

No moral theory has fulfilled this promise, however, because the project of codifying moral knowledge is fraught with peril. First, no simple principle is determinate and absolute. Any credible principle must be interpreted to clarify the meaning of the terms in which it is couched and qualified to countenance various generally recognized exceptions. Fully explicit statements of moral principles turn out to be lengthy, complicated, and unwieldy—a far cry from the succinct *Thou shalts* and *Thou shalt nots* of the Decalogue. In addition, it is doubtful that a fully explicit statement of any moral principle could ever be finalized.[26] New circumstances—brought about, for example, by scientific discoveries, demographic upheaval, unprecedented technology, or political or economic transformation—might point up the need for further amendment. Worse, even supposing that fully explicit and final statements of our moral principles could be obtained, these philosophical behemoths would be of little practical use to real-world moral subjects, whose cognitive capacities and time for deliberation are limited.

Second, no hierarchical ordering of principles is universal and absolute. Every principle can be trumped by another principle under some conceivable circumstances. Indeed, one reason why no single instantiation of the theoretical-juridical model has ever commanded wide assent among professional philosophers is that they are trained to dream up clever situations in which a seemingly inviolable principle would have to yield to more compelling moral considerations. This strategy casts doubt on the most enduring systems of rank-ordered principles. To defend their views against such challenges, some theorists limit the scope of applicability of their prioritized principles. John Rawls, for example, confines his theory of justice to pluralistic societies with democratic political traditions.[27] Rawls is vague about justice in other types of society. Other theorists give up on assessing the relative stringency of principles and assigning them fixed rankings. W. D. Ross, for instance, affirms that all principles hold prima facie—that is, each is binding unless some other principle overrides it—and that individuals must rely on intuition to determine which principle is binding in a given situation.[28] For moral theory, definitive systematization of principles is as elusive a goal as complete articulation of principles.

The rigidity of the theoretical-juridical model portends its downfall. But the deindividualization of moral life that moral codification entails is no less troubling. Intuitionism seems to furnish a more flexible alternative. However, its epistemology is unpersuasive. Intuitionists typically maintain that people share a common faculty of moral apprehension and that people whose faculties are not impaired by self-interest, bias, or some other distorting influence will reach the same moral conclusions. Not only does this claim rule out moral individuality, it also flies in the face of abundant evidence that many reasonable and conscientious people profoundly disagree about morality. Different people prioritize different values and have different styles of moral enactment. Yet most of these diverse individuals lead morally decent lives. A theory of moral knowledge should be able to explain how this is possible.

Plainly, these individuals are not complying with a universal moral code, nor are they following the dictates of a universal faculty of moral intuition. But neither are they impulsively doing whatever they happen to feel like doing or shrewdly calculating how to get whatever they happen to want most. They have values and interpersonal commitments; they make judgments about what they ought to do; they reproach themselves when they fall short of their ideals. Narrativity theorists maintain that these individuals are telling certain sorts of stories to themselves and to the people they associate with. They are anticipating what sort of story they will be able to tell if they do this or that;[29] they are recalling the story of a particular relationship in order to ascertain what the other person can legitimately expect of them;[30] they are crafting counterstories designed to resist a master narrative that depicts them in demeaning ways.[31] They are improvising, to be sure, but their creativity is constrained by narrative conventions, as well as by other people's willingness to accept their stories. Thus, narrative accounts offer an explanation of how moral knowledge can be both individualized and well justified, and this explanation positions these accounts to repudiate pernicious individual relativism along with the theoretical-juridical model. Since serious deficiencies have been found in every moral theory based on the theoretical-juridical model, and since glaring disparities separate this model's conception of moral deliberation from the ways in which moral subjects actually think as they go about their lives, it is no wonder that narrative accounts of moral knowledge are steadily attracting converts.

Moral Agency

The problem of moral agency is traditionally construed as a problem about free will and responsibility. Exercising moral agency requires free will. People can be held responsible for their conduct and for its foreseeable consequences provided that it arises from free will. Many philosophers take this much for granted. Where they differ is over the nature of free will. Followers of Kant maintain that persons are endowed with reason, a faculty said to transcend the nexus of causal determinism. Provided that reason can steer volition, the will is free. Followers of Hume contend that such transcendence is a fiction. According to this view, people have free will when no external force prevents them from doing what they want to do or compels them to do what they do not want to do. As long as the cause of an action is internal to the agent, that individual is free.

The dispute between Humean and Kantian accounts of moral agency has never been resolved. But in the twentieth century, Marxist insights into the impact of dominant ideologies on individuals' lives have complicated discussion of this topic. Specifically, it has become clear that a tenable theory of moral agency must contend with internalized oppression, for internalized oppression compromises self-determination.

Internalized oppression afflicts many members of systematically subordinated social groups. To internalize oppression is to incorporate the experience of occupying a subordinate social position into the structure of the self. Cramping norms and humiliating attitudes become embedded in the cognitive, emotional, and volitional capacities of affected individuals. As a result, their self-perception, their grasp of opportunities, their hopes for the future, and their choices comport with the social position to which they have been relegated rather than with their real abilities and rightful ambitions. People who have internalized oppression "voluntarily" replicate derogatory stereotypes and reproduce disadvantageous behavior patterns. They are acting on "their own" values and preferences, but they are also perpetuating their own oppression.

This paradox poses formidable problems for both the Kantian and the Humean approach to moral agency. Rationally willed transcendence is hardly an option for those who find themselves in the grip of internalized oppression. Yet they rationally gauge how best to cope with their lot in life. External coercion does not compel them to act as they do. Yet they are by no means *self*-determining agents. Holding members of subordinated social groups responsible for complicity in their own oppression would (literally) add insult to injury. Plainly, the problem of responsibility and agency must be reframed to take account of the menace of internalized oppression.

Claudia Card's approach accents the temporality of responsibility and displaces the issue of free will. In her view, an exclusively backward-looking conception of responsibility—one that focuses on imputing praise or blame for past actions—overlooks a more fundamental form of responsibility.[32] While acknowledging the need to place blame where it belongs, Card stresses how practices of taking responsibility—assuming the burdens of meeting needs or grappling with problems—pervade interpersonal relations and social life.[33] Many of these undertakings enact subordinating norms and may result from internalized oppression. However, some of them defy wrongful social norms and resist internalized oppression. One of Card's examples is her own refusal of her culturally sanctioned sexual identity and her taking responsibility for redefining her erotic identity as a lesbian.[34] As she points out, people who are not responsible for inflicting injustice may nevertheless need to take responsibility for ending it.[35] If those who are harmed do not band together and resist, no one else will.

Neither the Kantian nor the Humean conception of agency adequately addresses Card's forward-looking form of responsibility. Although taking responsibility need not involve overcoming internalized oppression, the kinds of responsibility taking that particularly interest feminists and other progressive philosophers often do. What is needed, then, is a theory of moral agency that appreciates the power of internalized oppression to subvert self-determination and that also explains how resistance is possible and why it is necessary. For Kantians, internalized oppression can have only a superficial impact on moral agency, for it cannot penetrate to and corrupt the individual's core rational capacity. For Humeans, internalized oppression may (perversely) reduce the urgency of resistance. Since people who have internalized oppression do not want to do anything that would challenge social norms and provoke an antagonistic response, individuals can be acting freely (doing as they want without external interference) in virtue of having internalized oppressive norms. An adequate theory of moral agency must distinguish genuine self-determination from choice dictated by internalized oppression, and it must explain resistance to injustice without underestimating the damage to agency that internalized oppression causes.

Autobiographical narrative provides a way to finesse philosophical impasses on the topic of free will and doubts about hyperindividualistic accounts of moral agency. Likewise, it provides a way to counteract philosophical worries that anti-individualistic accounts of moral agency, which emphasize enculturation and institutional constraints, gut self-determination. For purposes of explicating innovative moral thought and resistance to oppressive norms, narrative theories of moral agency invoke linguistic competence. To be a fluent speaker is to be capable of generating an indefinite number of different sentences. Since the potential for creativity is built into a commonplace human capability that also empowers people to tell their own life stories, it is to be expected that some people will project futures for themselves or for their society that overturn established values and conventions. People do not need a pure rational capacity that is insulated from social influence to conceive new options, for internalized oppression does not neutralize linguistic competence. Still, people need to be able to distinguish novel options that they really want to pursue from novel options that would be no more satisfying or worthwhile than those that subordinating norms prescribe. Here narrativity theorists often point to dissident discursive communities, such as friendships, political organizations, and support groups, that encourage people to revise their self-narratives and that facilitate critical scrutiny of unorthodox plot lines.[36] Although others' acceptance of one's self-narrative cannot serve as the sole criterion of its credibility, exchanging stories often helps people refine a basically convincing story or discard implausible ones.

Linking moral agency to autobiographical narrative renders taking responsibility for one's identity and resistance to internalized oppression intelligible. Not only can a modified self-narrative resignify the meaning of the protagonist's inveterate feelings, attitudes, desires, and behavior, but also it can project a continuation of the story that keeps faith with the protagonist but breaks with the past. The settings of the story may change and prompt different behavior, or the protagonist's changed interpretation of the same settings may lead to fresh ways of engaging with them. By tracking the protagonist's subjective responses along with her or his conduct, self-narratives expose moments of self-alienation and habits of self-

betrayal. By envisioning alternative episodes in which the protagonist feels different, acts differently, or both, self-narratives can bring behavior into accord with
subjectivity. The device of self-narrative can free up individuals' imaginations
without cutting them off from reality. Thus, narrativity clarifies how people can
be profoundly influenced by their social context and yet retain their capacity to
shape self-determined moral lives—to transvalue values, reroute their own path-
ways, and reconfigure their social ideals.

What's Missing from Narrative Accounts?

Recent philosophical treatments of narrativity are enormously edifying. They bring
out serious weaknesses in traditional philosophical formulations of the moral subject, moral knowledge, and moral agency. They impart density, nuance, and dyna-
mism to these concepts. Too often, philosophical abstraction and analysis squeeze
the life out of moral experience. Narrativity theory successfully resists this tendency. Still, narrative accounts retain their critical edge, for moral experience
includes reflexivity, exchanging rebukes and reassurances, and negotiating ways
to reconcile or live with moral disagreements. Narrativity theory preserves this
richness and vitality. However, I argue that, in explicating the epistemology of
narrativity, narrativity theory has paid insufficient heed to the processes through
which people generate and certify moral self-narratives.

    Narrativity theory's perilous proximity to poststructuralism is one reason why
this oversight concerns me. The poststructuralist subject is a discursively constructed
and reconstructed "nodal point" in the continual, sometimes turbulent interplay of
discursive currents.[37] This conception of subjectivity meshes well with the sheer
rush of experience, the transience of impulses, the effervescence of feelings, and the
fissures in consciousness. The splintering and instability that this conception en-
shrines make it a good antidote to conceptions that exaggerate coherence and
wholeness to the point of falsifying moral experience. However, these very strengths
concomitantly undercut its viability as an account of moral subjects, their knowledge, and their agency. Moral subjects must be capable of taking responsibility;
moral knowledge must schematize perception and shape action; moral agency must
express commitments (at a minimum, the commitment to refrain from committing).
If so, there must be limits to the extent and frequency of change that moral subjects,
moral knowledge, and moral agency can undergo. But continuity is anathema to
poststructuralism, for it can only be achieved through repression of difference.

    My reading of narrativity theory suggests that it can accommodate substantial
moral change without succumbing to the unfettered volatility that is fatal to the
poststructuralist model. To avoid the pitfalls of poststructuralism, narrativity theory
must posit (1) a narrator who is adept at using a set of skills that for the most part
generates accurate memory stories and plausible anticipatory stories and (2) an
independent interpersonal and institutional world in which narrators site their stories. Neither the narrator's autobiographical competence nor the narrator's world
can be reducible to discursive formations.

Many narrativity theorists insist on the distinctions between narrators and their autobiographies and between the worlds narrators inhabit and their stories about them.[38] They believe, as I do, that narrators can be deceived about themselves, suffer memory lapses, misread other people, acquiesce in the workings of unjust social structures, err in their moral judgments, and act badly. Consequently, these theorists seek to characterize credible stories. Although epistemologies of narrativity differ in specifics, two criteria recur in these accounts—coherence within self-narratives and consensus between oneself and others about one's self-narrative.

As Hilde Nelson maintains, vetting self-narratives often depends on assessing their coherence. To decide between conflicting stories of a particular relationship, for instance, it is useful to determine which coheres better with other uncontested stories about the individual.[39] Also, a story's correlation to past action and structuring of future action—that is, its coherence with personal recollections and with anticipatory self-narratives—adds to its credibility.[40] But an additional check on self-narratives is needed, for it is possible to produce a coherent self-narrative that contains more fantasy than reality. Thus, Margaret Walker cautions, individuals do not have the final say in assessing the merits of their self-narratives. Since moral values and justifications are "shared understandings," moral self-narratives are subject to others' challenges and sometimes their outright dismissal.[41] Yet, because auditors can be ill informed or biased, consensus can be misleading, too. Neither consensus nor coherence suffices as an epistemic standard for self-narratives. They complement and correct one another.

I am well aware that it would be preposterous to demand an epistemic metric to rule on the credibility of self-narratives. Moreover, I have no doubt that coherence and consensus are reasonable bases for evaluating them. Indeed, coherence and consensus are so deeply rooted in everyday practices of self-reflection and interpersonal arbitration that it is hard to imagine what it would be like to do without them. Yet, these criteria do not sit well with two insights into the self and social reality that narrativity theorists have helped to make philosophically salient.

Moral subjectivity, moral knowledge, and moral agency are never altogether coherent. Narrativity theorists accent the multiplicity within moral subjects. Their metaphors include "ensemble subjectivity" and a "small squad of Possible Selves."[42] Moreover, individuals rightly consider disparate values and behaviors appropriate to the widely divergent contexts in which they function, and there is no alchemy that can transmute their situated judgments into a consistent set of precepts. Since close observation of moral subjects, moral knowledge, and moral agency demonstrates that no strictly coherent, overarching narrative could credibly depict them, individuals must deploy the coherence criterion judiciously. It can alert them to confusion, rationalization, and other sources of distortion in their stories. But if it is applied indiscriminately and rigorously, it requires narrators to omit significant material that does not fit neatly with predominant autobiographical themes, motifs, tonalities, and so forth.[43] Unless people take the coherence criterion with a grain of salt, they will edit the unruly, disruptive incidents out of their self-narratives.

A major problem with the consensus criterion stems from the fact that auditors occupy social positions that are defined by multiple vectors of domination and subordination.[44] Because differently positioned auditors are equipped with and, perforce, listen through different interpretive frameworks, some are more likely to confirm, whereas others are more likely to dispute, the same self-narrative. Obtaining consensus for an episodic self-narrative involving people from different social spheres is seldom possible; obtaining intergroup consensus for a synoptic autobiographical narrative is virtually impossible. Nevertheless, like coherence, consensus seems indispensable to and inextricable from everyday practices of self-reflection and interpersonal arbitration. Just as people routinely ask themselves, "Does this make sense?" and mean "Is this story coherent?" so, too, they routinely do reality checks to solicit feedback and establish consensus. But successfully wielding the consensus criterion presupposes making wise decisions about whose feedback to trust, and these decisions are tricky. Auditors who hold power over the narrator often seem authoritative and command more deference than they deserve. Also the narrator's own self-destructive or self-aggrandizing proclivities are liable to skew perceptions of listeners' trustworthiness. Thus, many self-narratives that satisfy the consensus criterion encode internalized oppression or internalized privilege.

The intuitive plausibility of the coherence and consensus criteria rests on assumptions about the quality of narrators' discernment and judgment. Individuals need to select materials that can be organized into intelligible stories, but they also need to register the significance of anomalous information and to keep tabs on branching, parallel, and colliding plot lines. Narrators need social recognition for their stories. Still, they must filter out ignorant or hostile reactions while factoring in hard truths. Although people need to compile facts and recollect the past accurately, they must not neglect the future, which enlists them in composing aspirational self-narratives that express their ideals and hopes for themselves and for their societies. Seyla Benhabib alludes to the skills that enable individuals to juggle coherence, consensus, and the facts, both as they believe them to have been and as they want them to become, when she writes of the *"ability* to keep telling a story about who one is that makes sense to oneself and to others."[45] In my view, this utterly marvelous, extremely recondite, and blithely taken-for-granted ability is crucial to the epistemology of narrativity.

Narrativity is the output of processes that mobilize a wide range of human capacities—skills that enrich human experience and provide material for stories and skills that enable people to compose insightful stories and to revise stories that prove to misrepresent their experience and understandings. The following are among the skills that contribute to self-narrativity:

1. Introspection skills that sensitize individuals to their own feelings and desires, that enable them to interpret their subjective experience, and that help them judge how well a narrative conveys their sense of themselves
2. Communication and listening skills that enable individuals to get the benefit of others' perceptions, background knowledge, insights, advice, and support and that also enable them to expose flattery, bigotry, schadenfreude, and other sources of misleading feedback

3. Memory skills that enable individuals to recall relevant experiences and ap-
posite narrative devices—not only from their own lives but also from stories
that associates have told or that they have encountered in literature or other
art forms

4. Imagination skills that enable individuals to envisage feasible options—to
preview a variety of plot lines their lives might follow and to consider what
it would mean to be the protagonist of those stories

5. Analytical and reasoning skills that enable individuals to identify the advantages and disadvantages of different projections of the possible turns their
life stories could take

6. Self-nurturing skills that enable individuals to secure their physical and psychological equilibrium despite missteps and setbacks—that enable them to appreciate the overall worthiness of their self-portraits and their self-narratives, to
assure themselves of their capacity to carry on when they find their self-portraits
wanting or their self-narratives misguided, and to sustain their self-respect if
they need to correct their self-portraits or revise their self-narratives

7. Volition skills that enable individuals to resist pressure to capitulate to convention and that enable them to maintain their commitment to the continu-
ations of their autobiographies that they consider genuinely their own

8. Interpersonal skills that enable individuals to join forces to challenge and
change cultural regimes and institutional arrangements that pathologize or
marginalize their priorities and projects; that deprive them of accredited discursive means to represent themselves to themselves and to others as flourishing, self-respecting, valuable individuals; and that close off their opportunities to enact their self-narratives[46]

Now, it is important to bear in mind that people's competence with respect
to this repertoire of self-discovery, self-definition, and self-direction skills varies.
Individuals are more or less proficient in each skill, and they are more or less
adept at coordinating the skills they possess. My claim is that profiting from the
use of the coherence and consensus criteria is contingent on one's overall level
of competence in these skills and, therefore, that one's confidence in one's self-
narrative is justified if it is commensurate with one's overall level of competence
and if one has made good use of one's competence in developing this narrative.

It is tempting to look for properties that all credible self-narratives share, for
narratives are entities that can be inspected. Likewise, it is tempting to look for
interpersonal tests that credible self-narratives must pass, for stories are articulated
in the medium of language, and language is a medium of social intercourse.
However, neither coherence nor consensus can be made sufficiently precise to
obviate the need for judgment on the part of narrators, and good judgment hinges
on good self-discovery, self-definition, and self-direction skills.

There can be no foolproof method for vindicating self-narratives. But this is
no cause for regret. On the contrary, it builds respect for individuality into narrativity epistemology. It is advisable to give narrators plenty of discretion by leaving
the coherence and consensus criteria ambiguous, for putting teeth in them would

unduly regiment people's lives. Construed narrowly, coherence valorizes caution, control, and regularity. Thus, fidelity to this criterion could suppress spontaneity, experimentation, and yielding to lucky happenstance. Consensus can impose similar strictures. On the assumption that many of one's prospective interlocutors accept prevailing social norms and oppose radical change, consensus militates against dissent and nonconformity. To avoid capitulating to these convention-enforcing, opportunity-foreclosing subtexts, individuals must adapt coherence to their own values and styles of enactment, and they must seek consensus within communities of kindred but thoughtful and candid spirits. In other words, to apply these criteria well, narrators must individualize them, and they can only individualize them by exercising the self-discovery, self-definition, and self-direction skills I have sketched.

To ensure respect for the diversity of morally decent lives, narrativity theory must explicate the credibility of self-narratives in terms of this repertoire of skills. Self-narratives are not all equally valid, revealing, and conducive to flourishing, but there is no property internal to self-narratives nor any interpersonal test that can rank them. The best gauge of a self-narrative's credibility, then, is the narrator's overall degree of mastery of the self-discovery, self-definition, and self-direction skill repertoire and the extent to which the narrator made use of this competency in constructing a particular self-narrative.

Generic storytelling skills cannot be the sole resources that narratives laying claim to articulating moral subjectivity, moral knowledge, and moral agency draw on. Generic storytelling skills produce all sorts of fictions—fairy tales, negative utopias, science fiction, romances, and horror stories—as well as autobiographical narratives. Some superb storytellers are poor autobiographers. Notoriously, Ernest Hemingway's deficient self-discovery skills mar his autobiographical writing. A *Moveable Feast*, which contains some appallingly self-serving and arguably delusional passages, illustrates this failing. With the assistance of self-discovery, self-definition, and self-direction skills, though, storytelling skills become tools of moral individuality, moral insight, and moral self-determination. In many cases, it may be true, as Jerome Bruner claims, that "adventures happen to people who know how to tell it that way."[47] But it is also true that people can pad their self-narratives with adventures that did not happen and that people can suffer for want of the right words or framework in which to articulate how something actually occurred. To curb overactive imaginations, to overcome isolating silence, and to secure the credibility of self-narratives, the competency that keeps people attuned to themselves and alive to life's possibilities must underwrite the processes of self-narrating.

Notes

I am indebted, as usual, to several colleagues' astute comments on earlier drafts. Thanks to Sally Ruddick, Hilde Nelson, and Cheshire Calhoun.

1. Charles Taylor, *Sources of the Self* (Cambridge, Mass.: Harvard University Press, 1989); Martha Nussbaum, *Love's Knowledge* (New York: Oxford University Press, 1990); Richard Rorty, *Contingency, Irony, and Solidarity* (Cambridge: Cambridge University

Press, 1989); Alasdair MacIntyre, *After Virtue* (New York: Oxford University Press, 1984); and Alexander Nehamas, *Nietzsche, Life as Literature* (Cambridge, Mass.: Harvard University Press, 1985).

2. Marya Schechtman, *The Constitution of Selves* (Ithaca, N.Y.: Cornell University Press, 1996), 94.

3. Ibid.

4. Margaret Urban Walker, *Moral Understandings* (New York: Routledge, 1998), 110.

5. Ibid., 111.

6. Seyla Benhabib, "Sexual Difference and Collective Identities: The New Global Constellation," *Signs* 24 (1999): 335–361, 344. See also J. David Velleman, "The Self as Narrator," unpublished manuscript.

7. Hilde Lindemann Nelson, *Damaged Identities; Narrative Repair* (Ithaca, N.Y.: Cornell University Press, 2001), 20.

8. Ibid., 9.

9. John Christman, "Narrative Unity as a Condition of Personhood," unpublished manuscript.

10. Walker, *Moral Understandings*, 112–114, 129; Nelson, *Damaged Identities*, 158; and Benhabib, "Sexual Difference and Collective Identities," 348.

11. Schechtman, *Constitution of Selves*, 113, 116; and Nelson, *Damaged Identities*, 20.

12. Annette Baier, *Postures of the Mind* (Minneapolis: University of Minnesota Press, 1985), 84.

13. Sigmund Freud, "Introductory Lectures on Psychoanalysis," in *The Standard Edition of the Complete Psychological Works of Sigmund Freud*, vol. 16, ed. James Strachey (London: Hogarth Press and Institute of Psychoanalysis, 1915–1916), 285.

14. Here I am contrasting the classic biologistic conception of the divided self that Freud propounded with the relational self. However, it should be noted that the object relations school of psychoanalysis develops a nonbiologistic synthesis of the divided self and the relational self.

15. Walker, *Moral Understandings*, 108.

16. Susan Brison, "Outliving Oneself: Trauma, Memory, and Personal Identity," in *Feminists Rethink the Self*, ed. Diana Tietjens Meyers (Boulder, Col.: Westview, 1997), 17–18.

17. Lynne Taetzsch, "Fighting Natural," in *Minding the Body: Women Writers on Body and Soul*, ed. Patricia Foster (New York: Anchor Books, 1995), 233.

18. Ibid., 234.

19. Ibid., 235.

20. Ibid., 237, 239.

21. Ibid., 242–245.

22. Ibid., 242.

23. Ibid., 245–246.

24. Walker, *Moral Understandings*, chap. 2.

25. Ibid., 36.

26. Neo-Kantian Christine Korsgaard concedes this point by distinguishing provisional universality from absolute universality and by acknowledging that it is advisable to regard moral principles as provisionally universal, that is, to be prepared to add qualifications to them as need be. See Korsgaard, "Self-Constitution in the Ethics of Plato and Kant," *Journal of Ethics* 3 (1999): 1–29, 24–25; reprinted in this volume. However,

in this interpretation, as I argue below, the universality criterion ceases to be a practical guide to acting well and becomes a formal requirement of interest mainly to philosophers.

27. John Rawls, *Political Liberalism* (New York: Columbia University Press, 1993), 13–15.

28. William David Ross, *The Right and the Good* (London: Oxford at the Clarendon Press, 1930), 19, 41–42.

29. Richard Rorty, "Freud and Moral Reflection," in *Pragmatism's Freud*, ed. William Kerrigan and Joseph Smith (Baltimore, Md.: Johns Hopkins University Press, 1986), 18.

30. Walker, *Moral Understandings*, 111.

31. Nelson, *Damaged Identities*, 6–9.

32. Claudia Card, *The Unnatural Lottery* (Philadelphia: Temple University Press, 1996), 29.

33. Ibid., 28–29.

34. Ibid., chap. 7.

35. Ibid., 41.

36. For Example, Nelson, *Damaged Identities*, 1–6.

37. Chantal Mouffe, "Feminism, Citizenship, and Radical Democratic Politics," in *Feminist Social Thought: A Reader*, ed. Diana Tietjens Meyers (New York: Routledge, 1997), 534.

38. Walker, *Moral Understandings*, 120; Nelson, *Damaged Identities*, 102; and Schechtman, *Constitution of Selves*, 119.

39. Nelson, *Damaged Identities*, 94.

40. Ibid., 95. For related lines of thought, see Schechtman, *Constitution of Selves*, 97–98; and Walker, *Moral Understandings*, 75, 114.

41. Walker, *Moral Understandings*, 106, 113–114, 119–120. See also Schechtman, *Constitution of Selves*, 95; and Nelson, *Damaged Identities*, 81.

42. Walker, *Moral Understandings*, 119; and Jerome Bruner, "The 'Remembered' Self," in *The Remembering Self*, ed. Ulric Neisser and Robyn Fivush (Cambridge: Cambridge University Press, 1994), 46.

43. Walker, *Moral Understandings*, 144–148; and Nelson, *Damaged Identities*, 190.

44. Walker, *Moral Understandings*, chaps. 7 and 8; and Nelson, *Damaged Identities*, 92, 97.

45. Benhabib, "Sexual Difference and Collective Identities," 335–361, 346–347. See also Walker, *Moral Understandings*, 10, 66.

46. I have discussed these skills in some other works, including my *Self, Society, and Personal Choice* (New York: Columbia University Press, 1989), 78–84, 87; and my *Gender in the Mirror* (New York: Oxford University Press, 2002), 18–21.

47. Bruner, "'Remembered' Self," 48.

VI

Emotions, Reason, and Unreason

17

Self-Constitution in the Ethics
of Plato and Kant

Christine M. Korsgaard

I. Introduction

One of the most famous sections of David Hume's *Treatise* begins with these words:

> Nothing is more usual in philosophy, and even in common life, than to
> talk of the combat of passion and reason, to give the preference to reason,
> and to assert that men are only so far virtuous as they conform themselves
> to its dictates. Every rational creature, 'tis said, is oblig'd to regulate his
> actions by reason; and if any other motive or principle challenge the direc-
> tion of his conduct, he ought to oppose it, 'till it be entirely subdu'd, or at
> least brought to a conformity with that superior principle.[1]

As Hume understands these claims, reason and passion are two forces in the soul,
each a source of motives to act, and virtue consists in the person going along with
reason. Why should the person do that? Hume tells us that in philosophy, "[t]he
eternity, invariableness, and divine origin of [reason] have been display'd to the
best advantage: the blindness, unconstancy, and deceitfulness of [passion] have
been as strongly insisted on."[2] Hume proposes to "shew the fallacy of all this
philosophy," but in his demonstration he does not exactly deny what I will call
the Combat Model. He simply argues that reason is not a force, and therefore
that there is no combat.

I think that there are a few questions Hume should have asked first, for the
Combat Model makes very little sense. From the third person perspective, we do
sometimes explain a person's actions as the result of one motive being "stronger"
than another, for instance when the person has conflicting passions. But is the
difference between reason and passion then pretty much the same as the difference between one passion and another? And are a person's actions merely the
result of the play, or rather the combat, of these forces within her? How then
would actions be different from blushes or twitches or even biological processes?

Now we may try to solve this last problem by bringing the person, the agent, back into the picture—action is different from other physical movements because the person *chooses* to follow either reason or passion. But this makes the Combat Model even more perplexing. For what is the essence of this person, in whom reason and passion are both forces, *neither* of them identified with the person herself, and between which she is to choose? And if the person identifies neither with reason nor passion, then how—on what principle—can she possibly choose between them? The philosophers Hume describes here seem to be imagining that the person chooses between reason and passion by assessing their merits—reason is divine and reliable, passion blind and misleading. But surely that presupposes that the person *already* identifies with reason, which is what assesses merits. But how then could the person choose passion over reason? The combat model gives us no clear picture of the *person* who chooses between reason and passion.

The tradition supplies us with another model of the interaction of reason and passion in the soul, which makes better sense, because it assigns to them functional and structural differences.[3] I call it the Constitutional Model, because its clearest appearance is in Plato's *Republic*, where the human soul is compared to the constitution of a *polis* or city-state. I believe that the Constitutional Model has important implications for moral philosophy, and my project in this paper is to spell these implications out. Specifically, the Constitutional Model implies a certain view about what an *action* is, which in turn has implications about what makes an action good or bad. These implications are a little difficult to articulate clearly in advance of the argument, but the main idea is this: What distinguishes action from mere behavior and other physical movements is that it is *authored*—it is in a quite special way attributable to the person who does it, by which I mean, the *whole* person. The Constitutional Model tells us that what makes an action yours in this way is that it springs from and is in accordance with your constitution. But it also provides a standard for good action, a standard which tells us which actions are most truly a person's own, and therefore which actions are most truly *actions*. Now this is the hard part to say in advance of the argument: The actions which are most truly a person's own are precisely those actions which most fully unify her and therefore most fully constitute her as their author. They are those actions which both issue from, and give her, the kind of volitional unity which she must have if we are to attribute the action to her as a whole person. What makes an action bad, by contrast, is that it springs in part not from the person but from something at work *in* or *on* the person, something which threatens her volitional unity. I sum these claims up by saying that according to the Constitutional Model, action is self-constitution.

II. Plato

In Book I of the *Republic*, Socrates and his friends discuss the question what justice is. The discussion is interrupted by Thrasymachus, who asserts that the best life is the unjust life, the life lived by the strong, who impose the laws of justice on the weak, but ignore those laws themselves. The more completely un-just you are, Thrasymachus says, the better you will live, for pickpockets and thieves, who commit small injustices, get punished, while tyrants, who enslave whole cities and steal their treasuries, lead a glorious life, and are the envy of everyone (336b–334d).[4] Socrates, distracted by these claims, drops the discussion of what justice is, and takes up the question whether the just or the unjust life is best.

Socrates proceeds to construct three arguments designed to show that the just life is the best. The one that is central to my own argument goes like this (351b–352c): Socrates asks Thrasymachus whether a band of robbers and thieves with a common unjust purpose would be able to achieve that purpose if they were unjust to each other. Thrasymachus agrees that they could not do that. Justice, as Socra-tes says, is what brings a sense of common purpose to a group, while injustice causes hatred and civil war, and makes the group "incapable of achieving any-thing as a unit" (352a). Thrasymachus is then induced to agree that justice and injustice have the same effect wherever they occur, and therefore, the same effect within the individual human soul as they have in a group. Injustice, therefore, makes an individual "incapable of achieving anything, because he is in a state of civil war and not of one mind." The more complete this condition is the worse it is, for according to Socrates "those who are all bad and completely unjust are completely incapable of accomplishing anything" (352c).[5]

Now there's nothing obviously wrong with this argument, except of course that it flies in the teeth of the fact that we seem to see unjust people all around us, doing and accomplishing things right and left. So what is Socrates talking about? The argument leaves Socrates' audience puzzled and dissatisfied. So Plato's brothers, Glaucon and Adiemantus, demand that Socrates return to the aban-doned question, what justice is, and what effect it has on the soul. It is this demand that sets Plato off on his attempt to identify justice in a larger and more visible object, the ideal city, and his famous comparison between the constitution of the city and the constitution of the soul.

It will help to review the main elements of that comparison. Plato identifies three classes in the city. First there are the rulers, who make the laws and policies for the city, and handle its relations with other cities. Second, there are the auxilia-ries, a kind of combination soldier and police force, who enforce the laws within the city and also defend it from external enemies, following the orders of the rulers. The rulers are drawn from the ranks of these auxiliaries, and the two groups together are called the guardians. And finally there are the farmers, craftspeople, merchants, and so forth, who provide for the city's needs.

The virtues of the ideal city are then identified with certain properties of and relations between these parts. The wisdom of the city rests in the wisdom of its rulers (428b–429a). We aren't told much about this at first, except that the rulers of the ideal city, unlike Thrasymachus's rulers, rule with a view to the good of the city as a whole, and not to their own. The courage of the city rests in the courage of its auxiliaries, which is identified with their capacity to preserve certain beliefs, instilled in them by the rulers, about what is to be feared, in the face of temptation, pleasure, pain, and fear itself (429a–430c). The city's *sophrosyne*—its moderation or temperance—rests in the agreement of all the classes in the city about who should rule and be ruled (430e–432b). And its justice rests in the fact that each class in the city does its own work, and no one tries to meddle in the work of anyone else (433a ff.).

Plato then undertakes to find the same three parts in the human soul. The Constitutional Model, like the Combat Model, starts off from the experience of inner conflict. Socrates puts it forth as a principle that if we find in the soul opposite attitudes or reactions to a single thing at the same time, we must suppose that the soul has parts (436b–c). For example, the soul of a thirsty person is impelled by its thirst towards drinking. So if the soul at the very same time draws back from drinking, it must be with a different part. And this is an experience people actually have: there are thirsty people who decide not to drink. This happens when they judge that the drink will be bad for them. As Socrates says, "[i]sn't there something in their soul, bidding them to drink, and something different, forbidding them to do so, that overrules the thing that bids? . . . Doesn't that which forbids in such cases come into play as a result of rational calculation?" (439c–d). So reason and appetite must be two different parts of the soul.

In fact, however, Socrates' emphasis on conflict is slightly misleading, for even if there is no conflict, two parts of the soul may be discerned. Suppose instead that the drink has nothing wrong with it, and the person who is thirsty does drink. In this kind of case, Socrates says, "the soul of someone who has an appetite for a thing wants what he has an appetite for and takes to himself what it is his will to have, and . . . insofar as he wishes something to be given to him, his soul, since it desires this to come about, nods assent to it as if in answer to a question" (437c). The soul does not act directly from appetite, but from something that endorses the appetite and says yes to it. Even when conflict is absent, then, we can see that there are two parts of the soul.

Socrates next argues that there is a third part, *thymos* or spirit, which is distinct from both reason and appetite, although it is the natural ally of reason (439e–441c). That it is distinct from appetite shows up in the fact that anger and indignation, which are manifestations of spirit, are often directed against the appetites themselves. This is illustrated by the story of Leontius, who was disgusted at himself for wanting to look at some corpses, and berated his own eyes for their evil appetites (439e–440a). Socrates claims that spirit always fights on reason's side in a case of conflict between reason and appetite. Yet it is distinct from reason, for it is present in small children and animals, who don't have reason; and, furthermore, it sometimes needs to be controlled by reason (440e–441c).

By these arguments Socrates establishes that the soul has the same three parts as the city. Reason corresponds to the rulers and its function is to direct things, for the good of the whole person. Spirit corresponds to the auxiliaries and its function is to carry out the orders of reason. The appetites correspond to the rest of the citizens, and their business is to supply the person with whatever he needs.

Now if the soul has parts the question is going to arise what makes them one, what unifies them into a single soul. And part of the answer is that the parts of the soul must be unified—they *need* to be unified, like the people in a city—in order to act. Specifically, we can see the three parts of the soul as corresponding to three parts of a deliberative action. Deliberative action begins from the fact we have certain appetites and desires. We are conscious of these, and they invite us to do certain actions or seek certain ends. Since we are rational, however, we do not act on our appetites and desires automatically, but instead decide whether to satisfy them or not. As Socrates put it in a passage we looked at a moment ago, it is as if what appetite does is put a request to reason, and reason says yes or no. And then finally there is carrying the decision out—actually doing what we have decided to do. For of course we don't always do what we have decided to do, but are sometimes distracted by pleasure or pain or fear from the course we have set for ourselves. So we can identify three parts of a deliberative action corresponding to Plato's three parts of the soul, namely:

Appetite makes a proposal.
Reason decides whether to act on it or not.
Spirit carries reason's decision out.

This line of thought supports Plato's analogy between the city and the soul. For a city also engages in deliberative actions: it is not just a place to live, but rather a kind of agent which performs actions and so has a life and a history. And we can see the same dim parts in a political decision. The people of the city make a proposal: they say that there is something that they need. They ask for highways, or better health care, or more police protection. The rulers then decide whether to act on the proposal or not. They say either "yes" or "no" to the people. And then the auxiliaries carry the ruler's decisions out.

In fact, the main purpose of a literal political constitution is precisely to lay out the city's mode of deliberative action, the procedures by which its collective decisions are to be made and carried out. A constitution defines a set of roles and offices which together constitute a procedure for deliberative action, saying who shall perform each step and how it shall be done. It lays out the proper ways of making proposals (say by petition, or the introduction of bills, or whatever), of deciding whether to act on these proposals (the legislative function), and of carrying out the resulting decisions (the executive function). And in each case it says who is allowed to carry out the procedures it has specified. The constitution in this way makes it possible for the citizens to function as a single collective agent.

And this explains Socrates' puzzling definition of justice. Justice, he says, is "doing one's own work and not meddling with what isn't one's own" (433a–b). When Socrates first introduces this principle into the discussion (369e ff.), he's talking about the specialization of labor, and that's what the principle sounds like it's about.[6] But if we think of the constitution as laying out the procedures for deliberative action, and the roles and offices that constitute those procedures, we can see what Socrates' point is. For usurping the office of another in the constitutional procedures for collective action is *precisely* what we mean by injustice, or at least it is one thing we mean. For instance if the constitution says that the president cannot make war without the agreement of the congress, and yet he does, he has usurped congress's role in this decision, and that's unjust. If the constitution says that each citizen gets to cast one vote in the election, and through some fraud you manage to vote more than once, you are diminishing the voice of others in the election, and that's unjust. So injustice, in one of its most familiar senses, is usurping the role of another in the deliberative procedures that define collective action. It is meddling with somebody else's work.

I said in one sense, for this is very much what is sometimes called a *procedural* conception of justice, as opposed to a *substantive* one. This distinction represents an important tension in our concept of justice, and a standing cause of confusion about the source of its normativity. On the one hand, the idea of justice essentially involves the idea of following certain procedures. In the state, as I have been saying, these are the procedures which the constitution lays out for collective deliberative action: for making laws, waging wars, trying cases, collecting taxes, distributing services, and all of the various things that a state does. According to the procedural conception of justice, an action of the state is just if and only if it is the outcome of actually following these procedures. That is a *law* which has been passed in form by a duly constituted legislature; this law is *constitutional* if (say) the supreme court says that it is; a person is *innocent* of a certain crime when he has been deemed so by a jury; someone is *the president* if he meets the legal qualifications and has been duly voted in, and so forth. These are all normative judgments—the terms *law, constitutional, innocent,* and *president* all imply the existence of certain reasons for action—and their normativity *derives from* the carrying out of the procedures which have established them.

On the other hand, however, there are certainly cases in which we have some independent idea of what outcome the procedures ought to generate. These independent ideas serve as the criteria for our more substantive judgments—in some cases, of what is just, in other cases, simply of what is right or best. And these substantive judgments can come in conflict with the actual outcomes of carrying out the procedures. Perhaps the law is unconstitutional, though the legislature has passed it; perhaps the defendant is guilty, though the jury has set him free; perhaps the candidate elected is not the best person for the job, or even the best of those who ran, or perhaps due to the accidents of voter turnout he does not really represent the majority will. As this last example shows, the distinction between the procedurally just and the substantively just, right, or best, is a rough and ready one, and relative to the case under consideration. Who should be elected? The best person for the job, the best of those who actually run, the one preferred by the majority of the citizens, the one preferred by the majority of the registered voters, the one elected by the majority of those who actually turn out on election day. . . . As we go down the list, the answer to the question becomes increasingly procedural; the answer above it is, relatively, more substantive. We may try to design our procedures to secure the substantively right, best, or just outcome. But—and here is the important point—according to the procedural conception of justice the normativity of these procedures nevertheless does not spring from the efficiency, goodness, *or even the substantive justice* of the outcomes they produce. The reverse is true: it is the procedures themselves—or rather the actual carrying out of the procedures—that confers normativity on those outcomes. The person who gets elected holds the office, no matter how far he is from being the best person for the job. The jury's acquittal stands, though we later discover new evidence that after all the defendant was guilty.

Now if the normativity of the outcomes springs from the carrying out of the procedures, where, we may ask, does the normativity of the procedures themselves come from? And here we run into the cause of confusion I mentioned at the outset, for there is a standing temptation to believe that the procedures themselves must derive their normativity from the good quality of their outcomes. That cannot be right, as I've just been saying, for if the normativity of our procedures came from the substantive quality of their outcomes, we'd be prepared to set those procedures aside when we knew that their outcomes were going to be poor ones. And as I've just been saying, we don't do that. Where constitutional procedures are in place, substantive rightness, goodness, bestness, or even justice is neither necessary nor sufficient for the normative standing of their outcomes.

Perhaps we may now be tempted to say that what makes the procedures normative is the *usual* quality of their outcomes, the fact that they get it right most of the time. After all, even if we stand by the outcomes of our procedures though in this or that case they are bad, we would certainly change those procedures if their outcomes were bad *too often*. But this cannot be the whole answer, both because it isn't always true—think of the jury system—but also because, as act utilitarians have been telling us for years, it is irrational to follow a procedure merely because it usually gets a good outcome, when you know that this time it will get a bad one. So perhaps we should say that the normativity of the procedures comes from the usual quality of their outcomes *combined* with the fact that we must have some such procedures, and we must stand by their results. But why must we have such procedures? Because without them collective action is impossible. And now we've come around to Plato's view. In order to act together—to make laws and policies, apply them, enforce them—in a way that represents, not some of us tyrannizing over others, but all of us acting as a unit—we must have a constitution that defines the procedures for collective deliberative action, and we must stand by their results.[7]

According to Plato, the normative force of the constitution *consists* in the fact that it makes it possible for the city to function as a single unified agent. For a city without justice, according to Plato, above all lacks unity—it is not one city, he says, but many (422d–423c; see also 462a–e). When justice breaks down, the city falls into civil war, as the rulers, the soldiers, and the people all struggle for control. The deliberative procedures that unify the city into a single agent break down, and the city *as such* cannot act. The individual citizens and classes in it may still perform various actions, but the city cannot act as a unit.

And this applies to justice and injustice within the individual person as well. Socrates says:

One who is just does not allow any part of himself to do the work of another part or allow the various classes within him to meddle with each other. He regulates well what is really his own and rules himself. He puts himself in order, is his own friend, and harmonizes the three parts of himself like three limiting notes in a musical scale—high, low, and middle. He binds together those parts and any others there may be in between, and from having been many things he becomes entirely one, moderate and harmonious. Only then does he act. (443d–e)

But if justice is what makes it possible for a person to function as a single unified agent, then injustice makes it impossible. Civil war breaks out between appetite, spirit, and reason, each trying to usurp the roles and offices of the others. The deliberative procedures that unify the soul into a single agent break down, and the person *as such* cannot act. So Socrates' argument from Book I turns out to be true. Desires and impulses may operate within the unjust person, as individual citizens may operate within the unjust state. But the unjust *person* is "completely incapable of accomplishing anything" (352c) because the unjust *person* cannot act at all.

III. Kant

Now let's turn to Kant. The best way to see that Kant is thinking in terms of the Constitutional Model is to consider the argument he uses to establish that the categorical imperative is the law of a free will (G 4:446–448).[8] Kant argues that insofar as you are a rational being, you must act under the idea of freedom. And a free will is one which is not determined by any alien cause—by any law outside of itself. It is not, in Kant's language, "heteronomous." But Kant claims that the free will must be determined by some law or other—I will take up the argument for that in Section VII—and so it must be "autonomous." That is, it must act on a law which it gives to itself. And Kant says that this means that the categorical imperative *just is* the law of a free will.

To see why, we need only consider how a free will must deliberate. So here is the free will, completely self-governing, with nothing outside of it giving it any laws. And along comes an inclination, and presents the free will with a proposal. Now inclinations, according to Kant, are grounded in what he calls "incentives," which are the features of the objects of those inclinations that make them seem attractive and eligible.[9] Suppose that the incentive is that the object is pleasant. Then inclination says: end-E would be a very pleasant thing to bring about. So how about end-E? Doesn't that seem like an end to-be-produced? Now what the will chooses is, strictly speaking, actions, so before the proposal is complete, we need to make it a proposal for action. Instrumental reasoning determines that you could produce end-E by doing act-A. So the proposal is: that you should do act-A in order to produce this very pleasant end-E.

Now if your will were heteronomous, and pleasure were a law to you, this is all you would need to know, and you would straightaway do act-A in order to produce that pleasant end-E. But since you are autonomous, pleasure is not a law to you: nothing is a law to you except what you make a law for yourself. You therefore ask yourself a different question. The proposal is that you should do act-A in order to achieve pleasant end-E. Since nothing is a law to you except what you make a law for yourself, you ask yourself whether you could take *that* to be your law. Your question is whether you can will the maxim of doing act-A in order to produce end-E as a law. Your question, in other words, is whether your maxim passes the categorical imperative test. The categorical imperative is therefore the law of a free will.

Inclination presents the proposal; reason decides whether to act on it or not, and the decision takes the form of a *legislative act*. This is clearly the Constitutional Model.

IV. Standards for Action

The main point of resemblance between the theories of Plato and Kant shows up, however, in their treatment of bad action. On the Combat Model, what happens when a person acts badly? The answer must be that the person is overcome by passion. But on the Combat Model we could just as well say that when a person acts well, she is overcome by reason, for the two forces seem to be on a footing. According to the Constitutional Model, on the other hand, a person acts well when she acts in accordance with her constitution. If reason overrules passion, she should act in accordance with reason, not because she identifies with reason, but because she identifies with her constitution, and it says that reason should rule.[10] So what happens when a person acts badly? Here we run into what looks, at first, like a difficulty for the Constitutional Model. It turns out to be the source of its deepest insights.

The difficulty is, of course, that according to the account of Plato I just gave, an unjust person cannot act at all, because an unjust *person* is not unified by constitutional rule. When a city is in a state of civil war, it does not act, although the various factions within it may do various things. The analogy suggests that when a soul is in a state of civil war, and the various forces within it are fighting for control, what looks to the outside world like *the person's actions* are really just the manifestations of forces at work *within* the person. So it looks at first as if *nothing exactly counts as a bad action*.

And there's an *exact* analogy to this difficulty in Kantian ethics. For a well-known problem in the *Groundwork* is that Kant appears to say that only autonomous action, that is, action governed by the categorical imperative, is really free action, while bad or heteronomous "action" is behavior *caused* by the work of desires and inclinations in us (G 4:453–455). But if this were so, then it would be hard to see how we could be held responsible for bad or heteronomous action, or why we should even regard it as something we *do*. It seems more like something that happens in us or to us. This problem arises because of the argument by which Kant establishes the authority of the categorical imperative, the argument we just looked at. For that argument seems to show that action is *essentially* autonomous. Action must take place under the idea of freedom; and a free will must be autonomous. So it looks at first as if *nothing exactly counts as a bad action.*

It's important to observe that the *structure* of the problem in these two theories is exactly the same. Kant first identifies action with autonomous action, claiming that it is essential to action that it should be autonomous. He then identifies autonomous action with action governed by the categorical imperative, universalizable action. In exactly the same way, Plato first identifies action with action that emerges from constitutional procedure, claiming that it is essential to action that it should emerge from constitutional procedure. He then identifies action that emerges from constitutional procedure with just action. In other words, each argument first identifies an essential metaphysical property of action—autonomy in Kant's argument and constitutionality in Plato's—and then in turn identifies this metaphysical property with a normative property—universalizability in Kant's argument and justice in Plato's. And this is how the case for the normative requirement is made.

Furthermore, in both arguments the identification of the metaphysical property is an attempt to capture a specific feature of action, an important thing that distinguishes an action from a mere event, namely, that an action is *attributable* to the person who does it. The metaphysical property Plato and Kant are looking for is the one that makes it true that the action is not just something that happens in or to the person but rather is something that he as a person *does*. It is the property that makes the *person* the author of the action. Plato's explicit use of the Constitutional Model makes it clear he is trying to identify this property. For we certainly do distinguish the actions we attribute to a city as such from the actions we would attribute only to some of the individuals in it. And the basis of this distinction is whether the action was the outcome of following constitutional procedures or not. If a Spartan attacks an Athenian, for instance, we do not conclude that *Sparta* is making war on Athens unless the attack was made by a soldier acting under the direction of the rulers: that is, unless it issues from Sparta's constitutional procedures. By the analogy, we will only attribute an action to a person, rather than to something in him, if it was directed by his reason, his ruling part. In a similar way, Kant thinks that what makes an action attributable to the person is that it springs from the person's autonomy or self-government. The exercise of the person's autonomy is what makes the action *his*, and so what makes it an action.

And so we get the problem. It is the essential nature of action that it has a certain metaphysical property. But in order to have that metaphysical property it must have a certain normative property. This explains why the action must meet the normative standard: *it just isn't action* if it doesn't. But it also seems as if it explains it rather too well, for it seems to imply that only good action really is action, and that there is nothing left for bad action to be.

Now rather than finding in this a reason for rejecting these arguments, I think we should see it as our main reason for embracing them. For what we have just observed is that according to Plato and Kant, the moral standards we apply to actions are what I have elsewhere called "internal standards"—standards which a thing must meet in virtue of what it is.[11] An internal standard is one that arises from the nature of the object to which it applies, from the functional or teleological norms which make it the object that it is. Say that a house, for instance, is a habitable shelter. Then a good house is a house that has the features that enable it to serve as a habitable shelter—the corners are properly sealed, the roof is waterproof and tight, the rooms are tall enough to stand up in, and things like that. These internal standards are what make something *a good house*.

We need to distinguish here between something's being a good or bad *house* and its being a house that happens to be a good or bad *thing* because of some external standard. The large mansion that blocks the whole neighborhood's view of the lake may be a *bad thing* for the neighborhood, but it is not therefore a *bad house*. A house that does not successfully shelter, on the other hand, is a bad house. Let me give this kind of badness a special name. An entity which does not meet its internal standards is *defective*.

The distinction between internal and external standards is important, because internal standards meet challenges to their normativity with perfect ease. Suppose you are going to build a house. Why shouldn't you build a house that blocks the whole neighborhood's view of the lake? Perhaps because it will displease the neighbors. Now *there* is a consideration that you may simply set aside, if you are selfish or tough enough to brave the neighbors' displeasure. But because it does not make sense to ask why a house should serve as a habitable shelter, it also does not make sense to ask why the corners should be sealed and the roof should be waterproof and tight. For if you fall too far short of the internal standard for houses, what you produce will simply not be a house. And this means that there's a sense in which even the most venal and shoddy builder must try to build a good house, for the simple reason that there is no other way to try to build a house. Building a good house and building a house are not different activities: for both are activities in which we must be guided by the functional or teleological norms implicit in the idea of a house. Obviously, it doesn't follow that every house is a good house. It does, however, follow that building bad houses is not a different activity from building good ones. *It is the same activity, badly done.*

Just actions in Plato, universalizable actions in Kant, are actions that are good *as* actions, the way a house that shelters successfully is good as a house. And if this is right, we should get the same conclusions. If justice and universalizability are internal standards, then they are not extraneous considerations whose normativity may be doubted. An agent cannot simply set aside the question whether his action is universalizable or just, for if he falls too far short of the internal standards for actions, what he produces will simply not be an action. In effect this means that even the most venal and shoddy agent must try to perform a good action, for the simple reason that there is no other way to try to perform an action. Performing a good action and performing an action are not different activities: for both are activities in which we must be guided by the functional or teleological norms implicit in the idea of an action. Obviously, it doesn't follow that every action is a good action. It does, however, follow that performing bad actions is not a different activity from performing good ones. *It is the same activity, badly done.*

V. Defective Action

So if we could make these claims plausible, or even intelligible, we would have an important result here: an answer to the question why our actions must meet moral standards. Unjust or nonuniversalizable actions would be *defective*: they would be bad *as actions*. But how can actions be defective, and still *be* actions? The Constitutional Model again provides us with the resources for an answer. For we all know that the action of a city may be formally or procedurally constitutional and yet not substantively just. Indeed, nothing is more familiar: a law duly legislated by the congress and even upheld by the supreme court may for all that be unjust. So it's not as if there's no territory at all between a perfectly just city and the complete disintegration of a civil war. A city may be governed, and yet be governed by the wrong law. And so may a soul. This, according to Plato and Kant, explains how bad action is possible.

In Kant's work this emerges most clearly in the first part of *Religion within the Limits of Reason Alone*. There we learn that a bad person is not after all one who is pushed about, or caused to act, by desires and inclinations. Instead, a bad person is one who is governed by what Kant calls the principle of self-love, by a principle which subordinates moral considerations to those arising from inclination (R 6:36). The person who acts on the principle of self-love *chooses* to act as inclination prompts (R 6:32–39). Let me try to make it clear why Kant thinks that an action based on the principle of self-love is *defective*, rather than merely externally bad.

Imagine a person I'll call Harriet, who is, in any *formal* sense you like, an autonomous person. She has a human mind, is self-conscious, with the normal allotment of the powers of reflection. She is not a slave or an indentured servant, and we will place her—unlike the original after whom I am modeling her—in an advanced modern constitutional democracy, with the full rights of free citizenship and all her human rights legally guaranteed to her. In every formal legal and psychological sense, what Harriet does is *up to her*. Yet whenever she has to make any of the important decisions and choices of her life, the way that Harriet does that is to ask Emma what she should do, and then that's what she does.[12]

This is autonomous action and yet it is *defective* as autonomous action. Harriet is self-governed and yet she is not, for she allows herself to be governed by Emma. Harriet is heteronomous, not in the sense that her actions are caused by Emma rather than chosen by herself, but in the sense that she allows herself to be governed in her choices by a law outside of herself. It even helps my case here that Harriet does this because she is afraid to think for herself. For as I have argued elsewhere, this is how Kant envisions the operation of the principle of self-love.[13] Kant does not envision the person who acts from self-love as actively reflecting on what he has reason to do and arriving at the conclusion that he ought to do what he wants. Instead, Kant envisions him as one who simply follows the lead of desire, without sufficient reflection. He's heteronomous, and gets his law from nature, not in the sense that it causes his actions, but in the sense that he allows himself to be governed by its suggestions—just as Harriet allows herself to be governed by Emma's.

The analogous doctrine in Plato is much more elaborate, and this is to Plato's credit. For what Kant says here is incomplete and confusing. Minimally, it seems, Kant ought to have distinguished between a wanton principle of self-love—the principle of acting on the desire of the moment—and a prudent principle of self-love—which seeks, say, the greatest satisfaction of desires over time.[14] Both of these characters *are* found in Plato, and others besides. In Books VIII and IX of the *Republic*, Plato in fact distinguishes five different ways that the soul may be governed, comparing them to five different kinds of constitutions possible for a city: the good way, which is monarchy or aristocracy; and four bad ones, growing increasingly worse: timocracy, oligarchy, democracy, and worst of all, tyranny. In the three middle cases, what makes the constitution bad is that the unity of the person who lives under it depends upon contingent circumstances.

Nearest to the aristocratic soul is the timocratic person, who like the city he is named for, is ruled by considerations of honor. Such a person loves the outward form, the beauty, of goodness, almost as if it were goodness itself. This person goes wrong, and becomes divided against himself, in a certain kind of case—namely the kind of case in which the right thing is something which seems dishonorable. Suppose, for instance, the timocratic person is fighting for the good of the city, but we reach a point where really surrender is the better course. The timocratic person may be so fixed on the honorableness, the beauty, the glamour if you will, of this kind of action, of fighting-for-the-good-of-the-city that he may be unable to give up, even though it is really for the good of the city that he should do so.[15]

Next comes the oligarchic person, who appears to be ruled by prudence: he is cautious, non-luxurious, and concerned with long-term enrichment. In describing him Plato employs a distinction between necessary desires, whose satisfaction is beneficial or essential to survival, and unnecessary or luxurious desires, which are harmful and should not be indulged. The oligarchic person is attentive to the necessary desires and to money, while he represses his unnecessary desires. But he represses them because they are unprofitable, rather than because it is bad to indulge them. The result of this forceful repression, according to Socrates, is that "someone like that wouldn't be entirely free from internal civil war and wouldn't be one but in some way two." This kind of prudence rules despotically over the appetitive part, like the rich ruling over a discontented working class. Should some outside force—perhaps simply a sufficient temptation—strengthen and enliven his unnecessary desires, the oligarchic person may quite literally lose control of himself. If generally the oligarchic person manages to hang together, it is because he has the sort of imitation virtue which Socrates makes fun of in the *Phaedo*, the virtue of those who are able to master some of their pleasures and fears because they are in turn mastered by others.[16] Socrates has in mind here such arguments as that you should be temperate because that way you will get more pleasure on the whole. Generally Plato seems to think that honor and prudence are principles of choice sufficiently like true virtue to hold a soul together through most kinds of stress, although in an oligarchic person the fault lines are increasingly visible.[17]

Next in line is the democratic person, in whom the unnecessary desires are not repressed, and who as a result is a wanton. Socrates says that the democratic person, "puts his pleasures on an equal footing . . . always surrendering rule over himself to whichever desire comes along, as if it were chosen by lot. And when that is satisfied, he surrenders the rule to another, not disdaining any but satisfying them all equally" (561b). Democracy is a degenerate case of self-government, for such a person governs himself only in a minimal or formal sense, just as choosing by lot is different only in a minimal or formal sense from not choosing at all. The coherence of the democratic person's life is completely dependent on the accidental coherence of his desires. To see the problem, consider a story:

> Jeremy, a college student, settles down at his desk one evening to study for an examination. Finding himself a little too restless to concentrate, he decides to take a walk in the fresh air. His walk takes him past a nearby bookstore, where the sight of an enticing title draws him in to look at the book. Before he finds it, however, he meets his friend Neil, who invites him to join some of the other kids at the bar next door for a beer. Jeremy decides he can afford to have just one, and goes with Neil to the bar. While waiting for his beer, however, he finds that the noise gives him a headache, and he decides to return home without ever having the beer. He is now, however, in too much pain to study. So Jeremy doesn't study for his examination, hardly gets a walk, doesn't buy a book, and doesn't drink a beer.[18]

Of course democratic life doesn't have to be like this; it's only an accident that each of Jeremy's impulses leads him to an action which completely undercuts the satisfaction of the last one. But that's just the trouble, for it's also only an accident if this does *not* happen. The democratic person has no resources for shaping his desires to prevent this, and so he is at the mercy of accident. Like Jeremy, he may be almost completely *incapable of effective action*.

It is from the chaos resulting from this kind of life that the tyrannical soul emerges. This kind of soul is once again unified, but not under the government of reason looking to the good of the whole. According to Plato the tyrannical soul is governed by some erotic desire (572d–573a), which subordinates the entire soul to its purposes, leaving the person an absolute slave to a single dominating obsession (571a–580a).[19]

In Plato's story, as in Kant's, bad action is action governed by a principle of choice which is not reason's own: a principle of honor (timocracy), prudence (oligarchy), wantonness (democracy), or obsession (tyranny). It is action, because it is chosen in accordance with the exercise of a principle by which the agent rules himself and under whose rule he is—in a sense—unified. Yet it is defective, because it is not reason's own principle, and the unity which it produces is, at least in the three middle cases, contingent and unstable. And Plato can say with Kant that the person who governs himself in one of these ways isn't after all completely self-governed. For he is propped up, so to speak, by the fact that the circumstances which would create civil war in his soul don't happen to occur.

VI. Good Action and the Unity of the Platonic Soul

Now we are almost ready to talk about what makes action good. But first I want to take up a possible objection. I've just said that in the conditions of timocracy, oligarchy, and democracy, your unity and so your self-government are propped by external circumstances, by the absence of the conditions under which you would fall apart. But what, you might ask is so bad about that? The defect in these characters is like a geological fault line, a potential for disintegration that does not necessarily show up, and so long as it doesn't, these people have constitutional procedures and so they can act. So why not just go ahead and be, say, oligarchical? You'll hold together most of the time, you'll be able to perform actions, and you'll save all that money besides.

There is yet another way to ask this same question, which is to ask whether Glaucon's challenge is not too extreme. Glaucon wants Socrates to tell him what justice and injustice do to the soul. So he sets up the following challenge: take on the one hand a person who has a completely unjust soul, and give him all of the outward benefits of justice, that is, all the benefits that come from people believing you are just. And take on the other hand a person who has a completely just soul, and give him all of the outward disadvantages of injustice, all the disadvantages that come from people believing you are unjust (360d–361e). In particular the just person who is believed to be unjust will be—and I'm quoting now— "whipped, stretched on a rack, chained, [and] blinded with fire" (361e). Socrates is supposed to show that it is better to be just than unjust *even then*. But isn't that too much to ask?

In the context of the argument of the *Republic*, it is not. For the question of the *Republic* is asked as a *practical* question: it is the question of whether the just life is more worthy of *choice* than the unjust life. And if you choose to be a just person, and to live a just life, you are thereby choosing to do the just thing even if it means you will be whipped, stretched on the rack, chained, and blinded with fire. You can't make a conditional commitment to justice, a commitment to be just unless the going gets rough. Your justice rests in the nature of your commitments, and a commitment like that would not *be* a commitment to justice. So when deciding whether to be a just person, you've got to be convinced in advance that it'll be worth it even if things do turn out this way.

Suppose—for it's plausible enough—there's a person who lives a just life, is decent and upstanding, always does his share, never takes an unfair advantage, sticks to his word—all of that—but then, one day, he is put to the rack, and under stress of torture does something unjust. Say he divulges a military secret, or the whereabouts of a fugitive unjustly pursued. Am I saying that this shows that he was never really committed to justice, because his commitment must have been conditional? *Of course not.* What the case shows is that the range of things people can *be* is wider than the range of things they can choose, so to speak, *in advance* to be. This person was committed to keeping his secrets on the rack, but he failed, that's all—and very understandably too. But the fact that you can be a just person who in these circumstances will fail does not show that you can decide in advance to be a just person who in these circumstances will fail: that is, it doesn't show that you can make a conditional commitment to justice. For suppose you surprise yourself and you do hold out and you keep the secret even when they put you on the rack. Did you then fail to *keep* your conditional commitment?

So Glaucon's challenge is a fair one. But Plato more than meets it. For he doesn't merely prove that the just life is the one most worthy of choice. He proves the just life is the only one you can choose. Let me try to explain why.

Consider Plato's account of the principle of just or aristocratic action. Plato says of the aristocratic soul that:

> when he does anything, whether acquiring wealth, taking care of his body, engaging in politics, or in private contracts—in all of these, he believes that the action is just and fine that preserves this inner harmony and helps achieve it, and calls it so, and regards as wisdom the knowledge that oversees such actions. And he believes that the action that destroys this harmony is unjust, and calls it so, and regards the belief that oversees it as ignorance. (443e–444a)

In other words, the principle of justice directs us to perform those actions which establish and maintain our volitional unity. Now we have already seen that according to Plato volitional unity is essential if you are to act as a person, as a single unified agent. So reason's own principle *just is* the principle of acting in a way that constitutes you into a single unified agent. Deliberative action is self-constitution.

In fact, deliberative action by its very nature imposes constitutional order on the soul. When you deliberate about what to do and then do it, what you are doing is organizing your appetite, reason, and spirit, into the unified system that yields an action that can be attributed to you as a person. Deliberative action pulls the parts of the soul together into a unified system. Whatever else you are doing when you choose a deliberative action, you are also unifying yourself into a person. This means that Plato's principle of justice, reason's own principle, is the *formal* principle of deliberative action. It is as if Glaucon asked: what condition could this be, that enables the just person to stick to his principles even on the rack? And it is as if Plato replied: don't look for some *further* condition which has that as an *effect*. Justice is not some other or further condition that enables us to maintain our unity as agents. It is that very condition itself—the condition of being able to maintain our unity as agents.

To see that this is formal, consider the following comparison. One might ask Kant: what principle could this be, that enables the free person to be autonomous, to rule herself? And Kant would reply: don't look for some *further* principle which has that as an *effect*. The categorical imperative is not some other or further principle that enables us to rule ourselves. It is that very principle itself, the principle of giving laws to ourselves.

On the one hand, this account of the aristocratic soul shows us why the demands of Platonic justice are so high. On certain occasions, the people with the other constitutions fall apart. For the truly just person, the aristocratic soul, there are no such occasions. She is entirely self-governed, so that all of her actions, in every circumstance of her life, are really and fully her own: never merely the manifestations of forces at work in her or on her, but always the expression of her own choice. She is completely self-possessed: not necessarily happy on the rack — but *herself* on the rack, herself even there.

And yet at the same time, Plato's argument shows that this aristocratic constitution is the only one you can choose. For you can't, in the moment of deliberative action, choose to be something less than a single unified agent. And that means you can't exactly choose to act on any principle other than the principle of justice. Timocratic, oligarchic, and democratic souls disintegrate under certain conditions, so deciding to be one would be like making a conditional commitment to your own unity, to your own personhood. And that's not possible. For consider what happens when the conditions that cause disintegration in these constitutions actually occur. If you don't fall apart, have you failed to keep your commitment, like the conditionally just person who holds out on the rack after all? But if you do fall apart, *who is it* that has kept the commitment? If you fall apart, there is no person left. You can be a timocratic, oligarchic, or democratic person, in the same way that you can be a just person who fails on the rack. But you cannot decide in advance that this is what you will be.

Of course this doesn't mean that everyone chooses the just life. What it means is that choosing an unjust life is not a different activity from choosing a just one. It is the same activity — the activity of self-constitution — badly done.

VII. Good Action and the Unity of the Kantian Will

It remains to show that this is also Kant's view; and for that we need to revisit the argument by which Kant establishes that action must be in accordance with the categorical imperative, and fill in its missing step. Kant argues that insofar as you are a rational being, you must act under the idea of freedom — and this means that you do not think of yourself, or experience yourself, as being impelled into action, but rather as deciding what to do. You take *yourself*, rather than the incentive on which you choose to act, to be the *cause* of your action.[20] And Kant thinks that in order for this to be so, you must act on a universal law. You cannot regard yourself as the *cause* of your action — you cannot regard the action as the product of your will — unless you will universally.

To see why, let us consider what happens if we try to deny it.[21] If our reasons did not have to be universal then they could be completely particular — it would be possible to have a reason which applies only to the case before you, and has no implications for any other case. Willing to act on a reason of this kind would be what I will call "particularistic willing." If particularistic willing is impossible, then it follows that willing must be universal—that is, a maxim, in order to be willed at all, must be willed as a universal law.

Now there are two things to notice here. First of all, the question is not whether we can will a new maxim for each new occasion. We may very well do that, for every occasion may have relevant differences from the one we last encountered. Any difference in the situation that is actually relevant to the decision properly belongs in our maxim, and this means that our maxim may be quite specific to the situation at hand. The argument here is not supposed to show that reasons are general. It is supposed to show us that reasons are universal, and universality is quite compatible with—indeed it requires—a high degree of specificity.

The second point is that it will be enough for the argument if the principle that is willed be willed, as I will call it, as provisionally universal. To explain what I mean by that I will use a pair of contrasts. There are three different ways in which we can take our principles to range over a variety of cases, and it is important to keep them distinct. We treat a principle as *general* when we think it applies to a wide range of similar cases. We treat a principle as universal, or, as I will sometimes say, *absolutely universal*, when we think it applies to absolutely every case of a certain sort, but all the cases must be exactly of that sort. We treat a principle as *provisionally universal* when we think it applies to every case of a certain sort, unless there is some good reason why not. The difference between regarding a principle as universal, and regarding it as provisionally universal, is marginal. Treating a principle as only provisionally universal amounts to making a mental acknowledgment, to the effect that you might not have thought of everything needed to make the principle universal, and therefore might not have specified it completely. Treating principles as general, and treating them as provisionally universal, are superficially similar, because in both cases we admit that there might be exceptions. But in fact they are deeply and essentially different, and this shows up in what happens when we encounter the exceptions. If we think of a principle as merely general, and we encounter an exception, nothing happens. The principle was only general, and we expected there to be some exceptions. But if a principle was provisionally universal, and we encounter an exceptional case, we must now go back and revise it, bringing it a little closer to the absolute universality to which provisional universality essentially aspires.

The rough causal principles with which we operate in everyday life (I am not talking now about quantum physics) are provisionally universal, and we signal this sometimes by using the phrase "all else equal." The principle that striking a match causes a flame holds all else equal, where the things that have to be equal are that there is no gust of wind or splash of water or oddity in the chemical composition of the atmosphere that would interfere with the usual connection. There are background conditions for the operation of these laws, and without listing and possibly without knowing them all, we mention that they must be in place when we say "all else equal." Although there are certainly exceptions, natural law is not merely general, for whenever an exception occurs, we look for an explanation. Something must have made this case different: one of its background conditions was not met.

To see how it works in the practical case, consider a standard puzzle case for Kant's universalizability criterion. It may seem as if wanting to be a doctor is an adequate reason for becoming a doctor, for there's nothing wrong with being a doctor—in fact, really, it's rather admirable—and if you ask yourself if it could be a law that everyone who wants to be doctor should become one, it seems, superficially, fine. But then the objector comes along and says, but look, suppose *everyone* actually wanted to be a doctor and nobody wanted to be anything else. The whole economic system would go to pieces, and then you couldn't be a doctor, so your maxim would have contradicted itself! So does this show that it is wrong to be a doctor simply because you want to?

What it shows is that the mere desire to enter a certain profession is only a provisionally universal reason for doing so. There's a background condition for the rightness of being a doctor because you want to, which is that society has some need for people to enter this profession. In effect the case does show that it's wrong to be a doctor merely because you want to—the maxim needs revision, for it is not absolutely universal unless it mentions as part of your reason for becoming a doctor that there is a social need. Someone who decides to become a doctor in the full light of reflection also takes that into account.

That case is easy, but there's no general reason to suppose we can think in advance. When we adopt a maxim as a universal law, we know that there might be cases, cases we haven't thought of, which would show us that it is not universal after all. In that sense we can allow for exceptions. But so long as the commitment to revise in the face of exceptions is in place, the maxim is not merely general. It is provisionally universal.

So particularistic willing is neither a matter of willing a new maxim for each occasion, nor is it a matter of willing a maxim that you might have to change on another occasion. Both of those are compatible with regarding reasons as universal. Instead, particularistic willing would be a matter of willing a maxim for exactly this occasion without taking it to have any other implications of any kind for any other occasion. You will a maxim thinking that you can use it just this once and then so to speak discard it; you don't even need a reason to change your mind.

Now I'm going to argue that that sort of willing is impossible. The first step is this: To conceive yourself as the cause of your actions is to identify with the principle of choice on which you act. A rational will is a self-conscious causality, and a self-conscious causality is aware of itself as a cause. To be aware of yourself as a cause is to identify yourself with something in the scenario that gives rise to the action, and this must be the principle of choice. For instance, suppose you experience a conflict of desire: you have a desire to do both A and B, and they are incompatible. You have some principle which favors A over B, so you exercise this principle, and you choose to do A. In this kind of case, you do not regard yourself as a mere passive spectator to the battle between A and B. You regard the choice as yours, as the product of your own activity, because you regard the principle of choice as expressive, or representative, of yourself. You must do so, for the only alternative to identifying with the principle of choice is regarding the principle of choice as some third thing in you, another force on a par with the incentives to do A and to do B, which happened to throw in its weight in favor of A, in a battle at which you were, after all, a mere passive spectator. But then you are not the cause of the action. Self-conscious or rational agency, then, requires identification with the principle of choice on which you act.

The second step is to see that particularistic willing makes it impossible for you to distinguish yourself, your principle of choice, from the various incentives on which you act. According to Kant you must always act on some incentive or other, for every action, even action from duty, involves a decision on a proposal: something must suggest the action to you. And in order to will particularistically, you must in each case wholly identify with the incentive of your action. That incentive would be, for the moment, your law, the law that defined your agency or your will.

It's important to see that if you had a particularistic will you would not identify with the incentive as representative of any sort of type, since if you took it as a representative of a type you would be taking it as universal. For instance, you couldn't say that you decided to act on the inclination of the moment, *because you were so inclined.* Someone who takes "I shall do the things I am inclined to do, whatever they might be" as his maxim has adopted a universal principle, not a particular one: he has the principle of treating his inclinations *as such* as reasons. A truly particularistic will must embrace the incentive in its full particularity: it, in no way that is further describable, is the law of such a will. So someone who engages in particularistic willing does not even have a democratic soul. There is only the tyranny of the moment: the complete domination of the agent by something inside him.

Particularistic willing eradicates the distinction between a person and the incentives on which he acts. But then there is nothing left here that is the *person,* the agent, that is his will as distinct from the play of incentives within him. He is not one person, but a series, a mere conglomeration, of unrelated impulses. There is no difference between someone who has a particularistic will and someone who has no will at all. Particularistic willing lacks a subject, a person who is the cause of these actions. So particularistic willing isn't willing at all.

If a particularistic will is impossible, then when you will a maxim you must take it to be universal. If you do not, you are not operating as a self-conscious cause, and then you are not willing. To put the point in familiar Kantian terms, we can only attach the "I will" to our choices if we will our maxims as universal laws.[23] The categorical imperative is an internal standard for actions, because conformity to it is constitutive of an exercise of the will, of an action of a person as opposed to an action of something within him.

And this argument also shows that Kant's view is the same as Plato's. For if particularistic willing is what breaks us down, universal willing is what holds us together. For Kant, as for Plato, deliberative action by its very nature imposes unity on the will. It is only when you ask whether your maxim can be a universal law that you exercise the self-conscious causality, the autonomy, that yields an action that can be attributed to you as a whole person. So whatever else you are doing when you choose a deliberative action, you are also unifying yourself into a person. For Kant, as for Plato, action is self-constitution.

VIII. Conclusion

I will conclude by reviewing the course of the argument and saying what I take it to have established. I started by criticizing the Combat Model for failing to iden- tify the person who is the author of her actions. I hope that by now it is clear why it fails in that way. The Combat Model is not a picture of the human soul. It is a picture of the human soul in ruins, torn apart by civil war and therefore unable to act. According to the Constitutional Model, an action is yours when it is chosen in accordance with your constitution. Your constitution is what gives you the kind of volitional unity you need to be the author of your actions. And it is the person who acts in accordance with the best constitution, the most unified constitution, who is most truly the author of her actions. For Kant as for Plato, integrity is the metaphysical essence of morality.

The argument of this paper does not, by itself, get us all the way to the necessity of acting morally. The aim of the argument has been to establish that the Platonic principle of justice and Kant's categorical imperative are formal stan- dards of deliberative action. Both Kant and Plato believed that a certain content, the content of ordinary morality, could be derived from these formal principles. Plato's conviction appears at one of the most notorious moments of the *Republic*, when Socrates proposes to Glaucon that they can dispel any doubts they might have about their definition of justice "by appealing to ordinary cases" (442d–e). Accordingly, he asks Glaucon whether the just person as Socrates has described him would embezzle deposits, rob temples, steal, betray his friends or his city, violate his oaths or his other agreements, commit adultery, be disrespectful to his parents or neglect the gods, to all of which Glaucon says, with a complaisance startling to the reader, no, he would not, the just person Socrates has described him would not do these kinds of things. We are not told exactly why he is so sure. Kant, of course, does try to show us how content can be derived from his formal principle, and to that extent his version of the argument is superior to Plato's, although the success of his efforts is the subject of an old and famous debate. I think Kant's case can be made, but I haven't been trying to do that here.[24] Both Plato and Kant's arguments move (1) from the metaphysical property of action that makes it authored and so makes it action—autonomy in Kant's case, constitu- tionality in Plato's—to (2) a formal normative requirement that actions must meet if they are to have that property—universalizability in Kant's case, justice in Plato's—and then through (3) the derivation of content from the formal require- ment to arrive at ordinary moral requirements. It is the first two steps that have been my subject here.

At least in the formal sense, then, Platonic justice and Kant's categorical imperative, are internal standard for actions, because it is only insofar as your actions issue from your whole person, rather than something in you, that they can be actions. It doesn't exactly follow that we ought to choose actions justly and in accordance with the categorical imperative, for in a sense we cannot possibly choose in any other way. Choosing bad actions is not a different activity from choosing good ones. It is the same activity—the activity of self-constitution—badly done.

Notes

1. I have discussed this paper or the longer unpublished manuscript from which it is drawn with audiences at the inaugural meeting of The Society for Ethics, The University of Amsterdam, The University of Constance, The Humboldt University of Berlin, The University of Pittsburgh, the University of Virginia, The University of Salzburg, the University of Toronto, York University of Toronto, and the University of Zurich. I am grateful to all of these audiences for their interest, insightful comments, and challenging questions. I would like to thank Charlotte Brown, Barbara Herman, Govert den Hartogh, Anton Leist, Richard Moran, Amélie Rorty, and Theo van Willigenburg for reading and commenting on the manuscript.

2. David Hume, A *Treatise of Human Nature* (2nd Edition edited by L. A. Selby-Bigge and P. H. Nidditch; Oxford: Clarendon Press, 1978), Book II, Part III, Section III, 413.

3. Ibid.

4. One might think that Hume is also presenting a constitutional model, since his own argument suggests that the function of passion is to determine our ends and the function of reason is to discover means to ends. Elsewhere, however, I have argued that Hume does not really believe in a principle of instrumental *practical reason,* which instructs us to take the means to our ends, and which would be needed to integrate the two functions (the determination of the end and the identification of the means) into *a single system which produces actions.* Because of that, Hume is unable to work up a *person* out of these meager resources. What I've just said will become clearer as this essay proceeds, for it is actually, in a sense, a short version of the whole argument of this essay. For the argument that Hume does not believe in a principle of instrumental practical reason, see my "The Normativity of Instrumental Reason" in *Ethics and Practical Reason,* ed. Garrett Cullity and Berys Gaut (Oxford: Clarendon Press, 1997), 215–254; especially 220–234

5. References to Plato's *Republic* are inserted into the text, using the standard Stephanus numbers inserted into the margins of most editions and translations of Plato's works. Direct quotations come from the translation by G. M. A. Grube as revised by C. D. C. Reeve, which may be found in *Plato: Complete Works,* ed. John M. Cooper (Indianapolis, IN: Hackett Publishing Company, 1997).

6. The other two arguments are the "outdoing" argument used to establish that justice is a form of virtue and knowledge (349a–350d) and the function argument used to establish that the just person is happiest (352d–354a).

7. Socrates not only openly acknowledges this oddity later on, but actually suggests

that the principle of the specialization of labor is "beneficial" because it is "a sort of image of justice" (443c).

8. I have also discussed these points in "Taking the Law into Our Own Hands: Kant on the Right to Revolution" in *Reclaiming the History of Ethics: Essays for John Rawls*, ed. Andrews Reath, Barbara Herman, and Christine M. Korsgaard (Cambridge: Cambridge University Press, 1997), 308–309. The discussion here is in large part lifted from that discussion.

9. References to Kant's works are inserted into the text, using an abbreviation for the title followed by the volume and page numbers of the German Academy edition, which are found in the margins of most translations. The abbreviations and editions used are as follows:

> C2 = *Critique of Practical Reason*, ed. and trans. Mary Gregor, introduction Andrews Reath (Cambridge: Cambridge University Press, 1997).
>
> G = *Groundwork of the Metaphysics of Morals*, ed. and trans. Mary Gregor, introduction Christine M. Korsgaard (Cambridge: Cambridge University Press, 1998).
>
> R = *Religion within the Limits of Reason Alone*, ed. and trans. Theodore M. Greene and Hoyt H. Hudson, introduction John R. Silber (New York: Harper Torchbooks, 1960).

10. For a more complete account of these ideas and Kant's moral psychology generally see the first section of my "Motivation, Metaphysics, and the Value of the Self: A reply to Ginsborg, Guyer, and Schneewind," *Ethics* 109 (October 1998): 49–66.

11. Julia Annas and others have pointed out to me that there is some tension between this idea and certain passages in the latter books of the *Republic* which strongly suggest that Plato's view is that we should identify with reason—most notably the passage at 588b–e in which Plato compares the three parts of the soul to a many-headed beast (appetite), a lion (spirit), and a human being (reason). I agree, but I think that the tension is within the text of the *Republic* itself, that it is part of a general tension between the conceptions of the soul in the earlier and later books.

12. I discuss the conception of an internal standard in "The Normativity of Instrumental Reason," in *Ethics and Practical Reason*, ed. Garrett Cullity and Berys Gaut (Oxford: Clarendon Press, 1997), 215–254. See especially 249–250. There I argue that the hypothetical imperative is an internal standard for acts of the will.

13. The model for my Harriet is the persuadable Harriet Smith in Jane Austen's novel *Emma*. (Oxford: Oxford University Press, 1990).

14. See my "From Duty and for the Sake of the Noble: Kant and Aristotle on Morally Good Action" in *Aristotle, Kant, and the Stoics: Rethinking Happiness and Duty*, ed. Stephen Engstrom and Jennifer Whiting (New York: Cambridge University Press, 1996), 203–236; especially 208–212.

15. If I am right in saying that Kant sees self-love as operating unreflectively, this might seem to favor a wanton principle of self-love. Sometimes, however, it is clear that Kant has a prudent principle of self-love in mind—see for instance C2 5:35–36. While I think that the wanton principle does square better with Kant's arguments, I also think it should be possible to make the second *Critique* passages consistent with the view that those who act from self-love are unreflective. We just need to argue that there is a difference between being *reflective* and being *calculating*.

16. Although space constraints don't allow me to spell out the idea in sufficient detail here, I am tempted to say that the problem with the timocratic person is that he is

unable to deal with the contingencies that call for the application of what I have else-where called, following John Rawls, "non-ideal theory." See my "The Right to Lie: Kant on Dealing with Evil" in *Creating the Kingdom of Ends* (New York: Cambridge University Press, 1996), 133–158; especially 147–154. That is, he acts well, except in those moments when true goodness calls for concession, compromise, a less strict rule, or even—though this is rare—actions that are formally wrong. See my "Taking the Law into Our Own Hands: Kant on the Right to Revolution," in *Reclaiming the History of Ethics: Essays for John Rawls*, eds. Andrews Reath, Barbara Herman, and Christine M. Korsgaard (Cambridge: Cambridge University Press, 1997) for a discussion of this kind of case.

17. See Plato, *Phaedo* 68d–69c.

18. A number of people have argued that the problem described here would not arise for the rational egoist in the more ordinary modern sense, the person who seeks to maximize the satisfaction of his own interests. Indeed this is suggested by my own remarks about how imitation virtue can help hold the oligarch together, for modern egoism is much like Plato's imitation virtue. If correct, this objection would suggest that you can constitute yourself through the egoistic principle. A full response to this objection requires a full treatment of the claim that there is a coherently formulable principle of rational egoism. See my "The Myth of Egoism" available from the Department of Philosophy at the University of Kansas as the Lindley Lecture for 1999.

19. I have lifted this example from a footnote in my "The Normativity of Instrumental Reason," in *Ethics and Practical Reason*, ed. Garrett Cullity and Berys Gaut (Oxford: Clarendon Press, 1997), 215–254; 247, n. 64.

20. The problem with tyranny is not the same as that with timocracy, oligarchy, and democracy—it is not that the unity it produces in the soul is contingent. Plato envisions tyranny as a kind of madness (see 573c ff.). As I imagine the tyrant, his relation to his obsession is like a psychotic's relation to his delusion: he is able, and prepared, to organize everything else around it, but at the expense of a loss of his grip on reality, on the world. But that is only a sketch, and a fuller treatment of this principle, and of the question why a person cannot successful integrate himself under its governance, is required for the completeness of the argument of this paper.

21. To put it somewhat more strictly, you take yourself to be the cause of your intelligible movements, since it is only really an *action* if you are, or to the extent that you are, the cause. I think that there are important philosophical questions, yet to be worked out, about exactly how this point should be phrased, but for now I leave the more familiar formulation in the text. I am indebted to Sophia Reibetanz and Tamar Schapiro for discussions of these points.

22. The argument that follows made its first appearance in Section 1 of my "Reply" in *The Sources of Normativity* (Cambridge: Cambridge University Press, 1996), 225–233. I hope that the present version is clearer.

23. I owe this formulation of my point to Govert den Hartogh.

24. In Lecture 3 of *The Sources of Normativity* (Cambridge: Cambridge University Press, 1996), I give an argument that aims to move from the formal version of the categorical imperative to moral requirements by way of Kant's Formula of Humanity. See especially sections 3.3.7–3.4.10.

18

Emotional Rationality
as Practical Rationality

Karen Jones

In this essay I take as my target a messy set of intuitions about the extent to which and the dimensions along which emotions can be assessed for rationality. One strand in commonsense thinking puts emotions entirely outside the scope of rationality assessment. Everyone has heard such statements as, "But, that's how I feel"—uttered as if that ended the conversation. The view that emotions are outside the scope of rationality assessment gains strength from the perceived subjectivity of emotion—emotions vary so much from person to person and seem to depend so much on the agent's history that one can easily think that emotions can't be subject to rationality assessment,[1] that we can, at most, find emotions understandable (or not). But to say that emotions can be understandable (or not) is not to say that they can be rational (or not) since rationality is a normatively stronger notion than understandability.

Another strand in commonsense thinking is loquacious in its criticism of our own and of others' emotions and recognizes many kinds of assessment that seem to constitute rationality assessment. According to this strand, (1) a particular emotion might be ungrounded or insufficiently grounded in the evidence available to the agent. Jealousy often leaps ahead of the evidence in this way. Call this dimension of assessment *reasonableness*. (2) An emotion may fail to fit the features of the evoking situation and one may be, for example, angry when there is no slight. Call this dimension of assessment *aptness*. Aptness and reasonableness can come apart: one might, for example, have a panic attack that just happens to coincide with a nuclear catastrophe.[2] (3) Related to aptness, yet distinct from it, is *proportionality*: such a trifling slight merits only annoyance, not rage. That we separate emotions of different intensities shows the connection between proportionality and aptness, but they are distinct concepts. An evoking situation can merit not merely anger, rather than rage or irritation, but also only anger of such and such intensity. (4) Criticism of emotions can run even deeper: it can be objected that a kind of affective response, such as sexual jealousy, embodies an evaluative mistake. Or one might hold, as the Stoics did, that all emotions are in evaluative error. Call this dimension of assessment *evaluative correctness*. (5) Some emotions, in some contexts, are strategically unwise and lead the agent to fail to achieve her ends; emotions can thus be assessed according to the forward-looking dimension of *strategic wisdom*. Emotions that are out of proportion with their evoking situations will often be unwise, but they need not be (an extreme emotional response may be just what it takes to further the agent's ends),[3] and thus proportionality is not reducible to wisdom. For the same reason, strategic wisdom is not reducible to aptness or reasonableness.

These are not simply dimensions of assessment acknowledged in common-sense thinking; each has its advocate in philosophical discussion of the rationality of emotions. Jon Elster canvasses the idea of defining the rationality of emotion in terms of the reasonableness of the beliefs that cause the emotion; Ronald de Sousa rejects reasonableness and focuses on aptness; the Stoics focus on evaluative correctness; and Robert Solomon focuses on wisdom.[4] Not only is there no consensus on how to analyze the rationality conditions of emotions, but also there is no consensus on how even to approach the question. In addition to proposing and defending an account of rationality conditions for emotions, one of the goals of this essay is to get clearer about how to go about asking questions about the rationality of emotions.

A Slogan and a Constraint

My strategy in generating an account of the rationality conditions of emotions is to use a slogan and a methodological constraint to apply pressure to a substantive account of the nature of the emotions and thus extract from that account a picture of what makes an emotion rational. The conclusion of this essay is thus conditional: *if* you accept my preferred general account of the emotions, then this is what you *should* say about their rationality conditions, although—and I return to this—it is not what one advocate of a version of the preferred theory has in fact said.[5]

The slogan that provides the intuition behind my approach provides the title of this essay: emotional rationality is practical rationality. So as not to beg any questions, I could put the slogan in conditional form: if there is such a thing as emotional rationality, then it is a species of practical rationality. Put conditionally like this, it does not rule out the antirational assessment position, and those who think that emotions are subject to rationality assessment invariably think that such assessment has *something* to do with practical rationality. Of course, this agreement is a function of the slogan's vagueness: it is not at all clear what it means to say that emotional rationality is a species of practical rationality unless we further specify what we have in mind by practical rationality. As the argument progresses, the slogan will be given a more determinate meaning. By the end of the argument, it falls away as unnecessary since it has a heuristic function in helping us look in the right places to generate an account. The account, once generated, stands or falls on its own merits. The slogan is thus a starting point that will be transcended; so, in the end, no questions need be begged.

A slogan itself does not give us enough of a handle on the question of emotional rationality. Something else is needed to press against. That something else is a methodological constraint: your account of what emotions are constrains your account of their rationality conditions. If anything is a truism, this constraint is; nevertheless, truisms can have substantive implications. Consider, for example, Solomon's account of emotions and his story of their rationality conditions. Solomon, like the Stoics before him, identifies emotions with evaluative judgments.

> [E]motions are interestingly similar to beliefs. We can now explain this by claiming that emotions are judgments, normative and often moral judgments. "I am angry at John for taking . . . my car" *entails* that I believe that John has somehow wronged me. (This must be true even if, *all things considered*, I also believe that John was justified in taking my car.) The (moral) judgment entailed by my anger is not a judgment *about* my anger. . . . My anger *is* that judgment.[6]

Having identified emotions with evaluative judgments, Solomon claims that an emotion is rational to the extent that it functions to meet the subject's ego needs.[7] On this account, emotions are subject to forward-looking, instrumental rationality conditions. But this commits Solomon to the view that judgments (remember, emotions just are judgments) are assessable for instrumental rather than representational rationality.[8] The Stoics give the *kind* of answer Solomon should have given: they say that emotions are always irrational because they are mistaken evaluative judgments that confuse things that are merely among the so-called preferred indifferents with components of the agent's happiness. We might dispute the claim that emotions necessarily contain evaluative error, but this account at least recognizes that what you say emotions are constrains what you can say about their rationality conditions.[9]

Core Features of Quasi-Perceptual Accounts of the Emotions

The family of accounts for which I'm interested in generating rationality conditions can usefully be called quasi-perceptual. Although there are differences in the details, Cheshire Calhoun, Ronald de Sousa, and Amelie Rorty each develop an account of this sort.[10] The core intuition that drives such accounts and that unifies them so that they may properly be called a family of accounts is the intuition that emotions operate at a different level from beliefs and desires: emotions *shape* both cognition and motivation but are not themselves to be identified with either beliefs or desires.[11] Emotions are able to shape both cognition and motivation through their effects on what we experience as reasons for belief and reasons for action. Proponents of quasi-perceptual accounts variously describe emotions as "cognitive sets, interpretive frameworks, patterns of attention," and "species of determinate patterns of salience among objects of attention, lines of inquiry, and inferential strategies."[12]

According to quasi-perceptual accounts of the emotions, emotions have at least the following cognitive roles: they (1) focus attention, (2) direct inquiry, (3) shape interpretation, and (4) structure inference. Call a mental state that plays these four roles a *cognitive set*. These four characteristic ways in which emotions affect cognition interact: in the first instance, an emotion, such as fear, typically leads the agent to freeze and focus on the object (snake or stick?) that triggered the fear.[13] That focus may attach to specific features of the object (or evoking situation), features that are seen in evaluative terms.[14] Such evaluatively laden interpretations structure inference, making inferential moves come to seem compelling that would not have seemed compelling without the emotion: seen without anger, your remark might be quite innocent; seen with anger, it will be taken to reveal (yet again) your tendency toward superciliousness.

It is because of the control that emotions exert over perception and interpretation that they can "run away" with us. Evidence that might count against my anger will be interpreted through the lens of my anger. Thus the angry often—indeed, typically—have angry beliefs; that is, they typically form the evaluative judgments taken by judgmentalists to constitute the emotion. But they need not. An agent can resist these interpretative and inferential dispositions, reminding herself that there are other ways of interpreting the situation, that the inferences she experiences as compelling and has to struggle to resist would not seem compelling were she not angry. What the agent who assents to the emotional appearances and the agent who resists such appearances have in common are patterns of cognitive and desiderative focus.[15]

Generating Rationality Conditions

Preliminary Moves

Suppose—and I'm aware that I haven't given a defense of this claim—emotions shape both cognition and motivation and are constituted by patterns of salience, interpretation, and inference. When would it be rational for an agent to see the world through the lens of an emotion? Let me start by quickly canvassing two answers that might seem tempting but that are inadequate.

We might think that it is rational for an agent to see the world through the lens of an emotion only if she has an antecedently (or perhaps simultaneously) justified evaluative belief that the evoking situation instantiates the evaluative property that is the proper object of the emotion. For example, an agent's seeing the world through the interpretative schemata of righteous anger is rational only if that anger is grounded in a justified belief that the object of her anger has treated her disrespectfully. This proposal amounts to answering the question of the rationality of emotions in just the way a judgmentalist should—if you identify emotions with evaluative beliefs, then the emotion will be rational only if the evaluative belief is rational.

This answer rules out as irrational some emotional episodes involving so-called gut feelings that seem rational. No doubt gut feelings are sometimes irrational, but consider the following case. Suppose a woman has a firm belief that her partner is not having an affair. Moreover, she has excellent evidence to support this belief: she knows her partner and his character very well. In the past he has expressed sincere disapproval of such behavior on the part of others, and he is too much of a homebody to enjoy the intrigue that an affair would entail. Secure in this knowledge of his character, his partner has never felt jealous of his (many) friendships with women.

At a party to which they are both invited, the woman watches her partner interact with one of his women friends. She cannot articulate what it is about the interaction that bothers her; indeed, she can't be sure that it is anything at all about the interaction that does. She finds herself feeling insecure. She chides herself for this at first: "What is wrong with you? He has lots of friendships with women. This is no different." Nevertheless, her insecurity and the suspicion it generates lead her to focus closely on her partner's interaction with the friend and to go over in her mind various details of his recent interaction with her. As a result of following through with the patterns of attention and lines of inquiry characteristic of suspicious jealousy, she comes to the conclusion that probably he is being unfaithful. She is right. She is a pretty reliable detector of the subtle clues of body language and voice that indicate how things stand between people. Her distrust is well grounded in this evidence, though she could not have known that at first. Should we say, then, that had she believed at the outset that he was unfaithful, her belief would have been rational? It might indeed have been formed by a reliable ability to detect unfaithfulness, but it seems that it would not have been rational for her to form that belief on the basis of a vague hunch in the light of all the evidence that she had to support the belief that *of course* he couldn't be being unfaithful.[16] The evidence that would rebut the undermining belief that of course he's faithful is acquired as a consequence of having the emotion and is not in place when the agent first experiences the emotion. Yet it would seem that the emotion is rational from the start and doesn't just become rational when more evidence is in, for it would be odd to say that it is worthwhile to follow up on an irrational emotion, yet this is what we have to say if we suppose that the emotion becomes rational only when the evidence is in.

The suspicious jealousy case lets us see what is wrong with another answer that we might be tempted to give to the question of when it is rational for an agent to see the world through an affective lens. I've said that emotions give shape to the mind: they make some beliefs come to seem compelling and others not. They get us to focus on a partial field of evidence, and they get us to focus on this in a particular way, thereby supporting characteristic inferential patterns. In this way, emotional perception can become self-fulfilling: we see only what confirms our emotion because we see the world through the lens of the emotion. Even if the woman in our example had not been good at tracking unfaithfulness, she would, as likely as not, have found what *seemed* to *her* to be evidence for it once her suspicions were aroused. Twisting evidence in this way appears even more reprehensible once we remember that emotions also shape motivation and tend to give rise to characteristic sorts of action—I will want to retaliate against the persons whose action I see through anger. These observations might lead us to suspect that the answer we should give to the question of when it is rational to view the world through the lens of an emotion is *never*. There's a long tradition, both philosophical and commonsense, of associating emotions with incontinence and irrationality: the good reasoner is never emotional; the wise deliberator is always cool. In conceding that emotions get us to focus on a partial field of evidence and to interpret that evidence in patterned ways, quasi-perceptual accounts of the emotions might seem to have given up the game to those who are hostile toward emotions.

However, this response would be hasty. The shaping of cognitive terrain characteristic of cognitive sets is not limited to affective phenomena: there's evidence from cognitive science that such tendencies to interpret information are operative in many kinds of reasoning, including informal statistical reasoning, which proceeds by way of stereotype rather than the slower but more accurate set-inclusion method.[17] We might think that part of what happens when a scientist is inducted into a research tradition is that she comes not merely to acquire a set of beliefs and a set of abilities and skills but also to have the cognitive dispositions describable as cognitive sets.[18] If this is so, then the answer, "never," is indeed hasty. It is sometimes a good thing that the mind is prejudiced in its interpretation: sometimes such prejudices are exactly what we need to be able to see the evidence *aright* and thus to see the world *aright*.[19] Perhaps, then, we should say that a cognitive set is rational just in case having such a set, in the context in which it is had, nonaccidentally contributes to the formation, or confirmation of true beliefs. And, likewise but more precisely, an emotion E in situation S will be rational for agent A if and only if E nonaccidentally contributes to A's being able to arrive at or to confirm true evaluative beliefs. The partner in the suspicious jealousy case passes this test—she is a good tracker of signs of unfaithfulness, and her suspicions will tend to lead her to form true evaluative beliefs; thus this account lets us say that her emotion is rational.

The suggestion looks promising, but I want to argue that it is not quite right, that it forces a model of emotional rationality that remains too much patterned on the rationality of beliefs. In effect, the model asks us to reduce emotional rationality to the rationality of evaluative belief *formation*. However, emotions do much more than tend to give rise to evaluative beliefs, correct or otherwise. They also give rise to motives for acting—motives that cannot be reduced to the motives that follow from rational evaluative beliefs.[20]

If, however, emotions are to be assessed for rationality only according to whether they reliably produce correct evaluative beliefs, then we have to make the motivational aspect of rational emotions fit in under the heading of motives that follow from these evaluative beliefs. I argue that there can be cases in which an agent fails the test of having emotional states that reliably generate true evaluative beliefs but nonetheless has rational emotions, although this argument has to wait until we have in place some additional resources. In the meantime, I regard as live the hypothesis that emotions are rational to the extent that they tend to give rise to or confirm correct evaluative belief. It gives us one way of cashing out the "aright" as it occurs in the claim that emotions, like other cognitive sets, are rational to the extent that they let us see the world aright.

There is, though, another way of cashing out the "aright," a way that focuses more clearly on the issue of practical rationality. So far, only the methodological constraint has been active in shaping the discussion. The slogan lets us see a direction in which to look for an alternative account: perhaps the relevant sort of correct vision is not primarily, if at all, a matter of true belief but rather a matter of seeing the situation aright from the perspective of practical rationality; that is, perhaps emotional rationality is the rationality of good practical perception. The first step toward exploring this proposal is to get a better understanding of how emotions affect practical perception, which in turn requires an adequate understanding of the phenomenology of decision making.

Deliberation from the First-Person Perspective

In beginning to reflect about deliberation and choice from the first-person point of view, one notices three things:

1. During deliberation, one's attention as an agent is generally firmly directed outward toward features of the world, not inward toward one's own wants and desires. When we deliberate, we are trying to work out what we should want to do, not what to do given what we want. The features that claim an agent's attention during deliberation or that strike her as important when deliberation is unnecessary are reason-giving features. They are the kinds of considerations that could be cited in answer to the question "Why did you do that?" and they show the favorable light in which the agent viewed her chosen course of action. They can include considerations such as "She needed my help" and "It would be fun." They rarely include "I wanted to" because, except for actions undertaken on whimsy, it can always be asked, "Why did you want to?" and the answer to that will cite some alleged property of the chosen course of action.[21]

2. Deliberation proceeds on the basis of a restricted set of such features.[22] On any given occasion for choice, there will typically be a large number of considerations that could intelligibly count for or against a choice of action. But the agent does not have all these features in mind: certain features strike an agent as mattering; others do not; and thus an agent comes to inhabit a world that is shaped and structured into a world of reasons. Sometimes, indeed, frequently, the set of reason-giving considerations that are salient to an agent is restricted in such a way as to make it simply obvious what the agent is to do: only one consideration strikes the agent as mattering, or as having such importance that other considerations fall from view and the agent simply "sees" what to do. Considerations can be salient to an agent in three quite different ways: a consideration can be judged by the

agent to matter and so, to that extent, be salient to her without being experienced as having valence, that is, without being apprehended in a motivationally lively way. The dangers of cigarette smoking are typically salient to a smoker in this, rather abstract way. Alternatively, a consideration (the pleasures of spiteful revenge, say) can be salient in virtue of being apprehended in a motivationally lively way without being judged to be reason giving. Finally, a consideration can be salient, engage with the agent's motivational set, and at the same time, be judged to be of genuine reason-giving force in the situation at hand.

3. Deliberation may overrule some of the considerations that an agent takes to be reason giving and may also transform her understanding of how these reason-giving features provide reasons for acting. A consideration that might at first blush have seemed to be a reason for acting in ways that would conflict with, for example, a requirement of justice can come to be seen as a reason for modifying the way in which the requirement of justice is met. In this way, rather than merely determining which consideration is, in the circumstances, the most weighty and letting it outweigh the others, deliberation seeks to make compossible respect for each reason-giving feature that an agent takes to be present in a situation.[23]

Together these three observations show how important it is for an agent to arrive at the correct view of a choice situation: much of the work of deliberation is carried out *before* an agent sets out to deliberate about how the reason-giving considerations best support action. The way in which an agent interprets a situation, and so highlights certain considerations while overlooking others, crucially affects the outcome of her deliberation, for the world, so seen, sets the terms for what will count as an acceptable solution to a practical problem.

It will be useful to regiment the language in which we talk about the various stages of deliberation. Let's agree to call that set of considerations that the agent *takes to be reason giving*, and so to establish the parameters for a successful resolution to a deliberative problem, the *starting points of deliberation*.[24] The starting points of deliberation (or the features that will govern action when deliberation is unnecessary) are selected by a process that can be called framing: a situation framed in one way will highlight certain features; framed in another way, others will be highlighted. Framing is thus a process of interpretation that selects certain features as starting points for deliberation and rejects others as unimportant. A consideration rejected as unimportant can nonetheless continue to be salient to an agent. This tends to happen when the consideration is apprehended in a motivationally lively way. Such considerations clamor to be admitted into the starting points of deliberation and may affect the agent's deliberation and her ability to act on her decision.[25]

Rationality, Again

Armed with this phenomenology of deliberation, we can see at once the connection between emotions and practical rationality: it follows from a quasi-perceptual account of the emotions that emotions will tend to influence how an agent frames a choice situation. Emotions make us experience considerations as reason giving. Considerations that emotions lead us to experience as reason giving claim a place among the starting points of deliberation. That claim can be rejected, but often it isn't. Indeed, sometimes emotions preempt deliberation by presenting a single consideration as of overwhelming importance, and we act straightaway and without reflection. Sometimes this is to our deep regret: "How could I have lashed out so blindly? Why was I not cool enough to see all the reasons that counted against my taking revenge then, in that self-destructive way?" But sometimes it is to our advantage. In a flash we see a threat, and just as quickly we respond.

These remarks suggest a way of cashing out the thought that emotional rationality is practical rationality: emotional rationality is the rationality of good practical perception. More precisely:

> An emotion E in situation S is rational for agent A if and only if E enables A to form a rational framing of S.

We should not be troubled by the fact that the word "rational" occurs on both sides of the biconditional. What the proposal amounts to is the suggestion that we view the problem of emotional rationality as part of the larger problem of the rationality of framing, and as will be shown, in the particular case, the rationality of an agent's framing of a choice situation is not determined by whether the agent is experiencing a given emotion. Furthermore, although what constitutes a rational framing may be partly determined by facts about the agent's emotional life (e.g., by the fact that the other is her friend), on any plausible story of the nature of reasons what constitutes a rational framing is determined by a whole lot else besides — what else will become clearer in a moment. For these reasons, there is no problematic circularity, although as things stand the account is uninformative: we have no better handle on what makes for a rational framing than we have on what makes for a rational emotion.

In what follows, I want to make some suggestions about how to go about thinking about the rationality of framing. I will not be able to draw out all, or even most, of the implications of this way of thinking about the rationality of framing and its connection with the rationality of emotions. Instead, to have a manageable task, I focus on the ways in which the account lets us have a richer understanding of the rationality of emotions than the "generates true evaluative belief" model, as well as on how the account captures the grain of truth in the claim that emotions are subjective but does so without abandoning rationality assessment.

Progress can be made regarding the question of what makes a *framing* rational by thinking about what makes a *belief* rational. Although there is disagreement about what makes a belief rational, there's agreement on how to approach the question. You first identify success for a belief and then you ask what would make such success appropriately *nonaccidental*. A belief succeeds if and only if it represents the world as being the way the world actually is, that is, if and only if it is true. Rational beliefs are beliefs such that *if true*, it is no accident that they are true. Irrational beliefs might still be true and rational beliefs false, but it will be a lucky chance if an irrational belief is true and an unlucky chance if a rational one is false.

This suggests that we begin by asking what makes a framing successful and then identify rational framings as framings that pass a nonaccidentality test such that, if they succeed, it is not a lucky chance that they succeed. Unfortunately, whereas there's a clear answer to what makes a belief successful, there's legitimate dispute about what makes for a successful framing. What I want to argue, though, is that on the least controversial conception of what constitutes a successful framing—a conception that presupposes no more than what Bernard Williams calls "internal reasons"[26]—a successful framing is about more than latching onto considerations that mesh with concerns an agent currently recognizes as valuable. That claim alone is enough to set up the practical problem for arriving at *correct* framings that emotional rationality contributes to solving. The practical problem that, I argue, a rational agent faces is this: she aims to latch onto those considerations that she *should* recognize as reason giving, and yet what she has to go on in achieving this goal is nothing more than her own mechanisms and methods, reliable and otherwise, for detecting these considerations, together with her own best take on what is valuable and her own best take on the limits and liabilities of the methods she uses to work out what considerations matter. The rational agent aims to steer a course between, on the one hand, being closed off to recognizing new considerations as reason giving and, on the other hand, being too willing to recognize such considerations and so running the risk of incontinent or otherwise mistaken deliberation. *Rational* emotions help the agent solve this practical problem. Thus, we can make progress in our understanding of the rationality conditions for emotions even while bracketing the (important) metaphysical and substantive value questions concerning what considerations an agent *ought* to recognize as reason giving and what explains why such considerations ought to be so recognized.

Let's begin building up the picture by asking what a rational agent is trying to do when she faces a choice situation. She is not, I have already claimed, focusing inwardly on her desires, trying to work out what she wants. Instead, she is trying to work out what she *should* want. Her focus is thus outwardly directed toward features in the world. But which features is she interested in? Here's a first answer: insofar as an agent is rational, she is interested in latching onto those features that, in this particular situation, mesh with or answer to concerns she values. She wants all and only such considerations to be salient to her—"all" to be sure that she will not have occasion to regret her choice as having been made in ignorance of some important consideration, and "only" to be sure that her deliberation will not be derailed by considerations that she does not think matter claiming a place among those that will govern her search for an acceptable practical solution. I use the vague terms "mesh with or answer to" as a way of gesturing toward the complicated and open-ended way in which practical concerns (themselves natural features of the world) come to be attached to natural features of the world. Suppose an agent values the well-being of others; then, depending on the situation, she might wish any of the following properties to be salient to her and to engage her motivationally: that he is upset, that he has too many parcels to carry, that he is worried about his mother, and so on. Each of these, and each of the potentially open class of considerations that they illustrate, can be seen as a consideration that would support a helping response.

The suggestion that an agent is trying to latch onto those considerations that answer to valued concerns looks promising: it is able to capture one of the sources of regret that agents feel at having made bad choices. However, there's another important source of regret that it fails to capture, and this failure suggests that we haven't yet adequately characterized what it is the rational agent is trying to do. We regret missing considerations that mesh with our values, but we also regret choosing on the basis of values that we later come to repudiate as misguided and, equally, we regret choosing in ignorance of values. Just as we don't set out to work out what we want, but rather what we should want, we don't content ourselves with interpreting what we *should* want simply in the light of what we *happen* to value.[27] The agent's task is to latch onto those considerations that *really are reason giving* for her in S. That is, she wants to latch onto those considerations that mesh with what she, as a rational agent, *should* value.

If you hold that there are external reasons that agents are rationally required to take into account in their deliberation regardless of whether they in fact care or can be brought to care about the values and concerns that underwrite the reason-givingness of those considerations, then you will think that rational agents should aim at latching onto these external reasons. However, even on the view that what reasons an agent has extend only as far as the reasons she can be brought to care about, beginning from her current motivational set and correcting it by using the resources of practical deliberation, it still follows that a rational agent aims at more than latching onto those considerations that mesh with concerns that she currently has. Williams allows that the resources of practical deliberation are hard to characterize definitively:

> There is an essential indeterminacy in what can be counted a rational deliberative process. Practical reasoning is a heuristic process, and an imaginative one, and there are no fixed boundaries on the continuum from rational thought to inspiration and conversion. To someone who thinks that reasons for action are basically to be understood in terms of the internal model, this is not a difficulty. There is indeed a vagueness about 'A has reason to *phi*', in the internal sense, insofar as the process which could lead from A's present S [motivational set] to his being motivated to *phi* may be more or less ambitiously conceived.[28]

This concession is enough to set up the practical problem that emotional rationality contributes to solving. The rational agent aims to get things right, that is, to latch onto those considerations that she *should* recognize as reason giving. However, her own current understanding of what considerations she should recognize as reason giving is necessarily limited, both on account of failures of perception—of failures, that is, to see which considerations, in a concrete choice situation, mesh with her values—and on account of failures in evaluative judgment.

She needs to remain open to seeing ways in which previously recognized values might be implicated in new situations and to remain open to recognizing new values in the light of her practical experience. Yet she does not wish this openness to lead her into error.

In the light of the fact that the agent aims for something beyond merely latching onto those considerations that mesh with her current values and yet also has reason to be concerned about incontinent or mistaken deliberation, what should we say about the rationality of a framing? Correct framings capture considerations that obtain in the situation and that mesh with concerns that the agent *should* value. As a first pass, then, we can say that rational framings are framings produced by a mechanism or method reliable at latching onto these considerations. Such mechanisms or methods must be reliably keyed to the reason-giving features present in the situation. In contrast, irrational framings are framings that are produced by an unreliable mechanism—a mechanism not keyed to the reason-giving features present in the situation.

Rational emotions are thus emotions that enable an agent to form framings of choice situations that reliably latch onto the considerations that are—in the circumstances—reason giving for her. Irrational emotions, in contrast, are emotions that hinder the agent from perceiving the choice situation aright. (Thus, phobic emotions are paradigms of irrational emotions.) Because emotions structure interpretation and inference through shifts in perception of considerations as reason giving, emotions can help agents become aware of how their values are engaged by a particular choice situation (compassion, for example, highlights considerations that call for a helping response).[29] They can also help agents correct a mistaken evaluative judgment, as when, for example, compassion leads Huck Finn to perceive Jim, a runaway slave, as a human being, a friend, and someone worthy of his help, despite Huck's avowed moral beliefs according to which Jim is property and helping him is depriving his owner of her property rights.[30] Provided that Huck's compassion reliably latches onto reason-giving considerations he ought to recognize—and, as portrayed in the novel, Huck's compassion is indeed reliable—then compassion toward Jim counts as rational, even if it here conflicts with avowed evaluative beliefs.

It turns out that this account of the rationality of framing, and thus of emotion, in terms of reliability at latching onto reason-giving considerations, will have to be refined to cover cases in which the framings are undermined, as can happen, for example, when the agent reasonably believes that the mechanism she is using is not reliable. But I leave this to one side to return to the alternative account of rationality conditions according to which an emotion E in situation S will be rational for agent A if and only if E nonaccidentally contributes to A's being able to arrive at or to confirm *true evaluative beliefs*. Recall that, like my preferred account, this alternative account exploits the parallel between the kind of shaping of interpretation and inference that is characteristic of emotions on a quasi-perceptual account of them with similar shapings of the mental terrain found, for example, in a scientist's induction into a research paradigm. Such shapings create bias in interpretation and inference, but in other areas we recognize such biasing as rational when it contributes to the ability to "see the world aright." Both models accept this general-level description of the rationality conditions of emotions: where they differ is in how they cash out "aright," with the alternative model cashing this out in terms of reliably generating true evaluative beliefs, and my preferred model in terms of reliably latching on to reason-giving considerations. It turns out, however, that the two models are not extensionally equivalent; furthermore, I argue that the model that focuses on latching onto reasons offers a richer account of the rationality conditions for emotions and is one that recognizes their role in shaping motivation, as well as in shaping cognition.

The two models are best compared and contrasted by using some examples. The examples have two additional benefits: they let me bring out how my account responds to the objection that emotions are so subjective, so tied to particular facts about an agent's biography, that we can only talk of understandability and not of rationality; and they let me say something about the different dimensions of emotional evaluation and how we can see those dimensions as connected together.

Let's start with a trio of suspicion cases. Three women, Amy, Bethany, and Chandra each experience exactly similar encounters with Peter. Most people think Peter is charming, and indeed he is. But he is that sort of manipulative charmer who is, for some women, a hazard. In short, he is sleazy and would have a reputation were he not new in town. Amy, Bethany, and Chandra are each, in some degree, vulnerable to such men. That is, they would not find it amusing to try to out-manipulate a manipulator but would be harmed in some degree by an intimate friendship with such a person. All three value avoiding psychological harm, and presumably, any substantive account of the nature of reasons would include the avoidance of such harms among the considerations that an agent ought to take into account in her deliberation. Thus the cases do not introduce the complications that arise from allowing that the agent is trying to do more than latch onto considerations that mesh with concerns she currently values.

Peter's charms do not work on Amy, Bethany, or Chandra. They all react to them with wary suspicion—they feel that he isn't trustworthy. Amy, it turns out, is a genuine tracker of untrustworthiness in these sorts of contexts. Here's why: she has had the opportunity to watch her older brother, who is exactly like Peter. Perhaps she can't quite say why her brother and Peter are alike, but something in Peter's manner suggests a similarity. Immediately, she views Peter through the lens of her suspicion. She becomes attuned to the things in his manner that indicate that he is untrustworthy, forms the evaluative judgment that he is, and takes herself to have reason to avoid him. Both the models generate the answer that her emotion is rational: it reliably produces true evaluative belief, and it is no mere lucky chance that her emotion lets her latch onto the reason-giving features that are present for her in the situation.

Unlike Amy, Bethany and Chandra are not reliable trackers of untrustworthiness in this domain. Both return too many false positives to count as reliable. Bethany tends to be a suspicious person across a range of domains of interaction, both intimate and otherwise. We can tell a story about how this came to be so:

346 EMOTIONS, REASON, AND UNREASON

her parents were rather cold and untrusting people (and, if we like, we can tell another story about how her parents came to be like this—we could even tell a story in which their lack of trust was rational; but let's leave that to one side). Bethany's emotion is not keyed to features in the situation. What explains her response are facts, *not* about her situation, but about her. (In contrast, what explains Amy's response are facts about Amy—her history and the abilities it has honed—together with facts about the situation.) Bethany's suspicion has been insulated from confrontation with evidence that could undermine it: indeed, she seldom sees such evidence because, being a suspicious person, she interprets what might be evidence against her suspicion through the lens of her suspicion. She thus finds it difficult to form the kind of intimate relationships that might provide her with lessons in trusting, even though this is something she very much wants. Bethany forms the evaluative belief that Peter is not to be trusted as a result of interpreting his manner through the lens of her suspicion. As the case is described, it should be obvious that Bethany's suspicion is not rational. It is *apt*, since we are supposing that Peter really is untrustworthy, but it is only accidental that the emotion fits the evoking situation. Were Peter not sleazy, Bethany would still have responded to him with wary suspicion. Both my model and the "reliably produces true evaluative belief" model return the verdict that the emotion is irrational, and both models are surely right on this.

Now consider Chandra. Like Bethany, Chandra is not a reliable tracker of untrustworthiness in this domain. She doesn't invariably find men, or charming men, untrustworthy, but she returns too many false positives to count as a reliable detector of untrustworthiness. Here's why: Chandra is a survivor of sexual abuse and, as is quite common among survivors, tends to be quick to read sexual overtones into encounters in which others find no such overtones. However, as a result of this experience, Chandra is also exceptionally vulnerable to being manipulated and will suffer great psychological harm if she is. Chandra thus cannot afford false negatives in this domain. This is what separates her from both Amy and Bethany, who are only ordinarily vulnerable to men like Peter. Chandra provides the test case that lets us separate the two accounts of rationality conditions. Suppose Chandra, like Amy and Bethany, views Peter through the lens of suspicion and comes to form the belief that he is untrustworthy. The belief is formed by an unreliable mechanism: her emotion, like Bethany's is apt, but on the "reliably produces true evaluative belief" model of emotional rationality it is not rational. On the "rational framing" model, however, the emotion is rational. That is, her suspicion—though not reliable at producing beliefs about trustworthiness—does *reliably* latch onto considerations that ought to figure as reasons in her framing of this situation. How so? Given Chandra's vulnerability, Chandra has reasons that Bethany doesn't share. Chandra has a reason to avoid someone if there is a real, albeit small *possibility* that he is manipulative. Her suspicion, we are supposing, *is* keyed to *this* reason-giving feature, although it is also leading her to have false beliefs about trustworthiness.

Chandra's suspicion, we are supposing, is not distorting her perception of the *other* reasons that obtain for her in a situation. Her suspicion is hair-triggered but not invariably triggered. If it were, she would see reasons for self-protection when there weren't any and she would be disabled from seeing possibilities for intimate (and even ordinary) friendships when they existed. Bethany's suspicion, in contrast, is distorting—it prevents her from forming relationships that she would very much like. It is true that, in the case of Peter, her suspicion protects her, but she purchases that protection at a price it is not rational for her to pay since she does not have a reason to avoid somebody if there's only a small possibility that he is manipulative.[31]

Let's use these examples to return to the objection that emotions are so tied to the biography of the subject that the very enterprise of trying to talk about their rationality conditions is muddle-headed. This objection just conflates biographical subjectivity—that is, the fact that what emotions someone will experience in response to a situation is a function of her past affective experience—with epistemic subjectivity, or the idea that there can be no standards for assessment and that at most we can find emotions understandable (for an agent) or not.[32] The examples show that this objection is confused. The biographies of the three characters do indeed explain why they experience the emotional response that they do, when others similarly situated might not. But those biographies also contribute to explaining who has a rational emotion and why the emotion counts as rational. Past experience makes for reliable or unreliable affective mechanisms. And past experience makes for differing vulnerabilities and thus for differences in the reasons that the agents have, where such reasons follow from facts about that vulnerability. In this set of examples, the agents shared common ends (avoidance of psychological harm). Our next pair of examples show how biography affects the rationality of emotions through its influence on the ends that the agent has. But again, such influence is seen to be compatible with rationality assessment.

Consider two fathers, each with a standing emotion (i.e., an emotion of long duration) of grief at the loss of his child. Let us suppose that, with respect to their loss, they are similarly situated: both children were young, both deaths unexpected. Both deaths occurred a year ago, and so the first acute pain of grief has faded to standing but not yet to dispositional grief. Both men have correct evaluative beliefs about their situation—the loss resulting from death is irreparable, to die when so young is unfair, and to never again see their child is more than can be withstood. Their tendency to see the world through the lens of their loss only serves to confirm these evaluative beliefs. It reaffirms the permanence of the loss and the importance and wonderfulness of the person lost. The difference between the fathers is this: one lost his only child, the other is father to two more children. Both parents' grief is apt, let us agree (if anything merits grief, the early loss of your child does), but for all that, their grief need not be equally rational. Suppose I continue the story like this: the father with two living children is seeking out occasions that call his loss vividly to mind; he is reading situations as instantiating loss or the threat of loss. And this is beginning to affect his other children, who think, rightly, that they can't make up for their sibling's loss, but who are beginning to think that with all the faults of the living they can never win their father's attention and affection. This father's grief contributes to making him unable to see the reason-giving features that are present for him in virtue of his having other living children. His grief is apt, but he needs to find a different way to grieve. That need not be the case for the now childless father.

The alternative way of cashing out *aright* in terms of generating true evaluative beliefs does not capture a case of this kind, and this is so even if we stretch that model to cover beliefs about the reasons that one has. The grieving father may not form any mistaken *beliefs* about the reasons he has: he may well know that he has reasons to watch out for the well-being of his remaining children. His problem is rather that those reasons tend to get crowded out of his attention, which remains focused on the loss of his dead child. It might be objected that, in cases of this sort, the agent does indeed form mistaken beliefs about the reasons he has, and so these cases can be handled within an extended version of the "generates true evaluative belief" model that takes the beliefs in question to be beliefs about what reasons one has. The grieving father may not be mistaken about his *general* reasons (e.g., that he has reason to look out for the welfare of his remaining children), but he does form mistaken beliefs about his *particular* reasons, that is, about what, all-things-considered he should do here and now. Certainly, grief can lead to mistaken judgments of this kind, but it need not. The agent may be able to form all-things-considered judgments about what he ought to do, but he may find himself unable to act on those judgments: the irrationality of the emotion reveals itself by giving rise to framings that make it difficult for the agent to act on his all-things-considered judgment since competing considerations remain apprehended in a motivationally lively way, thus giving rise to distortions in how the choice situation is framed.

These two sets of examples show, I think, that in searching for the rationality conditions of emotions on a quasi-perceptual account of them, it is preferable to cash out arightness in terms of giving rise to rational practical perception rather than in terms of generating true evaluative beliefs. In addition, they show that the biographical subjectivity of emotions doesn't preclude rationality assessment.

The examples also help us understand the relationship between the account of rationality conditions defended here and the various dimensions of assessment identified in the introduction. The cases of Bethany and the grieving father with children show that it would be a mistake to identify the rationality of emotions with aptness; aptness may be accidental in a way that precludes rationality (Bethany), and in any case we look for more than nonaccidental aptness when we look for rational emotions (the grieving father). Of the theorists who have advanced quasi-perceptual accounts of the emotions, Ronald de Sousa is the only one to have attempted to give an account of their rationality conditions, and he identifies rationality with aptness: "true irrationality of an emotion involves the perception of a situation in terms of a scenario which it does not *objectively* resemble, in such cases we are well advised to see unconscious links and transformation rules that have turned one situation into another."[33] De Sousa's account of the rationality of emotions focuses on "fit" between the emotion and evoking situation at the expense of focusing on how such fit came about. Thus, accidental aptness appears to meet his criterion for rationality. Perhaps his reason for focusing on aptness is that "paying attention to certain things is a source of reasons, but comes before them";[34] and thus, since emotions are constituted by patterns of attention, emotions must come before reasons and so must not be subject to the "backward-looking" requirements of evidence or reliability. However, whether patterns of attention are rational depends, I have argued, on the etiology of such patterns and, thus, whether following up on them is likely or unlikely to reveal to us features of the world. An account like mine, which focuses on the distinctive contribution of affective cognitive sets to the perception of reason-giving features is more consistent with the intuitions behind a quasi-perceptual account and avoids confusing rationality with aptness.

What should we say about the dimension of strategic wisdom? Some accounts of rationality conditions reduce this dimension to fulfilling ego needs or to bringing the agent happiness. Such a reduction ignores altogether the role of evidence and reliability in the rationality of emotions. If all that matters is strategic wisdom understood in terms of fulfilling ego needs or producing happiness, then we can—*rationally*—feel whatever it is that will make us feel good. Although recognizing a role for something like strategic wisdom, my account does not reduce it to mere ego fulfillment, nor does it consider it an entirely independent dimension of assessment to be used in calculating (additively, perhaps?) the rationality of an emotion. Consider Chandra and the grieving father: what made Chandra's emotion rational was the cost to her of a false negative; what made the father's emotion irrational was the way it interfered with his ability to meet his other obligations. Rational framings will be framings that recognize the reason-giving considerations grounded in an agent's other ends. Deliberation based on rational framings will therefore be deliberation able to further such ends (in most cases; we can go wrong here). However, an emotion is not made rational just in virtue of it's being able to further the agent's ends. It must also pass a reliability test, though the reliability test is not that of generating true evaluative beliefs but rather of generating rational framings. Because such framings involve perception of considerations as reason giving and reasons are forward-looking insofar as they serve to justify action, my account incorporates something like a forward-looking dimension into the rationality assessment of emotions.

Notes

Many people have contributed to this essay: it has benefited from discussion by audiences at Cornell University, the Australian National University, the University of Auckland, and La Trobe University. Written comments from and discussion with Patricia Greenspan, Jay Wallace, and Al Mele helped shape its final form. Jennifer Whiting's advice about examples was invaluable. Carl Ginet introduced me to the philosophy of the emotions, and a symposium in his honor provided the occasion for writing this work.

1. For a discussion of the biographical subjectivity of emotions and its implications for the possibility of assessing emotions as appropriate, see Cheshire Calhoun, "Subjectivity and Emotion," *Philosophical Forum* 10 (1989): 195–210.

2. For this distinction between reasonableness and aptness, see Patricia Greenspan, *Emotions and Reasons: An Inquiry into Emotional Justification* (New York: Routledge, 1988), 83–85.

3. For example, being both prone to anger and willing to display one's anger can alter one's adversaries' expected utilities by increasing the anticipated cost of their non-compliance. For this argument and references to the larger literature, see Robert Frank, *Passions Within Reason* (New York: Norton, 1988).

4. Jon Elster, *Alchemies of the Mind: Rationality and the Emotions* (Cambridge: Cambridge University Press, 1999), 315–317; Ronald de Sousa, *The Rationality of Emotion* (Cambridge, Mass.: MIT Press, 1987), 184–198; A. Long and D. N. Sedley, *The Hellenistic Philosophers*, vol. 1 (Cambridge: Cambridge University Press, 1987), 412; Robert C. Solomon, "Emotions and Choice," in *Explaining Emotions*, ed. Amelie Oksenberg Rorty (Berkeley: University of California Press, 1980), 277–278; and Robert C. Solomon, *The Passions* (Garden City, N.Y.: Anchor/Doubleday, 1976), 191.

5. Theorists not persuaded by the merits of the preferred account can nonetheless take away the following lessons: (1) any account of the rationality of emotions needs to engage seriously with work on the rationality of deliberation; (2) any account of the rationality of emotions must recognize the constraints inherent in the best account of what emotions are.

6. Solomon, "Emotions and Choice," 258.

7. Solomon, *Passions*, 191.

8. I do not mean to claim that Solomon ignores the constraint, rather that the account he gives is not in fact compatible with it. In the appendix to "Emotions and Choice" (276–278), Solomon identifies the inference that would defend the move from emotions being judgments to their being subject to forward-looking rationality assessment. The missing premise is that judgments, being things we make, are things we do and therefore actions of a kind. From thus it would follow that they can be subject to forward-looking assessment. It is this inference, however, that I find implausible.

9. Furthermore, the account offers one way of explicating the slogan since the beliefs in question display a mistake in practical reason.

10. Cheshire Calhoun, "Cognitive Emotions?" in *What Is an Emotion? Classic Readings in Philosophical Psychology*, ed. Cheshire Calhoun and Robert Solomon (New York: Oxford University Press, 1984); Ronald de Sousa, "The Rationality of Emotions," in *Explaining Emotions*, ed. Amelie Oksenberg Rorty (Berkeley: University of California Press, 1980); and Amelie Oksenberg Rorty, "Explaining Emotions," in *Explaining Emotions*, ed. Amelie Oksenberg Rorty (Berkeley: University of California Press, 1980).

11. For discussions of the role of affect in cognition and references to the larger literature on this topic, see Joseph Forgas, ed., *Feeling and Thinking* (Cambridge: Cambridge University Press, 2000).

12. Calhoun, "Cognitive Emotions?" 340; and de Sousa, *Rationality of Emotion*, 197.

13. For a discussion of the role of the "low-road" fear system in focusing attention, see Joseph Le Doux, *The Emotional Brain* (New York: Simon & Schuster, 1996). There's evidence that not all responses that folk psychology labels fear are subserved by the same neurophysiological systems. A quasi-perceptual account of the emotions is thus committed to disputing Paul Griffith's account, in *What Emotions Really Are* (Chicago: Chicago University Press, 1997), of how to divide emotions into kinds: emotions are to be classified into kinds according to characteristic patterns of cognition and

motivation. Because these patterns of cognition and motivation are fundamentally *practical* orientations toward the world, emotions constitute what might be called practical kinds.

14. Quasi-perceptual accounts need not be committed to the view that such interpretations invariably involve the agent's entertaining thoughts that contain evaluative concepts—sometimes the fact that the evoking situation is interpreted in evaluative terms may reveal itself in the *pattern* of thoughts that the agent has about the situation. It may be up to interpreters to discern this pattern. Thus, to use an example from Calhoun, "Cognitive Emotions?," a woman may see her partner as a "manipulative exploiter" without those concepts figuring into her thinking; she may instead tend to dwell on the amount of free time he has compared with the amount she has, on the fact that he *never* vacuums, and so on. We see the unity or pattern in these tendencies to entertain thoughts when we subsume the case under the evaluative term "exploitative."

15. Thus quasi-perceptual accounts are able better to account for phobic emotions than are judgmentalist accounts, which require attributing to the agent inconsistent evaluative beliefs. See ibid., and Patricia Greenspan, *Emotions and Reasons*, 83–85.

16. For a related case but without tracking, see Greenspan, *Emotions and Reasons*, 5–11, on intuitive suspicion and the salesman.

17. For a summary of this empirical work on statistical reasoning, see Alvin Goldman, *Epistemology and Cognition* (Cambridge, Mass.: Harvard University Press, 1986), 307–311.

18. This analogy is proposed by Ronald de Sousa, "The Rationality of Emotions," 139.

19. For a defense of this claim and its significance for naturalistic epistemology, see Louise Antony, "Quine as Feminist: The Radical Import of Naturalized Epistemology," in A *Mind of One's Own*, ed. Louise Antony and Charlotte Witt (Boulder, Col.: Westview, 1993).

20. I take this to be a key insight of Greenspan's account, *Emotions and Reasons*, of the justification conditions of emotions.

21. Compare Derek Parfit, *Reasons and Persons* (Oxford: Oxford University Press, 1984), 121; Philip Pettit and Michael Smith, "Backgrounding Desire," *Philosophical Review* 99 (1990): 565–592; and T. M. Scanlon, *What We Owe to Each Other* (Cambridge, Mass.: Harvard University Press, 1998). This claim and, indeed, the rest of the essay, is intended to be neutral with respect to substantive accounts of that in virtue of which a consideration counts, for an agent, as a reason. What it rules out is the thought that the desires that an agent has are, in the typical case, in the forefront of her deliberation, but as becomes clearer in the following section, it says nothing about the relation between an agent's motivational set and whether a reason giving consideration is in fact reason giving for her.

22. Scanlon, *What We Owe to Each Other*, 46–47, observes that the class of consideration that comes to be on an agent's "deliberative agenda" is limited relative to the class of considerations that could engage the agent.

23. Both John McDowell, "Virtue and Reason," *Monist* 62 (1979): 331–350; and Barbara Herman, "Agency, Attachment and Difference," *Ethics* 101 (1991): 775–797, defend accounts that provide alternatives to a weighing model of deliberation. I need claim nothing as strong as a silencing model, however. It is enough if deliberation *seeks* to come up with an action option that respects all reason-giving considerations that are present.

24. The concept of the starting points of deliberation assigns a conceptual, rather

than a temporal, priority to the selection of considerations as reason giving. For example, if deliberation is unable to arrive at an action option that respects all the reason-giving considerations that the agent takes to be relevant, the agent might revisit the question of which considerations belong in the starting points of deliberation.

25. Amelie Oksenberg Rorty, "Where Does the Akratic Break Take Place?" *Mind in Action: Essays in the Philosophy of Mind* (Boston: Beacon, 1988).

26. Bernard Williams, "Internal and External Reasons," *Moral Luck: Philosophical Papers 1973–1980* (Cambridge: Cambridge University Press, 1981).

27. Compare Richard Moran, "Making Up Your Mind: Self-Interpretation and Self-Constitution," *Ratio* 1 (1988): 135–151. What the claim amounts to is that the rational agent's practical question of working out what she wants is transparent to the theoretical question of working out what there is best reason to want. One question is transparent to another just in case one cannot answer the first without thereby doing what one would need to do in order to answer the second.

28. Williams, "Internal and External Reasons."

29. For a defense of this claim, see Lawrence Blum, *Friendship, Altruism and Morality* (London: Routledge & Kegan Paul, 1980).

30. For a discussion of ways of resolving the conflict between compassion and bad moral theory, as well as of the Huck Finn case, see Jonathan Bennett, "The Conscience of Huckleberry Finn," *Philosophy* 49 (1974): 123–134.

31. It is worth briefly comparing the verdicts of this account of emotional rationality with that offered by Greenspan, *Emotions and Reasons*, with which it bears some similarity. According to Greenspan, an emotion is comfort or discomfort directed at an evaluative thought. Comfort or discomfort give spurs to action and thus provides the agent with reasons to act *additional* to those contained within the evaluative thought. The evaluative thought is the internal object of the emotion, and that which the thought is about is the external object of the emotion. An emotion is appropriate (what I'm calling rational) just in case (1) the internal object of the emotion is causally grounded in some significant pattern of perception (85–107) where the threshold for significance is a function of the adaptiveness of the kind of emotion in question; (2) the affective component of the emotion is proportionate to the role of holding the internal object of the emotion in mind. The accounts are not extentionally equivalent: Greenspan does not require that the agent be able to track reasons (85–86). If Bethany, though generally unreliable at detecting untrustworthiness, were to be able to latch onto a property that indicated untrustworthiness on account of some special feature of the situation, then the emotion could count as rational, even though in general her emotional responses prevent her from tracking her reasons (86). The account thus does not capture the thought that rational emotions enable an agent to *navigate* according to her reasons. On my preferred model, emotions' distinctive contribution to the agent's practical rationality lies in their ability to enable the agent reliably to latch onto her reasons and thus deliberate and act on the basis of them.

32. For this distinction, see Calhoun, "Subjectivity and Emotion," 195–210.

33. De Sousa, "Rationality of Emotions," 146.

34. Ibid., 139.

19

Killing in the Heat of Passion

Marcia Baron

Though the law condescends to human frailty, it will not indulge human ferocity. It considers man to be a rational being, and requires that he should exercise a reasonable control over his passions.

J. Coleridge, *Reg v. Kirkham* (1837) 8 c & P 115, 119

Hot-blooded killings are supposed to merit a lighter sentence than cold-blooded killings. Is the supposition warranted?[1] Should we have a heat of passion defense?

The supposition that, other things being equal, the "cooler" the homicide, the more culpable the killer, is well entrenched in the law. As Justice Powell observed in *Mullaney v. Wilbur*, "heat of passion 'has been, almost from the inception of the common law of homicide, the single most important factor in determining the degree of culpability attaching to an unlawful homicide.'"[2] Nonetheless, the defense is the subject of vigorous debate among legal scholars. Somewhat surprisingly, it has caught the attention of only a few philosophers.[3] I say "surprisingly" because it is a terrific topic for anyone interested in emotions and self-control, in how much we should ask of each other in the way of controlling anger, in the long-standing tradition of asking rather less of men in this regard than of women, and the related tradition of seeing aggression as a "natural" reaction to certain sorts of disturbing situations; and, of course, it is a great topic for all who are interested in excuses and justifications and, more broadly, in culpability.

The challenge for me in writing an essay on the provocation defense is that there is so much of philosophical interest that it is difficult to keep the chapter from becoming a book-length manuscript. I have to narrow my focus more than I like, but I try to touch on some of the issues that I won't have the space to discuss, in the hope that others will take them up. My focus is on two issues: first, whether the defense should be understood as a justification or as an excuse and, more generally, what the rationale is for having such a defense; second, whether there should be a provocation defense, and if so, what form it should take. But first, an overview of the defense and the many issues it raises.

The Provocation Defense

To qualify as a heat of passion killing, the "act of killing, though intentional" has to have been "committed under the influence of passion or in heat of blood, produced by an adequate or reasonable provocation, and before a reasonable time has elapsed for the blood to cool and reason to resume its habitual control."[4] The test has both a subjective and an objective component. The first asks whether the defendant was provoked (and did not "cool off" before committing the crime); the second asks whether a reasonable person would have been provoked to lose self-control (and would not have cooled off in the time that elapsed before the killing).[5] The objective test is not "Would a reasonable person have been provoked to kill?" The idea is not that killing in these circumstances was the (or even a) reasonable thing to do.[6] Rather, the idea is that a reasonable person would, in that situation, have "lost it"—but not to the point of killing the provoker.[7]

Already a host of questions comes to mind. What is it to lose self-control? Is there a continuum of self-control so that we can say that a reasonable person would lose it only somewhat, whereas the defendant lost it completely? Can one lose it without losing it entirely? What is it like to lose self-control, when the person losing it is a reasonable person, and how, if at all, does this differ from loss of self-control by people who can't qualify as "reasonable people"? Just what sort of standard is the reasonable person standard, anyway?[8] In addition, what link, if any, between loss of self-control and violence is implicit in the provocation defense? Does the objective test require that the situation would tempt even a reasonable person to go after the provoker with a weapon, rather than to weep or to write an angry letter? If so, is the reasonable person really just the reasonable man, renamed?

The history of the defense is relevant here. Whereas we now speak in law of the reasonable *person*, until very recently it was the reasonable *man* who set the standard in the heat of passion defense (and elsewhere in law). Any such change merits scrutiny: is only the name changed and do the gender presuppositions remain the same? In this instance there is added reason for wariness: first, because we are talking about emotion and self-control, subjects that are undeniably "gendered"; second, because of the history of the defense. Traditionally, the defense was defined in terms of certain circumstances that were regarded as "adequate" provocation. The circumstances were (1) an aggravated assault or battery, (2) mutual combat, (3) commission of a serious crime against a close relative of the defendant, (4) illegal arrest, and (5) observation by a husband of his wife (but not vice versa) committing adultery.[9] Someone who killed in any of those situations [and killed not just a bystander but an "offender"—the assailant in (1), the wife or lover in (5), etc.] was presumptively entitled to the provocation defense (if he did not cool off and a reasonable person would not have cooled off).

The defense is not commonly defined today in terms of this list—or any list—of circumstances that constitute adequate provocation. Nonetheless, certain situations are seen as paradigmatic of "provocation," and adultery is one such paradigm. Indeed, adultery is held by many to be the "archetypical illustration of adequate provocation,"[10] and one commentator remarks that "of all the traditional categories, adultery appears to have best resisted the changes brought about by time."[11] It has changed in one way: the defense is now available to a woman who, witnessing her husband in flagrante delicto, kills him (or his sexual partner). But although this gives the defense an air of gender neutrality, we should bear in mind that it is far more rare for women to kill in such a situation than it is for men to do so. Contrary to the popular view (reflected in so many films) that "Hell hath no fury like a woman scorned,"[12] a man scorned, or a man who believes himself cuckolded, tends to be far more dangerous to others than a woman in a comparable situation.[13]

My focus is on what the rationale is for having a provocation defense, keeping in mind the possibility that the defense is so tainted by background notions about (male) anger (and jealousy and possessiveness), assumptions to the effect that anger (on the part of men) finds its natural expression in violence and that it is a mark of masculinity not to control one's rage (and a mark of honor, if one's rage is appropriate, not to contain it) that the defense should simply be abandoned. The next section examines the distinction between justifications and excuses and attempts (but only attempts) to classify provocation as either a partial justification or a partial excuse.[14]

I've been speaking in the singular of "the defense," but this cloaks a complication. There is, in addition to the traditional heat of passion defense, a variation on it, put forward in the Model Penal Code and adopted by several states: the "extreme mental and emotional disturbance" (EMED) defense.[15] I focus on the heat of passion defense—and when I speak of "the defense," I'm referring to this defense—but I discuss EMED as well. When my claims apply to both the heat of passion defense and EMED, I use the broader term, encompassing both defenses: the "provocation defense."

Excuse or Justification?

Defenses are usually classified in philosophy of law and in criminal law as either excuses or justifications.[16] Insanity is an excuse; necessity is a justification. How should the provocation defense be categorized? Is it a partial excuse? Or is it (at least partly) a partial justification? Is the answer the same for both kinds of defenses: heat of passion and EMED?

Justifications differ from excuses in the following way. If I was justified in doing x, I did not act wrongly in doing x. Under the circumstances, doing x was not wrong. By contrast, to excuse my doing x is not to say that what I did was not wrong but only that (though I acted, and acted voluntarily)[17] I am not culpable for it. Be it because of something about me, something about the situation, or both, I could not be expected to act otherwise, and I am not, therefore, deserving of punishment.[18] The insanity defense clearly does not offer a justification, only an excuse. Self-defense offers a justification (though some cast self-defense as an excuse, saying that there is a natural instinct to defend oneself, and that therefore people cannot be expected to refrain from using violence when they believe it necessary for self-preservation).[19] How should provocation be classified?

If one has to choose—imagine that this is a multiple-choice exam question—between classifying it as a (partial) excuse and classifying it as a (partial) justification, the answer would have to be *excuse*.[20] The key idea in the heat of passion defense is that the defendant's agency was impaired by some provocation, sufficiently impaired to make us resistant to holding him fully responsible for the homicide but not so impaired that we deem him not to merit any punishment. The common-law rule, as noted above, is that the "act of killing, though intentional" must have been "committed under the influence of passion or in heat of blood, produced by an adequate or reasonable provocation, and before a reasonable time has elapsed for the blood to cool and reason to resume its habitual control." "Out of indulgence to the frailty of human nature, or rather, in recognition of the laws upon which human nature is constituted," the law regards such an offense as "of a less heinous character than murder," provided that it is "the result of the temporary excitement, by which the control of reason was disturbed."[21]

So far it sounds as if the defense is purely an excuse. The suggestion seems to be not that the person was justified in acting as he or she did, but rather that the situation was such that it was extremely difficult for the defendant to act otherwise. It sounds (so far) more like duress (an excuse) than like self-defense (a justification). This is even more strikingly the case with the EMED defense, as we'll see shortly.

A comment on excuses is in order. Excuses are not all of the same ilk, and they can be loosely divided into two groups:

1. Those (such as duress) that come into play because the *situation* was such that it was extremely difficult for that actor—and would be extremely difficult for most actors—to avoid acting wrongly or unlawfully.
2. Those (insanity being the paradigmatic instance) that come into play because of some peculiarity about the *actor* that makes it very difficult for him or her to act as the law requires

My assertion that provocation is more plausibly viewed as an excuse than as a justification will seem odd if one thinks of the second type of excuse. Provocation may fit into the first group (though I will question this) but not into the second.

Provocation is rather like duress: it requires a very special situation and does not require anything unusual about the actor; on the contrary, it has to be the case that a reasonable person in the defendant's situation would have been extremely upset, to the point, as it is sometimes put, that his or her reason is overcome. It is noteworthy that even in jurisdictions that have replaced the heat of passion defense with the EMED, courts have made it clear that this "objective component" remains part of the defense and that the defense is not a partial insanity defense. *Casassa* is illustrative.[22] The N.Y. Court of Appeals rejected Casassa's argument that the trial court erred in holding that in order to be entitled to the EED defense,[23] a defendant must show that his emotional reaction (not to be confused with the action arising from that reaction) was reasonable. The trial court "found that defendant's emotional reaction at the time of the commission of the crime was so peculiar to him that it could not be considered reasonable so as to reduce the conviction to manslaughter."[24] Casassa argued that the court erred in "refusing to apply a wholly subjective standard." The Appellate Division and the Court of Appeals disagreed and upheld his conviction.[25]

It is clear from the foregoing that the fact that the provocation defense has objective components and does not simply say, "He killed because he was very, very upset" does not preclude it from being a partial excuse. What distinguishes a justification from an excuse is not that only the former has objective components—the latter also can—but rather that if one was justified, one did not act wrongly. If one was partially justified, then one acted partly wrongly, partly rightly. If an excuse is in order, it is because it is too much to require someone in those circumstances to act rightly—or more precisely, too much to punish them if they do not. If a partial excuse is in order, it is too much to punish fully; one should be held accountable but not fully so.

Many cases and statutes lend support to the picture of the defense as purely an excuse. A 1991 Illinois appellate case cites approvingly, from a 1981 case, the following characterization of the distinction: "The distinction between murder and manslaughter is the recognition by law of human failings under stress and this distinction is designed to aid the person who, through no fault of his or her own, finds him or herself in a situation where one's judgment may be impaired."[26] Or consider the following, from a Wisconsin statute:

> "Heat of passion" which will reduce murder to manslaughter is such mental disturbance, caused by reasonable, adequate provocation, as would ordinarily so overcome and dominate or suspend exercise of judgment of ordinary man as to render his mind for the time being deaf to the voice of reason . . . and cause him, uncontrollably, to act from impelling force of the disturbing cause rather than from any real wickedness of heart or cruelty or recklessness of disposition.[27]

The idea in the Wisconsin statute seems to be that whereas what was done was wrong, the person could not help it. (Indeed, the wording makes one wonder why, if this is the rationale, it is not a complete defense rather than a partial one.)

But a closer look at the defense (in both heat of passion cases and manslaughter statutes) reveals that it is not purely an excuse; it is, somewhat confusedly, partly a justification. Although not indicated in the rule quoted above from *Maher*, it is assumed in common law that the provocation defense is available only if the provocation stemmed at least in part from the victim (or at least, the intended victim).[28] Some states have codified this assumption. Illinois, for instance, requires that at the time of the killing, the defendant was "acting under a sudden and intense passion resulting from serious provocation by the individual killed or another whom the offender [endeavored] to kill."[29] If the defense were purely an excuse, it would not matter whether the provocation came from the (intended) victim or from some other source. What would matter is only that the defendant was upset, perhaps that the provocation was adequate or reasonable (and perhaps that not enough time had elapsed for it to be the case that he should have "cooled off"). But whether or not the victim provoked the defendant could not matter.

The very words "provoke" and "provocation" are indications that the defense is probably not purely an excuse, for they suggest some degree of fault on the part of the "provoker," and this, in turn, suggests that the killer was partially justified in acting as he or she did. The meaning of the word "provoke" does not rule out saying (correctly) that someone provoked another unintentionally and without any fault at all; however, "He provoked me" generally carries with it an implication of fault.[30] If I am said to have provoked someone, I feel that I have been accused of something, not merely said to have been (quite possibly inadvertently) the occasion of someone's becoming very upset. Of course, the label could be a misnomer, or it could be that a long time ago there was a justificatory component but that it has disappeared. So the fact that it is called "provocation" is not decisive, but it is a clue.

Stronger evidence that the defense is not purely an excuse emerges when we examine appellate cases in which the appellant claims to have killed in the heat of passion. Arguments are frequently presented to show that the victim is somewhat at fault—to show, that is, that the victim "provoked" the defendant, even if not intentionally, at least culpably.[31] This would be otiose if the defense were purely an excuse.

Consider, for example, *State v. Thornton.*[32] James Thornton was convicted of murder for killing Mark McConkey, his wife's lover, after "discovering" them in bed together (discovering this after standing outside her window for hours, watching them as they ate dinner, read, did laundry, etc.). The Tennessee Supreme Court notes (twice) that Thornton's wife had met her lover just four days earlier and had had sex with him each night since then—details that would seem to be irrelevant (particularly when Thornton was not aware of these facts) unless the aim was to show that Thornton was not merely very upset but, in some sense, partially in the right in acting as he did.

That the heat of passion defense is not purely a partial excuse or purely a partial justification suggests that the defense needs to be abandoned or modified, or at least reconceptualized. What exactly is the rationale for it? Is it that the killer should not be held fully responsible for the killing, wrong though it unquestionably was? Or is it that the killing was not so very wrong? Can it somehow be both?[33]

The Model Penal Code (MPC) modifies the defense in a way that clears up the question of whether it is an excuse or a justification. Its version of the provocation defense—the EMED defense—makes it (as the label suggests) purely an excuse (a partial excuse, of course). The relevant portion of the MPC reads as follows:

Criminal homicide constitutes manslaughter when:
(a) it is committed recklessly; or
(b) a homicide which would otherwise be murder is committed under

the influence of extreme mental or emotional disturbance for which there is reasonable explanation or excuse. The reasonableness of such explanation or excuse shall be determined from the viewpoint of a person in the actor's situation under the circumstances as he believes them to be.[34]

The MPC drops the stipulation in the common law that there not have been a cooling-off period (i.e., that the killing have taken place "before a reasonable time has elapsed for the blood to cool and reason to resume its habitual control," in the language of *Maher*). Moreover, there need not be a discrete incident that provoked the killer. All that is required is (1) an emotional disturbance, under the influence of which the defendant committed the killing, and (2) a reasonable explanation or excuse for the disturbance. The explanation does not have to be a provoking incident. Nor must it be the case that the victim (or the intended victim) provoked the "disturbance." The MPC comments make this explicit: "Under the Code, mitigation may be appropriate . . . even where he [the actor] strikes out in a blinding rage and kills an innocent bystander."[35] The justificatory elements of the heat of passion defense are thus eliminated by the MPC.[36] For this reason one might hold that the extreme emotional disturbance defense is an improvement over the heat of passion defense. At least it is clear—clearly an excuse, rather than a confusing amalgam of justification and excuse.

I don't think that the EMED defense is an improvement, on the whole. Imagine someone deeply distraught over the loss of his job or his wife's announcement that she is filing for divorce (or both)—and imagine that he sprays bullets into a crowded fast-food restaurant, killing five people. That *that* should be considered a "provoked" set of killings seems preposterous. Either he is so mentally disturbed that he qualifies for an insanity (or temporary insanity or diminished capacity) defense, or he has to be said to have committed murder. I will have more to say in the next sections about the inadequacies of the EMED defense (and more generally, the excuse approach).

Some Reasons for Thinking the Defense Should Be Abolished

In this section I look into a possibility I hinted at in the first section: that the provocation defense is so fraught with background assumptions about gender and violence, domination, and control that it ought simply to be abolished.

The history of the defense certainly gives one pause, particularly when one reads such passages as the following, from an eighteenth-century English case:

> When a man is taken in adultery with another man's wife, if the husband shall stab the adulterer, or knock out his brains, this is bare manslaughter: for jealousy is the rage of the man, and adultery is the highest invasion of property, 1 Vent. 158 [citing a 1617 case]. . . . If a thief comes to rob another, it is lawful to kill him. And if a man comes to rob a man's posterity and his family, yet to kill him is manslaughter. So is the law

though it may seem hard, that the killing in the one case should not be as justifiable as the other.[37]

Notice all that this passage endorses. First, it favors punishing only lightly the killing of one's wife's lover and expresses some regret that the killing is punishable at all. Second, jealousy is the proper emotion for a man to feel here, and (though this is not made explicit) violence is the natural expression, for a man, of jealousy. Third and closely related, killing in such circumstances is akin to (and it is suggested, should be considered a form of) defense of one's property: adultery is the highest invasion of property.

That adultery is an invasion of property is a sentiment we rarely see articulated today, at least in those terms; but the view that "a man cannot receive a higher provocation," as Holt C. J. put it, seems not to have disappeared. Certainly there is strong sympathy for the "cuckold" who kills his wife or her lover. In 1995, upon sentencing a man to eighteen months imprisonment in a work-release program for intentionally killing his wife (killing her hours after discovering her adultery), Judge Robert Cahill said that he could imagine "nothing that would provoke 'an uncontrollable rage greater than this: for someone who is happily married to be betrayed in your personal life, when you're out working to support the spouse.'" He continued, "I seriously wonder how many men married five, four years would have the strength to walk away without inflicting some corporal punishment."[38]

The objection to retaining the defense is not simply that it sometimes leads to outrageously light sentences, and that this is especially likely to happen when men kill their wives. The point, rather, is that it reinforces attitudes and beliefs that need to be discouraged—or at the very least, not reinforced. Dressler summarizes feminist objections to the defense as follows:

Although the defense is supposedly founded on compassion for ordinary human infirmity, it is really a legal disguise to partially excuse male aggression by treating men "as natural aggressors, and in particular women's natural aggressors" . . . the defense simply reinforces precisely what the law should seek to eradicate, namely, "men's violence against women, and their violence in general."[39]

We might add that the defense reinforces a "Boys will be boys" mentality: it affirms a long-standing readiness to regard male aggression, male possessiveness toward females, and male channeling of anger into violence as inevitable, as at worst a "human frailty."[40]

I take these worries seriously but do not think that they are decisive—or anything close to decisive—reasons for abolishing the defense. They are strong reasons for *narrowing* the defense. Indeed, some jurisdictions have narrowed the heat of passion defense, restricting what can constitute adequate provocation. In response to the disturbing 1995 Maryland case noted above, the Maryland legislature in 1997 enacted the following: "The discovery of one's spouse engaged in sexual intercourse with another person does not constitute legally adequate provocation for the purpose of mitigating a killing from the crime of murder to voluntary manslaughter when the killing was provoked by that discovery."[41]

Narrowing the scope of the defense, and in particular, limiting what can constitute adequate provocation, is a plausible alternative to abolishing the defense. It also has many precedents. Various cases and statutes limit what can count as adequate provocation. A 1967 Illinois ruling held that the behavior of a two-year-old child cannot provide legally sufficient provocation to mitigate murder to manslaughter.[42] Minnesota's statute specifies that "the crying of a child does not constitute provocation."[43] Coker mentions that it is "an established principle of California voluntary manslaughter doctrine" that "the behavior of a resisting victim can *never* provide adequate provocation to mitigate murder to manslaughter."[44]

I can imagine someone finding the restriction enacted into law in Maryland too ad hoc. If that is a concern, an alternative would be a more general principle to restrict what counts as adequate provocation. We might stipulate that to count as adequate provocation, the provocation has to be at the very least illegal.[45] We might go further, requiring that to count as adequate provocation it has to be a felony (perhaps more specifically, a crime of violence; perhaps more narrowly still, that it either constitute serious bodily harm or be part of an ongoing pattern of physical and emotional abuse). This would rule out not only adultery (and crying or resisting an unlawful assault) but also petty theft; if we further require that it be a crime of violence, it would rule out theft more generally. (It might rule out too much: a provoker's intentionally burning down one's house probably should be considered adequate provocation, yet would not usually be classified as a violent crime, assuming that no one was injured by the arson and that the arsonist was not attempting to injure anyone.)

Another alternative to the heat of passion defense, of course, is the defense proposed in the Model Penal Code. But it will not help at all with the problems I've discussed in this section. As Nourse has documented, the effect of replacing the heat of passion defense with the EMED defense has been to allow a jury instruction on provocation in instances where a man killed his wife or girlfriend because she "left," "moved the furniture out," "planned a divorce," or "sought a protective order," as well as cases in which the defendant's "fiancée . . . danced with another," his girlfriend "decided to date someone else," or his ex-wife pursued a new relationship months after the final decree.[46] The reason for this is not hard to find. The EMED drops the traditional restrictions on what constitutes adequate provocation (along with other restrictions, such as the requirement that there not have been a cooling-off period) and does not propose new restrictions. Whereas in common law, adultery was considered adequate provocation only if witnessed by the killer,[47] the MPC drops that restriction, along with all other restrictions on what constitutes adequate provocation. The MPC framers explain:

> Section 210.3 . . . sweeps away the rigid rules that limited provocation to certain defined circumstances. . . . Where there is evidence of extreme mental or emotional disturbance, it is for the trier of fact to decide, in light of all the circumstances of the case, whether there exists a reason-

able explanation or excuse for the actor's mental condition. . . . This development reflects the trend of many modern decisions to abandon preconceived notions of what constitutes adequate provocation and to submit that question to the jury's deliberation.[48]

If we favor adding restrictions on what can constitute adequate provocation, the MPC approach is a step in the wrong direction.[49]

I have been suggesting that the heat of passion defense needs to be limited with respect to what constitutes adequate provocation, and I pointed out that the MPC approach has only made things worse. But why, it will be asked, not abolish the defense rather than merely limiting it? My reason is simply that there are many murder cases in which mitigation to manslaughter, on grounds along the lines of heat of passion, does seem to be in order. Here are a few examples:

1. *State v. Gounagias*, 153 P. 9 (Wash. 1915): V raped D (who was his "co-worker and at that time also his housemate") and, despite D's request, told others that he had done so. As a result, D was subjected to a series of insulting remarks. On the night of the killing (two and a half weeks after the assault) he was again insulted as he entered a coffeehouse. He returned home, retrieved a gun, went to V's house, and shot him five times.[50]

2. *People v. Ellie Nesler*: V, "who had previously been convicted on molestation charges in 1983, as a result of which he had served three months in jail," molested D's son (age six at the time) and three other boys. On the morning of V's preliminary hearing on the charges involving D's son, "the boy could not stop vomiting as he prepared to testify." As he entered the courtroom, V smirked at D and her son; later, another mother who had testified told D that V "'was going to walk.'" D retrieved a gun and fired five shots at V, who sat handcuffed at the defense table.

3. *State v. Furlough*, 1993 Tenn. Crim. App. LEXIS 769: D, a battered woman, awoke one morning to find her husband "'standing over their daughter with her diaper off, his pants down and his penis erect.'" The husband pushed D onto the bed "and told her to 'forget what she had seen.'" He threatened later that day "'to do it' with their baby" and said he was going to "'have (the child)' when they got home." D "went to their nearby truck, grabbed a gun, and shot him."[51]

I mention these cases to indicate that there are indeed cases in which a provocation defense seems highly desirable. In each instance, a murder conviction seems excessive, but at least in the first two cases, unless there happens to be evidence of insanity or diminished capacity (the latter being a defense that is available in very few jurisdictions), the provocation defense is the only available affirmative defense. The third case *might* possibly qualify as a killing in defense of another person, or as crime prevention.[52] Furlough might have believed that she could prevent the rape of their baby (and the serious injuries the rape would entail) only by killing the aggressor—indeed, she may have believed this on reasonable grounds, given her husband's history of violence, his apparent determination to rape the baby, and the likelihood that she will find doors closed in her face if she seeks help.[53] We can also imagine that she believes this but not on reasonable grounds, and in that case, she would not be able to argue that she killed in defense of another (though if she lives in a jurisdiction that recognizes imperfect self-defense, she would probably qualify for mitigation under that rubric).[54] But we can also imagine that she did not believe that killing her husband was the only way to protect the baby. Perhaps she killed out of a desire to protect the baby, together with rage at the father for not only desiring, and not only desiring and fantasizing acting on the desire, but actually intending to rape—indeed, having been, it appears, about to rape—their baby.[55] If so, then (again assuming for the sake of discussion that she did not believe that this was the only way to protect the baby) she would have no basis, were there no provocation defense, for arguing that she should be convicted of no more than manslaughter.

Although I take these cases to indicate a need for some version of the provocation defense, given how the judges ruled, I cannot not say that they provide reason for favoring the traditional heat of passion defense. In *Gounagias*, the court held that because two-and-a-half weeks had passed between the time that V raped Gounagias and Gounagias's killing of V, the trial judge had not acted improperly in excluding all evidence of provocation: "There was no sudden anger and resentment" but only "brooding thought, resulting in the design to kill."[56] In *Nesler*, the jury returned a verdict of voluntary manslaughter, but the judge imposed a ten-year sentence (unusually long for manslaughter), calling the crime an "execution."[57] His reasoning appears to be that this was not a sudden heat of passion; the molestings had occurred years ago (and even if Nesler did not learn of them right away, she could not have only recently made the discovery). In *Furlough*, the Tennessee Supreme Court (the court that overturned Thornton's conviction of murder, reducing his conviction to manslaughter) affirmed her first-degree murder conviction and life sentence. They explained: "assuming that the incident about which the appellant testified occurred, it occurred early that morning and the victim was not at the time of the shooting attempting to engage in any sort of sexual act with their daughter."[58] Apparently, the sight of her husband about to rape their baby, and hearing his repeated threats to rape the baby later, just can't compare with the sight of one's wife (even, as in *Thornton*, a wife from whom one is separated and who had announced her intention to date other men) having sex with another man. Hours later she should have cooled off (even though the threat has just been repeated).[59]

The rulings (in *Nesler*, the judge's comment) suggest (among other things!) that some rethinking is needed on the "no cooling-off" requirement.[60] On the one hand, there is a clear rationale for it: a desire for revenge is not supposed to mitigate; being very, very upset, and understandably so, is. But is a requirement that there be no cooling-off time a good way to distinguish between revenge killings and killings in the heat of passion? Just how should they be distinguished— and what evidence should be required for distinguishing them? Compare those, like Gounagias, who manage to contain their anger for a time but eventually explode, with those who do not manage to contain their anger at all (and perhaps do not even try). Why should the former be punished more harshly than the latter?[61] Shouldn't we recognize that heat of passion need not be sudden and that it can gradually build up? Finally, passions that cool down often remain vulnerable to rapid reheating. This seems to be the case with Nesler, whose rage at the man who (presumably) had molested her son very likely cooled and then reheated when she saw the boy vomiting repeatedly as he prepared to testify in court.

In addition to bringing out a need both to retain the provocation defense in some form and to try to improve it (perhaps abandoning the requirement that there not have been a cooling-off period), the examples may be helpful in another way: they may yield clues as to how best to understand the defense. Reflection on them and on other instances of (alleged) provocation suggests that the cases that most warrant mitigation are those in which the provoker acted egregiously, wronging the defendant (or someone close to the defendant)—so egregiously, in fact, that lethal force would have been legally permitted to thwart the attack, assuming that the defendant believed on reasonable grounds that lethal force was necessary for that purpose. (Lethal force after the attack is unlawful unless the defendant believe, and on reasonable grounds, that further seriously injurious attacks are impending and can only be prevented by the use of lethal force.) That these are the cases that most warrant mitigation underscores the centrality of the justificatory component. Does this tell us anything about how we should understand the rationale for the provocation defense?

The Rationale Revisited

It might seem that given the centrality of the justificatory component, the provocation defense should, despite what I said in the second section, be viewed as a justification rather than as an excuse (or a hybrid). But this won't work. Intense emotion is a crucial part of the provocation defense, but if the defense were purely a justification, it could not be. Killing coolly to get back at someone years later is not—and should not be considered—a "provoked" killing. Yet if the defense were purely a justification, what reason could there be for not putting revenge killings under the same rubric as killings in the heat of anger (provided that the offense being avenged is just as egregious)?

If the justification approach is out, should we reconsider the excuse approach? In discussing the extreme emotional disturbance defense, I indicated reasons for opposing the excuse model for provocation; in addition, reflection on the sorts of cases that seem most to warrant mitigation from murder to manslaughter strongly suggests that the defense cannot be purely a partial excuse. However, one might argue that even if these are the kinds of cases that most warrant mitigation, they are not the only ones that warrant it, and the provocation defense should therefore not be limited to them. On this basis, one could argue that the justificatory component is not essential to provocation and that provocation is a partial excuse, which sometimes has—but need not have—a justificatory component.

This is the position taken by Joshua Dressler, who sees the defense as purely a partial excuse.

Whether one is sympathetic to his position will depend on one's reaction to the cases that lack a justificatory component. Insofar as one thinks these should go to the jury—that the jury should be given a provocation instruction in such cases—one will be eager to treat the justificatory component as inessential to provocation. My own view is that they do not warrant mitigation on grounds of provocation. A case in which a distraught (and enraged) husband kills his wife or her lover, when she's announced that she's moving out in order to move in with her lover, may warrant a manslaughter rather than a murder conviction—but only, it seems to me, on grounds of diminished capacity or (temporary) insanity, not (without further detail, anyway) on grounds of provocation. By contrast, a case in which a distraught (and enraged) husband kills his wife because she caused the death of their infant by leaving her in the car for two hours, in the sun, with the windows rolled up, during a heat wave, does warrant a provocation defense. But setting this aside, let's examine Dressler's position.

Dressler holds that when there is a justificatory component, it lies not in the action taken but in the emotion behind the action. The emotion is either justified or excused, but "under no circumstances is the provoked killing justifiable in the slightest; indeed, the actor's violent loss of self-control is unjustifiable." The "modern defense," he writes, "is about excusable loss of self-control," not "about justifiable and controlled anger as outrage to honor."[62] The defense requires first that the defendant's anger or other intense emotion was either justifiable or excusable. But in addition, the "provocation must be so serious that we are prepared to say that an ordinary person in the actor's circumstances, even an ordinary law-abiding person of reasonable temperament, might become sufficiently upset by the provocation to experience substantial impairment of his capacity for self-control and, as a consequence, to act violently."[63]

This is (especially for those eager to classify as provocation some cases that lack a justificatory component) a promising solution to the problem of how to classify the provocation defense: the homicide itself is never justifiable in the slightest; the emotion may be either justified or excused. The difficulty lies in the connection between the impairment of capacity for self-control and the homicide. Notice that Dressler writes, "as a consequence." But why would acting violently be a consequence of substantial impairment of the capacity for self-control? Why suppose that there is so very tight a connection between losing self-control and acting violently? What about all the other things that people do when they lose self-control: scream at the provoker (or someone else), hurl the provoker's belongings out of the house (as in Spike Lee's *Jungle Fever*), or write an angry letter (or several such letters)?[64] Perhaps it will be argued that invariably when one loses self-control one loses the capacity to channel one's anger in one direction rather than another or to limit its severity.[65] On this picture, we can't count something as a loss of self-control if the agent acts violently but purposely keeps the violence within certain bounds, refrains from acting violently toward one particular person but not toward another (toward whom, let us imagine, one feels no less, or even differently, enraged), or refrains in a particular situation (where, say, a police officer is present). Much more needs to be said about loss of self-control (and how to distinguish between allowing oneself to engage in violence and engaging in violence because one has lost self-control) before an excuse approach can become plausible (if it can even then).[66] In trying to work this out, it will be important to keep in mind that provocation is only a partial defense. So if it is understood as an excuse, then the loss of self-control is either a somewhat culpable loss (unlike, say, the loss involved in involuntary intoxication) or a less than complete loss; if that were not the case, the defendant would be fully excusable and not just partly excusable. For this reason (even if for no other), it will be necessary to recognize either degrees of loss of self-control or degrees of culpability for loss of self-control (or both).

Is it possible to understand provocation as a hybrid of justification and excuse? Is it doomed to be incoherent? I am not sure, but I'll make a tentative suggestion of how it might work. To do so, I want to draw attention to a rationale that has received too little attention from philosophers and legal scholars, given how often it shows up in legal reasoning.

Suppose we were to step back and ask this question: why are cold-blooded killings considered more heinous than hot-blooded killings (and the perpetrators of the former more culpable)? A large part of the answer is that cold-blooded killings are thought to reflect more fully the real character of the killer than are hot-blooded killings. This is the idea behind resting the distinction between first- and second-degree murder on the presence or absence of premeditation, as well as distinguishing murder of both kinds from "hotter" homicides, designating the latter "voluntary manslaughter." It takes a more evil person to commit a cold-blooded killing than a hot-blooded one (setting aside the possibility of mental illness). The idea that cooler killings reflect more on the killer than do hot-blooded ones makes some sense. As Hume wrote, "Men are less blam'd for such evil actions, as they perform hastily and unpremeditatedly, than for such as proceed from thought and deliberation. For what reason? but because a hasty temper, tho' a constant cause in the mind, operates only by intervals, and infects not the whole character."[67] This much is fairly plausible, but the way it is expressed in provocation law is worrisome.

Let's first note a reason for not endorsing Hume's claim wholeheartedly: suppose someone is repeatedly violent but is violent hastily, without premeditation. That he is this way repeatedly—in particular if he does nothing to curb his aggressiveness, to avoid situations in which he acts violently, to redirect his hostility, and so on—surely does reflect on his character. So evildoing, even if unpremeditated, may indeed reflect on one's character.[68]

What particularly concerns me, however, is the direction that thoughts about character seem to take in connection with the distinction between murder and manslaughter. That someone intentionally killed another, and not in self-defense, is not enough, many people seem to feel, to warrant calling him a murderer, for *murderers are wicked people*. If we don't think this person is wicked, we don't want to call him a murderer and don't want to convict him of murder. This, I am suggesting, is one of the rationales for the provocation defense, though commentators rarely draw attention to it: we have before us someone who clearly has committed an unlawful homicide and has committed it intentionally, but we do not regard him as a murderer. So let's convict him of voluntary manslaughter instead. This motivation was, of course, particularly strong when a murder conviction carried with it a mandatory death penalty; but even now, and even when the death penalty is not an option at all, there is reluctance to convict someone of murder whom we just can't see as a murderer.

This rationale is loosely suggested in *Maher*. *Maher* explains that to count as murder, "the homicide must . . . be prompted by, or the circumstances indicate that it sprung from, a wicked, depraved or malignant mind—a mind which even in its habitual condition, and when excited by no provocation which would be liable to give undue control to passion in ordinary men, is cruel, wanton or malignant, reckless of human life, or regardless of social duty." By contrast, a killing in the heat of passion "is the result of . . . temporary excitement, by which the control of reason was disturbed, rather than of any wickedness of heart or cruelty or recklessness of disposition."[69] Blackstone's *Commentaries* draw a similar contrast: "manslaughter, when voluntary, arises from the sudden heat of the passions, murder from the wickedness of the heart."[70] Some statutes and cases I quoted earlier also emphasize that murder differs from manslaughter in that only the former reflects "wickedness of heart": *Wisconsin v. Hoyt* speaks of the person who killed in the heat of passion as acting "from impelling force of the disturbing cause rather than from any real wickedness of heart or cruelty or recklessness of disposition." In each instance, a key question in deciding whether a defendant is guilty of murder or only of manslaughter—whether the killing, in other words, merits the provocation defense—is this: how depraved does the killing show the defendant to be? Is the killing to be explained mainly by the killer's moral depravity or by the situation and the "sudden heat of passion" to which it gave rise?

This rarely examined rationale for the provocation defense explains some oddities in *Thornton*. I mentioned earlier that it was puzzling that the court would (twice) note that the deceased and Lavinia Thornton had met only four days prior to the shooting and had had sex every night since they met, and I noted that this would be of relevance insofar as the aim was to show that the killing was partially justified. But there is another explanation as well: the court is making an effort to show that James Clark Thornton is a good guy, not a murderer: "He visited the home almost daily . . . and there has been no suggestion that he was ever guilty of violence, physical misconduct or mistreatment toward his wife or son." Reporting that his wife testified that she had "told her husband she might want to 'date' someone else," the court says scornfully, "In that manner she sought to mitigate her infidelity and misconduct toward a husband who had never been unfaithful to her insofar as disclosed by the record."[71] Unlike his unfaithful wife (a woman so shameless as to have sex with a man the very day she met him), Thornton is a good person, the court is saying; and if this is relevant to the issue before them— whether he committed murder or only manslaughter—it is because murder is committed only by the wicked.

Does this notion—that only wicked people commit murder—provide a good rationale for the provocation defense? No. It is a dangerous approach to take in the law; we are all too familiar with the general readiness to be lenient on those who are viewed as "respectable citizens," and to find it very hard to think of them as criminals. I am reminded here of a case (never prosecuted) involving a man said by his children's babysitter to have raped her. The police asked her to repeat her story to them numerous times, answer such details as whether she was wearing perfume, what clothes she was wearing, and so on, and tried to find inconsistencies in her story. Having failed to find inconsistencies, they nonetheless expressed reluctance even to question the man, who after all was a respectable citizen and a family man. When I relayed this to my class, one of my students expressed sympathy with the police. After all, he said, the man was not "some thug."

To call a murder *manslaughter* because the perpetrator, though guilty of an intentional, unlawful homicide is not a wicked person sounds all too similar to calling a rape an "indiscretion" if committed by a "respectable, law-abiding citizen and a family man." Still, there is something to the idea of paying attention to character in distinguishing between murder and manslaughter, and I think it is roughly this: some situations are such that even good people are liable to get so enraged by them that many feel tempted to respond violently to the provoker: "The underlying judgment is . . . that some instances of intentional homicide may be as much attributable to the extraordinary nature of the situation as to the moral depravity of the actor."[72] We pay attention to the character of the defendant because we ask whether the homicide is to be explained mainly by reference to something depraved about the person or to something about the situation (and if the latter, the "something" would have affected many, perhaps most people similarly, albeit in a way that did not culminate in a homicide). The homicide does not reflect very badly on the killer; it reflects far less badly than do most unjustified homicides.

So far this sounds like the usual excuse approach to provocation, but I think a twist or two needs to be added: we mitigate insofar as we think that the situation was one in which the defendant (or someone very dear to the defendant) was *seriously wronged*, so that rage, and not merely deep disappointment, was understandable, and the rage would understandably be intense enough that it would be hard to control. (Compare here the husband whose wife announces that she is moving out and will be moving in with her lover to the husband whose wife caused the death of their infant by leaving her in a hot car with the windows closed.) In addition, we expect (and demand) more of each other by way of self-control when the (would-be) victim is innocent than when he or she wronged the other (and when the wrong was not trivial).

In the most compelling cases, there is another feature as well: taunting or arrogant flaunting on the part of the provoker or the provoker's friends. This was an element in the three cases discussed in the third section, and is present in many other provocation cases: for example, *Camplin* (who killed the man who had just forcibly sodomized him and was now gloating about it)[73] and the homicide in the film *Thelma and Louise* (committed by Louise, who having managed to stop a rape shoots and kills the rapist when, walking away, he says, "I shoulda gone ahead and fucked her").[74]

Without going so far as to deem the killing justifiable, we think, with regard to the anger itself, "This is how a good person would (or in other cases, might well) react." When there are taunts, it is not only understandable but also appropriate that the wronged person would want to bring home to the provoker the wrongness of what he has done. Thus the blend of excuse and justification: we are saying to the offender not only "I see why you were so upset" but also "You had every reason to be so upset"; not "Given how upset you were, I can see why you lost self-control" but "Most people in your situation would feel they had to show S how very horrible his action was, and many would have felt tempted to kill or at least seriously injure S." We are not saying, "You had half a right to do this"; but we are saying, "What you did does not reflect entirely badly on you."[75]

Clearly, my reluctance to regard the defense as purely a partial excuse and my preference for viewing it as a hybrid turn on my belief that it is best to limit the defense to cases in which the provocation was a clear wrong, and a serious wrong, rather than just upsetting. The cases in which someone was so very upset that a loss of self-control is, given the distress, understandable warrant a different type of defense, such as diminished capacity.[76]

Notes

Many thanks to Cheshire Calhoun, Claudia Card, Anthony Duff, Joshua Dressler, and David Sussman for their encouragement and their helpful comments on earlier drafts.

1. This question could be asked with deterrence reasons in mind, but in order to keep this essay to a manageable length, I will set such considerations aside. My focus is on considerations of culpability (with some attention to expressivist considerations as well).

2. *Mullaney v. Wilbur*, 421 U.S. 684 (1975), 696. Justice Powell repeats the observation in his dissent in *Patterson v. New York*, 432 U.S. 197 (1977). Temperature serves as the metric not only for distinguishing manslaughter from murder but also (albeit indirectly) for distinguishing second-degree murder from first-degree murder. Typically, the distinguishing mark of first-degree murder is that it is premeditated, and although courts differ over what constitutes premeditation, they seem to agree that it is of moral importance because it is a marker for cold-bloodedness. Premeditation "should be defined so as to distinguish 'ruthless, cold-blooded, calculated' killings from intentional killings that were spontaneous and nonreflective." Stephen A. Saltzburg, John L. Diamond, Kit Kinports, and Thomas H. Morawetz, eds., *Criminal Law: Cases and Materials*, 2nd ed. (New York: Matthew Bender & Co., 2000), 271–272, citing *State v. Guthrie*, 461 S.E. 2d 163, 182 (W. Va. 1995). Another court explains that "premeditation and deliberation characterize a thought process undisturbed by hot blood." *People v. Plummer*, 581 N.W. 2d 753, 757 (Mich. Ct. App. 1998); cited in Saltzburg et al., *Criminal Law*, 272.

3. The literature on provocation (very little of it by philosophers) includes Donna K. Coker, "Heat of Passion and Wife Killing: Men Who Batter/Men Who Kill," *Review of Law and Women's Studies* 2 (1992): 71–130; Joshua Dressler, "Rethinking Heat

of Passion: A Defense in Search of a Rationale," *Journal of Criminal Law and Crimi-nology* 73 (1982): 421–470; Joshua Dressler, "Why Keep the Provocation Defense?: Some Reflections on a Difficult Subject," *Minnesota Law Review* 86 (May 2002): 959–1002; Andrew von Hirsch and Nils Jareborg, "Provocation and Culpability," in *Responsibility, Character and the Emotions: New Essays in Moral Psychology*, ed. Ferdinand Schoeman (Cambridge: Cambridge University Press, 1987); Jeremy Horder, *Provocation and Responsibility* (Oxford: Oxford University Press, 1992); Dan M. Kahan and Martha C. Nussbaum, "Two Conceptions of Emotion in Criminal Law," *Columbia Law Review* 96, no. 2 (1996); and Victoria Nourse, "Passion's Progress: Modern Law Reform and the Provocation Defense," *Yale Law Journal* 106 (1997): 1331–1448. Although he only briefly discusses the provocation defense, J. L. Austin helped to spark interest in the topic, writing in his classic "A Plea for Excuses," in *Essays in Philosophical Psychology*, ed. Donald F. Gustafson (Garden City, N.Y.: Anchor Books, 1964), 3: "It is arguable that we do not use the terms justification and excuse as carefully as we might; a miscellany of even less clear terms, such as 'extenuation', 'palliation', 'mitigation', hovers uneasily between partial justification and partial excuse; and when we plead, say, provocation, there is genuine uncertainty or ambiguity as to what we mean—is he partly responsible, because he roused a violent impulse or passion in me, so that it wasn't truly or merely me acting 'of my own accord' (excuse)? Or is it rather that, he having done me such injury, I was entitled to retaliate (justification)?"

4. *Maher v. People*, 10 Michigan 212 (1862), 219.

5. American Law Institute, *Model Penal Code and Commentaries* (Philadelphia: American Law Institute, 1980), comments to 210.3, 55.

6. Curiously, British law actually does suggest that the test is "would a reasonable person have been provoked to kill?" Section 3 of the 1957 Homicide Act states, "Where on a charge of murder there is evidence on which the jury can find that the person charged was provoked (whether by things done or by things said or by both together) to lose his self-control, the question *whether the provocation was enough to make a reasonable man do as he did* shall be left to be determined by the jury; and in determining that question the jury shall take into account everything both done and said according to the effect which, in their opinion, it would have on a reasonable man." Quoted in *Director of Public Prosecutions v. Camplin* (1978), 2 All ER; italics are mine.) In section 3 at least the test is whether it was *enough* to make a reasonable man do as the defendant did—somewhat different from whether a reasonable person would have done as the defendant did. (I read the test as equivalent not to whether a reasonable man *would* have so acted but whether he *might* have so acted.) At Camplin's trial, according to *Camplin*, "the jury were directed that the criterion to apply where the defence of provocation was put forward was whether a reasonable man of full age would in like circumstances have acted as the respondent had done." The Court of Appeals, in a ruling affirmed by the House of Lords, took issue with "of full age" (Camplin having been only fifteen years old at the time of the crime) but not with "would . . . have acted as the respondent had done." See also the landmark decision *R. v. Smith (Morgan)* (2001) 1 AC 146.

7. Exactly how to articulate the standard is itself a challenge. *Maher*, considering to what extent the passions should have to be "aroused" and reason "obscured," proposes the following principle: "reason should, at the time of the act, be disturbed or obscured by passion to an extent which *might render* ordinary men, of fair average disposition, *liable* to act rashly or without due deliberation or reflection, and from passion,

rather than judgment" (*Maher v. People*, 220; cf. *Director of Public Prosecutions v. Camplin*). Although I am primarily drawing attention to the italicized words (italicized in the original), also worth noting is the choice of "ordinary" rather than "reasonable." This might be insignificant, but it might be that the judge favored a less normative term than "reasonable."

8. This encompasses several questions: how high a standard is it? What exactly is intended by "reasonable?" And just how "abstracted" or "notional" is the reasonable person? Framed differently, if we ask what a reasonable person in the actor's situation would have done, which features of the actor count as part of the situation? British cases are fascinating on this issue. See especially *R v Smith (Morgan)*.

9. Joshua Dressler, *Understanding Criminal Law*, 3rd ed. (LEXIS, 2001), 528–529. "Mutual combat" is "a fight or struggle which both parties enter willingly or in which two persons, upon a sudden quarrel, and in hot blood, mutually fight upon equal terms and death results from the combat." *People v. Neal*, 446 N.E. 2d 270, 274 (1983), cited ibid., 528.

10. *People v. Thompkins*, 240 Cal Rptr. 516, 518–519 (Ct. App. 1987); cited approvingly by Coker, "Heat of Passion," 71.

11. Laurie J. Taylor, Comment, "Provoked Reason in Men and Women: Heat-of-Passion Manslaughter and Imperfect Self-Defense," *UCLA Law Review* 33 (1986): 1679, n. 55.

12. This not very pretty saying reportedly dates to 1697, when William Congreve wrote in *The Mourning Bride* (1697), "Heaven has no rage, like love to hatred turned, Nor hell a fury, like a woman scorned." So reports *The Oxford Essential Quotations Dictionary*, American ed. (New York: Oxford University Press, 1998).

13. Coker, "Heat of Passion," emphasizes that in many murder cases in which the jury is read an instruction on provocation, the man had killed because he was "scorned"—because, that is, she had left him or had announced an intention to leave him or in some other way rejected him. See also Nourse, "Passion's Progress" and Martha Mahoney, "Legal Images of Battered Women: Redefining the Issue of Separation," *Michigan Law Review* 90 (October 1991): 1–94. In contrast to homicides by men of their female partners, homicides by women of their male partners are usually responses not to adultery or to the man's leaving or threatening to leave but to long-term physical and emotional abuse. See Saltzburg et al., *Criminal Law*, 751–752; and Taylor, Comment, 1697–1699.

14. The very idea of a partial defense is rejected by some scholars; for example, H. L. A. Hart, *Punishment and Responsibility* (New York: Oxford University Press, 1968), 15, claims, "Provocation is not a matter of Justification or Excuse for it does not exclude conviction or punishment." He classifies it under the heading of "'formal' Mitigation." For a discussion of partial defenses, see Douglas N. Husak, "Partial Defenses," *Canadian Journal of Law and Jurisprudence* 11 (January 1998): 167–192.

15. The Model Penal Code does not have legal force but is a blueprint that legislatures look to in drawing up or revising their statutes.

16. I am not taking into account failure-of-proof defenses, "offense modifications," or extrinsic defenses. See Paul H. Robinson, "Criminal Law Defenses: A Systematic Analysis," *Columbia Law Review* 82 (1982): 199; or Dressler, *Understanding Criminal Law*, chap. 16.

17. The requirement that to be convicted, one must have acted—have done something—and have acted voluntarily is sometimes confused with the absence of an ex-

cuse. If I act under duress, I still act voluntarily. (By contrast, if I commit a crime in my sleep, I do not act voluntarily.) The distinction between an action's being voluntary but excused and being involuntary bears striking similarities to Aristotle's account of voluntary action in *Nicomachean Ethics*. Aristotle says, for instance, that if a tyrant who has control over your parents and children tells you that unless you do *x*—something shameful—he'll kill them, if you then do *x* your action is more nearly voluntary than involuntary. But although your doing *x* does not count as involuntary, it might be wrong to blame you because you did it under "conditions of a sort that overstrain human nature, and that no one would endure." *Nicomachean Ethics*, trans. Terence Irwin, 2nd ed. (Indianapolis: Hackett, 1999), 1110a25. Unfortunately, provocation is sometimes explained in terms that suggest that the provoked person acted involuntarily. For an example, see the text accompanying note 27: "and cause him, uncontrollably, to act from impelling force of the disturbing cause."

18. I should note that the distinction between justifications and excuses is not as settled a matter as my remarks might suggest. In law, the distinction is often blurred, even ignored, and legal scholars who pay close attention—and urge that more attention be paid—to the distinction often disagree about how it should be understood. I discuss the disagreement in "Justifications and Excuses," forthcoming in the *Ohio State Journal of Criminal Law*, Spring 2005.

19. See, for example, Dolores A. Donovan and Stephanie M. Wildman, "Is the Reasonable Man Obsolete? A Critical Perspective on Self-Defense and Provocation," *Loyola of Los Angeles Law Review* 14 (1981): "A man who believes himself to be in imminent danger of death or great bodily injury and who therefore shoots and kills an antagonist who is advancing towards him with a gun in his hand commits the wrongful act of homicide voluntarily. He intended to pull the trigger and he voluntarily pulled the trigger. Yet, because he 'couldn't help himself,' the law will not view his act as morally 'voluntary.' His conduct is excused because he did not have a fair opportunity to choose between obeying the law prohibiting homicide or paying the penalty for violating that law" (453).

20. I insert "partial" as a reminder that it is neither a complete excuse nor a complete justification since, if successful, it results not in an acquittal but in a conviction for a lesser offense. Bear in mind that throughout this essay when I speak of provocation as an excuse, as a justification, or simply as a defense, the word "partial" should be understood.

21. *Maher v. People*, 219. The rationale of a concession to the frailty of human nature is frequently mentioned, both in connection with the common-law defense and with the MPC version. In *Camplin*, 171, Lord Diplock cites approvingly a statement in an earlier case (*R. v. Hayward*, 6 C & P 157, 1833) that the origin of the doctrine of provocation is "the law's compassion to human infirmity." The MPC comments state that the doctrine of provocation is "a concession to human weakness and . . . a recognition of the fact that one who kills in response to certain provoking events should be regarded as demonstrating a significantly different character deficiency than one who kills in their absence" (American Law Institute, *Model Penal Code*, 55).

22. *People v. Casassa*, 404 N.E. 2d 1310 (N.Y. 1980). Another illustrative case is *Connecticut v. Ortiz*, 588 A. 2d 127 (Conn. 1991).

23. In adopting a version of the MPC's EMED, the New York State Legislature dropped "mental" from the name of the defense—hence EED rather than EMED.

24. *People v. Casassa*, 1313.

25. In England, things have moved in the opposite—"subjective"—direction. See *R v. Smith (Morgan)*.

26. *People v. Williams* (1991), 215 Ill. App. 3d 800, 576 N.E. 2d 68, 159 Ill. Dec. 399, citing *People v. Monigan* (1981), 97 Ill. App. 3d 885, 53 Ill. Dec. 162, 423 N.E. 2d 546. Effective July 1, 1987, the term "voluntary manslaughter" was replaced by the term "second-degree murder," so the distinction at issue would not be murder versus manslaughter but first-degree versus second-degree murder. Since the crime was committed in 1986, the earlier statute applies.

27. Cited in *State v. Hoyt* 21 Wisc. 2d 284 (1964). The Wisconsin statute is no longer current. The current Wisconsin statute that concerns the provocation defense reads as follows:

> 939.44 Adequate Provocation
> (1) In this section:
> (a) "Adequate" means sufficient to cause complete lack of self-control in an ordinarily constituted person.
> (b) "Provocation" means something which the defendant reasonably believes the intended victim has done which causes the defendant to lack self-control completely at the time of causing death.
> (2) Adequate provocation is an affirmative defense only to first-degree intentional homicide and mitigates that offense to 2nd-degree intentional homicide.

28. Dressler, *Understanding Criminal Law*, 535; and Dressler, "Why Keep Provocation Defense," 968.

29. Pennsylvania has a very similar statute, as does Wisconsin. As noted above (note 26), Illinois classifies a heat of passion killing as second-degree murder. It defines first-degree murder more broadly than do most jurisdictions. (Compare Wisconsin; see note 27.) Pennsylvania, like most jurisdictions, classifies heat of passion killings as manslaughter. Apart from that, its treatment of heat of passion is virtually identical to that of Wisconsin.

30. The attribution of blame to the provoker colors the words "provocative" and "provocatively" as well. Think about the claim—made almost exclusively of women and teenage girls, never of males—that so-and-so dressed provocatively. See Lynne Henderson, "Rape and Responsibility," *Law and Philosophy* 11 (1992), for an excellent discussion of the assumption that women bear most of the responsibility for men's passions, especially their passions toward women. See also Coker, "Heat of Passion."

31. I am speaking in this and the previous paragraph only of the traditional heat of passion defense. The version of the defense put forward by the MPC and adopted by several states—the extreme emotional disturbance defense—is somewhat different, as will be explained shortly.

32. *State v. Thornton*, 730 S.W. 2d 309 (Tenn. 1987).

33. Kahan and Nussbaum, "Two Conceptions of Emotion," 319, take a different position: they say it is neither, and suggest that this reflects the inadequacy of the distinction itself. Their argument rests, however, on a questionable characterization of justifications. "Justifications," they write, "identify acts that produce morally preferred states of affairs." Unless one equates permissibility with the production of morally preferred states of affairs, there is no reason to understand justifications in this way.

34. Part (b) of section 210.3 of the Model Penal Code.

35. American Law Institute, *Model Penal Code*, 61.

36. Although the MPC rids the provocation defense of its justificatory components, the notion that the provocation should come from the victim (or intended victim) dies hard. Several jurisdictions have replaced the heat of passion defense with the EMED (or EED); even so, there have been few (if any) cases in which a defendant was deemed to have killed in EMED (or EED) when the provocation did not stem from the victim or intended victim.

37. *R. v. Mawgridge* (1707) Kel. 119, 137. The author of the opinion is Holt C. J., and the case is cited in Horder, *Provocation*, 39. Some state legislators in the United States apparently thought that such killings really were every bit as justifiable as killing in defense of one's property. Four states—Georgia, New Mexico, Texas, and Utah— treated the killing of a wife's lover as *justifiable* homicide, particularly if done to prevent consummation of an extramarital relationship. It was a complete, not merely a partial, defense to a murder charge. See Taylor, Comment, 1694. As late as 1956, a Georgia appellate case explains that if the defendant killed to "prevent its consummation," the conviction of voluntary manslaughter would have to be overturned; if, however, the defendant killed "as a result of a violent and sudden impulse of passion engendered by reason of it," the verdict of voluntary manslaughter was correct. *Scroggs v. State* (1956) 94 Ga. App. 28. Interestingly, in this case the defendant was female; she killed her husband's girlfriend. Traditionally, as noted above, a provocation defense was available only to men who killed their adulterous wives or the wife's lover; this was changed in the twentieth century in the United States. It is noteworthy that Georgia extended coverage of the "adultery prevention" defense to female killers before it dropped the defense. Texas repealed its "paramour statute" only in 1973. See Kahan and Nussbaum, "Two Conceptions of Emotion," 349.

38. Quoted in Kahan and Nussbaum, "Two Conceptions of Emotion," 346.

39. Dressler, "Why Keep Provocation Defense," 975–976, quoting Horder, *Provocation*, 192–194. I have omitted the parts of Dressler's summary that suggest that part of the objection is that the defense mainly benefits men. As a report of the objections, that may be accurate, but I am limiting my attention to the most serious objections.

40. I'm reminded here of some remarks by Camille Paglia about masculinity: "As a fan of football and rock music, I see in the simple, swaggering masculinity of the jock and in the noisy posturing of the heavy-metal guitarist certain fundamental, unchanging truths about sex. Masculinity is aggressive, unstable, combustible. It is also the most creative cultural force in history. Women must reorient themselves toward the elemental powers of sex, which can strengthen or destroy" (*Newsday*, January 27, 1991, 32).

41. Maryland Code 387A

42. *People v. Crews*, 231 N.E. 2d 45. Cited by Coker, "Heat of Passion," n. 130.

43. *State v. Thunberg*, 492 N.W. 2d (Minn. 1992).

44. Coker, "Heat of Passion," 126; her emphasis. She observes that *People v. Berry*, 556 P.2d (Cal. 1976) ran afoul of this requirement.

45. See Nourse's proposal in "Passion's Progress."

46. Ibid., 1332–1333.

47. This restriction in common law was entailed by the traditional doctrine that words alone are never adequate provocation. Interestingly, in many U.S. jurisdictions that have retained the traditional heat of passion defense, an exception to the doctrine has been made for . . . guess what? Adultery. Coker, "Heat of Passion," 73.

48. American Law Institute, *Model Penal Code*, 61.

49. One might, on the other hand, oppose adding restrictions, favoring instead (as

did the MPC drafters) that it be left to jurors to decide what constitutes adequate provocation. Dressler, "Why Keep Provocation Defense," 979–982, defends this position.
My disagreement with him reflects an underlying disagreement, I suspect, over
whether it is inappropriate to use the law as a tool to try to bring about societal (attitudinal) changes. My view is that the law has an expressive function—not only to express
the views of the general populace, but also to express to the general populace the
wrongness of, for example, treating one's spouse or one's children as one's property or
treating members of certain ethnic groups, interracial couples, or gays and lesbians as
socially or morally inferior. So whereas Dressler holds that jurors, not "law-trained persons" (980), should get to decide whether (say) a woman's filing for divorce can constitute adequate provocation (and thus warrant a jury instruction on the heat of passion
defense), I think it fine for judges to be restricted by laws, such as Maryland's, from giving an instruction to a jury that invites them to consider the possibility that the defendant, though guilty of an intentional homicide, should not be found guilty of murder
because he was "provoked" to kill. I regret that I do not have the space here to do justice to Dressler's arguments. For a discussion of the expressive function of criminal
law, see Kahan and Nussbaum, "Two Conceptions of Emotion," especially 351–353
and 359–365. Jean Hampton, "The Moral Education Theory of Punishment," *Philosophy and Public Affairs* (1984): 245–273; and Jeffrie G. Murphy and Jean Hampton, *Forgiveness and Mercy* (New York: Cambridge University Press, 1988), chap. 4, bring out
the importance of the expressive function. Kahan and Nussbaum also put forward
strong arguments in favor of restrictions on what can count as adequate provocation
and argue that in "the absence of legislative action, courts should take the lead in de-
claring that homosexual advances and like conduct are inadequate provocation as a
matter of law rather than permitting juries to decide this issue as a matter of fact. Likewise, they should declare that the infidelity of a man's wife is no longer legally sufficient to mitigate murder (of either the wife or the paramour) to manslaughter, given
the traditional and continuing nexus between anger in these circumstances and hierarchical conceptions of gender" (365).

50. I take Gounagias to be deeply upset and outraged by the violation and unable to
make any progress in getting over it because the insulting remarks are a constant reminder (perhaps with the effect that he feels as if the violation is ongoing). If one
reads it differently, it might seem that he is not primarily upset over the violation but is
humiliated at being sodomized like a gay man. If so, this would not be a compelling
case to cite as evidence that we need the provocation defense; what would be counted
as adequate provocation would be, in effect, antigay taunting. I thank Cheshire Calhoun for pointing out the need to clarify that I take the provocation to be constituted
by outrage and acute distress over the rape (distress that is repeatedly rekindled by the
insulting remarks).

51. Quotations are from the summaries in Saltzburg et al., *Criminal Law*, 289–291.
Their summary of Nesler's case is based on newspaper articles: *Los Angeles Times*, August 12, 1993, A1, and August 6, 1993, A3.

52. For an explanation of the crime prevention defense, see Dressler, *Understanding
Criminal Law*, 275–276.

53. For a vivid, detailed picture of the difficulties faced by battered women who
seek help (*hopefully* at least a little out of date, however), see Faith McNulty, *The
Burning Bed* (New York: Harcourt Brace Jovanovich, 1979). Appeals cases also give
one a sense of the difficulties, the most serious of which is probably the intensified

376 EMOTIONS, REASON, AND UNREASON

anger on the part of the batterer if the victim tries to leave. See, for example, *State v. Norman* 324 N.C. 253 (1989). See also Mahoney, "Legal Images of Battered Women."

54. Imperfect self-defense is a partial defense, recognized in a minority of jurisdictions. A defendant who unreasonably believed that self-defense was necessary would, if successful in pleading imperfect self-defense, be convicted of manslaughter rather than murder. See Dressler, *Understanding Criminal Law*, 232.

55. I have been discussing the case as if it were merely hypothetical. In actuality, the trial court judge refused to give a jury instruction on defense of another, and the Tennessee Supreme Court upheld this decision, saying that since at the time of the killing the child was not even present and the man was doing nothing to realize his threats, there was no justification for the homicide. The reasoning is interesting: "To excuse [*sic!*] a homicide on the ground that the appellant was defending another, the appellant must be making a bona fide effort to prevent a violent felony, with the honestly entertained, non-negligently held belief that there is no other way to prevent the commission of the felony." That makes sense, and if the facts were as the defendant claimed they were, she surely had a plausible enough case to warrant a jury instruction. The court continued, "Stated differently, a person must reasonably believe that the intervention is immediately necessary to protect the third party, and the third party would have had the right to invoke self-defense." Differently indeed! Why "immediately necessary"? Why not just "necessary"? Clearly, the addition of "immediately" poses obstacles to battered women's claims of self-defense (or defense of others). I discuss the problems the imminence requirement has caused for battered women who plead self-defense or defense of another after killing the batterer in "Self-Defense: The Reasonable Belief Requirement" (tentative title), unpublished manuscript.

56. The quote is taken from *Gounagias*, 14–15; cited in Saltzburg et al., *Criminal Law*, 290.

57. Ibid., 291, citing the *New York Times*, January 9, 1994, A20.

58. Ibid., 290, citing *Furlough*, *3.

59. Many heat of passion cases treat "suddenness" as a crucial element of the defense: the heat of passion has to be "sudden." There has been some movement away from this requirement, however. See *State v. Hoyt*. Note the parallel between the paradigms in self-defense and in heat of passion: in each case, "suddenness" was presumed to be an element of the defense, making it difficult for battered women to get the defense. In the case of self-defense, the imminence requirement continues to have this effect. I discuss this in my "Self-Defense."

60. The MPC in fact eliminates the requirement that the actor not have cooled off. This particular relaxation of requirements for the provocation defense strikes me as salutary.

61. The reasons for questioning the requirement of no cooling-off period also call for reconsideration of the traditional way of distinguishing first-degree murder from second-degree murder: by reference to the presence or absence of premeditation. Does premeditation always reflect greater culpability? As the drafters of the Model Penal Code observe, "Prior reflection may reveal the uncertainties of a tortured conscience rather than exceptional depravity." American Law Institute, *Model Penal Code*, 127.

62. Dressler, "Why Keep Provocation Defense," 974. The reference to honor is an allusion to Horder's account, which emphasizes the key role in the defense, at least historically, of the sense of honor. See Horder, *Provocation*, chaps. 2–3.

63. Dressler, "Why Keep Provocation Defense," 974.

64. One might say that it is part of losing self-control that one has no control whatsoever over what one does, but this is implausible. Debates about volitional incapacity (in connection with the insanity defense) are instructive here. In some jurisdictions, a person is not responsible for his criminal conduct if, at the time of the conduct, "as the result of mental disease or defect" he "lacked substantial capacity . . . to conform his conduct to the requirements of the law" [MPC 4.01(1)]. The word "substantial" was carefully chosen to avoid the implication that to pass the test one would have to lack any ability whatsoever to conform one's conduct to the law's requirements. At the time that the MPC was drafted, "volitional incapacity" required in military law that even in the presence of a policeman, the actor would not have been able to refrain from committing the act he saw to be illegal. The MPC drafters rejected this requirement, along with an even stricter requirement proposed in the previous century by J. Stephen, that "the impulse to commit a crime was so violent that the offender would not be prevented from doing the act by knowing that the greatest punishment permitted by law for the offence would be instantly inflicted" (American Law Institute, *Model Penal Code*, n. 18 and accompanying text).

65. Coker, "Heat of Passion," 96, assumes this to be the case when she claims that many physically abusive men who claim to have been "out of control" show by their own reports that they did not in fact lose self-control: "Statements made by abusive men directly contradict the loss of control excuse. For example, when asked why the violence wasn't more severe if they were 'out of control,' abusive men will frequently say that they did not want to hurt the woman seriously." By contrast, the requirement that for S to qualify for the heat of passion defense it must be the case that a reasonable person would also have been provoked by the situation to lose self-control, yet would not have killed, suggests that loss of self-control *is* compatible with some ability to channel the expression of one's rage (either that, or that the reasonable person is never tempted, no matter how enraged, to kill).

66. Something else will have to be explained: (why) is it so much harder to resist temptations to kill one who has provoked one than it is to, say, take the cash from an open, unattended cash register or from the purse of the person on the train who has fallen asleep [imagining a train compartment with no one else in it besides the (would-be) thief and the sleeping person, and imagine that the former will be disembarking at the very next stop]? Why the concession to certain human frailties (readiness to act violently in certain circumstances) but not others (e.g., greed)? This is a particularly pressing question given the law's virtual refusal to be forgiving when, say, a drug addict commits a crime because of a desperate need for another fix or a desperately hungry person commits a crime to get food. See Nourse, "Passion's Progress," on the question of why only some "human frailties" inspire the law's "compassion," and see Coker, "Heat of Passion," on what gets classified as a "human frailty."

67. David Hume, *A Treatise of Human Nature*, ed. L. A. Selby-Bigge, 2nd ed. with text rev. and variant readings by P. H. Nidditch (Oxford: Clarendon Press, 1978), 412. Hume holds that we blame someone for a particular action only insofar as we judge it to reflect a character deficiency: "When we require any action, or blame a person for not performing it, we always suppose, that one in that situation shou'd be influenc'd by the proper motives of that action, and we esteem it vicious in him to be regardless of it. If we find, upon enquiry, that the virtuous motive was still powerful over his breast, tho' check'd in its operation by some circumstances unknown to us, we retract our blame" (477–478). Aristotle also offers remarks that lend support to the view that one is

less culpable for actions committed in anger than for actions done coolly: "If he does it in knowledge, but without previous deliberation, it is an act of injustice; this is true, for instance, of actions caused by spirit and other feelings that are natural or necessary for human beings. For when someone inflicts these harms and commits these errors, he does injustice and these are acts of injustice; but he is not thereby unjust or wicked, since it is not vice that causes him to inflict the harm. But whenever his decision is the cause, he is unjust and vicious" (*Nicomachean Ethics* 1135b20–25).

68. Coker, "Heat of Passion," emphasizes that one rationale sometimes offered for the heat of passion defense—namely, that the killer is not dangerous and has killed only because of the highly unusual, highly disturbing situation—is poor at least with respect to a great many of the homicide cases for which a jury instruction on heat of passion is given: cases of husbands killing their wives because their wives were (allegedly) unfaithful, looking as if they'd soon be unfaithful, or planning to leave their respective husbands. A man who kills his wife or girlfriend, Coker emphasizes, typically has a history of violence—often chronic violence toward the woman he later killed and not infrequently toward other women with whom he has a "love relationship."

69. *Maher v. People*, 219.

70. W. Blackstone, Commentaries, cited in *Mullaney v. Wilbur*, 693.

71. *State v. Thornton*, 310.

72. American Law Institute, *Model Penal Code*, 56.

73. See *Director of Public Prosecutions v. Camplin.*

74. There was in the film no provocation defense, indeed, no arrest; but had there been a trial, a provocation defense would surely have been called for. This case lends additional support to the position that it is better to limit the provocation defense than to abolish it.

75. Cf. von Hirsch and Jareborg, "Provocation," 250: "Having been wronged, one is properly angry. Far from having a purely suppressing role, one's sense of right and wrong is part of what prompts and gives legitimacy to the anger. Not only is the feeling legitimate, but so are various forms of acting the feeling out: displaying outrage and taking a variety of steps against the instigator. It is only certain forms of acting out that are wrong and that one's moral sense should inhibit. Conscience thus has a divided role, of encouraging animus against the instigator, prompting one to take certain actions against him, and yet restraining one from making other kinds of responses . . . our sympathy for the provoked person—our sense of the appropriateness of extenuation—stems therefrom."

76. That diminished capacity defenses are available in very few jurisdictions does not seem to me a good reason to introduce them under the guise of a provocation defense. Merging the diminished capacity defenses with the provocation defense creates confusion. For discussion, see Dressler, "Why Keep Provocation Defense," 987–989.

Index

activity
  versus doing in Aristotle, 25
  and Florentine art interpretation, 27
  of good life within the grasp of ordinary
    persons, 38
  of ordinary life, 27–29
  sociopolitical conditions for, 34–35, 37,
    38–39
agency
  conditions for development of, 100–101
  defective, 320–323
  problems with Kantian and Humean ac-
    counts of, 296–298
  undermined by arrogance, 16, 209
agent
  Constitutional Model of, 18, 310, 312–313,
    316–318, 329
  hyperrational accounts of, 18
  minimally well-formed, 15, 128, 132,
    136–137
  models of, 5, 290–294
  value of narrative account of, 17, 293–
    294, 296, 298–299
  viewed in relation to its effects in the
    world, 121, 123, 126
Alexander, Meena, 247
Anderson, Benedict, 250
Apel, Karl-Otto, 234

Aristotle, 13, 14, 23–27, 285
  and the best life, 25–26, 31, 37
  on leisure, 32
arrogance, 16
  interpersonal, 193–196
  moral, 205–209
  primary, 196–209

Baier, Annette, 9, 16, 291
Baron, Marcia, 18
Baxandall, Michael, 13, 27–29
Beauvoir, Simone de, 10
Beck, Lewis White, 207
Bedau, Hugo Adam, 164, 167, 168
Bell, Diane, 236, 247
beneficence, 15, 93–97, 100, 182. *See also*
    benevolence; need
benevolence
  modeled in the Original Position, 78
Benhabib, Seyla, 289, 301
Bentham, Jeremy, 258, 264
blame
  and bitterness, 154
  and blameworthiness, 115–118, 125–126
Blum, Lawrence, 139
Bowden, Peta, 62
Broad, C. D., 257
Bruner, Jerome, 303

Printed in the United States
99629LV00001B/10/A

9 780195 154757